Ferrari

MEN FROM MARANELLO

Opposite: *The Ferrari Grand Prix story started in September 1948 and, 61 years later, no other manufacturer can claim a history approaching this length. The car shown is one of the first 1½-litre V12 supercharged cars that ran on the marque's Grand Prix debut in the 1948 Italian GP. This photograph was taken later at the International Trophy meeting at Silverstone in August 1949. (Guy Griffiths Collection)*

Ferrari
MEN FROM MARANELLO

THE BIOGRAPHICAL A-Z OF ALL SIGNIFICANT FERRARI RACING DRIVERS, ENGINEERS AND TEAM MANAGERS

Anthony Pritchard

Haynes Publishing Group

Published in June 2009

A catalogue record for this book is available from the
British Library

ISBN 978 1 84425 414 9

Library of Congress control no. 2008943643

Published by Haynes Publishing, Sparkford, Yeovil,
Somerset BA22 7JJ, UK

Tel: 01963 442030 Fax: 01963 440001
Int. tel: +44 1963 442030
Int. fax: +44 1963 440001
E-mail: sales@haynes.co.uk
Website: www.haynes.co.uk

Haynes North America, Inc., 861 Lawrence Drive,
Newbury Park, California 91320, USA

Printed and bound in Great Britain

CONTENTS

ACKNOWLEDGEMENTS

There are so many people to whom I have talked, and who have helped me in the preparation of this book. I am so very indebted to my Italian friends, and I am especially grateful to Mauro Forghieri, Julian Hunt, Gino Munaron, Dottore Matteo Panini, John Surtees, Peter Sutcliffe, and Romolo Tavoni, but there are also many written sources from which I have derived hope, inspiration, and information.

In my younger, halcyon days there were three books from which I could not be separated, and these have helped me throughout the time that I have been writing. I rely, especially on the results, in *Grand Prix Racing: Facts and Figures* by George Monkhouse and Roland King-Farlow. I wore out my first copy and now use what has become an increasingly tattered third edition (revised) published in May 1964 by G. T. Foulis.

The late Hans Tanner, despite the fact that he was off his egoistical head, remains the original and very valuable source of information on all matters Ferrari. Originally I relied on an early edition of *Ferrari*, circa 1961 (the book was first published in 1959). However, I now have the fifth edition published in October 1979. Hans Tanner committed suicide in 1975, poor man, and the fifth edition is extended and updated by Doug Nye.

Finally, one of the finest motoring books of all time, *Alfa Romeo: A History* by Peter Hull and Roy Slater, published by Cassell in 1964, is brilliantly informative about Alfa Romeo and, of course, Enzo Ferrari in his early days.

The Bibliography contains the full list of books I have referred to, but there are three more to which specific reference needs to be made here. In 1974, Robert Hale published my *Grand Prix Ferrari*, and in connection with this book I found it very useful for pinning down dates and specific events, together with specifications (when you have been around a long time, you tend to rely on your own books).

Alan Henry has also written two Ferrari books, which I found immensely helpful. His *Ferrari: The Grand Prix Cars*, published in its second edition in 1984 by Hazleton Publishing, has sat on the shelf within reach of my desk alongside my own Ferrari book for many years. Likewise, Alan's *Flat-12*, published by Motor Racing Publications in 1981, has also been a great help, especially anecdotally.

Anthony Pritchard
Wooburn Green, Buckinghamshire

INTRODUCTION

A problem in researching Ferrari people is describing precisely the position that they held within the Maranello organisation. Romolo Tavoni, Race Director 1957–61, has been of immense assistance in describing precisely the various roles that people played in the organisation in the 1950s. Another problem, not completely resolved, has been ascertaining the date and place of death of some of the Ferrari people.

Without having a concrete reason for doing so, I made the decision to omit certain people associated with Ferrari as drivers, mechanics, and technicians. What coloured my decision, I suppose, was largely sentiment. I have included Dudley Folland, primarily because he owned the first Ferrari imported into Britain, but I have excluded Mario Casoni because he was not a regular works driver and is, unfortunately, of minimal interest to an English-speaking audience.

There were always problems of balance within the entries, such as that relating to Pedro Rodriguez – since the most important parts of his career were with BRM and Gulf-Porsche, these are included, although they have nothing to do with Maranello.

There are gaps, which I regret, but I think have been unavoidable. Job descriptions generally are difficult to describe in current English. For example, when Vittorio Jano was 'offered the directorship of Lancia's experimental department', it means in normal-speak 'in charge of R&D'. Photographs have not been selected on the basis that they show the driver at the wheel of a Ferrari, but I have tried very hard to use photographs for their intrinsic quality.

It must be remembered that until 1960 the Indianapolis 500-Mile Race constituted a round in the Drivers' World Championship, even though Indianapolis drivers did not compete in F1 racing, and Indianapolis regulations were different. During 1952–3 the Drivers' World Championship was open to drivers with Formula 2 cars of 2000cc unsupercharged. The first Formula 1 World Constructors' Championship was not held until 1958.

I do need to clarify the use of the term Grande Épreuve, especially in relation to its use in the section about Tony Brooks. While no longer used today, at the time it meant, specifically, one of the traditional Grands Prix – of which there were very few – and later, more loosely, it came to mean races in the World Championship.

It needs to be remembered that from when the World Championship was introduced in 1950 up to and including 1959, points were awarded 8–6–4–3–2 for first, second, third, fourth, and fifth places respectively, plus one point awarded to the driver who set fastest lap. Up to 1957, where more than one driver shared a car, they also shared the points. This was changed in 1960, so that sixth place gained the single point. From 1961 nine points were awarded for first place, and later it became ten points.

Sir Henry Segrave, with a Sunbeam, won the 1923 French Grand Prix, and this was not just a Grande Épreuve, but the very first race to bear the title of 'Grand Prix'. The following year, Segrave, again with a Sunbeam, won the San Sebastian Grand Prix, but this was neither a Grande Épreuve nor, of course, was it a National Grand Prix. So, when Brooks won the 1955 Siracusa Grand Prix, it was a race that could be equated with Segrave and the San Sebastian Grand Prix, but not with the French Grand Prix.

The 1957 British Grand Prix was a Grande Épreuve, as it was a round in the World Championship, but its status was heightened by the fact that it also took its turn that year to be called the European Grand Prix – a title that was quite meaningless.

I have used certain abbreviations that are obvious (GP for Grand Prix, etc.), and others in car model designations – notably Ferrari, of course – for example, 246SP (246 Sport Prototipo or 246 SP), and Mercedes-Benz (300SL instead of the more correct 300 SL).

THE MEN FROM MARANELLO A–Z

Adamich, Andrea de

Works driver
Born: 3 October 1941 (Trieste, Italy)

A fine grounding in sports car and touring car racing preceded de Adamich's first appearance in F1. With Alfa Romeo Giulia GTA saloons entered by Autodelta, the Alfa Romeo works team, he won the 1966 European Touring Car Championship. The following year he was a regular driver of the very fleet, but decidedly fragile Autodelta Alfa Romeo Tipo 33 cars, and during the year, he scored one of the model's first successes, a win in the Ettore Bettoja Trophy at Vallelunga, Rome.

That same year he became one of the few men since Bob Gerard to compete in GP racing wearing spectacles, when Ferrari gave him a drive with a F1 car in the non-Championship Spanish GP at Jarama. He had a puncture and finished ninth after a wheel change. Ferrari then entered him in the 1968 South African GP, but he spun on oil and crashed. He was given another chance in the Race of Champions, but crashed in practice and suffered neck injuries that put him out of racing for much of the year.

In 1968 Ferrari had re-entered F2 with the Tipo 166 Dino, and de Adamich joined the team as soon as he was fit to race again. His first race with the team in F2 was the Rome GP on the Vallelunga circuit where he finished second to team-mate Ernesto Brambilla. After this race, the team travelled out to compete in the Argentinian series of F2 races. Andrea finished second in the first of two races at Buenos Aires, won at both Cordoba and San Juan, and then finished fifth in the second Buenos Aires race.

This marked the end of his career with Ferrari, who had decided not to retain his services. During 1970 he raced in F1, driving a works McLaren powered by Alfa

Left: *Young de Adamich, formerly an Autodelta driver, joined the Ferrari F1 team for 1968, but his career with the team came to an abrupt end when he crashed during practice for the Race of Champions at Brands Hatch.* (LAT Photographic)

Romeo. This continued into 1971 when there was a new deal between Alfa Romeo and March, but both were unsuccessful. From 1970 onwards through to 1974, he continued to race Sports Prototype Alfa Romeos. With these cars, his performances were especially good in 1971 when de Adamich won the BOAC 1,000km race (with Pescarolo) and the Watkins Glen Six Hours (with Peterson).

With sponsorship from the Italian company, Ceramica Pagnossin, he raced in F1 with Surtees in 1972 (best performance fourth in the Spanish race) and Brabham in 1973 (best performance fourth in the Belgian GP). Corrected eyesight is not satisfactory in racing drivers and, realistically, he had no serious chance of being successful. He retired from racing in 1973, but returned to the F1 scene the following year as a journalist and TV commentator. When his son Gordon took up racing, there was Andrea to support him.

Adamowicz, Tony

Driver for North American Racing Team
Born: 2 May 1941 (Port Henry, New York)

Tony Adamowicz was the son of Polish immigrants who owned a grocery store. After a spell in the army, Adamowicz spent five years at the White House as a communications aide to President Eisenhower, and subsequently worked with President Kennedy. He drove a Volvo PV544 saloon in East Coast Sports Car Club of America events between 1963 and 1965. For 1966 he joined Group 44 as a mechanic and driver, and raced Ford Lotus Cortinas. He won the under 2-litre TransAm category with a Porsche 911 in 1968, and he subsequently raced in the United States in CanAm and Formula 5000 (he won the Formula 5000 Championship in 1969).

In 1970 Adamowicz started to drive Ferraris for North American Racing Team. He co-drove one of the 312P coupés with David Piper in the 1970 Daytona 24 Hours, finishing fifth overall and second in the 3-litre Prototype class behind Parkes/Posey. At Sebring he co-drove a 312P with Luigi Chinetti Jr., but they retired because of engine overheating. He also drove one of these cars at Le Mans with Chuck Parsons, and they were running sixth on the Sunday morning when the 312P lost 45 minutes in the pits because of problems with the electrics, and at the finish they were too far behind to be classified.

Adamowicz shared a NART Ferrari 512S with Ronnie Bucknum at Daytona in 1971 and, mainly because the Porsche 917s had problems and there was a very small entry, they rose to second place. Then the car lost its tail section when going flat-out on the back straight. The Ferrari rejoined the race, and after a very competent drive they took second place, a lap behind the Gulf-Porsche 917 of Rodriguez/Oliver. Adamowicz missed the Sebring race, but he co-drove David Piper's Porsche 917 in the Monza 1,000km event where they retired because of gear-selector problems.

At Le Mans he shared with Posey a NART 512M, the improved 1971 version of the 5-litre car. The car was poorly prepared and, after it suffered a severe drop in oil pressure, they drove a good race to finish third, albeit 31 laps behind the winning 917. David Piper entered his private Porsche 917 for Adamowicz and Portuguese driver Mario Cabral in the Watkins Glen Six Hours race, but they retired because of an alternator failure.

There is no doubt that Adamowicz was a competent endurance sports car driver, but he had so little opportunity to mature. He continued to drive in US racing, and in 1981 he won the IMSA GTU Championship with an Electramotive Nissan 280ZX and, still with these cars, won the 1982 and 1983 GTO Championships. He retired after the 1989 Daytona 24 Hours.

Agnelli, Gianni

President of Fiat
Born: 12 March 1921 (Turin, Italy)
Died: 24 January 2003 (Turin)

After education at the Pierolo Cavalry Academy, and studying law at Turin University (but not qualifying as a lawyer), this member of Italy's most eminent family joined an Italian tank regiment when Italy entered the Second World War on the Axis side in June 1940. He fought on the Russian front and was wounded twice. He then joined an armoured car division in North Africa. (Of course, both tanks and armoured cars were products of the Fiat group.) It is said that he was shot in the arm by a German officer during a fight in a bar over a woman.

Agnelli married half-American Donna Marella Caracciolo di Castagneto on 19 November 1953. The marriage survived, despite his many extra-marital liaisons. In Italy he was always regarded as a man of great charm, and a leader of trends in male fashion. He

Above: *Gianni Agnelli was not slow in making his views known and here he lectures Piero Lardi Ferrari, who has no chance to escape.* (LAT)

became President of Fiat in 1966, and the Fiat Group, especially under his control, had a notorious reputation for acting in the interests of the Agnelli family rather than those of Italy. His son, Edoardo, who was not interested in the family business, suffered mental problems and committed suicide on 15 November 2000 by jumping off a bridge in Turin.

Gianni Agnelli was instrumental in pushing Fiat forward as a worldwide car manufacturer. He negotiated the acquisition of Alfa Romeo (to prevent it from falling into the hands of the American Ford company) and he engineered joint production arrangements in many countries, including Poland and Russia. Agnelli entered into the agreement on behalf of Fiat whereby the Turin-based group took a half-share in Ferrari in 1968, and assumed complete control of the company in 1988. For many years Agnelli was responsible for Fiat providing a lifeline to many Italian companies involved in motor sport.

Agnelli was appointed a senator for life in 1991, and he sat in the Italian parliament as an independent (or, perhaps more accurately, as the member for Fiat). He had close links with Juventus football club in Turin, and it is said he telephoned the Club's President, Giampiero Boniperi, every morning at 6am. He resigned as President of Fiat in 1996, but he remained honorary chairman. Agnelli's deteriorating health prevented him from being seriously involved in resolving Fiat Auto's financial and production problems. He died of cancer of the prostate gland in 2003.

Alboreto, Michele

Works driver
Born: 23 December 1956 (Milan, Italy)
Died: 25 April 2001 (Lausitzring, near Dresden, Germany)

Smooth, steady and very stylish, Alboreto rose to the top in motor racing swiftly and relatively easily. He was backed by Paolo Pavanello, who had been the March agent in Italy and a partner, with Walter Brun (Swiss slot-machine magnate), in the Eurobrun F1 project. After this folded, Pavanello concentrated on F3 and ran a very successful team. Alboreto was runner-up with Pavanello-entered cars in the 1979 Italian F3 Championship, and won the title the following year. He joined the Minardi F2 team in 1981 and won the race at Misano late in the season.

By this time he was already driving in F1 with the backing of Count Zanon, and after a trial drive with Tyrrell in the San Marino GP, the British team gave him a three-year contract. The Ford-powered Tyrrells were losing their competitiveness and were certainly no match for the latest turbocharged entries. In 1982

Alboreto took two fourth places early in the season; in Rio de Janeiro the first and second place cars in front of him had been disqualified, and at the United States GP at West Beach the third place driver was disqualified, so it was not as good as it sounds.

Later that year he finished third at Imola, fourth at Hockenheim, and then scored an unexpected win in the Caesars Palace GP, the result of so many of the faster runners falling by the wayside. Tyrrell secured Benetton sponsorship in 1983, but the team was still running normally aspirated Ford engines. A dreadful season was partially redeemed by Alboreto's remarkable win in the United States GP (Detroit) after Piquet's Brabham had a rear tyre deflate, and it was the Ford V8 engine's last GP win.

For 1984, Alboreto was offered a place in the Ferrari team, something no red-blooded Italian could turn down. Ferrari was going through one of its all too frequent poor patches, and the latest turbocharged cars were no real match for the McLarens, and about on a par with the BMW-powered Brabhams. Michele scored a good win at Zolder, and later in the year took a third in Austria and seconds at Monza and in the European GP at the Nürburgring. He netted fourth place in the Championship, which gave Ferrari some cause for hope.

The 1985 season witnessed a battle with Prost (McLaren) in the Drivers' Championship, but as the season progressed, so Ferrari faded and, for Alboreto, wins in Canada and Germany with seconds at Rio, Estoril, Monte Carlo, and Silverstone were counterbalanced by retirements in the last five races of the season. Prost won the Championship with 73 points to Alboreto's 53. Of Alboreto's driving that season, Nigel Roebuck commented:

'In the end he had to settle for runner-up, because the Ferrari wasn't as good a car as the McLaren – and also, truth be told, because neither was Michele as good as Alain. No disgrace in that.'

Alboreto remained with Ferrari for three more seasons, and although he seemed a permanent fixture at Maranello, it was not to be. Johansson was his team-mate in 1986 and Berger in 1987–8, but the team was just bouncing along the bottom, mediocre and uninspired. During these years Alboreto failed to win a single race. In 1986 he finished second in Austria, retired in 10 of the season's 16 races, and finished eighth in the World Championship.

The following year, second in Australia (after Senna, second on the road, was disqualified), meant a Ferrari 1–2 and signs of improvement, but Michele retired in 12

of the year's races, and he was seventh in the Championship. In 1988 he took a fifth place at Monza, and was third both at Monaco and in the French race. There was political turmoil at Maranello following Ferrari's death, and it was made clear to Michele that his contract would not be renewed.

Later, when he was discussing his years with Ferrari, Alboreto commented:

'The media in Italy are capable of convincing the Ferrari management about any aspect of the car's performance. The management, in turn, are prepared to believe the media far more than the drivers.

Below: *Alboreto learned his skills in Formula 3, and gained Formula 1 experience during three seasons with Tyrrell before moving on to Ferrari, for whom he drove for five seasons. He twice won Grands Prix for Tyrrell, the last to be achieved by this team that was so underfinanced in its latter days.* (LAT Photographic)

Throughout 1984–5 we kept saying that we hadn't enough power, but then some newspaper would come up with a statistic that we had the fastest speed in a straight line at some circuit or other. Then we would have to try explaining that the reason we were quick on the straight was because we were running no wing and the drivability of the engine is poor because there is no power at the bottom end of the rev range.' (Adapted from *Ferrari: The Grand Prix Cars* by Alan Henry)

In the summer of 1988 Frank Williams had offered a drive to Alboreto for 1989 and, as he had not heard anything by the autumn, he contacted Frank Williams and was assured that the team wanted him. In the end, Williams signed up Thierry Boutsen, and it seems that the Didcot team kept Michele 'dangling' until they were certain that they did not need him. Alboreto thought about retiring from racing, but managed to put together a deal with Tyrrell and returned to them for 1989.

Then, in mid-season, a sponsorship clash arose, because Tyrrell signed a deal with Camel, while Alboreto had a personal sponsorship deal with Marlboro. Alboreto lost both his Marlboro sponsorship and his drive with Tyrrell. He managed to sign up with Larrousse who entered a sponsorship deal with Camel, and this enabled the impoverished French team to pay Michele's wages. He stayed in F1 for another five seasons, spending three seasons with Arrows/Footwork and two with Scuderia Italia.

After Michele had left the F1 scene, he joined Alfa Romeo in the German Touring Car Championship, and he later raced Ferraris without success in the World Sportscar Championship. In 1996 he raced in the new Indy Racing League with Scandia/Simon Racing, driving in his only 500 race at the Brickyard. He also co-drove a Jöst Racing-entered Peugeot WSC-95 at Le Mans with Pierluigi Martini and Didier Theys, but they retired because of engine problems.

Resident with his wife and children in Monaco, Michele had no financial pressure to race and did so because of his love of the sport. In 1997 he agreed to drive the Peugeot again, along with Stefan Johansson (another former Ferrari driver) and Danish driver Tom Kristensen, who later broke Jacky Ickx's record of winning the most Le Mans races. He drove for Audi at Le Mans in 1999, but retired; he then shared a drive with an Audi to third place at Le Mans in 2000, and co-drove the winning car at Sebring in 2001.

In April 2001, Alboreto was conducting straight-line speed tests in an Audi R8 at the Lausitzring near Dresden in East Germany when a tyre blew, the car swerved off the track and crashed into a wall. Poor Alboreto was fatally injured and, as is so often the case with accidents in private test sessions, the circumstances of the accident were never published.

Aldrighetti, Giordano

Alfa Corse works driver
Born: 1905 (Milan, Italy)
Died: 12 August 1939 (Pescara, Italy)

Giordano 'Nando' Aldrighetti had a long and successful career racing motorcycles. His greatest success was as a works Gilera rider in the 1937 Italian GP at Monza, at the time a non-Championship race. After a slow start, a very slow refuelling stop and another pit stop to change a sparking plug, he came through to win the race from Ombono Tenni and set a new lap record of 111mph (179kph). He appeared regularly in the Isle of Man TT races, but in 1938 he had a very bad crash with a Gilera in the Swiss GP, and the injuries he suffered forced him to pull out of front-line motorcycle racing.

Nando joined the Alfa Corse team to race Tipo 158 Alfettas for 1939. He first raced one of these cars at Tripoli, where he retired. He did not appear for the team again until the Coppa Acerbo in August. During the Friday practice he crashed heavily and the car caught fire. Aldrighetti was thrown out and seemed to have escaped lightly. Sadly, though, he had suffered serious internal injuries and died shortly after midnight.

Alesi, 'Jean'

Works driver
Born: 11 June 1964 (Avignon, France)

When Giovanni 'Jean' Alesi entered the top ranks of F1 in 1991, it was initially announced that he would be joining Williams, but something undisclosed happened during protracted negotiations, and instead he appeared for Ferrari. Born in France of Sicilian parents, he was obvious and natural Ferrari material, although

he joined the team when its fortunes were abysmal.

Alesi entered racing with his own Alfa Romeo-powered Dallara in 1986, and he won the French F3 Championship for the ORECA team in 1987, but only after a mid-season change from Martini to Dallara chassis. He stayed with ORECA for F3000 in 1988, but he had a bad year, during which his relationship with the engineering staff failed to gel. For 1989, Marlboro decided to sponsor J J Lehto and Eddie Irvine at ORECA, leaving Alesi out in the cold. He switched to Eddie Jordan's team and won the F3000 Championship. During the year he was also offered a place in the Tyrrell F1 team as successor to Alboreto, who had joined the Larrousse team. Alesi's driving was a mixture of wildness, a marked lack of self-discipline, fantastic speed, and innate skill. The public wants to see an exciting driver, and Alesi supplied excitement in abundance.

The Tyrrells were uncompetitive, but Alesi took fourth place in his first race for the team, the French GP at Paul Ricard, and he was also fourth in the Spanish race at Jerez, albeit a lap in arrears after a stop for fresh tyres. Alesi stayed with Tyrrell for 1990. He finished a remarkable second behind Senna in the United States GP at Phoenix, and made it clear to the Brazilian that he would not be intimidated. There were more collisions during the year than there should have been, but these were balanced by his fine second place to Senna at Monaco.

It was not easy for Alesi when he joined Ferrari for 1991, although his Sicilian ancestry helped. In a year during which he became a much more controlled, self-disciplined driver, and built up his relationships with the team, his best performances were third places at

Above: *A fine view of Jean Alesi at the wheel of his F92A Ferrari in the 1992 Canadian GP at Montreal, in which he finished third. It was another poor year for Alesi, who finished seventh in the Drivers' Championship. When Alesi joined Ferrari in 1991, it seemed that he had the flair, drive, and natural talent to drag Ferrari out of the doldrums. Sadly, his great ability was never fully exploited, and his only race win for Ferrari was in the 1995 Canadian race.* **(LAT Photographic)**

Monaco, Hockenheim and Estoril. By 1992, Alesi's driving reflected his greater experience, and there were occasions that year when he displayed sheer brilliance, notably at Barcelona where he finished third, and the French race at Magny Cours where he drove magnificently until he retired because of engine problems. It was, however, a frustrating year, in which the Ferraris performed disappointingly.

Jean suffered even greater frustration in 1993, as it was only too clear that the Ferraris were not getting any more competitive or reliable. Berger had now joined the Ferrari team, and Alesi and he should have been a 'dream ticket'. Unfortunately, the main story was one of retirements, but Jean did manage a second place at Monza and a third at Monaco – despite colliding with team-mate Berger in the Principality.

Because of back injuries suffered in a testing accident, Alesi missed the second and third races of the 1994 season. The Ferraris were rather more competitive that year, and Berger won at Hockenheim and took two second places. Meanwhile, Alesi floundered, became

Above: *Jean Alesi, who seemed to be destined to drag Ferrari back to greatness when he joined the team for 1991 after two years in Formula 1 with Tyrrell. This photograph was taken in the Ferrari office building in Maranello.* (LAT Photographic)

Ferrari and Alesi had to go their separate ways following a major disagreement between Jean and Jean Todt. Alesi joined the Benetton team and, although he never won another GP, he finished fourth in the 1996 World Championship, and third in 1997. Once again he had been so close to really great success, but it slipped from his grasp, and at the end of 1997 he left for a two-year contract with the Sauber team. That his career was in decline was obvious.

After two largely unsuccessful seasons (best performance third in the 1998 Belgian race at Spa), he joined the struggling Prost team for 2000, leaving after the 2001 German GP to finish the year with Jordan. His last F1 race was that year's Japanese GP at Suzuka, where he collided with Kimi Räikkönen who had lost control of his Sauber, and his long career finished on a frustrating and disabling note.

Jean had married a Japanese girl, Kumiko, and she had put him under considerable pressure to retire from F1. He turned to touring car events with Mercedes-Benz, and then became involved in plans with a Japanese consortium to race a 'junior' McLaren team. These came to nothing and he is now concentrating his energies with the French Motor Sport Association to guide and develop young racing talent.

increasingly short fused, and failed to achieve a win. There were too many driver errors and engine failures, and while he should have won at Monza his gearbox was damaged during a refuelling stop – resulting in an uncontrolled outburst of Latin temper.

Alesi stayed with Ferrari for one more season, 1995. The great sadness is that, although he was a Ferrari man through and through and had all the talents and ability (temperament apart) for being a serious World Championship contender, it never came together. He achieved his only GP win, which was highly emotional and very popular, in Canada that year, and he also took second places at Buenos Aires, Imola, Silverstone, and the Nürburgring (European GP). At both Interlagos and the Nürburgring he turned in displays of virtuoso car control. He finished fifth in the World Championship for the second successive year.

Allison, Cliff

Driver
Born: 8 February 1932 (Brough, Westmorland, England)
Died: 7 April 2005 (Brough, Cumbria)

Allison's family ran a garage business in Brough, and after education at the local primary school and Appleby Grammar School, he joined the family business. At the age of 12 he started competing in local horse trotting and galloping events. From 16 he competed in motorcycle events, and then moved on to 500cc car racing. At first he drove an ancient JAP-powered Marwyn, and then raced Coopers. By 1955 he was racing a Mark X Cooper with disc rear brake.

Right: *Allison enjoyed a long run of consistent and successful driving with the works Lotus Team, but he joined Ferrari for 1959. He left the team after an accident in practice for the 1960 Monaco Grand Prix.* (LAT Photographic)

That year he was invited to join the Lotus sports car team and, although he received no money from Lotus, the team's main sponsor Esso paid him £2,000 per year by way of a retainer. His first race was the 1955 Goodwood Nine Hours in which he co-drove a Lotus Mark 9 with Ron Flockhart, but they retired because of oil leaking into the clutch, a common fault with early Coventry Climax FWA 1098cc engines. He crashed a Mark 9 in the 331-mile (356km) *Daily Herald* Trophy at Oulton Park the following weekend.

In Cliff's own words:

'The car looked as though it was very badly mangled, it was mainly the body, and the frame wasn't too bad. Colin [Chapman] wasn't too upset as I was leading all the Coopers except Ivor Bueb's [works driver], and as the Coopers were winning everything, it showed that at least we were on the right track.'

He rounded off the season by co-driving a Mark 9 with Colin Chapman in the Tourist Trophy on the Dundrod circuit in Northern Ireland and, after losing 11min while a broken oil pipe was changed, they finished 11th overall and second in class, only 50yd behind the works Cooper of Bueb/McDowell.

Cliff continued to race 500cc Coopers until the end of 1956, but most of his energies were concentrated on Lotus and the new Eleven. In international events he finished second with an 1100cc car behind Chapman, with a 1500cc model, in the Delamare Debouteville Cup at Rouen, and he and Keith Hall were leading the 1100cc class at Le Mans when he hit a large dog. He won the 1100cc class at Brands Hatch, Crystal Palace, Goodwood, Aintree, and Silverstone, and with a 1500cc sports car he finished fourth behind Salvadori, with the new Cooper single-seater, in the first 1500cc Formula 2 race at Silverstone in July 1956.

By 1957, Lotus was racing the new 12 Formula 2 car. Although it was generally unreliable, Cliff finished third in the Woodcote Cup at Goodwood on Easter Monday, and second behind Jack Brabham (Cooper) in the Gold Cup race at Oulton Park. Partnered again by Keith Hall, he won the 750cc class at Le Mans, and among other successes he won the 1500cc class of the Belgian Sports Car GP at Spa-Francorchamps.

Cliff stayed with Lotus in 1958. The team was racing the new 15, as well as competing in Formula 1 with the 12, now fitted with a 2-litre Coventry Climax engine. After winning the Formula 2 class of the International Trophy at Silverstone and finishing sixth overall with a 1500cc 12, he drove the 2-litre version at Monaco; the engine broke at Casino Square near the end of the race

and he pushed the car to the finishing line and sixth place. By the Dutch GP, Cliff had a 12 with a 2.2-litre engine and he finished sixth at Zandvoort, following this up with a fine fourth in the Belgian race.

During the rest of the 1958 season Cliff enjoyed little success, although he was now a mature and highly talented driver. He crashed the new 16 Formula 1 car in practice for the Portuguese GP; tarmac used to fill in tramlines at a roundabout on the Porto street circuit worked its way out and formed hard balls on which the Lotus lost adhesion and slid sideways into the scaffolding supports for a temporary footbridge, tearing off two wheels.

At the London Motor Show a Ferrari representative invited Cliff to attend a test session at Modena. As Cliff recalled:

'When I went for my test drive at Modena, Enzo Ferrari, technical director Carlo Chiti, and team manager Romolo Tavoni were all there. I drove Mike Hawthorn's lengthened Dino 246 on drum brakes. I wasn't nervous at all. It was just another day at the office. I thought that in driving for Ferrari I had really arrived, and this was true in those days.

Tavoni spoke good English, Chiti spoke no English, but it was possible to talk to him using schoolboy French, and while I am sure that Enzo Ferrari understood a lot of English, he wouldn't speak to you in English, but you could tell by the twinkle in his eye that he understood much of what was said, and he always had a lady interpreter with him. I covered only a few laps, and then it was home.'

After he arrived back in Brough, Cliff received the offer of a contract, and accepted.

'Ferrari paid 50 per cent of the start money to the driver, and with Ferrari there was usually about a thousand quid start money, so you got five hundred quid wherever you raced. They didn't pay me any retainer. Ferrari arranged all the transport, and I used to get a note from Tavoni just to be at Heathrow to catch an aeroplane at a certain time. The ticket was all done. At the end of the day I would get an account, and the air fare was taken off the start money. Sometimes what I received only just covered the costs of the trip.'

Brian Turle, the Shell competition manager, had agreed to pay Cliff a £2,000 retainer, but Shell reneged on the deal, claiming that Turle had no authority to agree it. Cliff

drove mainly in sports car races in the early part of 1959. He partnered Jean Behra at Sebring, and they finished second. He was at the wheel of a Formula 2 car in the Monaco GP and was eliminated in a multi-car accident triggered off by von Trips (Porsche). He and Dan Gurney took a less than satisfactory fifth place at the Nürburgring 1,000km race, and all three Ferraris retired at Le Mans.

Allison told the writer:

'I didn't like Le Mans at all. From the Ferrari driver's point of view, the idea was to break the car in your first session, and if you broke the car you could go home. So there was a lot of over-revving done. As the race wore on, if you got, say six hours over, then you started to think, 'Oh well, we'll probably have to nurse it through to the finish now.' I enjoyed some of the 1,000km races – they were OK because they didn't last too long – but Le Mans was just too dreary. On a fast circuit, a 1,000km race didn't last much more than six hours, so you only spent three hours at the wheel. In those days Grands Prix lasted three hours.'

Cliff retired in the German GP held on the banked Avus circuit, he shared the third place Testa Rossa in the Tourist Trophy, and retired again in the United States race at Sebring. He stayed with Ferrari for 1960, and in Formula 1 drove a Dino with slightly extended wheelbase, rather like the one the factory had built for Hawthorn. Cliff needed the extra length because he was well over six feet in height. Co-driving with Phil Hill, Cliff won the Buenos Aires 1,000km race, he was second in the Argentine GP, and shared the third-place Testa Rossa in the Nürburgring 1,000km race.

Above: *Originally, Allison drove only Ferrari sports cars, but he first appeared with a Formula 1 car in the 1959 German GP at Avus. By 1960, the front-engined Ferrari Dinos were completely obsolete and uncompetitive. Ferrari sent two of these cars to compete in that year's International Trophy at Silverstone. Phil Hill finished fifth, and Allison (seen here) took eighth place, both of them a lap in arrears. Allison crumpled the nose of his Dino in a start-line collision with his team-mate. Following Allison in this photograph is Joakim Bonnier with his rear-engined BRM. (Tom March Collection)*

His career, to all intents and purposes, came to an end at Monaco in 1960. He was third fastest in the first practice session, but after Cliff's Dino had been put on new tyres and the tank filled, it was announced that all the times were cancelled because of a fault in the timing mechanism. So Cliff had to go out to set a fast lap with the Dino in unsuitable configuration. This is how Cliff described his accident:

'Ferrari had changed the gear-selection mechanism round since we last raced the cars. Instead of being a conventional H-section, with the high gears on the right-hand side of the gate, it had the low gears on the right-hand side and the high gears on the left. First was an extension on the bottom right of the gate, with reverse above it; as you came out of first, a little flap dropped to prevent accidental engagement of reverse. The driver went left across the gate and up into second and then down into third. It was then across and up into fourth and down into fifth.

I had been used to changing from fifth to fourth by just banging the lever forward and keeping it over to the right-hand side. When I kept the lever to the right side of the gate with this gearbox, it went from fifth to second. So I locked the back wheels and ended up going hell for leather down the hill into the chicane, and in those days there was no escape road at all. You just had to go through the chicane. I touched the side of the kerb. The damage to the car was just to one wheel, but I was thrown out and went head-first into the straw bales at 100mph [160kph] plus.

I damaged my back and broke an arm. I spent a while in hospital and I was a long time on sticks. I wasn't able to drive for the rest of the year. To begin with, I thought that my racing days were over. Ferrari still wanted me to drive for them, but they had made it clear that it would be driving sports cars for a year and then having a test drive in a single-seater. If I proved up to it, I could drive in Formula 1 again. In retrospect this is what I should have done, but I was keen to drive in Formula 1. In those days there was no money at all in sports car racing.'

Cliff tested with Lotus at Silverstone in late 1960 and agreed to drive for the UDT-Laystall team in 1961. He practised for the Belgian GP with the team's Lotus 18, the handling of which he thought was very unpredictable. Whoever was faster in practice, he or Henry Taylor, was to drive the car in the race. It was a stupid arrangement that simply encouraged the driver to try too hard.

In this case it was especially stupid because the car was obsolete. Cliff ran out of opposite lock at Clubhouse Bend, the car hit the grass travelling sideways and he was thrown out of the car. Cliff suffered nerve damage to his legs and it was obvious that his racing career was at an end. As Cliff expressed it:

'I enjoyed racing. It was a wonderful time, not just the racing, but the whole circus. It's great when you start from the bottom, going up a step, up a step, but it's a nasty thing when you dive off the top.'

After he retired from racing, he buried himself in work in the family business. Many years later, Cliff's sons took over the running of the business. Cliff was a tall, powerful man who always seemed very fit, and gave the impression that he would outlive many of his peers. It was a terrible, unexpected blow to family and friends when he died of a massive heart attack at the age of 73.

Almondo, Mario

Technical Director
Born: 17 September 1964 (Turin, Italy)

After studying engineering and industrial management at the Politecnico di Milano until 1989, Almondo spent time as a lecturer, and followed this with his military service in the Carabinieri before joining Ferrari in 1991. After working for two years in the production car division, he was appointed Organisational and Personnel Manager 1993–4, Production and Quality Manager 1994–2000, and thereafter Racing Industrial Director/Engineer. In 2005 Almondo became Chief of Operations in the Motor Sport Division, and then Technical Director of the Motor Sport Division and Technical Director of the Formula 1 team in November 2006, following Ross Brawn's decision to leave Ferrari. Almondo became Operations Director in November 2007.

Below: *After Ross Brawn left Ferrari in 2006, his role as Technical Director was assumed by Almondo, who had been a very promising member of the Ferrari F1 team for some years.* (LAT Photographic)

Amon, Chris

Works driver
Born: 20 July 1943 (Bulls, New Zealand)

Son of a very successful New Zealand sheep farmer, Chris was a driver of immense talent, but totally without luck and just about every decision he made proved to be a wrong one. Despite his great ability, like Jean Behra and Roy Salvadori, he failed to win a single World Championship GP. At the age of 18 he was racing an old 250F Maserati in local events, and when Reg Parnell was out in New Zealand in 1962–3 he was very impressed by Chris's driving and invited him to join Reg Parnell Racing in the UK.

During 1963, Chris raced Parnell's Lola 4A, a car introduced the previous year when it displayed considerable potential, but without the benefit of any substantial development since then. Chris's best performances were seventh places at Reims and Silverstone. He stayed with the team for 1964, driving Lotus 25s (with BRM engines in all races except Zeltweg where his car had a Climax) and his best result was a fifth place, a lap in arrears, at the Dutch race. Reg Parnell died that year and for a while the team, now managed by son Tim Parnell, was chaotic.

Chris had a couple of drives with the Parnell team in 1965, but he was spending most of his time with fellow-New Zealander Bruce McLaren's young team. He raced McLaren Group 7 American-engined sports cars in 1965 and learned a great deal about controlling heavy, very fast cars. Plans for him to drive Ford-powered F1 cars in 1966 fell apart because of a shortage of engines, and so did a deal to race Cooper-Maseratis after John Surtees joined that team in mid-season. He finished eighth with a Cooper at Reims. He continued to race McLaren sports cars that year and he shared a victory drive with Bruce McLaren in a 7-litre Mark II Ford at Le Mans.

Ferrari signed Chris up for 1967, and the three years he was with the Maranello team were both very successful and immensely frustrating. The first year started well as, co-driving with Lorenzo Bandini, he won the Daytona 24 Hours and Monza 1,000km races. The Commendatore was delighted, but disaster struck when Bandini crashed at Monaco, suffering bad burns and a painful, lingering death. Enzo Ferrari, and Amon, and just about everyone else were devastated. Further serious problems followed, for Parkes crashed heavily at Spa, breaking both legs, while Scarfiotti picked a row with Ferrari management after the Belgian race and quit the F1 team.

Chris finished third at Monaco, fourth at Zandvoort, and third at Spa. As the sole works F1 driver, a massive burden fell on his shoulders, and although the V12 Ferrari was reasonably fast and reliable, it was not the best car on the grid. He retired in the French GP, but he took third place at Silverstone. He had retired his P4 Ferrari at Le Mans following a puncture out on the circuit, but he and Stewart drove a P4 into second place behind a Chaparral in the BOAC 500 race at Brands Hatch at the end of July. He finished third in the German race and sixth in Canada. Nothing was achieved in the last three races, but he was placed fourth in the Drivers' Championship.

Young Jacky Ickx joined the Ferrari team for 1968, and it gained fairly consistent success in the early part of the season – Ickx's win in the wet French GP was especially pleasing – although the cars still lacked a

Below: *Young New Zealand driver Chris Amon had immense talent, but his racing career was destroyed by a combination of poor judgement and bad luck. He joined Ferrari for 1967 and scored most of Ferrari's successes over the next three seasons. By 1969 he was thoroughly disenchanted by the performance of the obsolete V12 cars, and left the team to drive for March in 1970, instead of waiting for the latest flat-12 Ferrari 312B which was very successful that year.* (Klemantaski Collection)

Above: *At the 1968 British GP at Brands Hatch there was a tremendous fight between winner Jo Siffert and Ferrari drivers Chris Amon and Jacky Ickx. At the finish, Amon (seen here with his V12 Tipo 312) was 4.4sec behind the winner.* (Tom March Collection)

sufficiently competitive edge. Chris finished second in the British GP after battling with race-winner Siffert for the lead. As the season progressed, so the cars became less reliable, and Ickx crashed in practice for the Canadian GP, breaking a leg. By the 1969 season Chris was becoming disenchanted with Ferrari, increasingly so as hopes that the new 312B flat-12 F1 car would be ready to race that year faded.

Amon still fought hard, and at the Spanish race on the Montjuich Park circuit at Barcelona in May he took the lead after the works Lotus 49s crashed because of aerofoil failure, and he stayed in front convincingly until the engine broke late in the race. This failure handed victory to Jackie Stewart with his Ford-powered Matra MS80. For this race the Ferrari engineers had built a couple of special engines with revised camshafts and titanium connecting rods.

Chris held second place at Monaco until the differential failed on lap 17, but he achieved a good third place in the Dutch race with a car that had proved surprisingly durable, and in describing his performance in the French race at Clermont-Ferrand Chris said: 'I was screaming the guts out of it when a piston blew.' He

retired in the British GP and did not race again for the Ferrari team that year.

In 1969 Ferrari had also competed in Sports Prototype racing with the V12 312P cars, which were strikingly handsome and handled beautifully, but once again the problems were lack of sufficient power and reliability. The 312P made its debut at Sebring where Chris was partnered by Mario Andretti. They finished second after delays caused by debris from the wrecked tail of a Chevron being sucked into the air intake, causing overheating and an air lock.

Amon/Rodriguez finished fourth in the BOAC 500 race at Brands Hatch after they had been delayed by a puncture, and the car lost speed during the race because of a stretched throttle cable. At Monza, Chris again shared a 312P with Mario, but again delays were caused by a puncture and the engine blew up with Amon at the wheel when they were in fourth place. When he got back to the pits, he shouted at Mauro Forghieri, 'Why can't you build me an engine that lasts?'

Amon missed the Spa race because he was unwell, but he was back at the wheel of a 312P with Rodriguez at the Nürburgring. After holding second place, they dropped back to fourth, but further delays were caused by a front-wheel vibration. When he rejoined the race, he was really angry and wound up and set an outright circuit record. Then the engine stopped because of electrical problems. Chris opened the bonnet, investigated the problem and restarted the engine, only for it to cut out again after only a short distance. He shared a coupé version at Le Mans, but on the first lap he collided with the burning fuel tank from Woolfe's crashed Porsche 917.

Chris commented:

'The 312P was a car that promised much, but didn't ever really quite deliver. I think that, as much as anything, it was a victim of the chaos that was Ferrari at the time. In comparison to the Porsche 908, I felt that the Ferrari was the better car, but it lacked power. I think that we were also quite unlucky in 1969; there is no question that Mario and I would have won at Sebring had it not been for the problem with the debris. Equally, I think that we could have won at Monza had the engine stayed together. The same could be said of the two races that I did with Pedro Rodriguez – I think that we were in a position to win both had it not been for the problems that intervened.'

He had spent the whole season complaining about the lack of power and reliability of the V12 engine, and as for the long-awaited new car he said:

'Every time I drove that flat-12, the thing flew to pieces. It's not as though there were minor failures either … it was either blowing pistons or breaking its crankshaft. I thought to myself, "God, I can't stand any more of this."'

The 312B failed to appear in the Italian GP, and in this race an old V12 was driven by Pedro Rodriguez who took sixth place. Chris had left for pastures new.

For 1970, Chris joined the new March team and, although the March 701 was no match for either the Ferrari 312B flat-12 or the Lotus 72 (once teething problems had been resolved with both cars), he took second places at Spa and Clermont-Ferrand, but the real problem was the failure of March to pay him. He drove 512S Ferraris at Brands Hatch and the Nürburgring without success in 1970, although all the Ferrari team, including Mauro Forghieri and the 'Old Man' felt that he had come home.

Chris joined Matra for 1971, and a win in the two-part Argentine GP at the beginning of the first year of his two-year contract gave a very misleading impression of future performances. There were occasions when the Matra V12s showed great promise, but misfortune struck. Chris was leading the Italian GP at Monza in 1971, and the high-screeching V12 was running perfectly, but he lost his visor and, after a pit stop, finished sixth. His best performance that year was third in the Spanish race at Montjuich Park.

In 1972 he was leading the French GP at Clermont-Ferrand when his Matra punctured a tyre and he finished third after a pit stop for a wheel-change. Matra withdrew from racing at the end of the year and Chris signed up for March, but because of a disagreement he left the team before the 1973 season started. With his career entering a downward spiral, he drove for the Tecno team, which was a waste of his talents. In late 1973, Chris drove for Tyrrell in the Canadian GP, but finished at the tail of the field in tenth place because of tyre trouble. He was to have driven again for Tyrrell at Watkins Glen, but the team withdrew after Cevert's fatal crash in practice.

With substantial backing from John Dalton, Amon had formed a team to race a F1 car bearing his name. The design was over-complex and the car appeared at only four races. Poor Chris retired in Spain, failed to start at Monaco because of hub failure in practice, and failed to qualify in Germany and Italy. He drove BRMs in Canada and the United States without success. There were no drives in 1975 until late in the year when he was offered drives in Mo Nunn's Ensign team in Austria and Italy. On Amon's notorious bad luck, Andretti commented, 'I tell ya, if Amon became an undertaker, people would stop dying.'

Chris signed up with Ensign for 1976, and although the latest N176 car was fairly swift and very sweet-handling, it was prone to structural failures; as a result of these he crashed twice. He withdrew from the team and, after a practice accident with a Wolf-entered Williams in Canada, he retired from racing. He returned to New Zealand to manage the family farm and to marry his second wife – poor Chris was not lucky in marriage either. But he is regarded at Maranello as one of the very real and true members of the Ferrari team.

Anderloni, Felice Bianchi

Coachbuilder (founder of Touring)
Born: 1882 (Rome, Italy)
Died: 3 June 1948 (Milan, Italy)

Brought up in Milan, Anderloni had family connections with Isotta Fraschini and worked for them from about 1906. He left Isotta in 1925 and, with a friend, Gaetano Ponzoni, bought a small company known as Carrozzeria Falco that specialised in the construction of

Above: *Felice Anderloni built up Carrozzeria Touring into one of the greatest and most inspired of Italian coachbuilders. The company built bodies on many early Ferrari chassis.* (James Trigwell)

light body framework. Anderloni changed the name of the company to Carrozzeria Touring not long after his acquisition.

The name 'Touring' followed an Italian fashion at the time for adopting English names for even the most basic products, such as washing powder and floor polish. Interestingly, during Mussolini's dictatorship, Anglomania turned to Anglophobia and the company became known as Carrozzeria Turinga. It reverted to its old name after the collapse of Fascism, and added 'Superleggera'.

Carrozzeria Touring's success was founded on Alfa Romeo contracting with them to build bodies on the 6C 1500 and 6C 1750 chassis, and there was close rivalry between Touring and Zagato. Both built bodies of classic style, and while those made by Zagato were lighter, they were also far flimsier. By 1935, Touring had a separate section for the manufacture of bodies for industrial and military purposes. Later, the company expanded into the fabrication of aircraft components, notably light alloy welded seat frames.

Alfa Romeo car production was very small, so the bulk of Touring production was on rather staid and boring Bianchi and Fiat chassis, leavened by the delightful Lancias. Anderloni had been working on what he called the 'Superleggera' (extra-light) system of manufacture, and by 1937 this had been perfected. The system consisted of a framework of small-diameter steel tubing to which aluminium-alloy sheeting was attached by small wire clips that were bent round the tubing. The finest Touring bodies of the late 1930s were those built for the Alfa Romeo 8C 2900B cars entered in the 1938 Mille Miglia, and the superb aerodynamic bodies designed for the streamlined BMW 328s.

On Anderloni's death in 1948, his son Carlo Felice, who had worked with him for some while, took control. Business was difficult in early post-war days and, although Superleggera Touring built thousands of bodies on Alfa Romeo 1900 Sprint and Super Sprint chassis, margins were tight and profits small. Likewise, Touring built bodies on Ferrari chassis, but few were constructed and there was not much in the way of profit. Even so, Touring did steady business by taking on prototype work for Bristol and Aston Martin, and development work, coupled with a production run of 25 Italia cars, for Hudson.

Although no Ferrari had a Pininfarina body prior to 1953, this company secured a monopoly in building Ferrari bodies at the expense of the existing suppliers, notably Touring and Vignale. Carlo fought back, and in the early 1960s contracted with the Rootes Group to assemble its cars in quantity. These included the Sunbeam Alpine sports car (minus tail fins) and the Venezia, based on the Humber Sceptre chassis, but with a coupé body built in accordance with Superleggera principles.

The company had opened an additional factory and increased the workforce to around 220, but the Rootes cars were not a success – only 145 examples of the Venezia were built from 1963 onwards, and production ceased in 1965. By this time, Superleggera Touring was operating under administrative control pursuant to an order of the court in Milan made on 3 March 1964. The company secured a contract to build the bodies for the new Lamborghini of 1964 onwards, but the numbers were insufficient to save the company, which by 1966 had virtually ceased to trade.

A chemical group took over the Superleggera Touring premises in Milan and burnt most of the Touring drawings and artwork that, at the time, nobody wanted. Carlo Felice Anderloni joined Alfa Romeo as a design adviser and became responsible for styling, while many of the employees took jobs with Carrozzeria Marazzi, which built Maserati bodies, and in 2006 this concern acquired the rights to use the Superleggera Touring name.

Andretti, Mario

Works driver
Born: 28 February 1940 (Montona, Italy)

The Andretti family had the most difficult and humble of backgrounds, but collectively they are probably the most talented of all motor racing families. Mario and his twin brother Aldo were born to a farm manager and his wife in a part of Italy that was ceded to Yugoslavia after the Second World War and is now part of Croatia. The family moved in 1948 to a refugee camp in Lucca (Italy). They then emigrated to the United States where they settled in Nazareth, Pennsylvania. Mario's great hero was Alberto Ascari, and his great ambition was to emulate his hero's racing career.

After competing in sprints and midget car racing (winning the Midget Car Championship in 1964) and other American racing categories, he went on to win the Indianapolis 500-Mile race in 1969. Andretti was to prove exceptionally successful on both sides of the Atlantic. He first drove in F1 for Lotus in the 1968 United States GP, and raced three times for the team in 1969.

Andretti's greatest F1 racing successes were with Lotus, although he wanted to drive for Ferrari more often, and Enzo Ferrari wanted him to do so. The problem was that the 'Old Man' also wanted Andretti to live near the factory, so that he would be close by when needed. It seems that Ferrari had some sort of desire to control Andretti, probably because of his Italian background. He had certainly not taken this attitude, for example, with Cliff Allison, who lived in England and flew to Italy when he was needed.

During 1970 Mario drove a March 701 entered by the STP Corporation in F1, but he crashed heavily and wrecked the car in Austria. By 1971 he agreed with Ferrari to drive for the F1 team when his USAC commitments permitted, and although appearing in only seven races he won in South Africa and finished fourth at the Nürburgring, which was a pretty good effort. He drove for Ferrari in F1 again in a few races in 1972 and finished fourth in the South African Grand Prix. He was especially successful in Prototype racing and, co-driving with Ickx, won four events with flat-12 312PB 3-litre cars.

Mario concluded that he was stretching himself too much by competing in both American and European events. During 1973 he raced in F5000 and USAC with the Vel's Parnelli team in the United States. There was,

Above: *Over the years Mario Andretti proved that he was an exceptionally versatile driver. He drove for the Ferrari F1 team in 1970–1, but his best years in European-style GP racing were with Lotus. With the ground-effect 78 and 79 cars he won the Drivers' Championship in 1978.* (sutton-images.com)

however, no escaping the lure of F1, and from late 1973 through to early 1976 the Parnelli team competed in F1 with cars designed by Maurice Phillipe. These showed strong Lotus influence and Phillipe had, of course, designed the Lotus 72. The Parnelli team contested 16 F1 races during that time, with best performances by Andretti being fourth in Sweden and fifth in the French race in 1975. It had been a great waste of talent and money.

Andretti drove for Team Lotus from 1976 through to 1979 and enjoyed great success at a time of, initially, Lotus revival followed by triumph and decline – an almost inevitable cycle in F1. At the end of 1976 Andretti won the Japanese GP; he won four races in 1977 and finished third in the Drivers' Championship that year; then he won six races and the Championship with the supremely successful ground-effect Lotus 79 in 1978. Inevitably, triumph led to gloom, and Andretti stayed with Lotus for two more seasons without winning a single race.

In 1981 Mario signed for the Alfa Romeo team, and another year of failure ensued. After disaster struck Ferrari in 1982, with the death of Villeneuve and the serious injuries that put Pironi out of racing, he returned to the Ferrari team at Monza (where he drove very well to finish third) and at Las Vegas. Son Michael had started racing in 1980, and now Mario concentrated on Indy Car racing. By his last season in 1994 he had started 407 Indy Car races, taken 66 pole positions, and won 52 Indy races. He was one of the most successful drivers of all time.

Angelis, Elio de

Driver
Born: 26 March 1958 (Rome, Italy)
Died: 15 May 1986 (Marseille hospital, France)

The son of a wealthy powerboat racer, de Angelis made his career through karts and F3 to F2 in which he was racing a Ferrari-powered Ralt in 1978. The works Ferrari team was becoming increasingly concerned by the number of crashes that Villeneuve was having. Elio was invited to test-drive for Ferrari, and in all he covered about 1,000km at Fiorano. He later commented:

'I had no experience with F1 cars at the time, but I thought that the 312T3 was a good, conventional car, with excellent brakes.
    I also drove the 512BB built for Le Mans, but it seemed to me that it was a bit of a joke. The engine was good, but I was not impressed with the handling, and the brakes were finished after a dozen laps, let alone 24 hours. The 'Old Man' said to me, "If Villeneuve crashes again, the drive is yours."'

It was at this point that Villeneuve, who had no official knowledge (and maybe no knowledge at all) of plans to get rid of him, stopped having accidents and started achieving results.
    Elio de Angelis drove for Shadow in 1979, and for the Lotus team from 1980 to 1985, winning only two races. He joined Brabham for 1986, but, maybe because of structural failure, his car lost a wheel during routine testing at the Paul Ricard circuit in May 1986 and he received fatal injuries. Elio was immensely popular and it was a dreadful blow to the whole motor racing world.

Arcangeli, Luigi

Scuderia Ferrari driver
Born: 1902 (Forli, Italy)
Died: 23 May 1931 (Monza)

Arcangeli was a very experienced racing motorcycle rider and driver. In 1928 he won the Circuit of Senigallia with a Bugatti, and the following year he drove an OM without success in the Mille Miglia. He was a works Maserati driver in 1930, and he scored a number of successes that included 2nd Tripoli GP (Tipo 26B 2-litre), 1st Rome GP (8C-2500), and 2nd Monza GP (8C-2500). He signed up to drive for Scuderia Ferrari in 1931 and was killed with the twin-engined Tipo A in practice for the Italian GP. Peter Hull reminded us that his mother said of him affectionately in a Forlinese dialect, 'L'è un bon ragazzol, ma l'è matt da ligàr.' ('He's a fine lad, but he's crazy and ought to be locked up.')

Arnoux, René

Works driver
Born: 4 July 1948 (Pontcharra, near Grenoble, France)

During his early racing career Arnoux showed phenomenal potential, and like many whose potential is not fully realised, he became embittered and sour. The win of a Shell Volant award set him up in Formule Renault, but he had the opportunity to switch to the Elf team in 1974 and raced their Formula 2 car. Arnoux took an impressive fourth place at Nogaro on his debut with the Elf team; the following year he won the Formule Super Renault Championship; and in 1976 he drove for a full season for Elf in Formula 2, scoring three wins, but losing out in the Championship to Jean-Pierre Jabouille. The year after that he again won three races and took the Formula 2 Championship.
    The French Martini team moved up into Formula 1 in 1978, and Arnoux was an obvious choice of driver. The team had built a neat Cosworth/Ford DFV-powered car, but it was uncompetitive and its fate was inevitable in the highly sophisticated ground-effect era in which the team lacked the technology to compete. Arnoux finished ninth twice, but after eight races the team withdrew and Arnoux finished the year with two drives for Surtees. Then Renault, pioneers of the turbocharged

Above: *Arnoux was a driver of great talent, but was always somewhat inconsistent. He drove for Ferrari in 1983–4, but then, after a hopeless performance in the Brazilian race at the beginning of 1985, he split with the team fairly amicably. He joined Ligier in 1986 and stayed with them until the end of the 1989 season.* (LAT Photographic)

Formula 1 car that they had first introduced in 1977, offered Arnoux a drive for 1979.

He was to spend four seasons with Renault, and after two second places in 1979, Arnoux won two successive races – Interlagos and Kyalami – early in the 1980 season. As the season progressed, the Renaults lost their competitive edge, and prospects of a really good year evaporated, apart from a second place at Zandvoort. Prost joined Renault for 1981 and Arnoux was overshadowed. His last year with Renault in 1982 produced two race wins, one of which was highly controversial. Arnoux won the French GP that year, allegedly against team orders, and the atmosphere in the team made it obvious that Renault would not be renewing his contract.

Arnoux joined Patrick Tambay at Ferrari for 1983. He made an immediate and forceful impression with the team, and won three Grands Prix – Montreal, Hockenheim, and Zandvoort. It was not good enough, and he took third place in the Championship with 49 points to the 59 of winner Piquet (Brabham) and Prost (Renault). By 1984 it was clear that Arnoux's days at the top of the ladder were over; his performances were increasingly erratic, and his best performance was a brilliant drive to second place at Dallas after starting from the back of the grid.

He was still with Ferrari at the beginning of 1985, and finished fourth in Brazil. It was obvious that there was no longer a place for him in the team, and Ferrari did what they should have done at the end of 1984: they bought him off and brought in Johansson. It seemed that Arnoux's Formula 1 career was over, but after being out of racing for the remainder of 1985, he joined Ligier and stayed with them for four seasons. His generally erratic behaviour and inconsistent performances caused friction, and he failed to win a single race.

Because of René's criticisms in the press of the engine that Ligier was to use in 1987, Alfa Romeo withdrew its availability. Ligier was in decline and Arnoux did nothing to stop the rot. He and Ligier finally parted company at the end of 1989. He returned to racing to co-drive a Dodge Viper to 12th place at Le Mans in 1994, and then reappeared at the wheel of a Ferrari 333SP in 1995. He spent a lot of time acting as coach to Brazilian Pedro Diniz (his money was a multiple of his talent) and he did some work on Italian TV. He owns a number of kart tracks. Latterly he has been competing in Supertourisme, GT, and GPM racing.

Ascari, Alberto

Works driver
Born: 13 July 1918 (Milan, Italy)
Died: 26 May 1955 (Monza)

Ascari's life was overshadowed by the career and death of his father, Antonio, one of the great Italian drivers of the 1920s. Alberto was only seven when his father, a works Alfa Romeo driver, was killed in the 1925 French GP at Montlhéry. When he was 19, young Alberto, a big, strong lad for his age, began racing Bianchi motorcycles, but he soon moved on to a Maserati 6CM Voiturette and, partnered by cousin Giovanni Minozzi, he drove one of the Ferrari-built AutoAvio Tipo 815 sports cars in the 1940 Mille Miglia. They led their class until the Tipo 815 succumbed to mechanical problems at the end of the first lap.

During the Second World War, Ascari and Villoresi ran a transport business, and this kept Ascari out of the Italian army. By the end of the war he was decidedly beefy in a very muscular way, and he was always a driver of great stamina and resilience. Count 'Johnny' Lurani headed Scuderia Ambrosiana and had close ties with

Above: *This superb cockpit shot of Alberto Ascari was taken by Guy Griffiths during the International Trophy race at Silverstone in August 1949. He drove a good race with this works Ferrari Tipo 125 to win from Farina (Scuderia Milano Maserati) and Villoresi (works Ferrari).* (Guy Griffiths Collection)

the Maserati works. Luigi Villoresi, who became Alberto's friend and mentor, took Ascari with him when he agreed to drive GP Maseratis for Ambrosiana, and sports cars for the works. In 1948 Ascari had a particularly successful season, with a win from Villoresi in the San Remo GP, second to Villoresi in the British race, and third place with a 158 Alfetta in the French GP following a one-off invitation from Alfa Romeo.

At the beginning of 1949, Scuderia Ambrosiana contested the Formule Libre races held annually in Argentina, and Ascari won the first of these from team-mate Villoresi. Both drivers had signed up to appear for Ferrari once the European racing season started, but Ferrari struggled badly during its first three years in F1. Alfa Romeo had withdrawn from racing for 1949, wrongly expecting that the opposition would be too strong. Even so, the original short-wheelbase, supercharged 1500cc Ferraris fell far short of the

superiority expected of them, and they were barely a match for the overweight, underpowered 4500cc Talbot-Lagos that were blessed with very low fuel consumption and negligible tyre wear.

During 1949, Ascari was third in Belgium (behind Rosier, with a Talbot, and Villoresi); he won the Swiss race at Bremgarten from Villoresi (Sommer was third with a Talbot); he retired in the Dutch race; won the International Trophy at Silverstone; and finished second at Lausanne behind Farina (Maserati). Then, at Monza, the Ferrari team introduced an improved GP car with longer wheelbase and twin-stage supercharging. Ascari won the Italian GP with one of the new cars, but their advantage was short-lived, for Alfa Romeo returned to GP racing in 1950.

The next two years saw a fierce battle in which Alfa Romeo retained its dominance through to the 1951 British GP. Ferrari, acting on the advice of Aurelio Lampredi, concluded that he could never beat Alfa Romeo with supercharged cars, but the outcome could be very different if he followed the alternative offered by the GP formula: a 4500cc car could be as powerful as the Alfa Romeo 158, but with the advantages enjoyed by the underpowered Talbots, low tyre wear and fuel consumption.

So 1950 proved a year of experimentation and

development for Maranello, with a succession of poor performances succeeded by a very encouraging result in the Italian GP. The Alfa Romeos were immensely overdeveloped twin-stage supercharged anachronisms, with a gross power output of around 250bhp per litre, incredibly thirsty, often stopping to refuel twice during a race, and so very dependent on the durability of their Pirelli tyres. It was very difficult for Ferrari to match the Alfa Romeos on lap times, and the real Ferrari advantage was to lie in the saving of time in the pits.

At the beginning of the year, the Ferrari team ran supercharged 2000cc V12 cars in the Argentine Temporada races, and Ascari won just one of the three races, the General San Martin Trophy at Mar del Plata. In Europe, Ascari raced Ferrari F2 cars with some success, he struggled in GP racing with the twin-stage supercharged cars, and then raced the new unblown cars as they appeared. Retirements at Pau and San Remo were followed by a second place at Monaco (Fangio won for Alfa Romeo), retirement at Bremgarten, and then a fifth with the first of the unsupercharged cars, a 3.3-litre model, at Spa-Francorchamps.

Ferrari raced the first cars with unblown 4498cc engines at the Italian GP. Ascari blew up his engine while struggling to stay with the Alfa Romeos, and walked back to the pits to take over the 4498cc car

driven by Ferrari tester Dorino Serafini. Serafini was in sixth place, and despite gear-change problems Ascari brought this car through to finish second, just over 1min 18sec behind Farina. Ferrari had the low tyre wear and low fuel consumption needed for victory, but was still short of power. The last race in 1950 was the Penya Rhin GP at Barcelona. In the absence of the Alfa Romeos, Ascari won easily from Serafini – both Ferrari drivers were at the wheel of 4.5-litre cars.

Alfa Romeo had the more powerful Tipo 159 in 1951, but Ferrari responded with new twin-plug cylinder heads that, along with other changes, boosted power output by 50bhp. Ascari won the minor San Remo race in April with a single-plug car, and the first twin-plug cars ran in the Swiss GP at Bremgarten. It was a very wet race and Ascari, feeling unwell, finished sixth. Fangio

Above: *The Ferrari team at the 1951 Italian GP at Monza. Ascari, at the wheel of his Tipo 375 Formula 1 car, is pushed out, while work continues on González's car nearer the camera. This is a practice photograph, as Ascari is at the wheel of a single-plug car (identifiable by the evenly spaced exhaust pipes), and he drove a twin-plug car in the race. González's car has a twin-plug engine (identifiable by the pairing of the exhaust pipes) and the latest, higher Plexiglas aero-screen. Ascari and Villoresi took the first two places with their 375s, and González finished fourth. (Author's collection)*

Below: *Ascari with his four-cylinder 2-litre Tipo 500 Ferrari leads in the closing laps of the 1953 Italian GP at Monza. Behind him is Onofre Marimon (Maserati A6GCM), who was many laps behind after two pit stops, Nino Farina (Ferrari) and, a little further behind, Fangio (Maserati A6GCM). The race had a very dramatic finish. Ascari, who had dominated that year's World Championship, spun at the last corner, he was rammed by Marimon, Farina took to the grass to avoid a collision, and Fangio slipped though to score his only Championship race win of the year. (Author's collection)*

won the race from Taruffi (Ferrari) and Farina. Next on the calendar was the Belgian GP on the very fast Spa-Francorchamps circuit, and in this race Ascari was pretty well beaten before he started.

Changes to the track had made the circuit faster, which suited Alfa Romeo more than Ferrari, and lap speeds were now pushing 118/120mph (190/193kph). Also, the length of the race had been increased slightly to 315 miles (507km). This meant that the Ferrari needed to make an extra refuelling stop, while Alfa Romeo used supplementary fuel tanks so that they could scrape by with only one stop. The Alfa Romeos proved, as expected, faster than the Ferraris, and Farina and Fangio led from Ascari and Villoresi. Fangio lost 15min in the pits because a wheel jammed on the hub spline, and Ascari finished second, nearly three minutes behind Farina.

Reims was another very fast circuit that suited the Alfa Romeos, but both teams had mechanical problems and there were driver swaps as the slower drivers handed their cars over to the team-leaders. Initially, Ascari tigered with Fangio, but the Ferrari driver retired early in the race because of gearbox failure. Fangio was slowed by magneto trouble and he took over Fagioli's car when the third member of the Alfa Romeo team made a routine stop. New to the Ferrari team at this race was Argentinian Froilán González, and when he made a routine stop, his car was taken over by Ascari. At the end of this long, hard, and very hot race Fangio won from Ascari by a margin of just under a minute.

Silverstone, scene of the British GP – a bleak, characterless airfield perimeter road – made a grim contrast with the two previous races on European road circuits. Ascari retired his Ferrari because of gearbox trouble, but González, at the wheel of a single-plug Ferrari, defeated the might of Alfa Romeo and led Fangio across the finishing line by a margin of 50sec. González had offered his car to his team-leader, but Ascari had declined. Alfa Romeo's reign was ending: Ascari won the German GP at the Nürburgring and the Italian GP at Monza.

The last Championship race of the season was the Spanish GP at Barcelona. The Ferraris were plagued by tyre problems caused by the mistaken choice of 16in instead of the 17in covers used at most races during the year. Fangio won the race (and the World Championship), with González second, and Ascari a poor fourth. After this race Alfa Romeo announced their withdrawal from GP racing.

Ascari and Villoresi remained with Ferrari for another two seasons. It was only too obvious that there would be no serious opposition to the Ferraris in Formula 1, so the decision was made that World Championship

races – and many others – would be held to 2000cc unsupercharged F2 regulations until the commencement of a new 2500cc GP formula in 1954. Ferrari should have been strongly challenged by Maserati, but the effort from this team faded after team-leader Fangio crashed heavily in the Autodromo GP at Monza.

No other driver matched Ascari's performance in GP racing during 1952–3. He missed the Swiss GP because he competed at Indianapolis (where he retired), but he then won the remaining six rounds of the Drivers' Championship in 1952 and the first three rounds of the Drivers' Championship in 1953. With wins later in 1953 in the Swiss and British races, he won the Drivers' Championship in both years. In addition, he won four minor F2 races in 1952, plus wins in 1953 F2 races at Pau and Bordeaux. He set a new lap record at Le Mans and, partnered by Farina, he won the first Nürburgring 1,000km race in 1953.

It was gradually becoming obvious that, despite achieving so much in 1953, the Ferrari team was losing its sense of direction through its complete reliance, in single-seater racing, on a four-cylinder design that was becoming obsolete. Lancia were developing a new V8 Formula 1 car, typed the D50, and the Turin company offered Ascari and Villoresi exceedingly generous terms to join them. This they did, but the new car did not appear until the Spanish race in October, by which time it was still far from fully developed.

Ascari drove for Maserati in the French and British Grands Prix, and raced a works Ferrari at Monza. In 1951–3 Ascari possessed sheer brilliance, but his driving in 1954, with two exceptions, seemed brutally harsh on the car, and completely lacked inspiration. At Monza, his job was not to drive within the limits of his cars, but to beat Mercedes-Benz or break his car in his efforts. He did precisely what was asked of him.

It was the Mille Miglia that showed Ascari still possessed real greatness. He had, in fact, refused to drive in the road race following an accident in 1951 when he had gone off the road and killed a spectator. He claimed that a spectator had temporarily blinded him by shining a powerful flashlight on the Ferrari to read the number. There is no reason to disbelieve this. The race was specifically excluded from his contract, but he agreed to drive a Lancia D24 3.3-litre car in the 1954 race after Villoresi had been injured in an accident during training.

That the D24 was a beautifully balanced car, with power characteristics in complete harmony with the superb handling, is undoubted. The big 4.9-litre Ferraris fell by the wayside, and Ascari's Lancia was the only D24

Above: *After Ascari left Ferrari at the end of the 1953 season, almost a year elapsed before he first raced the new D50 Lancia. Ascari is seen in the Spanish Grand Prix in October 1954. He took pole position in practice, went into the lead on lap three, and then led for three laps before falling out of contention because of clutch failure.* (Author's collection)

to survive the race. It was the most gruelling, stressful race in his career, and he won by a margin of a little over half an hour from Vittorio Marzotto (works Ferrari Mondial 2-litre).

Ascari retired his Lancia D50 early in the Spanish GP, and the first few races of 1955 made it only too obvious that this V8 GP contender needed a great deal more development. This suited Ascari admirably, for he wanted neither a car with which he could win with consummate ease, nor to fight for victory against unreasonable odds. With the D50 he played a pivotal role in the development of a world-beater. The cars failed in the Argentine GP, in which Ascari led until he spun off on wet tar, and the team missed the Formule Libre Buenos Aires City GP, returning to Italy to continue development.

Lancia competed in three non-Championship races before the start of the main European season. Ascari was leading at Pau when a brake pipe broke, and after a pit stop he rejoined the race to finish fifth. He won at both Turin and Naples. The first round of the World Championship in Europe was the Monaco GP, and the race had all the prospects of a serious, straight fight between Mercedes-Benz and Lancia. Fangio (Mercedes-Benz) and Ascari were joint fastest in practice. All three Mercedes-Benz retired, and when Ascari took the lead from Moss, 19 laps from the finish, he would not know he was leading until he received a signal from the pits as he crossed the finishing line.

Brake trouble had plagued the Lancias throughout the race, and on that same lap, as he braked for the chicane, the brakes locked up and he ploughed through the barriers into the harbour. His blue crash helmet bobbed to the surface and he was rescued, apparently completely unharmed. Four days later Ascari was dead, killed in a practice accident at Monza, probably caused by a tyre coming off the rim, and the rim digging into the road surface. Ascari was known worldwide, and even in Britain newspaper sellers displayed posters reading 'Ascari killed'. He was a great loss in a terrible year.

Ascari, Antonio

Driver, Alfa Romeo

Born: 15 September 1888 (Bonferraro, near Mantua, Italy)

Died: 26 July 1925 (Montlhéry, Paris, France)

Son of a corn dealer, Antonio started racing in 1919 with a modified 1914 Fiat. He crashed in that year's Targa Florio (in which Enzo Ferrari also competed). In this race, so very important at an Italian national level, he again retired in 1920 (by which time he was a member of the works Alfa Romeo team), and again in 1921, but he took fourth in 1922. The following year he drove his Alfa Romeo to second place behind team-mate Sivocci in the Targa Florio, and he also won that year's Circuit of Cremona with a 3-litre car based on the Merosi-designed production RLS model.

In the 1924 Targa Florio race, Ascari had Ramponi as riding mechanic in his 3.6-litre Alfa Romeo, but the engine seized shortly before the finish, and the car was pushed across the finishing line to take second place. In this race it was fair enough for the driver and mechanic

Above: *This photograph was taken at the 1924 Italian GP just won by Antonio Ascari with the Jano-designed, Fiat-inspired Alfa Romeo P2. Ascari is second from the right. On the left is young Giulio Ramponi, who looks so very serious in every photograph, then an unidentified man in a cap, baby Alberto Ascari held by his mother, and next to Antonio Ascari is Nicola Romeo. Romeo's moustache was quite outstanding and – by today's fashions – decidedly unpleasant.* (**Tom March Collection**)

to push the car over the line, but spectators and soldiers helped, so Ascari was disqualified.

That year, Ascari was also racing the new Jano-designed, Fiat-derived P2 GP car, and on 9 June, for the second successive year, he won the Circuit of Cremona, a 200-mile (320km) race in which the team faced little opposition. In the words of Peter Hull, 'The race was an absolute walk-over for him'; he won at an average speed of 98.31mph (158.18kph), well ahead of Marconcini's Chiribiri and Malinverni's Bugatti. Five days later, partnered by Attilio Marinoni, he finished second with an RLS in the 24-hour Night GP (Gran Premio del Notte) at Monza behind a German NAG driven by Riecken/Berthold.

In August, Antonio drove a P2, with Ramponi as

mechanic, in the European GP at Lyon. They were leading from team-mate Campari and two of the V12 Delages, but, as in the Targa Florio, the engine of his car began to seize up, and he pulled into the pits. It would not start, either on the handle or being pushed, and water was running out of the exhaust pipe. They were 28 miles (45km) from the finish in this 500-mile (805km) race. After their retirement, Campari went on to win the race, the first time that a manufacturer had won in his very first GP (Cremona was not a GP, of course). In October, by way of consolation, Ascari won the Italian GP at Monza, and the team took the first four places in the absence of serious opposition.

Ascari's first race in 1925 – and that of the P2s – was at the end of June when three cars ran in the European GP at Spa. The race proved a fiasco because the complete Delage team retired through the engineers having failed to install blow-off valves in the supercharger inlet system, resulting in the build-up of pressure causing the inlet valves to stay open and hit the exhaust valves. This was the race in which it was said (and now denied) Jano invited Ascari and Campari to break off the race during a routine refuelling stop to have a five-minute meal, while the cars were cleaned and polished – to the hisses and jeers of the bored spectators. At the flag they were the only two finishers. It has been said that Giulio Ramponi always denied that this incident ever occurred.

The following month the team competed in the French GP held on the 7.7-mile (12.4km) permutation of the combined banked track and road circuit at Montlhéry, 'amid the purple heather and green trees of the St Eutrope plateau' (Hull). Ascari took the lead at the rolling start and he stayed in front for 169 miles (272km), over quarter-distance. Light rain had begun to fall, but Ascari did not abate his speed and at the long left-hand bend at the end of the straight before les Biscornes, it was obvious that he was travelling too fast for the conditions. The P2 started to slide and it went off the road, tearing down around 300m of fencing before it hit soft ground and overturned.

Ascari was taken by ambulance to hospital, but he died on the way. The other Alfa Romeo drivers, Campari and Brilli Peri, were in the pits when the news of Ascari's death filtered back. The order was given to rev up the engines and then shut them off. Following the withdrawal of the Alfa Romeos, the V12 Delage of Benoist/Divo won the race. Seen in many P2 photographs of the period is a young boy, obviously cosseted and doted on; this is Antonio's young son Alberto who was to win the World Championship in 1952–3 and was killed during practice with a Ferrari sports car at Monza in 1955.

Attwood, Richard

Driver for Maranello Concessionaires
Born: 4 April 1940 (Wolverhampton, England)

Apprenticed at Jaguar, Richard 'Dickie' Attwood (he dislikes being referred to as 'Dickie') first raced in 1960, and then in 1961 joined the Midland Racing Partnership to race Lola cars, which he did with considerable success. His best result was a win in the FJ race at the 1963 Monaco GP meeting. He shared the new Lola GT

Below: *Although Richard Attwood was never a works driver, he drove frequently and successfully for Maranello Concessionaires, and was a regular partner of David Piper, especially with Piper's 250LM.* **(LAT Photographic)**

with David Hobbs at Le Mans, and they ran well until Hobbs missed a gear and broke the engine. Attwood won the first Grovewood award that year, and in 1964 he joined the BRM team, but it was mainly a testing contract.

With Lola in 1964 F2 races, he won at Vienna and finished second at Pau, in the Eifelrennen, and at Albi. Poor Attwood raced for BRM only once, in the *News of the World*-sponsored Richmond Trophy at Goodwood on Easter Monday in which he finished fourth. He qualified the 4wd BRM P67 for the British GP at Brands Hatch, but the team decided not to race the car because it was purely experimental and unlikely to make a good impression. Attwood was a member of the works Ford GT40 that year, but the car he was sharing with Jo Schlesser retired at Le Mans because of a broken fuel line, and they were eliminated at Reims because of gearbox problems.

In 1965 he drove for Tim Parnell's private team, but their Lotus 25s with BRM V8 engines were uncompetitive. Through steady, sensible driving Richard took sixth places (and single points) in the Italian and Mexican races. He also took second place with a Lola to Clark (Lotus) in the F2 Pau GP, and won the Rome GP on the Vallelunga circuit.

At the end of the year he co-drove David Piper's Ferrari 365P2 in the Kyalami Nine Hours race. It was quite a sensational victory because Piper and Attwood had spent much of the race catching the lead Ford GT40 of Peter Sutcliffe/Innes Ireland. Half an hour before the finish, Sutcliffe (at the wheel of the GT40) slowed down because of what he suspected was wheel-bearing failure, but proved to be a wire-spoked wheel that was breaking up. Attwood pulled ahead ten minutes before the chequered flag to win by a very narrow margin. At the finish the Ferrari was almost out of fuel, and one of the rear tyres was through to the canvas.

Richard was a member of the BRM team in the Tasman Series at the beginning of 1966, and he won the Levin race. He drove in F2, but he was now appearing regularly at the wheel of Ferraris entered by Maranello Concessionaires, and at the end of the year he and Piper again won the Kyalami Nine Hours race. He drove again in the Tasman Series in 1967, as well as appearing for Maranello Concessionaires.

At Le Mans in 1968, David Piper offered him a drive in his 250LM Ferrari. Richard always enjoyed driving with Piper, especially at the wheel of the 250LM, which he thought was a superb car, with an unbreakable engine. However, it was no longer a suitable car for Le Mans, as it was not sufficiently

powerful. Although they finished the race, it was not the most pleasant of races. Richard recalls:

'David's car was on wire wheels, but NART had entered a 250LM for Masten Gregory/Kolb, and this was running on smaller disc wheels.

They were much faster than us down the straight, because their car was cleaner through the air, and then we would pass them through the corners because we had better grip. We didn't need the wide tyres at Le Mans – we just needed top speed. It was so frustrating, and then in the middle of the night it began to rain heavily. I would cheerfully have retired, but David had never completed the Le Mans race and was determined to make it to the finish. They had to virtually drag me out of bed for my stint early on the Sunday. We did finish the race in seventh place, and all the other 250LMs retired.'

Richard's racing career was not going anywhere, although after Mike Spence's death in 1968 he was given a place in the BRM team. He took a brilliant second place at Monaco behind Graham Hill (Lotus), but this was a circuit on which he always fared well. His performances waned during the year and he was dropped from the team after the German GP. In 1969 Rindt crashed his Lotus heavily in the Spanish race because of aerofoil failure and was unable to drive at Monaco. So Lotus gave Richard a drive and he finished a more than respectable fourth on a circuit that he knew and liked so much.

Although his single-seater days ended when he drove Frank Williams's F2 Brabham BT30 to sixth place and a class second in the 1969 German GP, his career with sports cars was anything but on the wane. After a 'try-out' in the 1968 Watkins Glen Six Hours race in 1968, Richard was a member of the works Porsche team in 1969 and drove for it again in 1970 when it masqueraded under the colours of Porsche Salzburg. With Hans Herrmann he scored a superb victory at Le Mans in 1970.

That summer he drove the camera car during the making of the *Le Mans* film, and retired from racing in 1971 – but not before a number of appearances with the Gulf-Porsche team. He took second place with Herbert Müller at the wheel of a Gulf 917 at Le Mans in 1971, and he and Pedro Rodriguez co-drove the winning 917 in the Austrian 1,000km race. Notwithstanding his retirement from racing, Richard continues to compete in historic events, usually at the wheel of David Piper's 250LM.

Badoer, Luca

Test driver
Born: 25 January 1971 (Montebelluna, Treviso, Italy)

As a young man, Luca Badoer was brilliantly successful, but his great potential rapidly crumbled and disappeared. He was a karting champion, and at the age of 19 he won the final round of the Italian F3 Championship, beating the leading contenders. The following year, 1991, he accepted the advice that he should start the season gently, but then he won four F3 races in succession – although he was disqualified from the last of these because his car had been fitted with a tyre that had not been through scrutineering.

In 1992 he drove a F3000 Reynard, entered and superbly prepared by Team Crypton. He drove

Below: *Disappointment followed disappointment in the career of Luca Badoer. He was a Ferrari test driver in 1998, but was dropped by the team at the end of the year.* **(LAT Photographic)**

exceptionally well, winning three early rounds, but then he had a bad crash at Spa. Despite this, he returned to F3000, and a victory at Nogaro clinched the Championship. For the next few seasons he wasted his life with three hopeless F1 teams – BMS Scuderia Italia (racing Lolas in 1993), 1994 was a blank year after an unsuccessful winter test with Benetton, and in 1995 he rejoined F1 with Minardi where his best performance was ninth in the Hungarian GP. In 1996 his ambitions had sunk sufficiently to enable him to accept a place with the hopeless Fortis Corsa team, which collapsed in mid-season.

During the next 18 months his only race appearances were a couple of drives in a GT Lotus. In 1998, however, he was offered – and accepted – a position as Ferrari test driver. Being a test driver means so often that there is a barrier to further progress. It was another bad year for the young Italian because he broke a wrist in an accident at Fiorano, and when Schumacher broke a leg in a crash at Silverstone, he was passed over for a temporary place in the team.

Ferrari did not renew Badoer's contract at the end of the season, but he – very much against the odds – returned to F1 as a member of the floundering Minardi team. It was another bad year for Badoer, made worse by his retirement because of gearbox failure when he was holding fourth place in the 1999 European GP at the Nürburgring. He stayed with Minardi until the season ended at Suzuka, but it was also the end of his F1 career.

Baghetti, Giancarlo

Driver
Born: 25 December 1934 (Milan, Italy)
Died: 27 November 1995 (Milan)

By winning his first three F1 races, Baghetti became a legend in Ferrari (and F1) history, but as he admitted himself, with a wry smile, he would have been a really great hero if he had retired from racing at the end of his first season.

Baghetti's racing career started in 1956 with an Alfa Romeo 1900 saloon, and with a rather faster 1900TI version of this model he finished second in the 1958 Mille Miglia, held as a rally. Later, he competed in sports car racing, and in 1960 drove a front-engined Dagrada FJ car with a Lancia Appia V4 engine. By this time the British rear-engined Lotus 18s were dominating the FJ category, making all the front-engined contenders obsolete, but Baghetti showed considerable promise. At Monza, the

British opposition was not the strongest, and he won both his heat and the final. Later, in the face of strong British opposition, he finished third in his heat at Albi, and took fourth place in the final. At this time the Fiat-powered Osca front-engined car was the most successful Italian FJ car, and Baghetti was putting up good performances with inadequate equipment. Dagrada pulled out of FJ before the end of the 1960 season.

On the strength of his performances with an underpowered car, Baghetti was invited to drive a F1 Ferrari in 1961. This was a works car, with works backing, but it was the older version with the V6 rear-mounted engine having the cylinders at an angle of 65°. The car was entered later in the 1961 season by Scuderia Sant'Ambroeus, the private team run by Eugenio Dragoni, who became Racing Director of the Ferrari works team for 1962.

Scuderia Sant'Ambroeus was a member of an organisation known as Federazione Italiane Scuderie Automobilistiche (Federation of Italian Automobile Teams/FISA), one of whose aims was to encourage and help young Italian motor racing hopefuls, and this organisation entered Baghetti in his first races. At the Syracuse GP on 25 April 1961 the British teams were out in force, but of course they were running on the old four-cylinder Coventry Climax FPF engines, and although it was heavier, Baghetti's Ferrari was some 25bhp more powerful.

The young Italian took the lead after five laps of this 195-mile (314km) race and won by a margin of five seconds from Dan Gurney (Porsche four-cylinder). Baghetti next drove the Ferrari in the 93-mile (150km)

Naples GP on 14 May. It took place the same day as Monaco, so the entry was weak. He took the lead on the fourth lap and stayed in front for the next 56 to win by a lap from Gerry Ashmore (Lotus).

Baghetti did not appear again with the Ferrari until the French GP. The race was run in exceptionally hot conditions. He survived the attrition of the first 41 laps that eliminated from contention all the works Ferraris, plus Moss's Lotus 18. For the last ten laps he fought off the works Porsche entries of Gurney and Bonnier in a slipstreaming battle that would prove too demanding for even much more experienced drivers. Bonnier dropped out of contention because of engine problems, and 300yd from the finishing line Baghetti pulled out of Gurney's slipstream and crossed the line a length ahead. Baghetti had displayed remarkable skill, superb timing, and incredible coolness.

Now Baghetti's career had nowhere to go but downhill, with very little respite. He spun off the wet track and damaged his Ferrari in the British GP at Aintree. He did not race the F1 car again until the Italian GP on the combined banked track and road circuit at Monza where he retired because of engine trouble. Respite in the downhill slide came in the minor Coppa Italia held on the Vallelunga circuit on 10 October. Scuderia Sant'Ambroeus entered Baghetti with a

Above: *Baghetti was the sensation of the 1961 season. He won the Syracuse GP with a Ferrari and went on to win that year's Naples and French Grands Prix. Here Baghetti is seen in the French race at Reims, battling to hold off the works four-cylinder Porsche cars of the vastly more experienced Bonnier (on the left) and Gurney. Baghetti won the race from Gurney by a margin of a tenth of a second. Bonnier had dropped back because of engine problems and finished seventh.* (Author's collection)

Below: *A superb cockpit shot of Giancarlo Baghetti at the wheel of his 65° Ferrari Tipo 156 in the 1961 French Grand Prix at Reims which he won after the failure of the works team cars.* (Author's collection)

Opposite: *In 1962 Baghetti became a member of the works Ferrari team, but it was a year in which the V6 Formula 1 cars were uncompetitive, and they proved no match for the latest V8 British opposition. Baghetti is seen at the banked Karussell corner in the German Grand Prix at the Nürburgring. He finished well down the field in tenth place. After this very disappointing season Baghetti's career was to all intents and purposes at an end, although he still made occasional racing appearances.* (Author's collection)

Porsche hired from the works, and he led throughout both heats to score an easy victory.

For 1962, Baghetti became a works Ferrari driver, but Ferrari had been temporarily emasculated by the departure of many of the team personnel. Young Mauro Forghieri became Technical Director, and in F1 Ferrari was forced to race the overweight, ill-handling V6 cars that had lost the power advantage that made them so successful in 1961. Baghetti ran in only four Championship races, and his best performances were fourth at Zandvoort and fifth at Monza, together with a second place in the non-Championship Mediterranean GP behind team-mate Bandini. In the 1962 Targa Florio he shared a 2-litre Dino 196 Ferrari with Bandini and they took another second place.

Both Phil Hill and Baghetti left the floundering Ferrari team at the end of 1962 to join the nascent ATS organisation (ATS stood for Automobili Turismo e Sport) headed by Count Giovanni Volpi, together with Ortiz Patino and Giorgio Billi, and with Carlo Chiti as technical director. The cars were hopelessly uncompetitive. A combination of penury and despair meant that the cars turned up at race meetings looking tatty and unkempt. The ATS team ran without success in only five races in 1963. For 1964, Baghetti joined the impoverished Scuderia Centro-Sud, and he raced V8 BRMs for 'Mimo' Dei without success.

In the 1965 Italian GP, Baghetti retired a works Brabham because of engine failure. He partnered Guichet in a works 206S Ferrari Dino in the 1966 Targa Florio, and they took second place. He drove Fiat-Abarths in the European Touring Car Championship, and he competed in F3 in Italy in 1967–8. He appeared with a works Lotus 49 in the 1967 Italian GP, but retired yet again. He also drove in the 1968 London–Sydney Marathon, but retired at Bombay after all his documents, including his passport, were stolen. Baghetti became a photo-journalist with a good reputation in Italy, and started the magazine *Auto Oggi* (*Motors Today*). He died of cancer at the age of 60.

entered drivers on a rather haphazard basis in 1962, and Bandini ran in only three Grands Prix, with a best performance of third in a nicely judged race at Monaco. In sports car racing he shared the second-place 2-litre Ferrari with Baghetti in the Targa Florio.

By 1963, Mauro Forghieri had found his feet as Technical Director of Ferrari and he decided that newcomer to the team John Surtees should be partnered in F1 by the very determined, but rather wild, Belgian driver Willy Mairesse. So, Bandini returned to Scuderia Centro-Sud for whom he drove the team's ex-works BRM P57, although he continued to race works Ferrari sports cars. Bandini's best result with the BRM was fifth place in the British race at Silverstone, while he shared the second-place Ferrari in the Targa Florio and the winning car at Le Mans.

After Mairesse crashed heavily at the Nürburgring at the beginning of August and put himself out of racing for the rest of the season, Bandini returned to the Ferrari F1 team. He retired in the Italian race at Monza, but he then finished fifth at Watkins Glen, retired in Mexico, took second place to Surtees in the non-Championship Rand GP at East London, and rounded off the season on 28 December by finishing fifth in the South African GP at East London.

Bandini's place in the Ferrari F1 team was now assured. The team raced the familiar V6 cars, but the new V8 appeared later in the season and the latest flat-12 Tipo 1512 was ready by the back end of the year. In 1964, Surtees won the Drivers' Championship by a single point from Graham Hill (BRM) and he was well backed-up by Bandini. Bandini won only one race, the Austrian GP on the bumpy Zeltweg circuit that took its toll of runners. He also finished third in Germany, Italy, and Mexico and took equal fourth place in the World Championship. In sports car racing he finished third, partnered by Surtees, at both Sebring and Le Mans.

The Ferraris performed indifferently in 1965, and Lorenzo's best performances were second at Monaco and fourth in the Italian and United States races. As the team went into 1966 and the new 3-litre GP Formula, it was obvious that relations between Bandini and Surtees were becoming strained. At Monaco, Bandini drove the team's V6 2.4-litre car – which was most suitable for this circuit – at the insistence of team manager Eugenio Dragoni and despite the protests of Surtees who had wanted to race this car. Bandini finished second to Stewart (2-litre BRM) and this indicates that Surtees would probably have won with it.

Surtees won at Spa, with Bandini third; and then came Le Mans, where Surtees left the team after a bitter disagreement. Bandini would have won the French race if his throttle cable had not snapped. He had no successes

Above: *During 1963, Lorenzo Bandini became number two in the Ferrari team to John Surtees. Bandini was no ace, but he was a hard worker and Italy's best driver at this time. Here he is seen helping to push his V8 Ferrari Tipo 158 to the start of the 1965 British GP at Silverstone. After only two laps of the race, Bandini retired because of piston failure. Although Surtees had won the 1964 Drivers' Championship, the team sank back into mediocrity again in 1965, and Ferrari failed to win a single GP.* (Tom March Collection)

for the remainder of the year. The 1967 season started well for the young Italian, who was emerging from Surtees's shadow, and, co-driving with new team-mate Chris Amon, he won both the Daytona 24 Hours and the Monza 1,000km races. He also took second place in the Race of Champions at Brands Hatch behind Dan Gurney (Eagle).

Bandini, with his V12 Ferrari, was second fastest in practice for Monaco, his favourite GP, and after leading in the early stages he dropped to second place behind Denis Hulme (Brabham). As the race drew to a close, he made a charge for the lead, but he was desperately tired, and on lap 82 of this 100-lap race he clipped a barrier on the harbour front. The Ferrari rolled over and burst into flames in the middle of the track with the driver trapped underneath. The emergency services were very slow to react, and by the time the driver was rescued he was terribly burnt, and without hope of survival. He lingered in dreadful pain for three days before dying.

Baracca, Francesco

Italian First World War fighter pilot (The Prancing Horse)
Born: 9 May 1888 (Lugo di Romagna, Italy)
Died: 19 June 1918 (shot down over Montello, Treviso)

Baracca's contribution to the story is the emblem of the Prancing Horse (in accounts of Baracca it is generally referred to as the 'Rearing Horse') that he had had painted on the fuselage of his aircraft. Baracca, the son of a gentleman farmer, joined the Italian army in 1909, rapidly became an officer in the Royal Piedmont Cavalry, and transferred to the Corpo Aeronautico Militare in 1912. By the time the First World War broke out, he was a very experienced pilot and instructor, but he did not gain his first combat victory with his Nieuport II until 7 April 1916.

Within two years he had a total of 34 'kills', but he was shot down by ground-fire on 19 June 1918 while flying a Spad VII. When Baracca's body was found, there was a bullet-hole in his forehead and he was clutching a pistol. Whether or not he committed suicide to avoid being burnt to death in his cockpit (or being captured) was unresolved.

In 1923 Enzo Ferrari adopted Baracca's Prancing/Rearing Horse symbol, and he said that he added the 'canary' yellow background, as this was the colour of Modena. One version of the story is that Baracca's family was sent the emblem on a piece of aircraft fabric, and later presented it to Ferrari as a symbol of his courage and audacity. Another is that Enzo's brother, Alfredo, was killed while he was a member of Baracca's squadron, and that the gift went direct to Enzo.

Below: *Francesco Baracca was an Italian First World War fighter pilot and – because of Ferrari – the only one known in Britain and the United States. Although there is some obfuscation of the background, the 'Prancing Horse' symbol of Baracca's squadron was adopted as the badge of Scuderia Ferrari.* **(Author's collection)**

Barnard, John

Engineer
Born: 1946 (Watford, Hertfordshire, England)

After gaining a diploma from Watford College of Technology, Barnard went to work for the General Electric Company, but then joined Lola Cars at Huntingdon as a junior designer. Barnard joined McLaren in 1972, working on a number of projects, including the M23 F1 car, and thereafter joined Vel's Parnelli Jones Racing to work alongside Maurice Phillipe on the team's F1 car raced in 1974–6. Subsequently, he worked on a number of Indy car designs, and in 1980 was responsible for the Chaparral 2K with which Rutherford won that year's 500 race and the CART Championship.

In 1980 Barnard returned to McLaren, now run by Ron Dennis, and worked on the McLaren MP4/1, which had the first carbon-fibre composite chassis. He joined Ferrari in 1987 and set up the Ferrari Guildford Technical Office in the UK, because he refused to live in Italy. His work for Maranello included the development of an electronic gear-change mechanism operated by two paddles on the steering wheel (and now usually described as a semi-automatic gearbox). It was a feature that was, in due course, adopted by all the teams. The Tipo 641 Ferrari with this gearbox is the only racing car in the permanent collection of the Museum of Modern Art in New York.

Ferrari success during the period of Barnard's technical supremacy at Maranello was very patchy, and all too often a very promising one-off result was followed by fairly consistent failure. In 1990, however, Alain Prost won five races with the Barnard-designed

Above: *Here, John Barnard is seen with Gerhard Berger. Barnard's days with Ferrari were largely unsuccessful because he insisted on working from England, and this caused time-lag and communication problems.* (LAT Photographic)

Ferrari 641/2, and the Frenchman finished second in the World Championship. Throughout the time that Barnard worked for Ferrari, the distance between Guildford and Maranello was too far for adequate liaison between design and construction/development.

Both sides felt that a change was needed, and Barnard moved to Benetton where his B191 scored a single victory in the hands of Nelson Piquet in the 1991 Canadian GP. He had completed the B192 that Schumacher raced in 1992, but left because of a disagreement over pay with Flavio Briatore. In 1993 Barnard worked on a F1 project for Toyota, which was never completed, and then returned to Ferrari. Despite the earlier problems, it was agreed that Barnard could continue to work in England from a Surrey-based technical office called Ferrari Design and Development, but his designs were largely unsuccessful.

When Jean Todt assumed control, he was unwilling to accept the situation of Barnard working from England, and the 1997 Tipo 310B was Barnard's last design for Ferrari. With this car Michael Schumacher won five races for the team, and scored 78 points compared to World Championship winner Jacques Villeneuve's total of 82. He was 36 points ahead of Heinz-Harald Frentzen, but all Schumacher's points were forfeited because of an incident at Jerez.

During the summer of 1997 Barnard bought the Ferrari Design Office in Surrey and renamed it B3 Technologies, which developed into a company supplying design and manufacturing services for F1 and other industries. In 1998 B3 contracted to work for the Arrows team, but there was a dispute and Barnard's organisation eventually worked for Prost's team, and Barnard became technical consultant to the Prost team until it folded in 2001. Barnard had developed an interest in motorcycle racing, and he became technical director of the Team KR Moto GP team.

On 29 February 2008, Barnard sold his shares in B3 Technologies to a small consortium headed by the company's former commercial director, John Minett. By this time Barnard had gone into partnership with Terence Woodgate to design and make a table called 'Surface' and marketed by Established & Sons, a company specialising in eye-catching limited editions by big-name designers. Surface is only 2mm thick and is a very advanced carbon-fibre structure with the 'unidirectional' skin wrapped round a hard foam core to make a 'biscuit' that is fatter in the middle, 92.5mm (where it's hidden by the top), very thin round the edges, and rigid, strong, and light all over. The price is likely to be upwards of £20,000.

In the *Telegraph Magazine* of 12 April 2008, Barnard is quoted as saying, with no-nonsense bluntness, 'It is a composite plank.' He is also quoted as saying, 'Two years ago I would have looked at Surface and said, "It's just a table with four legs."' This statement reflects the writer's reaction. The co-designers are threatening to make a chair using the same technology.

Barrichello, Rubens

Works driver
Born: 23 May 1972 (São Paulo, Brazil)

Although Rubens has never made it to the highest echelons of F1, after 16 years he remains a driver whose services are much in demand, and he is now the most experienced driver competing in F1. After winning the Brazilian Kart Championship five times, and having contested 11 Formula Ford races in Brazil, Rubens was still only 17, shy, and introspective when he came to race in Europe in 1990. He was backed by Brazilian food conglomerate Arisco, and in that first season he competed in the GM Lotus Euroseries, winning five races and the Championship with cars entered by Scuderia Salvati Draco.

This success earned him a place in F3 with West Surrey Racing, run by Dick Bennetts, and he won the British F3 Championship. There was talk of him progressing straight to F1, but wiser counsel prevailed and he drove in F3000 in 1992 for the Il Barone Rampante team. This had many internal and political problems, and Rubens could have been sucked into them. Instead, he fought his way through the season to finish third in that year's Championship.

Eddie Jordan was impressed by Rubens's talent, and brought him into his team which was using Hart V10 engines in 1993. It was not a competitive team, but Barrichello soon proved his worth in the European GP at Donington Park in April. It was a rain-soaked race on a slippery track, in which he held second place (assisted, admittedly, by traction control) until forced to retire because of fuel-pressure problems. His best result in a season with so many retirements was a fifth place at Suzuka.

He stayed with the team for 1994, and Imola proved the nadir and testing point of his season. A serious crash in practice, when he hit the wall at the Variante Bassa just before the start/finish line, turned the car over and knocked him unconscious. He nearly died because his tongue was blocking his airway. In the race, Ayrton Senna – Rubens's great hero, mentor, and friend – crashed at high speed and was fatally injured.

During 1994, Rubens scored a third, four fourths, and finished sixth in the Drivers' Championship. He stayed

Below: *After driving spells with Jordan and Stewart, Brazilian driver Barrichello joined Ferrari for 2000, and became a Maranello stalwart.* (LAT Photographic)

with the Jordan team, now using Peugeot engines, for two more seasons. Although the cars were very quick in qualifying, they were unreliable. After a second place in Canada in 1995, and a front-row start in Brazil in 1996, it became obvious that his career was progressing nowhere except into decline. It was time to move on, and he went to the Stewart team where it was mainly retirement after retirement, but he did take a brilliant second place to Schumacher (Ferrari) in the wet at Monaco in 1997. Rubens stayed with Stewart until the end of 1999.

In his final year with Stewart the cars were more reliable, and although the team's first, and rather improbable, win was achieved by Johnny Herbert, Rubens felt that his career progressed upwards during the year. His efforts were justified when he was invited to join Ferrari as number two to Schumacher. Throughout 2000, Rubens frequently achieved a podium finish, and his first GP win, for which he had waited and struggled so long, came in the German GP at Hockenheim.

It was also a year of long-awaited success for Ferrari. Schumacher scored nine wins and won the 2000 Championship, while Barrichello was fourth in the Championship and, in addition to his win, he took second places at Monaco, Montreal, and Indianapolis. Rubens was comfortable with the team, his team-mate and leader, and his own performances. In 2001 Schumacher again won eight races and the Championship, while Rubens finished second in five races, and third in four, to take third place.

The year 2002 provided another splendid season for both Ferrari drivers, but Rubens wanted to be winning races and there was a serious incident that reflected the feelings of both Ferrari drivers. In the Austrian GP he was leading the race, but team orders compelled him to give way to Schumacher on the final straight, and Michael came through and won. It was not as though the German needed the extra points. At the awards presentation on the podium, Schumacher exchanged places with Barrichello and gave him the winner's trophy. The outcome was that the drivers were fined for disrupting protocol on the podium, and for 2003 the FIA banned team orders.

In 2002 Rubens had won four races, and yet again he finished second in the Championship to his team-leader. The following year, Barrichello continued to support his team-leader and helped him fend off challenges. He won only the British and Japanese races and took fourth place in the Championship. It was all becoming rather tedious, and in 2004 the Brazilian again won only two races, but took second place to Schumacher in the Championship. The relationship between the two Ferrari drivers had always been good, but Rubens was becoming weary of what can only be described as his submissive secondary role in the team.

Ferrari's golden period had ended mainly because their Bridgestone tyres were less effective than the rival Michelins. In 2005 Barrichello managed no wins, only two second places, and he took eighth place in the Championship with only 38 points. Rubens had announced in August 2005 that he would be leaving Ferrari at the end of the year and was joining Honda. The team struggled to make progress in the face of very heavy opposition, and Rubens failed to achieve worthwhile results. Because of the world financial recession, Honda withdrew from racing at the end of 2008 and Ross Brawn took control of the team. The new Brawn car snatched a technical advantage at the beginning of 2009, and Barrichello finished second to team-mate Button in the year's first race in Australia.

Bazzi, Luigi

Engineer
Born: 1892 (Novara, Italy)
Died: 1986 (Italy)

Educated as an engineer, Bazzi worked for Fiat in Turin until Enzo Ferrari persuaded him to join Alfa Romeo in 1923. From that point onwards he spent his working life with Enzo Ferrari. He joined Scuderia Ferrari, and at their premises in Modena in 1935 he conceived the Bimotore (twin-engined) Alfa Romeos that were completed in four months. Two cars were built and they were based on Monoposto chassis, one with 3.2-litre engines mounted front and rear, and the other with 2.9-litre units.

The transmission incorporated a three-speed gearbox, and the procedure was to start one engine and then the other before connecting the drive. If one engine failed the car could continue on the other engine. These remarkable, and technically very successful, cars were driven by Nuvolari (two 3.2-litre engines) and Chiron (two 2.9-litre engines). The performance was outstanding, although tyre wear was excessive, and the tyres failed rapidly if the driver tried to use the full performance of the car.

When Alfa Corse was formed, Bazzi became chief engineer, while Enzo Ferrari was de facto racing manager. Ferrari left Alfa Romeo and Bazzi followed him and joined his new company. The creation of the Bimotore was somewhat exceptional, for Bazzi was

Above: *Luigi Bazzi (on right) with Tazio Nuvolari, the greatest Italian driver of all time, in 1936.* (Author's collection)

Below: *Seen here in 1961 is Luigi Bazzi, as always wearing a beret and probably Ferrari's greatest collaborator, with young Giancarlo Baghetti.* (LAT Photographic)

primarily a development engineer. Colombo designed the first Ferrari engine, the 1494cc Tipo 125, but it was Bazzi who cured its original faults and developed it into the 1903cc Tipo 159.

Throughout the 1940s and the 1950s Bazzi continued to carry out development work for Ferrari, but that changed after the 1960 Le Mans race. Bazzi had carried out a number of modifications to the exhausts and carburation of the team's Testa Rossa cars, without taking into account the effect on fuel consumption, and two of the team cars ran out of fuel early in the race. Every Tuesday, late in the afternoon, Ferrari held a meeting of senior staff. At the meeting following Le Mans, the 'Old Man' asked Bazzi for an explanation why the Testa Rossas ran out of fuel. There was a significant pause and then Bazzi said, 'Mr Ferrari, I cannot give an explanation.' Ferrari said that they would discuss the matter later, and although it is not known what discussions took place between Ferrari and Bazzi, it is not too difficult to guess. All responsibility was taken away from Bazzi, although he continued to work for the company and the total time he spent with Ferrari and working for him exceeded 60 years.

Behra, Jean

Driver
Born: 16 February 1921 (Nice, France)
Died: 1 August 1959 (Avus, Berlin)

The greatest French driver of early post-war years, Behra was fiery and determined, short on temper and patience, long on skill and driving tactics. He started his racing career on motorcycles and was three times French Champion before taking up car racing. He finished sixth with a Talbot-Lago in the 1949 Coupe du Salon held on a road circuit at Montlhéry near Paris.

Amédée Gordini invited Behra to drive one of his cars in the 1950 24-hour Bol d'Or race on a 3.1-mile (4.99km) banked track and road circuit at Montlhéry. The race was limited to 1500cc sports cars, and only one driver was allowed. Behra retired, but turned in a good enough performance to be asked to join Gordini on a regular basis for the 1951 season.

Behra remained a stalwart of the Gordini team until the end of 1954, but the fragile and modestly powered cars gave him little opportunity for success. His greatest triumph was in 1952 when he won the Formula 2 Grand Prix de France at Reims; he drove the car on the road

from Paris to the circuit because preparation was so late, and then defeated the works Ferrari team. There were rumours that the Gordini had an illegally oversize 2473cc engine, but there was no evidence either way. Another memorable performance was in the 1954 Pau GP in which he beat works Ferrari driver Maurice Trintignant by a margin of 60yd after three hours' racing.

Behra switched to Maserati for 1955, and he remained with the Italian team for three seasons. There was no hope of a Maserati defeating the works Mercedes-Benz W196 cars in Championship GPs that year, but he scored wins in the non-Championship Pau and Bordeaux races against weak opposition. He had a terrible accident in practice for the 1955 Tourist Trophy on the Dundrod circuit when he overturned his 300S Maserati and his head was trapped under the car as it ground along the road upside down.

The road surface wore through his crash helmet and then wore his right ear off. Cliff Allison shared hotel rooms with Behra when they were both driving for Ferrari in 1959, and he was fascinated by Behra's false ear. He commented that it was so realistic that it was not possible to tell it was plastic, and was astounded when Behra unscrewed it and put it on his bedside table at night. When he wanted a table in a crowded restaurant, Behra would go up to the table he wanted, remove his false ear and place it on the table. The diners quickly left!

Behra was number two to Moss in the Maserati for 1956, and his best F1 performances were second in Argentina and third at Monaco, Reims, Silverstone, and the Nürburgring. The following year he was number two to Juan Fangio, and apart from second place again in Argentina he achieved only a couple of sixth places. A Championship race win eluded him when he was leading the British GP at Aintree and the clutch of his 250F disintegrated. He had, however, achieved good results in non-Championship races. For Maserati, he won at Pau, Modena, and Ain-Diab (Morocco), and he won the Caen GP and the International Trophy at Silverstone with BRMs.

Maserati withdrew from racing at the end of 1957 and Behra joined BRM in Formula 1, and Porsche in F2 and sports car racing. BRM's chaotically unsuccessful career continued, although Behra's enthusiasm did much to lift the team's spirits. His best performance with a BRM was third at Zandvoort, but with Porsche cars he co-drove with Moss to third place in the Buenos Aires 1,000km races, won sports car races at the Nürburgring and Avus, and in Formula 2 won the Coupe de Vitesse at Reims and the F2 category of the German GP.

Ferrari, desperate for drivers after the loss of Collins, Hawthorn and Musso in 1958, made Behra an offer for

1959 that it was almost impossible for him to refuse. It was, however, a relationship that was cursed. Cliff Allison described Behra's temperament as 'being more like that of an Italian than a Frenchman, very excitable and uppity'. Behra despised team manager Romolo Tavoni, whom he regarded as a spineless sycophant. Trouble was inevitable. In sports car racing, Behra was second with Allison at Sebring and third with Brooks at the Nürburgring.

It was a different story in F1. Behra won the Aintree 200 race and finished second at Siracusa (F2) early in the season, but he retired at Monaco because of engine failure, and finished fifth in the Dutch race. At Reims he held third place with his Dino, setting a new lap record, later beaten by Moss with a BRM. Then Behra overshot a corner and rejoined the race in fourth place before pulling into the pits to retire because of engine problems. Behra was bitterly disillusioned with the standard of preparation of his cars.

He believed that he had been engaged as number one driver, but he was convinced that the preparation of his cars was inferior to that of the cars driven by other members of the Ferrari team. Ferrari in those days, of course, was not a team that recognised the role of 'number one driver'. Tavoni unwisely discussed the problem with Behra, and Jean exploded and punched the Ferrari team manager. Although some of his enemies would say that Tavoni merited a good whack, inevitably, and with some justification, the 'Old Man' sacked Behra from the team. What ensued was tragic, and many regarded Enzo Ferrari's attitude as unforgivable.

Jean was now free to drive again for Porsche, and the next meeting was at Avus where the German GP was held at the beginning of August. This was preceded by a

Above: *Behra was an outstanding driver for Gordini, and later for Maserati, and his only year with Ferrari was in 1959 when he was sacked from the team. Here he is seen at the wheel of his Gordini in the paddock at the International Trophy meeting at Silverstone in May 1952.* **(Guy Griffiths Collection)**

sports car race in which Behra drove a works Porsche. There are many accounts of what happened, and the writer is relying on that of his good friend Gino Munaron, who was a close friend of Behra.

'The banked curve at Avus was truly dangerous because it was not convex like other banked curves, but a level slope like tiled paving. At the top of the curve there ran a terrace, which during the Second World War served as the base for a battery of anti-aircraft guns defending Berlin. These guns had been fixed to a platform of concrete. There were also flagpoles mounted on the outer edge of the top of the banking.

On the fifth lap, Behra lost control of his Porsche; this slid up the banking and smashed against one of the platforms. He was catapulted out of the car against the flagpole bearing the Argentinian flag and was killed almost instantly. His body slid over the edge of the banking and fell into the paddock below.'

Ferrari sent neither tribute nor representative to the brave Frenchman's funeral. It was Enzo Ferrari at his most unpleasant.

Above: *Derek Bell was one of Britain's most successful drivers, but he had a poor career in F1 which he blamed on the Ferrari team for signing him up and then not using him. Here, Bell is at Silverstone for the 1969 British GP in which he drove the McLaren M9A.* (Guy Griffiths Collection)

Bell, Derek

Driver
Born: 31 October 1941 (Pinner, Middlesex, England)

Derek Bell MBE has had a very extensive racing career, starting with a Lotus Seven and leading to a Lotus Formula 3 car and a season with a Brabham BT23 in Formula 2. During the 1968 season with the Brabham, Bell was asked to test a Ferrari Dino Formula 2 car at Monza, and after a meeting the following day with Enzo Ferrari he joined the Ferrari team. His first race was the Monza Lottery Formula 2 event at Monza, and after taking pole position in practice, he was eliminated in the race in a multi-car accident. Despite the accident, Ferrari was pleased with his pole position, and Gozzi

gave him $1,000 in cash. It was only after he received this that he signed a contract with Ferrari.

There followed another Formula 2 race at Zandvoort. Bell was again fastest in practice and he won his heat. He was leading the final when it was stopped because of Chris Lambert's fatal crash. The race was restarted, but Bell retired when the gears jammed. Bell was given a F1 test at Maranello, and was warned by Mauro Forghieri that if he crashed the car he would never again drive a Ferrari. The test was in the wet, watched by the 'Old Man', who sat anonymously in a 2 + 2 GTE Ferrari. Bell drove really well and fast in difficult circumstances, and the result was a seat in the Formula 1 team.

Bell's first F1 race was the Gold Cup at Oulton Park, and although he ran well he retired because the gear-lever jammed in the gate. In the Italian GP at Monza he retired again, this time because of fuel pump failure. Yet another retirement followed because of engine failure in the United States GP at Watkins Glen. By this time Bell was becoming disillusioned by the lack of competitiveness of Ferrari cars, and by Ferrari politics. Bell went with Chris Amon to compete in the Tasman Series. The drivers each had a F2 car with 2.4-litre Dino engine (and no spare). Amon dominated the series, but Bell, although he failed to win a single race, took some good places and finished fourth in the Championship.

Back in Europe, Bell continued to drive Ferrari Dinos in F2, but they were never front-runners, and Bell's best performance was fifth at the Eifelrennen. Ferrari was in great difficulties, both financial and because of the poor performance of the cars, and was waiting closure of his deal with Fiat to buy into the company. Bell drove in one F1 race, the International Trophy at Silverstone, in which he finished ninth. Ferrari pulled out of F2, restricted his F1 entries to one car (except at the British race) and entered Bell in no more races.

Ironically, in 1969 Ferrari was also running the new 312P 3-litre Prototype, usually driven by Amon and Rodriguez, but there were no drives for Bell, and Ferrari refused to release him from his contract to drive a Gulf Ford GT40 at Le Mans. Ferrari completely screwed Bell's single-seater career, but he still drove for Maranello on two occasions in 1970.

Jacques Swaters invited Bell to drive his newly delivered Écurie Francorchamps 512S in the 1970 Spa 1,000km race, and he shared this yellow-painted car with Hughes de Fierlandt. At a refuelling stop the mechanics spilt a lot of petrol, and when Derek started the engine there was a loud whoosh and the car was enveloped in flames; photographers and pit staff fled as petrol running down the pits road ignited. Bell was trapped in the car because the interior door wire had broken. The fire was extinguished in less than a minute and Bell was uninjured apart from singed eyebrows. The car rejoined the race to finish eighth.

Bell drove a works 512S at Le Mans with Ronnie Peterson, but the Ferrari was eliminated after only 4½ hours. On the approach to White House, the battling trio of Bell, Regazzoni, and Parkes (all with 512S cars) caught Wisell, who had slowed down in his Filipinetti 512S because of oil on the windscreen. Bell swerved round Wisell's car, missed a gear, the engine revs went into the red, and he crawled back to the pits with a broken engine. Regazzoni rammed Wisell, and Parkes rammed Regazzoni's spinning 512S. It was one of the less praiseworthy episodes in Ferrari sports car racing.

Despite his lack of Formula 1 success, which included poor seasons with Tecno in 1972 and Surtees in 1974, Derek Bell enjoyed immense success in sports car racing. He had joined the Gulf-Porsche team in 1971, and stayed with Gulf, driving their Mirage cars, through to 1975. Bell was a consistent performer, and in 1975 when Gulf entered only Le Mans, the drivers of the winning car were Bell and Jacky Ickx.

Bell drove in a number of categories – including F5000, Formula Atlantic, and Touring cars – before

joining Porsche in 1982. With the Porsche team he won Le Mans another four times, and was twice joint Drivers' Champion with Hans Stuck. He continued racing well into the 1990s. After a career that was blighted by misfortune in its early years, Bell became one of the most successful British drivers of the late 1980s. He was awarded an MBE in 1986 for his services to motor racing.

Berger, Gerhard

Works driver
Born: 27 August 1959 (Wörgl, near Innsbruck, Austria)

Although he drove for other teams, Berger was one of those drivers whose name was inseparably linked to Ferrari, and during his successful GP career he scored

Below: *Gerhard Berger was another potentially great driver who stayed with Ferrari for four seasons, left for McLaren, and then returned to Maranello. He had great enthusiasm (and ambition), but he gradually became indifferent, and then despondent.* **(LAT Photographic)**

ten wins, of which five were for Maranello. That he was a fine driver, persistent, very talented, and hard-pushing is undoubted, but he was unlucky to be racing in a period when there were a number of greats – among them Piquet, Prost, and Senna – who overshadowed him. In another age he would have doubled his wins and, maybe, won the Drivers' Championship.

Gerhard's early racing was with Alfa Romeo Touring cars, and then in F3 in Germany before leaving his mark on the F3 scene in Europe generally. His reputation as a safe and fast driver led to him joining the ATS team in the latter part of 1984. ATS was a specialist wheel company headed by Hans Günther Schmid, who wasted a vast amount of the money he had earned doing something he knew a great deal about on something about which he knew very little.

ATS lasted eight seasons that were spent at the back of the grid among the also-rans, and earned a reputation second to none for poor organisation and autocratic management. Berger showed considerable promise by finishing sixth in the 1984 Italian race at Monza. ATS had been supplied by BMW with turbocharged engines, but the Munich company had lost patience with the team's incompetence and withdrew supplies. The result was that ATS pulled out of racing. During the winter, Berger had a testing accident that resulted in broken vertebrae in the neck, but he was fully recovered by the start of the 1985 season.

For 1985, Gerhard joined the Arrows team run by Jack Oliver and, in reality, another lost cause. Arrows, since 1984, had been using BMW turbocharged engines, and in 1985 they were tuned by Heini Mader, with the result that they were fairly competitive. In the many years that Arrows raced, they never won a single event, but in the 1985 Imola race the team was close to doing so. Thierry Boutsen was classified second (third on the road, but moving up a place after Prost's disqualification). After a slow, rather immature start to the season, Berger performed rather better later in the year and finished fifth in South Africa, and sixth in Australia.

The Benetton team signed Gerhard up for 1986, and part of his attraction to the team was that he had developed good relations with BMW who supplied his new team's engines. Berger enjoyed an excellent season, developing in skill and confidence. After sixth places in the Brazilian and Spanish races, he took a fine third place at Imola. Then his season went sour because of mechanical problems, but by Monza the team had reliability and Gerhard was on good form.

He finished fifth at Monza, but he collided with Johansson's Ferrari at Estoril – it was his fault and scotched any chance of winning the race. That first win came at Mexico City and was followed by an invitation to join Ferrari for 1987.

Gerhard gradually settled down at Ferrari after a hesitant start. He drove in 16 races during the year, retiring in nine, and in three of these he spun off. Suspension problems were the cause of the spin in France, but the other two were driver errors, including that at Estoril when he was leading. He recovered from the spin to finish second behind Prost (McLaren), and he also set fastest lap. Berger took fourth places at Rio, Monte Carlo, Detroit, and Monza. At the end of the season he proved his top echelon qualities by winning at Suzuka and Adelaide (setting fastest lap in the Australian race), and he finished fifth in the Drivers' Championship.

During Gerhard's second season with Ferrari in 1988, racing was dominated by Ayrton Senna and Alain Prost with their Honda-powered McLarens. Gerhard drove well and achieved a good measure of success. He won the Italian GP, with team-mate Alboreto second after Senna crashed and Prost retired because of engine trouble. In addition, Berger achieved two second places and two thirds, which with 41 points proved good enough for him to win third place in the Drivers' Championship behind Senna and Prost.

Nigel Mansell joined Ferrari for 1989, and for reasons that are far from clear Berger could not cope psychologically with the English driver's ebullient attitude. The days of turbocharged cars were now largely over and Maranello was racing the Tipo 640 V12 3.5-litre normally aspirated cars. At the first race of the year, in Brazil, Gerhard collided with Senna at the start. In the San Marino race at Imola he crashed badly at Tamburello corner, his car caught fire, and he sustained burns. Because of his injuries he missed the Monaco GP, but returned to race at Mexico City where he suffered the first of eight successive retirements.

He had a puncture in the German race at Hockenheim and crashed, and he spun off and out of the Belgian GP at Spa. It was only at the Italian GP in September that the season started to go right again, and Gerhard followed a second place there with a win and fastest lap in the Portuguese race at Estoril, and another second place in the Spanish race at Jerez. Berger finished the year at Adelaide by retiring after colliding with Philippe Alliot's Lola.

Berger entered into a three-year contract from 1990 to partner Ayrton Senna at McLaren, and the money paid was very generous. It meant being number two, supporting the team-leader, and having prospects of winning only if Senna retired or dropped right out of contention. It drained his morale and confidence, but Gerhard saw it as an interim situation and expected to get his career back on track again, preferably with Ferrari. Senna won the Championship for the second time in 1990, and Gerhard was joint third with Piquet (Benetton). He failed to win a GP, but despite being too hard on his Goodyear tyres, he finished second at Interlagos and Imola, and his retirements were few.

Senna won the World Championship again in 1991, while Gerhard took fourth place behind Williams drivers Mansell and Patrese. His one race victory of the season was at Suzuka where he was 'allowed' to win because Senna had such a substantial Championship lead, but he took second places at Imola, Silverstone, and Spa-Francorchamps. The McLaren team lost its dominant edge in 1992, and Senna slipped to fourth place in the Drivers' Championship behind Mansell and Patrese with Michael Schumacher (Benetton) third.

Gerhard was fifth in the Championship, a fairly low position, despite winning in Canada and Australia. In the latter GP, especially, he drove a finely judged race to beat Michael Schumacher with his Benetton by four-fifths of a second. Gerhard also took second places in Portugal and Japan. At this fairly late stage in his career, Berger was a completely dependable, steady driver upon whom the team could rely absolutely, or so it seemed.

Ferrari offered Berger exceptional financial terms for 1993, and he rejoined the team. He partnered Jean Alesi, who was now in his third year with Ferrari. It could have been a dream ticket, but the much-needed rapport between the two drivers was not there, and in any case the latest V12 F93A was not competitive enough to bring the team substantial success. The Austrian failed to win a race, his best performance being third place in Hungary, and he had great difficulty in coping with the new 'active' suspension system. Michael Andretti collided with him at the start in Brazil, he tangled with Damon Hill (Williams) at Monaco, and he had another accident with Martin Brundle (Ligier) at Spa.

Overall, Ferrari was more successful in 1994, and Berger's driving was rather more sure-footed. He took pole position in practice at Hockenheim and led throughout the race. He also took second places in the Pacific GP at Aida, the Italian race, and the Australian GP at Adelaide. With third places at Monaco

and Magny Cours, he took third place in the Championship with 41 points, a very long way behind the leaders Schumacher (Benetton, 92 points) and Damon Hill (Williams, 91 points). The gap between the best and the rest was enormous, and Ferrari was merely one of the rest.

Both Berger and Alesi stayed with Ferrari for a last year in 1995. There was now (again) a 3000cc capacity limit and there were 17 races during the year. The positions at the top of the Drivers' Championship were unchanged and Schumacher and Hill again took the first two places, but in 1995 Schumacher won by a margin of 33 points. Alesi, who won one race, took fifth place in the Drivers' Championship and Berger, who finished third six times, was sixth.

Obviously, the Ferrari team was making no progress and there was a clean sweep. Schumacher moved from Benetton to Ferrari and made history, while Berger and Alesi went to Benetton, now using Renault engines, and slipped into obscurity. Although Berger finished sixth in the Drivers' Championship in 1997, he did take pole position at Hockenheim and win the German GP. His performances were handicapped to an extent by the somewhat unpredictable handling of the Benetton chassis.

At the end of the year, Gerhard retired from racing, but joined BMW as head of their motor sport division in anticipation of the team's return to racing in 2000. Berger had taken over the road transport company, Berger Logistik, which his father had founded in 1961. Following his father's death in an aviation accident, he entered into a deal with Red Bull Chief Executive Dietrich Mateschitz in February 2006, whereby he acquired 50 per cent of Scuderia Toro Rosso, and Mateschitz acquired 50 per cent of Berger Logistik.

Bertolini, Andrea

Test driver
Born: 1 December 1973 (Sassuolo, Modena, Italy)

Bertolini started racing in 2001 with Porsche 996 GT-Rs, moving on to Ferrari 360 Modena and Maserati MC12 cars (the latter from 2004 onwards, and he took part in its development). In 2008 he became a Ferrari test driver, and from May onwards he extensively tested the new Ferrari A1GP car that was based on Ferrari's 2004 F1 Constructors' Championship-winning car.

Bertone, Giuseppe

Coachbuilder
Born: 4 July 1915 (Turin, Italy)
Died: 26 February 1997 (Turin)

Giovanni Bertone, born to a farming family in 1884, started his coachbuilding company in the early years of the 20th century. In pre-Second World War days he worked with most Italian manufacturers, notably Lancia, and when the Fascist government was in power, there was no shortage of work in building bodies for military vehicles, and manufacturing aircraft components. His son, Giuseppe, known as 'Nuccio', joined the company in the 1930s, and when he became general manager in 1950, the situation had changed completely; despite its fame, the Italian coachbuilding industry found the building of car bodies highly competitive and with very thin profit margins.

What the company tried to do under 'Nuccio' was to take orders for series of cars, and he succeeded in obtaining production runs from American dealer 'Wacky' Arnolt, for first 103 bodies on MG TD chassis, and then 142 bodies on Arnolt-Bristol chassis. Bertone also built very small numbers of bodies on Alfa Romeo chassis, and worked in close collaboration with Alfa Romeo in the development and construction of the bizarrely styled BAT (Berlina Aerodinamica Tecnica) cars with experimental aerodynamics.

The Bertone company invested heavily in the machinery for building bodies in quantity, and by 1961 it had 800 employees and built for Alfa Romeo many different bodies, including the 1750GTV and 2000GTV, together with the GT Junior. The company has also built many bodies for Lamborghini, notably the Miura and the Countach. Among its most successful mass-produced bodies were those for Fiat: the 850 Spider, the X1/9 mid-engined sports car, and the Punto drophead coupé. The company was also responsible for Iso Rivolta bodies, and styled the body fitted to the Innocenti version of the Mini Cooper.

The company has built very few bodies on Ferrari chassis, and the only early one of significance is that with the V-shaped nose on the 250GT chassis exhibited at the 1962 Geneva Show. Bertone has built only one body for Ferrari in quantity, and that is the four-seat Dino 308GT4 of which nearly 3,700 were made between 1973 and 1980.

Above: *Nuccio Bertone became head of the coachbuilding company his family founded, and under his direction the company grew immensely and achieved worldwide fame, with design contracts for many companies, and it built bodies in quantity for Fiat.* (Author's collection)

Below: *Before the company contracted to build the bodies for the 308GT4, Bertone did very little work for Ferrari. An exception was this body on the 250GT chassis exhibited at the 1962 Geneva Salon. John Bolster wrote in Autosport, 'Car of the Show – the Berlinetta Ferrari, with a divided nose like the Grand Prix car, a steeply raked windscreen, and an overall effect of speed, speed, and yet more speed.'* (LAT Photographic)

Binotto, Mattia

Engineer
Born: 3 November 1969 (Lausanne, Switzerland)

Binotto studied mechanical engineering at Lausanne, graduating in 1993, and then in 1994 he gained a Master's degree in car engineering at Modena University. In 1995 he joined Ferrari and worked in the Engine Test Team, holding the post until the end of 1996. Between 1997 and 2004 he was Race Team Engineer for Irvine, Barrichello and then, finally, Michael Schumacher. Since 2005, he has been the Chief Engineer of Race and Customer Engines.

Biondetti, Clemente

Works Scuderia Ferrari and Ferrari driver
Born: 18 August 1898 (Buddusó, Sardinia)
Died: 24 February 1955 (Florence, Italy)

This driver's main claim to fame was that he won the Mille Miglia road race four times. Like so many drivers, his motor sport career started on two wheels, back in 1923, but it ended abruptly three years later when he had a bad crash at Ostia and, if the reports are to be believed, he broke 24 bones. When he had recovered, he switched to four wheels and raced a miscellany of cars that included Salmson, Talbot, Bugatti, and works and private Maseratis – but with a conspicuous lack of success.

His first real impression on the motor racing scene came in the 1936 Mille Miglia in which he drove the Alfa Romeo Monoposto with which Pintacuda had won the race the previous year. He built up a lead on time over the Scuderia Ferrari 8C 2900S, but fell back to finish fourth because of a bungled refuelling stop at Perugia, and tyre problems. Scuderia Ferrari took him into the works team for the 1937 Mille Miglia, but he retired. With one of the works Touring-bodied cars, he was partnered by Stefani in 1938 and won the race at a speed that was not bettered until 1953.

Biondetti was a very provincial character without any pretensions or refinement, and Enzo Ferrari disliked him. Even so, his driving merited a place in the works

Above: *Even by bucolic Italian standards, Clemente Biondetti was a rough diamond. He was disliked by Enzo Ferrari, who was usually spot-on (and prejudiced) in his judgements of people. Biondetti's greatest claim to fame was his successes in the Mille Miglia, which he won four times, in 1938 with a Scuderia Ferrari Alfa Romeo, in 1947 with a private Alfa Romeo, and in 1948 and 1949 with works Ferraris.* (Tom March Collection)

team and he appeared regularly with Alfa Corse-entered Alfa Romeo 158s in Voiturette racing, and also made occasional appearances with Alfa Romeo GP cars during the period 1938–40. His successes included second place in the 1938 Coppa Ciano, wins in the following year's Coppa Acerbo and Prix de Berne (the Voiturette division of the Swiss GP), and he took second place in the 1940 Tripoli GP.

The Mille Miglia had been cancelled in 1939, but it was revived and held on a closed circuit in 1940. It was not revived in its original form until 1947 when it was a purely national race. Emilio Romano offered Biondetti a drive with his long-chassis Alfa Romeo 8C 2900B that had the supercharger removed to comply with the latest regulations. The Sardinian did the lion's share of the driving, and they won by a margin of just under 16 minutes from a 1100cc Cisitalia.

By 1948, Ferrari had emerged as a serious marque, and Biondetti drove Tipo 166 Ferraris to a win in both that year's Mille Miglia, and in 1949. In both years the strongest opposition came from Tazio Nuvolari. Biondetti also won the Tour of Sicily in 1948–9. In the 1950 Mille Miglia, now 51 years of age, he drove a Jaguar XK 120, finishing eighth. He built a GP 'special', combining a Jaguar twin-cam engine and a Ferrari chassis, and raced it without success in Grands Prix in 1950. He also drove it in the Mille Miglia without success in 1951–2. Biondetti was a member of the works Jaguar team at Le Mans in 1951, co-driving with Leslie Johnson, but they retired because of loss of oil pressure.

He shared Stagnoli's Ferrari in the 1952 Monaco GP, run as a sports car race, and they took third place. The same year he co-drove Cornacchia's Ferrari into second place in the Pescara 12 Hours race. Biondetti joined the Lancia team in 1953 and took eighth place in the Mille Miglia after a difficult race. His final Mille Miglia was in 1954 when he drove a borrowed 2.7-litre V12 Ferrari into fourth place. By this time he had been diagnosed as suffering from cancer, and this great Italian sports car driver died a slow, lingering death, not succumbing to the disease until February 1955.

Below: Bira's great days were in the 1930s, and in the post-war era he was seen mainly with private Maseratis. Here he is at the wheel of a Maserati 4CLT/48 fitted with a 4482cc V12 OSCA engine, a new hybrid, seen here on its debut at the international meeting at Goodwood in 1948. Bira drove F1 Ferraris on the model's debut in the 1948 Italian GP, and in the Penya Rhin race at Barcelona that year. (Guy Griffiths)

'B. Bira'

Works driver in 1948, but mainly privateer
Born: 15 July 1914 (Bangkok, Siam/Thailand)
Died: 23 December 1985 (Baron's Court, London)

Educated at Eton and Cambridge, and then a student of sculpture, Prince Birabongse Bhanutej Bhanubandh – known simply as 'Bira' – was supported by his older cousin Prince Chula in fulfilling his motor racing ambitions. Bira progressed from Riley Imp and MG Magnette to the three ERAs named Romulus, Remus, and Hanuman, together with the ex-Seaman straight-eight Delage and an 8CM-3000 Maserati. He was remarkably successful, and the adventures and successes of this Siamese driver were encapsulated in a series of books written by Chula.

Bira went on to marry an English society woman, Cheryl Heycock. He resumed racing with the ERAs after the Second World War, but the zest had disappeared. He switched to Maserati, then parted company with Prince Chula at the end of 1948. Towards the end of that season he enjoyed two drives in the new V12 F1 Ferraris, but retired because of transmission failure in both the Italian Grand Prix and the Penya Rhin races, held on the Pedralbes circuit at Barcelona.

Sadly, there were no more Ferrari drives for Bira. He joined de Graffenried to race a Maserati with Enrico Platé in 1949, and achieved a number of minor successes. For 1950 he went his own way again, and raced Maseratis over the next few years (including one with an OSCA V12 engine in 1951). He drove French Gordinis in 1952, he appeared in three races for Connaught in 1953, and because of its aerodynamic instability he crashed a works Aston Martin at Le Mans in 1954.

In early 1955 he won the New Zealand GP with his Maserati 250F and then returned to Europe. After only two more drives (that included third place in the International Trophy at Silverstone) he abruptly withdrew from racing. His marriage broke up, and he seemed lost without Chula's guidance. For a while he lived in Thailand, but he also had a home at Mandelieu on the French Riviera. He was living in a situation close to poverty when he collapsed because of a heart attack and died on a London Underground station in 1985.

Bizzarrini, Giotto

Engineer

Born: 6 June 1926 (Quercianella, near Livorno, Italy)

Bizzarrini read engineering at Pisa University, married Rosanna on 11 October 1953, and joined Alfa Romeo in August 1954. He worked in the experimental department, and also became a test driver before moving to Ferrari in February 1957. At Maranello, Bizzarrini again combined the roles of senior engineer and test driver. He worked on the development of the 3-litre Testa Rossa engine, and was responsible for the development of the 250GT SWB and 250GTO models. He was one of the management who left Ferrari at the end of 1961, and although he carried out very good work for the company, he appears to have been less than popular, and Ferrari conveniently forgets that he ever worked at Maranello.

From an engineering point of view Bizzarrini was remarkably talented, as he was able to design both chassis and engines. He had two real problems. The first was that he lacked concentration and staying power, and he always wanted to move on to the next project before he had completed the present one. He was also a lousy manager, especially so far as his personal affairs were concerned. After leaving Maranello, he conceived the 'bread van' version of the Ferrari 250GT built by Drogo, he acted as adviser to ASA (who were developing the 849cc version of the baby Ferrari, the 'Ferrarina'), and he worked for a short while on the ill-fated ATS F1 project.

Bizzarrini then set up his own engineering business, known as Società Autostar, at Livorno. He was commissioned by Ferruccio Lamborghini to design and build the original V12 Lamborghini engine, but this was partially redesigned by Dallara before the new car entered production, so as to achieve the lowest practical bonnet line. He then joined Renzo Rivolta's Iso Rivolta project and, after working on the original four-seater, he developed the staggeringly quick and alluringly beautiful Iso Grifo A3L coupé with 5.3-litre engine and 150mph (240kph) performance. Some cars were built under the Bizzarrini name, and in 1964 he left Iso to build Bizzarrini cars in his works at Livorno.

Bizzarrini continued to build cars under his own

Below: *Giotto Bizzarrini's inability to concentrate on projects for long periods was his biggest failing as an automobile engineer. Here, he is seen outside his house with his most successful creation after he left Ferrari – the Iso Grifo, but it is impossible to tell whether it is an Iso or a Bizzarrini-built car.* **(Klemantaski Collection)**

name until his company failed and he was made bankrupt. Thereafter, he worked as a consulting engineer, including the AMC AMX/3 project in 1969–71. He became Professor of Engineering at Pisa and Florence Universities until his retirement in 1985. Throughout this period and later, he continued design work. In 2009 he was still teaching at Rome University.

Bondurant, Bob

American Ferrari driver
Born: 27 April 1933 (Evanston, Illinois, USA)

Bob Bondurant initially indulged his enthusiasm for motor sport in his teens by riding an Indian motorcycle on dirt ovals, but then he moved to the west coast of

Below: *Bob Bondurant was a very able and very consistent driver of sports Ferraris, and went on to establish a successful racing drivers' school.* (LAT Photographic)

the United States where he raced a Morgan, and he then won the West Coast Production Championship, Class B, with a Chevrolet Corvette. A drive with Shelby American Cobra was the next step forward, and in 1964 he appeared regularly for the team, and his best performances were a class-win with a Daytona at Le Mans with Dan Gurney, and first in the class in the Sierra Montana Hill Climb (a round in the GT Championship).

Bob stayed with Shelby in 1965, finishing fourth overall and winning the class with Schlesser at Sebring, second in the GT class at Spa, winning the class in the Rossfeld Hill Climb, in the Reims 12 Hours race (with Schlesser), and the Enna Cup in Sicily. He was given a trial drive with a V8 Ferrari in the 1965 United States GP at Watkins Glen, where he finished ninth. In the Mexican GP he appeared with a Lotus 25 entered by the Reg Parnell (Racing) Team, but retired because of collapsed rear suspension. There were mixed feelings in Maranello about his performances, for he had proved his worth in GT racing with Cobras, while his GP showing was rather mediocre.

In the 1966 Daytona 24 Hours he co-drove a NART 250LM with Jochen Rindt, and they finished ninth overall, a none too satisfactory result, but the model was becoming obsolete. Ferrari brought Bondurant into the works team at Sebring to share the sole P3 entered with Mike Parkes. The Ferrari drivers fought hard against the Fords, holding second place at half-distance, but later Bondurant retired out on the circuit because of a seized gearbox. Bob was back at the wheel of a Ferrari at Le Mans, where he and Masten Gregory shared a NART-entered 365P2/3 with special long-tail Drogo body, but they retired after nine hours' racing because of a broken gearbox.

In 1966 he also acted as a technical consultant to John Frankenheimer in the making of the film *Grand Prix*. Bob had only two works Ferrari drives, but he rates these high on his CV – and who can blame him. During 1966 he also drove an obsolete BRM P261 entered by Team Chamaco Collect, and his results included a fourth (and admittedly, last) place at Monaco. During the year he also drove an Eagle in two races.

The following year, Bob tackled the CanAm series with a McLaren, but he suffered severe injuries in a crash at Watkins Glen. He made a successful comeback to CanAm racing in 1970–1, but after that he concentrated on running and developing his Bob Bondurant School of High Performance Motoring, now based at Phoenix International Raceway, Arizona, and sponsored by General Motors.

Above: *With his silly little hat and the pipe clenched between his teeth, Bonetto looks like a fugitive from a 'Popeye the Sailor' cartoon. He became a vastly experienced driver, but he was not popular with Enzo Ferrari, and never drove for the works team. He was killed at the wheel of a Lancia sports-racing car in the 1953 Carrera Panamericana Mexico.* (Author's collection)

Bonetto, Felice

Driver
Born: 9 June 1903 (Manerbio, near Brescia, Italy)
Died: 21 November 1953 (Silao, Mexico)

Bonetto never drove a works Ferrari. In post-war days he raced for Scuderia Milano (Maserati 4CLT and Milano F1 cars), he drove private Ferrari F2 cars in 1949, appeared for the Alfa Romeo works team with Tipo 159 cars (four races in 1951), the Maserati works team with A6GCM F2 cars (1952–3), and the Lancia works team with sports cars. He was at the wheel of a Lancia D24 team car in the 1953 Carrera Panamericana Mexico road race when he went off the road, hit a lamp-post and was killed.

There is a famous story about Bonetto. His only pre-war race was the 1934 Mille Miglia and with his old Alfa Romeo loaded up with fuel and tyres and without any practice, he started out from Brescia and, in fact, was setting a cracking pace. Scuderia Ferrari had entered Achille Varzi with a rather special 2632cc Alfa Romeo Monza, while the great Tazio Nuvolari, who had fallen out with Enzo Ferrari, was driving a 2336cc Monza entered and prepared by Scuderia Siena based at Como and with modifications that were said to be the work of Vittorio Jano.

Varzi was so obsessed with his rivalry with Nuvolari that he did not notice that both Tadini, with another Scuderia Ferrari Monza, and Bonetto, with his old car, were ahead of him and that Bonetto had taken the lead in the race. Scuderia Ferrari had set up a refuelling station at the top of the Futa Pass and Enzo Ferrari was watching keenly for the arrival of Varzi. He saw an Alfa Romeo approaching flat-out and he was convinced that it was Varzi, about to miss his refuelling stop.

Ferrari dashed into the road waving his arms furiously. Bonetto, it is said, looked him straight in the eye without lifting his foot off the accelerator, and Enzo had to throw himself into the roadside ditch from which he emerged plastered with mud. Varzi won the race from Nuvolari, while Bonetto's race ended in a collision with a tree. Few could hold a candle to Enzo Ferrari when it came to bearing a grudge, and it is obvious why Bonetto never drove for the team.

Borzacchini, Baconin

Scuderia Ferrari driver
Born: 28 September 1898 (Terni, Umbria, Italy)
Died: 10 September 1933 (Monza)

Borzacchini was named after Russian anarchist Mikhail Bakunin, who became a noted opponent of Karl Marx. His full name was Baconino Francesco Domenico Borzacchini, but he was sometimes known as Mario Umberto Borzacchini, allegedly having changed his name under pressure from elements of the Fascist Italian government.

Young Borzacchini started work in a garage as a trainee mechanic at the age of 14 and he served in the Italian army during the First World War. After the war he raced motorcycles, but he took up car racing in 1926. With a French Salmson light car he was very successful in Italian hill climbs, and after he had taken class wins in the Targa Florio in 1926 and 1927, he joined the Maserati works team, but achieved little success.

Borzacchini's most notable performance in this period was at Cremona in September 1929. With the Tipo V4 16-cylinder Maserati, he was timed during a private testing session over the 10km (6.214-mile) straight of this

Above: *Named after a Russian revolutionary, Borzacchini was one of the great Alfa Romeo drivers of the early 1930s. He drove for both Scuderia Ferrari and Maserati, and was killed at the wheel of a Maserati 8C 3000 at Monza in September 1933.* (Author's collection)

25km (15.54-mile) circuit at 152.90mph (246.17kph), a Class F World Record. In 1930 he won the Tripoli GP with a new 8C 2500 Maserati (it was his second win in this race), and he drove the V4 at Indianapolis with the superchargers removed to comply with the race regulations, but retired because of engine problems.

During the year, he left Maserati to join Alfa Romeo, and he finished third with a P2 in the Coppa Acerbo and second in the Monza GP. He drove a new 8C 2300 Alfa Romeo for Scuderia Ferrari in the 1931 Mille Miglia, but he crashed out of the race. Not long afterwards, he drove a 6C 1750 to second place in the Targa Florio. In the 10-hour European GP at Monza, the short-wheelbase 8C 2300s (which became known as 'Monzas' after the race), driven by Campari/Nuvolari and Minoia/Borzacchini, took the first two places. Later that year, Borzacchini, partnering Campari, took second place in the ten-hour French GP at Montlhéry.

In 1932 Borzacchini, partnered by Bignami, won the Mille Miglia and he finished second in the Targa Florio, driving 8C 2300s in both races. As a less favoured driver,

he was still at the wheel of a Monza in the Italian GP where Nuvolari and Campari appeared with the Monoposto on the model's debut. Nuvolari won, and Borzacchini finished third (behind Chiron with a 4.9-litre type 54 Bugatti). By the French GP held at Reims, for the first time Borzacchini was at the wheel of a Monoposto, and he finished second behind Nuvolari. Another second place followed in the Coppa Ciano. Overall, Borzacchini enjoyed an exceptional year.

At the beginning of 1933, Alfa Romeo withdrew from racing, so Nuvolari and Borzacchini became the leading drivers of Scuderia Ferrari, and in GP racing the team had to make do with the outdated Monzas. Borzacchini retired his Scuderia Ferrari 8C 2300 Alfa Romeo in the Mille Miglia because of a cracked cylinder head. In the Monaco GP, Borzacchini finished second despite the engine of his Monza making ominous clanking noises.

As the 1933 season progressed, so Borzacchini's fortunes suffered and the final, fatal, and terrible blow came in the Monza GP on 10 September, by which time he had returned to Maserati. With the two-seater 8C 3000 that Campari had driven to victory in the French GP, both he and Campari, with an Alfa Romeo Monoposto, crashed on the first lap of their heat of the Monza GP.

Both drivers skidded on oil dropped by Trossi's Ferrari-entered 4.5-litre V8 Duesenberg. The oil tank had split during an earlier heat and it spilled much of its oil on the track. The drivers had been warned about the oil, but it had not been stressed that the sand spread on the track was less than effective. Borzacchini survived a short while after the accident, while Campari was killed outright. Both drivers were Italian heroes and their deaths were terrible blows to Italian motor racing.

Bracco, Giovanni

Works sports car driver
Born: 6 June 1908 (Biella, Italy)
Died: 6 August 1968 (Biella)

Before and after the Second World War, Bracco drove Lancia Aprilias in Italian races, but his relatively short racing career was marked by two incidents, one of them a terrible disaster and the other a major triumph. In 1948 he entered a 3-litre Delage in the Circuit of Modena run on a very difficult 2-mile (3.2km) street circuit. The pits were rather foolishly situated on a curve. Cortese was making the second of two stops at the pits because of engine trouble and, as he slowed off, Bracco swerved to avoid him. He lost control of the Delage, which careered on into a packed spectator enclosure.

Bracco was flung out into the road, suffering a broken leg and broken ribs. Five spectators were killed and more than 15 were seriously injured. The race was stopped with 24 laps completed, and Ascari and Villoresi, with works 2-litre A6GCS Maseratis, were awarded the first two places. He had a reputation as a great clown, but he had a very temperamental personality that did not appeal to many team managers. It is a matter of fact that Bracco in later years drank heavily, even when racing, and the roots of this alcoholism may lie in the accident at Modena.

Bracco was a regular competitor in the Mille Miglia, but it is not always clear who owned the cars that he drove. In 1949 he raced a Tipo 166SC with Ansaloni spider body, and was partnered by young Umberto Maglioli, but they retired after holding sixth place overall at Livorno. Maglioli again partnered Bracco in 1950 when he drove a 166MM with Touring Barchetta body, and Bracco drove superbly to finish fourth overall.

The following year, Bracco was at the wheel of a 2-litre Lancia Aurelia B20 coupé, once again with Maglioli, and took a brilliant second place behind Villoresi with a works Tipo 340 Ferrari America. This Lancia was one of a number works-prepared for competition work, but they all belonged to the drivers. Shortly afterwards, Bracco won the Primavera Romana night race, and at Le Mans he and Count 'Johnny' Lurani, smartly attired with formal collars and ties, finished sixth with their B20 Aurelia and won the 2000cc class. With some sponsorship from Olivetti, Bracco drove his B20 in the Carrera Panamericana Mexico road race, but retired after spinning off.

In 1952 Ferrari had built the new 250 Sport powered by a much improved Colombo 2953cc V12 engine. Bracco, partnered by Alfonso Rolfo, was loaned one of these cars by Ferrari for the Mille Miglia. Throughout the race, Bracco swigged cognac from the flask that he always carried in a special mounting in the cockpit of his competition cars, and chain-smoked Nazionali cigarettes. In this race Ferrari faced immensely strong opposition from a team of Mercedes-Benz 300SL gull-wing coupés.

Bracco made Mille Miglia history by winning from Kling/Klenk, with a 300SL, by a margin of 4min 32sec after 12 hours of racing. If Bracco had the boost of tobacco and alcohol in the blood, Kling had the handicap of worn rear tyres (they could not be changed because one of the original wheels had jammed on the spline) and locking brakes. Later in the year, Bracco

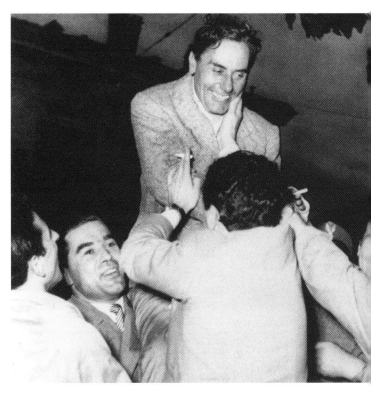

Above: *A smiling Bracco receives the appreciation of his supporters after his win in the 1952 Mille Miglia. He was an incredibly quick driver, who chain-smoked and sipped cognac while racing.* (Author's collection)

drove a 250 Sport in the Mexican road race and he again presented the 300SLs with stiff opposition, but he retired because of gearbox failure.

Although Bracco raced infrequently after 1952, he was again partnered by Rolfo in the 1953 Mille Miglia with a 250MM, the definitive version of the 250 Sport, now fitted with a very elegant Pinin Farina coupé body. They were in fifth place at Rome, but gradually fell back and retired because of various mechanical problems. He drove a 250MM Ferrari in the 1954 Carrera Panamericana Mexico road race – after saying that he would never run in the race again, following the death of his great friend Bonetto in the previous year's event.

As it was, he failed to complete the first stage because of mechanical problems. In the 1955 Targa Florio (so impressively dominated by the Mercedes-Benz 300SLRs that year) Bracco shared a new 200S 2-litre Maserati with Franco Bordoni, and it was probably his last race. Bracco crashed it very heavily in practice, and it was only fit to start the race because of extensive bodywork repairs carried out at a local garage. They failed to finish the race. Bracco died of cancer in 1968.

Brambilla, Ernesto

Works F2 driver
Born: 31 January 1934 (Monza, Italy)

Ernesto raced motorcycles, but in 1963 he drove a F1 Cooper-Maserati at the Italian GP for Scuderia Centro-Sud and, in 1968, Ferrari entered him in the team's Dino 166 F2 cars (1600cc). After a poor start he was very successful. He crashed in the Lottery GP at Monza in June, retired because of steering problems at Zandvoort, and then achieved a succession of excellent results: he finished third in the Mediterranean GP at Enna, and then he won at Hockenheim, Rome, and the first of two races at Buenos Aires. He retired in the last three races in the Argentinian series at Cordoba, San Juan, and at Buenos Aires for the second time.

He stayed with the team in 1969, finishing sixth at Thruxton and retiring because of engine problems in the Deutschland Trophy at Hockenheim; he pulled out of the Eifelrennen at the Nürburgring because he was unwell, took sixth place in the Madrid GP at Jarama, and retired again because of engine problems at Monza on 22 June. After this race, Ferrari withdrew the cars and, in due course, made an announcement that they would not return to F2 until they were competitive; they never did reappear.

Ernesto Brambilla made one more appearance for Ferrari, at the wheel of an F1 V12 Ferrari in practice for the Italian GP. He was abysmally slow, and Pedro Rodriguez took over the drive and finished sixth. Ernesto's racing career was at an end.

His younger brother Vittorio was born at Monza on 11 September 1937; he raced motorcycles and karts and worked his way up to driving a F2 Beta Tools-sponsored March 732 in 1973. In 1974_5 he drove for March in F1 and when the Austrian GP was stopped at half-distance because of rain, he was leading the race; as he crossed the finishing line, he waved both arms in the air in triumph, and promptly crashed, fairly lightly, into the barriers.

He retained his win after some argument, and for Vittorio it was just another in a long series of accidents, many of which were caused by 'red mist', loss of self-control. He was severely injured at the 1978 Italian GP in a separate incident from that which cost Peterson his life. After a slow recovery, he devoted his energies to his garage business in Monza; he died there on 26 May 2001.

Above: *Of the two Brambilla brothers, Ernesto was the less effervescent and more reliable. Although he drove the Dino F2 cars very successfully, there is a lingering doubt that Ferrari failed to give him a fair crack of the whip and the writer believes that he could have been a very successful driver of Sports Prototypes.* **(LAT Photographic)**

Brawn, Ross

Technical Director
Born: 23 November 1954 (Manchester, England)

After attending Reading School in Berkshire, Brawn became a trainee engineer at the Atomic Energy Research Establishment at Harwell, Oxfordshire. He worked for the March team from 1976, but two years later he moved to Williams. Subsequently, he worked at Haas Lola, Arrows and Jaguar.

He became Technical Director of the Benetton F1 team in 1991, the same year that Michael Schumacher joined the team. Throughout his Formula 1 career Brawn has displayed exceptional ability in exploiting regulations to the maximum, and at Benetton his contribution helped to transform the team's performances. In 1994 and '95 Schumacher won his

Above: *Ross Brawn left Ferrari for Honda and took complete control of the team – known as Brawn – after the Japanese company withdrew from racing at the end of 2008.* **(LAT Photographic)**

under almost any circumstances became legendary, as did his talent for motivating the entire team to perform consistently at the very highest level.

Thereafter Ferrari lost its dominant edge, and on 26 October 2006 it was announced that Brawn was leaving. It was originally believed that he would be taking a one-year 'sabbatical' to allow other team members to advance within the team, but at the end of 2007 came news that Brawn was joining the Honda F1 team. He had hoped for a more senior position at Ferrari, but he was passed over, probably a victim of the political infighting that has always been ever-present at Ferrari.

Facing the prospect of a dreadfully uncompetitive season with Honda in 2008, Brawn decided in April to start serious work on the following year's car – the design that was to become the Mercedes-powered Brawn which, following Honda's withdrawal at the end of 2008, took F1 by storm at the beginning of 2009.

Brivio, Antonio

Scuderia Ferrari driver
Born: 30 January 1905 (also recorded as 27 December 1905) (Biella, Italy)
Died: 20 January 1995 (Milan, Italy)

Marchese Antonio 'Tonino' Brivio (sometimes known as Marchese Sforza Brivio) was a member of the family that ruled Milan in the 15th and 16th centuries. He competed in the bobsleigh category of the Winter Olympics in 1936, as well proving to be an outstandingly able racing driver. He had started racing with a Darracq in 1928; prior to 1932 he drove Alfa Romeo sports cars for Scuderia Materassi. His first major success came in 1932 when he was partnered by Eugenio Siena, of the Scuderia Ferrari staff, in the winning 8C 2300 Alfa Romeo in the Spa 24 Hours race.

In August 1933, Brivio drove a 2.6 Monza to a win in the Swedish Summer GP held over 12 laps of the difficult 18-mile Vram circuit. One-hird of the circuit was narrow tarmac, but the rest was unmetalled. Brivio probably would not have won if team-mate Chiron had not been involved in a multi-car accident at the first corner after the start; it was a rather spectacular accident as a house on the corner caught fire and was burnt down.

Brivio drove a Type 59 Bugatti in the poorly supported 1934 Belgian GP and took second place to Dreyfus with another Type 59. Later that year, Brivio finished third with a Type 59 in the Coppa Acerbo, but

first two – and Benetton's only two – World Championship titles, and took nine race wins in each of the seasons.

For 1996 Schumacher left Benetton to drive for Ferrari, whose record in recent years had been deplorable. Schumacher was well aware that this first year would be spent developing the new V10 car into a potential race winner, but he nevertheless won the Spanish, Belgian and Italian races and took third place in the World Championship.

Brawn followed Schumacher to Ferrari a year later, becoming Technical Director. With Schumacher, Jean Todt and Rory Byrne, he plotted and achieved the team's fantastic run of successes. Together they formed what became known as the 'four-legged stool', the great powerhouse of F1 design and engineering that dominated racing and resisted the whims, demands and potential mistakes of Ferrari chairman Luca di Montezemolo. Schumacher and Ferrari won the Drivers' and Constructors' World Championships every year from 2000 to 2004. During this time, Brawn's ability to read a race and maximise the team's race strategy

Above: *Although he never made a great impression on the international scene, Brivio was a fast, consistent, and reliable driver of Scuderia Ferrari Alfa Romeos.* (Author's collection)

finished fourth in the Coppa Acerbo and an excellent third in the Vanderbilt Cup.

After Nuvolari non-started in the 1937 Turin race (full title Gran Premio Principe di Piemonte) because of an accident in practice, Brivio won from Farina and Biondetti. He achieved little else in the way of success in 1937 and he retired from racing in 1938 following a decision to marry. Enzo Ferrari thought that this was hilariously funny. In post-war days, Brivio became Chairman of the Sporting Commission of the Auto Club of Italy, and in 1948 a member of the Féderation Internationale de l'Automobile. He is believed to have been largely responsible for the introduction of the Drivers' World Championship in 1950.

Brooks, Tony

Works driver
Born: 25 February 1932 (Dukinfield, Cheshire, England)

As a dental student, Charles Anthony Brooks raced a Healey Silverstone with the full support of his parents, and he also drove Frazer Nash cars (for friend Dudley Hely and the works), together with a Connaught A-series belonging to another friend, John Riseley-Prichard. He scored a remarkable win with an unstreamlined B-series Connaught in the 1955 Syracuse GP, the first GP win by a British driver with a British car since Segrave's win at San Sebastian in 1924. Brooks qualified as a dentist, but never practised.

Tony was a member, along with Mike Hawthorn, of the disastrous BRM team in 1956, and the team's season was cut short after Brooks crashed heavily in the British GP at Silverstone because the throttle jammed open following a bodged repair in the pits. For 1957 Tony signed up to drive for Vanwall, and early success in the season included second place behind Fangio in the Monaco race after a multi-car crash eliminated team-mate Moss, together with Ferrari drivers Hawthorn and Collins. Shortly after this, partnered by Noel Cunningham-Reid, he showed such overwhelming skill in winning the Nürburgring 1,000km race with an Aston Martin that he became recognised as a truly great driver.

When Brooks crashed a works Aston Martin at Le Mans that year, he suffered injuries that resulted in him missing the French GP at Rouen and the non-championship Reims GP. He returned to racing in the European GP at Aintree, but he was not fully recovered

he had decided to leave Bugatti, and by the Circuit of Naples he had joined Scuderia Ferrari and took second place in this race. The Marchese decided to stay with Scuderia Ferrari for 1935 and he started the year with a third place at Monaco. At Tripoli that year he was hit in the face by a stone while overtaking Farina, and he went off the track at high speed. Race officials found him lying unconscious and semi-naked in the sand dunes some distance from his wrecked car.

He was treated in Professor Putti's clinic in the old monastery at Bologna, and did not race again until the end of June when he came fourth in the Penya Rhin GP at Barcelona. In August he finished second to Nuvolari in the Coppa Ciano, and he took third place behind two Auto Unions in the Coppa Acerbo. Brivio stayed with Scuderia Ferrari in 1936 and, partnered by Ongaro, won the Mille Miglia at record speed. In the German GP he drove a 12C 36 into third place behind two Auto Unions; he took second place in the Coppa Ciano,

Right: *Tony Brooks was a member of the Vanwall team in 1957–8, and drove for Ferrari in 1959. In July 1957, Brooks was still recovering from his bad crash at Le Mans, and in the European GP at Aintree he handed his Vanwall over to Stirling Moss, who scored the first World Championship race victory by a British car. Here, after their win, Brooks and Moss express their delight.* (Author's collection)

and he lapped gently to keep his car 'on the boil' if team-leader Stirling Moss required it. Stirling's Vanwall developed a bad misfire and he took over Brooks's car to fight his way back up the field, assisted by unexpected retirements, to score the first British victory in a Grande Épreuve since Sir Henry Segrave's win with a Sunbeam in the 1923 French GP.

By 1958, Brooks had become a highly polished, very, very safe driver, and he was undoubtedly one of the top six in F1. He remained with Vanwall and enjoyed a brilliant season, winning the Belgian, German, and Italian Grands Prix to take third place in the Championship behind Hawthorn and Moss. Vandervell withdrew from racing at the end of 1958 because of ill health, but Vanwall development continued. Tony Brooks signed up for Ferrari, and it seemed that the Dino GP cars would be dominant, certainly on the faster circuits. An advantage of this deal was that Tony was engaged to a young Italian girl, Pina, so he could spend time in Italy in a very worthwhile way.

Throughout 1959, Brooks was in serious contention for the Drivers' Championship, but the works Coopers driven by Brabham and McLaren provided a very serious threat. Despite being physically sick in the cockpit because of fumes, Tony was second to Brabham (Cooper) at Monaco, and he subsequently won the French GP on the fast Reims circuit, and the German race on the high-speed banked Avus track. Ferrari missed the British GP, and Vandervell provided Brooks with a rebuilt Vanwall of lower construction, but it retired early in the race because of ignition trouble.

When the teams arrived at Monza for the Italian GP, Brooks was second in the World Championship with 23 points to the 29 of Brabham. The Monza race, so well suited to Ferrari straight-line speed, destroyed Brooks's Championship prospects when he retired with clutch trouble at the start. In the United States race at Sebring Raceway, California, he was hit at the start by the Ferrari of team-mate von Trips, and after a pit stop for the car to be checked over he took third

Below: *In May 1959, Scuderia Ferrari entered Dino V6 cars for Tony Brooks and Phil Hill in the International Trophy race at Silverstone. Although these very powerful cars performed well on fast circuits, they were outclassed in this race. Phil Hill finished fourth, a lap in arrears, and Tony Brooks, seen here, retired early in the race because of valve failure.* (Tom March Collection)

place. He finished second in the Championship with 27 points to Brabham's 31.

By this time, Tony and Pina had married and settled in England, and he had increasing business interests and commitments. Although he was at the height of his powers as a driver, he elected to drive obsolete 1959 Coopers for the Yeoman Credit team in 1960. As might be expected, it was a poor year, and all that Tony achieved were a fourth place at Monaco, and fifths in the British and Portuguese races. Once again, Vandervell produced a new Vanwall, another lighter and lower car, which he drove at Reims, but he retired because of a transmission vibration.

The new 1500cc GP formula started in 1961, and the British teams were not ready. Tony drove for BRM, who raced cars that were too heavy and had the low-output Coventry Climax FPF engine. It was another pretty hopeless year in which his best performance was third place in the United States race at Watkins Glen. At this point Tony retired from racing to concentrate on his garage business at Weybridge and his family life. He had enjoyed three seasons at the top, two with Vanwall and one with Ferrari, and he certainly ranks in the top echelon of drivers ever to appear for Maranello.

Byrne, Rory

Engineer (Chief Designer)
Born: 10 January 1944 (Pretoria, South Africa)

After graduating from Witwatersrand University with a BSc in chemistry, Byrne worked for a company called Kolchem and became chief chemist. In 1969, with three friends, he founded 'Auto Drag and Spend Den', a company importing high-performance car parts, and then in 1973 he assisted a friend who was competing in the British Formula Ford Championships. In 1974 he became chief designer at Royale racing cars based at Park Royal in north-west London. In 1978 he joined the Toleman team, initially taking charge of team operations. He was substantially responsible for the design of the Toleman TG280 F2 car, which dominated the 1980 F2 Championship.

Between 1981 and 1985 he was the chief engineer at Toleman and was responsible for the design of the F1 cars, and there is no doubt that both Byrne and Toleman were in an immense learning curve at the time. The performance of Toleman F1 cars gradually

Above: *Born in South Africa, Rory Byrne has enjoyed a long and successful career as a race engineering designer. He was planning to leave Ferrari in 2009 and it is not certain whether he will do this.*
(LAT Photographic)

improved, and when Benetton took over the team in 1986 he remained as Chief Designer until 1991 when he moved to Reynard to work on their experimental F1 project.

He returned to Benetton Formula (as it had become known) in 1992 and was in charge of research and development. It was an immensely successful period, and Michael Schumacher won the Drivers' Championship in 1994 (Benetton was second in the Constructors' Championship), and again in 1995 when Benetton won the Constructors' Championship. Byrne retired to Thailand, but he was persuaded to join Ferrari in 1997 and was Chief Designer with the F1 team until the end of 2005. He became car design and development consultant in 2006 and then extended his stay with the team until 2009.

Campari, Giuseppe

Scuderia Ferrari driver
Born: 8 June 1892 (Lodi, near Milan, Italy)
Died: 10 September 1933 (Monza)

Motor racing with men like Arcangeli, Campari, and Sivocci was dangerous and delightful, as the Italian drivers lapped at high speed, and especially so in testing. Those drivers, associated with Alfa Romeo, broke off for a lunch with Lambrusco and pasta accompanied by vociferous arias. Campari had an ambition to be an opera singer, and he had apparently sung professionally at the Donizetti theatre in Bergamo, and was married to opera singer Lina Cavallero.

He was very popular with an affectionate Italian public and, according to some sources, he was known as 'Il Negher' ('The Darkie'), but the word 'Negher' is not a normal Italian word. He was a test driver with what was then known as ALFA, stayed with the company in post-First World War days and raced regularly for the Alfa Romeo works team, Alfa Corse, as part of their competition programme.

With P2 cars designed by Vittorio Jano, Campari won the 1924 French GP and finished third in the Italian GP at Monza behind Ascari and Wagner. The following year he was second to Ascari in the European GP at Spa-Francorchamps, and after Ascari's fatal accident in the French race Campari led until the team was withdrawn. He also finished second in the Italian GP. Campari bought his P2 from the works (it was believed to be the car with which he had won the French race at Lyon in 1924) and raced it with great success through to 1928. His wins included the Coppa Acerbo in 1927–8, together with FTD in a number of hill climbs.

With Alfa Romeos, Campari won the Mille Miglia, partnered by Ramponi, in 1928 (6C 1500 Super Sport) and in 1929 (6C 1750 Grand Sport), and he took third place, with Marinoni, at the wheel of a 6C 1750 Grand Sport in 1930. He was second on handicap with a 6C 1750 in both the 1930 Irish GP and the Tourist Trophy on the Ards circuit.

In 1931, one of Campari's best performances was in the Coppa Acerbo at Pescara, which he won with the twin-engined Tipo A Alfa Romeo, and he and Nuvolari shared the winning 8C 2300 in the Italian GP. Also, with Borzacchini, he finished second in the French GP, again with an 8C 2300. The following year Alfa Romeo introduced the new Monoposto, but while Nuvolari was on peak form, Campari achieved very little apart from winning one of the heats of the Monza GP in September. Because of financial problems, Alfa Romeo withdrew the Monopostos for racing in 1933, and Campari joined Maserati.

He won the French race with the two-seater 8C 3000 Maserati, and was third in the Coppa Ciano. By the Monza race on 10 September, Campari had returned to Alfa Romeo, and he drove a Monoposto for Scuderia Ferrari. He had announced that he would be retiring at the end of the season to devote himself to opera singing. It was not to be. On the first lap of the second heat, Campari and Borzacchini (with the 8C 3000 Maserati) were fighting for the lead when they skidded on a patch of oil. It seems that this had been dropped by Count Trossi's Scuderia Ferrari-entered 4½-litre Duesenberg in the first heat and had not been adequately sanded. Campari was killed instantly and Borzacchini died shortly afterwards.

Below: *Giuseppe Campari at the wheel of his Alfa Romeo P2, with riding mechanic Giulio Ramponi, at the 1924 Italian GP at Monza, where they finished third. For a short period during the race, Campari was relieved by Presenti, who was mainly a mechanic.* (Author's collection)

Above: *Ivan Capelli had a long career in Formula 1 with March and the Leyton House team before joining Ferrari in 1992. It proved to be a miserable season of almost complete failure, with an uncompetitive car, and he was dropped by Maranello before the end of the year.* (LAT Photographic)

retirements). For five seasons from 1987 he was a member of the Leyton House team in F1, and he became increasingly more mature and confident. In the main, retirement followed retirement, but he briefly led the 1988 Portuguese GP, before dropping back to finish second to Prost. He came second again to Prost in the French GP at the Paul Ricard circuit in 1990.

Although the 1991 season proved dreadful, with the cars uncompetitive, Capelli failing to finish a single race other than the Hungarian GP, in which he was classified sixth, and the team's South Korean owner arrested in Japan for financial irregularities, it could be described as Ivan's most successful season. Ferrari recognised his solid, proven talent, and signed him up for 1992. Sadly, Capelli flattered only to deceive. His season with the F92A was hopelessly unsuccessful; the car was rubbish, and his best performance was fifth place in Brazil. He was replaced by test driver Nicola Larini for the last two races of the season.

In 1993 his old boss at Leyton House, Ian Phillips, was running the Sasol Jordan team, and he brought in Capelli, but after only two races he was out again and his F1 and serious racing career was over. In 1995–6 he drove Primeras for the works Nissan team in the German Super Touring Championship, but after that he was rarely seen on the race track. For some while he commentated on GP racing in Italian digital broadcasts, and most recently he has been a commentator on the Italian TV station *Rai Uno*.

Capelli, Ivan

Works driver
Born: 24 May 1963 (Milan, Italy)

Capelli is a man who came so very close to being a great Italian champion, but foundered in his one season with Ferrari and rapidly disappeared from the ranks of F1 drivers. With a successful background in karting, Capelli entered F3 in 1982 and finished sixth in that year's Italian Championship. In 1984 he won the European F3 Championship for Enzo Coloni's Ralt-Alfa Romeo team, but there were suggestions that the cars were illegal and, although he was obviously not personally responsible for any infringements of the rules, his reputation was tainted.

Capelli missed races in 1985 because of his National Service, but, even so, he was entered in the 1985 F3000 series with a March. He drove in two F1 races for Tyrrell that year (fourth in Australia) and AGS in 1986 (two

Caracciola, Rudolf

Alfa Romeo works driver
Born: 30 January 1901 (Remagen, Germany)
Died: 28 September 1959 (Kassel, Germany)

For much of his racing life, Caracciola was a Mercedes-Benz driver, and his exploits with SSKL cars (including his win in the 1931 Mille Miglia) are legendary. The financial situation in Germany in 1931 was appalling, as the Weimar Republic was in its death throes. Mercedes-Benz could no longer afford to support him in 1932, and early in the season he joined Alfa Romeo. The team, not Caracciola, was adamant that his Monza should be painted German white and not Italian red (which meant that he was in fact running as an independent). During the season he scored quite a number of good places and, after he won the Italian GP, his car was painted red like the others.

By the end of 1932 Alfa Romeo was in serious financial difficulty and withdrew from racing. Caracciola and Chiron teamed up to race Alfa Romeo Monzas and Bugattis under the name Scuderia CC. The first race was to have been the Monaco GP in April, but Caracciola crashed his Monza on the second day of practice. It is not clear exactly what happened. Either, as Caracciola claimed, a brake locked on the downhill run from the tunnel to the chicane and he opted to hit the stone wall on the left rather than plunge into the harbour, or he made an error of judgement.

Rudi's right thigh was shattered and it seemed unlikely that he would race again. Even so, he was signed up for the re-formed Mercedes-Benz team for 1934 and, although it cannot be said that he made a full recovery, he was Germany's finest GP driver in the 1930s, despite the fact that he was at times in very considerable pain, and the personal tragedy that his wife Charly was trapped in an avalanche while skiing in 1933 and had died of a heart attack.

Later, Caracciola married Alice 'Baby' Hoffmann, and that they were happy together is undoubted. His premature death was hastened by the effects of two more bad accidents. He was seriously injured while driving an American car in qualifying at Indianapolis in 1946, and again suffered bad injuries when he crashed his 300SL Mercedes-Benz at Bremgarten in 1952 after a brake locked.

Above: *Rudolf Caracciola drove for Alfa Romeo during the 1932 season, winning the Italian Grand Prix.* (**LAT Photographic**)

Below: *Eugenio Castellotti in the pits at Reims in 1956. The young Italian was a great, dynamic, exhilarating driver, and his death early in 1957 was a terrible loss to Ferrari.* (**LAT Photographic**)

Castellotti, Eugenio

Works driver
Born: 10 October 1930 (Lodi, near Milan, Italy)
Died: 14 March 1957 (Modena Aerautodromo)

A driver fired by passion, with immense skill, very little self-control, and a burning ambition to succeed, Castellotti was one of the most promising and probably the fastest Italian driver of the 1950s. That he was wild was undoubted, but his driving was less wild than is often suggested by those who never saw him race. When he knew that his car would not last, he would turn in a magnificent 'balls to the wall' performance until it broke.

His race career started when he hired a Ferrari Tipo 166MM from Rome-based Scuderia Guastalla to drive in

the 1951 Mille Miglia and, partnered by Giuseppe Rota, he finished way down the field in 50th place. His performances rapidly improved, and in 1952 he scored a string of successes with a private Ferrari that included second place in the sports car Monaco GP, a win in the sports car Portuguese GP, and third place in the 86-mile (138km) sports car Bari GP behind other privately entered Ferrari drivers, Franco Landi and Tom Cole. He also drove lightweight Lancia Aurelia B20s in a number of races, including the Inter-Europa Cup at Monza.

The following year, 1953, partnered by Musitelli, Castellotti won the ten-hour Messina Night race in Sicily,

Below: *Castellotti is seen here at the wheel of the 4.4-litre six-cylinder Lampredi-designed Tipo 121 Ferrari that he drove at Le Mans in 1955 with Paolo Marzotto. It was one of the occasions when Castellotti was decried for driving wildly. He forced his way to the front and led at the end of the first hour. It is easily forgotten that Castellotti was a realist, and knew that his Ferrari would not last, so he ensured that he made an impressive show until he fell back because of engine problems and retired.* (Tom March Collection)

and he also won that year's Italian Mountain Championship (that is, hill climbs) with a Ferrari. He was brought into the Lancia team at some races, and after driving a 2-litre Aurelia B20 in the three-hour Inter-Europa Cup for saloons at Monza, he shared a D24 Spider in the Nürburgring 1,000km race, but retired because of battery failure. He then had the chance to display his outstanding talents in hill climbing.

With a D23 Spider he won the incredibly arduous (32km) Catania–Etna hill climb at a storming 62.14mph (99.98kph), and the following weekend was second to team-mate Bonetto in the Bologna–Raticosa event. He was then a member of the Lancia team in the Carrera Panamericana road race and drove a D23 Spider into third place behind Fangio and Taruffi with D24s. The Lancia effort in this race smacked of overkill, Bonetto was killed with his Lancia, and the Turin team dominated the results only because there was no serious opposition, once the Scuderia Guastalla team of 4.5-litre Ferraris had run into problems.

Castellotti became a regular Lancia team member in 1954, and his dark, handsome good looks featured prominently in publicity shoots. Along with Ascari and Villoresi, he was waiting to drive the new D50 GP car,

but for him this did not happen until 1955. His sports car appearances were fast and furious, and sometimes successful. He finished second in the sports car Porto GP, and in July he won the Bolzano–Mendola hill climb (a popular success because Lancia commercial vehicles were then built in a factory at Bolzano). He also won the Aôsta–Gran San Bernardo hill climb at the end of July, the Siena–Florence road race in September, and the Bologna–Raticosa hill climb in October.

The D50 GP car had appeared in the Spanish GP in October, and the two cars entered were driven by Ascari and Villoresi. Castellotti first raced the D50 in Argentina in January 1955, but had to hand his car over to Villoresi, who crashed. Back in Europe in non-Championship races, he finished fourth at Turin and second at Pau. Next on the calendar was the Championship Monaco GP. Brake problems caused Ascari to crash into the harbour, and Castellotti achieved one of his best F1 results by finishing second with his brakeless Lancia behind Trintignant (Ferrari).

A few days after Monaco, the great Alberto Ascari was killed in a practice accident at Monza. By now Lancia, having expended vast sums on their competition programme in the face of plummeting car sales, was insolvent and withdrew from racing. The team made one final entry, a single car for the ever-keen tiger of the team ran in the Belgian GP at Spa-Francorchamps on 5 June. Despite the all-powerful Mercedes-Benz team, Castellotti was fastest in practice, and the great Lancia engineer Vittorio Jano warned him to 'temper his enthusiasm with a modicum of restraint'.

After holding second place on the first lap, he dropped back to third and held that place until his gearbox failed out at Malmédy on lap 17. Eugenio now joined Ferrari, driving the fast, but unreliable 4.4-litre Tipo 121 car at Le Mans the following weekend, battling initially with Hawthorn and Fangio, leading at the end of the first hour, but dropping back to retire because of engine trouble in the fourth hour. It was a bad year for Ferrari, but Castellotti drove exceptionally well to take fifth place in the Dutch race, and a fine third behind the two surviving Mercedes-Benz cars at Monza.

For 1956, Luigi Musso joined Ferrari from Maserati, and there was immense rivalry between Musso and Castellotti, and not all that much amiability off the track. Sadly, it was one of Enzo Ferrari's weaknesses that he played drivers off against each other, and he did this with the two young Italians. Castellotti enjoyed an excellent season in sports cars; he co-drove the winning Ferrari at Sebring with Fangio; he drove brilliantly in the wet to win the Mille Miglia road race, one of the finest victories in the history of the race; and,

again partnering Fangio, he finished second in the Nürburgring 1,000km race.

In reality, there were too many top-drawer F1 drivers in the 1956 Ferrari team, and Eugenio's GP successes were limited. He took over Fangio's car to finish fourth at Monaco, and he came second in the French race at Reims, but otherwise retirement followed retirement. At Monza, while the more stable members of the Ferrari team tried their best to win the race, Castellotti and Musso, without team management restraint – Ugolini was now at Maserati – battled in a personal duel that was complete folly.

The Lancia-Ferraris were plagued by their Englebert tyres throwing treads and, although it was not appreciated until later, by fractured steering arms caused by the stress of the tyres. Fangio, who had urged them to take the race steadily, commented:

'But they said they wanted to run the race their way. From the start they forced the pace like madmen, locking wheels under braking and spinning their tyres everywhere. I could see that neither of them would be there at the finish…'

Castellotti spun off violently into a barrier and out of the race, but took over Fangio's original car to finish eighth, displaying the most incredible sangfroid. Musso was leading the race when the left-hand steering arm broke, the left front tyre burst, and he slid, completely out of control, across the vast start/finish apron and came to a halt just a few inches off the pit counter. Probably for the first time in his young and exciting life, he had been really frightened.

Eugenio was engaged to the young ballerina and actress Delia Scala. For the Italian paparazzi and their editors, it was a marriage made in Heaven, with the specific purpose of keeping the Jewish piano playing. Castellotti drove in the Argentine races at the beginning of the year, and on the team's return to Europe he and Delia went on holiday in March to the Adriatic coast. Delia wanted Eugenio to give up racing and it was something they were going to resolve while they were away.

Ferrari asked Castellotti to interrupt his holiday and to return to the factory for a testing session at the Modena Aerautodromo. During the tests Eugenio lost control, he was flung out of the car (some say for as far as 100yd, which seems improbable) and died of a fractured skull. It was a terrible loss to Italian racing. Enzo Ferrari is said to have commented that Castellotti was in 'a confused state of mind' because of the conflict between racing and retiring.

Cavey, Noël

Ferrari Test Engine Manager
Born: 10 January 1958 (Coutances, Manche, Normandy, France)

Much of Cavey's career has been with Renault, whom he joined in 1994. From then until 1998 he worked in Renault Research at Reueil Malmaison where he was a research and development engineer. He moved to Renault Sports at Viry-Châtillon, where he was in charge of F1 engine assembly and dyno bench tests, and he then became head of engine track testing with the Williams-Renault team. Cavey joined Ferrari in 1995, and for eight years he was responsible for test engines. He became Test Engine Manager in 2004, and a year later chief engineer responsible for Track and Bench Test engines. He is now Test Engine Manager. Ferrari job designations are never lucid.

Cheever, Eddie

Driver
Born: 10 January 1958 (Phoenix, Arizona, USA)

Edward McKay Cheever Jr. lived in Rome as a child (he became domiciled in Italy) and was soon gripped by a passionate interest in motor racing. His career started with karts, winning Italian and European Championships at the age of 15, and he raced for Ron Dennis's Project Four team in F2. On 15 September 1977 he tested a Ferrari 312T2 F1 car at Fiorano, with a view to driving one of these cars in a non-Championship race at Imola, which was cancelled. Subsequently Ferrari offered Cheever a contract, which he declined to accept.

   His racing career extended over many years with widely varying levels of success. Despite driving for nine different teams, being entered in 143 World Championship F1 races, and starting in 132, he never won a F1 race. He enjoyed many successes with the Jaguar sports car team in the years 1986–8. He switched to CART racing in 1990 – he has been a successful entrant, has done motor racing commentaries for television, and has driven in the GP Masters series of races.

Chinetti, Luigi

Private sports car driver, founder of NART
Born: 17 July 1901 (Milan, Italy)
Died: 17 August 1994 (Greenwich, Connecticut, USA)

Although not in any way a close collaborator of Enzo Ferrari, Chinetti made a major contribution to the success of Ferrari as a marque. He was the son of a gunsmith, worked in the family workshops, and after the First World War joined the Italian air force. After his discharge he joined Alfa Romeo, and was promoted to the racing department where he worked with Vittorio Jano and Enzo Ferrari, but it is not clear at what level. He went to France with the team for the 1925 French GP, the race in which Antonio Ascari was killed.

   After the race, he stayed in France to work on Alfa Romeo competition cars for the French agent. It is believed that Raymond Sommer owned the Alfa Romeo

Below: *Chinetti had a long career with Alfa Romeo in Europe, and raced the eight-cylinder cars regularly, especially at Le Mans where he won in 1932 with Raymond Sommer and in 1934 with Nuvolari. This photograph was taken in 1933 when he finished second, again with an Alfa Romeo. A rather smug Chinetti sits behind the wheel, while co-driver Varent has an arm around his shoulder.* **(Spitzley/Zagari Collection)**

8C 2300 that he entered at Le Mans in 1932; Chinetti probably sold him the car, and he co-drove it. It is likely that they got together because of an introduction from the factory. Six of these cars ran in the race, and there was a mighty battle that caused a high level of retirements.

Chinetti did very little driving in this, his first Le Mans, because he was unwell, but he was to make up for it in later years. Sommer/Chinetti won by a margin of just over 16 miles from Cortese/Guidotti with a works car. The following year at Le Mans he was partnered by Philippe Varent in an 8C 2300 Alfa Romeo which he – presumably – had sold to Varent. It was another hard-fought race and, although Chinetti/Varent led at one stage, they finished second, only 10sec behind the 2.3 Alfa of Sommer/Nuvolari.

Shortly afterwards, Chinetti partnered Chiron with an 8C 2300 in the Belgian 24 Hours race and, in the face of fairly weak opposition, they won this event from two other 2.3 Alfas. The following year, Chinetti, who was now a very well-established endurance racer, teamed up with French driver Philippe Etancelin. The race was run in very hot conditions, and retirements among the faster cars enabled them to build up a big lead, and they won from a 1.5-litre Riley by a margin of over 100 miles.

In 1935 Chinetti was partnered by Monégasque Jacques Gastaud, a giant of a man with a fatal attraction to ditches. Chinetti later commented:

'The first time we were able to effect a repair and restart, but the second time we could do nothing. As a matter of interest, we then held such a lead that it took the ultimate winners [Hindmarsh/Fontès with a 4.5-litre Lagonda] two hours to equal the distance that we had already run.'

There was no Le Mans in 1936. In 1937 Chinetti was partnered by Chiron with a French Talbot, but they failed to finish. Etancelin again partnered Chinetti in 1938, with a Talbot once more, but yet again they failed to finish. For the third successive year, Chinetti drove a Talbot at Le Mans in 1939, but on this occasion he was partnered by T A S O Mathieson. Once again they retired.

Following the death of Laurie Schell in a road accident in October 1939, Chinetti agreed to travel to the United States with his widow, Lucy O'Reilly Schell, to work on the two Delahayes entered by her team, Écurie Lucy O'Reilly Schell, at Indianapolis in 1940. Once Italy entered the Second World War on the Axis side, it was impossible for Chinetti to return to Europe. He married, stayed in the United States during the war years, and became an American citizen in 1946.

In about 1948, Chinetti returned to France and then travelled to Italy to see Enzo Ferrari. As a result of this visit he obtained the United States East Coast Agency for the new V12 Ferrari, and for some considerable while Chinetti International Motors, Inc was the sole Ferrari agent in North America. They were not the types of car that Americans bought readily, but Chinetti with Ferrari, and other importers with the British Jaguar and MG, and the German Mercedes-Benz, transformed thinking about European cars.

In early post-war days, Chinetti raced Tipo 166MM cars with Barchetta bodywork in European racing. With Lord Selsdon (a Scottish peer, formerly Peter Mitchell-Thomson), he won the 1948 Paris 12 Hours race at Montlhéry from Louveau/Brunet (Delage) and Folland/Connell (Aston Martin). The following year Chinetti and Selsdon ran a Tipo 166 Ferrari at Le Mans and, apart from 20min when Selsdon relieved his co-driver, Chinetti drove throughout. They won the race from Louveau/Jover (Delage) and Culpan/Aldington (Frazer Nash).

A little later that year Chinetti, partnered by Jean Lucas, won the Belgian 24 Hours race with a Tipo 166MM from Louveau/Mouche (Delage) and Johnson/

Below: *After the Second World War, Chinetti set up the American agency for Ferrari. Here he is seen with Piero Taruffi, for whom he acted as riding mechanic in the 1951 Carrera Panamericana road race across Mexico. Piero Taruffi, leaning against their Ferrari Tipo 212, won the race from Ascari/Villoresi (with another Ferrari 212 Export) and Stirling/Sandidge (Chrysler). (Tom March Collection)*

Brackenbury (Aston Martin). Chinetti, with the same co-driver, won the 1950 Paris 1,000km race. Interestingly, Chinetti competed in every Le Mans 24 Hours race between 1932 and 1952. He was also entered in the Carrera Panamericana Mexico road race in 1951 (first with Taruffi) and 1952 (third with Lucas), but it is not clear for how much of the race he drove.

In 1951 Chinetti had formed the North American Racing Team (NART) and it became the most important of the private Ferrari teams, although Enzo Ferrari did him few favours. What boosted NART in its early days was the money pumped in by Mexican building construction millionaire Don Pedro ('Papa') Rodriguez to enable sons Ricardo and Pedro to race Ferraris. Nothing pleased Chinetti and the Rodriguez brothers more than 'blowing off' the works cars, but they did so by overdriving their cars and suffered many mechanical failures.

NART developed a reputation for poor preparation work and poor performances in their later days, but they continued to enter Ferraris until 1982. Chinetti was also very active in encouraging Ferrari to develop models aimed especially for the North American market. Foremost among these was the Spider version of the Ferrari 275GTB/4. Luigi Chinetti died in 1994 after a long and very satisfying career.

Chiron, Louis

Pre-war Scuderia Ferrari driver
Born: 3 August 1899 (Monaco)
Died: 22 June 1979 (Monaco)

That Chiron was a great driver whose finest years were in the late 1920s and early 1930s is undoubted, as is the fact that he was a very unpleasant individual, with whom one would not trust one's dog, let alone one's wife. Early in his racing career he drove private Bugattis. Then, for two seasons, he raced for Alfred Hoffmann's Nerka sparking plug company's team, and

Below: *The Monégasque Louis Chiron was a thoroughly unpleasant, self-centred character, who exploited just about everyone he met. Although he was still racing in the 1950s, he was really a man of the late 1920s and the early 1930s. He was a very successful Bugatti driver, and a lounge lizard of mixed success. Here, he is seen at the wheel of a Bugatti Type 35 at Brooklands. His career with Scuderia Ferrari was short-lived.* (Author's collection)

also shared Hoffmann's wife, the lovely Alice 'Baby' Hoffmann-Trobeck.

He joined the Bugatti Molsheim works team in 1928, when it was at the height of its racing success, and stayed with them, winning around a dozen races and many good places, until the end of 1932 when Meo Constantini (Bugatti racing manager) sacked him. It was surprising that he had lasted with the team for so long, because he was bloody-minded, anti-social, and argumentative. It was during 1932 that Alfred Hoffmann and 'Baby' were divorced.

Plans for 1933 to run Scuderia CC with Caracciola fell apart when the German crashed in practice for the first race at Monaco, but Chiron continued to race his Alfa Romeo Monza and also co-drove, with Chinetti, the winning 8C 2300 at Le Mans. Chiron then joined Scuderia Ferrari and achieved many successes, including a win in the 1934 French GP at Montlhéry, three excellent second places that year, and second place with the 5.8-litre Bi-motore in the 1935 Avusrennen.

Chiron joined Mercedes-Benz for 1936 and achieved pretty well nothing of note on the race-track, apart from being involved in a multi-car crash at Monaco and crashing at high speed in the German GP. He did not race again for Mercedes-Benz, although his injuries were not serious, and it is pretty clear that Neubauer realised he had made a mistake in signing up Chiron, and persuaded him to move on. Caracciola had fallen deeply in love with 'Baby' Hoffmann, who then asked Chiron to marry her. He declined to do so, and when she married Caracciola, Chiron behaved as though he had been spurned.

In 1937 Chiron won the sports car French GP with a Talbot, and after the Second World War he raced the 1939 monoplace Talbot with great success. Subsequently, he drove a Talbot-Lago for Écurie France with considerable success. He seemed to have good relations with the Maserati brothers and frequently drove their OSCA cars. He created another less than savoury incident by accusing woman racer Hélène Delangle of being a Gestapo agent. It was an accusation founded on nothing except spite, and the impoverished 'Hellé Nice' could not afford to sue him for defamation.

Below: *In post-war days Chiron drove Talbot-Lagos for the Écurie France team. He is seen here at Silverstone in the 1949 British GP, struggling with the erratic brakes of the big French 4.5-litre unblown Talbot 'camion'.* **(Guy Griffiths)**

Chiron won the Monte Carlo Rally with a Lancia Aurelia B20 in 1955, and the eligibility of the car was protested by Georges Houel, motorcycle racer, in ninth place with an Alfa Romeo 1900. Although the win was upheld, later investigation by Lancia experts have established that the car was technically ineligible because it combined an earlier body shell for a 2-litre car with the latest 2451cc engine. This was obviously the responsibility of the Lancia factory, but it just happened to be part of a familiar pattern of sneaky behaviour.

After making his last racing appearance with a Citroën DS19 in the 1957 Mille Miglia, Chiron became director of Monaco's two sporting events, the Grand Prix and the Monte Carlo Rally. He performed these tasks satisfactorily and enthusiastically until the 1979 Monaco GP, held about a month before his death.

Chiti, Carlo

Technical director, Ferrari SpA
Born: 19 December 1924 (Pistoia, near Pisa, Italy)
Died: 7 July 1994 (Milan, Italy)

Chiti was a tubby, bespectacled, rather scruffy individual with eyes sparkling behind the thick lenses of his glasses. There are many stories about his eccentric behaviour, but although the writer knew him well in his Alfa Romeo days, he did not see his foibles. Chiti was hospitable, helpful, and competent, but not highly able. There are stories that Chiti adopted stray dogs (in some versions of the story it is cats), but when the writer visited him at the Autodelta works at Settimo Milanese, four-footed animals were conspicuously absent.

He was the son of a civil engineer, and as a slim young man he was a keen member of the Avanguardia Fascista (literally, Fascist Vanguard, the youth section of the Fascist movement). It has been said that they encouraged his aircraft modelling (his other interest was chemistry), but fascism appealed to those who liked order, and none like order more than the totally disorganised such as Chiti. He studied at Florence University, but graduated in aeronautical engineering at Pisa University.

Obtaining a job in early post-war Italy was difficult, but Chiti found employment with the Montecatini civil engineering company in Milan, and worked for them from 1948 to 1952. He took lodgings in the Via Scarlatti where he met his future wife, Lina Fumagalli. Chiti's work took him away from Milan, which upset Lina

greatly, and when Alfa Romeo invited applications for engineering jobs, she encouraged him to apply. Alfa Romeo offered him a job in Naples, and when he pointed out that he could not accept because his fiancée lived in Milan, he was appointed to the Reparto Sperimentale Corse (the experimental racing department).

Initially, Chiti had little to do with motor racing, but he was working with people totally committed to the sport, including Consalvo Sanesi, Giovanni Battista Guidotti, and Dr Orazio Satta, and he was soon gripped by enthusiasm. Later Chiti said, 'I had to struggle for acceptance. Every day I worked with people who had won championships and they thought that they alone knew the answers.' At this time, Alfa Romeo was developing six-cylinder sports cars, and he became race engineer on the 3-litre 6CM 3000 with which Fangio won the 1953 Supercortemaggiore GP at Merano. Chiti commented, 'It's easy to have a good relationship with a great driver, it's the mediocre drivers who are so difficult.'

Later, Alfa Romeo concentrated on racing modified cars, but in 1957 Chiti was introduced to Enzo Ferrari by Giotto Bizzarrini and offered a job. He thought Ferrari's offer was too vague and declined it. The men at Maranello have often said that Ferrari offers a job (or a drive) only once, but the years have proved this to be wrong. When engineer Andrea Fraschetti was killed in a testing accident at Modena in 1957, Ferrari contacted Chiti once more. Chiti joined Ferrari for a monthly salary of 185,000 lire, twice what he had been earning at Alfa Romeo, and he and his wife, and their baby daughter, occupied what had been Lampredi's Ferrari-owned apartment in Viale Trento e Trieste in Modena.

Among Chiti's greatest successes at Maranello was the development of the 3-litre V12 Testa Rossa sports-racing cars that dominated the World Sports Car Championship in 1958 and 1960. Efforts to modernise Ferrari engineering concepts met with stiff resistance from Enzo Ferrari and the engineering staff. He did, however, persuade Ferrari to adopt disc brakes on a trial basis in 1958 (Dunlop disc brakes were fitted on all F1 cars in 1959), and in 1959 the F1 cars also had Koni

Opposite: *Carlo Chiti, with sleeves rolled up, in the pits at the French GP at Reims in 1961. The car is the Tipo 156 1.5-litre GP model with the cylinders at an angle of 120°, and the driver was Richie Ginther seen in white overalls standing to the right of the cockpit. Any doubt about the location is dispelled by the member of the Police Civile standing in the background. The race was run in excessively hot conditions, and was won by Baghetti with an obsolete 65° car.* (**LAT Photographic**)

FERRARI: MEN FROM MARANELLO

telescopic dampers and coil springs in place of a transverse lead spring and Houdaille dampers. In secrecy, he redesigned the front-engined F1 Dino as the rear-engined 246MP and then developed a F2 version.

Ferrari front-engined cars had been hopelessly outclassed by the British Lotus 18s and Coopers in 1960, but it was a different story in 1961 with the start of the 1500cc GP formula. The latest V6 rear-engined Ferraris had aerodynamics developed in the first wind tunnel at Maranello, that Chiti had installed, and were distinguished by twin-nostril noses.

With the exception of Monaco and the Nürburgring (won by Moss with Rob Walker's underpowered four-cylinder Lotus 18), these cars won every round of the World Championship in 1961, but this was because they were so much more powerful than the British cars, and had little to do with either their aerodynamics or the roadholding, which was appalling. Chiti was also responsible for the very successful Dino 246SP rear-engined sports cars first raced in 1961.

The story of Laura Ferrari's eccentric interference in the running of the company is narrated elsewhere (see Appendix 4), but Chiti and Bizzarrini headed the defence of the senior staff, and all were dismissed in November 1961. Chiti became Technical Director to the ill-fated ATS project based at Pontevecchio Marconi (see Appendix 4). After this failed, he joined his old friend Ludovico Chizzola at his family's business in Udine. It had an agency for Innocenti cars (Minis built under licence by the company that also built Lambretta scooters). Chiti and Chizzola started a race preparation business and the firm, originally named Delta Auto, became Autodelta.

Chiti persuaded the chairman of Alfa Romeo, Giuseppe Luraghi, who had been his old boss at Portello, to contract them to prepare a batch of Alfa Romeo Giulia TZs for homologation. Alfa Romeo had other ideas, and bought out Chiti and Chizzola, and Chiti stayed for 20 years as head of the Autodelta concern. Autodelta developed competition versions of Alfa Romeo cars very successfully, but the pure competition cars that started with the first of the Prototype Tipo 33 cars, the 2-litre V8 of 1967, had a very chequered career. Autodelta later built 12-cylinder F1 engines and supplied Brabham before embarking on their own unsuccessful GP programme.

In 1983 the Euroracing organisation, an outside company, was given responsibility for Alfa Romeo's participation, and Chiti left Autodelta a year later. He set up Motori Moderni at Biandrate Novara, backed by Piero Mancini, Giacomo Caliri, and Giancarlo Minardi. Chiti developed a turbocharged 1½-litre V6, and from 1987 onwards he had close ties with the Japanese Subaru Corporation, part of Fuji Heavy Industries and builders of Subaru cars and Air Subaru light aircraft. This cooperation led in 1989 to the Subaru-Motori Moderni 3.5-litre flat-12 engine that powered the Dome Caspita 'supercar'. On 7 July 1994, Chiti suffered a massive, fatal heart attack.

Cole, Tom

Amateur driver
Died: 14 June 1953 (Le Mans)

Heir to the Vidor battery company, born British, but naturalised American, Cole had been crippled by spinal trouble when he was a youngster. He spent much of his early life bedridden, but once he was cured he wanted

Below: *Son and heir of the family who owned the Vidor battery company, Cole had an unhappy, illness-plagued childhood, but he showed signs of being a positive, successful amateur driver in the early part of 1953. This photograph was taken at the International Trophy meeting at Silverstone in May 1953, only a few weeks before his fatal accident with his private Ferrari at Le Mans. (Guy Griffiths Collection)*

Above: *Tom Cole is seen at the wheel of his Tipo 500 Formula 2 Ferrari in the International Trophy race at Silverstone in May 1953. He was a popular and successful privateer, and many were stunned by his death at Le Mans.* (Tom March Collection)

to catch up on everything that he had missed, and he became an enthusiastic pilot, yachtsman, skier, and motor racing driver. He teamed up with Peter Whitehead and they raced together in 1953 as Équipe Atlantic. Cole took delivery of a new Cooper Mark II-Bristol, painted white and blue. His first race was the Syracuse GP in March. Here his car burst a tyre, crashed into a wall, caught fire, and was burnt out.

A replacement was built, and in the International Trophy at Silverstone he drove Jack Swaters's Tipo 500 Ferrari, while Swaters drove the new Cooper-Bristol. Cole achieved no success with this Ferrari, but with his new Vignale-bodied Tipo 340 Mille Miglia Ferrari he finished second in the so-called Production Sports Car race at Silverstone.

The Tipo 340 then went back to the factory for modifications for Le Mans and was repainted white and blue. On 7 June 1953 Cole co-drove Peter Whitehead's Jaguar C-type to a win in the Hyères 12 Hours race. At Le Mans, six days later, Cole raced his 340MM, partnered by Luigi Chinetti. At 6.30am on the Sunday, Cole hit the straw bales at White House, the Ferrari overturned and, trapped under the car, he was crushed to death.

Collins, Peter

Works driver
Born: 6 November 1931 (Kidderminster, Worcestershire, England)
Died: 3 August 1958 (Bonn, Germany, in hospital)

One of the most charming men in British motor racing, Collins was exceptionally talented and able, but because of his charm and sexual appeal, his behaviour was sometimes oafish and foolish, simply because he knew that he could get away with it. His racing career started with 500cc cars, and the close, fast racing in small cars so close to the ground led to him becoming a driver who was also very fast, but very safe.

He first started racing a Cooper with a twin-cam Manx Norton engine in 1949 when he was only 17, and he achieved many successes, including wins in the 100-mile race at Silverstone and a race at Goodwood that year. He finished third in the final of the important 500cc race at the European GP meeting at Silverstone in 1950. After he switched from Cooper to JBS in 1951 he set BTD in his class at both Prescott and Shelsley Walsh hill climbs.

For 1952, Peter became a member of the HWM Formula 2 team run by John Heath. Although these Alta-powered cars had achieved some remarkable successes in 1950–1, they were very much in decline by this stage. The team still trailed round Europe, paying its way by earning starting money and, hopefully, prize money, but

Above: *During 1952–3 young Peter Collins gained experience in international racing at the wheel of HWM Formula 2 cars, but they were slow and uncompetitive. Here Collins is seen on the starting grid at the 1952 British GP at Silverstone. It was one of many poor races for the team that year, and Collins was delayed by engine problems that caused his ultimate retirement.* (Guy Griffiths Collection)

Below: *Collins joined the Ferrari team in 1956, and he is seen here at the wheel of his V8 Lancia-Ferrari in the International Trophy at Silverstone in May 1956. Fangio retired his own car and then took over this car, but retired because of clutch failure.* (Author's collection)

it became an increasingly uphill struggle. Peter's only performance worth mentioning in 1952 was sixth place, all of seven laps in arrears, in the French GP. The HWMs were becoming hopelessly slow, as well as unreliable, and in 1953 no success at all came Peter's way.

Peter also joined the Aston Martin sports car team in 1952 and he stayed with them until the end of 1956. The team's DB3 and, from mid-1953, DB3S cars, were underpowered, but nevertheless finished consistently well in international races. Peter achieved many successes, including a win with Pat Griffith as co-driver in the 1952 Goodwood Nine Hours race, and with the same co-driver he was second in the 1953 Nine Hours race. This successful pairing finished third in the 1,000km race at Buenos Aires in 1954, and Peter was second at Le Mans with Paul Frère in 1955, and with Stirling Moss in 1956.

Collins had driven the Vanwall Special for Tony Vandervell in 1954, and it was obvious that both car and driver had immense promise. Vandervell wanted Peter to continue to drive for him in 1955, but instead he switched to BRM – although, for reasons that have never been fully understood, he had indicated to Vandervell that he would take up his offer. He only turned down Vandervell after it was too late for the bearing maker to obtain a competitive alternative driver. It has been suggested that Collins was reluctant to drive in the same team as Hawthorn (at least, at this stage in his career) because it would be damaging to his career prospects.

The new Formula 1 BRM was not ready until late in the season, so Peter drove the team's Maserati 250F (winning the International Trophy at Silverstone), as well as competing with the monstrous V16 supercharged BRM. He was given a trial drive with Maserati in the 1955 Italian GP, but he was slowed by gearbox trouble that caused his eventual retirement.

Ferrari was very keen to have Peter in his team, so he signed up with Maranello in 1956, but for F1 only. Fangio was also in the Ferrari team and had an immense influence on Peter's attitude and career. Under Fangio's influence, Peter took his racing much more seriously, but still retained his great sense of fun. That year, Ferrari was racing the Lancia V8 cars, and they were more than a match for the rival Maserati 250Fs. Collins won the Belgian and French Grands Prix, and took over de Portago's car to finish second in the British race at Silverstone. As the season progressed, so Peter became increasingly Enzo Ferrari's favourite and almost a substitute son.

At Monza, Collins was holding third place and was in with a chance of winning the World Championship. But he handed his car over to Fangio when he stopped for a tyre change, and it has never been completely clear why he did this. The Argentinian finished second in the race behind

Moss (250F); he shared the six points with Collins, and won the Championship for the fourth time with 30 points from Moss, on 27 points, and Collins, with 25 points. It was not an official Ferrari request (Enzo Ferrari disliked Fangio); it has been claimed that the request was made by Fangio's manager, Marcello Giambertone, and also by Amorotti, who was to be Ferrari team manager in 1957.

Collins stayed with Ferrari in 1957, but began the year by marrying 26-year-old actress Louise King, who he had known for only a week, in the Plymouth Congregational Church, Coconut Grove, Miami, on 11 February. It seemed to be the sort of marriage that would not last, but all that can be said is that Peter and Louise were still deeply in love when he was killed in August the following year.

By 1957 the V8 Lancias were obsolescent, and the year turned into a battle between the Maseratis and the British Vanwalls. Peter had a poor year in F1, and his best results were third places in the French race at Rouen and in the German GP. He finished a poor joint eighth in the Drivers' Championship with eight points (with Hanks who had won at Indianapolis). Peter won the non-Championship Syracuse and Naples Grands Prix. Ferrari was developing the new V6 Dino cars, and in September 1957 Collins drove one of these cars in 1860cc form into fourth place in the non-Championship Modena GP.

At the beginning of the 1958 racing season Collins, partnered by Phil Hill and driving the new V12 3-litre Testa Rossa cars, won both the Buenos Aires 1,000km race and the Sebring 12 Hours. In F1, the Dino 246 was far from fully sorted early in the year. Peter's first win was in the non-Championship International Trophy at

Silverstone. He had retired in the Argentine GP, and was third at Monaco. Further retirements at Zandvoort and Spa-Francorchamps meant that he was trailing badly behind team-mate Hawthorn in the Championship, with only six points to the 19 of Hawthorn and the 22 of Moss, when the teams arrived for the British GP.

Collins drove a smooth, flawless race at Silverstone to win his first GP that year, with Hawthorn second and the Vanwall team outclassed. It all went horribly wrong at the Nürburgring where Brooks led for Vanwall, chased hard by Collins and Hawthorn. At the Pflanzgarten, Collins made a simple, but terrible error of judgement, clipped a bank at over 100mph (160kph) and the Ferrari rolled over a hedge and down into a field. Peter, thrown out of the car, suffered terrible head injuries and died without regaining consciousness soon after being flown by helicopter to Bonn hospital. Collins's death was a dreadful loss, but only one of many at a time when racing was so very dangerous.

Below: *Peter Collins achieved the peak of his ability in 1958, but a season that started with bad luck in major races culminated in disaster. Early in the season, he won the International Trophy at Silverstone where he is seen with his V6 Ferrari Dino. He achieved only a third at Monaco and a fifth in the French race at Reims, but was supreme in the British race, where he led throughout. He was leading the German GP at the Nürburgring when he made an error of judgement near the Pflanzgarten, and crashed, suffering injuries that proved fatal. (Tom March Collection)*

Colombo, Giaocchino

Engineer
Born: 9 January 1903 (Legnano, Italy)
Died: 24 April 1987 (Milan, Italy)

Colombo served an apprenticeship as a mechanical draftsman in the Technical Department of Officine Franco Tosi, a company in Legnano that manufactured diesel engines and steam turbines. That he was very able and talented is undoubted, and he won a competition organised by the Società Italiano Nicola Romeo. He joined Alfa Romeo on 7 January 1924 as a draftsman in the Special Design Department, in effect

the Racing Department, which was well advanced on the detail design and development of Jano's Alfa Romeo P2 racing car.

He and Jano came to work together very closely, and the young Colombo proved very adept in producing detailed drawings of Jano's design concepts. He had been promoted to head of the drawing office in 1928. Jano said of Colombo, 'He began to be my right arm.' He also said of him, 'He was a clever designer, who, too often, lacked the courage of his convictions.' After Jano left Alfa Romeo in 1936, Colombo went to the Scuderia Ferrari premises in Modena in May 1937, where he designed a range of cars on a very limited budget.

All were derived from Jano concepts, and the most successful was the Tipo 158 Voiturette, and in addition he did much of the design work on the Tipo 308, 312, and 316 3-litre GP cars raced from 1938. After Ferrari left Alfa Corse, Colombo stayed with Alfa Romeo during the war years. As a consultant he carried out much of the design work on the first V12 Ferrari engine while he was still working at Alfa Romeo. The Ferrari was a Jano concept, with development by Ricart and, of course, Colombo, and Bazzi carried out most of the practical work that eliminated its faults.

As a sports car in 2-litre Tipo 166M form, the Colombo engine was exceptionally successful. Unfortunately, the 1.5-litre supercharged version, used in the GP car that made its debut in the 1948 Italian GP, was dismally underpowered, and there was no easy

Below: *Giaocchino Colombo (on the right) with Aurelio Lampredi – two great Italian engineers together during the early years of the Ferrari company. Colombo was the first Ferrari engineer and responsible for the design of the original V12 engine. Lampredi started out as Colombo's assistant, but replaced him and was responsible for the design of the 'long-block' V12 engine. (The Geoffrey Goddard Collection)*

solution. So, Colombo was replaced by his assistant Lampredi, and he returned to Alfa Romeo.

Nevertheless, Ferrari relied on developments of the Colombo 'short-block' engine for many years, and these powered the long range of 250GT cars, together with the 3-litre Testa Rossa sports-racing cars and the 3.3-litre 250LM mid-engined Prototype of 1964 onwards. The sound of a later Colombo V12 on full song was – and still is – poetry set to music for many enthusiasts.

Colombo's work on his return to Alfa Romeo encompassed development of the later versions of the straight-eight Alfetta GP car and the Disco Volante sports-racing cars that appeared in 1952. In late 1952, Colombo became a technical consultant to Maserati and his brief was the design of the 250F GP car raced from 1954 onwards. His later work included the Bugatti Type 251 GP with transverse, rear-mounted, straight-eight engine, the failure of which was attributable to Pierre Marco's insistence on using an impractical layout, and shortage of funds, rather than failings on Colombo's part.

Later, Colombo worked on engine design for MV Agusta motorcycles (Meccanica Verghera). When Griff Borgeson met him at MV in 1964, he described him thus:

'He was short, just a bit rotund, bald, and full of high-strung vitality. Colombo was a very serious professional who laughed with easy spontaneity in talking about his three decades at the vortex of Alfa Romeo race-car engineering…'

Comotti, Franco

Scuderia Ferrari driver
Born: 24 July 1906 (Brescia, Italy)
Died: 10 May 1963 (Bergamo, Italy)

Gianfranco ('Franco') Alessandro Maria Comotti lived most of his life in Bergamo, and was in the main a very successful amateur driver. His early racing appearances include driving a Talbot of Scuderia Materassi in the 1928 European GP, but there is no record of him racing again until 1931 when he won the cyclecar division of the Circuit of Alessandria with a Salmson. In 1932 he married Anna Maria Peduzzi (born Olgiate, Italy, in 1912), a very slim, tall, and elegant lady racer who competed with Alfa Romeos in pre-war days, and after the Second World War raced 750cc Stanguellinis before moving on to a Ferrari Tipo 500 Testa Rossa in 1956 and retaining this through to 1959. She also raced OSCA cars in 1958–60.

Comotti had acquired an Alfa Romeo 8C 2300 Monza, as well as a wife, and the story is that he took the car to Scuderia Ferrari for servicing. Enzo Ferrari was far too

Below: *Gianfranco Comotti at the wheel of a mud-spattered Alfa Romeo Monoposto belonging to Scuderia Ferrari.* **(Spitzley/Zagari Collection)**

financially sharp to let a man with money slip from his grasp, and he gave Comotti a drive for the team, for which he presumably paid. He drove a 6C 1750 in minor races in 1932, finishing fourth in the 95-mile (153km) Targa Abruzzo at Pescara. It was much the same story in 1933, when he finished fourth with a 6C in the Circuit of Florence, and fourth again, with a 2.6-litre Monza, in the Targa Abruzzo.

By 1934 he was making occasional appearances in Grands Prix with a Scuderia Ferrari Monoposto. He took fourth place in the Circuit of Bordino at Alessandria and finished fifth at Casablanca; he shared the second place 6C 2300 with Rosa in the Circuit of Italy, won at Comminges, and took over Trossi's Monoposto to finish third in the Italian GP at Monza. He made even fewer appearances for the team in 1935, but finished fifth on home ground in the Circuit of Bergamo, and took third place in the three-hour Lorraine GP at Nancy; he gained fourth place in the Coppa Acerbo, and ended the year and his career with Ferrari by finishing second in the Circuit of Lucca.

Comotti was ardently anti-Fascist (not blowing with the wind like so many Italians), and in 1936 he moved to Paris. He gained employment with Antony Lago's Talbot concern where he tested customer cars prior to delivery, and was the reserve driver in the Talbot sports car team. He drove a works Talbot to a win in the handicap Tourist Trophy sports car race at Donington in 1937. He then joined the Lucy O'Reilly Schell Écurie Bleu racing Delahayes, but soon left the team. In the 1940 closed-circuit Mille Miglia, he drove the sole Watney-entered 3-litre Delage to start the race. He was in second place at the first lap, but retired after five laps, so co-driver Rosa never had a turn at the wheel.

During the latter part of the war in Italy, Comotti acted as an informer for the partisans in northern Italy, which was under German occupation. He was uncovered and sentenced to death, only to be reprieved after an Italian 'collaborator' interceded on his behalf. After the end of hostilities he returned to Paris and tested the new Talbot-Lago single-seater GP cars. He appeared regularly with one of these cars in 1948. He tested Milano-Maseratis and raced one in the 1950 Grand Prix des Nations at Geneva, where he retired.

Comotti also drove F2 Ferrari V12 cars for Scuderia Marzotto in 1952. His best result was third at Naples in a thin field. Much of Comotti's working career was in the oil business, and his last job was as representative for BP in North Africa and the Mediterranean. At the time of writing his widow was still going strong at the age of 95.

Cornacchia, Franco

Milan Ferrari and Maserati dealer
(Date of birth not known, but he died in 1999)

As the Ferrari and Maserati dealer for Milan and the surrounding area, Cornacchia, a wealthy man who had been a racing enthusiast for many years, sold competition cars in considerable numbers. He also raced himself and, like most Italian enthusiasts, competed in the Mille Miglia. In the 1950 race he was partnered by Mariani at the wheel of a Tipo 166MM Touring berlinetta, but they retired; the following year he and Mariani drove a 212 Export with Vignale coupé body into 17th place, and in 1952 he was partnered by Tinarelli and they finished tenth with a similar, but different car.

He ran a team called Scuderia Guastalla (Guastalla is a town to the north east of Parma and may have been his birth place), and in late 1953, when Ferrari was claiming that he was retiring from racing, Scuderia

Below: *Franco Cornacchia (on right), Ferrari distributor in Milan who ran Scuderia Guastalla, talking to Emilio Romano (winner of the 1947 Mille Miglia with Clemente Biondetti) in Brescia before the 1951 Mille Miglia.* (Author's collection)

Guastalla entered a team of what had been works cars in the 1953 Carrera Panamericana Mexico road race. These were the Le Mans coupés with beautiful bodies, one of which had finished fifth at Le Mans. These cars had won the Belgian 24 Hours and the Pescara 12 Hours events. The drivers in Mexico were Antonio Stagnoli, winner of the Italian 2-litre sports car Championship in 1951, partnered by Giuseppe Scotuzzi; Mario Ricci/Foresti; and Maglioli partnered by Pasquale Cassani.

It was a disastrous race for the Guastalla team. On the first stage, Stagnoli was travelling flat-out on a long straight when a front tyre burst, the Ferrari left the road, went down an embankment, turned end over end and was completely burnt out. Scotuzzi was killed instantly, while the mortally injured Stagnoli died later in hospital. In the opening stages of the race Maglioli was off-form, finishing fifth, fourth, and third in the first three stages, but then he won the fourth stage.

On stage five, Maglioli's Ferrari lost a wheel while he was travelling at about 120mph (193kph) and he was forced to abandon the car. A rest day followed and, as the regulations allowed drivers to swap cars, Maglioli took over Ricci's car and won stages six, seven, and eight from the very strong team of Lancias that were to be the overall winners. The 223-mile (359km) eighth stage was run on typical fast, abrasive Mexican roads constructed from volcanic rock, and Maglioli's average on this stage was 138.31mph (222.54km). It was a record speed for a stage in a race, and has never been bettered.

Cortese, Franco

Works sports car driver
Born: 10 February 1903 (Oggebbio Novara, Turin, Italy)
Died: 13 November 1986 (Turin)

Cortese was a very successful driver, with a career that ran from the 1920s through to the early post-war years. He competed in the first Mille Miglia road race in 1927, partnered by Barancini – the first of 14 appearances in the race, itself a record. He drove a 2-litre Tipo 61 Itala, finishing eighth, and he drove an Itala again the following year, partnered by Ciffi, but retired. Then he switched to Alfa Romeo for 1929 and, partnered by Guatta, he finished ninth. By 1930 he was driving for Scuderia Ferrari and, with Pietro Ghersi, finished fourth in that year's Mille Miglia.

In 1931, partnered by Balestrieri, he took 12th place with a 6C 1750 Alfa Romeo. In 1932 he partnered Marinoni in an 8C 2300, but they retired. Franco almost failed to make the start in 1933. To quote from this writer's *Mille Miglia* book:

'On the eve of the race an electric spark set fire to Cortese's Alfa Romeo while it was being refuelled in the company's works at Portello and an electrician was still working under the car. The damage was extensive and the fuel tank and pipes, the tail, the tyres, and electrics were all badly damaged.

Mechanic and test driver Bonini suffered severe burns. It seems that no one bothered to tell Cortese about the fire and he did not find out what had happened until four hours before the start of the race. Cortese insisted that the car be repaired in time for the start, and a frantic rush ensued. Most of the damage was to the rear of the car, and a combination of industry and frenzy ensured that it was repaired. Further problems followed when a mechanic poured a can of water into the fuel tank an hour before the start.

Below: *Cortese was a wealthy amateur who raced from the late 1920s through to post-war days, when he was frequently seen with private Ferraris. Here he is at the wheel of his works-entered Tipo 6CM Maserati Voiturette in the 1940 Targa Florio held in Palermo Park. He finished in this rather parochial event won by Luigi Villoresi.* (Spitzley/Zagari Collection)

Above: *Enzo Ferrari invited Cortese to test the unpainted Tipo 125 GP car before the model made its race debut at Monza in 1948. Here, Cortese is at the wheel on the cobblestones of the road from Maranello to Abetone. Also in the photograph are Lampredi and Enzo Ferrari (second and third from left).* (Author's collection)

Despite this, Cortese made the start only a few seconds late, after being called while the car was still being refuelled, and he insisted on driving for the entire race.'

He finished second, partnered by Castelbarco, but then missed the 1934 race. In 1935 he drove one of the new six-cylinder 6C 2300 saloons with Severi, and finished eighth. The following year he was once more at the wheel of an Alfa Romeo, but retired. He was partnered again by Guatta in 1937, and they finished sixth overall with a 6C 2300. Cortese's partner in 1938 was Fumagalli, and they drove a special Touring-bodied 6C 2300 into ninth place overall and a win in the National Sport category.

In the 1940 closed-circuit Mille Miglia, Cortese partnered Count Johnny Lurani at the wheel of a works BMW 328, but they covered only six laps and retired after a succession of pit stops because of a misfiring engine. In the late 1930s and the years leading up to the Second World War, Cortese drove Maserati 1500cc single-seater Voiturettes in a number of races, and perhaps his best performance was in the 1940 Targa

Florio held as a 142-mile Voiturette race in Palermo Park, where he took second place to Luigi Villoresi with another Maserati.

In post-war days, Cortese was closely involved with early Ferrari racing efforts. He drove a Tipo 125 with full-width body on the debut of the model at Piacenza on 11 May 1947, but retired because of what was said to be fuel pump failure. Later, Cortese drove – and retired with – a Tipo 125 in both the Circuit of the Baths of Caracalla at Rome on 25 May and at Vercelli on 1 June. He raced again at Rome on 15 June and won the race from Barbieri (Maserati). His next success was second place to Nuvolari with another Ferrari in a race at Parma on 13 July.

Cortese drove a works Ferrari in the 1948 Targa (which was combined with the 671-mile/1,000km Tour of Sicily), but retired for unknown mechanical reasons. He drove a Ferrari, partnered by Adelmo Marchetti, in that year's Mille Miglia, but again he retired. The following year he again drove a Tipo 166SC Ferrari, this time with Maglioli, in the Mille Miglia, but retired once more.

In 1950, partnered by Taravassi, he drove the Scuderia Ambrosiana Frazer Nash Le Mans Replica into sixth place in the 1,000-mile race; he raced the Frazer Nash again in the 1951 Mille Miglia, and his speed was higher, despite a broken pushrod, but he could only manage ninth place and a class second. The same year he won the Targa Florio with this car. As late as 1956 he won the Italian 2-litre Sports Car Championship with a Ferrari Tipo 500. He retired from racing in 1958 and became the agent in Italy for various car component manufacturers.

Costa, Aldo

Director of Chassis Development
Born: 5 June 1961 (Parma, Italy)

While at Bologna University, Costa wrote a thesis on F1 suspension with the aid of the Ferrari team. After graduating in mechanical engineering, he joined the Abarth division of Fiat and then moved on to the Minardi F1 team and spent seven years there. In 1995 he moved on to Ferrari, where his initial job was to coordinate John Barnard's design work with assembly at the factory. When Rory Byrne joined Ferrari at the end of 1996, Costa became the head of the vehicle design office. In 2005 he became the Chief Designer, and he was appointed Technical Director in 2007. He is married with two children.

Dallara, Gianpaolo

Engineer
Born: 16 November 1936 (Varano de' Melegari, Parma, Italy)

Dallara studied engineering at Parma University, but then, because of lack of adequate facilities, he completed his degree in the Polytechnic School in Milan. He had wanted to work in the aviation industry and had been expecting to obtain a job at Aer Macchi. What happened, however, was that Ferrari was recruiting graduates and making enquiries at Milan University. So Dallara went to work for Ferrari, joining the company in December 1959, and he initially worked for Carlo Chiti in the design department, mainly on stress engineering.

Below: *Dallara has built up an immensely successful racing car company in his home village of Varano de' Melegari after working for Ferrari, Lamborghini, and De Tomaso.* (Tom March Collection)

In February 1962, Dallara left Ferrari (probably because he had lost confidence after the departure of senior staff) and went to work for Maserati. He worked on a number of projects with Giulio Alfieri (whose father was a friend of Dallara's brother-in-law), especially the various 'Bird-cage' designs. While he was at Maserati, he was approached by Ferruccio Lamborghini – at the suggestion of Giotto Bizzarrini – who asked him if he wanted to join his new company as Chief Engineer. Dallara stayed with Lamborghini until 1968, when he joined De Tomaso.

He was responsible for the De Tomaso 505 F1 entered by Frank Williams for Piers Courage and others. Dallara stayed with De Tomaso for some years, but he realised that he wanted to build racing cars, so he left to set up his own works in his home village in 1975. In 1976 Dallara worked briefly for Lamborghini on the Countach project, but in the main Dallara has built only competition cars in a very substantial and modern factory with sophisticated wind tunnel facilities. Among the many cars built have been the BMS Dallaras raced in F1 by Scuderia Italia, F3 cars, and Indianapolis cars. Dallara also undertakes development work for other manufacturers.

Delli Colli, Gabrielle

Chief engineer, vehicle dynamics
Born: 19 October 1966

After obtaining a degree in mechanical engineering in 1992, Delli Colli went to work for the Fiat Research Centre, concentrating on suspension design. In 1995 he left to work for the Alfa racing team, Alfa Corse (a title that dates back to the early origins of the company) where he was International Touring Car race engineer to Nannini. In 1997 he moved to Minardi where he was race engineer to Tarso Marques (Brazilian) and then Jarno Trulli (Italian).

He moved on to Sauber where he was race engineer to Jean Alesi in 1998–9 (after Alesi's Ferrari days were over) and then with Pedro Diniz, still at Sauber in 2000. He followed Trulli to Jordan for the 2001 season and then joined Ferrari. Between 2002 and 2005 he was race engineer to Rubens Barrichello, and in 2006 he held the same position for Massa. In 2007 he was appointed chief engineer, vehicle dynamics.

Above: *Stefano Domenicali is one of the new breed of Italian motor racing engineers. He has played a variety of roles in the Ferrari organisation, but since January 2008 he has been officially designated 'Sporting Director'.* (LAT Photographic)

Above: *Not the most popular of Ferrari race managers, Eugenio Dragoni was a great friend of Enzo Ferrari, and his relations with John Surtees were appalling.* (LAT Photographic)

Domenicali, Stefano

Sporting Director
Born: 11 May 1965 (Imola, Italy)

After graduating in economics and business administration at Bologna University, he joined Ferrari in 1991 as a financial controller in the road car division. He was also appointed race director at the Ferrari-owned Mugello race circuit. Two years later, in 1993, he moved across to the racing team, still as a financial controller. He was placed in charge of human resources at Maranello in 1995. Stefano was appointed team manager in 1998 (he held the position until 2002). Following the departure of Ross Brawn, he became Sporting Director in January 2008, but as he had no factory duties, his was not the same job as that of Brawn.

Dragoni, Eugenio

Racing Director
Born: 1909
Died: 1974

A close friend and fervent supporter of Enzo Ferrari, Dragoni had connections with the Agnelli family and was a very successful businessman; among his interests was ownership of a company that manufactured cosmetics and perfumes. A great motor racing enthusiast, he was a director of Scuderia Sant'Ambroeus, which he controlled and managed. The Scuderia's earliest success in 1961 was entering Giancarlo Baghetti in F1 with a V6 65-degree Ferrari. After Romolo Tavoni left Ferrari at the end of 1961, Dragoni was asked to take on the position of racing director, which he did with great relish.

Like Tavoni, Dragoni was very much an Enzo Ferrari sycophant, but the difference was that Dragoni was a much harder, abrasive character, whereas Tavoni was softer, more pliant and generally much more pleasant. While Dragoni acted as racing director, Scuderia Sant'Ambroeus continued to enter cars, including the Dino that Scarfiotti drove in the European Hill Climb Championship in 1965. Dragoni introduced much-needed team discipline at Ferrari, but his uncommunicative, dictatorial attitude caused considerable friction within the team and many drivers of the period, notably Phil Hill, Chris Amon, and John Surtees, disliked him intensely.

Dragoni saw Ferrari as being a powerful Italian force, and believed that in an ideal world it should have only Italian drivers. He made a favourite of Lorenzo Bandini and argued that he was a better driver than John Surtees. Surtees was the mainstay of the Ferrari team during the years 1963–6 and believed that Ferrari should shed its parochialism and take a broad, international approach to racing. This, inevitably, led to conflict between them, and Dragoni was always working towards Surtees's downfall.

Although the loss of Surtees from the Ferrari team at Le Mans in 1966 was largely engineered by Dragoni, it was on Ferrari's instructions and his final decision. Subsequently, Ferrari, who was becoming a very confused old man, blamed Dragoni for Surtees's departure from the team and this was the main reason why he was replaced by Franco Lini for 1967.

Drogo, Piero

Racing driver and coachbuilder
Born: 8 August 1926 (Vignale Monferrato, near Alessandria, Italy)
Died: 28 April 1973 (Bologna, Italy)

Piero Drogo raced very little in Europe and the majority of his race performances were at the wheel of private Ferraris in South America. He finish seventh in the 1956 sports car Venezuelan GP at Caracas and, co-driving a Tipo 500 Testa Rossa with Jose Pola, he took another seventh place and won the 2000cc class of the 1957 Buenos Aires 1,000km race.

The following year he entered his own 3-litre V12 Testa Rossa in this race and, partnered by Sergio González, finished fourth. Shortly afterwards Drogo was classified 13th with this car in the Cuban GP, but it is far from clear why he was so far down the field. Drogo returned to Italy and drove another private Testa Rossa at Le Mans with Alfonso Gomez-Mena, but they retired because of clutch failure.

By this stage Drogo was out of funds, so he took a job as a mechanic at Stanguellini. After the British boycott of the Italian GP in 1960, the organisers were desperately short of runners, and Drogo secured a drive in a Formula 2 Cooper-Climax entered by Scuderia Colonia. He drove a slow race to finish eighth, five laps behind the winning Ferrari F1 car.

Drogo started Carrozzeria Sportscars, a coachbuilding company, in Modena circa 1961. He rebodied a number of Ferraris, including a Testa Rossa and several 250GT SWB cars, a couple of which had the dramatic 'breadvan' body that has become so famous. He also built bodies on works Ferrari Sports Prototypes and was responsible for the more aerodynamic 'Drogo' noses fitted to a number of Ferrari 250LMs. Drogo was killed in a road accident in 1973 when he ran into the back of a lorry that had broken down in a tunnel.

Dyer, Chris

Race engineer
Born: 12 February 1968 (Elmore, Australia)

After graduating in mechanical engineering in Australia in 1990, Dyer worked in 1991 for Packard Electric as a product engineer, but a year later moved to Holden Special Vehicles where he became a project engineer. Between 1994 and 1996 he was a project engineer with the Holden racing team. Between 1997 and 2000 he was with Arrows in F1, first as Data Analysis Engineer with Damon Hill and then as Race Engineer with Pedro Diniz (Brazilian), Toranosuke Takagi (Japanese), and then Jos Verstappen (Dutch).

In 2001 he joined Ferrari and for his first year he was Vehicle Engineer to Michael Schumacher, and this meant that while he had responsibility for the German driver's car, he did not attend races. Between 2003 and 2006 he was Schumacher's Race Engineer, and since then he has fulfilled the same role for Kimi Räikkönen. Dyer is married and has one daughter.

Englebert, Georges

Tyre manufacturer
(There is no available information as to the dates of his birth and death)

The Englebert company was founded in Belgium in 1895 by Oscar Englebert to make rubber goods, but soon became a manufacturer of tyres. In the 1930s the company started to supply tyres for sports car racing. In post-war days Georges Englebert, who had assumed control of the company, took a more substantial interest in motor racing. From 1950 Englebert supplied tyres to the Simca team (later Gordini). They were sometimes used by Mercedes-Benz in 1952 and, after using them occasionally, Ferrari contracted to use them exclusively in 1955.

During 1955, Ferrari took over the Lancia D50 cars that had run on specially developed Pirelli tyres. Four of these cars were entered in the Ferrari name in that year's Italian GP run in the combined road and banked track circuit. They were plagued by tyre failures in practice, and although Ferrari wanted to switch them to Pirelli tyres, Englebert objected on contractual grounds. Ferrari was forced to withdraw the D50s.

By 1956, Englebert had developed tyres that were suitable for the Lancia D50s at most circuits, but at the Italian race it became obvious that the Belgian company still could not provide tyres for these cars that would withstand the speed and bumps of the Monza banking. Ferrari continued to use Englebert tyres in 1957, but in that year's Mille Miglia road race the Marquis Alfonso de Portago crashed his works Ferrari, killing himself, his co-driver Eddie Nelson, and ten spectators.

Ferrari wanted to change tyre supplier, but there were difficulties other than the mere contractual. Pirelli had retired from racing at the end of 1956, although they had sufficient stocks to supply both Maserati and Vanwall in 1957. During 1958 Hawthorn tested a Dino 246 GP car on Dunlop tyres with promising lap times at the British GP at Silverstone. Then at Monza he raced a Dino with the disc brakes specially fitted to the late Peter Collins's Ferrari 250GT.

Once Ferrari was – finally – convinced of the merits of disc brakes, the advantages of a contract with Dunlop were immense; a supply of both tyres and brakes. For 1959 Ferrari contracted with Dunlop, and Englebert disappeared from the racing scene. Many years later the company changed its name to Uniroyal, and it is now part of the German Continental tyre group.

Below: Georges Englebert (on the left) seen here with French driver Jean Behra in about 1952 when the Belgian company was supplying tyres to Gordini, and Behra was driving for Gordini. (Author's collection)

Fagioli, Luigi

Pre-war Scuderia Ferrari driver
Born: 9 June 1898 (Osimo, Ancona, Italy)
Died: 20 June 1952 (Monte Carlo, Monaco)

This Italian was a driver with a racing career that was at various times interrupted by outbursts of violence and by illness, although, overall, he had a very varied and successful racing career. For reasons that seem to have been legendary rather than objective, he was known sometimes as 'the old Abruzzi robber'. Quite why is lost in the mists of time. Fagioli was a fighter, and was built like a bar brawler, for he had very broad shoulders, massively thick arms, and an immensely thick neck. The description makes him sound deformed, which he was not, and he was in his youth a very good-looking man.

Enzo Ferrari claimed that Fagioli raced purely as a hobby, but there are very serious questions about his real occupation. According to some stories, he owned a small pasta factory – and this sounds credible – but it has also been said that he was an accountant – which seems ludicrous. Incidentally, the name Fagioli translates into English as 'beans', but also as 'blockheads'. One thing about Fagioli is undoubted, and that is his antipathy towards Germans, notwithstanding the fact that during the years of the 750kg formula he drove for both Mercedes-Benz and Auto Union.

Fagioli started his racing career in 1926 with an 1100cc Salmson sports car. It was a shabby little car, badly prepared and unreliable, although he did achieve limited success.

It was good enough for Maserati to sign him up as a works driver in 1930 when Maserati was making a determined effort to break into international racing. With 8C 2500 cars, which at the time were pretty well unbeatable, Fagioli achieved a good run of success. He finished fourth in the 189-mile (304km) Circuit of Caserta (won by team-mate Arcangeli), and he went on to win the Coppa Ciano and the Circuit of Avellino, and to take fourth place in the Monza GP.

He stayed with Maserati through to 1933, winning the 149-mile (240km) Monza GP in 1931; the following year he won the Rome GP run in two 62-mile (100km) heats and a 149-mile (240km) final, and took second places in the five-hour Italian GP, the 308-mile (496km) Czechoslovakian GP, and the Monza GP. As has been recounted elsewhere, Nuvolari left Scuderia Ferrari in 1933 for a number of reasons, not least the failure of the factory to release the Monopostos, and joined Maserati, while Fagioli left Maserati and joined Scuderia Ferrari.

With obsolete Alfa Romeo Monzas, Fagioli achieved a great run of success in 1933 and scored wins at St Gaudens in the Comminges GP, the Coppa Acerbo, and the Italian GP. He also took second places in the Spanish, Marseille, and Czechoslovakian races. Early in 1934, the head of the Mercedes-Benz Rennabteilung (racing department), Alfred Neubauer, asked Fagioli to drive the new Mercedes-Benz W25 750kg GP cars. It was not that Mercedes-Benz really wanted Fagioli, but the team was in a desperate position because Caracciola was still not fit following his bad accident in practice at Monaco the previous year, and von Brauchitsch was not temperamentally suited to test driving.

During the time he was with Mercedes-Benz, Fagioli was invariably locked in argument with Neubauer. The famous team manager needed Fagioli and tolerated him, but he did not need to like him. Fagioli mistrusted Neubauer and hated both Caracciola and von Brauchitsch. With Mercedes-Benz cars Fagioli enjoyed a good run of success in 1934. He won the Coppa Acerbo and the Spanish GP, and in addition he took second places in the German and Czechoslovakian races.

The following year, Fagioli won at Monaco, Avus, and Barcelona, and he also took second places at Bremgarten and San Sebastian. In 1936 Mercedes-Benz had a terrible season and all that Fagioli could achieve

was a shared fourth place at Bremgarten. The team from Untertürkheim temporarily withdrew from racing before the end of the year. The Italian was developing bad rheumatoid arthritis, and as he had started to walk with the aid of a stick, it was generally believed that he was going to retire from racing.

Fagioli surprised everyone by joining Auto Union for 1937. At Tripoli, Fagioli and Caracciola battled for fifth place, but the Italian could not get past until just before the finish, with Fagioli third and Caracciola fourth. Fagioli was convinced – with good reason – that Caracciola had been baulking him deliberately. As soon as the race was over, he hurried as quickly as he could to the Mercedes-Benz pits and threw a wheel hammer at Caracciola, but missed him. It is said that Fagioli then 'grabbed' a knife, but it is more likely that he had one with him, and he tried to stab Caracciola and he was hauled off him by Neubauer and Wilhelm Sebastian.

Part of Fagioli's loss of control was caused by the pain from his worsening arthritis. During 1937 he missed six races, and his last race with Auto Union was the Swiss GP where he handed his car over to Nuvolari who finished seventh. The Italian now turned to

Below: *Although Fagioli was forced to retire from GP racing in pre-war days because of severe and crippling arthritis, in post-war days he returned to racing in much better health. He had enjoyed a long career in the 1930s driving for Scuderia Ferrari, Mercedes-Benz, and Auto Union. In 1950, when this photograph was taken, he was a member of the works Alfa Romeo GP team, alongside Farina and Fangio.* (Author's collection)

farming and he did not race again in pre-war days. When he returned to racing, it was not intended seriously. He partnered his nephew at the wheel of a Fiat 508S in the 1949 Mille Miglia, just to give him some support in his first race.

The arthritis (if it was really that) had nearly disappeared, and Fagioli was almost free of pain. Alfa Romeo returned to GP racing for 1950 after a season's absence, and following the deaths of Trossi, Varzi, and Wimille, they had great difficulty in forming a team. Fagioli was now 51, but he was brought in to drive alongside Farina and Fangio. The combined ages of the 'Three Fs' totalled over 130 years. Fagioli was content with Alfa Romeo, even though, age apart, he was the junior member of the team.

In 1950 he finished second in four rounds of the newly inaugurated Drivers' Championship, and also took a third place to score 24/28 points (net/gross) and gain third place in the Championship. The following year he drove for Alfa Romeo only at Reims, where he had to hand his car over to Fangio. He also drove an OSCA sports car in Italian races, and with one of these cars he won his class in the 1951 Mille Miglia. He raced Lancia Aurelia GTs in 1952 and finished third overall in the Mille Miglia behind Bracco (Ferrari) and Kling (Mercedes-Benz 300SL), but ahead of Caracciola with another 300SL, which must have given him considerable satisfaction.

That year the Monaco GP was held as two sports car races on 1 June. Fagioli was due to drive a Lancia in an event for cars up to 2000cc, but he never made the start. During practice, he touched the kerb as he exited from the tunnel; the Lancia ricocheted across the road and hit the wall. This veteran driver suffered terrible head injuries, together with a broken arm and leg, and almost three weeks later he died following the complete collapse of his nervous system.

Fainello, Marco

Car Performance Development Manager
Born: 12 September 1964 (Verona, Italy)

After graduating in 1990 from Milan Polytechnic University in mechanical engineering, Fainello joined the Fiat Research Centre, where he worked as a vehicle dynamics engineer. A year, later he was promoted to Vehicle Dynamics Manager. He joined Ferrari in 1995, and his first job was Support Race Engineer to Jean Alesi. A year later, in 1996, he became Support Race Engineer to Michael Schumacher. Marco was appointed Vehicle Dynamics Manager in 1997, and in 2004 he became Car Performance Development Manager. The department for which he is responsible includes research and development into both vehicle dynamics and tyres. He is married with two children.

Fangio, Juan Manuel

Works driver
Born: 24 June 1911 (Balcarce, Buenos Aires, Argentina)
Died: 17 July 1995 (Balcarce)

Although Fangio won the Drivers' World Championship five times, driving for four teams, in the main only his F1 career with Ferrari will be considered here in detail. There are a number of biographies of Fangio, and the writer particularly likes the Maestro's own, *My Twenty Years of Racing* (see Bibliography). Fangio was the son of impoverished Italian immigrants, and because of the family's financial situation he was forced to start work in a garage at the age of 11. Partly because of the atmosphere in which he worked, and partly because of his family's Italian background, Juan soon became a great motor racing enthusiast, but he was also a determined and skilled football player.

At the age of 16 he ran away to Mar del Plata, believing that he was a burden on the family, and determined to be self-sufficient. His father tracked him down and persuaded him to return home. Five years later, when he was 21, he was called up for military service, but once this was completed he returned to Balcarce and went into partnership running a very small garage with a friend, José Duffard. They were to enjoy a business relationship that lasted all their lives.

Like so many young men, he wanted to race but lacked not just the means, but the prospects of acquiring

Opposite: *A fine portrait of Juan Fangio, taken after one of his victories with the Mercedes-Benz W196 GP cars during the 1955 season. Fangio's position as the number one GP driver was taken for granted after his brilliant 1951 season, and his poor showings early in 1952 and his bad accident at Monza in June were simply ignored.* **(Daimler)**

Above: *Fangio's potential was recognised by Alfa Romeo team manager Juan-Battista Guidotti, and he was invited to join the F1 team for 1950. Here, he is seen at the wheel of his Tipo 158 in his wet heat of the International Trophy race at Silverstone in August 1950. He won the heat and finished second in the final to team-mate Farina.*
(Guy Griffiths Collection)

the means. His first opportunity came in 1934 when he raced a borrowed Ford Model A. Because a connecting rod broke, the owner demanded that he rebuild the engine – which he duly did. Later, Fangio was able to buy his own Ford Model A, which he developed for racing, and he then built a car that mated a Model A chassis with a Ford V8 engine. Over the next few years, Fangio competed with increasing success in those long-distance races with much-modified obsolete American cars that seem to have been peculiar to Argentina.

Fangio's consistent performances in these races led to the chance to drive one of the Maseratis imported in 1948 by the Automobile Club of Argentina, which was strongly supported by President Juan Perón who had been elected in 1946. Fangio was still racing a much-modified Chevrolet Special, but with the Maserati he finished fourth in his heat of the Buenos Aires GP (he retired in the final), and he was fourth again in the Mar del Plata GP. He also drove a Simca-Gordini bought by the Argentinian club, and he travelled to Europe to drive a Simca in the Coupe des Petites Cylindrées at

Reims, where he retired because of engine trouble.

In early 1949, Fangio again drove a Maserati in the races in Argentina. He took fourth and second places at Buenos Aires, and then, in February, won the Mar del Plata GP. The Argentine Automobile Club sent Fangio and Benedicto Campos to compete with Maseratis in Europe, entered in the name of Squadra Achille Varzi. He achieved an astonishing run of successes with his 4CLT/48 Maserati, and won the races at San Remo, Pau, Perpignan, and Albi. He also won the Marseille GP with a Simca and the Autodromo GP at Monza with a Ferrari. In other races, including the Belgian GP and French GP, he drove well, but retired.

Alfa Romeo had withdrawn from Grand Prix racing in 1949 because of the anticipated strength of the opposition, but this had failed to materialise and the team came back to racing again in 1950. The team faced a desperate shortage of drivers, and signed up Farina as team-leader, backed up by the relatively inexperienced Fangio (whose potential greatness was not widely appreciated), and the vastly experienced, but rather elderly Fagioli. Serious opposition to the Alfa Romeos did not emerge until the 4.5-litre unblown Ferrari appeared at the Italian GP. The Alfa Romeo drivers took the first three places in the Championship – Farina 30 points, Fangio 27 points, and Fagioli 24 points.

The first World Champion bitterly resented the serious challenge from the Argentinian, but the following year Fangio, driving with supreme accuracy, speed, and restraint, won his first Championship with three outright wins, two second places, and a total of 31 points (net), while a disgruntled, frustrated, and bad-tempered Farina displayed that he was past his best by dropping down the points table to fourth (19 points net) behind Ferrari drivers Ascari and González. At the end of the season Alfa Romeo withdrew from F1.

The Féderation Internationale de l'Automobile, the organising body of motor sport, in liaison with the various national organising clubs, decided that all World Championship races in 1952–3 would be to 2-litre Formula 2 rules. The reasoning was that, with the withdrawal of Alfa Romeo and the failure of the V16 BRM to become a serious force, Formula 1 would be dominated by Ferrari. In F2 there were competitors in profusion, but no company – Maserati, Gordini, or any of the British constructors – could produce sufficiently competitive cars, and Ferrari dominated GP racing for another two years.

Fangio went to drive for the Maserati team, but Modena's new A6GCM six-cylinder model was not ready at the beginning of the season and the full team was due to make its debut in the Autodromo GP at Monza on 8 June. The V16 BRMs were still not reliable, but they were immensely powerful; the handling was difficult and they offered a challenge to the top drivers. BRM also paid very well, and both Fangio and González contracted to drive these V16 F1 cars in 1952. After retiring his BRM in the Albi GP on 1 June, Fangio drove a V16 car again in the Ulster Trophy on the Dundrod circuit on 7 June, and again retired.

While Fangio was in Northern Ireland, he received a telegram from the Maserati works pleading with him to get back in time to drive for the team in the Monza race the following day. Fangio, very foolishly, decided that he would be in Italy in time to drive the Maserati. He flew from Belfast to Le Bourget, Paris, where he learned all flights to Italy had been cancelled because of bad weather. So, knowing that he was making a mistake, he drove a Renault 750 overnight the 500-plus miles to Monza.

Because he had not practised, the Argentinian started from the back of the grid at Monza. On the second lap, as he was making his way up the field, he lost concentration, hit the kerb at Serraglio Corner and was thrown out of the car. He was taken to hospital unconscious, and it was discovered that he had broken vertebrae in the neck. This accident put Fangio in a plaster cast up to his chin, and he was out of racing for the rest of the year. He went back to Balcarce to recover, rest, and convalesce.

Fangio returned to lead Maserati in 1953, and although, by the end of the season, the latest versions of the six-cylinder A6GCM developed 190bhp (some 10bhp more than the rival four-cylinder Tipo 500 Ferrari), they

retained a rigid rear axle, and the handling was generally inferior. Ascari dominated racing to win his second successive World Championship, while Fangio finished second in the French, British, and German races, and won the Italian GP after Ascari spun on the last corner.

Apart from minor F2 wins, and drives in four races for BRM, Fangio drove one of the latest Alfa Romeo 6C 34 3.6-litre coupés into second place in the Mille Miglia road race despite a steering defect; he retired with one of these Alfa Romeos at Le Mans, and won the sports car Supercortemaggiore GP at Merano with a new 3-litre Alfa Romeo Spider. In addition, he won the Carrera Panamericana Mexico road race with a Lancia D24.

Below: *Fangio acknowledges the applause of his supporters after winning the 1954 Italian GP with this streamlined Mercedes-Benz W196. It was not one of Fangio's better victories, and he won only after race-leader Stirling Moss, driving his Maserati as part of the works team, dropped out because of a leaking oil tank.* (Daimler)

Above: *In 1956, Fangio drove for Ferrari and it proved one of the most miserable seasons in his racing career. Fangio expected to be treated as team-leader on the basis of his three World Championships, but Enzo Ferrari tried to pretend that all drivers in the team were equal. Here, at the British GP at Silverstone, the World Champion discusses compounds with the mechanic from Englebert, the Belgian company that supplied Ferrari's tyres.* (Tom March Collection)

The new 2500cc Formula 1 came into force for 1954, and it was to prove one of the most successful of all GP formulae. Fangio stayed with Maserati until the new Mercedes-Benz W196 streamlined F1 car was ready. He won the Argentine and Belgian races before switching to the German cars. With wins at the wheel of the W196s in the French, German, Swiss, and Italian races, he gained his second Drivers' Championship.

He stayed with Mercedes-Benz in 1955 and won the Argentine, Belgian, Dutch and Italian Grands Prix, finishing second to team-mate Moss in the British race. He won the Drivers' Championship for the third time. Fangio also drove the team's 300SLR sports-racing cars. He finished second in the Mille Miglia road race and, co-driving with Karl Kling, he took second places in the Tourist Trophy and Targa Florio sports car races.

Fangio had difficulty in finding a satisfactory works drive in 1956. The British teams were still not competitive (although that was to change within 18 months) and Moss had signed up to lead Maserati. Fangio did not want to drive for Ferrari, but either he did drive for Maranello or he retired for a season. Ferrari did not pay very well,

he would not recognise Fangio (or anyone else) as a team-leader, and the Argentinian was convinced that his cars were not well prepared. During 1955 Ferrari had taken over the V8 Lancias and raced these as Ferraris, while trying to modify the design (but only succeeded in making these very competitive cars less potent).

In the Argentinian race, Fangio took over from Musso to win, and he subsequently relieved Collins to take second place behind Moss at Monaco. He retired in Belgium, finished fourth in the French race at Reims, and then won at Silverstone and the Nürburgring. The 1956 Italian race was marked by the refusal of the young Italian driver Musso to hand his car over to Fangio, and Collins's very willingness to do so when asked by Fangio's racing manager Marcello Giambertone (if this happened). Fangio won his fourth World Championship from Stirling Moss, but the race raised the very clear issue that Collins acted like a gentleman and Musso did not.

In a team where there was no discipline, and very little self-discipline, it is not difficult to see why Musso looked after himself, and this writer would urge that Collins should have done the same. Racing was a matter of life and death to the Italian young tigers (and was to prove so for Collins) and there was no room for the 'After you Claude' nonsense. Furthermore, Fangio had no moral or other rights to his team-mates' cars, and should not have expected deference of this kind, although he clearly did. All season, Fangio was unhappy and depressed and he was forced to take psychiatric treatment. He was not the right man for the Ferrari team.

By way of contrast, Fangio formed a good working partnership in sports car racing with Eugenio Castellotti, and they won the Sebring 12 Hours race, were second in the Nürburgring 1,000km race, and third in the Supercortemaggiore GP. The World Champion had a thoroughly miserable time driving solo in the rain-soaked Mille Miglia, and because of the position of holes in the bodywork to draw in air to cool the front brakes of his car, water thrown up by the wheels flooded the cockpit every time he braked. It was obvious that he would have liked to retire, but he struggled on to finish fourth.

In a sense, all the leading drivers found their natural homes in 1957. All the young tigers, Castellotti, Collins, Hawthorn, and Musso, at Ferrari, Moss and Brooks at Vanwall, while Fangio returned to Maserati where Behra remained as number two driver. Maserati started the season as the strongest team, but Vanwall achieved its first victory at Aintree, and Moss went on to win for the British team at both Pescara and Monza (Fangio was second in both races).

During the year, Fangio won four Championship races: Buenos Aires, Monaco, Rouen, and the Nürburgring. He drove two of his greatest races, the French GP and German GP, but performed miserably in the British race. He won the Championship with 40 points to the 25 of second-place man Moss. During the year he also won the Sebring 12 Hours race, co-driving with Behra, and sports car races in Cuba, Portugal, Interlagos, and Rio de Janeiro.

In 1958 Fangio retired, although it seemed at the beginning of the season that he was unsure about his future. Maserati had withdrawn from racing because of financial problems, and the Maestro and his manager arranged to field their own team of ex-works 250Fs in the Argentine GP, in which he was fourth, and in the non-Championship Buenos Aires City GP, which he won. His final racing appearance was with a one-off works Maserati entry of the prototype lightweight 'piccolo' 250F in the French GP at Reims, and he drove a steady race to take fourth place.

Fangio returned to Argentina to pursue his business interests, which included a Mercedes-Benz dealership and, subsequently, he opened a motor museum in Balcarce. The Maserati factory had wanted to present a 250F to Fangio to commemorate his fifth World Championship. At the time they could not afford to do this, and eventually Fangio bought one of the Cameron Millar reproductions.

How does Fangio rank in the hierarchy of World Champions? As usual, comparisons with the great drivers outside his era are vague and invidious. Fangio was a vastly experienced, mature driver when he won his later Championships. During this period he had very few accidents because he so rarely made a mistake. He drove consistently within his limits, displaying outstanding accuracy and exceptional car control. Above all, he coupled speed with restraint.

Above: *Seen here, at the Maserati factory in 1947, are coachbuilder Medardo Fantuzzi (right) and Luigi Villoresi at the wheel of an early post-war Maserati sports car. After Maserati withdrew from racing at the end of 1957, Fantuzzi did work for Ferrari.* (Author's collection)

Fantuzzi, Medardo

Coachbuilder (after Maserati withdrew from racing)
Born: 1906 (Bologna, Italy)
Died: 1986 (Modena, Italy)

Fantuzzi was an exceptionally skilled panel-beater, whose skills extended to styling in addition to mere construction. He and his brother Gino Fantuzzi worked together, and they forged a close relationship with Maserati that dated back to the formation of Officine Alfieri Maserati in 1926. Without doubt the most famous bodies built by Fantuzzi were those on the ACGCS/53 sports-racing car chassis of which there were 44 with Fantuzzi bodies.

After Maserati withdrew from racing at the end of the 1957 season, Fantuzzi worked with Ferrari and, in addition to the bodies of later Ferrari TR250 Testa Rossas, he built a number of other bodies on Ferrari chassis, including one-offs on 250GTE and 330 chassis. Fantuzzi also worked for De Tomaso, Serenissima, and Tecno. After he gave up the business, the running of it was taken over by his son, Fiorenzo Fantuzzi.

Above: *Vastly experienced, immensely tough, and as hard as granite, 'Nino' Farina was a man whose racing career was irreparably damaged by the Second World War. Here, he is seen after winning the International Trophy race at Silverstone in August 1950. He was driving for Alfa Romeo and won the first ever Drivers' World Championship with these cars.* (Guy Griffiths Collection)

Farina, Giuseppe

Works driver
Born: 30 October 1906 (Turin, Italy)
Died: 30 June 1966 Chambéry, France)

Giuseppe 'Nino' Farina's parents were wealthy, and he and his brother were brought up in comfortable surroundings and were well educated. Giuseppe's father, cousin of Pinin Farina, ran the Stablimenti Farina coachbuilding firm. Farina studied law at Turin University, and in due course he was awarded a doctorate. Farina's earliest motor racing efforts met with bad crashes. Exuberance overcoming innate skill was a fault that dogged him throughout his racing career.

By late 1934 he was driving Maserati voiturettes for Scuderia Sub-Alpina, a team closely involved with the works. Soon he moved on to GP Maseratis, but these were uncompetitive, and no match for the German opposition or the contemporary Alfa Romeos. During this learning curve Farina was very much influenced by his friendship with the great Tazio Nuvolari. It was an unusual friendship because Farina was so detached from normal relationships, and lacked the warmth to attract friends. Partly because of Nuvolari's influence, he adopted the driving style for which he became famous, the inclined, relaxed position with outstretched arms that influenced a generation of drivers.

Enzo Ferrari recognised the intelligence that Farina applied to his driving, and for 1936 signed him up to drive Alfa Romeos for Scuderia Ferrari. In the Deauville GP, a minor race, he was leading with his 8C 35 Alfa Romeo, and when he lapped Marcel Lehoux's ERA, the two cars collided; the ERA was pushed off the road, caught fire, and its driver perished. Farina was injured, but not badly. At the time, the incident was accepted as just another accident in a dangerous sport. It was, however, to prove part of Farina's ruthless pattern of collisions and crashes. During 1936 he finished third in the Penya Rhin GP, fourth in the Eifelrennen, and third at Milan.

In 1937 Scuderia Ferrari continued the struggle to beat the Silver Arrows, and although the Alfa Romeos were significantly inferior, good results were achieved on occasions. Farina started the season with second place behind team-mate Brivio in the Circuit of Turin, and later he won the Circuit of Naples. He finished second in the Circuit of Milan, a race in which the Alfa Romeo drivers beat Hasse, with the sole Auto Union entered, into fourth place.

In 1938 Farina's first GP was at Tripoli where he drove the latest supercharged V12 3-litre Alfa Romeo. The race was run concurrently with the class for 1500cc Voiturettes, and Farina turned in a strong performance, holding fourth place behind the three works Mercedes-Benz entries. When he came up to lap Laszlo Hartmann, with a 1500cc Maserati, the Hungarian unintentionally baulked him. Farina rammed the Maserati. Both cars went off the road and Hartmann suffered injuries from which he died the following day. Farina was also quite badly hurt.

Later in 1938, Farina with the V12 Alfa Romeo took second places in the Coppa Ciano at Livorno (behind Lang's Mercedes), in the Coppa Acerbo at Pescara (behind Caracciola's Stuttgart entry), and in the Italian GP (behind Nuvolari's Auto Union). If the crash at Tripoli is brushed under the carpet, Farina had a very good year, and he won the Italian Championship for the first time.

In the Tripoli race in May 1939, Mercedes-Benz took the first two places with their new 1500cc W165 cars. Farina, at the wheel of an Alfa Romeo Tipo 158 Alfetta, held second place behind Caracciola's Mercedes until his over-driven engine gave up after nine laps. Farina performed well with 158s later in 1939; he led throughout to win the Coppa Ciano at Livorno, and finished third in the Coppa Acerbo at Pescara behind Alfa Romeo team-mates Biondetti and Pintacuda. There was no strong opposition to the Alfettas in these races, and Farina won the Italian Championship for the second time.

On 3 September 1939, Great Britain and France declared war on Germany following the invasion of Poland two days' previously. In most of Europe, motor racing ground to a halt, but not in Italy where Benito Mussolini did not declare for the Axis until 10 June 1940. The Mille Miglia road race was staged over nine laps of a closed 103-mile circuit between Bologna, Mantua, and Cremona. Farina drove well with his 6C 2500 Alfa to finish second, 7½ minutes behind von Hanstein (streamlined BMW 328).

With the declaration of war, the Italian Champion joined the army to fight for El Duce and country. Like so many other fine drivers of his generation, the war years were when Farina would have been at his greatest and most successful. They were wasted years, and he never achieved the pinnacle of his ability. In post-war days he was embittered, his mood swings were more marked, his lack of mental stability more evident.

When international racing was resumed in 1946, Alfa Romeo re-entered the fray. Farina and former works Bugatti driver Jean-Pierre Wimille were at the wheel of Alfettas in the team's first post-war race, the 112-mile (180km) St Cloud GP in June, but the 158s had suffered during their long hibernation and both retired because of clutch problems.

In July, the 158s ran in the GP des Nations held on a street circuit at Geneva. The race saw a fair amount of bumping and baulking by Tazio Nuvolari, at the wheel of a Maserati, but Farina and Nuvolari had been friends for many years (Nuvolari was the grand old man of Italian motor racing and he was also very unwell). Farina showed a different, theatrical side to his personality.

Tazio took the lead on the first lap of his heat, followed by Farina, who was gesticulating dramatically to make it quite clear how badly he was being baulked. On the second lap 'Nino' forced his way into the lead, but with none of the viciousness that he had shown on other occasions. In the final, Nuvolari rammed Wimille's leading 158, which spun off, and the Frenchman rejoined to finish third behind Farina and Trossi.

Farina won his heat at Milan, but was penalised a minute for jumping the start. Team orders dictated that Trossi should win the final, and after a few laps Achille Varzi allowed Trossi to slip into the lead. 'Nino' was not putting up with this and was determined to get ahead of Varzi and catch Trossi. There was mutual hostility between Varzi and Farina, and a bitter duel developed, which ended when Farina spun off because a brake locked. He kept the engine running, but he drove into the pits and pulled out of the race with a look on his face that was one of the blackest ever seen at a motor racing circuit. Farina was sacked from the Alfa Romeo team.

Farina was absent from racing in 1947, but returned in 1948 with Maseratis entered by Scuderia Milano. It proved a poor year as 'Nino' was over-driving cars that were not prepared to the highest standards, and his one real success was his win in the Monaco GP. The new V12 1.5-litre GP Ferrari made its debut in the rain-soaked Italian race held in Valentino Park, Turin, in September 1948. Farina had been brought into the testing programme and was asked to drive the new car in its races that year. At Turin he lost control and smacked the front of the car against the straw bales. Later he won the minor Circuit of Garda, but he retired at both Monza and Barcelona.

'Nino' had high hopes of being invited to lead Ferrari's 1949 GP team, but instead Enzo opted for Maserati drivers Alberto Ascari and Luigi Villoresi. So, frustrated and more embittered than ever, Farina carried on with Scuderia Milano. It was another season without substantial success, but he finished second, splitting the Ferraris, in the International Trophy at Silverstone – and could have won but for a wild spin – and he beat Ascari (Ferrari) into second place in the Lausanne GP.

At the 1949 European GP at Monza, Ferrari introduced improved, twin-stage supercharged cars, while Scuderia Milano produced their latest Maserati-based Milano. In the early laps of the race Farina, with the Milano, chased the new Ferraris hard, but then pulled into the pits, complaining that his car was too slow, and withdrew from the race. It was petulance of the worst kind, and very foolish. Villoresi retired his Ferrari, and if Farina had kept going he would probably have finished second.

After a year's absence, Alfa Romeo returned to racing in 1950. Their biggest problem was the lack of suitable drivers. Racing manager Giovanni Battista ('John the Baptist') Guidotti and the directors saw no alternative but to ask Farina, now 43, to rejoin the team. Alongside him were 38-year-old Argentinian Juan Fangio, in his second season of European racing, and 51-year-old veteran Luigi Fagioli. The 'Three Fs', as they became known, had a combined age of over 130.

Now that 'Nino' was leader of the top Formula 1 team, in some ways he mellowed into his security. Alfa Romeo did not need to choose the race winner; it was sufficient to give Farina the fastest car and leave the rest to his burning determination. This was Farina's right as team leader, and whatever Fangio and his manager, Marcello Giambertone, thought, Fangio was 'the new kid on the block'.

Farina could still be vicious and lethal, all too ready to ram another driver if he did not get out of the way quickly enough. During practice at Silverstone in 1950, a young British driver – destined for greatness – nipped past Farina on the inside of corners several times. Farina accelerated ahead again once they were clear of the corner, but to onlookers who knew him it was obvious that he was becoming angrier and angrier. After the British driver had returned to the paddock, the kind and vastly experienced Villoresi told the lad, 'You've never met anyone like Farina. He's a killer. Keep out of his way or he'll push you off.'

The 'Three Fs' proved to be one of the most successful teams of all time. Alfa Romeo entered 11 races and won them all – and had now won every race entered since the failure at St Cloud in 1946. Farina took the newly inaugurated Drivers' Championship with 30 points to the 27 of Fangio and 24 of Fagioli. Ferrari driver Ascari, in fourth place, accumulated only 12 points. 'Nino' won the British, Swiss, and Italian races and set fastest lap at both Bremgarten and Silverstone. He also scored wins in the non-Championship Bari GP and the International Trophy at Silverstone.

The Championship was in the balance until the Italian GP at Monza. Farina bitterly resented the Argentinian's challenge to his role as team leader and, although Fangio was a man who preferred to avoid confrontation, their relationship had become increasingly strained. Farina, with the fastest Alfa at Monza, led throughout, while Fangio retired because of gearbox failure.

Farina and Fangio remained with Alfa Romeo in 1951, but Fangio had benefited from experience and his driving was now vastly superior to that of Farina, and the latest unsupercharged 4.5-litre Ferraris presented a much greater challenge. Farina won at Spa, and the rest of his season combined bad luck with the occasional lack-lustre performance. He led at Reims, but over-drove the Alfetta and twice the left front tyre failed. At the Silverstone circuit, González won with his Ferrari – the long-awaited Ferrari breakthrough – and Ascari won for Ferrari again at both the Nürburgring and Monza.

In the Italian race 'Nino' retired his Alfa with engine problems and took over Bonetto's car. In one of his finest drives, he struggled to bring the Alfetta up through the field. The Alfetta developed a fuel leak, and

Above: *Giuseppe Farina, the first World Champion, poses with his Tipo 158 Alfa Romeo before the Italian GP at Monza in 1950. Farina won the race from the Ferrari Tipo 375 shared by Serafini and Ascari.* **(Author's collection)**

as 'Nino' accelerated away from the pits, fuel could be seen spewing from the tail. Despite the fire risk, Farina was not black-flagged and he brought the car through to finish third behind the Ferraris of Ascari and González. Denis Jenkinson wrote:

'The scream of that supercharged engine running continuously at 9,000rpm in a vain attempt to win remains in my memory as one of the landmarks of motor racing.'

In the last round of the Championship, the Spanish GP, the Ferraris were plagued by tyre problems, and Fangio and Farina took first and third places. For Farina it had not been a fulfilling year and he finished a despondent fourth in the Championship with 19 points, behind Fangio (31 points), Ascari (25 points), and González (24 points). Alfa Romeo now withdrew from GP racing, and it was the end of an era both in motor racing and for Farina himself.

All major races in 1952 were held to 2000cc ormula 2 rules, and Farina joined Ferrari, where he was

overshadowed by Ascari. Farina always expected more of his car than it was capable of, and his crash record worsened. In Championship events he was second at Spa, Rouen, the Nürburgring, and Zandvoort. He finished second in the World Championship with 24 points to the 36 of Ascari.

Farina's last full season was in 1953. It started appallingly. The first Championship race was the Argentine GP at Buenos Aires in January. It was estimated that there were 500,000 spectators and the crowd control was abysmal. Farina was in fifth place when he lost control and ploughed into spectators gathered in a prohibited area on a corner.

It was carnage, although full details were never published. Five spectators were killed outright, and it is believed that another five died from their injuries. Farina suffered leg injuries, but not sufficiently bad to prevent him from reappearing at the same circuit a fortnight later. With a 2.5-litre Ferrari, he won the Formule Libre Buenos Aires City GP from team-mates Villoresi and Hawthorn.

Farina had a good European season, although he continued to play a secondary role to Ascari. He was second in the Dutch race behind Ascari, was fifth in the French GP, a closely fought race in which he was only a couple of seconds behind the winner, Mike Hawthorn, and he finished third at Silverstone. In the German race, Ascari's leading Ferrari lost a wheel, and Farina, recapturing some of his former mastery, surged through

Above: *An Alfa Romeo mechanic is on the left in this photograph; then the order is Consalvo Sanesi, Giuseppe Farina, Felice Bonetto, Juan-Manuel Fangio, and Giovanni Battista ('John the Baptist') Guidotti, who remained with Alfa Romeo in pre-war days and did not join Ferrari. He had been Alfa Romeo's racing manager since 1946. This photograph was taken at the International Trophy meeting at Silverstone 1951.* (**Guy Griffiths Collection**)

to win, passing Fangio (Maserati) and Ferrari team-mate Hawthorn. It was his last Championship race win. He was second in the Swiss and Italian races, and he finished third in the World Championship behind Ascari and Fangio.

The 1954 season started well for Farina, with second place in the Argentine GP, a win, co-driving with Umberto Maglioli, in the Buenos Aires 1,000km race, and a win in the first race of the European season at Siracusa. In the Mille Miglia he drove one of the 4.9-litre Tipo 375 Plus cars, which were notoriously difficult to control. At Peschiera, shortly after the start, he went off the road, badly injuring riding mechanic Presenti and several spectators, as well as breaking his right arm.

It was after this accident that Farina admitted that he could not remember how many crashes he had been involved in. The 1954 Mille Miglia marked the end of Farina's serious racing career. He reappeared at the

Belgian GP where he led initially with his Squalo Ferrari, but retired because of rear axle problems. Another crash with a 3-litre sports Ferrari followed during practice at Monza and he suffered bad burns.

Approaching his 49th birthday Farina decided to retire from racing, but he wanted to cap his career by competing at Indianapolis. He failed to qualify in both 1956 and 1957 with special Ferraris entered by Luigi Chinetti. Farina continued to maintain close links with the motor trade – and motor racing. On 30 June 1966 he was driving his Lotus-Cortina to the French GP at Reims when he lost control on a slippery road near Chambéry. His car demolished two telegraph poles and he was killed instantly. He was not a man who would have wanted to die in bed.

Despite the oddness of his personality, Farina was a happily married man with an exceptionally attractive wife. It was a great sadness to them that they had no children. To rate Farina is difficult. He was not a great World Champion, but he could drive with the most tremendous flair and inspiration. He was very much an outsider, just as though he had stepped out of the pages of an existentialist novel by Jean-Paul Sartre or Albert Camus.

Below: *Dino Ferrari on the left and his father, Enzo Ferrari, second from right. It is clearly a (badly) posed photograph and it is common knowledge that Ferrari junior had nothing more than a rudimentary knowledge of motor racing matters.* (LAT Photographic)

Ferrari, Dino

Enzo Ferrari's only legitimate son
Born: January 1932 (Modena, Italy)
Died: 30 June 1956 (Modena)

Enzo Ferrari's son Alfredo, commonly known as 'Dino' (or 'Alfredino') was his greatest love and, after the successful foundation of the Ferrari company, it was his intention to groom him as his successor. Unfortunately, Dino always suffered from bad health, but Enzo sent him to study engineering in Switzerland – and bearing in mind his very real delicacy this was not a good idea.

Ferrari always attributed the concept of Maranello's V6 engine to Dino, and named it after him. This was pretty silly and fooled few, for Vittorio Jano and his colleagues at Lancia were recognised as the pioneers of the V6 layout, and the Maranello factory only became interested in it after Jano and his colleagues joined Ferrari from Lancia.

Of course, Dino was interested in most things mechanical, and there is no reason to doubt that Dino was excited about the concept and discussed it with Jano at Maranello and in hospital. Dino had developed muscular dystrophy, which resulted in his death. At the French GP at Reims on 1 July, the Ferrari drivers wore black armbands as a token of mourning for Dino. The name 'Dino' was used by Ferrari for all cars with the V6 engine layout.

Ferrari, Laura

Enzo Ferrari's wife
Born: circa 1900 (Racconigi, about 20 miles/32km south of Turin, Italy)
Died: 27 January 1978 (Modena, Italy)

Very little is known about Laura Dominica Garello Ferrari, although a number of highly inaccurate and scurrilous statements have been published. She is said to have come from a rather poor background, but nothing else is certain apart from the fact that she is believed to have been around 21 when they met. Enzo Ferrari claimed that he had thrown away papers relating to their early life together. They married on 28 April 1923, and their only child Alfredo was born in 1932.

It was not until about 1960 that Laura started to attend races (which, of course, Enzo never did following Guy Moll's death). The late Cliff Allison told the writer that she would turn up accompanied by former team manager Girolimo Amorotti. It has also to be remembered that Enzo Ferrari had a terrible conscience, and he always believed that he had treated Laura badly over his relationship with Lina Lardi.

As Tavoni put it:

'Laura Ferrari was suffering from mental problems and she was constantly interfering in the management of the company. Some of these were very slight matters, some much more important. For example, she harassed Chiti to pay rent on the Ferrari-owned apartment that he occupied, but it was part of his package that he occupied it rent-free.

We were all desperate, and eight of us, the principal managers in the company, agreed that we had to do something about it. There was absolutely no alternative. So we took legal advice from a lawyer in Modena, and as a result we wrote a collective letter to Enzo Ferrari, explaining the position and the problem. But the truth of the matter was that he knew about the problem, and there was absolutely nothing that he could do about it. We had no problems with Enzo Ferrari personally, only the way in which Laura Ferrari was behaving, undermining the conduct of the company's business.

At the time, Enzo Ferrari was not a well man. You could see it in his face, the way he looked, and he made matters worse by forgetting to take his medicine. I kept reminding him, and it angered him that he had forgotten. We were convinced that this failure to take the medicine affected the way he was thinking. We sent the letter about the problems on the Saturday before the last Tuesday in October 1961. On that Tuesday we had our usual 5pm meeting with Enzo Ferrari. Our letter was not discussed.

At the exit on the ground floor of the building, the Assistant Secretary, who worked for me, was standing at the door. He told each of us, 'This is your money and you must sign for it or, if you wish, it will be paid into your bank. Then you are out of Ferrari.' Each of us was handed a letter terminating our employment, together with a cheque for what each of us was owed. I told him that I wanted to talk to Ferrari, but this was refused.'

Despite this reaction and all the problems that ensued, Ferrari was well aware of the situation and dealt with it in his own way and in his own time. In February 1962 the Ferrari company issued a statement that, 'Signora Ferrari will no longer be connected with the Ferrari racing équipe.'

Below: *Laura Ferrari (wife of Enzo and 'the great meddler' who caused so much dissension at Maranello) at the 1961 Dutch GP. On the left, with trophy, is works Ferrari driver Wolfgang von Trips, who won the race with his Tipo 156, and on the right is Phil Hill, who finished second with his Tipo 156.* (LAT Photographic)

Ferrari, Piero Lardi

Enzo Ferrari's illegitimate son
Born: 22 May 1945 (Modena, Italy)

Piero is the son of Lina Lardi, whom Ferrari always referred to as 'the other woman'. The situation was such in Italy, and with Laura Ferrari, that Enzo could not recognise him as his son until after his wife's death. In 1968 Piero married Floriana Nalin. Now, Lina lives with Piero in a house near the centre of Modena formerly occupied by Enzo and Laura Ferrari. Piero Lardi Ferrari continues to own 10 per cent of the shares of Ferrari and is an honorary president of the company. He gained a degree in engineering when he was 62.

Below: *Piero Lardi Ferrari.* (LAT Photographic)

Filipinetti, Georges

Ferrari dealer and entrant
Born: 8 August 1907 (Carouge, near Geneva, Switzerland)
Died: 3 May 1973 (Geneva)

Filipinetti was the son of Italians from Domodossola in northern Italy who settled in Geneva. His father ran a business selling major electrical appliances, air-conditioning, and heating equipment based near Geneva's Central Station. Georges studied engineering in Germany and worked as an inspector for Chrysler and Bugatti before taking over the management of his father's business in 1936.

He opened up several car agencies and, after the Second World War, set up a company known as Société Anonyme pour la Vente des Automobiles Ferrari (SAVAF) in partnership with Californian John von Neumann. He also invested and dealt in property and became a very wealthy man. Nominally, at least, he was the Swiss ambassador to San Marino. He purchased the enormous and luxurious Schloss Grandson at Neuchâtel (Neuenburgersee).

It was from there that Filipinetti managed his business activities, and when Scuderia Filipinetti was founded in 1961, it was based there. Scuderia Filipinetti was one of the leading private Ferrari teams, and among the last cars raced was the very special modified 512M Ferrari with a narrower 'greenhouse' developed by Mike Parkes and which ran at Le Mans in 1971.

The Filipinetti team also raced Ford GT40s extensively. Peter Sutcliffe told the writer of his experiences of driving for Filipinetti:

'I first drove for the team in 1965 when Peter Harper and I were entered with a Cobra Daytona coupé loaned by Shelby American and painted Swiss colours of red with white stripes. It was very fast, it handled dreadfully, but we went well until the engine broke on the Mulsanne Straight during the night.

Filipinetti was a lovely man; he was Swiss-Italian and he had connections all over the place. We were put up in the most wonderful chateau some 15km out of Le Mans; we were superbly looked after. He had excellent mechanics (although one of these was seconded to us from Alan Mann Racing), his own chefs, and a team doctor – the doctor was called Monsieur Pilule ('Mr Pill').

The following year I drove a Ford GT40 with Dieter Spoerry, who was not desperately fast, but ultra-reliable. We ran well and were the only GT40 not to be eliminated by engine trouble. On the Sunday morning we were in fifth place, and as I braked in the Esses, fuel from a loose filler cap, that the plombeur had failed to close properly, allowed around 30 gallons to spill over the front of the car and spray on the tyres. They were cold and the car did not catch fire. It was because of this race that Filipinetti recommended me to Enzo Ferrari, and I was invited to drive P4s twice in 1967.'

Filipinetti helped a number of Swiss drivers, including Jo Siffert (who raced Lotus 21 and 24 Formula 1 cars with Filipinetti sponsorship), Herbert Müller, and Tommy Spychiger (sadly killed when he crashed the Filipinetti 365P in the 1965 Monza 1,000km race). Both Dallara and Mike Parkes worked for Filipinetti at his factory in Formigine in Italy to develop a version of the Fiat X1/9 with 16-valve cylinder head for European Touring Car racing, and a car competed in the Six Hours race at the Nürburgring in 1973.

Following Filipinetti's death because of a diabetic condition, from which he had suffered for many years, the project was abandoned, and while Dallara set up his own factory and took over development of the 16-valve head, Parkes later joined Lancia.

Fiorio, Cesare

Racing Manager
Born: 5 May 1939 (Turin, Italy)

This very able team manager was the son of Sandro Fiorio, who had been the head of public relations at Lancia. Cesare raced a Fiat and won his class of the Italian Touring Car Championship in 1961. He also competed in the Monte Carlo Rally in 1962, but crashed, and this proved to be his only rally drive. With the support and input of friends, Cesare established a team called HF Squadra Corse in 1963; it was dedicated to competing with Lancias and received a degree of support from the factory. In late 1964, the Lancia factory took over HF

Squadra Corse, but Cesare remained as team manager.

The team achieved major successes in 1967 when Ove Andersson won the Spanish Rally and Sandro Munari was victor in the Tour de Corse (Corsica). Two years later, HF Squadra Corse was fully integrated as Lancia's official motor sport division. After Fiat's takeover of Lancia, Munari won the 1972 Monte Carlo Rally, and the marque won the World Rally Championship in 1974, 1975, and 1976. Fiorio continued to manage the Lancia team when it competed in Group C sports car racing from 1982 onwards. In 1984 he was appointed head of Fiat's motor sport activities, and in 1988 he took control of the Alfa Romeo works team, Squadra Corse Alfa Romeo.

He became sports director (racing manager) of Ferrari in 1989, and the year started well with a victory by Mansell in Brazil. Later that year, Mansell won in Hungary and Portugal, but overall the cars lacked reliability and Ferrari finished third in the Constructors'

Below: *Cesare Fiorio was the founder of the Lancia team called HF Squadra Corse. He was Sporting Director of Ferrari from 1989 to 1991.* (LAT Photographic)

Championship. The following year, Prost joined the Ferrari team and, although he won five races and took second place in the Drivers' Championship with 71 points to the 78 of Senna (McLaren), there was dissatisfaction with Fiorio's achievements.

Fiorio was sacked at the beginning of 1991, but as there was no one to replace him immediately, he stayed until after the disastrous San Marino GP at Imola. At this race, heavy rain started to fall before the start. Prost spun off in a deep puddle and never made it to the grid, while Alesi had his own spin after ten laps because of gearbox trouble, and retired. In 1994, Fiorio managed the Ligier team (then owned by Flavio Briatore) and that year was made a Cavalieri della Repubblica Italiana (Knight of the Republic of Italy).

He was sacked the following year by Ligier's new owner, Tom Walkinshaw, but after a spell with the short-lived Forti team, he rejoined Ligier when it was taken over by Alain Prost. He was team manager for Minardi during the years 1998 to 2000, and has latterly worked as a TV commentator. Although Fiorio was a brilliantly successful manager in his early, rallying days, his later years in GP racing were dismal failures.

Below: *Here, Fischer is congratulated on his sixth place in the 1951 German GP, which was a good result in a World Championship race dominated by the 4.5-litre unblown Ferraris and the supercharged 1.5-litre Alfa Romeo Tipo 159s. Ascari won the race for Ferrari, and Fangio was second with his Alfa Romeo.* (Author's collection)

Fischer, Rudi

Driver
Born: 19 May 1912 (Stuttgart, Germany)
Died: 30 December 1976 (Lucerne, Switzerland)

German-born Rudolph 'Rudi' Fischer became a Swiss resident, and he ran a very successful restaurant in Lucerne. He was into his late thirties before he took up motor racing. His early racing performances included a sixth place at the wheel of an HWM in the 1950 Prix de Berne, and a retirement immediately after the start of that year's F2 Rome GP. Fischer had demanded 700 X 16 tyres, to which a courteous but unwise John Heath agreed, and the result, as predicted by Alf Francis, was a broken driveshaft.

For 1951, Fischer was sufficiently encouraged to buy a Ferrari F2 chassis with 2562cc V12 engine from the works. Ferrari built a small number of these cars, which were eligible for F1, and Fischer ran his in the name of Écurie Espadon (Espadon is French for a two-handed sword or a swordfish – take your pick!). He enjoyed a very successful season with what was a fast, tough, and fairly safe car.

Rudi finished second to Villoresi's 4.5-litre V12 Tipo 375 F1 car in the Syracuse GP, he was sixth on the difficult Pau circuit, finished third at San Remo, and he was second again at Bordeaux. In the Championship Swiss GP he was a poor 11th, he took fourth place in the Dutch GP (a non-Championship event at this time), and in the German GP at the Nürburgring on 29 July he took sixth place. He crashed in practice for the Italian GP, but overall it was a season that most private entrants would have envied.

Ferrari sold a number of Tipo 500 four-cylinder 2-litre cars in 1952, and these were sometimes known as 'Starlets'. Fischer bought one of these cars, which he again ran in the name of Écurie Espadon. World Championship races were now held to 2-litre Formula 2 rules, but there were still a number of Formula 1 races. So, Rudi ran the Tipo 500 in F2 and the Tipo 212 in F1.

Once again, he was the most successful private entrant. He started the season with fourth place at Siracusa behind three works F2 Ferraris. In the F1 Turin GP at Valentino Park he finished third behind the works Ferraris of Villoresi (Tipo 375) and Taruffi (Tipo 212). Retirements followed at Pau and in the International Trophy at Silverstone.

Ascari was absent from the Ferrari team at the Swiss GP, because he was qualifying for Indianapolis. Two of

FERRARI: MEN FROM MARANELLO

the works Ferraris retired at Bremgarten because of magneto failure and Fischer took a fine second place behind surviving works Ferrari driver Taruffi. A week later, Fischer won the Eifelrennen at the Nürburgring from Moss with the much less powerful HWM. Rudi followed this up with sixth place at the wheel of the Tipo 212 in the F1 Albi GP. The works Ferraris of Ascari and Villoresi retired because of engine problems in the Autodromo GP at Monza, and Fischer took third place behind the surviving works Ferraris of Farina and Simon.

Rudi was a poor 11th in the French GP at Rouen, retired in the minor race at Les Sables d'Olonne, and took 14th place in the British GP at Silverstone. Another remarkable performance followed in the German GP, in which he finished third behind two works Ferraris. An engine failure occurred in the Italian GP, but then it was fifth place in the non-Championship Modena GP. In the final race in his circuit career, Fischer won the Avusrennen on the banked Berlin track from

Above: *In 1951 Swiss driver Fischer raced a 'hybrid' Ferrari for Écurie Espadon. This combined a Formula 2 chassis, usually powered by a 2-litre V12 engine, with a larger 2.6-litre V12 sports car engine. He scored a large number of good placings with this red and white-painted car, and is seen here in the German GP at the Nürburgring where he took sixth place.* (Author's collection)

Hans Klenk and Theo Helfrich, both at the wheel of Veritas cars.

Rudi Fischer retired from international racing at the end of 1952 after two very remarkable racing seasons. He continued to appear in minor events, mostly hill climbs, until the late 1950s. Quite why he pulled out of racing at the end of 1952 is not known for sure, but it is probable that he knew that he was not going to progress further, and it is almost certain that his retirement was partly because of this and partly because of his business commitments.

Folland, Dudley

Driver
Born: 28 November 1912 (Brondeg Glanamam, Carmarthenshire, Wales)
Died: 1979 (Abergavenny, Wales)

In 1948 Folland, who had raced in pre-war days as 'Tim Davies' because of the opposition of his family, bought Peter Monkhouse's shares in Monaco Motors, based at Watford and specialising in the preparation of competition cars. The managing director was John Wyer, and the other shareholder was Ian Connell. Folland owned and raced the 2-litre Aston Martin that had originally been delivered to Dick Seaman, and this was ultimately developed into the very potent sports-racing car called 'Red Dragon'. He also owned an MG K3 Magnette.

Folland had, however, seen the Ferrari that Giulio Ramponi had brought to the UK, and he decided that he wanted one. John Wyer wrote in *The Certain Sound: Thirty Years of Motor Racing*:

'During the winter of 1948/9 I went, with Dudley, to Modena, where he bought a type 166 Ferrari [it was a Tipo 166 Spider Corsa]... The memory of testing that little car and taking it up to 7,000rpm on the straight but narrow road from the Ferrari factory at Maranello back towards Modena, on a bright but very cold morning in January, will always remain with me. I met, for the first time, Enzo Ferrari and his Chief Engineer, Aurelio Lampredi.'

It was the first British-owned Ferrari and it was painted British racing green. Folland first raced his new acquisition at Goodwood on Easter Monday 1949. He shared Peter Whitehead's F1 Ferrari in the British GP in May, finishing ninth, and retired his Ferrari in the Manx Cup on the Douglas circuit on the Isle of Man because of a burnt-out clutch. He later ran his car in a couple of Formula 2 races on mainland Europe, including Angoulême (fifth in the Circuit des Remparts) and Reims (fourth in the Coupe des Petites Cylindrées). For 1949, Ferrari had introduced a single-seater F2 car, and Folland's car was already obsolete when he bought it. It was later sold back to the factory.

Below: *Dudley Folland is seen at the wheel of the Ferrari Tipo 125 supercharged GP car that he shared with owner Peter Whitehead in the 1949 British GP at Silverstone. Whitehead turned in some stirring performances with this car, but on this occasion they finished a mediocre eighth.* (Guy Griffiths Collection)

Forghieri, Mauro

Technical Director
Born: 13 January 1935 (Modena, Italy)

The full story of Forghieri and his long career in racing is told in Appendix 5. It suffices to reproduce here two comments by Jody Scheckter, who drove for Ferrari in 1979–80.

'Mauro Forghieri was the technical boss at Ferrari, but for me he was more the team manager. Marco Piccinini was the political team manager, but Forghieri made things happen. But he has some very awkward ideas about design, and didn't want to understand the wing car concept.

At Silverstone [in 1979] we were slow: I qualified 11th, Gilles 13th. The problem was that the V8s were getting more air through the underside of the car, their ground-effects worked properly, whereas we had our wide flat-12 – which was made worse by having the exhaust pipes going through the only place that the air could come in through.

But Forghieri didn't want to do anything about it. After Silverstone the Italian press were going mad, like they always did, and so Mr Ferrari called a meeting. I said to Gilles, 'Let's speak with one voice on this; the car needs to be modified.' In the meeting I said, 'We shouldn't be fighting among ourselves, we should be fighting the other teams.' Gilles said the same, and Mr Ferrari agreed with us, so Forghieri modified the exhausts. We took it to Monza and we had another 300rpm, and more performance. It was a performance jump.' (Jody Scheckter, *Motor Sport*, May 2008)

Fraschetti, Andrea

Engineer
Born: 1928 (Florence, Italy)
Died: 29 August 1957 (Modena, Italy)

When the Lancia racing équipe was taken over by Ferrari in 1955, Jano joined Ferrari as consultant, and Fraschetti, who had worked with Jano in Turin, went with him. Fraschetti had very considerable experience in the design and development of competition cars, and he became a senior engineer; Ferrari entrusted him with the design and development of a new competition sports car. The decision had been made to revert to the V12 layout, and the result was the 3490cc Tipo 290MM, which retained single overhead camshafts, and (apart from a de Dion rear axle) the chassis was similar to that of the early 250GTs.

In most respects it was a completely new design of relatively low weight, and Fraschetti immediately began working on twin overhead camshaft cylinder heads – his design for these first appeared in early 1957. Soon, Fraschetti was at work on the very potent 3780cc Tipo 315 Sport and 3023cc Tipo 335 Sport cars. He was a designer who believed strongly in driving the cars himself, but sadly during testing on 29 August 1957 he lost control at the Monza Aerautodromo and crashed with fatal results.

Above: *Throughout his career, young Mauro Forghieri often looked as though he carried the entire burden of the world on his shoulders. As Technical Director of Ferrari, that is a close approximation of his duties. In this photograph he is seen with racing driver 'Gentleman Jack' Sears at the 1969 British GP meeting at Silverstone.* (Guy Griffiths Collection)

Below: *A very happy-looking Mauro Forghieri photographed at the opening of Fiorano in 1972.* (LAT Photographic)

Frère, Paul

Driver, journalist
Born: 30 January 1917 (Le Havre, France)
Died: 23 February 2008 (Brussels, Belgium)

Although he was born in France, Frère's parents were Belgian, and his racing career started on motorcycles in early post-war days. In 1948 he co-drove a special-bodied MG PB with Jacques Swaters in the Belgian 24 Hours race, and they finished fourth in their class but well down the field. Paul drove regularly in production car races, and he was also service manager of the Belgian Jaguar distributors until he left to concentrate on motoring journalism. In 1952 he won the Eifelrennen at the wheel of an HWM, and was then invited by HWM to drive these Alta-powered cars in a number of races, including the rain-soaked 1952 European GP at Spa, in which he took fifth place.

Paul won the Touring Car class of the 1953 Mille Miglia with a Chrysler Saratoga, and he finished second with an HWM, only feet behind de Graffenried (Maserati) in that year's Eifelrennen. Frère has always been grateful for the opportunities to race given to him by John Heath, who ran the HWM Formula 2 team, and he regards Heath as the man who made his racing career, along with those of Stirling Moss and Lance Macklin. He drove Gordinis in three GPs in 1954, but retired in all three races.

His first drive at Le Mans was in 1954 when he shared Shelby's DB3S Aston Martin. He took over Taruffi's Tipo 555 Ferrari at Monaco in 1955 to finish eighth, and he was fourth with a 555 in that year's Belgian GP. In the disastrous 1955 Le Mans race he co-drove the second-place Aston Martin DB3S with Peter Collins. In 1956 he enjoyed both the climax and nadir of his racing career. Ferrari asked him to drive in the Belgian GP because Musso had been injured at the Nürburgring. Paul was reluctant to accept as he had not raced an F1 car for a year, and only agreed after trying the Lancia-Ferrari in practice. He drove a magnificent race to take second place behind team-mate Collins.

In 1956 Paul was a member of the works Jaguar team, but it was an unlucky year. He crashed a D-type in practice at the Nürburgring, he took second place at Reims with Hawthorn (Hamilton was sacked from the team for winning against team orders), and at Le Mans he slid off and wrecked his D-type on the slippery track through the Esses on the second lap of the race.

Success for Frère at Le Mans was finally achieved in

Above: *A very youthful Paul Frère, photographed in the 1950s when he was at the peak of his powers as a racing driver, and his career as a motoring journalist was about to take off.* (Author's collection)

1960 when he co-drove the winning works Ferrari Testa Rossa. That same year he drove in a few minor F1 races, and with an Équipe Nationale Belge Cooper-Climax he won the 1960 non-Championship South African GP from Stirling Moss (Cooper-Borgward). It was Paul's last racing season, and during the 1970s and 1980s he became known for his close collaboration with the Porsche factory, which resulted in a number of highly technical, authoritative books on the Porsche 911 and on Porsche competition cars.

For some years Paul had lived in Monaco, and his last book was a treatise on the Porsche Boxster. In 2006, at the Nürburgring, he was involved in an accident while road-testing a Honda Civic Type-R. His injuries included a shattered pelvis and several broken ribs, as well as puncturing both lungs. For an 89-year-old his recovery was remarkable, but his health suffered, and barely 18 months later he died at the age of 91. Paul was a great friend to the writer, and his help, support, and encouragement will be very greatly missed.

Galli, 'Nanni'

One-off works driver
Born: 2 October 1940 (Bologna, Italy)

Giovanni 'Nanni' Galli adopted his rather transparent *nom de plume* when he started racing at the quite late age of 24. He anticipated opposition from the family, and when his father, a wealthy textile merchant, found out about it, he announced that he thought that young Giovanni should have something better to do with his time. He started racing with a Mini Cooper, moved on to an Alfa Romeo GTA, and became a protégé of Carlo Chiti once Alfa Romeo introduced the 2-litre Tipo33 V8 sports prototype in 1967. Over the years 'Nanni' was primarily an Alfa Romeo driver, and he achieved some good results despite the frailty of the machinery.

After driving in F2 for Tecno, he was sponsored by Autodelta in a one-off deal with McLaren at Monza in 1970 (failed to qualify) and a works March 721 with Alfa Romeo engine and Autodelta money in 1971. It was a hopelessly poor season, and for 1972 'Nanni' joined the well-funded, but unsuccessful, Tecno F1 team. He finished third in the non-Championship Gran Premio Reppublica Italiana on the Vallelunga circuit at Rome, but there were only eight starters and five finishers, so this result did not mean very much.

Clay Regazzoni was unable to drive for Ferrari in the French GP at Clermont-Ferrand because he had fallen and broken a bone in his left wrist while playing football with the mechanics, so Galli was asked to join the team. Of his performance, Alan Henry wrote:

> 'Whether this was meant as a lesson to Clay not to be a silly boy in future is not clear, but Galli certainly proved no threat to Regazzoni's place in the team. Hopelessly wild in practice, he qualified 19th and he finished a lapped 13th…'

This was Galli's only drive for Ferrari. He finished the year with Tecno, drove – badly – for Williams early in 1973, and then retired from racing, apart from a works drive in an Abarth sports car in 1974.

Right: *Gendebien was one of the greatest sports car drivers of all time, and he won at Le Mans on four occasions, three with Phil Hill, and in 1960, the year pictured here, with Paul Frère at the wheel of a Ferrari Testa Rossa.* (**LAT Photographic**)

Gendebien, Olivier

Works sports car driver
Born: 12 January 1924 (Brussels, Belgium)
Died: 2 October 1998 (Les Baux de Provence, France)

Said to be from an aristocratic background, Gendebien was a paratrooper during the Second World War. After hostilities ceased he worked in forestry in the Belgian Congo (now the Democratic Republic of the Congo). It was in the Congo that he first met rally driver Charles Fraikin who was looking for a co-driver. On his return to Europe he drove a Veritas into sixth place in the 1952 GP des Frontières at Chimay, and thereafter he partnered Fraikin in a Jaguar. They twice finished second in the Liège–Rome–Liège Rally.

In 1953 Gendebien competed in the Production Car races at Spa-Francorchamps with a three-year-old Ferrari Tipo 166MM lent to him by a friend, Jerry

d'Hendecourt. He won the race, and of his performance Paul Frère wrote in *On the Starting Grid*:

> 'Having got his hands on a decent car, Gendebien showed that he was a born driver, head and shoulders above the rest of the entry.'

For 1955, Gendebien acquired a Mercedes-Benz 300SL coupé and, after driving this to seventh place overall and a class second with his brother-in-law Wascher in the Mille Miglia road race, he and Stasse won the Liège–Rome–Liège Rally outright.

During 1955 he also drove works Ferraris in a few events, but his season ended in September with a crash that could have been a lot worse. Shortly after the start of practice for the 1955 Tourist Trophy at Dundrod, he crashed his 3-litre Monza Ferrari at the exit of the bend known as 'Wheeler's Corner'. Olivier was taken to hospital suffering from a very badly bruised arm and concussion.

Gendebien became a regular works Ferrari driver in 1956, but the majority of his drives were with sports cars, and his few single-seater drives were mainly unsuccessful. Only five single-seater appearances are worth mentioning. After starting with fifth place at the wheel of an experimental 555 SuperSqualo Ferrari with Lancia V8 engine in the Argentine GP, he retired in the French race that year, and made no further GP appearances until 1958. That year he took sixth place in the Belgian race, and in 1959 he finished fourth in the French GP at Reims, and sixth at Monza.

His main successes were in sports cars, and he frequently partnered American Phil Hill. They were smooth, fast, unflustered, and persistent race winners. The successes were numerous, and those mentioned in the following paragraphs were the more important. Except where indicated, all were with Hill as co-driver. The first of these was the 1956 Buenos Aires 1,000km race in which he and Hill finished second. His great success of the year was the rain-soaked Mille Miglia in which, partnered by Wascher, he finished fifth overall with his leaky, near-flooded 250GT Ferrari and won the GT class, defeating the vast number of Mercedes-Benz 300SLs entered.

He co-drove the winning Ferrari in the Targa Florio three times, with Musso in 1958, with von Trips in 1961, and with Mairesse and Ricardo Rodriguez in 1962. Gendebien won the Reims 12 Hours race twice, in 1957 and 1958, when it was held as a race for Grand Touring cars, and he was partnered by Paul Frère. Gendebien was co-winner in the Sebring 12 Hours race three times: in 1959, in 1960 with Herrmann (at the wheel of a Porsche), and back at the wheel of a Ferrari in 1961.

Co-driving with Phil Hill he was again second in 1962.

Gendebien's greatest run of success was at Le Mans where he won four times with Ferraris, three times with Phil Hill (1958, 1961, and 1962) and once with Paul Frère (1960). He competed in three F1 races in 1961 and, with a yellow-painted works Ferrari Tipo 156 nominally entered in the name of Équipe Nationale Belge, he took fourth place in the Belgian race. In 1962 he won the Nürburgring 1,000km race with Hill. Gendebien retired from racing at the end of 1962.

Gené, Marc

Test driver
Born: 29 May 1974 (Sababel, Catalonia, Spain)

Although Marc Guerrero Gené was a very successful driver in his early days, his competitive edge petered out, and the early promise has not been fulfilled. In 1987, at the age of 13, he was a runner-up in the Junior Spanish Kart Championship, and he won the Spanish

Below: *After an unsuccessful F1 career, Marc Gené became a test driver for Ferrari, and in this role he has proved very successful.* (LAT Photographic)

Senior Kart Championship the following year. He moved on to Formula Ford and took fifth place in the 1992 Spanish Championship. He has a degree in economics and trained as an accountant. He is married and speaks four languages.

Gené drove in Formula 3 during the period 1993–6, but he found that raising the necessary funding for his racing was proving increasingly difficult. In 1997 he secured a drive with Keith Wiggins's Pacific F3000 team. Unfortunately, he had a bad accident on the second lap of the Pau street race and suffered fractured vertebrae. After recovering, he drove for Nordic Racing in a couple of events, but there was no real future with the team. Because of lack of racing opportunities, he worked as an accountant in 1998, but also drove for Nissan in the Spanish Open Fortuna series.

For 1999 Gené obtained sponsorship from the Spanish Telefonica giant, and he was able to buy a drive with the Fondmetal Minardi F1 team alongside Luc Badoer. This team was uncompetitive, although they showed reasonable form in the European GP at the Nürburgring in September. Badoer rose to fourth place, but fell back and retired because of gearbox trouble, while Gené turned in his best performance of the season to take sixth place and a single point. This was good enough for the Minardi team to retain their travel bonuses. Gené stayed with Minardi in 2000, but he lost the Telefonica sponsorship and the drive at the end of the year.

That Gené had talent was widely recognised, and for 2001 he obtained a testing contract with the Williams team on the basis that he was first reserve if either of the regular team members was unable to race. He stood in for Ralf Schumacher at the Italian race at Monza in 2003, qualifying fifth and finishing fifth. Schumacher missed much of 2004 because he had to rest to enable his back injuries to heal. Gené drove for Williams in the French race at Magny-Cours (qualified eighth, finished tenth) and in the British race at Silverstone (qualified 11th and finished 12th). The team was not satisfied, and Antonio Pizzonia took his place in the next four races.

In November 2004 Gené signed a testing contract with Ferrari, and he again drove alongside Luc Badoer. The need for dedicated and very able test drivers reflected the changing face of GP racing, but latterly the situation has changed again and the amount of testing that teams can do is severely restricted. Despite this, both test drivers have been retained by Ferrari, and the arrangement is that Gené does most of the testing at Fiorano and Mugello, while Badoer travels with the team to Grands Prix and test sessions at other circuits. In 2007–8 Gené also drove sports cars for Peugeot in the Le Mans series.

Above: *Taken at Maranello in 1949, this photograph shows, left to right, Bonetto, Ferrari, Giberti, and Villoresi.* (Author's collection)

Giberti, Federico

(There is no available information as to the dates of his birth and death)

Giberti joined Enzo Ferrari at Scuderia Ferrari very soon after it was set up. He was a very able technician, but he was one of the employees who Ferrari valued, yet failed to appreciate, and he could undertake with great competence just about any job that the 'Old Man' required of him. Back in 1934 he was Scuderia Ferrari's racing manager, and it is obvious that he had stepped in to fill a vacancy as a matter of urgency. In the main he worked on the technical side of Ferrari activities, but when Ferrari became a manufacturer he once again assumed the position of racing manager, and he held this from 1947 to 1951.

During that period were two of Ferraris most critical years, 1950 and 1951, when the team was struggling to beat Alfa Romeo and achieve GP supremacy. Later, Giberti became head of the department of Ferrari that placed orders for materials and ensured that supplies of these flowed smoothly. In late 1961, Giberti was one of the senior staff who collaborated in writing a letter to Ferrari pleading with him to stop Laura Ferrari from meddling in the running of the team. He was peremptorily sacked, but asked Ferrari to take him back and he rejoined the company after a couple of weeks.

Ginther, Richie

Works driver
Born: 5 August 1930 (Granada Hills, California, USA)
Died: 20 September 1989 (France)

A dynamic driver, who was so close to being in the top rank, Richie spent only two seasons with Ferrari. He was a small, freckle-faced individual with a broad grin, a high level of optimism, and someone who gave very much to the sport that he loved. He was born in the same town in California as Phil Hill, and it was through Hill, a friend of Richie's older brother, that he took up racing. When he left school in 1948, he went to work for Douglas Aircraft in the tool and die shop, and he helped Hill by working on his cars.

Richie started racing in 1951 with an MG, but then went off to endure his military service during the Korean War. He only became seriously involved in racing when he partnered Phil Hill with a Tipo 340 4.1-litre Ferrari in the 1953 Carrera Panamericana Mexico road race. Hill ran well until he lost control and crashed, seriously damaging the car, but both occupants escaped unharmed. In 1954 Ginther raced an Austin-Healey that he prepared himself, and he again partnered Phil Hill in his drive to second place with a Ferrari in the Mexican road race behind Maglioli with a works 4.9-litre car.

Above: *As well as being a member of the works team in 1961, Californian Richie Ginther became chief development driver. Ginther is seen here at the wheel of a Ferrari Tipo 156 rear-engined F1 car in 1961, and his best performance that year was second at Monaco. He was very unlucky not to have won a GP in his years with Ferrari, or his three seasons with BRM.* **(LAT Photographic)**

Below: *Here, Ginther is seen with the rear-engined Formula 1 Dino prototype alongside the harbour wall in the 1960 Monaco GP. This Ferrari was an ill-handling brute, and Richie did well to drive it to sixth place.* **(Author's collection)**

During 1955 he raced a Porsche in the United States for VW and Porsche dealer John von Neumann. In 1956 von Neumann started dealing in Ferraris and Ginther was able to race these. Luigi Chinetti recognised Ginther's ability, and he drove Ferraris for him as well. He was asked to share a 2-litre Ferrari with Picard at Le Mans in 1957, and they ran well, rising as high as 11th place before water pump failure caused their retirement. Co-driving with von Trips, he finished second in the 1960 Buenos Aires 1,000km race.

This resulted in a four-race contract from Ferrari, and it was enough to persuade Ginther to give up his job and move with his wife to Europe. He drove in more than four races and, although he was out of success in sports car events, he turned in excellent single-seater performances with uncompetitive machinery. He finished sixth at Monaco with the experimental rear-engined Ferrari, took second place in the Italian GP (held on the full banked track and road circuit and boycotted by the British teams), and with the older front-engined F2 Ferrari he finished second at Modena. Ferrari signed Ginther up for 1961 and, because of his engineering ability, he also became chief development driver.

He failed to win a GP when Ferrari was largely dominant, or in the three seasons with BRM that followed, although he was joint second in the Drivers' Championship in 1963. In 1961 he was second at Monaco where he shared fastest lap with Moss, and took third places in the Belgian and British races. In sports car racing, Richie drove a 246SP rear-engined car in most events and was largely unsuccessful. His best performance was at Sebring where he and von Trips retired their 246SP, because of broken suspension, and took over the fifth-place Testa Rossa which they brought through to finish second.

For reasons that partially explained on page 340, Ginther's contract with Ferrari was not renewed for 1962. In addition, when Forghieri was appointed Technical Director following the departure of many of the team personnel, he had insisted that Ferrari give him a free hand, and to Mauro that meant the power to make decisions uninfluenced by other technical staff. Richie was welcomed as number two to Graham Hill at BRM, and he played an important role in the development of the latest V8 cars and the non-stop battle between BRM and Lotus. His own racing successes over the three seasons included six second and three third places.

Ginther was engaged by Honda for 1965 to drive and assist in the development of their very complex F1 car with transverse V12 engine. He was backed up by the existing Honda driver, Ronnie Bucknum. A year of hard development work resulted in Ginther winning the 1965 Mexican GP, the last race of the 1500cc formula. It was ironic that a car that had proved a race-winner had become obsolete the moment that it won and, in effect, Honda had to start all over again with a new 3-litre design.

Until the new car was ready, Ginther drove a works Cooper-Maserati without success in two races, and the new 3-litre V12 Honda eventually appeared at Monza. Ginther was lucky to escape without serious injury when a rear tyre deflated in the Italian race and the Honda left the track and ploughed through the trees. Ginther finished fourth for Honda in the last race of the year at Mexico City. He left Honda, reluctant to face another year of sustained development work, and joined Dan Gurney's Eagle team. After failing to qualify at Monaco, he decided during practice for the Indianapolis 500 race to retire from racing.

There were medical factors involved in Richie's decision, but initially he maintained close contacts with motor sport, and managed minor teams before going off to live in a camper in the desert. He attended the German GP at Hockenheim in 1977, looking unfamiliar with long hair and moustache, and he presented the winner, Niki Lauda, with a special prize to mark Goodyear's 100th GP win. Richie was not seen again until BRM's 40th anniversary at Donington Park in 1989. He looked frail and ill and, sadly, he died of a heart attack shortly afterwards while he and his family were on holiday in France.

Giunti, Ignazio

Works driver
Born: 30 August 1941 (Rome, Italy)
Died: 10 January 1971 (Buenos Aires, Argentina)

During the period 1969–70, young Giunti was the great Italian hope in motor racing, and it was believed that he had a fine future ahead of him. Ignazio had wealthy parents who were prepared to support his motor racing ambitions, and as a teenager he competed in sprints, hill climbs, and other club events with Alfa Romeos. For 1966 Carlo Chiti invited him to join the Autodelta team, and the following year he won the Touring Car division of the European Mountain Championship.

In 1967 Autodelta introduced the 2-litre Tipo 33 Sports Prototype, and Giunti, partnered by 'Nanni' Galli, drove these very unreliable cars regularly. Nothing was gained that year, but Giunti's fortunes at Autodelta

Above: *Giunti was a driver of great promise, and his terrible death at Buenos Aires in January 1971 was a massive blow to both Ferrari and Alfa Romeo – he had driven for the Milan team for some years.* (Author's collection)

changed for the better in 1968 when they raced the well-developed Tipo 33/2 coupés. Partnered again by Galli, Ignazio led the Targa Florio, but they fell back to finish second to a Porsche 907. Giunti and Galli then finished fifth in the Nürburgring 1,000km race, winning the 2000cc class.

Giunti partnered Vaccarella and Bianchi in the surviving works 33/2 to score a hollow victory in the Circuit of Mugello in the face of weak opposition, and after the other three Autodelta 33/2s had retired. At Le Mans the 33/3s finished fourth, fifth, and sixth overall, and took the first three places in the 2000cc Prototype class; Giunti and Galli shared the class-winning car. Autodelta raced the 3-litre Tipo 33/3 in 1969, but this model lacked both speed and reliability, and the season was an almost complete disaster for which Carlo Chiti has to be held responsible.

When the writer visited Autodelta in September 1969, Giunti and his fiancée joined Chiti, Bussinello, 'Nanni' Galli, and myself for lunch at the bistro across the road from the works. He was a very pleasant,

intelligent young man and his fiancée was exceptionally pretty. It seemed that he was well settled at Autodelta, despite the season's problems, and it was something of a surprise when he joined Ferrari for 1970.

There is no doubt that his steady, skilful driving was a great asset to the Ferrari sports car team. Throughout the year, the 512S 5-litre Ferrari was no real match in the Sports Car Manufacturers' Championship for the much more highly developed opposition. Even so, Giunti turned in some splendid, cool-headed, precise drives. He shared the winning 512S Competition Sports Car in the Sebring 12 Hours race (the only Championship race that the model won) and he was second at Monza co-driving with Vaccarella and Amon.

The big, bulky 512S was an unsuitable car for the twisting, badly surfaced roads of the Targa Florio, but with what was only a token entry, Giunti and Vaccarella brought their Ferrari to the finish in third place. They came in behind two Gulf-Porsche 908.03 Prototypes that had been specially developed for this race and the Nürburgring 1,000km event. Ignazio drove well again in the Six Hours race at Watkins Glen, where he and Andretti took third place behind Gulf Porsche 917s.

Ferrari gave Ignazio his chance in F1, and in his first race, the 1970 Belgian GP, he finished fourth after a pit stop caused by an oil leak. He drove in three other F1 races, but he was out of luck; he took seventh place in the Austrian race because of a pit stop for a wheel change; due to mechanical problems he finished 14th in the French GP at Clermont-Ferrand; and he retired in the Italian race at Monza because of engine problems.

It had been made clear that, for 1971, Clay Regazzoni was the preferred number two to Jacky Ickx in F1, but Giunti stayed with the team, mainly to race the new 312PB 3-litre Prototype. The first race of the year, held in January, was the Buenos Aires 1,000km event, in which the single Ferrari was driven by Giunti and Arturo Merzario.

Giunti was leading the race when he collided with the Matra of Jean-Pierre Beltoise. Beltoise's Matra had run out of fuel about a quarter-mile from the pits. The Frenchman started to push it back, and the marshals did nothing to stop him, even when he crossed over the track at corners to take advantage of the camber. As the drivers lapped the course, they knew roughly where Beltoise was, but Giunti pulled out of the slipstream of Parkes's Ferrari 512M to overtake and found Beltoise in his path, and he had no chance to avoid it. The two cars collided, and the Ferrari somersaulted down the track for about 200yd and burst into flames before coming to rest in front of the pits.

His co-driver, Arturo Merzario, was waiting in the pits in overalls, gloves, and helmet to take the wheel.

Merzario vaulted over the pit barrier, and heedless of his own safety, rushed into the inferno in an effort to rescue the man who was a good friend, as well as his co-driver. Giunti, who had 70 per cent burns and multiple injuries, died some two hours later. Of this terrible accident, Mauro Forghieri said to the writer:

'Giunti was one of the few very promising Italian drivers at the time, and his death was a big shock to Enzo Ferrari. Racing is dangerous, but when a driver is killed because of something like that, it is not acceptable.'

Gobbato, Ugo

Alfa Romeo Managing Director
Born: 16 July 1888 (Volpago del Montello, Treviso, Italy)
Died: 28 April 1945 (Milan, Italy)

The son of a farmer with only a smallholding of land, Gobbato obtained a diploma in electricity and mechanics and he went to Germany where he worked as a draftsman. He returned to Italy for his compulsory military service in 1909, and afterwards worked at the Marelli electrical factory near Milan. Subsequently, he joined Fiat where he worked on fitting out and commissioning the new Lingotto factory. After completion of these works, he held the position of plant manager. In 1929 he reorganised the NSU factory at Neckarsulm in Germany, which had been bought by Fiat, and the following year he took over the setting up of Fiat Espana, working with Hispano-Suiza. It was while he was in Spain that he first met Wifredo Ricart.

Fiat had put in a bid for the construction of a ball and roller-bearing factory in Moscow. This was to be the largest factory of its kind outside the United States and was part of Russia's first five-year plan. It was a very demanding job in near-impossible circumstances. The Russians with whom he had to work were constantly being changed for political reasons, and the standard of living was so bad and food so difficult to obtain that two of Gobbato's Italian staff contracted scurvy. Following this, Gobbato sent his wife and family (there were six children) back to Italy. The job lasted two years, from 1931 to 1933.

In 1933 Alfa Romeo had been taken over by the government Instituto Ricostruzione Industriale (IRI). The company was in dire financial circumstances, with

Above: *Gobbato was a very able company manager, and restored Alfa Romeo's fortunes. He was, however, a Fascisti and he was assassinated by Communist Party supporters on 28 April 1945.* **(Author's collection)**

mounting losses, and there were many who thought that it should be liquidated. Mussolini strongly believed that Alfa Romeo should survive, because of its prestigious products and history. Gobbato accepted the position of Managing Director with the assurance that there would be adequate funds available for future development of the company. Under Gobbato's management, very few cars were built, but the company's main production was military trucks and aero-engines.

Alfa Romeo continued to finance a racing programme, but – in the main, for there were exceptions – the cars were raced by Scuderia Ferrari. There were two main problems with the racing programme: the finance was not adequate to compete on even terms with the German teams in GP racing and, at this time, Vittorio Jano was a burnt-out case lacking design initiative. Relations between Gobbato and Jano were not good, and in 1936 Gobbato dismissed him following his failure to design an adequate chassis for the new V12 Tipo 12C 36 GP car. Very shortly afterwards, Alfa Romeo bought an 80 per cent interest in Scuderia Ferrari.

Gobbato conducted Alfa Romeo's fortunes with great confidence and considerable success. Car production rose slightly (270 in 1937, 542 in 1938, and 372 units in 1939), racing continued and with greater success internationally following the introduction of the Tipo 158 and the formation of the new Alfa Corse team. So, Ferrari worked directly for Alfa Romeo and enjoyed terrible relations with Spaniard Wifredo Ricart who had become engineering supremo. It has been said by Borgeson and others that Ferrari exploited the bad relations with Ricart to ensure his dismissal with enough financial compensation for him to set up on his own again in Modena.

With the main production still concentrated on lorries and aero-engines, the number of employees rose from under 1,000 in 1933 to 9,500 in 1943. Such was the confidence of the Italian government in Gobbato's management that the company was given the go-ahead to build a massive new factory with the latest production methods for the manufacture of aero-engines and complete aircraft at Pomigliano d'Arco near Naples. The project was, of course, very welcome – as was the Alfasud factory in post-war days – because of the poverty in the south of Italy. Mussolini laid the foundation stone on 1 April 1939 and it was completed very rapidly.

The main Portello factory was around 90 per cent destroyed by Allied bombing, most of the damage being done on 29 October 1944. The Pomigliano works survived largely unscathed despite Allied bombing in September 1943, but they were razed to the ground by the German military forces retreating to the north. Italy was nominally liberated from the Germans on 25 April 1945. Anarchy in the form of the Italian resistance (Communist of course) assumed power. As a supporter of the former Fascist government, Gobbato – as so many others – was exposed to retribution by the Communists.

On 27 April he was tried by the 'People's Courts' (that is, a 'kangaroo court') on charges of criminal collaboration with the Germans, but, astonishingly, found not guilty. The following morning, as he was walking from the Portello factory to his home a short distance away, a blue Lancia Augusta braked to a stop alongside him. Gobbato saluted the occupants of the car, whom he obviously knew. Two men got out of the car; one held a sub-machine gun and the other a shotgun, and they killed him with a fusillade of fire. They got back into the car and were driven away. Despite witnesses, the murderers were never identified or caught.

His son, Dottore Piero Gobbato, worked for Fiat, but he was appointed General Manager of Ferrari, except for the company's racing activities, in June 1965.

Above: *José Froilán González, perched on the front wheel of his works Ferrari at the British GP at Silverstone in July 1951. He drove a brilliant race to win, beating Fangio (Alfa Romeo) who finished behind him in second place.* (Guy Griffiths Collection)

González, José Froilán

Driver
Born: 5 October 1922 (Arrecifes, Buenos Aires, Argentina)

During the 1950s quite a number of South American drivers appeared in European races and, Fangio apart, the most successful was González. His birthplace was a small town to the north-west of Buenos Aires, and he was a man of considerable bulk. There is no evidence as to his weight during his racing years in Europe, but the writer would suggest a figure of around 16 stones (224lb/101kg). In Europe the press called him 'The Pampas Bull' (and, all too often, referred, wrongly, to

Above: *Froilán González became a works Ferrari driver in 1951, and his greatest success came in the British GP at Silverstone. With his 4.5-litre unsupercharged Tipo 375 car in less powerful single-plug form he scored a brilliant win, giving the works Alfa Romeos their first defeat since their failure in the St Cloud GP in France in 1946. González did not have an attractive driving style, hunched over the wheel, grim-faced, foot flat to the floor, and sliding the car rather than drifting it. Here, he leads his team-leader Ascari, who retired because of transmission problems.* (Guy Griffiths Collection)

Below: *González's next race was the German GP at the Nürburgring, and the Alfa Romeos were again defeated. Ascari won for Ferrari from Fangio (Alfa Romeo) and then, in third place, came González. Here, González is making a slow pit stop while his Tipo 375 is refuelled from churns.* (Author's collection)

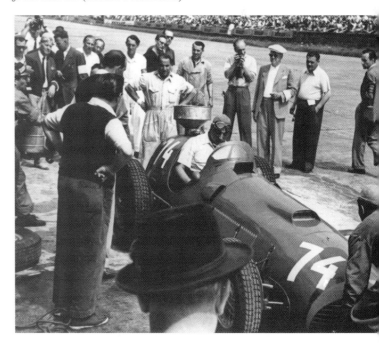

his surname as 'Gonzales'), while his friends called him Pepe.

Despite his bulk, González was a competent swimmer, soccer player, and cyclist before moving on to motorcycle sport and those arduous South American cross-country races. After driving a Maserati in Argentina, he came to Europe in 1950 as a member of the Argentinian government-sponsored Squadra Achille Varzi and raced alongside Fangio. He was out of luck in Europe, apart from Albi where he took second place. In the Formule Libre races in Buenos Aires in January 1951 he drove a supercharged 2-litre Ferrari and defeated the pre-war 3-litre supercharged Mercedes-Benz W163s that the works had entered as a means of testing the water before making a full racing comeback.

In 1951 the Ferrari F1 team was mounting its full-scale attack on the ageing supercharged Alfa Romeos that had won every race entered since 1946. González was in Europe, but without a drive until Taruffi was unwell and unable to appear with one of the unblown 4.5-litre Tipo 375 Ferraris in the French race at Reims. At Reims the Argentinian was given one of the less powerful single-plug cars, but he worked his way up to second place. When he stopped to refuel, team-leader Ascari took over González's car and went on to finish second behind Fangio (Alfa Romeo).

González, still with a single-plug car, was included in the Ferrari team at the British GP at Silverstone, and it proved a momentous race. 'Pepe' took the lead early in the race, Fangio passed him on lap ten, and the Ferrari driver pressured him until lap 38 when he went ahead again. It was becoming increasingly obvious that all was not well with Fangio's Alfa Romeo, and it was wilting

Below: *At the end of 1951, González left Ferrari and spent two seasons with Maserati. He returned to Ferrari for 1954, and this was to prove his last serious season of racing. Here he is at the wheel of his Tipo 553 Ferrari Squalo before the start of his wet heat of the International Trophy at Silverstone in August. He won his heat and then switched to a Tipo 625 Ferrari to win the final.* (Tom March Collection)

under pressure from the Ferrari. González did not make his refuelling stop until lap 60 of this 90-lap race, and he was expecting Ascari to take over his car.

Instead, Ascari, only too well aware that this was González's day, simply gave him a reassuring pat on the shoulder, and after a refuelling stop that lasted only 23sec the Argentinian was on his way again. Fangio's stop took 65sec because the Alfas were incredibly thirsty (at racing speeds their fuel consumption was 1½mpg) and González went on to win the race by a margin of 50sec. It was a momentous victory that changed the face of motor racing. Later that year, González finished third in the German race and second in both Italy and Spain. He took third place in the Drivers' Championship.

For 1952 both Fangio and González joined Maserati to drive the Modena team's new A6GCM F2 cars. All World Championship races (except Indianapolis) were held to F2 rules in 1952, but Maserati provided little opposition to Ferrari, for Fangio was badly injured in a crash at the Autodromo GP at Monza in June, which put him out of racing for the rest of the year, and their new six-cylinder cars were uncompetitive. González's only World Championship race appearance was in the Italian GP where he drove a new and much more potent twin-plug version of the A6GCM, and finished second to Ascari.

Both Fangio and González stayed with Maserati in 1953, but the Maseratis were still no match for the Ferraris. González took third places in Argentina, Holland (where he took over Bonetto's car), and

FERRARI: MEN FROM MARANELLO

France, together with a fourth in Britain. In his next race after Silverstone, the sports car Lisbon GP, he drove a Lancia, but crashed heavily, fracturing a vertebra and putting himself out of racing for the rest of the year.

González returned to Ferrari in 1954 and, although the team's F1 cars were obsolescent and no real match for the new W196 Mercedes-Benz when Fangio was at the wheel, he turned in some fine performances. His real triumph was his win in the British GP at Silverstone, where the streamlined W196 was a tremendous handful, and he won with a Tipo 625, a three-year-old design, and Hawthorn took second place with a similar car. He also finished third in Argentina and second in the Swiss GP, as well as winning the non-Championship International Trophy, the Bari GP, and the Bordeaux GP.

In sports car racing, Ferrari had introduced the Tipo 375 Plus 4.9-litre V12 car, with an engine that was patently too powerful for the chassis. The Mille Miglia, in which all three 375 Plus cars retired, and that driven by Farina crashed badly, reinforced the view that these cars had no future. González soon proved otherwise. In the sports race run in heavy rain at the International Trophy meeting at Silverstone 'Pepe' drove a 375 Plus with sheer mastery of car and conditions, and scored an easy win. Le Mans was a repeat performance on a much grander scale, and once again González drove brilliantly in the wet. He was partnered by Trintignant, and they won the race by a narrow margin.

At the Tourist Trophy on the Dundrod circuit in Northern Ireland in September, the unlucky González crashed heavily, and badly injured an arm. He went back to Argentina for the winter, but never reappeared in Europe except to drive Tony Vandervell's Vanwall in the 1956 British GP. He continued to race in his own country, and finally retired from racing in 1960 to concentrate on running his motor business. In later years he lived in Montevideo, the capital of Uruguay, but he then returned to Argentina once the political climate had become more acceptable.

Gozzi, Franco

Ferrari's personal assistant and team manager
Born: 29 November 1932 (Ghirlandina, Modena, Italy)

The son of a shoemaker, Gozzi studied jurisprudence and graduated in 1958. He married the daughter of Enzo Ferrari's barber, Antonio D'Elia, who put a word in for Franco with the 'Old Man'. Ferrari spoke to the

Above: *Gozzi was a 'jack of all trades' and was employed by Ferrari in a large number of different roles. Here, he is seen at the Daytona 24 Hours race at the end of 1970 with, on his left, driver Arturo Merzario and Mauro Forghieri.* (LAT Photographic)

manager of the San Geminiano bank, who assured Enzo Ferrari that he could offer the young Gozzi a job, but it would not be available for about four months. So, Ferrari decided to employ Gozzi himself, and his first job was to draft Ferrari's thesis for the honorary degree he was shortly to be awarded by Milan University. As a result of his successful accomplishment of this task, his employment with Ferrari started in August 1960.

He was initially appointed assistant to the sales director Gerolamo Gardini, and he held this position until 1961. That year, Ferrari appointed him Chief Press Officer. This also meant being Enzo Ferrari's personal assistant and confidant. He became incredibly close to Ferrari, and acted as his eyes and ears. Unlike other members of Ferrari's close clique, he was essentially a modest and reserved person. He became Team Manager ('motor sport director of the Racing Department') in 1968, and held this position until 1970.

After this spell as racing manager, he returned to the role of Ferrari's personal assistant and confidant. Following Ferrari's death in 1988, he began to attend races again as consultant to the motor sport director Pier Giorgio Capelli. When Luca di Montezemolo became the new President of Ferrari in 1993, he acted as his assistant for two years. He worked for Ferrari as a consultant for another 12 months and retired in 1996. His memoirs were published in 2002 (see Bibliography).

Above: *Kansan driver Masten Gregory sits on the pit counter at the Italian GP at Monza in September 1958. Alongside him is Marie-Teresa de Filippis, who competed, without success, at the wheel of an elderly Maserati 250F in a number of Grands Prix. Both gave a lot to motor racing, but received little in return.* (Author's collection)

Gregory, Masten

Occasional works and regular private sports car driver
Born: 29 February 1932 (Kansas City, Missouri, USA)
Died: 8 November 1985 (Porto Ecole, near Rome, Italy)

Masten's family owned a chain of bowling halls, managed by his mother after the death of his father when Masten was very young. After his mother sold the business, the young Kansan bought and raced Allard and Jaguar cars. He received an offer to run in the 1954 Buenos Aires 1,000km race, and he entered his C-type Jaguar with Dale Duncan as co-driver. They were plagued by mechanical problems and finished 14th.

The race was won by Giuseppe Farina and Umberto Maglioli with a magnificent Ferrari Tipo 375 4.5-litre V12 car with Pinin Farina Spider body. Gregory bought the Buenos Aires winner and decided to bring it to Europe. Ferrari, Maserati, and other manufacturers were often

delighted if they could sell one of the works cars in North or South America, as it gave them a nice profit as well as saving them shipping the car back to Italy.

Gregory's first race with his new acquisition was the Reims 12 Hours event. The car was still painted red and, with Clemente Biondetti as co-driver, they took an excellent fourth place. By the sports car Portuguese GP on the Monsanto circuit in July, the Ferrari had been painted in American white and blue colours, and in this 202-mile (325km) race he finished third behind González and Hawthorn with new 3-litre four-cylinder Ferraris. In the Tourist Trophy on the Dundrod circuit, Masten co-drove 'Bob' Said's 2-litre Ferrari Mondial. They finished ninth, and second in the 2000cc class behind the A6GCS Maserati of Musso/Mantovani.

Masten drove the big Ferrari in the wet at the international hill climb at Prescott in September, and although the car was a tremendous handful he managed second place in the over 3000cc sports class behind Alex Francis with a 4.3-litre Mercury-powered HRG. He followed this success by taking second place to Roy Salvadori (Écurie Ecosse C-type Jaguar) in the unlimited-capacity sports car race at the Goodwood meeting on 25 September.

At the beginning of October he drove the Ferrari to a win in the over 2500cc sports car race at Aintree from Peter Collins and Reg Parnell with works DB3S Aston Martins, and then travelled to Montlhéry where he took second place in the Coupe du Salon. He finished off a very successful season by winning the Nassau Trophy in the Bahamas in December. With very good reason, Masten considered this Ferrari to be one of the finest cars that he raced.

For 1955 Gregory acquired a 3-litre Ferrari Monza and raced it with success that year and in 1956. Masten was brought into the works Ferrari team at the Buenos Aires 1,000km race in January 1957, and he won the race driving a 3.5-litre V12 car with Perdisa and Castellotti. Gregory's racing days with Ferraris were now over. He raced an obsolete Maserati 250F for Scuderia Centro-Sud in 1957 and achieved a remarkable third place at Monaco because of the high level of retirements. He drove F1 Maseratis a few times in 1958, but was also a regular driver for Écurie Ecosse.

He became number three in the Cooper F1 team in 1959 and achieved two good results, a third at Zandvoort and second, albeit a lap in arrears, in Portugal. He suffered bad shoulder and rib injuries when he lost control of his Écurie Ecosse Tojeiro in the Tourist Trophy at Goodwood, and jumped off the tail just before it hit the bank. When he had recovered in 1960, he found that Cooper no longer wanted him. Over the next few seasons he raced less and less competitive machinery in F1, but in 1965 he and Jochen Rindt scored a superb win at Le Mans with a Ferrari 250LM entered by North American Racing Team.

This win rejuvenated Masten's flagging career and he was in demand by private sports car teams throughout the late 1960s. He continued to drive Ferraris occasionally for NART, and he appeared with works Alfa Romeo 33/3s in a few events in 1970; he finally retired from racing in 1972. Gregory was a very highly strung, nervous person, and this has led some writers, in my opinion quite wrongly, to accuse him of being a drugs user. He certainly smoked very heavily, and he died at the age of 53 following a major heart attack.

Guichet, Jean

Works and private sports car driver
Born: 10 August 1927 (Marseille, France)

Essentially an amateur driver who ran a very successful ship repair company, Guichet bought a Ferrari Mondial in 1956 and first competed with it in a local hill climb. He was a regular Ferrari customer and sometimes works sports car driver. His greatest success was in the 1964 Le Mans race, which he won at the wheel of a works

275P, co-driving with Nino Vaccarella. Guichet and Giancarlo Baghetti co-drove a works Dino 206S on carburettors to second place in the 1966 Targa Florio behind a Porsche 906. In that year's Spa 1,000km race he co-drove a 206S Dino entered by Maranello Concessionaires with Richard Attwood, and they finished sixth, winning their class.

Attwood had a rather low opinion of Guichet, and commented to the writer:

'He wasn't that fast and I thought that he was probably a rich guy who managed to buy his way into a car or two.'

Mauro Forghieri told the writer:

'He was a gentleman driver who later became a very good performer.'

Guichet's last Ferrari drive was at Le Mans in 1967 where he and Herbert Müller shared a Scuderia Filipinetti-entered 330P3/4. He had been planning to drive a 512S at Le Mans in 1970, but he had been injured in a testing accident in the Camargue and retired from racing.

Below: *Guichet, who was from Marseille, was a very consistent, very dependable driver in endurance racing, and he was highly regarded by Enzo Ferrari.*
(LAT Photographic)

Gurney, Dan

Works driver
Born: 13 April 1931 (Port Jefferson, New York, USA)

The son of an opera singer, Gurney over the years proved to be one of the most able and most affable of American drivers. He started his competition career with a Triumph TR2 in 1955 and then moved on to a Porsche with which he achieved considerable success. He drove a Ferrari for Frank Arciero, a building contractor, in 1957, and he was still driving a Lotus 19 for Arciero as late as 1963. Dan's talents were recognised by Luigi Chinetti, who offered him a drive in a NART Testa Rossa at Le Mans in 1958, but his co-driver Bruce Kessler and Jaguar driver Brousselet collided at Tertre Rouge and the latter was killed in the accident.

Dan joined the works Ferrari team for 1959 and,

Below: *In terms of personality and character, Dan Gurney was one of the greatest drivers of the 1960s. Although he had raced private Ferraris in many American races, his only season with the works team was in 1959, when he drove in four GP races. His most successful year in Europe was 1967 when he won Le Mans with a 7-litre Ford (co-driving with A. J. Foyt with whom he is seen here), and the Belgian GP with one of his own Eagles.* (Ford Motor Company)

although he did not race for the F1 team until the French race at Reims where he retired because of a holed radiator, he finished second in the German race at Avus, third in Portugal, and fourth at Monza. In sports car racing he shared the winning car at Sebring, retired in the Targa Florio and Le Mans and took fifth places with Allison at the Nürburgring, and with Brooks in the Tourist Trophy at Goodwood. The atmosphere at Maranello did not suit Dan, and he left to drive for BRM in 1960, but a poor year with a succession of retirements turned to tragedy at Zandvoort where the brakes of his Ferrari failed and a small boy was killed.

At the end of the season, Dan moved on again to Porsche, where he stayed two years. With the new flat-eight air-cooled F1 car, Gurney won both the 1962 French GP at Rouen and the Solitude GP. Dan then joined the Brabham team where he partnered Jack Brabham for three seasons, and although success was rather thin on the ground, he won the 1964 French and Mexican races. Gurney ran his own F1 Eagle team in 1966–8 and won the Belgian GP in 1967.

In 1969 he quit F1 for USAC racing, finishing second at Indianapolis (he had also been second there in 1967), but he returned to Europe and drove in three races for the McLaren team after the death of Bruce in a testing accident. Gurney continued to enter his Eagles in USAC races, and won at Indianapolis in 1973 (Gordon Johncock) and 1975 (Bobby Unser). He re-entered CART racing in 1996 and, although the original effort with Toyota was unsuccessful, he has continued to enter racing on a regular basis.

Hamilton, Duncan

Driver
Born: 30 April 1920 (Cork, Ireland)
Died: 13 May 1994 (Sherbourne, Dorset, England)

Hamilton was an effusive, gregarious, arrogant personality, with a strong sense of humour, highly opinionated, but a very fine driver. The family moved to West London when he was six, and during the Second World War he served with distinction in the Fleet Air Arm. He was even allowed to have his own personal Seafire (a navalised Spitfire) when he was based at Port Reitz, near Mombassa, Kenya. In early post-war days he worked as a salesman for Henlys, at one time the largest distributor of Jaguar cars, and later he ran his own very successful business in Byfleet, Surrey, specialising in second-hand Rolls-Royce and Bentley cars.

Initially, he raced an 'R'-type supercharged MG and a Bugatti Type 35B before moving on to a Maserati for the 1948 season. In 1951 he acquired a French Talbot-Lago GP car, but his real successes were to come in sports car racing. He co-drove Nash-Healey cars at Le Mans with Tony Rolt, and they finished fourth in 1950 and sixth in 1951. By 1952, Rolt and Hamilton were both members of the works Jaguar team, and Hamilton had taken delivery of the first production C-type.

Rolt and Hamilton won at Le Mans in 1953 with their disc-braked, lightweight works C-type – it was a remarkable performance by the Jaguar team, which finished first, second, and fourth. The following year, Rolt and Hamilton were at the wheel of the new D-type, and after a race-long battle they took second place, only 2½ miles behind the winning 4.9-litre Ferrari 375 Plus of González/Trintignant.

The Ferrari team had, however, breached the race regulations in two important respects: more than the permitted number of mechanics had worked on the car, and a mechanic had started the car from under the bonnet while González sat at the wheel. If William Lyons of Jaguar had protested the win, there is no doubt that his protest would have been upheld.

Hamilton stayed with Jaguar for another two seasons, but team manager 'Lofty' England sacked him after the 1956 Reims 12 Hours race. Hamilton had broken team orders by setting a new lap record and overtaking team-mate Paul Frère to win the race.

Subsequently, Ferrari asked Hamilton to drive for the sports car team, but he was entered at only two 1956 races. These were Le Mans, where de Portago wrote off their car very early in the race and Hamilton missed out on a drive; and the Swedish GP where he co-drove a Tipo 860 Monza with de Portago and Hawthorn into third place. Ferrari never regarded Hamilton as a serious prospect for the works team, but these drives assuaged his *amour propre*.

Hamilton maintained good relations with Jaguar, and for 1957 bought one of the previous year's team cars. Partnered by Masten Gregory, he finished sixth with this at Le Mans in 1957. The following year at Le Mans, Hamilton was partnered in the D-type by Ivor Bueb and they were running strongly in second place, challenging the leading Ferrari until Sunday lunchtime when Hamilton collided with a French car that had stopped on the track in heavy rain. The D-type spun, hit a bank, and overturned into a ditch. Hamilton was lucky to escape with severe bruising. He retired from racing at the end of the 1959 season.

Below: *After 'Lofty' England sacked Duncan Hamilton from the Jaguar team at the 1956 Reims 12 Hours race, his* amour propre *was satisfied by Ferrari offering him, only briefly, a place in the works team. Here Hamilton is seen at the wheel of his private Talbot-Lago at the International Trophy meeting at Silverstone in May 1951.* (Guy Griffiths)

Hawthorn, Mike

Driver
Born: 10 April 1929 (Mexborough, near Doncaster, Yorkshire, England)
Died: 22 January 1959 (Guildford bypass, Surrey, England)

Below: *Young Mike Hawthorn joined the Ferrari team for 1953. It took him a while to settle down in the team, but he scored a fantastic, hard-fought win in the French GP at Reims, beating Fangio (Maserati) by a margin of less than a second. Next came the British GP, and Hawthorn is seen with his Tipo 500 four-cylinder 2-litre Ferrari on the starting grid before the race. Behind the car is Basil Cardew, motoring correspondent of the Daily Express. After a wild spin, Hawthorn finished fifth.* (Guy Griffiths)

In the 1950s, young motor racing enthusiasts were divided in their support for Mike Hawthorn and Stirling Moss. Hawthorn supporters favoured a green anorak – just as worn by their hero – but to have adopted the bow tie that Hawthorn wore as a sort of caricature of himself, a calculated attempt to be different, would have been a step too far and, even if Mike got away with it, would have sent all the wrong signals.

In his first season of racing he won the *Motor Sport* Brooklands Trophy for his performances with a Riley at Goodwood Club meetings. The difficult decision was what Mike was going to race in his second season. Bob Chase (described by Chris Nixon, rather unfairly, as an eccentric, alcoholic motor racing enthusiast) was a family friend of the Hawthorns who ran a garage at Shoreham.

Chase offered to buy a new Cooper-Bristol F2 car for Mike to drive in 1952. Mike had tested for Connaught and HWM, but there was no future for him with either team, and the Cooper was the perfect answer. On paper, the Cooper was uncompetitive because power output of the Bristol engine, derived from the pre-war

BMW 328 and featuring Fritz Fiedler's cross-over push-rods, to avoid the need for twin camshafts, was only 140/150bhp compared with the 175/180bhp of the works Ferraris. But the Cooper was of very light construction, and the engine of Hawthorn's car was very carefully tuned and, running on nitromethane fuel additive, almost certainly had a power output in excess of 150bhp.

The 1952–3 seasons were a golden period for Hawthorn, who had a very unhappy life. After a sensational debut with the Cooper on Easter Monday, when he won two races and finished second in the main race of the day, a Formule Libre event won by Froilán González with Tony Vandervell's 4.5-litre Ferrari Thin Wall Special. The Cooper's gear-lever broke off in the International Trophy at Silverstone, but after that the run of success started once more. Mike won a Formule Libre race at Boreham and finished second in the Formule Libre Ulster Trophy at Dundrod.

Mike then ran in the Belgian GP at Spa where he finished fourth, he took third place in the British GP,

and fourth place in the Dutch GP. He was far too behind in the Italian GP to be classified because of magneto problems. The ten points that he gained was sufficient to give him joint fourth place in the World Championship in only his second season of racing. It was the intention that Mike should drive a works Ferrari in the non-Championship Modena GP a week after Monza, but he took the Cooper round in practice because his Ferrari was not ready. He crashed the Cooper, but Ferrari signed him up for the 1953 season.

Initially, Mike found great difficulty in adjusting to life

Below: *The development of Mike Hawthorn's racing career was carefully monitored and organised by father Leslie. It was he who chose the early cars and took responsibility for their development and preparation. In this photograph Mike is seen at the wheel of his ex-works 1100cc Riley Ulster Imp on his first competition appearance in the 1950 Brighton Speed Trials, in which he won his class.* (Guy Griffiths Collection)

Above: *There was also a Formule Libre race at the British GP meeting in 1953, and Hawthorn drove a Tipo 625 car, the 2490cc version of the Formula 2 model. On the starting grid he was alongside the incredibly noisy V16 BRM of Ken Wharton, and he put his hands over his ears to try to shut out some of the noise. Hawthorn retired in this race because of engine overheating.* (Guy Griffiths)

in Italy, and Enzo Ferrari was disappointed with his early performances. However, his ability soon showed through. In those days, points were only awarded for the first five places with a single point for fastest lap, and Mike scored Championship points in every race except the Belgian GP in which he finished sixth. He was fourth in the Argentine and Dutch races, and then came the Belgian. In the next race, the French GP at Reims, Mike fought a race-long 300-mile (483km) wheel-to-wheel battle with Fangio (Maserati) and won by a margin of one second. In fairness, it has to be mentioned that Fangio had gearbox problems in the closing stages of the race.

In the British race at Silverstone, Mike was fifth after a wild spin at Woodcote. He was third in both the German and Swiss races, and he finished fourth at Monza. He took fourth place in the Drivers' Championship. Mike also won the International Trophy at Silverstone, the Ulster Trophy at Dundrod, and he shared the winning 4.5-litre sports cars with Farina in the Belgian 24 Hours and Maglioli in the Pescara 12 Hours. It was an exceptionally successful year by any standard.

Mike was 'off the leash' when he lived in Modena – too far from home for his father's influence to have effect – and, of course, all restraints disappeared following his father's death. He then had the chance to live life to the full, quaffing his ale, partying, womanising, and quaffing more ale. While researching his book *Mon Ami Mate* about the lives of Mike Hawthorn and Peter Collins, Chris Nixon learned that when Hawthorn was in France for the 1953 French GP his illegitimate son Arnaud Delaunay was conceived. It was an incident in Mike's life that was previously unknown.

There was no question of Mike not staying with Ferrari for 1954, but it was a very unhappy year. In the Argentine GP, first round of the Championship, he was disqualified for being push-started after a spin. Then Mike faced an inquisition in parliament and the press about his failure to be called up for military National

Service, then compulsory in Britain save for medical exemption. In fact, he suffered a kidney complaint, and medical exemption would have been inevitable.

The first European race was the Syracuse GP, and here, blinded by straw thrown by Marimon as his Maserati clouted the straw bales in his effort to stay ahead of the young British driver, Hawthorn hit a stone wall. The fuel filler came open, petrol slopping on to the hot exhaust was ignited, and Mike suffered serious burns despite González's efforts to haul him out of the cockpit. He was due to return to racing at Le Mans in June, but came back to England when he received news that his father had been fatally injured in a car crash on his way home from the Whit Monday Goodwood race meeting.

Mike was forced to pull into the pits in the Belgian GP because he was being overcome by fumes from an exhaust leak. González took the car over, and after a further stop for repairs he brought the car across the finishing line in fourth place. The new Mercedes-Benz W196 cars made their race debut in streamlined form in the French GP at Reims at the beginning of July. All three Ferraris retired because of engine failure in vain pursuit of the German Stromlinienwagen, which took the first two places.

In the British GP at Silverstone, the streamlined W196s displayed their unsuitability for anything but the fastest circuits. González won for Ferrari, and Mike took second place, his first real success of the year. In the German race, the Mercedes-Benz team introduced an unstreamlined version of the W196, and with this model Fangio won at both the Nürburgring and Bremgarten. Hawthorn retired his own car in the German race because of final drive problems, and took over from González to finish second.

Another retirement followed in Switzerland, but Mike took second place behind Fangio in the Italian race at Monza. He drove a 3-litre Ferrari Monza in the Tourist Trophy at Dundrod later in September and, partnered by Trintignant, won the race on scratch despite strong opposition from Jaguar and Lancia. The last Championship race of the year was the Spanish GP held on the Pedralbes street circuit at Barcelona.

Mike drove a new version of the 553 Squalo with coil spring front suspension, and he was very satisfied with the handling and general performance. He took the lead at just over a quarter race-distance and won from Musso (Maserati) and an oil-soaked Fangio, whose ailing Mercedes-Benz was making peculiar wailing noises. Juan Fangio won the World Championship with 42 points from González (Ferrari, second on 25 points), and with Mike in third place with 24½ points. It was a good result in an unhappy year.

For 1955, Mike decided that he should devote more time to the family business, Tourist Trophy Garage, so he signed up with the British Vanwall team in F1, and Jaguar in sports car racing. Mike soon realised that the Vanwall still needed a great deal of development work and that the team's organisation was poor. After retiring in both the Monaco GP and Belgian GP, he returned to Ferrari. That year the Ferraris were completely outclassed by Mercedes-Benz, who won all the Championship races except Monaco where all three W196s retired and Trintignant won for Ferrari by default. Mike's only finishes were in the Dutch race (seventh) and at Aintree where Castellotti took over his car to take sixth place.

The worst race for Hawthorn in 1955 was Le Mans in which he and Ivor Bueb scored a tragic triumph. Mike was accused of triggering off the accident that caused the death of Mercedes-Benz driver Pierre Levegh and more than 80 spectators. Although film footage produced by the Jaguar team's race photographers vindicated him, he was never completely exonerated in France and Germany, where he was a convenient scapegoat for Levegh's poor reactions and the deficiencies of the Le Mans circuit.

In the Tourist Trophy a single works D-type Jaguar was driven by Hawthorn and Desmond Titterington and they faced three Mercedes-Benz 300SLRs. The Jaguar drivers turned in a magnificent performance, holding second place on the penultimate lap when the D-type broke its crankshaft and spun on its own oil. By entering a single car to take on the might of Mercedes-Benz, Jaguar gained immense publicity, win or lose.

Hawthorn wanted to stay with the Jaguar team in 1956 and remain close to the garage business, so he agreed to drive the new four-cylinder P25 BRM that had first raced in the Gold Cup at Oulton Park in September 1955. Number two in the team was Tony Brooks. At the start of the year, Hawthorn drove the Maserati 250F owned by the Owen Racing Organisation, builders of the BRM, into third place in the Argentine GP. This was his only single-seater success of the year. During the year the BRMs suffered major brake problems and were unsafe. They first ran in the International Trophy at Silverstone in May of that year, but both cars retired.

Mike non-started at Monaco because of engine problems, but two BRMs ran in the British GP, and although they were tremendously fast, they were disgracefully unreliable. Hawthorn retired because of oil leaking from a universal joint, and Brooks had a dreadful crash after the throttle jammed open following a bodged repair in the pits. Mike drove a Vanwall in the French race at Reims, but handed it over to Schell early in the race because he was too tired after driving a Jaguar in the 12 Hours race.

BRM had withdrawn from racing after the British race in July to try to resolve their problems. Hawthorn was offered a drive by Ferrari in the German GP at the Nürburgring, but, in a vicious hark back to the 1955 Le Mans, the Automobil Club von Deutschland's insurers refused to insure him for the race. It was Jaguar's last year in sports car racing, but Mike's only success was second place with Paul Frère in the Reims 12 Hours race.

In 1957 Ferrari was racing the V8 Lancia-derived cars in modified Tipo 801 form, but they were no match for the latest Maserati 250Fs or, as the season progressed, the Vanwalls that had become much more reliable. Ferrari failed to win a single World Championship race, and Mike's best performances were fourth in the French GP at Rouen, third in the British race at Aintree, and second in the German GP. Despite a relatively unsuccessful year, Hawthorn was very glad to be back in the Ferrari team, and his friendship with fellow-driver Peter Collins was very close.

During 1958, Ferrari raced the new Dino 246 cars and he had an especially strong team of drivers with Peter Collins, Mike Hawthorn, and Luigi Musso all vying for a Championship win. It was much the same in the Vanwall team, where both Moss and Brooks won races

Below: *Ferrari raced the Lancia V8 cars in much-modified form in 1957, but they were no longer a match for either the works Maserati 250Fs or the Vanwalls. Behra was leading the British GP at Aintree with his Maserati when the clutch exploded, scattering pieces of metal over the track. Hawthorn, seen here, punctured a tyre on this debris, and after a pit stop rejoined the race to finish third.* (Tom March Collection)

throughout the year, and effectively this prevented Moss from winning the Championship that he deserved.

Maserati had withdrawn from racing, and although the rear-engined Coopers won the first two Championship races in Argentina and Monaco, the season was largely a straight fight between Ferrari and Vanwall. It was another tragic year for Ferrari and Hawthorn, for Musso was killed in the French GP, and Collins suffered fatal injuries when he crashed in the German GP. Although sad, these deaths opened the door for Hawthorn to win the World Championship unchallenged by any other Ferrari driver.

During the year, the Vanwall team won six races (fine from the point of view of the Manufacturers' Championship, but Moss and Brooks each won three of these). In addition, Moss won the Argentine race with a Cooper and finished second to Hawthorn in the French race. Ferrari drivers won only two races, Hawthorn in France and Collins at Silverstone, but Hawthorn scored points consistently, at eight races in total.

The Moroccan GP, the last in the 1958 series, settled the outcome, and Hawthorn's second place behind Moss (who also took a point for fastest lap), was good enough to clinch the Championship for the Ferrari driver with 42 points net (49 gross) to the 41 gross and net of Moss. The great irony of the 1958 season was that at the Portuguese race in August, Moss, who was the winner, gave evidence to the stewards that Hawthorn, who finished second, should not be disqualified.

On his last lap, Hawthorn spun and stalled the Ferrari and push-started it. It was claimed that he had pushed the car in the opposite way to the direction of the circuit, and if this had been established, disqualification would follow. Moss confirmed that Hawthorn had pushed the car on the footpath and not the track. If Hawthorn had been disqualified he would have lost seven points (including that for fastest lap) and his grand total on the best six performances would then have been 39 and Moss would have won the Championship.

Hawthorn retired from racing at the end of the 1958 season. He was planning marriage to his fiancée, Jean Howarth, and also to expand Tourist Trophy Garage. On 22 January 1959 he was driving his extensively modified Jaguar 3.4 saloon on the Guildford bypass at the Hogg's Back when he lost control in dreadfully wet weather and was killed outright in the crash. There were suggestions that Hawthorn and racing entrant Rob Walker, at the wheel of his 140mph (225kph) Mercedes-Benz 300SL, were racing, but Walker denied this. Walker claimed that Hawthorn overtook him and that he was close behind the Jaguar when it crashed. Walker, who is dead, never changed that account.

Hill, Phil

Works driver
Born: 20 April 1927 (Miami, Florida, USA)
Died: 28 August 2008 (Santa Monica, California, USA)

Although Hill won the 1961 F1 Drivers' Championship, his long-term fame is as a sports car driver. With a father who was a dedicated Democrat supporter and a mother who was a fierce Republican, the Hill household – consisting of Phil, his parents, and his two siblings – was riven by strife in a way that is difficult to imagine in England. The family had moved from Miami to Santa Monica, and Phil lived in the family house for his entire life. It appears that both his parents were alcoholics. As a result of this he spent much of the time with his divorced aunt, Helen. Phil's father was first foreman of the Los Angeles Grand Jury (apparently a permanent position) and then local postmaster.

In 1935 he began three years' study at the Hollywood Military Academy, and played alto horn and drums in the Academy's band. All his life he suffered from sinus trouble, and because of his breathing difficulties he often raced with his mouth open. He went to work at the Douglas

Above: *After winning the World Championship in 1961, Phil Hill stayed with Ferrari for another season. The V6 cars had been so much more powerful than the opposition in 1961 that they were challenged on very few occasions. By 1962, though, they were no match for the latest British V8 cars that were just as powerful, but lighter. Here, Hill is seen on the starting grid at the British GP at Aintree. His was the only Ferrari in the race, and he retired because of ignition problems.*
(Tom March Collection)

aircraft factory, and then, to please his father, he studied business administration at the University of California between 1945 and 1947. Even so, the main attraction was always cars, and he took a job helping a mechanic, Rudi Sumpter, who raced a midget speedway car.

Phil started racing and rallying an MG TC in the late 1940s. He had bought the car new from International Motors in Beverly Hills, and he went to work for this company as a mechanic. It was as a mechanic that he came to Europe to attend service courses at Jaguar, MG, Rolls-Royce, and SU Carburettors. He returned to the United States with a Jaguar XK 120 that he soon disposed of in favour of an 8C 2900B Alfa Romeo Corto. He started to drive regularly for private owners, and he

returned to Europe for the Le Mans race in 1952, but a drive failed to materialise.

It was the chance to drive Ferraris for Alan Guiberson in the United States, and Chinetti's influence, that put Hill in a position where he could prove his great worth. Partnered by Richie Ginther, he finished second with a Guiberson Ferrari to Umberto Maglioli in the 1954 Carrera Panamericana road race, and the following year he was partnered by Carroll Shelby at the wheel of Guiberson's Ferrari Monza when they took second place to the Hawthorn/Walters Jaguar D-type in the Sebring 12 Hours race.

Prompted by Luigi Chinetti, Ferrari invited Hill to drive a works Tipo 121 Ferrari at Le Mans in 1955. He partnered Umberto Maglioli, and although they rose as high as third place at one point, they retired in the seventh hour because of clutch and radiator problems. At Buenos Aires in 1956, Hill partnered Olivier Gendebien at the wheel of the second-place Ferrari in the 1,000km sports car race. That year he joined the works Ferrari team on a fairly regular basis, and his successes included taking second place with Peter Collins in the sports car Swedish GP and winning the five-hour Messina Night race.

The following year he and Peter Collins headed a Ferrari 1–2–3 in the 1,000km sports car Venezuelan GP. In early 1958, they co-drove sports Ferraris to victory in the Buenos Aires 1,000km, and he won the Sebring 12 Hours race, also with Collins. He and Gendebien also won at Le Mans that year. The 'Old Man' took the view that Hill was so effective as a sports car driver – and served the Scuderia best in that role – that he would not seriously consider him as a GP driver.

An exception was the 1958 Buenos Aires City GP, a Formule Libre race, and the intention was that von Trips should drive a Ferrari in the first heat and Phil in the second. The young German crashed, and that stymied Phil's GP aspirations in the short term. Phil was getting desperate for a F1 drive, so he arranged an entry with an obsolete Maserati 250F, belonging to Joakim Bonnier, in the French GP, and finished a mediocre seventh. (Not a bad performance for a very uncompetitive car.)

The 'Old Man' relented – somewhat – by entering him with a F2 car in the German GP at the Nürburgring

at the beginning of August. Hill led the F2 class comfortably until he spun on a patch of oil, and he was unaware that in his off-course excursion the oil breather pipe running under the car was torn away. So, he was spraying his back tyres with his own oil mist, and he fell back to finish ninth overall and fifth in the F2 category.

By the next F1 race, the Portuguese GP, Ferrari was short of drivers following the death of Musso at Reims and Collins at the Nürburgring. Hawthorn (Ferrari) was battling with Moss (Vanwall) for the Drivers' World Championship, and now Hill had an important role to play. He retired at Lisbon, but he took third place in the Italian race, after falling back to let Hawthorn move ahead to finish second. In the final round of the Championship at Casablanca he again finished third, having eased off to let Hawthorn finish second and win the Championship.

In 1959 the GP Ferraris were increasingly outclassed by the rear-engined Coopers, but for Phil it was a good enough season, for he was polishing his skills and constantly improving his performance. With second places at Reims and Monza, he finished fourth in the Drivers' Championship. Aston Martin won the World Sports Car Championship in 1959, but Phil shared the winning Ferrari at Sebring. By 1960 the GP Ferraris were becoming obsolete, and Phil's only GP win was in the Italian race held on the combined banked track and road circuit at Monza – the race boycotted by the British teams running rear-engined cars.

Ferrari was still holding its own in sports car racing, and was the dominant marque in 1960. Phil won the last 1,000km race at Buenos Aires with Cliff Allison, was second in the Targa Florio with von Trips, and he shared third place at the Nürburgring. Ferrari largely dominated F1 in 1961 when the team ran their new rear-engined V6 cars, and when the British teams' new V8 engines were not ready in this the first year of the new 1500cc GP formula. Phil had finished third at Monaco, but he won in Belgium, and he was second in the Dutch and British races.

When the teams arrived at Monza for the Italian GP, Phil had 29 points gross (25 net for the best five performances) and von Trips's total was 33 net. On the second lap of the race, Jim Clark (Lotus) and von Trips collided. Wolfgang von Trips and 14 spectators were killed. Hill went on to win the World Championship with 34 points, and it was an immensely sad result that hung over Hill all his life.

By 1962, most of the leading Ferrari executives had been sacked and the V6 cars were outclassed by the British V8 entries. Despite the strength of the opposition, Hill finished second at Monaco and third in

Above: *For 1963, Phil Hill left Ferrari, which faced a very uphill struggle to become competitive again, and joined the ill-fated ATS team who raced V8 cars designed by Carlo Chiti. Here, Hill is seen in the Belgian GP on the debut of the new car. He retired because of gearbox trouble after a slow race.* (The British Petroleum Company)

the Belgian and German races. It was a far better effort against the odds than it seems. In addition, in Prototype racing (as sports car racing was known), Hill won the Nürburgring 1,000km race with Gendebien, and he won at Le Mans for the third time, again partnered by Gendebien. During these years they were the most formidable sports car partnership.

At the end of the 1962 season, it was made clear to both Hill and Baghetti that their contracts would not be renewed, and both signed up to drive the new Chiti-designed ATS GP car. It was a superb design, very advanced in certain respects, but the execution was hopelessly shoddy, the preparation was abysmal, and

the failure of these cars effectively destroyed the F1 careers of both drivers. Phil signed up for Cooper in 1964 and had a thoroughly miserable and unsuccessful season, and the nadir was at Zeltweg where he wrote off two cars.

Phil's F1 career was now over, apart from his failure to qualify with an Eagle at the Italian GP at Monza in 1966. He still had a fine career ahead of him in sports car racing, and he raced with great skill and maturity for Ford in 1964–5 and Chaparral in 1966–7. His successes included wins with Jo Bonnier at the Nürburgring in 1966 and with Mike Spence in the BOAC race at Brands Hatch in 1967. When Phil retired from racing on a high note after the Brands Hatch win, he did not know that the best parts of his life were still to come.

After retiring from racing, he set up what became the leading car restoration company in the United States. He also became a television commentator and, over a period in excess of 30 years, he worked with John Lamm on track tests for *Road & Track* magazine.

His other interests included antique clocks, mechanical music, steam trains, and photography (a book with a collection of his photographs is currently in production).

Throughout his racing career he had appeared to be a confirmed bachelor, but he fell instantly in love with Alma Varanowski, a schoolteacher who knocked on his door to ask him to participate in a school project. He has been quoted as saying, 'I opened the door and thought, "Thank you Heaven."' They married in 1971 and they had a son and daughter. In 2002 he succeeded Toulo de Graffenried as President of the Club International des Anciens Pilotes de Grand Prix and he and his wife were frequent guests at classic car events worldwide.

Hoare, Colonel 'Ronnie'

British Ferrari agent through Maranello Concessionaires and owner of Maranello Concessionaires Racing Team
Born: 31 August 1913 (London)
Died: 1989 (Monte Carlo)

A fascinating, talented, and successful businessman – and womaniser – Ronald John Hoare (born as Ronald Jack Hoare) put Ferrari very much on the map in the UK. He was educated at Collett Court (the Prep school for St Paul's school) and subsequently at St Paul's. His godfather, Lord Aberconway, arranged for him to be apprenticed at the Metropolitan Railway.

He worked as a salesman at University Motors, the London MG distributors, and after joining the Army Supplementary Reserve, he was commissioned following the outbreak of war. He enjoyed a distinguished army career that included becoming a full colonel on General Montgomery's staff in North Africa and playing an important role in the planning of the invasion of Sicily.

It was not until 1955 that Hoare resigned his commission and bought a one-third share in F. English Limited, the Ford main dealers in Poole, where he and his third wife Anne settled. He was elected a Conservative councillor on Dorset County Council and became Chairman of Hurn (Bournemouth) Airport Management Committee. In 1959 he and Bob Gibson-

Above: *A formal portrait of Ronnie Hoare, taken in the 1960s.* (Author's collection)

Jarvie set up the United Racing Stable, entering Formula 2 cars, but the partnership was not a success and was dissolved at the end of the season.

Hoare had always owned exotic cars, including C- and D-type Jaguars and a Ferrari Testa Rossa. The British Ferrari agency was originally vested in Brooklands Motors in Bond Street, but they were not seriously interested, and after he became a works driver Mike Hawthorn took over the agency at his Tourist Trophy Garage in Surrey. Hoare acquired his first touring Ferrari, a 250GT, from Tommy Sopwith, who had bought it off the Tourist Trophy Garage stand at the 1958 London Motor Show. Tourist Trophy Garage lost the agency after the death of Mike Hawthorn.

In 1960 Hoare went to Maranello to see Enzo Ferrari, and in response to Ferrari's question, 'How many cars a year do you think you can sell?' Hoare said, 'Four', and the 'Old Man' was delighted. Ferrari had only sold four cars in Britain in the previous ten years. Initially, the new importer, Maranello Concessionaires Ltd, conducted sales from two bays of F. E. English's premises in Poole Road, Bournemouth.

During 1961, Hoare and Tommy Sopwith split the costs of racing a 250GT (originally a standard model replaced during the year by a 'Competizione'). They shared the entry of a 250GTO in 1962, and after Sopwith retired from racing, Maranello Concessionaires raced its own GT and Prototype Ferraris through to the end of 1967.

Maranello Concessionaires opened a London service depot at Wellesley Road, Chiswick, in 1964, Shaun Bealey became managing director and a shareholder in mid-1967, and the company took over Tower Garage in January 1968. Hoare and Bealey sold out to the TDK Group in 1968, mainly because of Hoare's health problems. Ronnie Hoare was a very heavy pipe smoker and suffered from emphysema, and he went to live in Monte Carlo for tax and health reasons. Hoare became very unhappy there and he wanted to return home, but he was too ill to do so. He died in Monte Carlo in 1989.

This section is an abbreviated version of the chapter 'Colonel Ronnie Hoare, Founder of Maranello Concessionaires' in the writer's book *Scarlet Passion: Ferrari's famed sports prototype and competition sports cars, 1962–73* (Haynes Publishing, 2004). The full story of the racing activities of Maranello Concessionaires is told in *The Colonel's Ferraris* by Doug Nye (Ampersand Press, 1980)

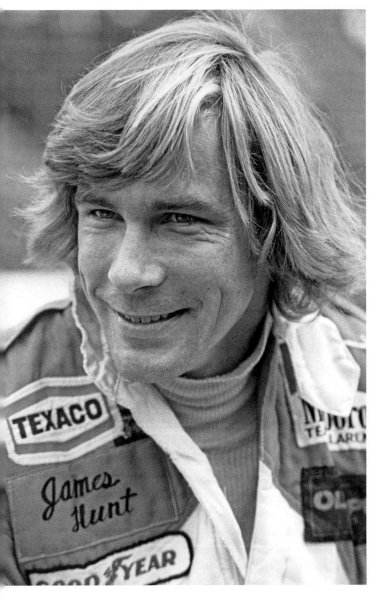

Below: *James Hunt, who won the Drivers' World Championship in 1976, was a 'hippy' type of free spirit and a great individualist who always did what he – and no one else – wanted. He never drove for Ferrari, but this came close to happening, and the repercussions make fascinating speculation.* (LAT Photographic)

Hunt, James

Racing driver
Born: 29 August 1947 (Belmont, Sutton, Surrey, England)
Died: 15 June 1993 (Wimbledon, London, England)

As Hunt never drove for Ferrari, it is purposeless to narrate his racing career, but there is good cause to mention why he did not race for Maranello. Because of the 'Old Man's' concerns about the stability of drivers Villeneuve and Reutemann in 1977, Daniele Audetto and Piero Lardi Ferrari had a secret meeting in 1978 with Hunt at a villa near Monaco and reached agreement that Hunt would drive for Ferrari in 1979. What prevented Hunt driving for Ferrari was a promotional contract with Vauxhall. Gianni Agnelli of Fiat, who owned a controlling interest in Ferrari, wished to avoid conflict with General Motors, and the agreement was abandoned. Instead, Hunt signed up for Wolf for 1979, but walked away from his car at Monaco and announced that he was retiring from racing immediately.

Ickx, Jacky

Works driver
Born: 1 January 1945 (Brussels, Belgium)

Jacky's interest in motor sport was encouraged from an early age by his father Jacques Ickx, a renowned motoring author and journalist. At Ferrari, Jacky built up a close relationship with Mauro Forghieri, just as Chris Amon had done, and his fate was very similar. The succession of inadequate cars led to a loss of enthusiasm and a breakdown of relations with Enzo Ferrari.

He started his competition career with a Zündapp 50cc motorcycle, and he rode in the International Six Days Trial at the age of 17. His career on four wheels began with a loaned BMW, which he drove in a few circuit races and hill climbs. In 1963 he drove a standard Lotus-Cortina in hill climbs for Ford Belgium, and the following year he raced a modified Lotus-Cortina for the same entrant. This led to drives for Alan Mann Racing, including Budapest in 1965 when he met Ken Tyrrell.

Tyrrell was one of the greatest judges of motor racing talent, and he offered Jacky a place in his team driving a F3 car. Ickx could not accept immediately because of his National Service, which lasted 15 months. When he was on leave from the Belgian army, he continued to drive for Ford Belgium and he took second place in the Marathon de la Route with a Mustang. He had a trial with a Tyrrell Cooper-BRM F2 car in the latter part of 1965, and entered into a three-year contract. His drives with Tyrrell's F2 and F3 Matras proved largely unsuccessful, apart from second places at Silverstone and Zandvoort.

Co-driving a BMW with Hubert Hahne, he won the 1966 Belgian 24 Hours Touring Car race, and he also won the 1966 Marathon de la Route with a Lotus-Cortina. He was much more successful in 1967, winning the European F2 Championship with Tyrrell-entered Matras; he scored four victories with John Wyer's Gulf-sponsored Ford GT40-based Mirage Sports Prototypes, and he also drove F1 Cooper-Maseratis in a couple of races. The intention was that he should drive a Tyrrell-entered F1 Matra alongside Stewart in 1968, but the team's finances would not extend to a second car.

Instead, Ferrari signed Ickx up for 1968, but as they were competing only in F1 (and F2), he was free to continue driving Ford GT40s and Mirages for Wyer's Gulf team. Although Ferrari was to race V12 F1 cars until the end of 1969, the team was struggling to remain competitive, but Ickx was superb. He drove brilliantly in the wet to win the French GP at Rouen, and he also took third places at Spa, Brands Hatch, and Monza, together with fourths in Holland and Germany. Slim prospects of a win in the World Championship evaporated when Ickx crashed in practice for the Canadian race because the throttle had jammed open, and he broke a leg.

**Right:** Jacky Ickx drove for Ferrari in 1968, but then left to join the Brabham team. He rejoined Ferrari for 1970, and stayed with Maranello until mid-1973. He was thoroughly fed up with poor cars, and the 'Old Man' thought Ickx was becoming 'too political' (which meant critical!). Ickx is seen at the 1968 German Grand Prix, where he finished fourth in his 312. (sutton-images.com)

His drives for the Gulf team were outstanding, and he shared the winning Ford GT40s in the Championship races at Brands Hatch, Spa (for the second year in succession), and Watkins Glen, but missed Le Mans because of his crash at St Jovite. He returned to the Gulf team to share the winning car in the Kyalami Nine Hours race. Wyer and Gulf were anxious to retain Ickx's services for 1969, so it was agreed that he would leave Ferrari to drive for Brabham in F1 and stay with Wyer in sports car racing.

In 1969 the latest Ford-powered Brabhams were very competitive and Ickx won the German GP at the Nürburgring, beating Stewart who won that year's Drivers' Championship with Matra cars. Ickx also won the Canadian GP, and he took second place to Stewart in the British race at Silverstone, after running out of fuel on the last lap and being classified a lap in arrears. He took second place in the Drivers' Championship with 37 points to the 63 of Stewart, all-conquering with the latest Matra MS80.

Below: *Ickx was one of the greatest drivers of his generation, but his successes never quite matched the fine potential. Here, Ickx is seen at the wheel of his 312B2 Ferrari in the wet 1972 Monaco GP. Beltoise (BRM) made a superb start, and visibility through the spray thrown up by the BRM was so bad that Ickx could not see enough to mount a challenge. He settled for second place, a little under 40sec behind the winner.* (Author's collection)

Ickx achieved the finest sports car drive of his career at Le Mans where he brought the winning GT40 across the line 100yd ahead of Herrmann with the second-place, but raggedly running Porsche 908. Although Le Mans was different, by 1969 the GT40s were too old, too heavy, and too slow in most races to defeat the latest 3-litre Porsche 908s, while the new Ford-powered Mirage was unreliable. Even so, Ickx won the Imola 500km race that year with the Ford-powered Mirage.

For 1970, Ickx returned to Ferrari and has commented:

'I only left Ferrari at the end of 1968 because of the conflict over my Gulf Oil contract. Gulf did not want me driving an F1 Ferrari contracted to Shell for fuel and oil at the same time as I was driving for them. At the time I rejoined Ferrari it was clear that Fiat and, also, Gianni Agnelli personally, were having more influence. I first drove the 312B at Vallelunga in October 1969. I found that it had a great deal of promise. The engine felt strong, it was smooth and it had a lot of torque.'

Ickx enjoyed a very successful year in F1, although it was tinged by tragedy and ultimate failure to win the Drivers' Championship. Ickx worked closely with Forghieri on development of the 312B1 flat-12 F1 which improved in both speed and reliability as the season progressed. At Lotus, Jochen Rindt was working closely with Maurice Philippe and the other members of the

engineering staff on the development of the 72. The British team had the edge because Rindt was driving at an exceptional peak of ability and the car was fully sorted earlier in the season.

Ferrari was, of course, trying to do the impossible by running a team in sports car racing in parallel with the F1 programme. The result was that both Ferrari teams suffered, and in any event the 512S Competition Sports cars were markedly inferior to the Gulf-Porsche 917s. In the Spanish GP, the second Championship race of the season, a collision between Ickx and Oliver (BRM) resulted in the Ferrari catching fire and Ickx suffering quite severe burns. The writer vividly recalls the strained expression on the young Belgian's face as he struggled to cope with the pain from the burns and, later, the skin irritation as they healed.

When Jochen Rindt crashed his Lotus 72 with fatal results in practice for the Italian GP, Ickx was in second place in the Championship and with reasonable prospects of overtaking the deceased Austrian's points total. Wins in the Austrian race (before Rindt's death) and in the Canadian and Mexican races, coupled with that at Hockenheim, third at Zandvoort and fourth at Watkins Glen, brought him a total of 40 points to the 45 of Rindt.

In sports car racing, the only Ferrari Championship win was at Sebring (Ickx was not a driver of the winning car), and Ickx was involved in a tragedy at Le Mans. At around 1.35am on the Sunday, a brake locked on Ickx's 512S and he spun over a sandbank, killing a marshal. His only sports car success was a second place with Surtees, making a guest reappearance with the team, in the Spa 1,000km race. Ickx was the one Ferrari driver capable of taking on the Gulf-Porsche team on even terms, but the 512S Ferraris were not up to the job. At the end of the year, Ickx, partnered by Regazzoni, won the Kyalami Nine Hours with the improved 512M car.

Following his marriage, Ickx had considered retiring from racing, but he stayed with Ferrari for another three years. Forghieri's team had developed the improved 312B2 cars, but throughout the year their performance was inconsistent. Ickx won one GP, the Dutch race – a brilliant drive on a wet track – and his only other finishes in the points were second in Spain and third at Monaco, although his outstanding win in the non-Championship Jochen Rindt Gedächtnisrennen must be mentioned. In Prototype racing, Ickx and Regazzoni raced the new 312PB car, but although it was tremendously fast, it was very unreliable and finished in only one Championship race, second place at Brands Hatch.

In 1972 Ickx had an exceptionally successful year in Prototype racing in the absence of serious opposition –

the Alfa Romeos were uncompetitive, and Matra ran only at Le Mans, which Ferrari missed. Altogether Ickx was the winner in the Daytona Six Hours, Sebring 12 Hours, BOAC 1,000km (all with Andretti), and second at Monza and Spa (with Regazzoni), and then rounded off the season with wins in the Austrian 1,000km (with Redman) and Watkins Glen Six Hours (with Andretti).

Forghieri had been moved sideways by 1973, and a new engineer from Fiat, Sandro Colombo, produced the extensively redesigned 312B3, which made a hopeless debut in the Spanish GP at Montjuich Park, Barcelona. Forghieri was brought back to redesign what had been a redesign of his own car. In Prototype racing, Ickx and the other Ferrari drivers battled for supremacy with Matra, and in a closely fought year, in which the Championship was won by the French team, Ickx, partnered by Brian Redman, won only at Monza.

When Ferrari missed the German GP, Ickx drove a works McLaren M23 into a sound third place. The Italian GP, in which he took eighth place, was his last race with Ferrari. Ickx had fought tirelessly and sometimes hopelessly for Ferrari, but he cared too much for the team, and this led him to speak too frankly. Enzo Ferrari no longer wanted the Belgian in the team because he had become 'too political' – he spoke his mind.

Ickx drove for Frank Williams in the 1973 United States GP, and then signed up with Lotus for 1974. Team Lotus was racing the obsolete 72E and the new, but hopelessly flawed, 76. Ickx won the Race of Champions in the wet at Brands Hatch. But otherwise his best performances were third at Interlagos and the British GP at Brands Hatch. Jacky stayed with Lotus for 1975, but his confidence had been shattered by racing inadequate cars, and he left the team in mid-season.

The remaining years of Ickx's GP career were disappointing and largely pointless. In 1976 three races with Williams were followed by five races with its successor Walter Wolf Racing Team (these included two failures to qualify). Ironically, Ickx then replaced Amon at the small Ensign team, but in his fourth race with this team in 1976, the United States GP East at Watkins Glen, he crashed, suffering a broken ankle and burns. He made a few further appearances for Ensign in 1977–8, and mid-season in 1979 he replaced the injured Patrick Depailler at Ligier.

Ickx had been forging a new and very successful racing career with Porsche in Group 'C'. He co-drove the winning car at Le Mans in 1975–7, won many races in the World Championship of Makes, partnered by Jochen Mass, and won again at Le Mans for the fifth and sixth times in 1981–2. Even so, his really great years were at Ferrari where he was so badly treated.

Iley, John

Head of Aerodynamics
Born: 29 September 1967 (Stratford-upon-Avon, Warwickshire, England)

In 1990 John graduated from the Lanchester Polytechnic, Coventry, with a degree in Automotive Design. He went to work in 1990–1 for Brun Technics on vehicle dynamics and aerodynamics for a Group C Prototype competition sports car. During 1991–2 he worked as an aerodynamicist for Allard Motorsport and Spice Cars in relation to cars for various sports categories, including IMSA GTP and IMSA Camel Lights.

By 1997 he was employed to work on aerodynamics by the HRS Consultancy for Newman Haas Racing for Lola and Swift Indy cars. John joined the Jordan team as senior aerodynamicist in 1997, and later became the Head of Aerodynamics. Between 2002 and 2003 he was Head of Aerodynamics at Renault F1, and since November 2004 he has been employed by Scuderia Ferrari as Head of Aerodynamics. He is married with two children.

Below: *A deeply concentrating Innes is seen at the wheel of a Team Lotus 18 in the Gold Cup race at Oulton Park in 1960. He drove a good race, but the gearbox failed, which resulted in his retirement.* (**Tom March Collection**)

Ireland, Innes

Driver
Born: 12 June 1930 (Mytholmroyd, near Todmorden, Yorkshire, England)
Died: 22 October 1993 (Reading, England)

The son of a veterinary surgeon, Ireland was an engineering apprentice at Rolls-Royce in Glasgow, and he served his National Service in the Parachute Regiment (he claimed to have enjoyed it!). In 1953 he started club racing with a 3-litre Bentley, but it was his acquisition of a Lotus Eleven in 1956 that pointed his racing career in the right direction. He started a garage business, which was geared towards the preparation of Lotus cars for private owners. For 1959 he joined Team Lotus in F1, and he stayed with Colin Chapman until the end of 1961. It was then that Chapman decided that he did not want both Ireland and Jim Clark in his team.

Ireland joined the UDT Laystall Racing Team in 1962, and from this point onwards there was nowhere to go except down. An exception was the decision of Ferrari Technical Director Mauro Forghieri to make a 120° V6 F1 car available to the team for Ireland to drive in the International Trophy and provide an assessment. The drive also represented a tribute to Stirling Moss who had been critically injured in a crash at Goodwood on Easter Monday. He never again drove a works Ferrari,

but he stayed in F1 with the British Racing Partnership and Reg Parnell (Racing) until the end of 1965.

In addition, Ireland won the 1962 Tourist Trophy with a UDT-Laystall-entered Ferrari 250GTO, drove a Ferrari-engined Lotus 19 for American Team Rosebud, and raced Ford GT40s for Colonel Ronnie Hoare. His final F1 races were two appearances (and retirements) with a 2-litre BRM entered by the very amateur, but fun-loving, Bernard White Racing in the United States and Mexican Grands Prix in 1966. Ireland's later career encompassed a spell as Sports Editor of *Autocar* magazine, and he was then European correspondent for *Road & Track*. He married Jean Howarth, who had been Mike Hawthorn's fiancée, only a year before his death from cancer at the age of 63.

Irvine, Eddie

Works driver
Born: 10 November 1965 (Newtownards, County Down, Northern Ireland)

Although born in Newtownards, Edmund 'Eddie' Irvine grew up in Conlig, County Down, and he was supported in his motor racing ambitions by an enthusiastic family. With works Van Diemen cars, he won both the RAC British and Esso FF1600 Championships in 1987, a year in which he scored 14 race wins. He also won the FF1600 race at the Brands Hatch Formula Ford Festival and raced in F3 in 1988.

Above: *Although he drove sports Ferraris for private owners on a number of occasions, Innes Ireland only drove a single-seater once. The occasion was the 1962 International Trophy race at Silverstone in May when Mauro Forghieri made one of the later 120° V6 cars available to the UDT-Laystall Racing team. Innes Ireland drove the Ferrari into fourth place.* (The British Petroleum Company)

Excellent, but never quite outstanding, performances followed, and he progressed to F3000 for 1990 with Eddie Jordan's team; he won at Hockenheim and finished third in the Championship. He then drove in Japanese F3000 and performed well. In addition, he drove for Toyota in Japan and at Le Mans where he shared the fourth-place car and set fastest lap in 1993, and finished second in 1994.

Eddie Jordan gave him a chance in his F1 team at Suzuka in 1993 and his drive in that race was such that many enthusiasts said, 'Good on you, son', even if his actual performance was not praiseworthy. Steve Small described it succinctly and dramatically in his famous *Grand Prix Who's Who*:

'… rarely can a Grand Prix debut have brought so much controversy. As, revelling in the tricky conditions, he battled with Damon Hill for sixth place, he first baulked and then had the temerity to repass the race leader, Ayrton Senna, who was attempting to lap him; in the closing stages he punted Derek Warwick off to claim his first Championship point; and then he suffered a physical and verbal [ie oral] assault from the irate Brazilian after the race. It certainly moved the self-assured Ulsterman to centre stage, if only for a weekend.'

Jordan signed Eddie for a full season, but at the beginning of 1994 he was blamed for a multi-car crash and given a one-race ban. He appealed and, for his temerity in so doing, the ban was extended to three races. If the organisers disapproved of appeals, they should abolish the appeal system! Even those who make the most transparent, facetious appeals have the right to be heard fairly. That goes to the very essence of any system of justice. Eddie drove well in poor cars both that year and in 1995 – in the latter year his best performances were a third in Canada and a fourth in Suzuka.

For 1996 it was announced that Irvine was joining Schumacher in the Ferrari team, and that astounded just about everyone. Clearly, the Ferrari team saw him as being the right man to drive in a supporting role and it was a wonderful learning curve for the Irish driver. It was a year in which Ferrari – and Schumacher – were trying to find their way back to the top of the GP scene.

The promise was there, so was the commitment; it was all a matter of well-directed effort. Schumacher finished third in the Drivers' Championship, while Irvine was an invisible tenth, having retired in 11 of the year's 16 races and with best performances of third at the beginning of the season in Australia, fourth at Imola, and fifths at Buenos Aires and Estoril.

Part of the problem was that he had insufficient opportunity for testing, and the Ferrari engineers were not yet the leaders in F1 technology. In the 1997 World Championship, Schumacher finished second to Villeneuve with 78 points to the French-Canadian Williams driver's 81, but then he was disqualified from the overall placings for a title challenge to Villeneuve at Jerez that was unreasonable and dangerous.

Irvine had consolidated his position with the team and, although he failed to win a single race, his support of his team leader was consistent and confident. He finished seventh in the Championship, and his performances during the year included a second at Buenos Aires, plus third places at Imola, Monte Carlo, Magny Cours, and Suzuka.

In 1998 Ferrari was still struggling for success and was only just beginning to emerge at the forefront of racing. That year's Champion was Mika Häkkinen of McLaren, with a total of 100 points to Schumacher's 86. Coulthard (McLaren) was third with 56 points, and Irvine fourth with 47. Eddie enjoyed a very consistent year, with only three retirements, three second places,

Above: *Irishman Irvine drove for Ferrari for four seasons and his career with the team ended with second place to Häkkinen in the 1999 Drivers' Championship. He then joined the Jaguar team.* (LAT Photographic)

and five thirds. Irvine's first win came at Melbourne in 1999, and then he finished second at Monaco, third at Montreal and second at Silverstone.

Ferrari team-leader Schumacher had an accident on the first lap of the British race that resulted in a broken leg, and he was out of racing until the Malayan GP at Sepang, the penultimate race of the year. Now Irvine had no alternative but to take up the battle with the McLaren drivers. He fought hard and, with the full backing of the Ferrari team, he won the Austrian, German, and Malaysian races, and was third in the last race at Suzuka. He took second place in the Championship with 74 points to the 76 of Häkkinen.

For 2000, Irvine left Ferrari to lead the Jaguar team. The combination of a high income and being able to emerge from Schumacher's shadow were great attractions. Sadly, the Jaguars proved unreliable and uncompetitive, and in three seasons his best performances were third places at Monaco in 2001 and Italy in 2002. His rather too public criticisms of Jaguar, because of the team's slow progress in becoming competitive, and the poor financial position of the Jordan team who could not afford to take him on again, left him without a drive for 2003. So Eddie retired from F1 and has not raced since. He is not short of money; he has business interests and has had his own television programme.

Jano, Vittorio

Engineer

Born: 22 April 1891 (San Giorgio Canavese, Piedmont, Italy)

Died: 13 March 1965 (Turin, Italy)

Vittorio Jano was born Viktor János, of Hungarian parents who had taken up residence in Italy, and his father was the technical head of one of the two arsenals in Turin. By 1909, when he was 18, Jano had completed his studies at the artisan's professional college (Instituto Professionale Operaio) in Turin and obtained a job as a trainee draughtsman at the Rapid factory, a Ceirano-owned company. Less than two years later he moved to Fiat where he worked in the competition department on all the post-First World War competition cars up to and including the Tipo 805 GP car.

His position at Fiat was quite junior, but even so, he was well worth poaching by Alfa Romeo. The company wanted to make its mark in racing and originally relied on engineer Merosi, who had been with ALFA since the company had first been reorganised independently of Darracq in 1909, and had been responsible for the very successful series of RL and RM push-rod ohv touring and sports cars.

Merosi had designed the P1 six-cylinder twin overhead camshaft cars complying with the requirements of the GP formula that was in force between 1922 and 1925. The P1 Alfa Romeo had an in-line six-cylinder twin overhead camshaft engine developing an uncompetitive 115bhp. Three of these cars were entered in the 1923 Italian GP, but Ugo Sivocci crashed in practice with fatal results, and the cars were withdrawn. Apart from this tragedy, they were unlikely to prove race-winners. They were never entered in another race, and were broken up.

Jano may have had no engineering qualifications, but he was to prove to be one of the greatest designers in the history of motor sport. It was almost an act of desperation by Alfa Romeo that led to the poaching of Jano. First, Enzo Ferrari visited him with the Alfa Romeo proposal, but – not surprisingly – he did not trust Ferrari, and told him that he would be willing to entertain a serious proposal from someone in authority at Alfa Romeo. A second visit was paid by Eduardo Fucito, who was a vice-president.

In designing the Alfa Romeo P2, Jano in effect built a straight-eight Fiat 805 with substantial improvements, notably much stronger, but no less flexible valve springs, the engine built up in two blocks of four cylinders (the 405 had four blocks of two cylinders), and the camshafts driven by spur gears. These cars were immensely successful, despite Antonio Ascari's fatal crash in the 1925 French GP. Once he had designed the P2, Jano laid down the series of six-cylinder sports cars, in single and twin cam forms, with engine capacity ranging from 1487cc through to 1752cc (with a final series of 1920cc engines built as late as 1932).

The first of these cars went into production in 1927, and they set a standard for all others to imitate. Jano started the development of the eight-cylinder 8C 2300 competition sports car in 1930, and these first ran in the 1931 Mille Miglia. It was suggested by Luigi Chinetti, who was working at Alfa Romeo at this time, that Jano, in designing the 8C 2300, was strongly influenced by Émile Petit's straight-eight Salmson design. Later, Jano adopted a supercharger for each cylinder block, as Petit

Below: *Vittorio Jano, the 'genius in overalls', is seen during his days at Alfa Romeo standing in front of a P2 GP car. Giulio Ramponi is on the extreme right of the photograph.* (Guy Griffiths Collection)

had done with the Salmson. (See page 78 of *The Alfa Romeo Tradition* by Griffith Borgeson.)

During the 1930s, Alfa Romeo produced a brilliant range of racing cars. After the 1931 Tipo A, powered by two 1752cc engines (mounted side-by-side, but with separate crankcases), the Monoposto followed in 1932 and was raced by the works until 1935. In 1934 Ugo Gobbato, Alfa Romeo's new managing director, reduced Jano's role from being chief engineer of all Alfa Romeo divisions, to the automotive division alone.

The first Monoposto-derived sports car, the Tipo 2900A, was built in small number from 1934, and Jano's first V12 GP cars appeared in 1936. There were times Nuvolari and the other Scuderia Ferrari drivers turned in magnificent performances and humbled the German teams, but these were infrequent – increasingly so from 1936 onwards.

Jano faced the impossible task of trying to defeat the German teams on a very limited budget, and he was also, as others at the Alfa Romeo factory commented, 'a squeezed lemon'. As Borgeson quite rightly points out:

'He achieved fine things in the future, but he did not achieve them essentially alone, as in the past.'

Jano left Alfa Romeo in the latter part of 1937, but as the door at Portello closed, another at Turin opened for him.

Lancia was a highly innovative company, and Vincenzo Lancia had shown great technical leadership. He had died in late 1936 and left a tremendous void at the company he had founded. The Lancia company offered Jano a directorship, and he would be in charge of the experimental department. The position suited Jano especially well, as it meant that he could return to live in his home town of Turin after an absence of 13 years.

Jano's early work at Lancia was on improvements to the existing V4 Aprilia, and finalisation of the specification of the 903cc Ardea that entered production in 1939. Jano's major achievement in his early years with Lancia was the development of the V6 engine. This layout had previously been ignored because of theoretical balancing problems, but Jano and his assistant, Francesco de Virgilio, resolved these, and the V6 1754cc Aurelia B10 that entered production in 1950 proved to be an engine of impeccable smoothness and balance.

The ultimate heir of the Lancia company was Giovanni (Gianni) Lancia, Vincenzo's son born in Turin on 16 November 1924. The Lancia family held 90 per cent of the shares in the company, and when Gianni became general manager in 1948, only they could have put a ban on his excesses. The company was solvent, free of bankers' restraints and interference, and the managing director, Panagadi, had no real influence.

Lancia was essentially an old-fashioned company with outdated production methods, and it needed capital investment to modernise production (thereby improving the profit margin on each car), and to increase production. It also desperately needed new models, especially a small family car, to supersede the existing delightful, but rather staid range. What happened was that Gianni was lured by motor racing, and started the competition activities in a very modest way.

The company achieved remarkable successes with the 1991cc B20 GT version of the Aurelia, and then embarked on a very expensive racing programme that, together with the cost of erecting a tower office block straddling the Via Vincenzo Lancia in Turin, brought the company to insolvency. Gianni's motor sport ambitions for Lancia were, of course, stoked by having the services of one of the greatest Italian automobile engineers of all time. Automobile experts in Italy looked aghast at the company's spiralling costs and diminishing sales, and concluded that Lancia's downfall was inevitable.

First of the new cars was the D20, a four overhead camshaft 2.9-litre V6 coupé designed and developed by Jano and his assistants, principally Ettore Zaccone, who was responsible for engine design. The model made its debut in the 1953 Mille Miglia, and Bonetto finished third overall. Lancia developed open 3.3-litre versions, and they had an excellent power to weight ratio and superb handling. Although these cars failed because of minor problems in the first Nürburgring 1,000km race at the end of August, the team had a good run of success in minor Italian events, and in November 1953 took the first three places in the Carrera Panamericana Mexico.

Jano was working hard on a new Formula 1 car, together with his assistants, Zaccone (engine) and Falco (chassis). The new car, typed the D50, was powered by a 90° V8, with the engine forming a stressed member with the chassis (a concept reinvented by Colin Chapman 13 years later) and angled in the frame to give a low seating position. Gianni Lancia succeeded in obtaining the services of Alberto Ascari and Luigi Villoresi who had been with Ferrari for the last five years.

Development of the new car was slow, and it did not appear until the Spanish GP in 1954. In the meantime, the team continued to race the latest version of the competition sports car, the 3.3-litre D24. Although, as explained elsewhere, the Mille Miglia was excluded from Ascari's contract, he drove in the race in place of Villoresi and scored an outstanding win. Overall, however, save in Italian events, the sports Lancias had a poor year, and the GP cars failed on their debut at Barcelona. The team then withdrew from sports car racing to concentrate on Formula 1.

During the early part of 1955, the Lancia D50s had mixed fortunes. After failing in Argentina, the team had a good run of successes in minor events, with Ascari winning at Turin, Castellotti finishing second at Pau, and Ascari winning at Naples. At Monaco the Mercedes-Benz entries failed, and Ascari had just taken the lead when the brakes locked at the chicane and he plunged into Monte Carlo harbour. He was rescued – apparently unhurt – and Castellotti with his D50 finished second behind Trintignant (Ferrari). Only a few days later Ascari was killed when his Ferrari rolled in practice at Monza.

By this time, Lancia was hopelessly insolvent and at least had a vaguely face-saving reason for withdrawing from racing. Castellotti was at the wheel of the sole Lancia that started in the Belgian race, but retired because of gearbox problems after an impressive drive. The Lancia company was taken over by the Presenti family, who controlled the giant Italcimenti Corporation, for little more than its debts. The entire team D50 cars and parts, together with the team's transporter, were handed over to Ferrari, and the racing staff joined Ferrari.

At Maranello, Jano acted as consultant, and his main achievement was to introduce Ferrari to the practicalities of the V6 engine. Enzo Ferrari called the V6 engines 'Dino' in memory of his son, who died in 1956, and always promoted the notion that Dino was responsible for the concept. Jano was kind and generous, and there is no doubt that he discussed the V6 layout with the very sick young man, but that is as far as it went. For a few years Jano travelled to Maranello when his services were required, but he attended less with the passing of the years. He became very depressed with the death of his own son. He, too, became seriously ill, and he committed suicide in 1965.

Johansson, Stefan

Works driver
Born: 8 September 1956 (Växjö, Sweden)

Lively, full of good humour, and from a family already steeped in motor racing (his father raced Mini Coopers), Stefan Nils Edwin Johansson came close to reaching the very top of the motor racing tree, but although he had great opportunities with two leading teams, it never quite worked out and he slipped back into mediocrity. Stefan raced karts in Sweden, and in 1976 moved on to European Championship F3 where

Above: *Swedish driver Stefan Johansson is seen here shortly after he was brought into the Ferrari team to replace Arnoux. He joined Ferrari at a time when its fortunes were at a very low ebb, and struggled against the odds for two seasons before the team dispensed with his services.* (LAT Photographic)

his driving proved very fast and very wild, and an element of relief was felt when his money ran out.

In 1979 he campaigned in the British F3 Championship, starting with a Chevron, but his year did not take off until he switched to a March chassis. In 1980 the Shadow team, which was in its last painful throes, offered him a drive. It was all too soon, driving dud cars for a team whose hopes had long evaporated into the ether, and after Stefan failed to qualify at Buenos Aires and Interlagos, he and Shadow parted company, leaving the Swedish driver with a damaged reputation. Motor racing ambition has destroyed many a good man. For the record it needs to be said that Teddy Yip bought into the Shadow team during the year, quickly realised his mistake, and by the French GP wound it up.

Stefan overcame this embarrassment, returned to F3 with the Project Four team and won the 1980 Vandervell F3 Championship after a season-long battle with Kenny Acheson. He was invited to join the Toleman team in F2, and after a good year with this developing outfit, he moved back to F1 in 1983 with Spirit-Honda. The team was very much in the learning curve, the cars were a long way from being fully sorted, and although he did not achieve much, it seemed that driver and team were building a good future. But Honda cancelled their engine contract at the end of 1983 and thereafter they were engine suppliers to Williams alone.

Spirit stayed in business by switching to the Hart turbocharged engine and selling the drive, which was bought for Mauro Baldi by his sponsor. Johansson decided to drive anything anywhere and, although it sounded like a bad idea, it worked. Martin Brundle crashed the works Tyrrell during practice at Dallas, and Stefan was offered his place in the team. At this time

Below: *Johansson was enthusiastic and full of determination, even when the odds were stacked high against him. He is seen here with Ferrari engineer Dr Harvey Postlethwaite, third from left.* (LAT Photographic)

Tyrrell was in dispute with FISA over allegations of illegal additions to the fuel. The team was allowed to race until its appeal against suspension and forfeiture of points was heard. After four races the Tyrrell appeal was heard and dismissed, and Stefan was on the street once more.

GP racing was going through a very odd period. The Toleman team had suspended Ayrton Senna for signing up – allegedly in breach of contract – with Lotus for 1985. So, another drive fell into Stefan's lap, and his appearances for Toleman in the last three races in the season netted for him a fourth place, two laps in arrears in the Italian GP. Johansson signed up for Toleman for 1985, but the team now had no tyre supplies. Their supplier, Michelin, had withdrawn from racing, Goodyear would not take on any more teams, and Pirelli would not help Toleman because of open criticisms by this team in the past.

In the first race of 1985, Stefan drove for Tyrrell, and after this, the Brazilian GP, Arnoux had parted company with Ferrari. Johansson was summoned to Maranello for an interview with Enzo Ferrari. The 'Old Man' was pretty senile by this stage, and if it is true that he asked the Swede, 'Are you a fighter?', he must have read the words off a piece of paper. Stefan is said to have replied, 'I've had to fight for everything I've had.' Again, if it were true, which is very improbable, it would have been a lie!

Stefan's task at Ferrari was to back up Michele Alboreto in his bid to win the Drivers' Championship. Sadly, the Ferrari Tipo 156/85s were pretty mediocre cars, and the team was in decline. In the Championship the winner was Prost (McLaren), but Alboreto pushed hard until Ferrari reliability worsened and he took second place. Stefan finished seventh with a car that he considered felt 'nervous', and his best performances were second places at Canada and Detroit.

Ferrari signed the Swedish driver again for 1986, and although he finished fifth in the Championship, the Ferraris were again unreliable and Stefan's best performances were third places at Spa, the Hungaroring, Austria, Monza, and Adelaide. His contract was not renewed for 1987, but he was lucky enough to obtain a drive at McLaren alongside Prost. Overall Stefan drove adequately, but he was often too slow in qualifying and this left him having to fight his way up too many places during the race. In any event, McLaren saw Prost and Senna as their dream ticket for 1988, and once again Stefan was out in the cold.

He drove for Ligier in 1988 (no points!) and Onyx from the start of 1989 through to 1990, but the team dumped him in favour of Gregor Foitek after two races of 1990 because the Swiss newcomer could pay for his seat. It may have been some consolation that it was not long before Onyx succumbed to financial collapse.

There were no more F1 races for Stefan in 1990, and his F1 career came to halt in 1991 after two races for AGS (in both he failed to qualify) and four for Footwork (a retirement and three failures to qualify).

In 1992 he joined Tony Bettenhausen's small Indy Team and he stayed with them until 1996 without achieving much. In 1997 he had two significant successes, co-driving the winning Ferrari Tipo 333SP in the Sebring 12 Hours race and the winning Jöst Racing Porsche WSC95 at Le Mans. He has continued racing from time to time, and runs several successful businesses. Someone has turned up the statistic that he is the F1 driver who has gained the most podium finishes without winning a race.

Klass, 'Bobby'

Works driver
Born: 25 January 1936 (Stuttgart, Germany)
Died: 22 July 1967 (Mugello, Italy)

Günther 'Bobby' Klass was the son of a wealthy industrialist, and he proved to be a very successful businessman himself. He married at the age of 19 and built up his own commercial empire consisting of a chain of launderettes, a night club, and a wholesale business. He first competed in 1961, moving on to his first Porsche in 1952, running initially in rallies and then taking up circuit racing. He joined the works Porsche team in 1965 and his limited successes included fifth place with Antonio Pucci in the Targa Florio and sixth with Peter Nöcker at Nürburgring.

Little success came Klass's way in 1966, although he drove Ferrari, Ford GT40, and Porsche cars for Scuderia Filipinetti. Ferrari saw that Klass would be a very suitable driver to assist in the Dino Sports Prototype programme, so he was asked to join Maranello for 1967. He made few race appearances for Ferrari; co-driving with Jonathan Williams, he retired his Dino because of overheating at Monza, and he crashed the Dino that he was sharing with private entrant Mario Casoni in the Targa Florio.

At Le Mans he was partnered with Peter Sutcliffe, and they worked their way up to fourth place, but their P4 was eliminated because of the failure of a badly cut gear driving the camshafts in the 18th hour. Klass was due to drive a 2-litre Dino in the Circuit of Mugello, but during practice he crashed into a tree on a very difficult winding section of the course and was killed. By this time he was divorced, and he left an 11-year-old son.

Above: *Klass had joined Ferrari for 1967, and development testing of the Dino was part of his duties. Sadly, he was killed in practice for the 1967 Circuit of Mugello, and his death was one of the reasons why Maranello abandoned development of these delightful challengers to Porsche in the 2-litre class.* (Porsche-Werkfoto)

Lampredi, Aurelio

Technical Director
Born: 16 June 1917 (Livorno, Italy)
Died: 1 June 1989 (Livorno)

In pre-Second World War days Lampredi worked in the military shipyards at Livorno, but then joined Piaggio, which was primarily engaged in aircraft manufacture. He then moved to Reggiane, aircraft manufacturers, during the war years and worked on a number of advance projects, including an inverted 18-cylinder engine of W configuration, with direct fuel injection and three-stage supercharging. After the Second World War there was no future in aero-engine development in Italy.

Lampredi joined Ferrari in September 1946 and worked as a junior design engineer under Colombo's supervision. He was unhappy with this situation at Maranello and left for Isotta Fraschini early in 1947. By the end of 1947 Ferrari had persuaded Lampredi to return to Maranello. Colombo

Above: *During his years with Ferrari, Technical Director Aurelio Lampredi carried out development work of considerable importance, especially his redesign of the Colombo V12 engine, and the introduction of a four-cylinder design built in many forms between 1951 and 1956. This photograph was taken at the 1954 Syracuse GP, and Lampredi is seen in the cockpit of a Tipo 625, warming up the engine.* (Author's collection)

had developed for Ferrari a V12 engine based on pre-war Alfa Romeo designs that originated with Vittorio Jano. The first Ferrari V12 had a capacity of 1498cc, and later original Colombo versions were increased in size to an ultimate 2715cc. The 1498cc engine, in supercharged form, powered the first GP Ferraris of 1948 onwards.

Colombo was increasingly a consultant who spent less and less time at the Ferrari factory, and left altogether in 1949. Much of Lampredi's energies had been directed at development of Colombo's V12 design. It was used in Ferraris in improved form for many years, but Lampredi urged Ferrari that the way forward in F1 was to build an unsupercharged 4.5-litre engine. This necessitated redesigning the V12 engine in what became known as the 'long-block' form with greater overall length to permit adequate spacing of the increased cylinder bores. In 1951 Ferraris powered by this engine in both single and twin-plug forms finally defeated the Alfa Romeos that dominated post-war GP racing.

The 1500cc supercharged/4500cc unsupercharged GP formula remained in force until the end of 1953, but following the withdrawal of Alfa Romeo from racing, it

was obvious that there was no marque that could offer a threat to Ferrari supremacy. Accordingly, World Championship races in 1952–3 were held to Formula 2 2000cc unsupercharged rules. Racing was still dominated by Ferrari, and Alberto Ascari won the Drivers' Championship both years with Ferrari Tipo 500 four-cylinder cars designed by Lampredi, with excellent torque at low rpm and the advanced feature of the four-speed gearbox mounted at the rear in unit with the final drive.

Lampredi developed sports cars with the four-cylinder engine in both 2-litre and 3-litre forms. In 3-litre form these cars were known as the 'Monza', and the handling was especially difficult. Although Lampredi was a very successful engineer, he had no personal racing experience or experience with very fast cars, and the biggest weakness of the design was its difficult handling when in the hands of drivers of limited ability. In all, there were 39 3-litre Monza and 2-litre Mondial/Testa Rossa cars (the last-named so called because the cam covers were painted red). Of the 39, 33 cars crashed and 17 drivers were killed.

For 1954 onwards there was a new F1 with a capacity limit of 2500cc, and Ferrari raced 2.5-litre versions of the four-cylinder cars. In the first season, the racing was closely fought and the Ferraris, Maseratis and the new straight-eight Mercedes-Benz W196 cars were all very competitive, but the Germans had the edge because of the superior driving of Juan Fangio. Ferrari won two of the year's Championship races, González in the British event at Silverstone and Hawthorn in the Spanish race held on the Pedralbes street circuit in Barcelona. Mercedes-Benz almost completely dominated F1, and it was obvious that Ferrari had fallen out of serious contention.

The four-cylinder GP cars were no longer competitive, and a six-cylinder version was still on the drawing board. Lampredi had persuaded Ferrari that a twin-cylinder car was needed for the tortuous Monaco street circuit, because it would have excellent low-speed torque and acceleration. It would also have very swift throttle response. The result was the Tipo 116F with in-line engine of 2493cc (118 x 114mm) with four valves per cylinder and developing a very modest 174bhp at 4,800rpm. The apocryphal story is that it vibrated so badly that it rang the bells in the tower of the Maranello parish church. The six-cylinder sports cars designed by Lampredi for the 1955 World Sports Car Championship were underdeveloped and unreliable.

After his early successes, nothing that Lampredi did was right. Ferrari was anxious to terminate Lampredi's services, and the opportunity came when the Lancia company withdrew from racing. The D50 GP cars were given to

Ferrari, the Lancia technical personnel came with the cars, and Fiat offered to sponsor Ferrari. In addition, as part of the deal, Fiat offered a job to Lampredi at their Turin factory where he designed a very successful range of single and twin overhead cam engines. In addition, Lampredi was also manager of Fiat's Abarth subsidiary between 1973 and his retirement in 1982.

Landi, 'Chico'

Brazilian private F1 driver
Born: 14 July 1907 (Sao Paulo, Brazil)
Died: 7 June 1989 (Sao Paulo)

Francisco Sacco 'Chico' Landi raced in Brazil and achieved a good measure of success. He first came to Europe in 1948 and he raced in the Bari GP, a 202-mile (325km) race for F2 cars (known at the time as Formula B) and, at the wheel of a Tipo 166 Ferrari, won the race from Bonetto and Varzi, both of whom were driving 1100cc Cisitalias. He was entered by the works Ferrari team in the 1951 Italian GP. In practice he drove the prototype Tipo 625 2.5-litre car, but it was decided that he should handle a single-plug V12 4.5-litre car in the race, and he retired this because of mechanical problems.

Early in 1952, he raced a supercharged V12 2-litre Ferrari in South America, finishing fifth at Sao Paulo, second in both Rio de Janeiro races on the Gavea and Boavista circuits. There were two races at Buenos Aires in March,

Above: Landi is seen here at the wheel of his Tipo 375 Ferrari in the Formule Libre race at the British GP meeting at Silverstone in July 1952. The race was won by Piero Taruffi with Tony Vandervell's Ferrari Thin Wall Special from Luigi Villoresi, but Landi drove a good race to finish third. (Guy Griffiths)

and in both of these Landi finished third with the Tipo 166; Fangio won both races, with González second in the first of these and Menditeguy second in the second race.

Landi bought a Tipo 375 from the factory (it could well have been the car that he raced at Monza) and he ran this in the two Piriapolis GPs in Uruguay in May (Piriapolis is on the Atlantic coastline to the east of the capital Montevideo); he finished second to Fangio in the first, and retired in the second.

Then Landi came back to Europe and raced the 375 in a few races. All World Championship races in 1952–3 were held to F2 (2000cc unsupercharged) rules, but there were still a few races to the old F1 4500cc unsupercharged/1500cc supercharged rules. One of these was the Albi GP, and Landi finished second to Rosier after the V16 BRMs ran into problems.

Later, Landi, with the Tipo 375, finished third in the Formule Libre race at Silverstone in July 1952, and second at Boreham at the beginning of August. Landi was also a member of the Brazilian Escuderia Bandeirantes, which raced a team of beige-painted A6GCM F2 Maseratis in a few races in Europe without success in 1952. As late as 1956, he drove a works Maserati 250F in the Argentine GP. Italian Gerino Gerini shared the driving, and they took fourth place.

Larini, Nicola

Test driver
Born: 19 March 1964 (Lido di Camaiore, Tuscany, Italy)

Larini's racing career developed in a rocket-like manner. His ascent to F1 was rapid and his decline to touring car events almost as swift. After driving in Formula Italia in 1983 and Formula Abarth and F3 in 1984, Larini joined the Coloni team for 1985. In 1986 he won the Italian F3 Championship for Coloni with a Nova-Alfa Romeo-powered Dallara, and he drove for this team in a couple of F3000 races in 1986. The same year he drove in F1 for Coloni in the Spanish GP (failed to qualify) and the Italian GP (retired).

In 1988–9 he raced for Osella, very much at the bottom of the pile and struggling to pre-qualify. Against

Below: *Nicola Larini was a very talented Italian driver, who raced in F1 for Coloni, Osella, Ligier, and the Modena team, before becoming a Ferrari test driver to participate in the development of their active suspension system. He never fulfilled the promise expected, but later achieved very good results in touring car racing.* (LAT Photographic)

the odds, Larini often showed tremendous promise, working his way up to a good place only to retire because of his car's mechanical frailty. In the 16 races in 1989, Larini failed to pre-qualify seven times, retired seven times, was excluded once because the team missed the weight check, and disqualified once for starting from the wrong grid position.

For 1990, Larini joined Ligier, and a miserable, unsuccessful season ensued. In 1991 he drove for the Modena team running Lamborghinis and failing to qualify/ pre-qualify (ten races), and with one reasonable finish, seventh at Phoenix. In touring car racing his stock was rising, for he won the 1992 Italian Touring Car Championship for Alfa Romeo, and he moved with Alfa Romeo into the more prestigious German Championship.

In F1 he had a short-lived lucky break. Ferrari gave him a testing contract in 1992 to develop their active suspension. At the end of the year he was brought into the team for two races. He started from the back of the grid because of technical problems, was left behind at the start, but finished 12th in Japan and 11th in Australia. Larini had done what was required, to test the traction control under race conditions, and his testing contract continued. He was given another chance by Ferrari in 1994 when Alesi was unable to drive because of a back injury sustained during testing.

In the Pacific GP, where he qualified seventh, he and Senna were both pushed off the track at the first corner by Häkkinen. With a complete change of fortune, Larini drove a brilliant race to finish second just under a minute behind Schumacher (Benetton) at Imola. He continued to race Alfa Romeos, and do some testing for Ferrari, and this led to a place in the Sauber Petronas team who were using Ferrari engines bearing the Petronas name. From day one, it all went badly wrong, and Larini survived only five races before the arguments and disputes proved too much. He returned to racing Alfa Romeo touring cars, but later raced Chevrolets.

Lauda, Niki

Works driver
Born: 22 February 1949 (Vienna, Austria)

Andreas Nikolaus 'Niki' Lauda, or 'The Rat' as he was known at one time because of his protruding teeth, was one of the hardest-pushing drivers both on and off track. He struggled in F3 during his first couple of seasons in racing, and also tried, but again struggled

Above: *A very youthful Lauda is seen here at the 1975 Belgian GP. Lauda won his first Drivers' World Championship with 64½ points to the 45 of Emerson Fittipaldi (McLaren).* (LAT Photographic)

with, a Porsche 908. He was a man of the most incredible determination who succeeded in becoming a champion in the face of his own shortcomings as a racing driver. He obtained a works drive with March by paying for it with a cheque on the bank of which his grandfather was a director.

When a driver buys a seat with a F1 team (rather rare these days but very common 30 years ago) it is like a second or third marriage, a triumph of optimism over experience. The entrant expects nothing and hopes for cleared cheques, while the driver also expects nothing, but hopes for the world. In 1972 Lauda drove for March alongside Ronnie Peterson, and that year's 712X car was a notorious disaster. He achieved some success with March F2 cars, but March was an unsavoury company, and when they dumped him at the end of the year he was not surprised.

Lauda bought a seat with the BRM team, who had doubts as to whether he could meet the monthly payments. He held third place at Monaco before his gearbox broke, and he finished fifth in the Belgian race at Zolder. BRM was faring badly, but still had Marlboro money, and Lauda bailed himself out of his difficulties by signing a three-year contract with the team. He was not aware that he was being stalked by Ferrari, who wanted a young man who would work closely with the team and stay with them through thick and thin (or at least until they discarded him).

In addition, Lauda had his own ideas about his future in motor racing, and he wanted to be with a team that placed a major emphasis on development and testing. Luca di Montezemolo, who had been brought in to rebuild the Ferrari team to its former glories, gave Lauda what he wanted. No one expected miracles of Lauda, but even in his first year with the team he came close to achieving them. The latest version of the 312B3 Ferrari was a much-improved car, and it improved further as the season progressed. Despite the debacle at Brands Hatch (see Appendix 5), Lauda finished fourth in the 1974 Drivers' Championship.

The following year, driving the latest 312T cars, Lauda won the Monaco, Belgian, Swedish, French, and Watkins Glen races and took the Drivers' Championship with 64½ points to the 45 of Fittipaldi (McLaren). Lauda stayed with Ferrari in 1976, and early in the season it seemed likely that he would repeat his win in the Championship. With the 1975 312T car, he won the first two races at Interlagos and Kyalami. By the Zolder race, the Ferrari drivers were driving the latest 312T2 cars, and with these Lauda won at Zolder and Monaco.

Disaster struck at the Nürburgring, and Lauda came close to death after setting second fastest time in practice to James Hunt (McLaren). The race started in depressingly gloomy and misty conditions on a wet track. On the first lap, most of the drivers found that the circuit was drying out rapidly and many – among them Lauda – stopped to change to slicks at the end of the lap. Lauda rushed off to make up lost ground. As he went flat-out into the left kink before the right-hand Bergwerk, the Ferrari twitched suddenly and violently. It slid to the right, then the slide snapped back, and the tail slid to the left.

The Ferrari charged through the catch-fencing on the right of the circuit, cannoned into a rocky outcrop behind the fencing and started to burn furiously as the fuel cell and deformable structure on the left side of the car were torn off. The Ferrari ricocheted off the catch-fencing, and the whiplash was so bad that Lauda's helmet was torn off and a cheekbone fractured.

On a circuit that was flooded with burning fuel, American driver Brett Lunger, who was unable to avoid hitting the Ferrari with his Surtees, together with other drivers and a marshal dashed into the flames and rescued Lauda. After he was rescued, Lauda was able to stand and staggered to the edge of the circuit where he collapsed.

When Lauda was examined in hospital, it was ascertained that he had inhaled toxic fumes from the Ferrari's burning glass-fibre body panels. He was so very close to death for several days, but then he started a remarkable recovery, accelerated, it is said, by the mental terror of being administered the last rites by a German Catholic priest. Lauda worked hard at recovering his fitness, and at ensuring that he fulfilled his promise to Enzo Ferrari to be ready to race again at the Italian GP at Monza on 12 September. The precise cause of this terrible accident was never ascertained.

James Hunt (McLaren) had been accruing points in his bid to win the World Championship. At the start of the Japanese race, Lauda still led with 68 points to the 65 of the British driver. The Japanese race at Mount Fuji was another race that started in gloomy, wet, misty conditions. After two laps, Lauda pulled out of the race, but Hunt led until a tyre punctured on a drying track and, after a stop to fit new tyres, he resumed the race to finish third and take the Championship by one point. This whole episode was not motor racing at its best, but certainly at its most dramatic.

After withdrawing from the Japanese GP, Lauda said of himself:

'All right, so I made a mistake by stopping in the rain. OK, so I lost the Championship. But I stand by what I did, even though I was wrong. Some people called me a great driver who knew all the answers. They were wrong, as well! It is complete rubbish to talk like that because I didn't know everything, but I knew myself!

I always forced myself to be honest with my conscience. When I look back on Japan, I still think that I made the right choice. I think that the conditions were so appalling that we were all mad to be out there. But just think again. Suppose that the situation had turned out differently and somebody had been killed. If I'd pulled out as I did and kept my title, then everyone would have been jumping around saying, 'Lauda's fantastic, he's a genius, a wonderful technician.' But that, of course, would have been nonsense as well.'

In 1977 Lauda was partnered at Ferrari by Reutemann, and it seems that he did not rate the Argentinian very highly. The Ferrari 312T2s were still very competitive and, after a poor start to the year, Lauda won at Kyalami, finished second at Long Beach, withdrew from the Spanish race (see Appendix 5) and then took second place at Monaco, won in Sweden, finished second in the British race at Brands Hatch, and third at Zandvoort.

The Austrian had made it clear that he would be leaving Ferrari at the end of 1977 to join Brabham. Lauda later commented:

Above: *Niki Lauda shows the scars from his near-fatal accident at the Nürburgring in 1976. This photograph was taken in 1984 after Lauda had returned from retirement to drive for McLaren.* (LAT Photographic)

'The magic had gone out of my relationship with Ferrari. I felt that I had put an enormous effort into winning races and championships, but their attitude had changed. First, they wanted to run a third car for Cheever in the planned non-Championship race at Imola in September, a critical moment in the Championship.

After that, they told me that they would be running a third car for Villeneuve in North America. That was absurd, because they made their decision before we had won the Championship, and I was aware that the decision might seriously jeopardise our chance of doing so.'

Lauda was able to finish second at Monza, while Reutemann retired. The Austrian had been dissatisfied by racing manager Nosetto's inability to clarify what would be team orders if Reutemann were ahead of him in the closing laps at Monza – common sense dictated that Reutemann, who had no chance of winning the

Opposite: *Niki Lauda is seen here at the wheel of his 312T2 Ferrari at the 1976 British Grand Prix in which he finished second to Hunt after a restart following a first-lap accident. Crouched alongside the car is his personal mechanic, Ermanno Cuoghi.* (LAT Photographic)

Championship, should allow Lauda to go ahead. Niki needed every point that he could get to clinch the World Championship.

The next race was the United States GP at Watkins Glen on 2 October. Lauda's fourth place in the wet gave him a total of 72 points and his second win in the World Championship because he was unbeatable by the next two (Andretti who had 47 points and gained no more) and Scheckter (Wolf) who won in Canada and finished the year in second place in the Championship with 55 points. Lauda now sent a telegram to Enzo Ferrari, thanking him for his help in winning the Championship for the second time.

He expressed his regrets, however, that his ill-health prevented him from driving Ferraris in the last two races of the year, Canada and Japan. It matched the 'Old Man' for arrogance and was well deserved. Niki stayed with Brabham for two years, winning two races in 1978 and finishing fourth in the Championship that year. In 1979 the Brabham team was hopelessly unsuccessful, and after driving the Ford-powered BT49 in practice for the Canadian race he made the on-the-spot decision to retire from racing.

Lauda spent the next two years building up his airline business, and then returned to F1 in 1982 driving for McLaren. The team badly needed experience and someone who would dedicate themselves to testing and development. Lauda was their man and he stayed with the team for four seasons, during which he won eight races, and in 1984 won his third World Championship. After retiring from racing, Lauda acted as adviser to Jaguar, and also to Ferrari on a relatively informal basis.

There is a postscript to the story of Lauda's relationship with Ferrari and this relates to his mechanic Ermanno Cuoghi. Cuoghi had been head mechanic at John Wyer's Gulf-Porsche team, but he joined Ferrari as joint head mechanic in 1972 and, after Lauda joined Ferrari, it was agreed that Cuoghi would be employed by Ferrari as the mechanic responsible for Lauda's car. After Lauda had informed Ferrari that he would be leaving to drive for Brabham in 1978, Cuoghi indicated that he too would be leaving to work with Lauda at Brabham.

Ferrari's reaction was one of those exceptionally unpleasant, vicious responses that have always marred the image of the 'Old Man' with the general public. At the Watkins Glen race, the racing manager Nosetto fired Cuoghi, thereby leaving him alone and without sufficient funds to return home. After the Watkins Glen race, Lauda took the winner's rostrum because his fourth place had clinched his World Championship. As a pointed gesture aimed at Ferrari, he made Cuoghi, who had been sacked the previous evening, join him on the rostrum.

Above: *Lewis-Evans was a natural in 500cc racing, helped by his father, Lewis ('Pop') Lewis-Evans, who backed his motor racing ambitions to the hilt, and his slim, light figure was a great advantage in this class of racing. He is seen here in the paddock at Castle Combe in Wiltshire in 1952 when he was racing a Cooper-Norton. (Guy Griffiths Collection)*

Lewis-Evans, Stuart

Works sports car driver
Born: 20 April 1930 (Luton, Bedfordshire, England)
Died: 25 October 1958 (East Grinstead, Sussex, England)

Stuart Nigel Lewis-Evans was one of those drivers whom Ferrari let slip from his grasp. His father, Lewis ('Pop') Lewis-Evans was a stalwart of British Formula 3 racing, and Stuart joined him in this category in 1951, racing a Cooper-Norton. Physically, he was very slight, he seemed to lack stamina, and he suffered from stomach ulcers – but in some ways he was very tough and he was very determined.

He was offered a drive by Connaught at Brands Hatch in October 1956, and appeared for the team in 1957 before it withdrew after the Monaco race. He won the Richmond Trophy at Goodwood on Easter Monday, held third place at Naples before retiring because of mechanical failure, and took fourth place at Monaco.

Ferrari was sufficiently impressed to offer Lewis-Evans a drive at Le Mans that year, and he and Severi brought their Tipo 290 home in fifth place behind four D-type Jaguars. Stuart turned up for the French GP at Rouen, expecting a drive with Ferrari, but there was no car for him. So Tony Vandervell, short of drivers, snapped him up on a temporary basis, and after he had led in the French race and finished third in the Reims GP, he became a permanent member of the Vanwall team.

Lewis-Evans was consistent and brave, achieving modest success in both 1957 and 1958. It all went wrong when the engine of his Vanwall seized in the last race of the Moroccan GP; he collided with a tree and suffered terrible burns. He was flown back to England for treatment, but he died in the burns unit at the East Grinstead Hospital six days after the race.

Above: *A journalist by profession, Franco Lini acted as racing manager for Ferrari in one year only, 1967, following the departure of Eugenio Dragoni.* (**LAT Photographic**)

Lini, Franco

Racing Manager, journalist
Born: 1924 (Mantua, Italy)
Died: 22 July 1996

Ferrari had once previously employed a journalist, Sculati, as race manager and he lasted only a year, before being replaced because he claimed too much credit for himself. Ferrari failed to learn that lesson and appointed Lini racing manager for 1967. Lini worked in his father's machine tool business, but unsurprisingly he was happier racing bikes, writing race reports, and after a bad accident he concentrated on journalism. As a journalist he worked for *L'Équipe* and *Auto Italiano*.

Of Lini, Mauro Forghieri said:

'He was a nice person, but I have to say that controlling a racing team was not his job. He had good relations with the press, which Enzo Ferrari wanted after the Dragoni era.'

After a year, he left the team and returned to journalism. He died of lung cancer.

Lloyd, David

Test team engineer
Born: 6 April 1967 (England – further information not disclosed)

After driving in Karting and Formula Ford during his formative years, Lloyd graduated in microelectronics, computing, and instrumentation. He became an engineer in Formula Vauxhall Lotus in 1991. Between 1992 and 1996 he ran his own team in European Formula Opel, and then from 1997 to 1998 was an electronics engineer in F1 with Tyrrell. In 1999 he joined the BAR Honda F1 team as an assistant track engineer, and he was a track engineer for the same team from 2000 to 2002. From 2003 to 2006 he was test team engineer with Ferrari, and in 2007 he became the Ferrari F1 team Race Operations Manager.

Mackay-Fraser, Herbert

Driver
Born: 23 June 1927 (Connecticut, USA)
Died: 14 July 1957 (Reims circuit, France)

Sometimes, what is published about drivers, especially those from an allegedly wealthy family, is fiction to conceal an impecunious background. We cannot be absolutely certain about Mackay-Fraser, so we need to rely partially on his own account of his background. His father is said to have been a businessman with interests in Brazil, including a coffee plantation in Pernambuco in the north-east of the country.

Herbert raced in SCCA events in the United States before moving to Rio de Janeiro, presumably in connection with his father's business interests. It was there that he came across a Ferrari that was for sale. It was an early 3-litre four-cylinder Tipo 735 Sport model

Below: *Herbert Mackay-Fraser came from South America to Britain to race his 3-litre four-cylinder Ferrari. He soon made his mark in European racing and became a works Lotus driver. He was killed when he crashed a stripped Eleven sports car in the F2 Coupe de Vitesse at Reims in 1958.* (LAT Photographic)

raced by the works in 1954, with 2942cc (102 x 90mm) engine and Pinin Farina-styled body.

Mackay-Fraser brought the car to Europe and raced it at both the Boxing Day 1955 Brands Hatch meeting and the British Empire Trophy at Oulton Park in 1956. After the engine blew up, the car went back to the factory for the latest 2999.6cc (103 x 90mm) engine to be installed. He first raced the car painted red, but it was later repainted in United States white and blue racing colours.

During 1956, Mackay-Fraser co-drove Bonnier's Maserati 300S in a few races, and he was also co-driver of Ivor Bueb's Lotus Eleven with Climax FWB 1460cc engine in the 1500cc Reims 12 Hours race. The Lotus displayed tremendous speed, and led the race in its early stages, but gradually fell back because of gearbox problems that caused its eventual retirement.

For 1957, he became a regular member of Team Lotus, driving both the sports cars and the new 12 F2 car. He co-drove the class-winning 1100cc Lotus at Le Mans and was impressive in his first F1 drive with a BRM in the French GP at Rouen. He learned a great deal in practice, and was very fast in the race until he retired because of a drive-shaft joint failure.

A week later, Mackay-Fraser was dead; Lotus had entered a stripped Eleven sports car with faired-in cockpit and twin-cam FPF 1475cc engine in the F2 Coupe de Vitesse at Reims. In practice, Cliff Allison concluded that this Lotus was aerodynamically unstable and 'kept trying to take off'. As number one driver he opted to race the 12 and advised Herbert to start the race for the money and then park the Eleven up. The young American ignored the advice, lost control on the main straight on the approach to Garenne Corner and was killed.

Maglioli, Umberto

Works driver
Born: 5 June 1928 (Bioglio, Vercelli, Italy)
Died: 7 February 1999 (Monza, Italy)

Famed as a sports car driver, Maglioli had a long career with some very fine successes. His experience of the Mille Miglia road race started in 1950 when he was riding mechanic to Giovanni Bracco in a 2-litre Ferrari Tipo 166. If he could survive being a passenger to this exceedingly mad Italian, then he could survive just about anything. In 1952 Umberto drove Lancias in the

Italian National Production Car Championship, and this led to an invitation to drive for Ferrari in 1953. Early in the year, however, he drove a Lancia to a win in the Targa Florio.

Maglioli shared a Tipo 375 4.5-litre car in the Reims 12 Hours race with Piero Carini, but they were disqualified for infringements of the race regulations caused by electrical problems (turning off the headlamps before the permitted hour on the Sunday morning and receiving a push start in the pits). This was not the sort of disqualification that would have happened in Italy, and there was a near riot as Ugolini threatened to withdraw the F1 cars from the French GP later that day. It was all a Ferrari bluff, and the cars were pushed out at the last moment.

Later that year, Maglioli shared the winning 375 with Mike Hawthorn in the Pescara 12 Hours race. Maglioli and Carini, the 'cub' members of the Ferrari team, were entered in the Italian GP with the latest, but ill-handling Tipo 553 Squalo cars. Umberto brought his car across the line in eighth place. Scuderia Guastalla, run by Ferrari's Milan agent, Franco Cornacchia, entered a team of five Tipo 375 coupés in the Carrera Panamericana road race. It proved disastrous. Stagnoli crashed on the straight after a tyre burst and was killed. Maglioli's own car shed a wheel, and he took over Ricci's car to finish sixth. Mancini finished fourth with his Guastalla entry behind three works Lancias.

Maglioli drove sports cars for Ferrari regularly in 1954, but he also ran in four F1 races. The new 2500cc GP formula had started, and in the first Championship race at Buenos Aires he finished a poor ninth, and he was eighth in the Formule Libre Buenos Aires City GP a fortnight later. Umberto drove a Tipo 625 in the International Trophy race at Silverstone, but had to give the car to Trintignant for the final. He did not drive a F1 Ferrari again until the Swiss race where he finished seventh with a Tipo 553 Squalo, and in the Italian race González took over his Tipo 625 and brought it across the line third.

Umberto enjoyed a very active, if not especially successful, sports car season in 1954, and his bulky, amiable figure, with pipe in mouth, became very familiar. In January he partnered Giuseppe Farina at the wheel of a works 4.5-litre Tipo 375MM in the Buenos Aires 1,000km race, which they won from a private 3-litre Tipo 250MM driven by Schell/ de Portago. By the start of the European season, Ferrari had ready the monstrous 4954cc V12 Tipo 375 Plus cars that were so difficult to drive well. Maglioli drove and crashed these cars in both the Tour of Sicily

Above: *Maglioli was an exceptional sports car driver, and one of his best performances was in the 1955 Mille Miglia when he drove this Tipo 118 six-cylinder Ferrari into third place behind the Mercedes-Benz 300SLRs of Moss and Fangio.* (Author's collection)

and the Mille Miglia, and the example he shared with Paolo Marzotto at Le Mans retired because of mechanical problems.

He was due to race one of the new four-cylinder 3-litre Monza cars in the Tourist Trophy at Dundrod, but returned to Italy after news came through that his mother had died. Maglioli's last race in 1954 was the Carrera Panamericana Mexico in which he again drove a works Tipo 375 Plus Ferrari. He had quite a battle with Phil Hill, who won three of the eight stages, but at the finish he was around 25min on time ahead of the American.

In 1955 the Mille Miglia was dominated by the Mercedes-Benz 300SLRs which took the first two places. Ferrari was racing the hopelessly unreliable Lampredi-designed six-cylinder cars and, with a 3.7-litre Tipo 118LM version, Maglioli drove an exceptional race to finish third. At Le Mans he co-drove a 4.4-litre Tipo 121 version with Phil Hill, but they retired because of overheating, the same malady that affected the other two Ferrari team cars. He was a poor eighth, co-driving with Trintignant, at Dundrod in the Tourist Trophy, and he was eliminated in the Targa Florio in October when the Ferrari he was sharing with chief tester Sighinolfi lost a wheel.

Although Ferrari did not see Maglioli as F1 material, he shared the third-place Ferrari with Farina and Trintignant in the Argentine GP in 1955. This was the exceptionally hot race in which only two drivers, Fangio and Mieres, both Argentinians, drove through without relief. He finished at the tail of the field in the Formule Libre Buenos Aires City GP, and his only other F1 drive was with a Tipo 555 SuperSqualo at Monza in September when he finished sixth. At this point Umberto decided that he had experienced enough frustration at Ferrari, and joined Porsche for 1956 to drive sports cars only. He also drove rather decrepit 250F Maseratis in three races in 1956, and retired in all three.

Maglioli was a very real asset to the Porsche team, and he enjoyed good relations with team manager Huschke von Hanstein. His greatest success in 1956 was an outright win, driving solo, in the Targa Florio, and the following year he won his class in the final Mille Miglia. Later in 1957 he crashed very heavily during practice at the Salzburgring. This put him out of action for some while, although he appeared for Porsche in a few events in 1959. He returned to Ferrari in 1963 sharing the third-place 250P with Parkes at Le Mans that year, and he won with Parkes at the wheel of a 275P at Sebring in 1964.

Later, Maglioli drove Ford GT40s for Scuderia Filipinetti, and very occasionally he raced for Porsche. His last substantial success was a win with Vic Elford at the wheel of a Porsche 907 in the 1968 Targa Florio. It seemed that they had lost all chance of winning after a rear wheel worked loose on the first lap, and in all this cost them about 15min. Instead, they achieved an improbable victory; they both drove brilliantly, making up lost ground and benefiting from the retirement of other drivers to win by a margin of 2min 40sec from 'Nanni' Galli/Ignazio Giunti with an Alfa Romeo Tipo 33/2. Maglioli ran a specialist watchmaking business, and he died of cancer in 1999 after a long illness.

Mairesse, Willy

Works driver
Born: 1 October 1928 (Momminges, Hainault, Belgium)
Died: 2 September 1969 (Ostend, Belgium)

Mairesse's motor sport career started in 1953 when he co-drove a Porsche 356 in the Liège–Rome–Liège Rally. He rallied a Peugeot 203 in 1954–5, and in 1955 acquired a Mercedes-Benz 300SL Gullwing. Belgian Ferrari importer Jacques Swaters asked Mairesse to drive for his Écurie Francorchamps, and he appeared regularly for the team in 1957–9, although he achieved little success apart from second place, with Haldeaux, at the wheel of a Ferrari in the 1958 Reims 12 Hours race for GT cars.

For 1960, Mairesse joined the works Ferrari team on the insistence of Jacques Swaters. He drove in only three Formula 1 races, retiring twice and taking third place in the Italian GP, which was boycotted by the British teams. With Berger, he also won the Tour de France, a rally that was more like an endurance race, and at the finish they had been off the road so many times that there was hardly a panel unbent on their Ferrari 250GT SWB. Because of his hard driving he was known at the factory as the 'Tigre' (Tiger).

The following year, Mairesse made the occasional, unsuccessful Formula 1 appearance, and in one race only, the German GP, he drove for the works, but spun off. The young Belgian did rather better with sports cars in 1961, finishing second with Parkes at Le Mans in a works Ferrari, and again winning the Tour de France partnered by Berger (and it was Ferrari's sixth successive win in the events).

Ferrari's Formula 1 cars were uncompetitive in 1962, but Mairesse won the non-Championship Brussels and Naples races. He was also fourth in the Italian race, and at Spa-Francorchamps (a circuit which he knew so very well) the Belgian led briefly, but a fierce battle with Trevor Taylor (Lotus) ended in a heavy crash on the straight. The Ferrari overturned and caught fire, while the Lotus demolished a telegraph pole. Two very lucky drivers were able to stagger away from the accident largely unscathed. It seems that it was neither driver's fault, but apparently the Lotus jumped out of gear and slewed sideways into the Ferrari.

Mairesse fared rather better in sports car racing. In Sicily, driving with Gendebien and Ricardo Rodriguez, he won the Targa Florio (Ferrari 246SP), and he was second at the Nürburgring with Parkes (Ferrari 250GTO 4-litre).

Mairesse was a regular member of the Ferrari team in

1963. With Vaccarella, he drove a 250P to second place in the Sebring 12 Hours; after a spin on the last lap of the Targa Florio cost him victory with the 2-litre Ferrari that he was sharing with Scarfiotti, he rejoined the race to finish second; and then Surtees and he scored a fine victory in the Nürburgring 1,000km race. For Mairesse, disaster struck at Le Mans when he and Surtees were leading on the Sunday morning. As the 250P, with Mairesse at the wheel, swept under the Dunlop Bridge a flash of fire could be seen from the rear end.

Mairesse exited from the Esses with the car enveloped in flames – the fire had spread to the fuel tank, which had exploded. He aimed for the straw bales and jumped out, but he had suffered bad burns to his face, shoulders and right arm. Inspection of the car at the factory revealed that a poorly fitted rubber gasket had failed to seal one of the filler caps, although the cap itself fitted properly. At speed, fuel splashed on to the rear lamp switch, which started the fire.

Despite his injuries, Mairesse was back in the F1 team at the German GP at the Nürburgring. At the Flugplatz on the second lap he failed to keep the steering straight while airborne, landed with the wheels slightly askew and crashed into the ditch. Sadly, he killed a medical attendant on duty at this point and he suffered a broken arm, which put him out of racing until the end of 1964. The accident also brought an end to his career as a works driver.

In 1965 he was to have driven a BRM V8 entered by Scuderia Centro-Sud in the Belgian race at Spa, but during practice he withdrew and went off to race a saloon car elsewhere. The BRM was uncompetitive and he could not face what he saw as the humiliation of racing such a bad car. The following weekend he shared an Écurie Francorchamps Ferrari 250LM at Le Mans with

Above: *Mairesse was a very hard, difficult man, who was a superb driver and devoted his life to his motor racing career. One of the tragedies of his life was that he fully realised that his skills were great, but not the greatest, and that he would never achieve the goals at which he was aiming.* **(LAT Photographic)**

'Beurlys' (Jean Blaton), and they finished third behind two other private 250LMs after all the works Ferraris and works Fords retired.

Mairesse was a sad, embittered, but talented man who found it difficult to forge social relationships. He had started a business that was proving to have considerable potential, but he was constantly torn between facing the reality that he was now 37 with his best racing days behind him, and the romance of the racetrack. He shared a Scuderia Filipinetti-entered Porsche 906 with Herbert Müller in the 1966 Targa Florio, and they achieved a superb victory. The following year, again co-driving with 'Beurlys', he took third place with a P4, nominally entered by Écurie Francorchamps, at Le Mans.

His last major race was Le Mans in 1968 when he shared a Ford GT40, yet again with 'Beurlys', and entered by Claude Dubois. At the start of the race, Mairesse failed to close the driver's door properly; it flew open and the Belgian lost control of the car, crashing heavily into a barrier. He was two weeks in a coma and, although he came round, he never made a full recovery physically or mentally. If ever a man needed psychiatric help and support, it was Mairesse. Sick, depressed, and purposeless, he committed suicide in a hotel room in Ostend in Septermber of the following year.

Mansell, Nigel

Works driver

Born: 8 August 1953 (Baughton, Upton-upon-Severn, Worcestershire, England)

In a long racing career, much of which was spent with Lotus, Mansell earned a dreadful 'Essex man' reputation as a whinger and whiner, always moaning and

Below: *For most of his racing life, Nigel Mansell drove for Lotus, but he had two years with Ferrari in 1989–90. In his first season his performances were encouraging for a team that was in the doldrums, but when Prost joined him at Maranello in 1990 he was overshadowed and lost confidence.* (LAT Photographic)

complaining, but he simply was not like that. True, his manner and attitude were against him (and so was that awful moustache!), but so, very much, were the press. Mansell fought a steep uphill struggle to earn a drive in F1, and he first appeared in a couple of races for Lotus in 1980. He was a regular member of the Lotus team from 1981 though to 1984, and then, for 1985, he joined Williams, staying with them for four seasons.

Ferrari offered Mansell a very remunerative drive in 1989 – it was one of those occasions when they were floundering badly, and Fiat decided that the team should try to buy its way out of trouble. The real problem was the might of McLaren, and the formidable skills of its drivers Senna and Prost. Driving alongside Gerhard Berger, Mansell proved a sensation in his first race for Ferrari, and won the Brazilian GP from Prost. A series of retirements led to disqualification at Montreal where he had to start from the pits, but did so too soon.

Some good places followed – second in the French and British races, and third at Hockenheim – and Mansell scored his second win of the season in Hungary in what was described by Steve Small as 'a stunning bit of opportunism in traffic'. In Portugal, Mansell and Senna collided and the British driver was disqualified for receiving outside assistance to rejoin the race. Because of the collision he was suspended from the Spanish race a week later. He retired in both Japan and Australia and finished fourth in the Drivers' Championship.

For 1990, Alain Prost joined Ferrari from McLaren, won five races during the year, finished second in the Championship and monopolised the team's efforts. A completely overshadowed and demoralised Mansell announced his retirement, but Frank Williams persuaded him to join the Canon Williams Team. After a slow start to the season, he won five races during the year and was a very real Championship contender. He spun off in Japan because of brake problems; he was beaten by Senna into second place in Australia, and finished second in the Championship.

It all came together at long last in 1992. Driving what was undoubtedly the best car, he won nine races with Williams-Renault and took the Championship with a lead of over 50 points from team-mate Patrese in second place. Mansell pulled out of F1 in 1993 and came very close to winning the Indianapolis 500 race that year. He drove for Williams in four races in 1994, winning at Adelaide, and finally retired from racing altogether after two unhappy appearances for McLaren in 1995.

Manzon, Robert

Works driver Le Mans 1954
Born: 12 April 1917 (Marseille, France)

Manzon ran a business that distributed and sold diesel equipment. After racing his own 1100cc Cisitalia in 1947, taking wins in rather parochial French events at Angoulême and Comminges, Manzon was invited to join Amédée Gordini's Simca team during the 1948 season, and he spent most of his racing career with Gordini. He was one of the best French racing drivers in post-World War Two days and, although the Simcas (they became Gordinis for 1952) were fragile and often uncompetitive, Manzon always drove with determination and confidence.

He was lying second in the 1953 Argentine GP, a round in the Drivers' Championship, and all set to gain six points, when his Gordini lost a wheel.

The fragility and, thus, danger of Gordini cars was blatant; they were too light and, because of lack of funds, components were used well beyond their safe life. After the Argentine race there was a very Gallic argument, and Manzon left the team on its return to France.

During the rest of 1953 he drove works Lancia sports cars. For 1954, he joined Louis Rosier's private team, racing Ferrari Tipo 625 cars. When Rosier was asked to drive a works Tipo 375 Plus at Le Mans that year, Manzon was chosen as his co-driver. They were well up with the leaders, holding second or third place for many hours, but in the 15th hour they retired because of gearbox failure.

In the French GP the new Mercedes-Benz W196 cars took the first two places, and many cars retired, overstressed by their drivers' efforts to stay with the *Stromlinienwagen*, but Manzon's steady drive brought him a well-deserved third place. Reward came in the invitation from Ferrari to try a Tipo 553 Squalo in practice at the Swiss GP at Bremgarten. Manzon crashed – it seems to have been pure driver error – and the car was a write-off.

There was no second chance, and a saddened Manzon returned to Gordini for 1955. He ran in only three Championship races and retired in them all. He stayed with Gordini for 1956, and he was holding third place at Monaco when his gearbox failed, but he did achieve two morale-boosting successes. He won the non-Championship Naples GP, taking the lead after the failure of the works Ferraris, and, with a Gordini, beat Taruffi (Ferrari) into second place in the 224-mile (360km) 2-litre Pescara sports car race. Manzon retired from racing at the end of the year to concentrate on family and business, but Gordini was at the end of the road and retired from racing early in 1957.

Marinoni, Attilio

Pre-war Scuderia Ferrari and Alfa Corse driver/tester
Born: 1896
Died: 18 June 1940 (Milan, Italy)

According to some versions, Marinoni was a riding mechanic for Alfa Romeo as early as 1919. Certainly,

Below: *Previously employed by Alfa Romeo, Marinoni joined Scuderia Ferrari as chief mechanic and reserve driver in 1934. When Alfa Corse took over Scuderia Ferrari, Marinoni moved to the works team, and he was killed on 18 June 1940 in a collision with a lorry while testing an Alfa Romeo 158. (Author's collection)*

from the mid-1920s onwards he worked for the Alfa Romeo racing team. It is believed that he was head mechanic in the racing department. He occasionally drove works cars in races, and in the first Mille Miglia road race in 1927 he was at the wheel of a modified pushrod RLSS and partnered by the great Giulio Ramponi. They rose to third place behind two OMs, but retired near the finish because the exhaust pipe had sagged on to the final drive, which caused the transmission to overheat.

He drove for the works in a number of other events, and his greatest success was in the 1928 Belgian 24 Hours Touring Car GP in which he and Boris Ivanowski, a former officer of the Russian Imperial Guard, won with a supercharged 6C 1500 Alfa Romeo by a margin of 145 miles (233km) from a 4.1-litre Chrysler driven by de Vere/Mongin. The same year he finished third, partnered by Perfetti, behind Ivanowski (Alfa Romeo) and Rousseau (Salmson) in the handicap Georges Boillot Cup at Boulogne.

In 1929 Marinoni drove a 6C 1500 to seventh place in the Tourist Trophy on the Ards circuit. At Spa that year he was paired with Robert Benoist at the wheel of a 6C 1750 and, after a strong entry of Minervas had run into problems, they headed an Alfa Romeo 1–2–3. In the Mille Miglia in 1930 he acted as riding mechanic to Campari, who brought his 6C 1750 Alfa Romeo home in third place.

At Spa he co-drove in the 24 Hours race with racing motorcyclist Pietro Ghersi. Their car was a 6C 1750 Alfa Romeo, and because Ghersi had injured a knee while riding his Motor Guzzi in the Isle of Man TT races, Marinoni was forced to drive single-handed for much of the race. Marinoni won the race for the third successive year, and again Alfa Romeos took the first three places.

Later that year he partnered Kaye Don with a 6C 1500 in the Double-Twelve race at Brooklands. They led on handicap, but the timing gears stripped. Marinoni drove to the premises of the concessionaires, Alfa Romeo (British Sales) Limited, to obtain the parts needed to repair the car, drove back to Brooklands, mended the car and, after three hours, they rejoined the race. At the finish they were 16th, but at least they finished and had a good race.

The following year Marinoni again partnered Campari in the Mille Miglia, and they took second place behind Caracciola/Sebastian with their 7-litre Mercedes-Benz SSKL. After he became senior works test driver, part of Marinoni's job included demonstrating cars to prospective purchasers, and he would sometimes act as co-driver when a customer bought a competition car and wanted some back-up in racing it.

His drive in the 1932 Le Mans race was memorable for not exactly the right reasons. Early in the race he was battling with Schumann, at the wheel of another 8C 2300, when he went off the road just before Indianapolis, ploughed through the undergrowth and rejoined the race; some hours later he went into the ditch at White House and was forced to abandon his car.

From 1934 onwards he acted as reserve driver for Scuderia Ferrari and in that year's Italian GP at Monza, he took over Comotti's car, that had caught fire, and finished sixth. The following year he relieved an exhausted Dreyfus three laps from the finish of the Belgian GP and brought the Monoposto across the line in fourth place. He drove a Scuderia Ferrari Monoposto in the 1935 Italian GP, finishing an excellent fourth, albeit five laps in arrears.

In 1936 Scuderia Ferrari sent Pintacuda and Marinoni to drive 8C 2900A sports cars in the 178-mile (286km) Rio de Janeiro GP. Marinoni retired because of engine trouble on the first lap, and team-mate Pintacuda also retired because of engine problems while leading easily. Both Alfa Romeo drivers stayed in Brazil to compete in the 140-mile (225km) São Paulo GP held on public roads through a residential part of the city. Marinoni had a race full of incident; he spun twice, and the second time he stalled his engine and was unable to restart it. Pintacuda slowed right off and gave Marinoni a push-start. The Alfa Romeo drivers took the first two places.

Marinoni was increasingly taking charge of Scuderia Ferrari entries, and he managed the entries in the second Vanderbilt Cup in 1937, and in that year's Swiss GP. When Alfa Romeo was developing the Tipo 158 Alfetta, Marinoni played an important role in development testing. Alongside Severi, Sommer, and Emilio Villoresi, he drove one of these cars in the Voiturette Premio di Milan that preceded the Italian GP at Monza in 1938. He was included in the team so as to test modifications under racing conditions, and he retired shortly before the finish. This was the only race in which Marinoni drove a Tipo 158.

He tested Alfa Romeos on a regular basis, and development of the competition cars continued after Mussolini brought Italy into the Second World War on the side of the Axis on 10 June 1940. Only eight days later Marinoni was killed in a testing accident on the Como-Milano autostrada. He was driving a 158B fitted experimentally with semi-de Dion torsion bar rear suspension designed by Wifredo Ricart. The road was a two-lane main highway, and Alfa Romeo took cars out without having the road closed, as it was usually fairly quiet and free of traffic. A lorry-driver fell asleep, crossed over and hit the 158 head-on. Marinoni was killed, and the Alfa Romeo, which caught fire, was burnt out.

Martinelli, Paolo

Engineer
Born: 29 September 1952 (Modena, Italy)

From a young boy, Martinelli's ambition was to work for Ferrari, and it was quickly achieved. He studied mechanical engineering at Bologna University and graduated in 1978. He obtained employment with Ferrari immediately, and worked on the development of production car engines. In 1994 he was put in charge of F1 engine design and development. It was his decision to cease use of the traditional V12 engines and to adopt the V10 configuration that has proved so successful. On 1 November 2006 Martinelli moved to another executive engineering position in the Fiat Group, and Gilles Simon took over his position as chief competition engine designer.

Below: *Paolo Martinelli was responsible for Ferrari's adoption of the V10 engine arrangement for 1996.* **(LAT Photographic)**

Martini, Giancarlo

Driver for Scuderia Everest
Born: 16 August 1947 (Lavezzola, Italy)

Giancarlo Minardi, who later ran his own F1 Minardi team, owned a racing team called Scuderia dell Passatore, which competed in Formula Italia and was based at Faenza; their lead driver was Giancarlo Martini. After Martini had finished second in the Formula Italia Championship in 1972, and won it in 1973, Minardi changed the name of the team to Scuderia Everest, and it was financed by the Italian Everest industrial rubber-manufacturing company. For 1974, the team acquired two March-BMW 742 cars to compete in the European F2 Championship, and the drivers were Martini and Lamberto Leoni.

Enzo Ferrari had been under pressure to encourage and promote young Italian drivers, and at the beginning of 1976 he made an obsolete 312T available to Scuderia Everest. The team entered the car for Martini in the Race of Champions at Brands Hatch on 14 March, but he crashed on the warming-up lap. Despite this discouraging performance, Martini was then entered in the International Trophy race at Silverstone on 11 April. He finished tenth, and at this point Ferrari terminated the experiment.

Scuderia Everest concentrated on F2, and Martini finished seventh in that year's Championship (his best result was third at Pau) with the team's March 762-BMW. This team raced Ferrari-powered Ralts in 1977 and, in addition, Giancarlo Martini drove a French Renault-powered Martini Mk 22 for the Everest team, and thereafter withdrew from racing.

Marzotto, Giannino

Driver and Mille Miglia winner
Born: 13 April 1928 (Valdano Castelvecchio, Trissino, near Vicenza, Italy)

Twice winner of the Mille Miglia, arrogant (but delightfully so), opinionated, charming, and hospitable, Count Giannino Marzotto is one of four brothers, all of whom competed in motor racing. The family, which has ancient ties with the textiles industry and runs a chain of hotels, has considerable wealth. Money was not short when they were racing, and they had close ties with Ferrari.

Giannino first competed with a Lancia Aprilia in 1947, and when his brothers told him that his driving was 'not too bad', he took part in more events, including the Tour of Sicily (run with the Targa Florio) and the Mille Miglia in 1948. Enzo Ferrari gave him a Tipo 166MM car in October 1949 (Gino says he does not know why Ferrari did this), and he drove it to a win in the Vermicino–Rocca di Papa hill climb near Rome and set FTD. Then Ferrari made available to him a Tipo 195S Berlinetta, and he entered this in the 1950 Mille Miglia accompanied by Marco Crosara, a close friend from his schooldays.

Ascari and Villoresi retired their new 3.3-litre Ferraris, and Marzotto beat Serafini (with another Tipo 195S) after a race-long tussle. At 22, Gino was the youngest ever winner of the race, and he became famed as the

Below: *This photograph of Giannino Marzotto (on the right), and his 'riding mechanic' Marco Crosara, was taken in a bar in Valdagno shortly after Marzotto's second win in the Mille Miglia in 1953. They were old school friends, and Crosara was brave (foolish?) enough to ride with Giannino in several 1,000-mile races.* (Author's collection)

man who took part in this arduous race wearing a suit and silk tie. Gino told the writer:

> 'I am tired and bored with questions about me wearing a suit in the race. The suit was the one I used to go to work in every day.'

In 1951 he had built by a coachbuilder called Fontana a special streamlined coupé body on a modified 212 Export chassis and, again partnered by Crosara, he ran this car, known as 'the egg', in the Mille Miglia. The race was not a success, and Gino retired because of a chunked rear tyre that he incorrectly identified as a possible problem with the prop-shaft. That year, Ferrari had serious financial problems, and to help him out Gino bought the works V12 F2 cars, which were raced in the name of Scuderia Marzotto. Gino finished third in the Prix de Rome on the Caracalla circuit, and won the Rouen GP. These cars were obsolescent, as Ferrari introduced his new four-cylinder F2 car in September 1951.

Over the next year or so, Gino raced very little because of business commitments, although he managed Scuderia Marzotto. Ferrari made available to him a 4.1-litre Ferrari for the 1953 Mille Miglia and he raced this, again partnered by Crosara. He won the race, beating Fangio with the 6CM Alfa Romeo into second place. This was the famous race in which it was claimed that Fangio carried on racing despite a broken track rod. This was most definitely untrue and was said for publicity reasons. Although the Alfa Romeo's steering was not perfect, there was nothing wrong with it except a touch of wheel shimmy.

At Le Mans, Gino and brother Paolo drove one of the delightful new Tipo 340 Ferraris with Pinin Farina coupé body. The Ferraris were no match for the disc-braked Jaguars, but the Marzottos drove steadily to finish fifth. Giannino raced only once more, in the 1954 Mille Miglia with a Ferrari 4.9-litre Tipo 375 Plus and sister-in-law Gioia ('Joy') Tortima as passenger. They retired because the car developed a bad vibration that caused part of the bodywork and the mounting for the oil tank to break away. Gino was not prepared to drive the car at 140–150mph (225–240kph) in this condition.

Since the death of his wife, Gino has continued to live alone in the family home at Trissino. Well, not quite alone, as he has adopted a delightful collie-cross born on a local farm. The dog dotes on him, and when I was there Gino was feeding him pieces of the finest Scottish roast beef passed under the table. He eats very little himself, and seems to keep going by chain-smoking Gitanes Blondes and drinking single-malt Scotch whisky as though it were mineral water.

Marzotto, Paolo

Occasional works sports car driver
Born: 9 September 1930 (Valdano Castelvecchio,
Trissino, near Vicenza, Italy)

Paolo first competed in 1948, when he ran in the Mille
Miglia at the age of 17 and failed to finish after running out
of road. He did not race again until 1950 when he had a
Ferrari Tipo 166MM, and retired in both the Tour of Sicily
(incorporating the Targa Florio) and in the Mille Miglia.
With the same car the following year, he took second place
in the Sicilian Gold Cup, finished sixth in the Tour of Sicily,
and was fourth overall in the Mille Miglia.

At the beginning of 1952, Paolo was still racing the
Tipo 166MM, and with this he won the Tour of Sicily. He
was at the wheel of a Tipo 225S by the Mille Miglia, but
he retired because of engine trouble. He went on to win
the Dolomite Gold Cup, the Circuit of Calabria, the
Circuit of Senigallia, and the Circuit of Pescara.

In 1953 he retired his Tipo 250MM in the Circuit of
Sicily and the Mille Miglia. At Le Mans he shared a works
Tipo 340 4.1-litre works Ferrari with brother Gino, and
they finished fifth in a steady drive against strong
opposition. Later that year, he won the Dolomite Gold
Cup with his 250MM, and then drove a works Tipo
375MM coupé to a win in the Circuit of Senigallia and,
with the same car, won the Circuit of Pescara.

He drove a works 3-litre Ferrari Tipo 735 Sport with
2941cc engine and Pinin Farina spider body in the
Tuscany Cup, but retired. He was at the wheel of his
own, works-prepared Tipo 375 Ferrari in the 1954 Mille
Miglia and rose to fourth place before retiring because
of gearbox failure. Later in May he retired again in the
sports car Naples GP, and he also retired at Le Mans
where he shared a Tipo 375 Plus with Maglioli.

Paolo's final drives were two appearances for the
works with the team's latest six-cylinder cars. He drove
a 3.7-litre Tipo 118 in the 1955 Mille Miglia. Ferrari was
running on Englebert tyres, but the drivers, especially
he and Taruffi, were worried whether the tyres could
stand up to the higher speeds the cars were now
attaining. At the last moment, Ferrari relented and fitted
Pirellis. They were no better than the Engleberts and
tyre failure caused his retirement.

His last drive was at Le Mans, where he was entered as
co-driver to Eugenio Castellotti with a Tipo 121 4412cc.
The car was well up with the leaders, but both drivers
knew that it would not last. They retired in the fifth hour
because of engine failure. Like Gino, Paolo was a very fine

Above: *Paolo Marzotto drove for the works Ferrari team
more often than his brothers. In Italy, cartoonists made
fun of his rather long nose. He is seen here at his wedding
to Florence David at Baden-Baden on 22 September 1955.*
(Author's collection)

driver in endurance sports car races, but his business
commitments brought his racing to an end.

Marzotto, Umberto

Private sports car driver
Born: 12 April 1926 (Valdano Castelvecchio, Trissino,
near Vicenza, Italy)

After driving a Lancia Aprilia in the 1948 Mille Miglia,
Umberto bought a beautiful Cisitalia Tipo 202 with Pinin
Farina coupé body that he ran in a few minor events.
For 1950, he bought a Ferrari Tipo 166MM. With this he
hit a tree in the 1950 Mille Miglia and tore the car in
two, but suffered only minor injuries. The photograph
of the front part of the car on the edge of a ditch is one
of the most famous images taken in the 1,000-mile race.

For 1951, he acquired a 212 Export Ferrari and with this
he finished 11th in the Dolomite Gold Cup and won the
poorly supported Trieste–Opicina hill climb. He was a great
enthusiast, but not in the same league as his more talented

Opposite: *Umberto Marzotto poses here with a female friend and the Cisitalia 202 coupé that he drove in the 1948 Dolomite Gold Cup.* (Author's collection)

brothers. He raced through to the end of 1953, and his last few races were with a Lancia Aurelia B20 GT car. His final competition drive was in the 1953 Dolomite Gold Cup, and he took sixth place and a class win with the Lancia.

Marzotto, Vittorio

Occasional works sports car driver
Born: 13 June 1922 (Valdano Castelvecchio, Trissino, near Vicenza, Italy)
Died: 4 February 1999

The eldest of the brothers, Vittorio started competing in 1948, driving and retiring a Lancia Aprilia in the Mille Miglia, and racing on a fairly occasional basis until 1955. During this period, he achieved quite a number of successes, albeit mainly in rather parochial Italian events. In 1951 he raced a Ferrari Tipo 212 Export, and on the basis of an outright win in the Tour of Sicily, a second place in the Tuscany Cup, and despite a retirement in the Dolomite Gold Cup, he won the Italian Championship in the 2000cc sports class. That year he also finished second in the Circuit of Porto.

For 1952, Vittorio moved on to a Tipo 225S Ferrari, and he was the unexpected winner of the Monaco GP, run that year as a sports car race. There were a large number of retirements, including Moss who crashed on a patch of oil with a works C-type, and this helped Marzotto's cause considerably. Perhaps Vittorio's greatest success was his second place overall and a class win in the 1954 Mille Miglia with a 2-litre Ferrari Mondial. Driving solo, he was a little over half an hour behind Ascari (Lancia D24) and beat Musso (Maserati) in the 2000cc class by nine seconds.

Opposite: *Another fascinating Mille Miglia photograph taken at the 1951 race showing, left to right, Clemente Biondetti (about to replace an envelope in his Jaguar-engined Ferrari Tipo 166SC), Mille Miglia organiser Renzo Castagneto, and Vittorio Marzotto.* (Author's collection)

Massa, Felipe

Works driver
Born: 25 April 1981 (Sao Paulo, Brazil)

During 1990–7 Massa drove very successfully in karting at both a national and international level. He competed in the Brazilian Chevrolet Championship in 1997, finishing fifth, and won the Championship in 1990. Felipe then went to Italy, and in 2000 won both the Italian and European Formula Renault Championship. He moved on to F3000 for 2001, and won the European Championship by gaining six race wins from the eight races in which he competed.

He joined the Sauber-Petronas team (which used Ferrari engines under the Sauber name) in 2002, and he took 13th place in the Championship. He became a Ferrari F1 test driver, but returned to Sauber-Petronas,

Below: *The works driver is seen at the Spanish GP in 2008.* (LAT Photographic)

finishing 12th in the 2004 Championship and 13th in 2005. When Massa was racing for the Sauber-Petronas team, he was known within the team – affectionately – as 'Little Brazilian Bastard' in contrast with Johnny Herbert, another cheerful and sunny character, who in earlier, happier days had been referred to as 'Little British Bastard'.

Massa became team-mate to Michael Schumacher in 2006 and won the Brazilian and Turkish races, finishing third in the Drivers' Championship that year with 80 points. Remaining with Ferrari in 2007, he won in Bahrain, Spain, and Turkey, and gained 94 points, but dropped to fourth in the Championship. Still with Ferrari in 2008, and after a poor start to the 18-race season, he went on to another ten podium finishes, including wins in Bahrain, Turkey, France, Valencia, Spa-Francorchamps (from Hamilton's retrospective penalty), and Brazil – just missing the World Championship by one point to Lewis Hamilton (McLaren) in the last race.

Massimino, Alberto

Engineer
Born: 1895 (Turin, Italy)
Died: 1975 (Modena, Italy)

After studying mechanical engineering in Switzerland, Massimino worked at Fiat from 1924 to 1928; he then worked briefly at Alfa Romeo and the coachbuilder Stablimenti Farina. He joined Scuderia Ferrari in 1938 just before it was taken over by Alfa Corse. He carried out some development work on the Alfa Romeo 158 before moving to Enzo Ferrari's new AutoAvio concern where he worked on the Tipo 815 that ran in the 1940 Mille Miglia.

He went to Maserati in 1944, where his work included development of the six-cylinder cars conceived by Ernesto Maserati, the 4CLT/48 'San Remo' GP car and the F2 A6GCM of 1952. He also worked on the 250F GP car. In 1955 Massimino rejoined Ferrari, and he was responsible for the improved version of the GP SuperSqualo 555 car with five-speed gearbox and revised suspension that ran in the 1955 Italian GP. At Ferrari he also worked on the Tipo 500 Testa Rossa sports-racing car. At various times Massimino also worked for De Tomaso, Moretti, Serenissima, and Stanguellini.

Mazzola, Luigi

Test Team Manager
Born: 16 February 1962 (Ferrara, Italy)

Mazzola joined Ferrari in 1988, and became a Testing Race Engineer the following year. In 1990–1 he was Race Engineer to Alain Prost, but left Ferrari in 1992 to work for Sauber, where he was employed as Track Manager, and he added to his duties in 1993 acting as Race Manager for J J Lehto (Finnish). He returned to Ferrari in 1994, and initially was Race Engineer to Gerhard Berger, but since 1995 he has been Test Team Manager. He is married with two children and breeds German Shepherd dogs.

Left: *Alberto Massimino was an engineer with all the leading Italian teams. He is seen here with an early Maserati A6GCS.* (Author's collection)

Merzario, Arturo

Works driver

Born: 11 March 1943 (Civenna, Como, Italy)
(Note: there was apparently an error in the registration of his birth and his first name should have been registered as Arturio.)

The diminutive Merzario had a very extensive F1 career, which was largely unsuccessful. He had drives with works F1 Ferraris in 1972–3 (see below), but later he appeared at the wheel of cars entered by Frank Williams and Walter Wolf before entering March, Shadow and his own Merzario cars in 1977–9. He first drove works Ferrari 512S competition sports cars in 1970; he shared the winning car at Sebring with Andretti and Ickx (the only Championship win by the 512S, which was consistently beaten by the Porsche 917s); subsequently he finished fifth at Brands Hatch with Amon, fourth at Monza with Amon, and third at the Nürburgring with Surtees.

When the new 312PB flat-12 Prototype appeared at Buenos Aires on 10 January 1971, Merzario partnered Giunti. After the dreadful collision when Giunti hit Beltoise's Matra, it was Merzario who sprinted to the Italian car, burning furiously, and struggled to release his team-mate from the inferno. During the remainder of the year the 312PB was raced by Ickx, partnered by Regazzoni or Andretti, but little Arturo was back in 1972 when Ferrari was running a full team, and the make dominated the year's Prototype racing.

Arturo achieved two major successes; he shared the winning car with Redman at Spa where they averaged what was a phenomenal speed for a 3-litre car: 145.05mph (233.39kph); in the Targa Florio with the sole 312PB entered, he and rally driver Sandro Munari defeated a team of four Alfa Romeos. Ferrari also gave Merzario a chance in F1, and on his debut in this category in the British race at Brands Hatch his sixth place was commendable; Merzario then appeared in the German race at the Nürburgring and finished 12th.

In 1973 the Ferrari team struggled to beat Matra in Prototype racing, and generally the Matras were faster and handled better. Partnering Carlos Pace, Merzario finished second to team-mates Ickx/Redman in the Nürburgring 1,000km race, but his behaviour in Germany was odd and unacceptable. During the final quarter of the race he struggled to wrest the lead from team-mate Ickx, and three times he ignored the 'Come In' signal. When he eventually did come into the pits, he sat in the car, gripping the wheel fiercely and

Below: *The diminutive Merzario was a long-serving Ferrari driver, who had an exceptionally successful season in sports car racing in 1972, and then drove in F1 with the team in 1973. Merzario's main problem was his difficult temperament.* (LAT Photographic)

refusing to look the pit staff in the eye. Eventually, Ing Caliri, who was running the team, grabbed him bodily and lifted him out of the car.

Arturo then walked out of the pit without saying a word to anyone. Ferrari was somewhat reluctant to include him in the team at Le Mans, but because of a shortage of drivers there was not much choice. At the Sarthe circuit, Merzario turned up looking bright, breezy, and nonchalant, wearing his cowboy hat with Marlboro logos, and he fulfilled his task of acting as the hare to the letter. He was leading when he came in to hand over to Pace, but six laps were lost while the mechanics sorted out a leaking auxiliary fuel tank, and at the finish they took second place, 40 miles behind the Matra of Pescarolo/Larrousse.

In F1, the Ferrari team fared far from well, although another renaissance was on the horizon. Merzario drove regularly for the team, and his best results were fourth places in Brazil and South Africa. Ferrari did not consider his performances merited a place in the 1974 F1 team, and Maranello had withdrawn from Prototype racing. He joined the Autodelta team for Prototype racing in 1975 and, in the absence of serious opposition, he co-drove to win six races, including a final, parochial version of the Targa Florio. Merzario was and is eccentric, but it seems to be nothing serious!

Above: *Seen here at the Monaco GP in 1934 is Algerian driver Guy Moll, one of the most promising young drivers of his generation. He crashed his Scuderia Ferrari Alfa Romeo Monoposto with fatal results in that year's Coppa Acerbo after Enzo Ferrari had urged him to drive harder.* (Spitzley/Zagari Collection)

Moll, Guy

Scuderia Ferrari driver
Born: 28 May 1910 (Algiers)
Died: 15 August 1934 (Coppa Acerbo, Pescara, Italy)

That Guillaume Laurent 'Guy' Moll was one of the most promising drivers of the 1930s is undoubted. His father was French and his mother Spanish, and their financial position was very comfortable. The family lived in Algeria, which had been under French control since a colonial campaign and invasion in 1902. Having completed his studies in 1932, young Moll drove a Lorraine-Dietrich in a very minor, local race. His natural talent impressed fellow-Algerian Marcel Lehoux, who saw the young man's driving and decided to encourage his career.

During that year, Lehoux provided Moll with a Bugatti Type 35C for a couple of local races. In the three-hour Oran GP held on the Mediterranean coast, Moll led away at the start, but retired because of

mechanical problems, and shortly afterwards he retired again in Morocco in the 258-mile (415km) Casablanca GP on the Anfa circuit. At Marseille he finished third behind Nuvolari and Sommer with Alfa Romeos.

In February 1933, Moll drove an elderly Bugatti in the inaugural Pau GP held over a distance of 132 miles (212km) on this 1.5-mile (2.4km) street circuit in the shadow of the Pyrenees. It snowed overnight before the race, which was held in terrible conditions, and Lehoux won from Moll, with Etancelin third in his Alfa Romeo Monza – 'Phi-phi' was slowed by an engine misfire caused by melting snow on the plug leads.

With money from his parents, Moll had bought an Alfa Romeo Monza, and he first appeared with this in the Nîmes GP held in June 1933, finishing third. He next appeared in the French GP at Montlhéry, where he took fifth place (a good result in a race in which he faced the Scuderia Ferrari-entered Alfa Romeos). Moll then retired at Le Mans, where he shared a long-wheelbase 8C 2300 with Clôitre.

Then came the Marne GP at Reims, where Moll drove an inspiring race and would have finished third, but he was disqualified for receiving outside assistance during refuelling. A succession of third places followed for Moll: Nice, Comminges, and Marseille in France; then he was second in the Monza GP (the disastrous race that cost the lives of Borzacchini, Campari, and Czaykowski).

Moll was contracted by Scuderia Ferrari in 1934, and it was the first year of the 750kg GP formula marked by the debut of the 'Silver Arrows' and the start of Alfa Romeo's decline. He won the Monaco GP, but only after Chiron, all set for victory and nearly a lap ahead with his Monoposto, hit the sandbags at the Station Hairpin and lost three minutes before he rejoined the race.

In the Tripoli race, he finished second after a tussle with Varzi at the last corner, and he claimed that the Italian was trying to run him off the road. In the Avus race, he drove the special streamlined Monoposto designed by Professor Pallavicino of the Breda Aircraft company, and won the race from Varzi with another Scuderia Ferrari Alfa Romeo and Momberger (Auto Union).

His performances all season had been outstandingly good, and he was obviously a champion in the making. In the French GP at Montlhéry, he took over Count Trossi's Maserati to finish third. Shortly afterwards he finished second in the Coppa Ciano. The next race for the Ferrari team was the Coppa Acerbo at Pescara, which Moll led at half-distance from Henne (Mercedes-Benz) and Varzi (Alfa Romeo). While he was stationary in the pits, Enzo Ferrari urged him to drive faster and, back in the race, he began to close on Fagioli (Mercedes-Benz) who was now leading.

On lap 17, Moll started to lap Henne at about 160mph (257kph) as the two cars passed through the timed kilometre on the Montesilvano Straight. Then there was a sudden break in the exhaust note of the Monoposto, as Moll tried to hold the rear end slide when the tail swung sideways, the car uprooted trees and finished up against the side of a house. The Algerian suffered terrible injuries, to which he succumbed very shortly afterwards. Ferrari blamed himself for this accident, and it was because of this that he ceased attending races. Moll was the promising driver of his generation, and his death was a terrible tragedy. He is buried in the cemetery of Maison Carrée Alger, Algeria.

Montezemolo, Luca di

Chairman of Fiat, President of Ferrari
Born: 31 August 1947 (Bologna, Italy)

In Italian society and business, Luca Cordero di Montezemolo had all the right family, and he was most definitely 'born with a field marshal's baton in his knapsack'. After studying at the University of Rome

Above: *A member of the Agnelli family, di Montezemolo joined Ferrari as the liaison man at the circuits, with the brief of keeping Enzo Ferrari fully informed of the team's performances in an impartial way. He came to have a considerable influence on the management of the team, and he worked closely with Niki Lauda, seen here on the right.* (Author's collection)

La Sapienza ('Learning') and taking a degree in law, he attended Columbia University in New York as a visiting student studying international trade law. Briefly, he drove for the private Lancia rally team HF Squadra Corse. After completing his tertiary education, he joined the management team at Fiat in Turin.

In 1973 he was transferred to Ferrari as assistant to Enzo Ferrari. He settled into a position whereby he acted as racing manager (and had a superb relationship with Forghieri and the drivers), and he also acted in a liaison role with Enzo Ferrari and the Fiat management in Turin. By the time he left Ferrari at the end of 1975 he had transformed the team into a leading F1 contender. On his return to Fiat, he was appointed manager in charge of all the group's motor sport activities.

His climb through the Fiat management structure was rapid. In November 1991 (three years after Enzo Ferrari's death) he was appointed President of Ferrari, and succeeded in transforming the company. He brought back Niki Lauda as consultant, and appointed Claudio Lombardi as racing manager. Under

Above: *A recent photograph of di Montezemolo, now Chief Executive of Fiat Auto and President of Ferrari.* **(LAT Photographic)**

Above: *The greatest British driver only occasionally appeared with Ferraris, mainly because of a well-based grudge arising from Enzo Ferrari's promise of a car at the 1951 Bari GP. After travelling all the way to Italy, he found that there was no car available. Here, Moss is seen with Juan Fangio at the meeting on Easter Monday 1952 at Goodwood* **(Guy Griffiths Collection)**

Montezemolo's direction, the production car division regained its profitability and, after a long uphill struggle, Ferrari reverted to its proper role as one of the most successful F1 teams. It has to be repeated that it was slow, as it was not until 1999 that Ferrari won the Constructors' Championship, and Michael Schumacher did not win the first of his Drivers' Championships with Ferrari until 2000.

Moss, Stirling

Driver
Born: 17 September 1929 (West Kensington, London, England)

Stirling Moss's inclusion in this book results from the fact that he did not race a works Ferrari. He met Ferrari at Maranello in 1951, and was invited to drive the new Tipo 625 2.5-litre car in the Bari GP if it was ready in time or, failing that, in the Italian GP. Stirling travelled to the Bari race, saw the new car, but was told that it was for Piero Taruffi and there was no drive for

him. He then arranged to drive David Murray's old 2-litre V12 Ferrari in this race, but he was confused by the central throttle and crashed in practice. Although the car was repaired, it blew its engine in practice the following day.

As Stirling later wrote in *My Cars, My Career*:

'… Ferrari … had really dropped us all in a hole. I did not forget, and I would not forgive, and because of that it would always give me great pleasure to beat those red cars – Grand Prix, sports and GT alike…'

This was not quite the end of Stirling's Ferrari experiences. He drove a Tipo 290S 3.5-litre V12 sports car for one Jack de Vroom in the Bahamas in 1957 and won the 252-mile (405km) Nassau Trophy. Two months later, in February 1958, he won the Cuban GP with a Tipo 335S 4.1-litre Ferrari entered by North American Racing Team. The race had to be stopped after five laps because of a fatal accident.

Nardi, Enrico

Engineer, constructor
Born: 1907 (Bologna, Italy)
Died: 23 August 1966 (Turin, Italy)

During the 1920s Enrico worked for the Lancia company, and he became a close adviser to Vincenzo Lancia. During this time he built the first Nardi car, a special powered by a British JAP motorcycle engine, and he competed with it in hill climbs. Following Lancia's death in late 1936, he left the Lancia company in 1937 and, after a very short spell at Scuderia Ferrari (soon to be absorbed into Alfa Corse), he joined Enzo Ferrari's new company to work on the new 1500cc Tipo 815 car. He rode with Lotario Rangoni (q.v.) in one of these cars in the 1940 Mille Miglia, and he worked in Ferrari's machine-tool factory during the war years. In 1946 he left to set up his own company with Renato Danese, and this was based in Turin.

The Nardi company manufactured speed equipment, such as crankshafts and manifolds, for Fiats, and became famous for its very light and very strong steering wheels with a wood rim on a light alloy frame. Nardi continued to build cars in small numbers, and perhaps the most important of these were the single-seaters for the Italian national 750cc formula, the Formula 2 single-seater with rear-mounted 1991cc Aurelia engine built in 1952 (it proved too underpowered to be worth racing), and the twin-boom car, the last Nardi, that ran at Le Mans in 1955.

Nuvolari, Tazio

Pre-war Scuderia Ferrari driver
Born: 16 November 1892 (Castel d'Ario, near Mantua, Italy)
Died: 11 August 1953 (Mantua)

During the years Scuderia Ferrari was racing Alfa Romeos, Tazio Giorgio Nuvolari was not simply the greatest Italian driver and one of the greatest drivers in the world – that is, the driver with the most talent and most determination, but all 5ft 5in of him was such a formidable character on and off track that even Enzo Ferrari had to defer to him. Varzi and Nuvolari were great friends, although they did not have much in common – save that they both had tremendous talent and determination.

Above: *A typical view of one of the greatest racing drivers of all time. Tazio Nuvolari ('The Flying Mantuan') is seen here in pre-war days. He is wearing his usual yellow jersey under his overcoat, and is grimacing with concentration.* (Author's collection)

Tazio raced bikes and started racing cars in 1925, and he was given a trial by Alfa Romeo with a P2 at Monza that year. It set a pattern that was to repeat itself over the years. Tazio crashed, not because he was trying too hard, but because the gearbox seized up. Nuvolari's racing career seemed to be punctuated by crashes, following which he raced wearing a corset, or strapped up beneath his yellow jersey. In reality, it happened only very occasionally and his accidents were relatively few.

By 1930, both Nuvolari and Varzi were in the works Alfa Romeo team. From 1931 they were driving the Jano-designed 8C 2300 cars that ran well, almost but not quite dominating the races in which they competed. By 1932, the top Italian drivers were appearing at the

Opposite: *The great Italian, seen here after scoring his last win, with a Maserati in the 1946 Albi GP. The young lad, bottom right, seems disconcerted by Nuvolari's choice of language.* (Author's collection)

wheel of the latest Tipo B straight-eight Monoposto introduced that year. Alfa Romeo had the best cars and the worst finances. Alfa Romeo withdrew from racing at the end of 1932 because of financial difficulties, and Enzo Ferrari expected the factory to make the Monopostos available to him.

When Alfa Romeo failed to release the Monopostos to Scuderia Ferrari, the Modena team had to fall back on the less powerful, less competitive Monzas. So, Nuvolari left to drive for Maserati, which upset Ferrari very much. Nuvolari's pursuit of personal success overrode what Ferrari saw as being the common – and team – interest. Tazio was consistently successful with the Bologna cars, but in 1934 the Monoposto Alfa Romeos were released to Scuderia Ferrari.

Nuvolari drove an Alfa Romeo Monza entered by Scuderia Siena in the 1934 Mille Miglia road race, and took second place to his mate Varzi who drove a Scuderia Ferrari entry. Shortly after the 1,000-mile race, Tazio drove a Maserati 8CM 3000 in the Bordino GP at Alessandria. The race was run in the wet in two qualifying heats and a final, and in the concluding run on a lethally slippery track the Mantuan was trying too hard with inadequate machinery, and went off the track and hit a tree. His extensive injuries included a leg broken in two places.

Although there were no immediate repercussions, in 1934 GP racing was run to a new 750kg formula, and while Alfa Romeo and Maserati, working on very limited budgets, continued to race the Monopostos and developments of these, the German teams, Mercedes-Benz and Auto Union (the latter recently formed by the amalgamation of four companies) received subsidies from the German government and built cars of exceptional performance.

Nuvolari stayed with Maserati for the rest of 1934, and then returned to Scuderia Ferrari. The Italian cars continued to do well in minor single-seater races and sports car events, but as the German teams developed their cars to increasing levels of power and reliability, so they increasingly dominated GP racing, apart from the occasional surprise performance by Nuvolari and his team-mates. The most astonishing performance was Nuvolari's in the 1935 German GP at the Nürburgring.

It was an incredible victory that deserves to be described fully. Caracciola (Mercedes-Benz) led initially, with Nuvolari second about 12sec behind. On the second

lap, Bernd Rosemeyer (Auto Union) pushed his way through to second place, and Nuvolari, showing signs of struggling against the odds, dropped back to fifth. Then Tazio fought back, he sped up, and on lap 11 he moved briefly into the lead ahead of Caracciola. At the end of that lap, half-distance, the four leading cars stopped to refuel.

Mercedes-Benz driver von Brauchitsch spent only 47sec in the pits while his car was refuelled. Neubauer, the Mercedes-Benz team manager, made a bad error of judgement by not instructing the mechanics to change von Brauchitsch's tyres. In contrast to the smooth operation in the Mercedes-Benz pit, chaos reigned in the Alfa Romeo pit. The handle of Scuderia Ferrari's fuel pump had broken and the team had to resort to refuelling Nuvolari's Alfa Romeo from churns. Nuvolari's Alfa Romeo was stationary for 2min 14sec, and the Mantuan, hyped up and over-excited was waving his arms in a frenzy, and dancing round his car.

While the leading cars were stopped, Fagioli went by and into the lead. Nuvolari rejoined in third place, 1min 47sec behind von Brauchitsch. Then Fagioli stopped, and von Brauchitsch and Nuvolari moved up to first and second places. Von Brauchitsch set a new lap record and seemed sublimely unaware of any possibility of Nuvolari catching him. But one of von Brauchitsch's tyres was showing the breaker strip as he started the last lap 35sec ahead of the Alfa Romeo. Inevitably, the Mercedes driver suffered a puncture, and Nuvolari won by a margin of over 1½min from Stuck (Auto Union).

It was a magnificent victory for Alfa Romeo and a humiliating defeat for Mercedes-Benz. Victories in major races for Alfa Romeo were becoming very rare. Nuvolari stayed with Alfa Romeo until 1938, when he joined Auto Union. Over the next two seasons he won three races. After the Second World War Nuvolari was a sick man, already both his sons had died, and he was suffering major bronchial problems because of a life of heavy smoking. For political reasons his health problems have all too often been attributed – wrongly – to exhaust fumes. His last win was with a Maserati in the 1946 Albi GP; he finished second with a Cisitalia in the 1947 Mille Miglia.

The following year he had been convalescing in a sanatorium on Lake Como, and when he began to feel well enough to race, he travelled to the Ferrari factory at Maranello, where he arranged to drive a 2-litre Ferrari. He was accompanied in the race by Sergio Scapinelli, who must have been petrified by Tazio's driving. Through sheer over-driving the Ferrari fell apart and, of Scapinelli, Count Johnny Lurani wrote, 'His white-faced mechanic swore that never again would he sit beside this devil incarnate.' Nuvolari died at his home on 11 August 1953.

Above: *In F1, this fine Brazilian driver was a member of the Williams, Surtees, and Brabham teams, but for Ferrari he drove only in sports car races in 1973, teaming up with Arturo Merzario.* (LAT Photographic)

Pace, Carlos

Works sports car driver
Born: 6 October 1944 (São Paulo, Brazil)
Died: 18 March 1977 (near São Paulo)

Carlos José Pace was a good friend of the Fittipaldi brothers, and raced in Brazil for much of the latter part of the 1960s, driving Formula Vee cars, Renault Gordini saloons, and an Alfa Romeo 33/2, and winning the Brazilian National Championship each year, 1967–9. In 1970 he came to Europe with Wilson Fittipaldi to run in F3, and he soon became a front-runner. He left the European winter for the Brazilian summer, but he then came back to Europe with very adequate sponsorship that enabled him to secure a place in the Williams F1 team alongside Pescarolo. For 1973, Pace was a member of both the Surtees F1 team and the Ferrari Prototype team.

The Ferraris had handling problems throughout the year, and they faced a stiff task trying to beat the French Matras in their latest and more powerful form. Pace finished fourth at the Vallelunga Six Hours race, where he co-drove with Merzario, and they finished fourth again at Dijon. In the Monza 1,000km race, Pace/

Merzario led for a couple of hours but dropped out of contention because of a leaking fuel collector tank. Pace again partnered Merzario in the Spa 1,000km race, and the Brazilian did most of the driving. Their 312PB had an oil pipe come loose; the gearbox lost most of its oil and a couple of its ratios, and they finished fourth.

Pace was left out of the team at the Targa Florio (only two cars were entered, and the team naturally favoured drivers with local knowledge), but he returned to the team at the Nürburgring where he again co-drove with Merzario to finish a hectic second after the little Italian fought to take the lead from team-mate Ickx. At Le Mans, the 312PB of Merzario/Pace acted as the hare of the Ferrari team, and they eventually finished second to the Matra of Larrousse/Pescarolo. The team's last Prototype race of the season was the Watkins Glen Six Hours, and Pace/Merzario finished third. Ferrari withdrew from Prototype racing and, sadly, Pace never again drove for Maranello.

In F1 in 1973, Pace drove for Surtees (best result: fastest lap and third place in the Austrian race) and he stayed with them for 1974, but the cars had a lot of problems and, frustrated, Pace quit the team in mid-season. He was quickly taken on by Brabham, and at the end of the season he set fastest lap at Watkins Glen and took second place. The rest of his short career was spent at Brabham, and in 1975 he won his home GP.

For 1976, Brabham switched to using flat-12 Alfa Romeo engines which were heavy, less powerful than claimed, and possessed poor reliability. Pace achieved little that year, but he started the 1977 season well enough with second place in Argentina. That Pace had immense prospects was undoubted, and Bernie Ecclestone of Brabham believed that he had the makings of a truly great driver. Sadly, he was killed in Brazil in a light aircraft accident shortly after the South African GP.

Parkes, Mike

Works engineer and driver
Born: 24 September 1931 (Richmond, Surrey, England)
Died: 28 August 1977 (near Turin, Italy)

Mike's father was chairman of Alvis Limited, of Holyhead Road, Coventry, builders of Alvis cars, aero-engines and military vehicles, and it gave impetus to a man who was to prove both a fine driver and a brilliant engineer. He was educated at Haileybury School and joined the Rootes Group as a trainee engineer. At Rootes he was later very

Above: *Mike Parkes was a superb engineer, as well as a fine driver. The one man with whom he had bad relations was John Surtees.* (LAT Photographic)

deeply involved in the development of the rear-engined Hillman Imp saloon, powered by an 875cc version of the all-alloy Coventry Climax FWA engine, and this new car entered production in 1963.

His earliest competition work was in Club racing, but in 1959 he agreed to drive the F2 Fry, designed and built by David Fry. It was originally planned that Stuart Lewis-Evans would race it, but, sadly, Lewis-Evans was fatally injured in a crash in the 1958 Moroccan GP. Parkes raced this rather unorthodox car through 1959, but it was unsuccessful and the project was abandoned.

Tommy Sopwith, together with his friend Sir Gawaine Baillie, had been racing Jaguar saloons. Tommy retired at the end of 1959, but continued to manage the team, which raced under the name Équipe Endeavour. Mike Parkes joined the team in 1961, and Tommy explained how this came about:

'In 1958 I had driven for the Rootes Group in rallying, and this included the Alpine Rally in which I drove a Sunbeam Alpine with a Dr Deane, and finished second in the up to 1600cc class. Some time later I was invited to a Sunbeam-Talbot Owners Club dinner/dance and there I met Mike Parkes. We got on well, and our friendship led to me asking him to drive for Équipe Endeavour.'

In 1961 Sopwith's Équipe Endeavour ran a Ferrari 250GT SWB in partnership with Maranello Concessionaires. Mike Parkes drove this during the year and won the GT race at the international meeting at Brands Hatch in August. And he also finished second to Moss in the Tourist Trophy that month. At Le Mans he shared an Écurie Francorchamps-entered Ferrari 250 Testa Rossa with Willy Mairesse, and they took second place.

The following year, Sopwith and Maranello Concessionaires bought a 250GTO, and at the wheel of this car Parkes was first in the GT class at the Easter Goodwood meeting, won the GT races at the international meeting at Silverstone in May, and in the wet at Brands Hatch in August, and took third place in the Tourist Trophy at Goodwood after a spin. Also in May 1962, Parkes had driven a works Ferrari 4-litre coupé with Mairesse in the Nürburgring 1,000km race, and they had taken a superb second place behind Phil Hill/Olivier Gendebien with another Ferrari.

For 1963, Ferrari invited Parkes to work for the Maranello organisation in the dual roles of development engineer and reserve driver. It was the year that Surtees joined Ferrari. Surtees and Parkes did not get on, and it would not be going too far to say that they disliked each other. In addition, racing manager Dragoni liked and supported Parkes, while his antipathy towards Surtees grew very rapidly. It was a time when the Ferrari sports car team was at its strongest, and Parkes rapidly developed into a fine sports car driver.

At Sebring in 1963 he drove a 4-litre 330LMB with Bandini, and because of its power and tyres, speed had to be restricted. Parkes spun off and hit a tree, and although he was able to crawl back to the pits, the car was wrecked fair and square, and had to be withdrawn. In the Targa Florio he shared a 250P with Surtees, but it was Surtees's turn to wreck the car. He went straight on at a slow corner, wrecking the bodywork and splitting the fuel tank. At the Nürburgring, Parkes spun into a bridge abutment, destroying the 250P that he was driving with Scarfiotti – but he may have been nudged by Mairesse who was following very closely. Parkes shared a 250P with Maglioli at Le Mans and, after delays caused by mechanical problems, they finished third.

It was not exactly an outstanding performance, but at the Ferrari Press Conference in January 1964 there were presentations of gold medals to both John Surtees and Mike Parkes for their contribution to Ferrari racing successes in 1963. At the start of the 1964 season, Parkes shared the winning 275P with Maglioli in the Sebring 12 Hours; with Guichet he drove a 250GTO into second place in the Nürburgring 1,000km race;

Above: *At Le Mans in 1963 are, left to right, John Surtees, Willy Mairesse, Mike Parkes, Lorenzo Bandini, and Ludovico Scarfiotti. In that year's race Ferrari entered a team of 250P cars. With these cars, Scarfiotti/Bandini won the race, Parkes/Maglioli finished third, and Surtees/Mairesse were eliminated by a fire while leading the race.* (LAT Photographic)

and at Le Mans, driving with Scarfiotti, he retired because of oil-pump failure. His season was cut short because of a testing accident.

The following season, 1965, proved very successful once again. Parkes won the Monza 1,000km race with Guichet; Scarfiotti crashed the car that he and Parkes were sharing in the Targa Florio; but he had another good result at the Nürburgring where he and Guichet finished second with a 275P2. All the works Ferraris retired at Le Mans, and after the 24 Hours race he drove the 365P2 of Maranello Concessionaires in a few events.

By the start of 1966, the Fords were largely sorted. They were often proving to be reliable, and were providing stiff opposition to the Ferraris. Parkes and Bob Bondurant drove a P3 in the Sebring 12 Hours, but after battling with the Fords, one works Ferrari against four 7-litre Mk IIs, the

P3's gearbox gave up. In the Monza 1,000km race, held on a streaming wet track, Parkes and Surtees won in the absence of the Fords. In the Targa Florio, Parkes crashed the Dino he was sharing with Scarfiotti. Then, co-driving again with Scarfiotti, they won at Spa in what was to prove Ferrari's last Prototype win of the year.

At Le Mans there was the appalling incident when Surtees left the Ferrari team and, in any event, the works P3s failed. As a result, Parkes was brought into the F1 team at the French GP at Reims and drove a V12 Tipo 312 car with the cockpit and front section lengthened to accommodate his height of 6ft 4in. Parkes drove a good race to finish second to Brabham with one of his own cars. Later he took another second place in the Italian GP.

It looked as if 1967 would prove Parkes's best season so far. He started the season with a second place with Scarfiotti in the Daytona 24 Hours; finished second in the Monza 1,000km with the same driver; and then drove his V12 F1 car to a remarkable and very satisfying win in the International Trophy at Silverstone. In May, he and Bandini won the non-Championship Siracusa GP in a dead heat, and Mike finished fifth in the Dutch race at the beginning of June. Another second place with Scarfiotti followed at Le Mans. Then disaster for Mike struck in the Belgian race.

On the first lap of the race at Spa-Francorchamps, the Ferrari driver lost control through the fast left-hand bend at Blanchimont. It was a bad accident and Mike broke both legs. Already Enzo Ferrari had marked him down as his successor, and he would have given him the world (or, at least, a substantial share in SEFAC Ferrari) if he gave up racing. Tommy Sopwith told the writer:

'I pleaded with him, I begged him on bended knee to give up racing – Ferrari had offered him a fantastic future in recognition of his engineering skills.'

Instead, Mike insisted on continuing racing once he had recovered from the accident, and a parting of the ways with Ferrari was inevitable. He returned to racing in the 1969 Paris 1,000km race and in 1970–1 drove for NART and Scuderia Filipinetti (and for the latter team developed the narrower and more aerodynamic 512 Ferrari, informally typed the 512F that ran at Le Mans in 1971).

In 1972 he shared a Lola T212 2-litre car with Peter Westbury in the Targa Florio. Mike worked on the Fiat 128 Touring Car programme, and then moved to Lancia to work on development of the Stratos. He was killed in August 1977 when his car was in collision with a lorry near Turin. At the time he was engaged to be married, and his best man was to have been Tommy Sopwith.

Parnell, Reg

Driver
Born: 27 July 1911 (Derby, England)
Died: 7 January 1964 (Derby)

By occupation a pig farmer and a transport contractor, Parnell raced extensively in pre-war days, but a bad accident at Brooklands in late 1937 resulted in the suspension of his licence until 1939. Parnell was practising with his MG Magnette for the BRDC 500 race, and was high on the banking, lapping a young woman driver, Kay Petre, who was driving fairly slowly,

Below: *Apart from his own car, which he drove in 1954, Parnell only appeared in Europe with one other Ferrari. This was Tony Vandervell's Thin Wall Special, which Parnell drove in a number of races during 1951. Here, Parnell battles with the Thin Wall in his heat of the International Trophy at Silverstone in May. He finished second to Fangio (Alfa Romeo) in the heat, and he was leading the field in the final when the race was abandoned due to torrential rain.* (Tom March Collection)

familiarising herself with her works Austin Seven single-seater. Parnell was too high up the banking for the speed at which he was travelling, the MG started to slide, and although Reg tried to control it, there was a loss of momentum and he swerved down the banking and into the side of Petre's car.

She was thrown out of the car, was knocked unconscious, and suffered serious head injuries. Although she had plastic surgery, and had to overcome partial paralysis, she eventually made an almost full recovery. She always insisted that what had happened was just a motor racing accident, but the RAC, the organising body of British motor sport who imposed the suspension, seemed to be swayed by the fact that the accident involved a woman, and one who enjoyed great popularity, and that Parnell came from the wrong social background.

During the war years, Parnell acquired a large collection of racing cars, and the money raised by selling them afterwards went a long way towards financing his

Below: *For 1954 Reg Parnell bought the late Bobby Baird's Tipo 500 Ferrari from his widow in a deal brokered by Hans Tanner. The car was returned to the factory where it was rebuilt with a 2490cc engine. Parnell is seen here in the International Trophy at Silverstone in May 1954 when he finished second in his heat, but retired in the final because of prop-shaft problems.* (Tom March Collection)

racing career in post-war days. He raced the ex-Wakefield 16-valve Maserati and an ERA. In September 1948, Parnell took delivery of a new 4CLT/48 Maserati, which was entered in the name of Scuderia Ambrosiana, a Milan-based team headed by Count Lurani. To take the funds out of the country to buy such a car would have been a breach of the British government's currency regulations, that limited British citizens to spending no more than £25 abroad in each year.

In his biography of Reg Parnell, Graham Gauld recounts that Joe Ashmore, a friend and contemporary of Parnell, bought his 4CLT/48 by paying the money to an Italian ice cream salesman based in London. The inference is that he took the money to Italy on one of his trips to visit his family. Parnell raced his 4CLT/48 regularly through to 1951. He became the leading member of the Aston Martin sports car team from 1950 onwards, and he drove Tony Vandervell's Ferrari Thin Wall Special in 1951, and the V16 BRM during the years 1951–2.

In 1953 Northern Irish driver Bobby Baird was killed at the wheel of his 4.1-litre Ferrari sports car at Snetterton. There was a scramble to buy Baird's Ferraris from his widow, and Parnell secured the Tipo 500 2-litre single-seater. It went back to the factory where it was fitted with a new body and a 2490cc engine for the 2500cc F1 that came into force for 1954. What is interesting is that this car was also entered at races by Scuderia Ambrosiana, and there was obviously another illicit financial arrangement. Parnell enjoyed a fairly successful season with this car in 1954, and won five British races.

Parnell raced for the Aston Martin team until the end of 1956, and then became team manager. He also raced Connaught F1 cars for both the works and Rob Walker, and it was a crash with Walker's car at Crystal Palace in May 1956 that was the prime cause of his decision to retire from racing before the 1957 European season. Both Parnell and Peter Whitehead negotiated with the factory to buy Ferrari SuperSqualo cars with Tipo 860 3.4-litre Monza engines, and they raced these in the 1957 Tasman series. Parnell won all three of his races, the New Zealand GP at Ardmore, the Lady Wigram Trophy at Christchurch, and the Dunedin Trophy. Parnell then sold his Ferrari to a local driver.

In 1960–1 Parnell managed the private Yeoman Credit Racing Team of F1 Coopers, with John Surtees as number one driver. For 1962, this became the Bowmaker team, with John Surtees as number one, and raced F1 Lolas. When the Samengo Turner brothers (owners of the Bowmaker finance company) withdrew from racing at the end of 1962, Parnell took over the team, which then ran as Reg Parnell (Racing). In January 1963, Parnell developed peritonitis, and died of a blood clot at the age of 53. His son Tim took over the racing team.

Above: *An entrant and driver with a long and successful career, Penske's connections with Ferrari were limited to the development and entry of the so very promising Sunoco-Ferrari that ran in a few Sports Car races in 1971.* **(LAT Photographic)**

Penske, Roger

Developed and entered the Sunoco-Ferrari
Born: 20 February 1937 (Shaker Heights, Ohio, USA)

Penske started racing in 1958 and, apart from other very successful business interests, he has operated racing teams in F1, Indy racing, and CART. His only racing contacts with Ferrari have been in connection with the Ferrari 512S 5-litre Competition Sports Car that he developed into the much more potent and competitive Sunoco-Ferrari. For the 1971 season, Mauro Forghieri had developed an improved Competition Sports Car typed the 512M. For reasons that have not been made clear, Enzo Ferrari decided not to race the 512M, but instead to run a development programme, entering a 312PB 3-litre car in Prototype racing in 1971, with a view to running a full team the following year.

Mauro Forghieri explained what happened with regard to Roger Penske and the Sunoco-Ferrari:

'Mark Donohue and his entrant Roger Penske came to Italy, and they were planning to run the car that became the Sunoco-Ferrari. The car originated as a 1970 512S that had run in a few CanAm races, and it was owned by Kirk White, a businessman in Philadelphia. With the help of Luigi Chinetti, I asked Enzo Ferrari if I could give all the drawings for the 512M to Donohue, and he agreed. I had explained to the 'Old Man', 'Mark Donohue is a good driver, he is also a good engineer, and so is Roger Penske; they can do a 512M even better than ours.' It was a miracle that Ferrari agreed.'

After Penske's team had rebuilt the 512S to 512M specification, they added a special pressurised fuel refuelling system, provision for filling the oil and water reservoirs by compressed air to save time during pit stops, and a vacuum device on the brake master cylinders to draw the fluid back from the brakes and to pull the pistons back into the calipers so as to speed up brake pad changes. Another feature, to speed up driver changes, was that the drivers wore seat buckles strapped to their waists.

Penske sent two Ferrari 5-litre engines to Traco, the Chevrolet engine development specialists, and this company rebuilt them completely and made a number of minor modifications. Power output was boosted to in excess of 600bhp, which was at least as much as the works cars were developing, probably quite a bit more. Penske turned out the Ferrari in metallic blue, and it had yellow wheels with polished rims. Unfortunately, what had started out as a short-term project was in reality no such thing, and much more development time was needed.

It was the best turned-out Ferrari in Sports Car/Prototype racing in 1971, but lack of development coupled with bad luck meant that it achieved very little success. Mark Donohue was partnered through the year by David Hobbs. They finished third in the Daytona 24 Hours race, despite a very long time spent in the pits to carry out emergency repairs after a collision with a Porsche 911, and at Sebring the Sunoco-Ferrari collided with one of the Gulf-Porsche 917s and eventually finished sixth. It rose to second place at Le Mans, but the engine seized up, and it retired because of suspension problems at Watkins Glen. That was the end of the road for the Sunoco-Ferrari, but Penske had a long and successful career entering cars in Indy racing and elsewhere.

Perdisa, Cesare

Works driver
Born: 21 October 1932 (Bologna, Italy)
Died: 10 May 1998 (Bologna)

One of a group of wealthy and talented Italian drivers, Perdisa was a close friend of both Castellotti and Musso. In his early days he raced Maserati sports cars, but he joined the Maserati works team in 1955, and appeared in most of that year's World Championship Grands Prix. The Monaco GP in 1955 was a hard-fought race with a high level of retirements, and Perdisa was called in to the pits to swap cars with Jean Behra to improve the Maserati team leader's chances of finishing higher up the field. Behra had clutch trouble with Perdisa's car, spun, and stalled, while Perdisa carried on with Behra's car to finish third.

Perdisa was out of luck in other races that year, but he stayed with the team for 1956, and his main duty was to keep his 250F single-seater 'on the boil' in case new team-leader Moss needed it. For this reason, Perdisa drove a 250F with the throttle on the right, instead of the usual central mounting. In the Belgian race, Moss's 250F lost a wheel and Perdisa was called in to hand over to Moss, who brought this car through to finish third. He also handed his car over to Moss in the French GP at Reims after the gear-lever broke on the team-leader's car. Moss took fifth place.

For 1957, Perdisa joined Ferrari where he would be driving alongside his friends Castellotti and Musso. Perdisa drove a Lancia-Ferrari in torrid conditions in the Argentine race, finishing sixth, sharing his car with Collins and von Trips. After Castellotti was killed in a testing accident at Modena Aerautodromo, Perdisa withdrew from racing, but he regularly attended races, playing poker with Musso and other drivers. Perdisa's family business was the Calderini publishing house, and in 1956 while he was still with Maserati, he founded the magazine *Velocitas*, which survived until 1964. He became Maserati agent in Bologna and, after his father's death, he ran Calderini.

Left: *Perdisa was part of the same immensely wealthy set as Castellotti and Musso, and he gave up racing after Castellotti's death. This photograph was taken at the 1955 Monaco GP.* (LAT Photographic)

Peterson, Ronnie

Works sports car driver
Born: 14 February 1944 (Orebro, Sweden)
Died: 11 September 1978 (Niguarda hospital, Milan, Italy)

Along with Villeneuve, Peterson was one of the most exciting drivers of his generation. He was Swedish karting champion between 1963 and 1966. Then he raced a home-built F3 special, but once he had got over aspirations that this might be a race-winner, he worked his way up through Formula 3 with a Tecno, becoming a works Tecno driver in 1969. He was offered a three-year contract with March from 1970. In 1971 he was the number one March driver and, despite failure to win a Championship race, four second places ensured second place in the Championship.

Although he joined the Ferrari sports car team in 1972, Ronnie never drove F1 cars for Maranello. In sports car racing he was partnered with Tim Schenken, and as well as winning the Buenos Aires and Nürburgring 1,000km races, they took second places in the Daytona 24 Hours, Sebring 12 Hours, BOAC 1,000km, and Watkins Glen Six Hours races.

For 1973, Peterson joined Lotus, and from now most of his successes were with this team. In 1973 he won the French, Austrian, and Italian races, and finished third in the Championship; the following year he won the Monaco, French, and Italian races, and was fifth in the Championship. By 1975 Lotus was in its sixth season with the faithful old 72 model, and Peterson failed to win a single race. The following year he returned to

March after a collision with team-mate Andretti at Interlagos at the beginning of the season. His only success was a win in the Italian race.

Ronnie joined Tyrrell for 1977, but his driving style and the handling characteristics of the six-wheel P34 Tyrrell were incompatible. After a season in which he was consistently slower than team-mate Patrick Depailler, he rejoined Lotus, strictly as number two to Andretti. In my opinion, Peterson was a superior driver to Andretti and it was sad that the Swede should be humiliated in this way.

During the year, Peterson won the South African and Austrian races, as well as finishing second in the Belgian, Spanish, Swedish, French, and Dutch races. Disaster struck at Monza. He had crashed his 79 car in the warm-up session because of brake failure, and took over an old 78. There was a massive accident just after the start, involving ten cars, and Peterson's car caught fire. The race was stopped, and drivers Hunt and Regazzoni – not marshals – were first on the scene attempting to rescue Peterson.

The Swedish driver lay on the track for 18 minutes before an ambulance arrived. Initially, reports from the hospital were good, although he had broken both legs. Following an operation, his condition deteriorated and on the Monday morning he died because of fat embolism: that is fat leaking into the blood system. Peterson was one of the most popular drivers of all time, and many enthusiasts cherish his memory.

Above: *Piccinini is a very wealthy man and lives in Monaco. He is a banker, and his company held Ferrari's business. He was very close to Enzo Ferrari and he held the position of Racing Manager for a period of ten years from 1978 to 1988. He lost the position as part of the 'clean sweep' after Ferrari's death, but returned briefly to Maranello in 1991. Here, he is seen (right) with John Barnard.*
(LAT Photographic)

settled in Monaco. It is understood that in Monaco his father took over a private bank called the Principe Societé de Banque de Monaco (where Enzo Ferrari was a customer).

Marco has, himself, Monégasque nationality (he lives in Monaco). He studied architecture in Rome and started his close interest in motor racing by becoming involved with De Sanctis, which built competition cars in small numbers, and in the 1970s was successful in Formula Ford and the Italian National Formula 850. Marco was joint founder of a small competition car company based in Monaco and, after his father's death, he took over running of the bank.

Piccinini had come to know Enzo Ferrari, and for 1978 he was asked to join Ferrari as Sporting Director (Racing Manager). After the Imola incident in 1982, when Pironi passed and beat Villeneuve against team orders, he made a rare mistake. He inadvertently heightened Villeneuve's anger by confirming to members of the press, who asked him, that there were no team orders. It was one of his few mistakes, and everyone in the team knew that he was covering for Pironi, and even Enzo Ferrari made a comment, showing his sympathy for the French-Canadian.

Piccinini became a director of Ferrari, and he stayed with the team until after Enzo Ferrari's death in 1988, when Fiat, who now had full control of Ferrari, decided that a 'clean sweep' was needed. Even so, he returned briefly to Ferrari in 1991, and in 1992 he took over the running of CSAI, the Italian National Sporting Authority. In 1998 he was elected Deputy President of the FIA and he was re-elected in 2001 and 2005.

He is a director of a number of different companies, including Finter Bank Zurich and Church's Shoes (a member of the PRADA Group).

Piccinini, Marco

Racing manager
Born: 1952 (Rome, Italy)

Marco is the son of a wealthy electronics manufacturer (his industrial group included such brands as Voxson and Videocolor). In the late 1960s his father had sold his business interests because of poor health and

Pininfarina, Battista

Coachbuilder to Ferrari
Born: 2 November 1893 (Turin, Italy)
Died: 3 April 1966 (Turin)

Born Giovanni Battista Farina, the tenth of 11 children, he was nicknamed 'Pinin', which in colloquial Piedmontese means the youngest or smallest brother.

At the age of 12 he started to work in the body shop known as Stabilimenti Industriali Farina, owned by his older brother, who, confusingly, was also called Giovanni. In 1930 'Pinin' formed Carrozzeria Pininfarina. Some clarification is needed, for although the business was called Pininfarina, it was not until 1961 that Farina changed his name to Pininfarina (apparently, with the authorisation of the President of the Republic of Italy), so it is correct to refer to all bodies as by the Pininfarina company.

The company rapidly became one of the most respected and innovative of Italian coachbuilders, and during the 1950s it absorbed Stabilimenti Industriali Farina. For reasons that remain unclear, Pininfarina built no bodies on Ferrari chassis until 1953, when the company was commissioned to build coupé bodies on 250MM and 340MM/375LM chassis. These bodies had a remarkable smoothness, symmetry of line, and balance, and very quickly Pininfarina was styling almost all Ferrari bodies.

It soon became the pattern that Pininfarina designed bodies and carried out all prototype work, but actual construction of production bodies was carried out by Scaglietti. As well as building bodies, the company conducted design work for mass manufacturers, notably the British Motor Company (which managed to destroy all Pininfarina symmetry and balance to create designs of extreme ugliness), and Peugeot. It is believed that the last body that Battista Farina himself designed was the 1600 Duetto Spider built by Alfa Romeo and exhibited at the Geneva Salon in March 1966.

Above: *The great stylist had little to do with Ferrari prior to 1953, but then became the main coachbuilder on Ferrari chassis. Born Battista Farina, he called himself Pininfarina from 1961 onwards.* (Author's collection)

Pininfarina, Sergio

Coachbuilder to Ferrari
Born: 8 September 1926 (Turin, Italy)

Born Sergio Farina, he followed his father, Battista Pininfarina, and became a renowned automobile stylist and body designer. After the death of his father in 1966, Sergio became Chairman of the Pininfarina company. On 23 September 2005 he was named Senator for Life of the Italian Republic. He became Honorary Chairman of Pininfarina in 2006 when his son Andrea succeeded him as Chief Executive Officer.

Pininfarina, Andrea

Coachbuilder to Ferrari
Born: 1957 (Turin, Italy)
Died: 7 August 2008 (Trofarello, near Turin)

Andrea was the third generation of the family to head this highly successful coachbuilding company with Ferrari and Fiat, and took over as chief executive in 2001; he also became Chairman of the board of directors in 2006. He was killed on his Vespa scooter when he collided with a motorist at crossroads where the car driver on the minor road failed to see him and crossed into his path; he left a wife and three children.

Pintacuda, Carlo

Pre-war Scuderia Ferrari driver
Born: 18 September 1900 (Florence, Italy)
Died: 8 March 1971 (Buenos Aires, Argentina)

Sometimes described as a member of the 'Florentine school of racing drivers', Carlo Maria Pintacuda was one of a number of very successful drivers born in that city (others were Biondetti, Brilli Peri, Masetti and Materassi). The exact details of how he started racing are unclear, but it is said that he received an inheritance that funded his early competition entries. He was never a great driver and his career can be summarised by saying that while he had many successes with Alfa Romeos in the 1930s, he was not good enough to interest the German teams in the 1930s, nor for Alfa Romeo to sign him up again in post-war days.

During the period 1925 to 1928 Pintacuda paid his way, racing in minor events and then one of the Bornigia brothers asked him to co-drive his 6C 1750 in the 1929 Mille Miglia. It was not a works entry as such, and they drove reasonably well to finished tenth overall. For various reasons, quite possibly financial, he dropped out of the racing scene and reappeared in the 1934 Mille Miglia. It seems that it was Bornigia, by this time a Lancia dealer in Rome, who provided him with an Astura saloon, and in a race marred by sustained heavy rain, Pintacuda, partnered by Nardilli, had a warm, snug race to finish tenth overall again and win the over 3000cc class.

There followed a test drive with a Monoposto Alfa Romeo provided by Scuderia Ferrari and, as a result of this, Pintacuda was entered in the 1935 Mille Miglia by Scuderia Ferrari with a Monoposto modified to sports trim and a cockpit that two people could just about squeeze into. It seems that this car was Pintacuda's own property. Because it was so cramped, there was a limited choice of co-drivers, and Pintacuda settled for a jockey, the Marchese della Stufa. Pintacuda gave everyone a bit of a fright by trailing Tadini and Varzi (3.7-litre Maserati) in the early stages of the race.

After Varzi retired, he threw to the winds Ferrari's advice to drive with restraint, and by Siena he had built up a lead of 17min. On the run back north, rain began to fall, and he drove much more steadily, almost too slowly, and won from Tadini by a margin of just over a minute. After this race, Pintacuda became a minor celebrity in Italy and a regular member of Scuderia Ferrari.

Pintacuda drove the two-seat Monoposto again in the Targa Florio on 28 April, but retired, and he retired with

Above: *Pintacuda was one of the most successful of pre-war Scuderia Ferrari drivers, and he competed regularly in both GP and sports car racing. In post-war days he moved to Buenos Aires, and he died there in 1971.* **(Author's collection)**

this car yet again in the Tripoli GP. By the Bergamo race on 19 May, Pintacuda was at the wheel of the latest version of the Monoposto with Dubonnet motifs and a 3.2-litre engine, and he finished third. On the same day as the French GP at Montlhéry, Brivio with his 'Biposti' Alfa Romeo set third FTD in the Sorrento Sant'Agata hill climb, and the following weekend he was fourth fastest at Kesselberg mountain hill climb.

Next came a third place at Turin, and he was second to Tadini in the Grossglockner mountain hill climb. Later in the year, Pintacuda finished third in an Alfa Romeo 1–2–3 at Modena, and he was third again in the Circuit of Lucca. Pintacuda stayed with the Scuderia in 1936. He was partnered by Stefani in the Mille Miglia, and they finished third with an 8C 2900A behind similar cars driven by Brivio/Ongaro and Farina/Meazza. In the face of the usual strong German opposition, Pintacuda drove a good race with an 8C 35 to finish fifth at Tripoli, and the following weekend, again with an 8C 35, he was second in the Tunisian GP.

Then Pintacuda and Marinoni embarked for Brazil with two 8C 2900A cars. They ran in the Rio de Janeiro GP on the Gavéa circuit on 7 June, but both cars retired because of transmission problems. Pintacuda won from Marinoni at São Paulo on 12 July, following which the cars were sold. Back in Europe, Pintacuda finished fourth in a poorly supported Italian GP; he had been brought back into the team to drive a spare 8C 35 after Farina crashed in practice.

In the 1937 Mille Miglia road race, Pintacuda, partnered by Mambelli, was at the wheel of the latest 8C 2900B and, despite failure of the headlights, he won by a margin of just under 20 minutes from Farina with a similar car. Scuderia Ferrari returned to Brazil in 1937, and shipped out on the *Conte Grande* two 8C 35s for Pintacuda and Brivio; Federico Giberti was in charge of technical matters, and he was assisted by mechanics Meazza and Stefano. Stuck was also entered with an Auto Union, but he did not have the easy race that he and everyone else was expecting.

There was only the one race, the 173-mile (278km) Rio de Janeiro GP on the Gavéa circuit, also known as the *Trampolin do Diablo* (Devil's springboard) because of the succession of hairpin bends. The race was run before a crowd estimated at 700,000, and started in heavy rain. A dirty plug cleared itself, and Pintacuda, in third place, passed Brivio and set off in pursuit of the Auto Union. The Alfa Romeos could run through the race non-stop, but Stuck had to stop to refuel, which enabled Pintacuda to go ahead and win by four seconds.

When Alfa Corse took over Alfa Romeo racing activities, they were not initially interested in the services of Pintacuda, but with an 8C 2900 he did take an excellent second place, partnered by Mambelli, in the 1938 Mille Miglia behind Biondetti/Stefani. Both he and Tadini travelled out to Brazil again to drive the latest 3-litre supercharged cars in the 1938 Rio de Janeiro GP on 12 June. Pintacuda had an eight-cylinder car, and Tadini drove a 12-cylinder. In the face of weak opposition, Pintacuda won the race again by a margin of 6½ minutes from local driver Arzani with an 8C 35. Tadini was delayed by an engine misfire and, after several pit stops for plug changes, he finished a poor sixth.

Pintacuda also drove Tipo 158 Voiturettes in 1939 at Tripoli (where he retired), the Coppa Ciano (he handed his car over to Biondetti, who finished third), and the Coppa Acerbo (second), and once in 1940 at Tripoli

where he finished a poor fifth. There was no place for Pintacuda in post-war days, but professional entrant Enrico Plate based in Milan offered him a drive with a Maserati in an early post-war Temporada race in Argentina. Pintacuda liked Argentina very much and settled with the large Italian community to run an antiques business which he called 'La Spiga'; it is a word with a number of meanings in Italian, but in this context the most likely is 'ear of corn'.

Piper, David

Private entrant
Born: 2 December 1930 (Edgware, Middlesex, England)

Piper has been one of the most consistent – and persistent – Ferrari drivers. His competition career started in 1954 with the supercharged 746cc J4 MG that

Below: *Another driver of great ability who only appeared with works Ferrari sports cars on a couple of occasions. Generally, David Piper was content to race as a privateer, and he scored many successes with his own cars.* **(LAT Photographic)**

had originally been raced by Hugh Hamilton, and he ran this in sprints and hill climbs. He moved on to the 'Empire Special' Lotus in 1955, a Mark VI fitted with a supercharged 746cc MG engine. From 1956 through to 1958 he and Bob Hicks raced Lotus Eleven sports cars with Coventry Climax FWA 1098cc single-cam engines, weekend after weekend, on the European mainland, living on their starting and prize money.

David moved on to a 1500cc Lotus 15 sports-racing car, and this was followed by a 16 front-engined single-seater with which he failed to achieve any success. During 1961 and early 1962, David raced a Formula Junior Lotus 20, but he soon realised that there was not much of a future as a Lotus privateer at an international level. So, in 1962, he bought his first Ferrari, a 250GTO, and because he liked bright colours and thought that BRG was rather sombre and gloomy, he started to have his cars painted light green. It had nothing to do with BP, who sponsored him quite early on in his career.

This was replaced by another 250GTO in 1963, and then in 1964 he bought a 250LM (chassis number 5897). He crashed the 250LM very heavily at Snetterton in September 1964, and for the rest of the season he raced a 250LM borrowed from Maranello Concessionaires. The factory supplied a replacement chassis, and after he had rebuilt the car he and Tony Maggs drove it to third place in the 1965 Sebring 12 Hours race. He raced this 250LM throughout 1966, in which year he acquired chassis 8165, the last 250LM to be built. He was also racing a 4.4-litre Tipo 365, which he upgraded to 365P2 specification before crashing it heavily at the Crystal Palace circuit in 1967.

From 1966 he drove for Maranello Concessionaires and he bought this team's P3/4 at the end of 1967. In 1969 the Ferrari team brought him in to drive 312Ps in the Spa 1,000km race (second with Pedro Rodriguez), and at Le Mans (again with Rodriguez, but they retired because of a tightening gearbox and oil consumption problems). At that year's Nürburgring 1,000km race he shared a works Porsche 917 with Frank Gardner. These big 4.5-litre cars were far from developed, the Porsche works driver did not want to handle them, and Piper/Gardner did well to finish eighth with what was an unwieldy monster at this stage in its development.

In late 1969, Piper bought a Porsche 917 from the factory and, with Richard Attwood as co-driver, won the Kyalami Nine Hours race yet again. Starting in 1962, Piper had won this race five times, and he was partnered by Attwood in these victories three times. During the making of Steve McQueen's film, *Le Mans*, Piper crashed, quite possibly because of loss of concentration, injuring his right leg. The injury was not

serious, but he caught an infection in a French hospital and the leg had to be amputated. Over the years, David has owned many Ferraris, and has run both the 917 and the 250LM regularly at historic meetings. He has also built three 'replicas' of the 1966 Ferrari P3 Prototypes.

Pironi, Didier

Works driver
Born: 26 March 1952 (Villecresnes, Val-de-Marne, France)
Died: 23 August 1987 (English Channel, off Isle of Wight, UK)

Pironi's ambitions to be a racing driver started when he attended a race meeting with his half-brother, racing driver José Dolhem. Didier and Dolhem (born 1944) shared the same father, and their mothers were sisters. As soon as he was old enough, Didier attended the Winfield racing school at Magny Cours, and he was so talented that he won a place in an Elf-sponsored drive with Martini in 1973.

In 1975 he entered French Formula Renault, and he won the 1976 Championship. He went into F2 with Martini, and was second place in the team to René Arnoux in 1977. During that season he ran in the important Monaco F3, which he won, and before the end of the year he had won his first F2 race at Estoril.

This led to a contract with Tyrrell in 1978. Tyrrell was not a team in decline, but one that had declined and was stuck firmly at the bottom of the F1 ladder. Drivers were on a learning curve, and they did, at least, have the opportunity to show unexpected talent. During this time, Didier's greatest success was not with Tyrrell, but the Renault-Alpine team at Le Mans when he and Jean-Pierre Jaussaud won the 24 hours race in 1978. In his two seasons with Tyrrell his best results were third places at Zolder and Watkins Glen in 1979.

In 1980 he joined Ligier, which was a strong team at this time. Pironi out-drove his team-mate Lafitte, who had been with Ligier since 1976. He scored a first World Championship race win at Zolder, finished second in the French race, and in the British race at Brands Hatch he worked his way up through the field to lead, and looked like winning until he went off and damaged a wheel after a tyre punctured.

Following Scheckter's retirement at the end of 1980, Pironi joined Gilles Villeneuve at Ferrari and, initially at least, played 'second fiddle' to the emotional French-

Canadian. After a hopeless 1980, the team had the V6 126CK turbocharged cars, which were unrefined and experimental and which Forghieri believed would take a considerable while to develop to race-winners. They proved to be not that bad, for Villeneuve won the Monaco and Spanish races, Pironi drove steadily and cautiously, respecting his team-mate and the raw, undisciplined power of the new cars.

Initially, the 1982 season followed the same pattern, but everything fell apart at the San Remo GP at Imola on 25 April. The British teams (with the exception of Tyrrell and Toleman) boycotted the race because of an Appeal Court decision relating to disposable ballast. It was a time when the technical disputes were often more interesting than the racing, but what happened at Imola went a long way towards changing that. It was generally recognised that Villeneuve and Pironi were the strongest driver pairing in F1 at the time. Maybe Pironi was seething and not showing it, but there was nothing obviously amiss until Imola.

Under the adoring, faithful lapdog gaze of the Tifosi, watching the race in their thousands, there was an exciting, forceful battle between the two red Ferraris and the yellow Renault of Arnoux; the three cars constantly swapped places until Arnoux retired because

Above: *Seen here during the 1982 season are the two great rivals in the Ferrari team, Didier Pironi and Gilles Villeneuve. After an incident at Imola, that same year Villeneuve was killed in practice at Zolder, and Pironi suffered severe injuries in a practice crash at the German GP at Hockenheim.* (LAT Photographic)

of engine failure on lap 44 of this 60-lap race. At this point the Ferraris were running in the order Villeneuve, Pironi. It has been established clearly that Ferrari team instructions were, and always had been, for the two drivers to hold station and finish in the order that they held when they assumed first and second paces.

This did not mean that Pironi could not pass Villeneuve (if he wanted to put on a show), but he had to cede the lead before the finish. At the start of the last lap, Villeneuve was leading, but Pironi went ahead, and by the time Villeneuve took on board that Pironi had passed him for real, there was nothing that he could do about it. That was the order in which they took the chequered flag. On the rostrum Villeneuve's face was flushed with indignation and resentment, and he never spoke to Pironi again. Both drivers paid the price of the most terrible hubris.

Two weeks later Villeneuve was killed in practice at Zolder. There was so much anger and so much resentment about Pironi's win, and directed at him – totally out of proportion to the importance of the Imola race or the significance of the deed – that Pironi was driven in self-protection to a stance of callous insouciance about Villeneuve's death. He was given the choice of whether or not he drove at Monaco. He chose to drive, and was classified second after his car failed in the tunnel on the last lap because of a battery fault.

Pironi was still the only Ferrari driver at Detroit and Montreal and, very sadly, he was involved in a fatal accident through no direct fault of his own in the Canadian race. As Didier waited for the green light, holding the Ferrari on the brakes to prevent it from creeping, he stalled the engine. Behind him was Riccardo Paletti (Oselli) who drove into the back of the Ferrari and was killed by the impact. Then Pironi had a bad crash in a testing accident at the Paul Ricard shortly before the Dutch race, and was very lucky to escape injury. The cause was a broken suspension wishbone, and these were replaced by strengthened wishbones before Zandvoort.

The Frenchman won the Dutch race (newcomer to the team Tambay finished eighth), Pironi and Tambay finished second and third in the British race, and then, out-powered by the Renaults on the Paul Ricard circuit, they took third and fourth places in the French race. There is no doubt that at the next race, the German GP at Hockenheim, Pironi was very hyped up, and, as events were to prove, dangerously so. Despite excellent results, he felt constant criticism ('if Gilles were still alive, he would have done better than that') and parts of the Italian press were insinuating that he was driving for points, not to win.

On the Friday, Pironi had taken pole position and then, during untimed practising in pouring rain on the Saturday morning, he was simply trying too hard and losing concentration; he ran up the back of Prost's Renault RE30. The Ferrari was launched over the Renault's right rear wheel, glanced off the guard rail and came to rest on the grass at the side of the track. The front of the Ferrari's monocoque had been smashed, and Pironi lay in the wreckage with two broken legs.

Pironi recovered well, after initial fears that amputation would be necessary, but he never regained enough feel and movement to resume racing. He took up powerboat racing, just as dangerous a sport as motor racing, and he and his two crew members were killed in an accident off the Isle of Wight in August 1987. Only weeks after his death, his girlfriend gave birth to twins that he had fathered, and she named them 'Didier' and 'Gilles'.

Pola, Julio

Works driver
(There is no available information as to the dates of his birth and death)

Spaniard Julio González Pola raced just the once for Ferrari, driving a Tipo 125 GP car in the Penya Rhin GP on the Pedralbes street circuit in Barcelona on 31 October 1948. Depending on how you look at it, Pola broke his engine or Pola's engine broke. He is said to have been involved in a murder in Spain, presumably some grudge left over from the Civil War, which was common enough at the time. He fled to Venezuela where he continued to race occasionally.

Piero Drogo (q.v.) lived in Venezuela, and Pola partnered him in the 1957 Buenos Aires 1,000km race in which they finished seventh with a 2-litre Ferrari. The following year, Pola finished second with a Ferrari 250GT to Jean Behra (also with a Ferrari 250GT) in the fourth and last Venezuelan GP run as a road race over a distance of 469 miles (755km) in November 1958.

Portago, Alfonso de

Works driver
Born: 11 October 1928 (London)
Died: 12 May 1957 (Guidizzolo, near Brescia, Italy)

His full name was Alfonso Antonio Vicente Eduardo Angel Blas Francisco de Borja Cabeza de Vaca y Leighton Marquis de Portago. As can be seen from one of those names, de Portago's Spanish ancestry was not complete, for his mother was an Irish former nurse. The de Portago family had a house in the Avenue Foch, one of the smartest addresses in Paris, and the family settled there after the start of the Spanish Civil War. This had been brewing for a long time and, although the

Opposite: *Fag in mouth, Alfonso de Portago is seen at the wheel of a D50 Lancia-Ferrari at the 1956 French GP at Reims. He retired because of gearbox problems.*
(LAT Photographic)

FERRARI: MEN FROM MARANELLO

family opposed the challenge of the peasantry and wished to maintain traditional standards and roles, they also were contemptuous of the Nationalist generals, above all Franco whose background and class were totally unacceptable.

Of course, the de Portagos had too much money and many would say that the Marquis Alfonso had inherited wealth and status too early in life. He was also a very handsome, somewhat disreputable-looking individual of considerable sexual allure, coupled with sexual drive that would have made the proverbial alley cat seem restrained. There is a story that, when he was 17, he won a $500 bet by flying a light aircraft under a bridge across the Seine.

Alfonso quickly made his mark as an outstanding sportsman. He was Champion French amateur jockey three times, he twice rode in the Grand National at Aintree as a 'Gentleman' (amateur), he was a superb swimmer, and he became an exceptional bob-sleigher. Prior to his marriage he had a son, Kim, by an American so-called 'supermodel' Dorian Leigh. He was married to Carroll McDaniel, an American showgirl, and they had two children, but in 1957, at the time of his death he was courting actress Linda Christian, Tyrone Power's ex-wife.

He first raced with Luigi Chinetti in the Carrera Panamericana Mexico road race in November 1953, and the car was a Tipo 375 Ferrari, which they retired after the first stage of the race. In January 1954 Roy Salvadori flew on an Aerolineas Argentinas Douglas DC-4 from Paris via Lisbon and just about everywhere on the South American seaboard to Buenos Aires. Of the flight, Roy commented:

'I palled up with a very scruffy individual, who obviously needed a shave, and I assumed he was an Italian mechanic.

We played poker and, fortunately, my losses were very small, but he seemed too well informed. He spoke several languages – which surprised me – but it was only later that I learned that he was the Marquis de Portago, a very well known international horseman and playboy and – later – a member of the works Ferrari team.'

At Buenos Aires the young Spaniard drove a 3-litre V12 Ferrari Tipo 250MM spider that Chinetti had sold him; he shared this with Harry Schell and they both drove exceptionally well to finish second.

Later in 1954, de Portago and Schell drove the 250MM Ferrari in the Sebring 12 Hours race, but retired because of transmission failure. He also bought a new Maserati A6GCS 2-litre sports car from the factory in 1954 and entered it at Le Mans with Argentinian Carlos Tomasi as co-driver. They ran well, but retired on the Sunday morning because of loss of oil pressure. In July, de Portago won the 2-litre class of the Circuit of Metz with the Maserati. Later in the year, de Portago drove a Tipo 375 Ferrari in the Mexican road race, but retired because of a broken oil pipe. That year at the Nassau Speed week he finished second in the Nassau Trophy with this car and won the Bahamas Trophy.

For the 1955 season de Portago approached Enzo Ferrari about driving works cars. The 'Old Man' had far too much sense to turn away de Portago's money, but did not – at that stage – want him in the works team. They came to an arrangement that at some races the team would prepare and enter a Tipo 625 F1 car for him, and de Portago also bought a 3-litre Monza sports car. Maglioli partnered de Portago at the wheel of the Monza at Sebring where they retired because of a broken oil pipe.

In the Coupe de Paris held on the 3.9-mile (6.28km) combined road and banked track circuit at Montlhéry on 17 April, the Marquis drove a very unusual Ferrari. This was the ex-Louis Rosier Tipo 375 GP car that Rosier had rebuilt as a central-seater sports car for the 1954 Buenos Aires 1,000km race. The car was too heavy, it was outclassed by the new 3-litre, and de Portago finished fourth. He drove the Tipo 625 at Turin and Bordeaux, retiring in both races, and he crashed in practice for the International Trophy at Silverstone, breaking a leg.

Mike Hawthorn partnered de Portago at the wheel of his Monza sports car in the Goodwood Nine Hours race, but although the car was very fast, it succumbed to transmission problems. De Portago was back at the wheel of the Tipo 625 in the *Daily Dispatch* Gold Cup race at Oulton Park, but crashed again. It seems that it was this car that Peter Collins persuaded the factory to sell to Donald Healey. The engine was tried in an Austin-Healey sports car and then installed again in the Tipo 625, which was bought by Ian Sievewright. Later de Portago finished second with the Monza in the Venezuelan GP, and in the Bahamas took second place in the Nassau Trophy and won the Governor's Cup.

For 1956 de Portago graduated to membership of the works team and he achieved a fair amount of success in less important sports car races. He won the 184-mile (296km) Porto GP with a Monza from Phil Hill (Monza) and Benôit Musy (Maserati 300S). He finished fourth,

Above: *Ferrari battled in early post-war days to defeat the Alfa Romeo 'Alfettas' which seemed invincible. The breakthrough came at the 1951 British GP at Silverstone where González won the race for Ferrari from Fangio (Alfa Romeo). Seen here, before the race, is the Tipo 375 Ferrari of Luigi Villoresi, who finished in third place.* (Guy Griffiths Collection)

Below: *Swiss driver Rudi Fischer was entered with this red and white Tipo 500 by Écurie Espadon in 1952. He was remarkably successful with the car; after finishing fourth here in the International Trophy at Silverstone, he took second place in the Swiss GP, and won both the Eifelrennen and the Avusrennen.* (Tom March Collection)

Left: *This very interesting photograph shows part of the starting grid at the 1952 British GP at Silverstone. Numbers 16 and 17 are the works Tipo 500 Ferraris of Giuseppe Farina and Piero Taruffi, while number 34 is the Maserati A6GCM of Bianco entered by the Brazilian team Escuderia Bandeirantes.* (Guy Griffiths Collection)

Below: *In 1952, Ferrari built a small number of four-cylinder 2-litre Tipo 500 cars, sometimes known as 'Starlets', for sale to private owners. In that year's British GP, Roy Salvadori took over the red Tipo 500 belonging to Ulster driver Bobby Baird, and is seen here leading Reg Parnell (Cooper-Bristol). Parnell finished seventh, and Salvadori eighth.* (Tom March Collection)

Above: *At the International Trophy meeting at Silverstone in May 1953 there was a race for what were very loosely described as 'Production Sports Cars'. The race was won by Mike Hawthorn, seen here with this Touring-bodied Tipo 340MM 4.1-litre Ferrari. It was a delightful car, and another one, but with Vignale body, was driven into second place by private entrant Tom Cole.* (Tom March Collection)

Below: *Alberto Ascari, 1952–3 Drivers' World Champion, drove this Tipo 500 Ferrari to a win in the 1953 British GP at Silverstone, from Fangio (Maserati) and Farina (Ferrari). Between the 1952 Belgian GP and the 1953 British race Ascari won nine successive rounds of the World Championship, a feat that remains unmatched nearly 60 years later.* (Tom March Collection)

Left: *In 1955, both Ferrari and Maserati were completely overshadowed by Mercedes-Benz, and Ferrari's only Championship race win was at Monaco by Trintignant with his Tipo 625. Here, in the British race at Aintree, Castellotti, with his Tipo 625 Ferrari, leads Roy Salvadori (Gilby-entered Maserati 250F). Castellotti, in fifth place, was the highest-placed Ferrari driver. Salvadori retired because of a broken gearbox. (Tom March Collection)*

Below: *The Ferrari 801s are lined up in front of Ferrari's pit at the 1957 British GP at Aintree. Number 10 is Hawthorn's car, number 12 that of Collins, and (behind them) number 14 driven by Musso. The fourth car, driven by Trintignant, is not visible in this photograph. (Tom March Collection)*

FERRARI: THE MEN FROM MARANELLO

Right: *In 1957, Peter Collins was in his second season with the Ferrari team. At the wheel of the Ferrari-entered Lancia D50s in 1956 he had won the Belgian and French Grands Prix, and had finished third in the Drivers' Championship. By 1957 the latest Ferrari Tipo 801 version of the Lancia was uncompetitive, and the only races that Ferrari won were non-Championship events – Collins at Siracusa and Musso at Reims. Collins is seen here at Aintree where he retired because of a leaking radiator. (Tom March Collection)*

Below: *Peter Collins at the wheel of his Ferrari before the start of the 1958 British GP at Silverstone. He drove in masterly fashion to win the race from team-mate and close friend Mike Hawthorn. A fortnight later, Collins was killed when, through an error of judgement, he crashed his Dino in the German GP at the Nürburgring. (Tom March Collection)*

Above: *Mike Hawthorn being pushed out in his Ferrari Dino to the start at the British GP at Silverstone in 1958. Mike is wearing his favourite green anorak, and his preferred wood-rim, four-spoked steering wheel can be seen clearly. He finished second in this race, and despite a distinctly patchy season he won the Drivers' Championship, beating Stirling Moss by a single point.* (Tom March Collection)

Below: *Wolfgang von Trips was still very much a junior driver at Ferrari, and at Silverstone in 1958 had become a regular member of the F1 team following the death of Musso at Reims. Collins led throughout, and Hawthorn finished second, despite a stop to take on more oil. Von Trips battled with Cooper drivers Salvadori and Brabham, but retired his Ferrari Dino on lap 59 when it ran its engine bearings.* (Tom March Collection)

Right: *Stirling Moss and Jackie Stewart are the two greatest names not to have signed to drive for Ferrari. Stirling had a grudge that went back to 1951 when Ferrari made a serious blunder, offering to provide a car for him in an Italian race, only for the British driver to discover when he arrived at the circuit that it was to be driven by someone else. Stirling did, of course, drive Ferrari GT and sports cars from time to time. Here, Stirling is seen at Silverstone in 1958, the year that he came so very close to winning the Drivers' Championship. (Tom March Collection)*

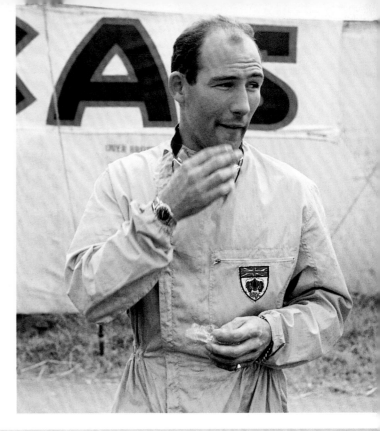

Below: *Tony Brooks drove for Ferrari for only a single season in 1959 and was very highly rated by the team. He is seen in the Portuguese GP on the Monsanto circuit where he was completely off-form and complained that his engine was down on power. He finished ninth and ultimately took second place in the Drivers' Championship, which he came very close to winning. (LAT Photographic)*

Above: *Throughout 1960 the Ferrari drivers struggled with their uncompetitive front-engined Dino V6 GP cars. Phil Hill is seen here in the Monaco GP where he finished third behind Stirling Moss (Lotus) and Bruce McLaren (Cooper). Later in the year he won the Italian GP, which the British teams boycotted because it was held on the combined banked track and road circuit at Monza.* (Tom March Collection)

Below: *By 1960, Enzo Ferrari was beginning to realise that his maxim 'the horse always pulls the cart' was no longer true, and Carlo Chiti persuaded him to agree to the construction of a rear-engined car that aped the Coopers. Richie Ginther drove this experimental rear-engined Formula 1 Dino in the Monaco GP. He finished a poor sixth, but it was all part of Ferrari's learning curve.* (Tom March Collection)

Opposite: *In 1961, Giancarlo Baghetti was a Ferrari sensation, winning his first three Grands Prix – the Syracuse, Naples and French races – with a nominally privately entered 65° V6 car. Here, he is seen with his Ferrari in practice for the 1961 Italian GP held on the 6.214-mile combined road and banked track Monza circuit. In this race, Baghetti retired because of engine trouble.* (Tom March Collection)

Above: *Because the British teams were unprepared for the new 1500cc GP formula that came into force in 1961, Ferrari dominated the season, except for the Monaco and German races, which Stirling Moss won with Rob Walker's outdated Lotus. Here, in the Dutch GP at Zandvoort, is race-winner Wolfgang von Trips with his 120° Tipo 156 Ferrari. Phil Hill took second place with a similar car. Von Trips was all set to win that year's Drivers' Championship, but he was killed in an accident at Monza.* (Tom March Collection)

Below: *After Ferrari's brilliantly successful 1961 season, the V6 cars proved no match for the British opposition in 1962, and Maranello failed to win a single round in the World Championship. Here, 1961 World Champion Phil Hill is seen with his Tipo 156 Ferrari in the 1962 British GP at Aintree. His was the only Ferrari entry, and after struggling up the field to hold ninth place, he retired because of ignition problems.* (Tom March Collection)

Above: *John Surtees joined Ferrari at the start of 1963, after the team had just endured one of its worst-ever seasons. The team made a gradual come-back, in both Prototype and GP racing, that culminated in Surtees winning the Formula 1 World Drivers' Championship in 1964. Surtees drove this V8 Tipo 158 car into third place in the 1964 British GP at Brands Hatch behind Jim Clark (Lotus) and Graham Hill (BRM).* (Tom March Collection)

Below: *Despite the 1964 Championship victory, the Ferraris had lost their competitive edge in 1965, a year in which Jim Clark (Lotus) dominated the World Championship. Here, in the French GP at Clermont-Ferrand, Ferrari number two driver Lorenzo Bandini is at the wheel of a flat-12 Tipo 1512 car. Three laps from the finish and in fifth place, Bandini slid off the road and hit a bank. He carried on, but a wheel fell off and he retired in a shower of sparks.* (Tom March Collection)

Above: *John Surtees had driven the V8 car during the early part of the 1965 season, but he appeared at the wheel of a flat-12 Tipo 1512 car in the British GP at Silverstone and took third place behind Jim Clark (Lotus) and Graham Hill (BRM). Surtees crashed very badly with a Lola in practice for a CanAm race later in the year, and missed the United States and Mexican races. At first there had been doubts as to whether he would recover sufficiently to continue racing. (Tom March Collection)*

Below: *With the introduction of the 3-litre GP formula in 1966, Ferrari adopted a 3-litre V12 design once again, but the engines were down on power. Here, John Surtees is seen in the 1966 International Trophy race at Silverstone in which he finished second behind Jack Brabham (Brabham). Surtees left Ferrari in acrimonious circumstances in June 1966. (Tom March Collection)*

Above: *Lorenzo Bandini is seen in the 1966 French GP at the wheel of his V12 Ferrari. The throttle linkage broke while he was in the lead and, although he rejoined the race after a long pit stop, he was too far behind to be classified. Jack Brabham won the race from Mike Parkes with another Ferrari. (Tom March Collection)*

Right: *This is a fine view of Bandini, with the 2.4-litre V6 Ferrari, leading Surtees (Honda) in the 1967 Monaco GP, but it is also very sad. As the race progressed, Bandini became very tired, and he lost concentration at the chicane on lap 82 of this 100-lap race, struck the barriers and overturned his car. The Ferrari caught fire after it was turned back on to its wheels and the young Italian suffered severe burns to which he succumbed in hospital. (Tom March Collection)*

Opposite: *Here, in the Mexican GP in 1967, young Chris Amon, with his V12 Ferrari, leads Jack Brabham (Brabham-Repco V8). Amon was in second place two laps from the finish when his engine cut out. He got out of his car, took off his crash helmet and heard the electric fuel pumps ticking. So he put his helmet back on, got back into the car, and fired up the engine. After this he finished fifth on the road, two laps in arrears. Under an obscure rule, the last lap had to be completed within twice the time of the winner's fastest lap, so his last lap was disregarded and he was classified eighth. Typical Amon luck! (Tom March Collection)*

Above: *Ferrari made a strong three-car entry in the non-Championship Gold Cup race at Oulton Park in August 1968. Chris Amon finished second with his Ferrari behind Jackie Stewart (Matra), but the other two Maranello entries retired. This is Derek Bell, whose Ferrari was eliminated by engine problems. (Tom March Collection)*

Above: *Here Jacky Ickx is seen at the wheel of his 312B at the 1970 Spanish GP at Jarama. The Belgian suffered bad burns in an accident. Jackie Oliver lost control of his BRM because of braking problems and collided with Ickx, whose Ferrari caught fire.* (LAT Photographic)

Below: *Jacky Ickx won only the one grand prix in 1972, the German race at the Nürburgring, where he is seen here. The 312B2 was a good car, but not good enough to achieve consistent success.* (LAT Photographic)

Above: *Lauda's first season with Ferrari was in 1974 and he is pictured in the Dutch Grand Prix at Zandvoort, where he and Regazzoni took the first two places with the much-improved 312B3.* (LAT Photographic)

Below: *Regazzoni drove works Ferraris from 1970 to 1976, when he was dropped from the team without any real regard for his long and faithful service to Maranello. He is seen in the 1975 Italian Grand Prix at Monza, where he scored a fine win from Fittipaldi (McLaren).* (LAT Photographic)

Above: *In 1976, Ferrari raced the 312T2, a version of the flat-12 car with transverse gearbox. Here, Lauda is at the wheel at the Monaco GP, where he took pole position, led throughout the 78 laps, and won by a margin of a little over ten seconds from Scheckter (Tyrrell P34 six-wheel car). The 312T2 was an exceptionally handsome car, as were most Formula 1 Ferraris of this era. (LAT Photographic)*

Below: *After his horrific accident at the Nürburgring in 1976, Niki Lauda made a near-miraculous recovery and return to racing. He drove this 312T2 car, with transverse gearbox, to a win in the 1977 Dutch GP at Zandvoort. Lauda won his second Drivers' World Championship by a comfortable margin from Jody Scheckter (Wolf). (Tom March Collection)*

Above: *In 1978, Ferrari had a good, but not outstanding year. The make was second in the Constructors' Championship, and Argentinian driver Reutemann was third in the Drivers' Championship. Reutemann won four races, including the United States GP at Watkins Glen. Here, he is seen during qualifying at the United States race with that year's 312T3 car.* (LAT Photographic)

Below: *At Monaco in 1979, Jody Scheckter leads Gilles Villeneuve. It was a year in which the Ferrari in latest 312T4 form proved largely unbeatable. Each driver won three races, and Scheckter won the Drivers' Championship with 51 points to the 47 of Villeneuve. The following year was a disaster, and the team failed to win a single race.* (Tom March Collection)

Left: *In 1981, Ferrari raced turbocharged cars drive by that brilliant pair of drivers Gilles Villeneuve and Didier Pironi. Pironi is seen in the Spanish GP at Jarama. Villeneuve won the race, while Pironi had mechanical problems and finished at the tail of the field in 15th place.* (Tom March Collection)

Below: *In the 1982 San Marino GP at Imola there was the fall-out between Gilles Villeneuve and Didier Pironi. Here, Villeneuve leads Pironi, but after Pironi won the race against team instructions, Villeneuve never again spoke to him. Thirteen days later Villeneuve was killed in an accident during practice for the Belgian GP. Pironi's racing career ended when he crashed, smashing his legs very badly in a practice accident at Hockenheim later that year.* (LAT Photographic)

Above: *Patrick Tambay joined the Ferrari team after Villeneuve's death. This photograph of Tambay with a Ferrari 126C3 was taken during the 1983 Dutch GP. It was a brilliant race for Ferrari, and Arnoux and Tambay took the first two places.* (LAT Photographic)

Below: *A stalwart of the Ferrari team over many seasons was Michele Alboreto, seen here with his turbocharged Tipo 156/85 car in the 1985 Brazilian GP. He took pole position in practice, led the race for a few laps, and finished second just over three seconds behind race-winner Prost (McLaren).* (LAT Photographic)

Above: *Throughout the years of turbocharged cars, Ferrari struggled to remain competitive. The 1987 cars were designated the F1/87, and here, in the San Marino GP at Imola, Michele Alboreto leads Gerhard Berger. Alboreto took third place behind Mansell (Williams) and Senna (Lotus), but Gerhard retired because of electronics problems.* (Tom March Collection)

Below: *Sparks fly from Jean Alesi's Ferrari F93A as he bounces across the kerb marking the inside of the circuit in the 1993 South African GP. He retired in this race because of engine problems.* (LAT Photographic)

Above: *This brilliant photograph was taken at the 1995 Spanish GP, and shows Gerhard Berger with his Ferrari 412T2 during a routine pit stop for fuel. Berger finished third behind Michael Schumacher and Johnny Herbert with their Benetton B195 cars.* (LAT Photographic)

Below: *When Jean Alesi first joined the Ferrari team, it seemed that he had immense promise and that he was the man most likely to revive the team's fortunes. Here he is at the wheel of the Tipo 412T2 Ferrari that he drove to a win in the 1995 Canadian GP at Montreal ahead of Rubens Barrichello and Eddie Irvine with Jordan cars.* (LAT Photographic)

Left: *Michael Schumacher was not just the greatest Formula 1 driver of recent years, but he was also a successful footballer and played for a Swiss Third Division team. He is seen playing in the annual football match at the Spanish GP in 2005. (LAT Photographic)*

Below: *Michael Schumacher ploughs through the spray in the 1996 Spanish Grand Prix to take his first win for Ferrari. Schumacher went on to win a total of 72 grand prix for Ferrari over a ten-year period – a remarkable achievement. (LAT Photographic)*

partnering Gendebien in the 1,000km (621-mile) Supercortemaggiore GP at Monza limited to 2-litre sports cars. He blotted his copybook at Le Mans by spinning off on the second lap on the very greasy road through the Esses and wanged into Fairman's works D-type, which had already spun off, and ensured that both cars were out of the race.

In August he co-drove the third-place Ferrari Tipo 860 Monza with Hawthorn and Duncan Hamilton in the 1,000km (621-mile) Swedish GP at Kristianstâd, a round in the World Sports Car Championship. That de Portago was a much more mature driver, who had followed a patient learning curve, was evident, and he had become an asset to the Ferrari team.

'Fon' also turned in some very good performances with the Ferrari-entered Lancia D50s in F1 and backed his team-mates up very well. With Fangio unofficially leading the team, de Portago was very much the sorcerer's apprentice. He first drove for the F1 team in the French GP at Reims where he retired because of gearbox failure, but at Silverstone he was well placed enough for Collins to take over his car and finish second. In the German GP he rose to fourth place and was called into the pits for Collins to take over his car. Shortly afterwards Collins spun the Lancia-Ferrari into a ditch and out of the race.

After the race de Portago suggested that Collins could have pushed the car back on to the track – so they put this to the test, but found that it needed Collins's Ford Zephyr as tow-car and six people as pushers to get the car back on the road. 'Fon's' last F1 race in 1956 was the European GP at Monza. It was not a good race for the Spaniard, as the D50s were throwing treads on their Englebert tyres. This happened on de Portago's car and he was forced to retire because the suspension had been damaged by a flailing tread.

A fortnight later de Portago competed in the Tour de France, a high-speed rally that was a race spread over seven days and with speed tests at venues that included Mont Ventoux, Le Mans, Rouen-les-Essarts, Reims, and Montlhéry. The Marquis was accompanied by his 'ski instructor' Ed Nelson and they won the event from Stirling Moss/Georges Houel (Mercedes-Benz 300SL Gullwing). Who and what was Ed Nelson really? Edmond Nelson was aged 42 when he and 'Fon' met; he was an American air force veteran, and at the time he was working as a lift operator in the Plaza Hotel in New York.

There is no suggestion that there was anything sexual between them, but there was a deep and close relationship, not unusual with heterosexual men who have a strong sex drive and sporting ability, for they tend to bond easily. Something clicked between them, and it was irrelevant that Nelson was a redneck from Hicksville, South Dakota. 'Fon' put together a Spanish bobsleigh team for that year's Winter Olympics and they finished fourth. After running the 250GT in a couple of races, he drove a factory Tipo 860 Monza in the Bahamas, finishing second in the Governor's Cup and third in the Nassau Trophy.

In early 1957 de Portago shared the third-place Ferrari in the Buenos Aires 1,000km race, took third place in the Cuba GP, and won the Coupe de Vitesse at Montlhéry. The next event was the Mille Miglia 1,000-mile road race, and Alfonso drove a 4.1-litre Tipo 335 Sport partnered by Ed Nelson. He was holding third place when the accident occurred, and comment about this was worldwide. One of the simplest, most accurate, and balanced accounts was given in the American magazine, *Road & Track* which said:

'Alas the joy [of Taruffi's win] was too great to last, and was soon dispersed by the terrible news that only 25 miles [40km] away from the finish, drama had struck brutally. In one of the long stretches before Brescia, the Marquis de Portago, driving contentedly in third place at a speed of 165mph [265kph], suddenly left the road and crashed first into a series of stone markers and then plunged into the crowd after cutting a telephone pole in two.

The car literally flew into the air for 150 yards [148 metres] before plunging into a small canal. Both de Portago and his inseparable companion Nelson were instantly killed by the impact, which also took the lives of ten other people. Two wonderful persons had just disappeared from the scene of our lives. It was not de Portago's fault: by the irony of destiny, for once he had been driving a smooth, well-planned race, taking no chances.'

That de Portago's car went out of control because of a punctured tyre was undoubted. On the Tipo 335 Sport, there was a protective metal skin round the fuel tank and on de Portago's car this had broken away. Some have said that this was the cause of the accident because it punctured the side wall of a rear tyre, but this was not the case. The incident was thoroughly investigated by Ferrari and the company was satisfied that the puncture was caused by something lying in the road, possibly a piece of metal.

Postlethwaite, Harvey

Ferrari engineer
Born: 4 March 1944 (England)
Died: 15 April 1999 (Barcelona, Spain)

After education at the Royal Masonic School for Boys at Bushey in Hertfordshire, Postlethwaite studied engineering at Birmingham University, and gained a doctorate in mechanical engineering in 1965. As a boy, his ambition was to become a pilot, but this was thwarted because he was colour-blind. He worked as a research scientist in the petrochemical department of

Below: *Postlethwaite was a fine engineer, best known for his work at Tyrrell, where he evolved the sloping nose (adopted by all the other constructors), and for his design and development work on the turbocharged Ferraris raced from 1981.* (LAT Photographic)

ICI and, as a motor sport enthusiast, he competed in club racing with a Mallock. He concluded that he was not 'cut out' to be a racing driver, and after the March company was set up in 1969, Postlethwaite joined them in 1970 to work on the F2 and F3 programme.

Harvey moved to the amateur and very eccentric Hesketh team in 1973, modifying the team's March 731 F1 car to make it a competitive proposition, and then designing the Hesketh 308.

'In this car Postlethwaite extended his 'developed March' theme, laying out a car that was sensible, in that there were no design ventures into the unknown.' [Mike Lawrence, *A–Z of Formula Racing Cars*]

After a promising first season with James Hunt at the wheel, Hunt drove the improved 1975 car to a win in the Dutch GP, and three second places.

Hesketh gave up racing at the end of 1975, when two of the latest 308C cars were sold to Walter Wolf, who was setting up his own team. Postlethwaite joined Wolf for 1977, and for them he designed the WR7 to WR9 cars with honeycomb-construction monocoques. The Wolf team's problem was that it had no answer to the Lotus ground-effect cars, and multimillionaire owner Walter Wolf was losing interest rapidly. Fittipaldi absorbed Wolf in 1979, and Harvey joined this team, designing the Fittipaldi F8, which was raced in 1980.

In mid-1981, Postlethwaite went to Ferrari and was given carte blanche to develop a completely new chassis for the Tipo 126 engines on which the team was to rely in 1982. Those who knew the 'Old Man' were well aware that 'carte blanche' today could mean 'the sack' tomorrow. Harvey wanted to build a carbon-fibre composite chassis, which he had the experience and knowledge to do, but concluded that the team lacked the ability to tackle this kind of construction.

He persuaded Enzo Ferrari that they should build cars with honeycomb-construction monocoques to avoid being dependent on an outside supplier, and it was his intention that Ferrari should build its own carbon-fibre structures at a later date.

During this first spell with Ferrari he was given leave by the 'Old Man', in mid-season, to attend the motorcycle Tourist Trophy races on the Isle of Man, and he rode over from Italy on his MV Agusta motorcycle. Villeneuve's death at Zolder at this time was a terrible blow, for not only was he a person for whom Postlethwaite had great affection, but also was one whose press-on enthusiasm he particularly admired.

The accident raised questions about the structural

integrity of the 126C2 cars, and the comments of rivals and other critics caused him great concern. Ferrari carried out tests to destruction on both the 1981 126CK and the 1982 C2 cars on static rigs. These revealed that there were no deficiencies in the structural integrity of the cars, rather they highlighted the very high forces that they could withstand in accidents of this kind.

Postlethwaite remained with Ferrari until 1987 when Gustav Brunner (formerly with ATS) joined the chassis design team. He then moved to Tyrrell, where he worked for four years, and his time with this team was marked by an improvement in results. In 1991 he moved from Tyrrell to Sauber as Technical Director, but left before the Swiss team entered F1 with his new design in 1993, and returned to Tyrrell to stay with them until the team was sold to British American Racing in 1998.

Honda was planning a new F1 car to be built completely in-house. This was designed by Postlethwaite, but built by the Dallara concern in Italy. During testing at Barcelona, Harvey suffered a fatal heart attack. Honda began supplying engines again to other constructors in 1990, but did not run their own team until they took over British American Racing for 2006.

Prost, Alain

Works driver
Born: 24 February 1955 (Lorette, Saint-Chamond, near St Etienne, Loire, France)

Although they were born in France, Alain Marie Pascal Prost's parents were of Armenian descent. He started karting when he was 14, and when he moved on to serious motor racing he won the French and European F3 Championships. He joined the McLaren F1 team in 1980. They were going through a bad patch, but it worked as a season's learning curve, during which he

Below: *Alain Prost made his reputation with the Renault team during the years 1981–3 and he came close to winning the Drivers' Championship with one of these turbocharged cars in 1983 when he took second place, two points behind Nelson Piquet (Brabham), and he won the Drivers' Championship for McLaren in 1985–6. This photograph was taken when he joined Ferrari in 1990.* (LAT Photographic)

finished in the points four times. He moved on to Renault for 1981, and he was to stay with the French turbocharged racing cars for three seasons.

The Renaults lacked reliability, but Prost completely out-drove his team-mate René Arnoux. During 1981 he won the French, Dutch, and Italian races, and finished fifth in the Drivers' Championship. Reliability was still the problem in 1982, although Alain again won races, at Kyalami and Rio de Janeiro, and took fourth place in the Championship. The following year he won in France, Belgium, Britain, and Austria, and was set to clinch a Championship win in South Africa when turbocharger failure forced him to retire, and he lost out to Piquet (Brabham) by two points.

Prost spent the next six seasons back with McLaren, establishing his greatness as a driver by winning the World Championship in 1985, 1986, and 1989, and finishing second in 1984 (to team-mate Lauda) and 1988 (to team-mate Senna). At McLaren, relations with Senna became very fraught, and Prost decided to leave to drive for Ferrari in 1990. He stayed at Maranello for two seasons. In his first season with them he finished second in the Championship, winning five races with 71 points

(net) to the 78 of Senna, after Senna's McLaren had run into the back of the Ferrari at the start in Suzuka.

Ferrari raced the improved 642 during 1991, but the team's intrigues, backbiting, and disputes reached new heights. Prost failed to win a race, but finished second three times, took fifth place in the Championship, and was sacked at the end of the year. He was under great pressure to join Ligier, but insisted on a year's break from racing. For 1993 he joined Williams, and the original intention was that he should partner Mansell. Mansell decided not to take up his place in the team, thereby giving Prost a good run at the World Championship, which he gained for the fifth time.

He left Williams at the end of 1993 rather than have Senna as a team-mate and, although he tested a McLaren-Peugeot in 1994, he decided to retire from racing. He took over the ailing Ligier team in 1997, and he ran it as 'Prost Grand Prix' until it went bust in 2001. Prost was an exceptionally able driver, known as 'The Professor' because of his intellectual approach to the sport. He was described by Denis Jenkinson as, 'a very warm and uncomplicated man who doesn't rely on passion or inspiration'.

Below: Räikkönen's F1 career started with the Sauber-Petronas team in 2001, and the following year he moved to McLaren where he stayed until 2006. He joined Ferrari in 2007, and he and Massa provide very stiff opposition to the latest generation of McLaren drivers.
(LAT Photographic)

Räikkönen, Kimi

Works driver
Born: 17 October 1979 (Espoo, Finland)

In his young days, Kimi contested karting with great success, starting in 1988 and scoring many class wins in Finland in a career that lasted through to 1999. By that time he was driving in Formula Renault (FR), and in 2000 he won the British Formula Renault Championship, as well as three races in the British FR Euro 2000 series. The same year he tested with Sauber-Petronas, and as a result gained a place in the team for 2001 when he finished tenth in the Drivers' Championship with nine points.

Kimi's potential was immense, and it was recognised by Ron Dennis who brought him in to the McLaren-Mercedes-Benz team. After finishing sixth in the Championship with 24 points in 2002, he took second place in 2003 with 91 points to the winner Schumacher (Ferrari). He was seventh (45 points) in 2004, second again (112 points) to Alonso (Renault) in 2005, and finished fifth in 2006. He joined Ferrari for 2007, and that year, with 110 points, took the World Championship by one point from Hamilton and Alonso (both McLaren) scoring wins in Australia, France, Britain, Belgium, China and Brazil, second places in Hungary and Turkey, and third places in Malaysia, Bahrain, Italy and Japan. He did not enjoy such a good season in 2008 and, although team leader, often had to play second fiddle to his team-mate Filipe Massa. He only managed two wins (Malaysia and Spain), finishing third in the Championship table with 75 points, behind Massa's 97 points and new World Champion Lewis Hamilton's 98 points.

He and his wife live in Switzerland.

Ramponi, Giulio

Scuderia Ferrari mechanic
Born: 8 January 1902 (Milan, Italy)
Died: December 1986 (South Africa)

Giulio Ramponi was one of the greatest motor racing personalities whose biography was never written. While he was a young boy, first his father and then his stepfather died. He was keenly interested in automobiles and he was still very young when he attended a course on automobile mechanics at the Arti e Mestieri (art and business) School in the Via Santa Maria in Milan. After completing the course, he worked for the Florentia car company (the company had been manufacturers, but they were not listed as such after 1912), and then joined the Pelizzola fuel pump company as an apprentice.

It has been suggested that he was Campari's nephew, but this seems not to have been the case. For whatever reasons, Campari took a shine to the young Milanese lad. Apart from sheer enthusiasm, his slim build made him an ideal riding mechanic. So Giulio started an apprenticeship with Alfa Romeo where he worked – and learned as he worked – in the engine test section, on the assembly of running gear, and then in the experimental department headed by Luigi Bazzi.

Back in 1919, Ramponi had ridden with Campari in the Parma–Poggia di Berceto mountain hill climb, and he rode regularly with Alfa Romeo drivers. He was assigned to work on the P2 of the team's fastest driver, Antonio Ascari. He rode with him in the 1924 Targa Florio. They were leading close to the finish when the Alfa Romeo's engine seized. Both Ascari and Ramponi tried to restart the car on the handle, but without success, and they then pushed the car to the finishing line with the help of soldiers and spectators. They

dropped to second place behind Werner (Mercedes), but a protest was entered that only the car's own crew could push it, and this was upheld by the stewards.

In the French GP at Lyon they were again leading, with victory in sight, when the engine seized. Once again, they tried desperately to restart it, once again they failed, and Campari won the race with his P2. Ascari, partnered by Ramponi, won the Italian GP at Monza. Ramponi remained in charge of preparation of Ascari's car, but because of a change in the regulations, mechanics were no longer carried. After the 1925 season, Ramponi continued to work in the racing department of Alfa Romeo, but he was now chief test driver on Jano's latest design, the 6C 1500 production car.

Ramponi's first competition appearance was with a 6C 1500 in the 1926 Cuneo–Maddalena hill climb, and with strict instructions from Jano to complete the course safely, he was third fastest. That there was still a place in the world for riding mechanics was established by the Mille Miglia 1,000-mile sports car race first held in 1927. In this, Ramponi acted regularly as riding mechanic, first with works-entered Alfa Romeos and later with Scuderia Ferrari entries.

In the 1927 race, Ramponi rode with Marinoni in an

Below: *At the 1924 Monza GP, Giulio Ramponi, then a young mechanic with the Alfa Romeo team, stands on the left of the P2, while driver Antonio Ascari stands on the right with the infant Alberto clutching the steering wheel.* (Spitzley/Zagari Collection)

RLSS Alfa, but they retired because of transmission problems; he partnered Campari in the winning experimental supercharged 6C 1500 Super Sport in 1928, and they won the race. Later that year F. W. Stiles, the British agent, entered Ramponi with a supercharged 6C 1500 in the Essex Motor Club Six Hours race at Brooklands. Ramponi won the race, and Peter Hull and Roy Slater recount, in *Alfa Romeo, a History*, an incident in the pits after Ramponi left following a tyre change while leading on handicap:

'[Because of] lack of knowledge of the English language, he failed to realise he had to replace the tools in the pit. When, after much gesticulating, he did understand, he hurled the jacks into the pits as if they were so many hand grenades, and everyone had to take cover under the pit counter.'

Ramponi won the race on handicap. In 1929 Campari, partnered by Ramponi, won the Mille Miglia yet again, but now with a 6C 1750 Gran Sport.

That year the first Double Twelve race was held at Brooklands, and Stiles entered four of the latest 6C 1500 cars. There were difficulties in scrutineering, and certainly the engine in the car supposedly to be driven by Ramponi/Lurani had a non-standard fixed head.

'It has been said that this particular engine was soon brought up to standard specification by welding some dummy nuts in the appropriate places on top of the head.'

Ramponi, who had insisted on driving single-handed, won the race by a narrow margin on handicap from the Bentley 4½-litre of Davis/Gunter. After the race, Ramponi wanted Alfa Romeo to give a percentage of the share money to his mechanic, Perfetti, but this they refused to do.

The story rumbles on with some confusion. Alfa Romeo would not agree to what was proposed, so Giulio left the company and went to work for OM (Officine Meccaniche) at Brescia. OM had won the first Mille Miglia in 1927 with their remarkably potent 'Superba' six-cylinder side-valve cars (side-valve? – yes and they were fantastic, but in rapid decline by this time). Ramponi raced for OM and the British agents, L. C. Rawlence & Co. Limited, with little success. He also drove a supercharged Bentley for the Hon. Dorothy Paget's team at Le Mans in 1930, but he was ill and, until a piston failed, co-driver Dr J D Benjafield had to both drive and nurse his Italian colleague.

Giulio was now really short of work. He partnered George Eyston in the 1931 Double Twelve race at the wheel of a four-seater 8C Maserati, but they retired at the end of the first day because of rear axle failure. It was later in the year that Ramponi was asked by Alfa Romeo to return to the company to help with the development and race preparation of the new Tipo B Monoposto racing car. This was a peculiar time with, simultaneously, an overlap and a parting of the ways between Alfa Romeo and Scuderia Ferrari.

Both teams entered cars in the 1932 Mille Miglia, and Giulio partnered Pietro Ghersi at the wheel of a Zagato-bodied car entered by Scuderia Ferrari. In Florence, Ghersi underestimated the speed at which he was travelling, he skidded wildly as he attempted to take a right-hand bend, and hit a post, with serious damage to the car, slight injuries to himself, and a broken arm for Ramponi. Relations with Ferrari became even more strained when it was learned that he had failed to take out insurance cover for his drivers and riding mechanics. Alfa Romeo withdrew from racing because of financial problems, and at first would not make the Monopostos available to Ferrari. By the Coppa Acerbo that year, Alfa Romeo relented, but it was too late for Ramponi, who had left the team.

After he departed Ferrari, Ramponi initially stayed in Milan to look after the Italian aspects of Whitney Straight's motor racing team. Then, in 1934, he came to London and did not return to Italy until after the Second World War. It appears that this was because of something disastrous that had happened in his home country. So far as the writer is aware, he never discussed the reasons for this sudden departure from Italy. (The writer was Ramponi's UK solicitor after Ramponi went to live in South Africa, and we met regularly when he was in the UK.)

We are left to surmise, but there are two quite possible scenarios. It has been suggested that he was deeply implicated in the 1933 Tripoli GP lottery scandal, and if he had stayed in Italy he would have faced criminal proceedings. The other (and, in the writer's opinion, much more likely reason) was his deep antipathy to fascism. This accounts more than anything for his disagreements with Alfa Romeo, and it has been said that he was threatened with death if he returned to Italy.

Straight decided to withdraw from racing at the end of 1934, and a final job that Ramponi carried out for him was the rebuild of one of the team's 8CM Maseratis into a sports two-seater. This work was carried out in a garage (formerly a stable) in Lancaster Mews, London W2. By 1935, Ramponi was quite well acquainted with

Dick Seaman, probably because of Seaman's racing appearances in Italy with his MG Magnette. This year Ramponi supervised the rebuild of the engine of Seaman's black ERA, R1B, although it seems that Jock Finlayson did most of the actual work.

Ramponi advised Seaman that he would do better in 1936 Voiturette racing at the wheel of rebuilt and modernised versions of the 1927 Delage 1.5-litre straight-eights, originally raced by the works. Seaman agreed and, in addition to buying a car from Earl Howe, he acquired a second example raced by Senéchal and stored in the Delage factory. So successful were these cars in rebuilt form that they clinched Seaman's acceptance as a member of the GP Mercedes-Benz team in 1937.

In the meantime, Giulio and Billy Rockell (a former Bentley mechanic) went into partnership and opened a small Alfa Romeo specialist business in the garage premises in Lancaster Mews. In the late 1960s onwards, the writer used to own and drive modern Alfa Romeos on a regular basis. It was suggested that I should have my cars serviced by Ramponi, Rockell, and that was how I first met Giulio.

With the outbreak of the Second World War, Giulio was interned as an enemy alien in a camp on the Isle of Man. It was a particularly bad time for him because his wife died of peritonitis, and being interned in this way came as a terrible blow to a man who liked, and had trusted, the British. Following his release in 1944, he worked for a while at Bristol-Siddeley engines in Coventry.

Ramponi remarried, and he was employed for some years as a trade representative for component manufacturers that included Ferodo, Girling, Lockheed, Lodge, and Vandervell bearings. Relations with Ferrari were resumed on a fairly amicable basis, and he brought an early Ferrari to Britain in 1948. He retired to South Africa in 1973, but Ramponi, Rockell flourished for many years.

Below: *When Mike Anthony was racing a Lotus 10, Giulio Ramponi helped him sort out the carburation. Here, Giulio is working on the Bristol engine in the paddock at the British GP meeting at Aintree on 16 July 1955.* (Author's collection)

Above: *In this not unfamiliar photograph, the Marquis Lotario Rangoni, partnered by Enrico Nardi, is seen at the wheel of his AutoAvia Costruzioni Tipo 815 in the closed-circuit 1940 Mille Miglia. They failed to finish the race.* (Spitzley/Zagari Collection)

Rangoni, Lotario

Driver and part financier of the AutoAvio Costruzioni cars
Born: 1913 (Florence, Italy)
Died: 2 October 1942 (Pistoia, Italy)

It is claimed that Marquis Lotario Rangoni Machiavelli was a scion of both Florentine and Modenese nobility. He managed the family's agricultural holdings at Spilamberto, near Modena, and raced Alfa Romeo and Fiat Balilla cars. He bought one of the two Tipo 815 cars built by Ferrari in 1939–40 and raced it in the 1940 Mille Miglia, partnered by Enrico Nardi. He led the 1500cc class for much of the race, but he retired because of transmission problems. Rangoni became a test pilot for Savoia-Marchetti and was killed when he crashed in one of this company's three-engined aircraft in 1942.

Redman, Brian

Works F2 and sports car driver
Born: 9 March 1937 (Burnley, Lancashire, England)

During a long racing career, Brian Hermon Thomas Redman established a superb reputation as a sports car driver, although he drove just about every category of car at one time or another. Brian has said that his 'education is best described as minimal'. He was the scion of the family that ran the Redmans chain of grocers' shops, together with two cafés, and initially he worked in the business. After progressing through the ex-Coombs 'Lightweight' Jaguar E-type entered by the Red Rose Team, a Lola T70-Chevrolet, an F2 Brabham, and a Lola, by 1968 he was driving Ford GT40s for the Gulf team, and, partnered with Jacky Ickx, he won at Brands Hatch and Spa.

In 1968 Brian received a telephone call from Forghieri inviting him to test drive a Dino F2 car at Modena Aerautodromo, and following this Brian drove one of these cars into fourth place in the Eifelrennen held on the short Sudschleife at the Nürburgring, despite a stone thrown up by Ahrens's Brabham smashing his goggles. He was asked to drive the F2 cars

Above: *Brian Redman was another outstanding sports car driver who partnered Jo Siffert in the Porsche and Gulf teams during 1969–70. He was a leading member of the Ferrari sports team in 1972–3. In the latter years he partnered Jacky Ickx, and they made an exceptionally compatible and successful combination. In this photograph he is seen with Jody Scheckter. (LAT Photographic)*

for the rest of the season, but good sense prevailed and Brian refused.

Redman was invited to drive in the Ferrari Prototype team from late 1971. He and Regazzoni won the Kyalami Nine Hours race, and during 1972 he shared two good wins in the 312PB, at Spa (with Merzario) and the Austrian 1,000km race (with Ickx). Brian stayed with the team for 1973 when Ferrari was struggling, none too successfully, to beat the Matras. During this difficult year, he partnered Ickx to a win in the Nürburgring 1,000km race, but this was his only success.

Brian enjoyed a long and successful racing career. He had driven in F1 for Cooper (he survived a bad crash at Spa in 1968 when the suspension broke), Surtees (one race in 1971), McLaren (three races in 1972), and four races with the Shadow team in 1973–4. During 1970 he had partnered Siffert in the Gulf-Porsche team, and he had a long career in F5000 in the United States.

Regazzoni, Clay

Works driver

Born: 5 September 1939 (Mendrisio, near Lugano, Switzerland)

Died: 15 December 2006 (motorway accident near Parma, Italy)

After an early racing career driving F2 and F3 Brabhams in partnership with fellow-Swiss Silvio Moser in 1965–6, Gianclaudio 'Clay' Regazzoni became a member of the works Tecno team in 1968. He was a hard-pushing, unforgiving driver who made no allowances for the shortcomings of his opponents, and his attitude put off some who would have otherwise supported him. Clay moved on to works Dino 166 F2 cars in 1969, but this first relationship with Maranello was short-lived, and he soon returned to Tecno.

Clay became an occasional F1 Ferrari driver in 1970, and when he won a remarkable and determined victory in that year's Italian GP, following Rindt's fatal accident in practice with his works Lotus, there was a change of attitude at Maranello. It was, after all, fine having nice young men like Amon, Ickx and 'Nanni' Galli at the wheel of the red cars, but there was also a place for a bit

Above: *During the years 1970 to 1972, Swiss-born Regazzoni was a brilliant member of the Ferrari team. Apart from partnering Jacky Ickx at the wheel of the new 312PB Sports Prototype in 1970, he won the Italian GP that year and took second places in Austria, Canada, and Mexico. There was no place for him in the Ferrari team in 1973, when he drove for BRM, but returned to Maranello the following year and won the German GP, as well as finishing second in Brazil, Spain, Holland, and Canada.* (Author's collection)

of the rough. He had showed this in the Monza race by pulling out a lead and then holding on to it by darting to and fro across the track.

This prevented Stewart from getting back into Clay's slipstream, and caused the PC Scotsman to trumpet: 'That driving was unethical, unsporting, and dangerous.' One thing that we know for sure is that Clay did not care a Swiss centime what Stewart thought. So Regazzoni stayed with Ickx at Ferrari in 1971–2 and the Swiss driver revelled in being a member of the Ferrari team.

The F1 312Bs achieved far less success during the early 1970s than anticipated or deserved. Regazzoni's best performances in F1 in 1971 were third places at Kyalami, Zandvoort, and the Nürburgring. The following year he was just as unsuccessful, with a third at Jarama and second at the Nürburgring. In only one Prototype race in 1971 did Ickx/Regazzoni finish with the new 312PB, the BOAC 1,000km at Brands Hatch where they were third. In 1972 the Ferraris dominated Prototype

racing, but Clay's only win was at Monza where he again co-drove with Ickx.

Ferrari was in dire trouble at the start of the 1973 season. Enzo Ferrari told Regazzoni that the team would be running only one car in F1 (which was not strictly true) and, although his contract would not be renewed, it was hoped to re-engage him again for 1974. For a season Regazzoni drove for BRM in F1, and Alfa Romeo in Prototype racing, and proved that he had been a very useful spy when he returned to Ferrari as had been promised. Although Regazzoni was nominally number one driver, it soon became evident that his role was to support young Austrian Niki Lauda, who had also joined the team from BRM.

Clay was consistently at the front during 1974. He was second four times, rounded off the season with a win at Watkins Glen, and finished second in the World Championship with 52 points to the 54 of Emerson Fittipaldi (McLaren). He scored a fine win in the 1975 Italian GP (fifth in the Championship won by Lauda), and in 1976 he was still competitive. He won the United States GP West at Long Beach, but his position in the team weakened after Lauda's terrible crash at the Nürburgring. Ferrari missed the Austrian race, but Regazzoni drove into second place the sole Ferrari entered at Zandvoort.

Lauda had recovered sufficiently to drive again at Monza, where Reutemann made his first appearance for the team. The Austrian's phenomenal recovery, coupled with Reutemann's presence in the team, made it clear that Regazzoni's career with Ferrari was coming to an end, and it was unrealistic to expect it to last indefinitely. Regazzoni has said that he didn't know how his career with Ferrari came to an end, but that was being very naïve.

Just before the 1976 Italian GP, Regazzoni went to the works to talk to Enzo Ferrari and said to him:

> 'I have heard rumours that my position at Ferrari as a driver is over.'

If Regazzoni reported Ferrari's reply accurately, it is obvious that Ferrari was being ingenuous and lying:

> 'As far as I'm concerned, there is no problem, but you must remember that I am only a member of the Board of Directors. Fiat will have an input in any decision, but no decision will be made until after the Japanese race [held on 24 October 1976].'

Regazzoni spoke again to Ferrari after the Italian GP and – apparently – the 'Old Man' was even vaguer. At this time, Regazzoni had offers from Brabham and McLaren, but he turned both down. Then, just before he departed for the United States GP East at Watkins Glen on 10 October, he received a telegram informing him that he was free to negotiate with other teams.

Clay was left without a competitive drive for 1977. He signed up for the impoverished Ensign team and drove for them all season, with best results being fifths at Monza and Watkins Glen. A year with the sinking Shadow team in 1978 netted another two fifth places. His last full season was with Williams in 1979, and it was a good year, for he won the British race (the Williams team's first ever win), took second places at Monaco and Hockenheim, and finished third at both Monza and Montreal.

To put it bluntly, Regazzoni had achieved all that could be expected of him at Williams, and there was no sentiment at Didcot to keep him in the team. He returned to Ensign for 1980, and in only the fourth race of the season at Long Beach the Ensign's brake pedal snapped off and he charged down the escape road into a parked Brabham.

He suffered serious spinal injuries that resulted in him being confined to a wheelchair. Despite this dreadful finale to his career in motor sport, his enthusiasm was undiminished. For more than ten years he commentated on motor sport for TV, he was fully involved in the development of hand-control systems for cars, and he even competed in saloon car racing with cars adapted this way. Regazzoni was killed in a collision with a lorry on an autostrada near Parma.

Reutemann, Carlos

Works driver
Born: 12 April 1942 (Santa Fe, Argentina)

Known as 'Lole', Reutemann was of very mixed ancestry, for one of his grandparents was a German-speaking Swiss, his mother Italian, and his father was an Argentinian cattle-rancher. He raced touring cars, and in F2, in Argentina before being chosen by the Automovil Club Argentino for a sponsored season in Europe with a Brabham BT30 F2 car in 1970. He performed well, but not conspicuously so, and returned to Europe in 1971 to take second place on 40 points in the F2 Championship (Peterson won with 54 points). Bernie Ecclestone acquired Brabham for 1972, and Reutemann

signed up with him that year and stayed with the team for several seasons.

During 1973, Reutemann drove Ferrari 312PB Sports Prototypes at Monza, Le Mans, and Watkins Glen, and Ferrari's knowledge of his sports car skills was to pay

Below: *Argentinian Carlos Reutemann was always regarded as an enigma because his race performances were so inconsistent, ranging from the brilliant to the abysmal. He drove for Ferrari in sports car racing in 1973, and then joined the Formula 1 team for 1977–8. He then spent a year with Lotus, enjoyed two full seasons with Williams and after the first two races of 1982 withdrew from racing and returned to Argentina. Quite why is not certain, but it may have been the embarrassment and discomfort caused to him on the world stage by the Argentine invasion of the Falkland Islands.* (LAT Photographic)

good dividends in the future. In 1974 Reutemann had a very successful year with the Brabham team and won the South African, Austrian, and United States races. He won the German race at the Nürburgring in 1975, but soon afterwards he started to become disenchanted with the team because of the contract to use Alfa Romeo engines.

The Argentinian has said that it was agreed that the Brabham team would take a Cosworth DFV-powered car to Brazil for the start of the 1976 season, if the Alfa Romeo-powered cars proved more than two seconds slower during winter testing. With the Alfa Romeo engine, the Brabham was more than two seconds slower, but there was no Cosworth-powered car at Interlagos. Reutemann retired at race after race during 1976, and his best performance was fourth at Jarama.

After Lauda's bad accident with a Ferrari in the German GP, the Fiat directors wanted to bring Reutemann into the Maranello team. Reutemann had to buy his way out of his Brabham contract by repaying all that he had earned so far in 1976, together with a penalty. Later he said:

'I finalised my deal with Ferrari, the Tuesday before Monza, with the help of Luca di Montezemolo.

On the Thursday, the day before the start of official practice, I drove the 312T2 for the first time. It was fantastic – it had an incredible feeling of strength, with vast torque and an excellent gearbox. I raced the car only in the Italian GP. During the race it became obvious that I was far too tall to fit into the cockpit, and I suffered bad cramp. As a result I finished ninth. It was my only race with Ferrari that year, and for the rest of the season I tested at Fiorano.'

Reutemann's racing career with Ferrari was fairly short-lived. He won only the Brazilian race in 1977, but he finished second in Spain and Japan, and took third places at Buenos Aires, Monaco and Anderstorp. Alan Henry wrote in *Ferrari Flat-12*:

'Carlos would be the first to admit that he was a driver who could be out-psyched by a strong team-mate and, in retrospect, one should remember that when assessing the Argentinian's performance in 1977.'

The following year, Carlos was promoted to team-leader, following the departure of Lauda, and he finished a strong third in the Drivers' Championship with wins in Brazil, at Long Beach, Brands Hatch, and Watkins Glen. Reutemann decided to leave Ferrari for 1979, and a deal was put together whereby he joined Mario Andretti at Lotus. The new 80 was a disaster, and Reutemann struggled with the obsolescent 79. Although he turned in some fine drives, his frequent poor finishes masked the effort and determination that he had put into his drives. His best performances were in the Argentine and Spanish races, in which he finished second.

After the single year with Lotus, Carlos joined Williams, and in 1980 he finished third in the Championship, winning at Monaco and taking second places at Hockenheim, Montreal, and Watkins Glen. After battling throughout the year with Piquet (Brabham), the outcome of the Championship was not settled until the last race at Caesars Palace, Las Vegas; after falling back to take eighth place because of handling problems that were not apparent until the warm-up, Carlos finished second in the Championship.

He reappeared in 1982, still driving for Williams. After finishing second at Kyalami, he was eliminated in Brazil by a collision with Arnoux. Carlos made the decision to withdraw from racing immediately. Whether this was because the unfair outcome at Caesars Palace still weighed on his mind, or whether it resulted from the conflicts and problems that arose from the Argentine invasion of the Falkland Islands has never been made clear.

Ricart, Wifredo

Engineer
Born: 15 May 1897 (Barcelona, Spain)
Died: 19 August 1974 (Majorca)

Much of what we know about Wifredo Playa y Medina Ricart comes from Enzo Ferrari's deep-rooted prejudices. He remains an enigmatic and much maligned engineer. The early years of his working life were spent in his Spanish homeland, in a backward motor industry. He was engineering supremo at Alfa Romeo during one of the bleakest periods in its long history. Later, in post-Second World War days, he was responsible for the creation of one of the most exclusive and exotic ranges of Grand Touring cars.

Ricart was born in Barcelona on 15 May 1897. He was about 5ft 10in in height, with dark hair, very pale skin, and green eyes. He came from an upper-class military background and is said to have been an engaging, charming, and persuasive speaker. Ricart spoke five languages, was devoted to music, and his interests extended to astronomy and drawing.

Above: *Spanish engineer Wifredo Ricart is best known for the hatred in which he was held by Enzo Ferrari who, in his autobiography, describes his alleged eccentricities in florid, incredible terms. Ricart was very able and carried out significant design work, and it is ironic that the first Ferrari engines had design features introduced by Ricart at Alfa Romeo.* (Author's collection)

The first Ricart cars were built to compete in the 1922 Voiturette Penya Rhin GP at Villafranca. Ricart was strongly influenced by Ernest Henry, the greatest automobile engineer of the early 1920s, and his work on twin overhead camshaft engines at Ballot. The Ricart engine was a four-cylinder of 1,498cc (75 x 84mm) and, like the contemporary Ballot, featured twin overhead camshafts, together with four valves and two plugs per cylinder. It is believed that power output was 58bhp at 5,600rpm.

There was the usual channel-section chassis, semi-elliptic springs, rigid axles front and rear, and an exceptionally neat two-seater body. It was reckoned that the maximum speed was about 85mph (137kph). Two cars ran at Villafranca, but both retired because of engine problems. K. Lee Guinness (Talbot) was the winner. The Ricarts ran in a number of other Spanish events with success, and in 1923 one of these cars, driven by Gaston, won its class in the Rabassada hill climb near Barcelona.

In speedboat racing the Ricart engine powered the craft that won both the Barcelona GP and the Spanish Championship. In 1926 Ricart exhibited a new model at the Paris Salon. This featured a six-cylinder, twin overhead camshaft 1485cc (64 x 77mm) engine with two valves per cylinder and twin carburettors. This car was never raced, nor did it enter production. Ricart y Perez did, however, build a small number of production cars with 1600cc side-valve engines at around this time.

Later, Ricart went into partnership with Dr Felipe Battlo y Godo, a textile engineer said to have limited racing experience, who had been building 1,600cc and 3,690cc cars in Barcelona under the name Automoviles Espana. Together, they marketed cars under the name Ricart-Espana. During the years 1930–4 Ricart worked as a freelance designer, mainly on the development of two-stroke diesel engines. In 1935 he was appointed General Manager of the Valencia public transport system, with especial responsibility for bus operations.

Although Ricart's home, Barcelona, was strongly Republican, he was an ardent Fascist. Valencia supported the Fascists in the Spanish Civil War. Generalissimo Franco, as he became in 1936, made Ricart an honorary captain in the Nationalist air force. It is said that Ricart had helped Alfa Romeo's Fascist managing director, Ugo Gobbato, when he was in Spain on business. Ricart had all the right credentials, and his departure in October 1936 to act as a technical adviser on a consultancy basis to Alfa Romeo was no mere coincidence. There is little doubt that Gobbato initially failed to realise the potential of the man he was taking on board.

Ricart was glad to escape from the horrors of the Spanish Civil War and – together with his wife, a half-French woman of exceptional good looks, his three sons, and his parents – he moved to Italy. Initially Ricart worked at the Portello factory on a V6 diesel engine. In 1937 Alfa Romeo entered into a consultancy agreement with Harry Ricardo's engine development company. This followed a visit by Ricardo to Milan that year and led to a close relationship between two men with confusingly similar names and the same intensive interest in the internal combustion engine; they not only worked together well, but became good friends.

With managing director Ugo Gobbato's support and approval, Ricart imposed a sense of order and purpose at Alfa Romeo, but this contributed to a great extent to the prejudice, which he encountered at the time, and the hatred of Enzo Ferrari and others in later years. In April 1940, Ricart was appointed Technical Consultant to the General Management and head of the Special Projects Section at Alfa Romeo. He had overall responsibility for three racing car designs, work on two of which was well advanced in 1938, and he was also working on the 28-cylinder Tipo 1101 aircraft engine.

What is clear is that the Alfa Romeo management regarded both the Tipo 316 V16 3-litre supercharged GP car and the Tipo 158 straight-eight Voiturette as interim models – even though the 158 was to prove one of the most long-lived and most successful racing cars of all time. Both were the work of Giaocchino Colombo, both followed the design principles of the great Vittorio Jano, who had been forced out of the company, and both were dear to the heart of Enzo Ferrari. Ferrari even described the 158 as a 'racing machine entirely mine'.

While Ferrari and his cronies inside and outside Alfa Romeo ridiculed Ricart as a man and an engineer, he was not too proud – as we shall see – to adopt aspects of Ricart's designs and regard them as his own. John Reynolds, in his biography of Harry Ricardo, *Engines and Enterprise: The Life and Work of Sir Harry Ricardo* claims (relying on correspondence in the Ricardo archives) that the V16 engine of Ricart's Tipo 162 projected GP car was substantially the work of Ricardo, and that Ricardo was responsible for the choice of its very wide, 135° cylinder layout.

It is clear that Ricart sought the advice of Ricardo, as consultant to Alfa Romeo, on design aspects of the 162 and followed the advice that he received. It is equally clear that Ricart was responsible for the overall design of the 162, and the fact that he sought the advice of Ricardo does not diminish his achievement, but is in fact a testimony to his open mind and common sense.

Cadillac used the angle of 135° between cylinders for their 16-cylinder model introduced in 1930. It was a very satisfactory layout for a racing engine; the balancing forces were excellent, it was compact if a little on the wide side, and the wide 'V' gave room for the installation of the superchargers and carburettors, while maintaining a low overall height. The capacity of the engine was 2,995cc (62 x 62mm). Griff Borgeson pointed out that this was the first use of a 'square' engine in GP racing since the early years of the century, and the shortest stroke ever used on a GP car up until that time.

There were two light alloy cylinder blocks with wet liners, and these incorporated split crankcases that were bolted together. The crankshaft ran in ten plain bearings, and there were roller-bearing big ends. Each of the detachable cylinder heads had twin overhead camshafts operating four valves per cylinder, not used previously by Alfa Romeo, through fingers, and with hairpin springs. These valve springs were another

suggestion by Ricardo, and previous racing Alfa Romeos had used conventional springs.

Designers were generally contemplating the use of twin-stage supercharging in pursuit of increased power output, and it was first seen in GP racing on the 1939 Mercedes-Benz W163. Ricart adopted twin-stage supercharging on the Tipo 162, with two single-stage and two twin-stage blowers mounted in the 'V' of the engine. The design of the Tipo 162 was largely settled in 1938, so it is clear that Ricart and Uhlenhaut (at Daimler-Benz) had adopted similar concepts independently.

Alfa Romeo laid down six Tipo 162 cars, but only one was completed. It was claimed that during the first bench-test in March 1940 the engine developed 490bhp at 7,800rpm. A four-speed gearbox was mounted behind and in unit with the final drive. The chassis was of tubular construction, with front suspension by trailing links and coil springs, and at the rear a de Dion axle was suspended on longitudinal torsion bars. The 162 first ran on 19 April 1940, and it was tested more intensively in June. On 10 June, Mussolini had dragged a reluctant Italy into the Second World War, so the Tipo 162 was never raced.

Ricart's second racing car project was probably of greater significance. This was the rear-engined Tipo 512, which reflected Auto Union design practice, by having a rear-mounted engine. In many respects – number and angle of cylinders apart – the design of the 512 closely followed that of the 162. The 512 had a horizontally opposed 12-cylinder engine of 1,490cc (54 x 54.2mm). The engine was cast as two magnesium-alloy, wet-liner cylinder blocks, joined on the centre-line, and had detachable cylinder heads.

Twin overhead camshafts per bank of cylinders, driven by a train of spur gears from the front of the engine, operated two valves per cylinder through fingers and hairpin valve springs, as on the 162. Although there were plain bearings at the outer ends of the crankshaft, the five inside main bearings and the big-ends were of the roller-type. Twin-stage supercharging was again used, with one low-pressure primary supercharger, one high-pressure secondary supercharger, and a single triple-choke carburettor mounted on top of the engine.

Transmission was by a five-speed gearbox in unit with the final drive. The chassis was a tubular structure, front suspension was by unequal-length double wishbones and longitudinal torsion bars, and at the rear there was a de Dion layout similar to that of the 162. Between the engine and the cockpit there was a very large saddle-shaped fuel tank that fitted snugly round the driver. Ricart pioneered the use of three-shoe brakes on the 512. These were retained on later production Alfa

Romeos, and many considered them superior to early disc brakes.

Ricart also installed twin-stage supercharging on an Alfa Romeo 158, and fitted one of these cars with Tipo 512 front and rear suspension. On 18 June 1940 Attilio Marinoni was testing the 158 with 512 suspension on the Milan–Varese autostrada when he collided with a lorry, the driver of which had fallen asleep and drifted across the centre-line of the road. The 158 caught fire and Marinoni was killed. Ricart's critics spread the story that the car involved in the accident was a 512, and it was a very simple and effective means of discrediting him.

The Tipo 512, described rather unkindly by one critic as 'looking like a 158 going backwards', ran as a complete car for the first time in September 1940. The prospects of it ever being raced were bleak indeed, for Italy had entered the Second World War three months earlier. The power output was claimed to be 335bhp at 8,600rpm – 225bhp per litre – and even if this figure was somewhat exaggerated it was still the highest power output per litre of any car built up until that time. In contrast the power output of the Tipo 158 at this time was 152bhp per litre.

Consalvo Sanesi, who had succeeded Attilio Marinoni as chief test driver, tested the 512 extensively, but was two seconds a lap slower at Monza than with the 158. The 512 suffered from major handling problems, not unexpected with such a new and radical time, but it was some while before Sanesi could persuade Ricart of the car's shortcomings. Apart from other deficiencies, the roll-axis was too high and the 'old guard' at Alfa Romeo were content to let Ricart and his aides struggle with these problems rather than contribute the benefit of their long experience.

Yet another Ricart project in 1941 was the Tipo 163 sports-racing coupé, which was to be powered by a version of the Tipo 162 GP engine in normally aspirated 190bhp form and with very streamlined body, complete with wheel valances. Although one car was built, it was never completed because of the imminent departure of Ricart and his team from Milan.

Ricart was also working on the Tipo 1101 liquid-cooled radial aero engine, with 28 cylinders in seven banks of four and a capacity of 50 litres. Despite all the difficulties at the factory, this engine was running on a test rig in 1942 and by November of that year it was producing around 2000hp. Ricart was planning a turbocharged version, which, it was anticipated, would develop 2500hp at 23,000ft. While Italy was at war, there was the possibility of this engine powering both fighter and bomber aircraft.

Because of Allied bombing raids on Milan in October 1942, Ricart had moved the special projects, design, and development departments to Lago d'Orta, to the north of Milan, and the experimental workshops were set up at nearby Arimeno. During the time that he spent at Lago d'Orta, Ricart worked on the design of the 6C 2000 Gazzella saloon prototype, with 2-litre six-cylinder engine, unit construction, and the gearbox in unit with the rear axle. Bomb damage to the Alfa Romeo factory prevented this design from entering mass production.

As the war progressed in the Allies' favour, support for the Fascist cause became less and less acceptable, and Ricart's popularity waned even further. On 28 April 1945, an unknown assailant, probably a Communist supporter, shot to death Fascist managing director Ugo Gobbato. Ricart almost certainly was on the list for assassination, but when his contract expired on 31 March 1945, it was simply allowed to lapse and he quickly left Italy.

No one hated Ricart more than Enzo Ferrari, who regarded Ricart as an eccentric showman, and his comments about him stretch credulity. In his autobiography Ferrari wrote of him:

'Ricart affected jackets with sleeves that came down far below his wrists and shoes with enormously thick soles. When he shook hands, it was like grasping the cold, lifeless hand of a corpse.'

Ferrari had a personal axe to grind, and he was, wittingly, guilty of copying certain of Ricart's design features, which Colombo incorporated in the first V12 Ferraris. In his memoirs, Enzo Ferrari claims that he chose a V12 layout for his first cars because he had been so impressed by the pre-war V12 Packard Twin Six.

It is a fatuous statement, for Ferrari was intimately familiar with the Jano- and Colombo-designed Alfa Romeo V12 GP engines, and the technology of these and Ricart's work was there for the taking. Engine design is an evolutionary process, rather than a revolutionary one, and Ferrari's sin was not the copying of the ideas of Jano and Ricart, but his open contempt for a man whom he should have respected.

Ricart returned to Spain, and in 1946 he was appointed Director General of Centro de Estudios de Automocion, a body that determined the future products of Empresa Nacional de Autocamiones SA (ENASA), a company which it had formed to manufacture commercial vehicles. It was a well-timed move by Franco's non-combatant government, when the rest of Europe's motor industry was struggling to rebuild bomb-shattered factories or build up production lines to meet peacetime orders.

The main factory was at Barajas, Madrid, but the company also occupied the old Hispano-Suiza factory at

Sagrera, Barcelona, which had continued making cars until 1943. Ricart did not entirely lack support in Italy, and around 25 former Alfa Romeo and Fiat engineers joined him in the new venture. In March 1947, the ENASA board appointed Ricart adviser on technical matters. Nearly two years later, in January 1949, Ricart became what amounted to Director General of ENASA. Initially all vehicles were built under licence, and the company built up close ties with Leyland. The range included buses, coaches, trolleybuses, and tractors.

The tractors were marketed under the name 'Empresa', but all the other products were sold under the name 'Pegaso', the Spanish for Pegasus, the mythical winged horse that arose from the blood spilt when Perseus struck off the head of Medusa. Between 1951 and 1957 ENASA built a mere 84 very high-priced V8 cars, the majority of which had four overhead camshaft engines. The company adopted a handsome flying horse badge that, at least when applied to the V8 cars, appeared to be a mockery of Ferrari's prancing horse.

Rodriguez, Pedro

Works driver
Born: 18 January 1940 (Polanco, Mexico City)
Died: 11 July 1971 (Norisring, Germany)

The two Mexican racing drivers, Pedro and Ricardo Rodriguez, were the sons of Don 'Pedro' Hermanos Rodriguez. Jo Ramirez wrote of him at some length:

'"Don Pedro", as he used to be known, owned several businesses and was well connected with the government, so that his products were those that the government chose whenever it needed the particular items he manufactured. He therefore never lacked sales.

In Europe and the United States there were all sorts of different versions of where and how Don Pedro came by his money: it was said, for instance, that he was the strong man of the Mexican City police force, and that he was the right-hand man of President Lázaro Cárdenas in the 1930s [he was president 1934–40], and therefore had the necessary connections to make a huge profit from property and land in Mexico City and Acapulco. It was even suggested that he owned the biggest chain of bordellos in Mexico City….

Don Pedro had been a motorcycle racer in his youth, and was a great racing enthusiast who wanted his sons to shine in the sport. He therefore started them early, on motorcycles and in karts. By the time they were in their teens they were already driving big powerful race cars – Ricardo raced a Porsche RSK Spyder, while Pedro had a Chevrolet Corvette and a Ferrari Testa Rossa, even though they weren't old enough to drive on public roads.'

In their early racing careers, the two brothers gained drives in Luigi Chinetti's North American Racing Team, which Rodriguez Senior financed to a certain extent. With a NART Ferrari, they took second place in the 1958 Nassau Trophy and, later, in 1961 the brothers finished third in the 12 Hours race at Sebring. Then the brothers came to Europe, still racing NART cars, and in 1961 in the Nürburgring 1,000km race they took second place, and they won the Paris 1,000km event. Rodriguez achieved very little in 1962, the year of his brother's death, but he recovered from the blow sufficiently to continue racing. For several years, however, it seemed that his career was going absolutely nowhere.

He drove Ferraris in North America in 1963–4, and he appeared with Team Lotus 25s at Watkins Glen and Mexico City in 1963, but retired at both circuits. Because Ferrari was at war with the Italian Motor Sport Association before they failed to support him over the

Left: *Seen here at the 1969 British GP at Silverstone where he drove a Tipo 312 V12 Ferrari, the young Pedro Rodriguez was a brilliant sports car driver, one of the greatest ever, but he never quite made it to the top in the rarefied atmosphere of Formula 1.* **(Guy Griffiths Collection)**

homologation of the 250LM, NART entered the works
F1 Ferraris in the 1964 North American races in
American white and blue colours, and Pedro drove a V6
to sixth place and his first World Championship point.

In 1965 he again drove Ferraris in the two North
American F1 races following Surtees's bad accident in
practice for the sports car Canadian GP. They were in
American colours and entered in NART's name, but
were works cars. Pedro retired his Tipo 1512 in both
races. The following year, he raced Lotus 33s a few
times, and in 1967 Roy Salvadori, Cooper racing
manager, brought him into the team, and he scored a
surprise win in the South African race. What had been
intended as a one-off appearance for Cooper became
the start of his first season as a full works driver, but the
team's Maserati-powered cars were in marked decline,
and all that Pedro could achieve later that year were a
couple of fifth and sixth places.

Pedro joined BRM in 1968, and after the team did
well in the Tasman series with 2.5-litre versions of their
V12s, the performance of the V12s in full 3-litre form
during the year was mediocre. Rodriguez achieved a
very lucky second place at Spa behind Bruce McLaren
(McLaren) after Stewart had to stop for fuel in his Matra.
Pedro also finished third at Zandvoort and third at
St Jovite. The team failed to appreciate his efforts, and
for 1969 he was replaced by John Surtees. Rodriguez
also joined John Wyer's Gulf team at Le Mans in 1968
because the team was desperately short of drivers, and,
partnered by Lucien Bianchi, won the race with a Ford
GT40 from the Porsche 907 of Steinemann/Spoerry.

Pedro drove a BRM for Tim Parnell's team in the early
part of 1969, but in mid-season moved to Ferrari. The
V12s were obsolete, and his best performances were
sixth in Italy and fifth (entered by NART) at Watkins
Glen. That year the Mexican had also driven for Ferrari
in Prototype racing, and although he turned in some
magnificent efforts, there was little success because of
the strength of the Porsche 908 opposition and the
poor reliability of the Ferrari 312Ps.

Pedro's greatness came into its own in 1970–1. He
returned to BRM who had succeeded in producing a
decent development of the V12, the P153, and there was
no shortage of money because of Yardley sponsorship.
With the P153, Pedro won the Belgian GP at Spa, and also
finished second at Watkins Glen after a late stop to top
up the fuel cost him the lead to Emerson Fittipaldi. He
stayed with BRM for 1971, but generally the season was
harder, and his best performance was second in the
Dutch race after leading in the wet much of the race –
when his engine developed a misfire, there was no way
that he could hold off Ickx.

Above: *'Papa' (Hermanos) Rodriguez is seen here in the
pits at Le Mans in 1961 with younger son Pedro. They are
awaiting the arrival of Ricardo, overdue with the 250TR
Testa Rossa that the brothers were driving. The engine had
failed, and he coasted into the pits to retire a few seconds
after this photograph was taken.* (Author's collection)

At the Gulf-Porsche team in 1970–1 Pedro was a
leading protagonist in the battle between the 917s and
the 512S Ferraris; his performance was stimulated by
his rivalry with Jo Siffert, who also raced for the team,
and although they were team-mates, their battles were
exciting, sometimes frightening, to watch. Partnered by
Kinnunen, Rodriguez won four of the ten rounds in the
Sports Car Championship, and his driving was
exceptionally fast and sure-footed in the wet. In the race
at Brands Hatch, wet for most of its distance, the
Mexican was driving in torrential rain at almost
undiminished speed, when John Wyer, Gulf team boss,
looked up from his lap charts and snapped, 'Will
someone tell Pedro it's raining.'

Ferrari had pulled out of racing Competition Sports
Cars in 1971, and was entering only a new 3-litre
Prototype, although the 917s continued to battle with
this and the 3-litre Alfa Romeos. Early in the season,
partnered by Jack Oliver, Pedro won at Daytona, Monza,
and Spa. Any reasonable driver would have concluded
that he had enough on his hands with BRM and Gulf-
Porsche, but Pedro lived for racing, and he agreed to
drive a 5-litre Ferrari 512M for Herbert Müller at the
Norisring on 11 July 1971. He crashed heavily –
probably because of tyre failure – the car caught fire,
and by the time Pedro had been released from the
wreckage he had died because of multiple injuries.

Rodriguez, Ricardo

Works driver
Born: 14 February 1942 (Polanco, Mexico City)
Died: 1 November 1962 (Mexico City)

Jo Ramirez, who knew the family well, wrote:

> 'I remember one particular weekend when Ricardo went to California with his RSK Porsche, to drive in a couple of races at Riverside racetrack. He was, naturally, not allowed to drive on the Californian roads, so Don Pedro did the chauffeuring.
>
> When they got to the circuit and met all the other drivers – people of the calibre of Ken Miles, Richie Ginther, and John von Neumann – they took one look at this Mexican boy and had wry smiles on their faces. Well, Ricardo may have been just a boy, but he went on to win both the Saturday and Sunday races.
>
> OK, the Rodriguez brothers had money and the best equipment, but there was no doubt that they were good, especially Ricardo. He was a born racer who didn't have to work at it – it all came naturally. He had a talent for speed and was completely fearless. In short, he had all the ingredients of a World Champion.
>
> On another occasion I saw him driving in six different races on a Sunday at the Mexican Autodromo Magdalena Mixhuca, now renamed the Autodromo Hermanos Rodriguez. The first race was for small saloon cars (which he won in a Renault Dauphine), then came a race for bigger saloon cars, then sports cars, and so on to the main event, Formula Junior. Ricardo proved his versatility by winning all of them.'

In 1960 Ricardo shared a NART-entered 250GT SWB at Le Mans with André Pilette, and they drove an outstanding race to finish second. Chinetti had obtained for the Rodriguez family a special version of the Testa Rossa. It had originated as the V6 3-litre car that Hawthorn raced at the International Trophy meeting at Silverstone in May 1958, and thereafter was rebuilt as a V12 works car. After the 1958 Nürburgring 1,000km race in which von Trips/Gendebien had finished third, it stood in a corner at the factory. It was rebuilt with a TR60-type

Below: *A driver of immense promise, Ricardo Rodriguez drove Ferraris on a regular basis. In the main, these were Sports Prototypes, but he was at the wheel of this 65° Formula 1 car in the 1962 Pau GP. The race was dominated by Maurice Trintignant, who won the race with a Rob Walker-entered Lotus, but Ricardo finished second after a battle with private entrant Jack Lewis at the wheel of a V8 BRM.* (Author's collection)

body and right-hand drive. The Rodriguez brothers had driven it into second place in the 1960 Nassau Trophy and then finished third with it at Sebring in 1961.

At the 1961 Italian GP the 'Old Man' gave Ricardo what amounted to a test drive under racing conditions. Ricardo drove one of the older V6 cars with the cylinders at an angle of 65° instead of the 120° of the later, more powerful cars. Rodriguez was second fastest in practice, a quite incredible performance, 1/10sec slower than von Trips. In the early stages of the race Rodriguez held third place, but he retired because of fuel pump failure.

Ricardo joined the works Ferrari team in 1962 and, despite the team's serious lack of competitiveness in F1, Ricardo turned in some very impressive performances. In Prototype racing, as it was now called, he shared the winning 246SP V6 sports car with Willy Mairesse and Olivier Gendebien in the Targa Florio. Although he achieved no other Prototype/ sports car successes, he performed well in F1, but constantly carped at Ferrari about the shortcomings of the cars.

In the Pau GP on 23 April, Easter Monday, Ricardo finished second, about a minute behind Maurice Trintignant with a four-cylinder Lotus-Climax. He drove the car that Phil Hill had raced at Monza in September 1961, and all the way to the finish Ricardo scrapped with Jack Lewis at the wheel of his private V8 BRM. In reality, Ferrari had too many drivers, so Ricardo appeared with the F1 team rather inconsistently. He crashed in the Dutch race, finished fourth at Spa, took sixth place with a 65° car at the Nürburgring, and retired because of ignition problems at Monza.

Ferrari missed the North American races, but Ricardo arranged a drive at the wheel of the Rob Walker-entered Lotus 24 with Climax V8 engine in the first Mexican GP, a non-Championship race. Ramirez was at the race and in his book he recounts a telephone call with a friend, Roberto Ayala, who was present at the circuit:

'Ricardo lost control at the entrance of the Peraltada [a tight, but fast right-hand corner] where there's an undulation right across the track.

It's difficult to know what happened, but it could have been a chassis failure. He hit the outside guard rail and then bounced back into the inside one, where he was thrown against the rail and practically cut in half. He was conscious, but in deep pain, crying: 'I don't want to die, please don't let me die!' But all of the paramedics' efforts were in vain, and he died on the way to the hospital.'

Although Ricardo was only 20, approaching 21, he was already married to Sarita Cardosa, whom he had known

for a long time. Jo Ramirez remembers when Ricardo was courting Sarita. She lived very close to Jo, and he recalls Ricardo parking his metallic-gold Oldsmobile outside Jo's house when he visited. His death was a national disaster in Mexico; the family were completely shattered and, although he was determined to continue racing, Pedro was mentally crucified by his brother's death.

Rosier, Louis

Private Ferrari driver and works driver at Le Mans in 1954

Born: 5 November 1905 (Chapdes-Beaufort, Auvergne, France)

Died: 29 October 1956 (Neuilly-sur-Seine in hospital, Paris, France)

Essentially a private entrant, and no 'ace', Rosier was a hard-slogging driver, who loved the sport, drove as

Below: *Several times Champion of France, Louis Rosier enjoyed a long and relatively successful career as a private entrant of Ferraris and, later, Maseratis. Here, the consistent and determined French driver is seen at the wheel of his 4½-litre unsupercharged Talbot-Lago at the International Trophy meeting at Silverstone in May 1951.* **(Tom March Collection)**

often as possible and was several times French Champion. He was the son of a wine merchant. He started competition work with a Harley-Davidson motorcycle in 1927, and later opened his own garage, which became one of the biggest Renault agents (in addition to selling Talbot cars). According to some sources, Rosier worked with the Resistance, and his wife and daughter were taken to Germany as hostages. He went there in 1945 after the end of hostilities, found them, and brought them back to France.

In early post-war days he competed with a Talbot Type 26C F1 car which was normally entered in the name of Écurie Rosier. With this car he raced internationally, but also won many French races, which were held regularly in France in much the same way as travelling circuses. For 1952 he acquired a Tipo 375 Ferrari GP car (which he raced only on a limited number of occasions because of the change in the formula for GP racing) and a Tipo 500 F2 car. The Tipo 375 was rebuilt in 1954 as a sports car with central driving position, but it was not a success.

His results included wins at Montlhéry (1948), Albi (1950, 1952–3, the last of these years with the Ferrari), Bordeaux (1951), Cadours (1952, Ferrari), and Les Sables d'Olonne (1953, Ferrari). Although he achieved very little success in World Championship races, it has been calculated that he drove in 38 of these events, starting with the first, the British GP (also called the European GP) at Silverstone on 13 May 1950). Partnered by his son Jean-Louis (who drove only briefly), he won at Le Mans in 1950 with a two-seater 4.5-litre Talbot.

For 1954, Rosier acquired a second Tipo 500 Ferrari, and both of his cars were rebuilt at the factory with 2.5-litre engines to comply with the GP formula that came into force that year. Maurice Trintignant scored a surprise victory with one of these cars in the Formule Libre Buenos Aires City GP, and thereafter joined the works Ferrari team. Rosier also joined the works Ferrari team at Le Mans sharing a 4.9-litre Tipo 375 Plus with Robert Manzon, and although they held second place at one stage, they retired because of gearbox problems.

Rosier ordered a Tipo 250F Maserati and, after running as a works entry in the 1955 Italian GP, he drove his ex-Marimon 250F, chassis number 2506, in European events through 1956, with a best result of fifth in the 1956 German GP. He also raced a private Ferrari Monza sports-racing car in 1955, and for 1956 took delivery of a new Maserati 300S sports-racing car. On 7 October 1956, Rosier crashed on the first lap of the Coupe du Salon on the 3.9-mile (6.28km) combined road and banked track circuit at Montlhéry. He lingered in Arpajon hospital until he died on 29 October. Hygiene in French hospitals was very bad at the time and it can be surmised that an infection contributed to his death.

At his Renault dealership in Clermont-Ferrand, he had developed and manufactured, in small numbers, sporting cars based on 4CV and Frégate components. Italian coachbuilder Rocco Motto was responsible for the bodywork, and the later car based on the Frégate had a multi-tubular chassis. The cars were assembled by a company called Brissoneau. Rosier was also closely involved in the project to develop the race-track on public roads at Clermont-Ferrand, and when this eventually opened in 1958 it was known as Circuit de Charade Louis Rosier.

Ruesch, Hans

Driver
Born: 17 May 1913 (Naples, Italy)
Died: 27 August 2007 (Lugano, Switzerland)

A late survivor among drivers who raced in pre-war days, Hans Ruesch was born in Naples to a German-speaking Swiss textile industrialist and a Swiss mother who spoke Neapolitan. After education in Switzerland, he attended Zurich University where he read law. He lived in Paris and, subsequently, the United States. He started motor racing in 1932 with an Alfa Romeo and, in the motor racing world, he was constantly buying cars and selling them on at a profit. He was a regular competitor in the Mille Miglia, and in 1936 he bought one of the Tipo 8C 35 GP cars from Scuderia Ferrari. With Dick Seaman as co-driver, he won the 1936 Donington GP with this car.

Later, in 1936, he finished second to Raymond Mays (ERA) in the Mountain Championship at Brooklands. In 1937 his successes included wins in the GP des Frontières and the Bucharest GP. Against much stronger opposition, he took eighth place in the German GP at the Nürburgring and in the Milan GP. Later the same year he won the Brooklands Mountain Championship from Kenneth Evans (2.9-litre Alfa Romeo Monoposto).

It has been calculated that between 1932 and 1937 Ruesch achieved 27 wins, three second places, and five thirds. He withdrew from racing in 1937 and turned to authorship. He wrote a novel, *Top of the World* that sold a million copies, and was later filmed as *The Savage Innocents*, starring Anthony Quinn and Peter O'Toole. He married Maria Luisa de la Feld in 1949 and they had

Above: *Hans Ruesch always ran as a privateer, and also acted as a trader in racing cars. He had many interests outside motor racing, but even so he turned in some fine drives.* (LAT Photographic)

Salo, Mika

Racing driver
Born: 30 November 1966 (Helsinki, Finland)

In his early years, Salo achieved great success in karts and FF1600, and he came to Britain in 1989 to drive F3 Reynard-Toyota cars for Alan Docking Racing. He continued to drive Ralts for this team in 1990, but during the year he was convicted of driving over the alcohol limit. As this damaged the prospects of him being issued with a FIA Super Licence, he moved to Japan where he tested and raced on behalf of Yokohama tyres.

He was in Japan for four years, but at the end of 1994 he was offered drives in the last two races by Lotus (a tenth place and a retirement), and then in 1995 he joined the Tyrrell team whose Yamaha-powered cars brought him only two fifth places in the Italian and Australian races. Salo stayed for another two seasons with Tyrrell, with best results of: in 1996, fifth in the Brazilian and Monaco GPs (in the latter race he retired because of a collision, but was still classified), and in 1997, fifth in the Monaco GP.

For 1998, he moved to Arrows, the most consistently unsuccessful F1 team and, in simple terms, it was another wasted year with a succession of retirements and dreadful placings, relieved by one finish in the points – a fourth place at Monaco. That Salo's career was going nowhere was all too obvious. There was no longer a seat for him at Arrows because of lack of sponsorship, but he drove in three races in the BAR team, following Zonta suffering a foot injury.

After Schumacher's accident at Silverstone, Salo was brought into the Ferrari team. Much of the team's energies were expended on supporting Irvine in his battle to beat the McLarens in the World Championship, but Salo took a brilliant second place in the German GP, after relinquishing the lead to Irvine on instructions from the pit. He also took an excellent third place in the Italian race at Monza, and deserved better than being abandoned in the wilderness once more.

For 2000, Salo joined Sauber (11th in the Championship), but for the following year he went to Toyota, who were preparing to enter F1, and he drove regularly for them during their debut year in 2002. Followers of F1 were astonished when Toyota dropped him at the end of the year. Salo dropped out of F1 completely, but he has raced in endurance events, driving Maseratis and Ferraris. He lives in Monaco with a Japanese wife and their two children, and believes that one day – not too far away – his F1 career will work out.

three children. In 1953 his novel *The Racer* was published and was made into a film of the same name (but also shown under the title *Such Men are Dangerous*) starring Kirk Douglas.

Ruesch returned briefly to racing in 1953 at the wheel of a Ferrari Tipo 340MM car with Touring spider body. He drove an inspired race in the British Empire Trophy race held on the difficult Isle of Man road circuit, and in the handicap final took third place with this very unsuitable car, beating Moss with a C-type Jaguar. In September 1953 he drove the same car in the Supercortemaggiore GP at Merano, but spun off into a spectator area, killing a policeman and injuring a number of people. He withdrew from racing once more. In the 1970s he became a significant figure in the anti-vivisection movement, and wrote many books and papers on animal rights and natural medicines.

Salvadori, Roy

Racing Driver
Born: 12 May 1922 (Dovercourt, Essex, England)

Although Roy Francesco Salvadori raced just about every make of European car between 1946 and his eventual retirement in 1965, he drove Ferraris only rarely. In 1952 Bobby Baird offered him a drive with his Tipo 500 Ferrari in the British GP, and Roy drove steadily, if not spectacularly, to finish eighth, three laps behind race-winner Ascari. Shortly afterwards, Baird asked Roy to attend a test session at Snetterton and there he drove both the Tipo 500 and Baird's Tipo 225 2.7-litre sports car. He was consistently quicker than the owner, and as a result was invited to drive in a number of races during the remainder of that season.

After finishing fourth overall with the sports Ferrari in the over 2000cc sports car race at the international meeting at Boreham on the Saturday of the August Bank Holiday weekend, he shared the Tipo 225 with the owner in the Goodwood Nine Hours race. After pit stop delays and with Roy doing most of the driving, they eventually finished third behind the winning Aston Martin and another Ferrari driven by Tom Cole and Graham Whitehead.

Later, Roy drove Baird's F2 car at Goodwood in September (fifth and sixth places in the two short races entered) and won the F2 race at Castle Combe the following weekend, as well as finishing fourth in the Formule Libre race. It was back again at the wheel of the sports car a week later, and Roy took third place in the race for unlimited-capacity sports cars at Charterhall near Berwick-upon-Tweed the following weekend. Originally Roy was going to drive Baird's cars in most races in 1953, but Baird changed his mind, so Roy signed up as a works Connaught driver.

He did not race a Ferrari again until August 1962 when he drove John Coombs's new 250GTO into second place behind Mike Parkes with the Maranello Concessionaires' car. He drove 250LMs twice for Maranello Concessionaires in his last full season of racing in 1964: second in the 100-mile Archie Scott-Brown Memorial Trophy at Snetterton in July, and second in the Coppa Inter-Europa at Monza in September – both races were for Prototypes and GT cars.

Below: *Roy Salvadori in the cockpit of his Frazer Nash Le Mans Replica at the International Trophy meeting at Silverstone in 1952. Despite a near-fatal crash at this circuit with his Frazer Nash the previous year, Roy bounced back to finish sixth overall and win the 2000cc class.* (Guy Griffiths Collection)

Scaglietti, Sergio

Coachbuilder
Born: 1920 (Modena, Italy)

Sergio entered the motor trade at the age of 13 following the death of his father, aided by his older brother who lied about Sergio's age so as to get him a job at the coachbuilders where he worked. Only four years later Sergio's brother, together with a friend, set up their own bodyshop opposite the premises of Scuderia Ferrari in Modena, and Sergio went along with them. Their standards of work were high, they were conveniently situated, and Scuderia Ferrari was soon bringing in cars for body repairs.

In post-war days the small Scaglietti workshop received occasional work on Ferraris, and Enzo Ferrari noted the high standards that the small firm adopted. Ferrari gave Scaglietti the chance to build competition bodies, both to Pininfarina's and his own designs. The Scaglietti works gradually expanded, and the sheer convenience of having a body-builder so close was immense. It increasingly became the practice with the company's GT cars that Pininfarina created the design at their works in Turin, and that the production bodies were built by Scaglietti close to the Maranello factory.

In the early 1960s, the Scaglietti concern was taken over by Ferrari to ensure that the company always had its own supplier and was not dependent on outside companies whose production could be disrupted by the strikes so often implemented by the metalworkers' union. Control of the Scaglietti company passed with Ferrari to Fiat, and it remains Ferrari's in-house coachbuilder.

Scarfiotti, Ludovico

Works driver
Born: 18 October 1933 (Rome, Italy)
Died: 8 June 1968 (Rossfeld, Germany)

Described by Steve Small as 'A great all-rounder who wasn't out of the top drawer', 'Ludo' Scarfiotti nevertheless developed into a very successful member of the Ferrari team in both racing and sports car events. He belonged to one of the founding families of Fiat, lived in Rome, and the family ran a very substantial construction business. Like so many Italians, he had a

Above: *Ludovico Scarfiotti drove for Ferrari in sports and F1 races on various occasions between 1964 and 1968, but he was much more successful at the wheel of Sports Prototypes and sports cars. His greatest success was his win in the 1966 Italian GP. He was killed while practising with a Porsche for the Rossfeld hill climb in 1968. (LAT Photographic)*

great love of motor racing and, like so many Italians, his racing career started in the Mille Miglia 1,000-mile road race in which he won the 1100cc Touring and Gran Turismo class with a Fiat in 1956. He drove a Fiat in the race again in 1957, but failed to finish.

He was tested by Ferrari in 1958, but, clearly, the team was not impressed and he went on racing an OSCA, said to be a 2-litre, of which a few examples were built. With this car he finished second to Cabianca, a long-serving OSCA driver, in the 62-mile (100km) Naples GP held that year on the Posillipo circuit. He continued to race the OSCA in 1959, but a year later, in 1960, he shared the driving of a 2-litre V6 Dino works Ferrari with Cabianca and Mairesse in the Targa Florio, and they finished fourth.

Later that year, he shared a Testa Rossa TR60 at Le Mans with Pedro Rodriguez, but that was the year that two of the works Ferraris ran out of fuel early in the race because of a monumental error made by Luigi Bazzi, who failed to take account of changes made to the cars after the practice weekend. Scarfiotti was still not a member of the works team in 1962 when he won the European Hill Climb Championship with a mid-engined 2-litre Dino 196SP prepared at the works and entered by Scuderia Sant'Ambroeus.

It was not until 1963 that Scarfiotti became a works driver on a regular basis. He drove a Tipo 156 F1 car in the Dutch GP and finished sixth, but he was seen rather more frequently driving Ferraris in the Prototype class. At this time the team was racing the 3-litre V12 Tipo 250P which was virtually unbeatable. Scarfiotti partnered Mairesse at the wheel of a 250P in the 1963 Targa Florio, but they were eliminated by a rather odd occurrence. Ludovico made a rather heavy landing with the car and had flattened the outward bulge at the bottom of the fuel system, which housed the inlet for the fuel line, and this partly cut off the fuel supply.

The car was retired because of a badly misfiring engine. At the Nürburgring 1,000km race that year, Scarfiotti partnered Mike Parkes, but Parkes spun their 250P into a bridge and it was too badly damaged to continue. 'Ludo's' greatest success that year was in the Le Mans 24 Hours race in which he partnered Bandini at the wheel of a 250P. They took the lead and won after the retirement of Surtees/Mairesse with a similar car.

In 1964 Ludovico partnered Nino Vaccarella with a 275P in the Sebring 12 Hours race and, after delays caused by a defective rear light and a faulty clutch, they finished second behind Parkes/Maglioli, who were also driving a 275P. The next Prototype race for the works team was the Nürburgring 1,000km, which Scarfiotti/Parkes won with their 275P. Scarfiotti was partnered with Parkes, again at the wheel of a 275P, at Le Mans, but they had a lot of problems in this race and retired because of oil pump failure. Later in the year, Scarfiotti finished second with a 330P in the sports car Canadian GP. He drove only in one F1 race, the Italian GP, in September, in which he finished ninth.

Ludovico's first Prototype race in 1965 was in the Monza 1,000km in which he partnered Surtees in a 330P2 (4-litre car with twin overhead camshafts per bank of cylinders). A tyre failed while Surtees was at the wheel, they dropped to seventh and then climbed back to finish second to team-mates Parkes/Guichet. Scarfiotti partnered Parkes in the Targa Florio, but he crashed early in the race. He co-drove with Surtees in both the Nürburgring 1,000km race, where they led throughout with the 330P2 except for routine pit stops, and Le Mans, where they retired because of gearbox failure. All the works Ferraris and all the Fords retired in the 1965 24 Hours race.

The 1966 season saw Scarfiotti's greatest achievement in winning the Italian GP with a 3-litre V12 Ferrari, leading team-mate Parkes and Denis Hulme (Brabham) across the line. At Sebring he co-drove a Dino 206S with Bandini, and they finished fifth, second in class. It was a lucky victory on a fast circuit, and Ludovico had been able to benefit from a high level of retirements.

Scarfiotti had a good run of success with Ferraris in Prototype racing, despite the strength of the Ford opposition. He partnered Parkes again with a 330P3 in the Spa 1,000km race, and they won easily from the Fords of Whitmore/Gardner and Scott/Revson. These two drivers were paired again at Le Mans, but Scarfiotti collided with a Matra-BRM shortly before midnight. Scarfiotti defended his European Hill Climb Championship, but his efforts were disrupted by strikes in Italy, and Mitter and Herrmann took the first two places with lightweight Porsche flat-eight cars.

After testing at Daytona with the new P4 in late 1966, Ferrari was in a strong position in the 24 Hours race at the beginning of February. The Fords were plagued by gearbox problems, and the works Ferraris took the first two places, with Bandini/Amon winning from Parkes/Scarfiotti. It was a good start to a season of Ford versus Ferrari battles. Ferrari missed the Sebring race, and in the Monza 1,000km race (which Ford missed) the P4s again took the first two places, with Amon/Bandini leading Scarfiotti/Parkes across the line. Then Ferrari entered only a single P4 for Scarfiotti/Parkes in the Spa 1,000km race, but they were delayed by gear-selector problems and finished a poor fifth.

In the meantime, Scarfiotti had finished fourth with a V12 F1 Ferrari in the Race of Champions at Brands Hatch, and then, in a prearranged finish, Scarfiotti and Parkes dead-heated in the non-Championship Siracusa GP. Shortly afterwards, Bandini was killed at Monaco, which was a terrible blow to the team's morale. Maranello pulled out of the Nürburgring 1,000km race and, although Ford won at Le Mans, Scarfiotti/Parkes finished second. Shortly afterwards, Parkes was badly injured at Spa, and Klass was killed at Mugello.

Ferrari clinched the Prototype Championship at the end of July when Amon/Stewart finished second to the Chaparral of Phil Hill/Spence in the newly inaugurated BOAC 500 race at Brands Hatch, with Scarfiotti/Sutcliffe taking fifth place. The run of disasters suffered by the Maranello team had disheartened 'Ludo', and after a dispute with Lini and Forghieri, in which he was criticised for not driving hard enough at Brands Hatch, he left the team. He drove an Eagle for Dan Gurney at the Italian GP, but retired because of engine problems.

For 1968, Scarfiotti signed up for F1 with Cooper, to drive their V12 BRM-powered cars. He retired in South

Africa, and took fourth places at Jarama and Monaco, which was quite encouraging. He also occasionally drove for Porsche, and negotiated with Cooper for their consent on an individual event basis. He finished well down the field at Sebring, but partnered Mitter in the second-place 907 at Monza, and retired in the Targa Florio.

Jonathan Sieff, a director of the Cooper Car Company, recalled:

'Ludo asked me if he could be released from his contract with us to drive a Porsche in the Rossfeld Hill Climb on 2 June. There was no GP that weekend, so I didn't have any objection. Although Roy Salvadori was no longer racing manager, we were still close. He became quite heated by my decision, banging the table and telling me that Ludo was under contract to Cooper and we should not allow him to break it in this way. Roy was quite right, for Scarfiotti was, tragically, killed in practice at Rossfeld. For no obvious reason, he went straight on at a corner, was killed outright and his body flung out of the car.'

Scheckter, Jody

Works driver
Born: 29 January 1950 (East London, South Africa)

Jody is the younger brother of Ian Scheckter (born 1947) who had a dreadful year with the totally disorganised March team in 1977, and then returned to South Africa where he continued to race with success. As a youngster, Jody David Scheckter showed great promise as a racer in South Africa, starting with karts at the age of 12, progressing to motorcycles and saloons (including a home-prepared Renault) before disappearing off to do his National Service.

Once this was over, he returned to racing, and his successes in the Formula Ford Sunshine series led to him winning the 'Driver to Europe' prize. In the UK he drove in Formula Ford and raced a Ford Mexico, trying hard to impress, and McLaren signed him up for their F2 season. It was a thin season as far as results were concerned, but he won the Greater London Trophy at the Crystal Palace circuit.

Scheckter drove for McLaren in F1 at Watkins Glen in 1972 (ninth), and appeared in five races for the team

Above: *After several seasons with Tyrrell, and a year with Wolf, South African Jody Scheckter joined Ferrari for 1979. He is seen here at the British GP where he finished fifth, but he went on to win that year's Drivers' Championship. Scheckter stayed with Ferrari for 1980, but it was a hopelessly unsuccessful year and at the end of it he retired from racing.* (Author's collection)

the following year. He achieved nothing apart from a sensation at the British GP when he spun at the end of the first lap, eliminated a good number of the runners, and caused the race to be stopped and restarted. Just as it was to be with Gilles Villeneuve four years later, Scheckter obviously possessed immense talent, but it needed discipline and direction.

In September 1973, at the United States GP at Watkins Glen, Scheckter agreed to drive for Tyrrell the following year. The intention was that he would partner François Cevert. He recounted what happened in *Motor Sport* magazine:

'Next day, ten minutes before the end of morning practice, as I accelerated out of the pits, Cevert came past. When I got to the Esses, the front of his car was in the middle of the track. The rest of it was in the guardrail on the left, sort of wrapped over it.

I stopped and jumped out of my car and ran over to him, because a fire was a big thing, so it was an automatic reaction. I got to the battery and I remember that it was sparking like anything, so I went to grab his seat belt buckle. And immediately I turned around and walked away. I'll never know what I saw in the cockpit; to this day I don't remember because it's just blanked out of my mind. Other drivers had pulled up and were running over and I stopped them and said, 'No, it's finished.'

Jody stayed with the Tyrrell team for three seasons and performed exceptionally well. In 1974 he won two races and took two second places to finish third in the Championship. The following year he won only one race, was second once and finished seventh in the Championship as the Tyrrell began to lose its competitive edge. In 1976 Tyrrell was racing the P34 six-wheel cars and again Scheckter won once, but finished second four times, and took third place in the Drivers' Championship.

The time had come for a change, and he signed up to drive for the new team being entered by Canadian oil millionaire Walter Wolf. In his first race with the team, the Argentine GP at Buenos Aires, he scored an unexpected win. Scheckter respected the way that the Wolf team was run and appreciated the amount of attention that he received as sole driver. Later, he finished second in South Africa, won at Monaco, finished second at Hockenheim and, with victory in the Canadian race, took second place in the Championship with 55 points to the 72 of Lauda (Ferrari).

The design of the 1977 Wolf cars had been comparatively simple and straightforward with relatively few development problems, as well as being very satisfying to race. The following year's car was a much more complex 'wing' design, still the work of Dr Harvey Postlethwaite, but no real match for the latest Lotus ground-effect opposition. Jody's best performances were second places in the German and Canadian races, together with a couple of thirds, which earned him a poor seventh place in the Championship.

For 1979, Jody moved on to join Gilles Villeneuve at Ferrari. Initially this appeared to be a serious mistake. It was thought unlikely that Jody could fit happily into Ferrari's management style, even more unlikely that this cool and calculating driver could work easily with the exciting and excitable French-Canadian, and doubtful whether Ferrari could build a satisfactory and effective flat-12 ground-effect car. The critics were wrong on all counts. For the first two races of 1979 Ferrari relied on the previous year's 312T3 car, but the latest 312T4 appeared at the South African GP and is described more fully in Appendix 5.

It proved the most effective racing car in 1979, and Scheckter and Villeneuve vied with each other all season. Scheckter won the Belgian and Monaco races, and took second places at Kyalami, Long Beach, and Zandvoort. At Monza, Ferrari produced the improved 312T4B with many changes, including new rear suspension. The two Ferrari drivers fought off the French opposition and took the first two places at the end of this very exciting race. Scheckter clinched his World Championship 51 points (net) and Villeneuve was second with 47 points (net).

'Winning the title for Ferrari at Monza – I remember the sea of people at the end, but what I really felt after a year of being up and down was the relief. It was just a relief to get it over. I didn't get too emotional or excited when the crowd were going mad, and that maybe helped me the following season, when they weren't going mad.' (*Motor Sport*, May 2008)

At Maranello, the Ferrari engineers, headed by Forghieri, were concentrating on development of the turbocharged cars for 1981, but the factory rebuilt the 1979 cars for 1980 in 312T5 form. Everything had been done in a rush, the latest cars were very unreliable and, as the Michelin tyres became more and more suited to the needs of the turbocharged Renaults, so they were less and less programmed to Ferrari suspension characteristics. It was an abysmally unsuccessful year for Ferrari, and the best performances were a few hard-won fifth places, and the worst at Montreal where Scheckter failed to qualify. Scheckter had planned to retire after one more year, but he had not been expecting anything so dreadful.

After his retirement from racing, Scheckter started a business from scratch in the United States, known as Firearm Training Systems, Inc., for developing weapon training systems for law enforcement and the military. Having developed the company into a multi-million dollar business, he sold out after 12 years and came to the UK, where he bought the 2,500-acre estate known as Laverstoke Park in Hampshire. Here, with his second wife Clare, he has concentrated on organic farming, with especial emphasis on buffalo, of which he had, as at 2008, a herd of 1,000, together with pure uncrossed Angus and Hereford cattle, which are now extremely rare.

Schell, Harry

Works driver
Born: 29 June 1921 (Paris, France)
Died: 13 May 1960 (Silverstone circuit,
      Northamptonshire, England)

Harry enjoyed his motor racing in a truly sporting,
enthusiastic way, but he also enjoyed running his bar in
Paris – when he was driving for Tony Vandervell's Vanwall
team, the 'Guv'nor' even had the effrontery to complain
about the prices. Harry had been involved in motor
racing from adolescence. His father, Selim Laurence
Schell ('Laurie') had American parents and was born in
Geneva. 'Laurie' Schell, who lived in Paris, was married to
Lucy O'Reilly Schell, a wealthy heiress of Irish
background. They built close ties with the Delahaye
factory, funded the construction of the V12 Competition
cars, which they raced extensively under the name Écurie
Bleue, and then bought the two Maserati 8CTF 3-litre
supercharged F1 cars from the factory.

'Laurie' was killed in a road accident near Paris on
18 October 1939, so Lucy, son Harry, Luigi Chinetti (who
looked after the cars), together with the cars, sailed for
the United States. They ran the Delahayes at
Indianapolis without success, and once Italy declared
war on the Axis side Chinetti was trapped in the United
States for the duration. Harry served in the American
armed forces during the war, and once Europe had
settled down after the war he travelled back. He raced
an 1100cc Cooper-JAP in the 1950 Monaco GP, but he
was eliminated in a multi-car accident, and he drove and
retired a Talbot in that year's Swiss GP.

For 1951, Harry agreed to drive a Maserati 4CLT/48
for Enrico Plate and, still with the same entrant, drove
4CLT/48s rebuilt in unblown 2-litre form in 1952. These
cars were unsuccessful, as were the Gordinis that he
raced in 1953. During 1954, Harry raced a 1953 Maserati
A6GCM powered by the latest 250F 2.5-litre, but still
without notable success. In sports car racing he
co-drove de Portago's Ferrari 250MM early in the year.
They finished second behind a works 4.5-litre Ferrari in
the Buenos Aires 1,000km race, but retired at Sebring.

Harry appeared at the Spanish GP at Barcelona in
October 1954 with his own 250F. The Maserati factory
offered him an appropriate pourboire, if he started with
a half-full tank and drove flat-out. This he gladly
accepted, accelerated into the distance, but spun off,
and after a refuelling stop retired because of failure of
the de Dion rear axle, a common shortcoming with

Above: *Franco-American driver Harry Schell (left) with
Raymond Sommer at the International Trophy meeting at
Silverstone in 1950. Schell, who was to become a fine, if
not top rank, GP driver was competing here with a
Cooper 500cc car.* (Guy Griffiths Collection)

early 250Fs. In 1955 Schell drove for Maserati in
Argentina, and then he appeared with a works Ferrari at
Monaco, where he retired with engine problems. He
was going to drive for Ferrari again at Spa, but Ferrari
changed his mind and offered the drive to Trintignant.

Tony Vandervell signed him up in mid-1955, and he
stayed with the British Vanwall team until the end of
1956. Schell gave his all to the Vanwall, but sadly,
Schell's all was not enough for the man who's obsession
was to beat 'the bloody red cars'. Dropped from the
team, he joined Maserati for the 1957 season, drove as
determinedly as ever, and his best performance was
third to Moss (Vanwall) and Fangio (250F) in the
Pescara GP held on a difficult road circuit.

BRM signed him for 1958, and he stayed until the
end of the 1959 season. Schell had the guts and
determination so badly needed by this unsuccessful
British team. His best performance was second place in
the 1958 Dutch GP, with team-mate Behra third. For the
1960 season, he joined Yeoman Credit, and he was
practising with one of this team's Cooper F1 cars in the
wet at the International Trophy meeting at Silverstone
when he lost control on a fast bend and was killed.

Schenken, Tim

Works sports car driver
Born: 26 September 1943 (Sydney, Australia)

Schenken was a driver of very considerable promise. He first competed with an Austin A35 in the Tempelstowe hill climb and rapidly progressed to a Lotus 18. He came to the UK in 1965, won both F Ford and F3 Championships, and gained a Grovewood award in 1968. His F1 career started in 1970 when he drove a De Tomaso 505 for Frank Williams in four races, with promise but no success. The following year he was number two to Graham Hill in the Brabham team, and his best place was a third in Austria.

Below: *Schenken was a driver with immense talent that was never fulfilled. He drove for Ferrari only in 1972 when he was paired in sports car racing with Ronnie Peterson. They won at Buenos Aires and the Nürburgring, and also took four second places.* **(LAT Photographic)**

For 1972, he joined the Surtees F1 team, and it is probably fair comment that the poor performance of the Surtees F1 cars (and the team's limited finances) spelt an effective end to his F1 prospects. In contrast, an important development for Schenken was his contract to drive the Ferrari 312PB Prototypes and, partnered with Ronnie Peterson, he achieved the following: 2nd, Daytona Continental Six Hours; 2nd (and fastest lap) Sebring 12 Hours; 2nd, BOAC 1,000km, Brands Hatch; 3rd, Monza 1,000km; 1st, Nürburgring 1,000km; 3rd, Austrian 1,000km; 2nd, Watkins Glen Six Hours.

Peterson hit a damp patch and crashed at Spa; the team entered only a single car for Merzario/Munari in the Targa Florio, and did not run at Le Mans. Schenken stayed with the team for 1973, but it was a much more difficult and hard-fought year, for the cars were inferior to the French Matras. Schenken drove in fewer races and Peterson was no longer in the team. With Reutemann, Schenken finished second in the Vallelunga Six Hours, and was second again in the Monza 1,000km. He was not in the team at Spa or in the Targa Florio. He drove with Reutemann again at Le Mans, but retired because of engine failure while leading in the sixth hour. Schenken and Reutemann also retired at Watkins Glen.

In 1973 Schenken drove in a single F1 race for Frank Williams – the Canadian GP where he ended up in 14th place. The following year, Ron Tauranac designed a F1 car for Trojan (builders of production McLarens), and Schenken drove the car in an unsuccessful low-budget exercise that was terminated before the North American races.

Schenken co-founded Tiga cars in 1974, with New Zealand driver Howden Ganley. He raced Porsche sports and GT cars for the George Loos concern in 1975–7 and shared a Jaguar X12C in the 1977 European GT Championship. At the end of the year he retired to concentrate on Tiga. He moved back to Australia where he lives with his wife and three children, and each year he acts as Race Director for the Australian V8 Supercar Championship series.

Schetty, Peter

Works sports car driver and team manager
Born: 1942 (Basle, Switzerland)

Son and heir to a family textile manufacturer, Peter Schetty competed as an amateur in motor sport, and in 1966 he came second driving a Ford Mustang in the GT

category of the European Mountain Championship. As a result of this he joined the Abarth company for 1967, carried out development testing, and then drove their latest 2-litre car, finishing third in the Mountain Championship behind works Porsche 910s driven by Gerhard Mitter and Rolf Stommelen.

As a result of this success, Ferrari invited Schetty to work at Maranello on development of a new car to compete in the Mountain Championship. This car was the Tipo 212 E (Esperimentale/Sperimentale) 'Montagna', a quite remarkable flat-12 car developed by engineer Stefano Jacaponi. The engine was developed from the Tipo 1512 F1 unit of 1964–5 and had a capacity of 1991cc (65 x 50mm) and a power output of 280bhp at 11,000rpm. The chassis was a modified Dino 206, probably Dino chassis 020 renumbered 0862, and was fitted with right-hand drive.

There were seven rounds in the 1969 Mountain Championship, and Schetty won them all. For 1970, he became a works driver and appeared regularly at the wheel of Tipo 512S cars. He achieved no success worth mentioning in 1970. He then worked on the development of the 312PB, and was Ferrari team manager in 1972. He returned to the family business at the end of the year, but in 1973, when Ferrari was struggling badly, he responded to a request from the 'Old Man' and travelled to Dijon to act as team manager at this 1,000km race on a one-off basis.

Above: *Peter Schetty was at the wheel of the flat-12 212 Montagna car when he won the European Hill Climb Championship for Ferrari in 1969. He drove the works 512S cars in 1970, and was team manager in 1972.* (LAT Photographic)

Schumacher, Michael

Works driver
Born: 3 January 1969 (Hürth Hermülheim, Germany)

The rise of Schumacher from a working-class background to a reign as the most successful GP driver of all time is a very remarkable story. In his very early days, his parents backed his childhood racing expectations with karts to what many would think were ridiculous degrees. When he was four, his bricklayer father modified his pedal kart by fitting a small two-stroke engine. Young Michael crashed this, so it was decided that the safest thing would be for him to join the local kart club, where he became the youngest member.

Above: *Michael Schumacher became the most successful driver in the history of GP racing, because of a combination of great natural talent and vast experience coupled with what were the best cars of their era, and the organisational skills of Luca di Montezemolo.* (LAT Photographic)

It was straining the family finances, so his father set up a business, in addition to his job, repairing karts and hiring them out. His mother started to work in the café of the kart club. It was still not enough, and Michael began to receive financial support from local businessmen, who – presumably – treated it as tax-deductible. Michael won the German Junior Kart Championship in 1983, and four years later he was both German and European kart champion. By 1988 he had left school to be apprenticed as a motor mechanic, and that year he won both the German Formula Ford and Formula König Championships.

Michael joined the F3 WTS Team run by Willi Weber in 1989, competing regularly and winning the German F3 Championship in 1990. Along with Heinz-Harald Frentzen and Karl Wendlinger, in late 1990, he joined the Mercedes-Benz Junior Racing Programme in the World Sports Prototype Championship. He competed regularly with Sauber-Mercedes cars, and his F1 debut came with a Jordan in the 1991 Belgian GP where he substituted for Bertrand Gachot (imprisoned in the UK after assaulting a London taxi driver with CS gas in a traffic altercation).

Opposite: *The great Schumacher seen during his last year as a Ferrari driver. He is celebrating on the podium with his trademark leap after winning the 2006 German GP at Hockenheim from team-mate Massa and Räikkönen (McLaren).* (LAT Photographic)

That Michael was sensational was undoubted, and he was of course under contract to Mercedes-Benz who then moved him into the Benetton team, and an attempted injunction by Jordan failed. During 1992, Schumacher drove Benetton cars to a third place in Mexico and a win in the wet Spa race, to take third place in the World Championship.

A fraught 1994 season, that culminated in a collision with rival Damon Hill (whom he led by a single point) brought him the World Championship, the first by a German driver, and made it clear to the world that his manners and behaviour were completely Teutonic. In 1995, despite several collisions with Hill, he won his second World Championship.

For 1996, Schumacher joined Ferrari. He was followed by many of the Benetton technicians, and the Benetton team won only one more GP before it was taken over by Renault in 2000. It was money, and the opportunity for fame (primarily the former) that attracted Schumacher to Ferrari, for the team was jogging along in mid-field and had shown no real promise for some while. All that was to change, even though it took a very long time and meant altering completely Ferrari's approach to racing. No Ferrari driver had won the Championship since Scheckter in 1979, and the team had not won the Constructors' Cup since 1983.

During 1996, Schumacher won three races, although the team still suffered from reliability problems, and he took third place in the Championship. The 1997 Championship was fought out between Schumacher and Jacques Villeneuve (Williams), but the German had a one-point lead at the last race of the season at Jerez.

When Villeneuve passed him, the two drivers collided. Schumacher, who retired, was held responsible and was ordered to forfeit all points gained during the season. Villeneuve finished the race and won the Championship. FISA, quite rightly, was appalled by drivers resorting to physical tactics if they could not win fairly, and the punishment very much fitted the crime.

In 1998 the season was fought out between Schumacher and Häkkinen (McLaren), but the McLarens were much superior in the early part of the season and Ferrari was only able to close the gap in the later races. The McLaren driver went on to win the

FERRARI: MEN FROM MARANELLO

Championship by a margin of 14 points. In 1999 Häkkinen again won the Championship after Schumacher crashed at Stowe in the British race after his brakes failed and he suffered a broken leg.

It was not until 2000 that Schumacher first won the Drivers' Championship with Ferrari, and it proved to be the start of a period of domination by the German driver. When Schumacher won the 2000 Italian GP, he matched Ayrton Senna's total of 41 GP wins. It had been another year of battling with Häkkinen, but Schumacher won the Championship by a margin of 19 points. Throughout 2001 the Ferrari team carried out a sustained challenge, and Schumacher won nine races to gain the Championship by the enormous margin of 68 points from McLaren driver Coulthard.

The year 2002 was remarkable for Schumacher's near domination, and the superiority of the latest F2002 Ferrari model. Of the 17 rounds of the Championship, Schumacher won nine, and he finished in the first three at all the year's races. He won the Championship with 144 points to the 77 of his team-mate Barrichello in second place. Schumacher won again in 2003, but by a margin of only two points from McLaren driver Kimi Räikkönen. Schumacher clinched a record seven World Championship victories in 2004, again with Barrichello second at the wheel of the other Ferrari.

By 2005, the cycle of Ferrari supremacy was over. Rule changes had given users of Michelin tyres a definite advantage, and Ferrari was running on Bridgestones. That year, Schumacher and Ferrari won only one race, the United States GP at Indianapolis, where safety problems with Michelin tyres were experienced, and all but the six users of Bridgestone tyres dropped out after the formation lap. Schumacher finished the season in third place in the Championship with 62 points. He drove one more season for Ferrari in 2006, finishing second in the Championship, and then retired from racing. Since then, Schumacher has acted as consultant and test driver for the Ferrari team.

Scotti, Piero

Private sports car driver
Born: 11 November 1909 (Florence, Italy)
Died: 14 February 1976 (Florence)

Below: *Piero Scotti was a very keen and often successful driver of private sports Ferraris, and he also had the distinction of racing – albeit very briefly – a Connaught GP. Scotti, who was a big bulky chap, is seen here at the start of the 1953 Mille Miglia at the wheel of his Vignale-bodied 250MM Ferrari. He is partnered by Giulio Cantoni, and they retired at Ferrara very early in the race.* **(Author's collection)**

Scotti, who ran a mineral-water bottling plant, was primarily a private sports car driver with Ferraris. He was very competent, and finished third overall with his Tipo 212 Export, partnered by Ruspaggiari, in the 1951 Mille Miglia. He moved on to a Tipo 225 Sport in 1952, and raced a 3-litre 250MM in 1953. By 1954 he was racing a new Tipo 375 4.5-litre car with Pininfarina spider body and achieved a good measure of success with it in minor Italian events. He was out of luck, however, in the Mille Miglia in which he drove solo, and he retired with this car in both 1954 and 1955. During 1954, with the Tipo 375, he finished third in the Circuit of Agadir, won the Tuscany Cup race, and later in the year won the Tuscany Cup race.

Tony Brooks's victory with a B-series Connaught in the 1955 Syracuse GP impressed Scotti considerably. He learned that a B-series was available for immediate delivery (chassis B7) and he arranged to buy it on hire-purchase. The car was repainted red. Idiosyncratically, the Connaught chief engineer opted for a matt maroon, while Scotti was expecting a glossy Italian racing red, and this was a bad start to the relationship. The whole concept of an Italian buying a British GP car was, of course, pretty loopy, certainly at this time.

Scotti drove the car in only two races. In the International Trophy at Silverstone in May he finished seventh on the road, but he was too far behind to be classified. He then drove the Connaught in the Belgian GP, but retired because of loss of oil pressure. By this stage, Scotti believed that he had endured more than enough problems with the Connaught, which was returned to the works at Send in Surrey. Scotti's racing career was finished, and the Connaught ended up in the Science Museum in South Kensington, London, where it languished for many years.

Sculati, Eraldo

Journalist, team manager
Born: December 1918
Died: Not known

Sculati was a journalist who agreed to act as team manager for a year from the start of the 1956 season. At the end of the year he offered to carry on, but Ferrari declined his services. Sculati had been a good team manager, but he talked a lot to the press, and too often took personal credit, which Enzo Ferrari thought should be his.

Sears, Jack

Racing driver
Born: 16 February 1930 (Northampton, England)

Son of Stanley Sears, well known for the Sears, Truform, and Freeman, Hardy & Willis shoe shops, and a collector of veteran and classic cars (especially Rolls-Royces), Jack combined two interests, his love of farming and his motor racing. Jack's early racing career was centred on rallying and racing works Austins and Austin-Healeys, but later he became very well known for driving Jaguar 3.8s for Tommy Sopwith's Équipe Endeavour team. He moved on to a Ford Galaxie entered by John Willment and, with this and a Ford Cortina GT, won the British Touring Car Championship in 1963.

That year, he was invited to drive at Le Mans by Colonel Ronnie Hoare of Maranello Concessionaires, and the car was a Ferrari 4-litre Prototype coupé known as the Tipo 330LMB ('Le Mans Berlinetta') which he shared with Mike Salmon. They finished fifth overall, and won the over 3000cc Prototype class. He then drove the Maranello Concessionaires' Ferrari 250GTO at Mallory Park on 13 July, when he finished second to Graham Hill with John Coombs's lightweight Jaguar E-type. Three weeks later, he drove Coombs's 250GTO in the Guards Trophy at Brands Hatch, and won the GT class.

Jack again drove Coombs's 250GT0 in the *Autosport* Three Hours race at Snetterton on 27 September, and finished fourth overall, second to Mike Parkes with another 250GTO in the Grand Touring class. As Jack commented:

> 'I was very lucky to be able to drive such a wide variety of cars. I had wonderful times driving these special cars, which today are so highly sought after.'

Later, Jack drove Cobras for John Willment, works Shelby American Cobras in the European rounds of the 1965 World Championship GT races, and Team Lotus Lotus-Cortinas in the British Saloon Car Championship. Sears's racing career came to an end during testing at Silverstone in late 1965 when he had a bad crash with a Lotus.

Seidel, Wolfgang

Works sports car driver
Born: 4 July 1926 (Dresden, Germany)
Died: 1 March 1987 (Munich, Germany)

In the main, Seidel was a private entrant, notably of Porsche sports-racing cars, although he drove for the Porsche works team based at Zuffenhausen, Stuttgart, on occasion. He was an above-average driver, very dependable and quite fast, if no ace. Because of his reliability, Ferrari brought him into the sports car team on a number of occasions. In the Reims 12 Hours race for GT cars in July 1957, he partnered Wolfgang von Trips and they finished third. Later in 1957 he shared the second V12 3-litre Testa Rossa prototype in the Swedish GP with Masten Gregory, but they retired.

Seidel partnered Gino Munaron with a prototype Testa Rossa in the 1958 Targa Florio, and was holding a good fourth place on the last lap when he slid off the

Below: *Although not an especially talented driver, Seidel was predictable, dependable, and reasonably quick. He drove for Porsche fairly regularly, and also made occasional appearances as a member of the Ferrari sports car team.* (Author's collection)

road and rejoined the race, unaware that the sump had split and the oil was running out. He retired just a few kilometres down the road when the engine seized. He again partnered Munaron in the Nürburgring 1,000km race, and drove steadily to finish fifth.

At Le Mans, he partnered von Trips and they were holding third place in a very wet race when he spun at Arnage in a heavy shower and got stuck in the mud. He struggled for more than an hour to get the car back on the road, but without success, and he made his way back to the pits to be berated by Tavoni. In the four-hour Rouen GP for sports cars, held in June 1960, he drove a new Ferrari prototype 250GT SWB, with disc brakes, into third place behind Jack Fairman (ex-works Aston Martin DBR1 sports-racer) and Jo Schlesser (with an older type 250GT Ferrari).

Two years later, in 1962, he and Peter Nöcker finished fifth overall, and first in the GT class, in the Nürburgring 1,000km race. Seidel had been driving single-seaters from time to time, but without much success. In 1962 he raced his own Lotus 24 with BRM V8 engine, entered in the name of his Autosport Team, but he retired in the British race at Aintree because of brake problems and overheating, and failed to qualify as a starter.

Serafini, Teodoro

Works driver and tester
Born: 22 July 1909 (Pesaro, Italy)
Died: 5 July 2000 (Pesaro)

In his early days, Teodoro 'Dorino' Serafini raced motorcycles and, as a member of the Gilera team, he won the 500cc European Championship in 1939. Although he continued to race motorcycles in post-war days, he was switching to cars. He drove a 4CL Maserati in the Comminges GP on the St Gaudens circuit on 10 August 1947. The steering wheel and column came away in his hands when he was in second place, travelling at about 120mph (193kph). The car went off the road into a wood, rebounding from tree to tree, before coming to rest a crumpled heap and catching fire. In addition to burns, Serafini's injuries included broken arms, legs, and ribs.

It took some while for Serafini to recover from the accident, but when he was recovered, Ferrari, who knew a man when he saw one, invited him to join his company. He became the Ferrari chief tester, and also raced occasionally. He joined the team late in 1949 and first raced in Argentina in December.

With a private Tipo 125 car, he took a poor eighth place in the Perón Cup race on the Palermo Park circuit, Buenos Aires, in December, but by the beginning of 1950 he was driving a 2-litre supercharged car, and he finished second to Villoresi in the Eva Perón Cup race on the same circuit in January. Later that month, Serafini drove a Tipo 125 in the General San Martin Trophy at Mar del Plata and the Coppa Accion de San Lorenzo at Rosario, but he retired in both of these races because of mechanical problems.

Back in Europe, Serafini tested regularly, but he also raced on a number of occasions. He retired with a works single-stage supercharged Tipo 125 in the San Remo GP in April, finished third in the F2 Autodrome GP at Monza at the end of May, and was a poor seventh with a single-stage Tipo 125 at Bari in July. At Monza in September, Ferrari introduced his Lampredi-designed unblown V12 car, and Serafini drove one of the new cars. He was in sixth place when he came in for new tyres, but was told to hand the car over to team-leader Ascari, who brought it through to finish second to new World Champion Giuseppe Farina.

The non-Championship Penya Rhin GP at Barcelona the following month was the last F1 race of the year, and Serafini took a good second place behind Ascari. Partnered by Salami, he finished second overall with a Tipo 195 Ferrari in the 1950 Mille Miglia. Serafini also drove in sports car races, and at Le Mans he shared a Tipo 195 Ferrari with Raymond Sommer. They led for the first

Above: *Dorino Serafini at Silverstone in August 1950 when he was entered in the Production Sports Car race with a works Ferrari.* (Guy Griffiths Collection)

Below: *Dorino Serafini drove this works Tipo 166MM Ferrari with Touring Barchetta body into second place behind team-leader Alberto Ascari with a similar car in the 2-litre Production Sports Car race at Silverstone in August 1950.* (Tom March Collection)

couple of hours, but gradually dropped back and retired shortly after half-distance because a dynamo support bracket fractured. He came to Britain in August and drove a Tipo 166 Ferrari into second place in the 2-litre Production Sports Car race at Silverstone behind Ascari.

In 1951 Serafini made a number of F1 appearances early in the year. He finished second with a 2.6-litre single-seater in the Syracuse GP in Sicily, and again with a 375 at San Remo. In the Mille Miglia 1,000-mile road race he drove a 4.1-litre Tipo 340 Ferrari, partnered once again by Ettore Salami, but he crashed heavily at his home town of Pesaro because spectators crowding on to the road obscured his line through a bend. On the wet road the Ferrari mounted a bank and crashed through trees before dropping into a field. Serafini suffered a broken arm and leg. Although he continued to test for Ferrari, this marked the end of his serious racing career.

Severi, Francesco

Pre-war Scuderia Ferrari driver
Born: 28 May 1907
Died: 20 May 1980

Severi was an occasional driver for Scuderia Ferrari. In 1934 he partnered Cortese in one of the new unsupercharged 6C 2300 2.3-litre cars in the Targa Abruzzo 24 Hours race at Pescara. There were problems with the 6C's wheels, as they were breaking up under cornering stresses. The Scuderia Ferrari mechanics resolved this by going to the team's garage in central Pescara to borrow the wheels of the Monoposto that the team was running in the Coppa Acerbo the next day. It worked, and Cortese/Severi won the race at 64.26mph (103.39kph) from the similar cars of Tadini/Barbieri and Rosa/Comotti.

The following year, Severi partnered Cortese at the wheel of a 6C 2300 in the Mille Miglia, and they finished eighth overall. They drove together again at the wheel of a 6C 2300 in that year's 24-hour Targa Abruzzo, and won again at the higher speed of 66.73mph (107.74kph). This year Rosa/Comotti with a similar car finished second, and Mongin/Paris took third place. Severi drove an Alfa Romeo 8C 35 in the 1936 Eifelrennen, but after trailing at the back of the field he retired because of oil pump failure.

Severi partnered Raymond Sommer in his private Alfa Romeo 8C 2900A in the Belgian 24 Hours race in July, and they won the race easily at 77.67mph (124.97kph) – a

Above: *Franco Severi had a fine track record in pre-war days, and his successes included a win with a Maserati in the 1937 Targa Florio held as a Voiturette race in Palermo Park. Post-war he raced private Ferraris with considerable success.* (Author's collection)

speed not bettered until the 1949 race. In 1937 Severi was listed among the official Scuderia Ferrari reserve drivers, but his appearances for the team were infrequent. In the 1938 Belgian 24 Hours race, run in atrociously wet conditions, he shared an Alfa Corse-entered 8C2900B sports car with Pintacuda and, after the retirement of Sommer/Biondetti because of transmission problems, they took the lead and won at 76.44mph (122.99kph) from the Delage of Gérard/Monneret.

By June 1938 Severi had graduated to the Alfa Corse Tipo 158 Voiturette team. He finished fourth in the 1938 Coppa Ciano (Emilio Villoresi and Biondetti took the first two places ahead of Marazza with a Maserati), fourth in the Coppa Acerbo (he was the only 158 finisher), second to Emilio Villoresi by a mere second in the Circuit of Milan, and retired at Modena. Severi remained a reserve driver in 1939, and seems to have appeared for the team only twice.

In the Coppa Ciano, held as a 1500cc race, Biondetti had mechanical problems with his Tipo 158. He took over Pintacuda's car, while Severi took over Biondetti's car, once it had been repaired, and finished fifth, five laps in arrears. He also drove in the Coppa Acerbo, where he took fourth place. There are no other records of him driving for the Alfa Corse team.

Siena, Eugenio

Scuderia Ferrari Chief Mechanic and private driver
Born: 1 April 1905 (Milan, Italy)
Died: 15 May 1938 (Mellaha, Tripoli, Libya)

It is said that Siena was Campari's cousin and, if so, this would have facilitated his acceptance as an apprentice at Alfa Romeo, and he later became head of the tuning shops. After Enzo Ferrari had formed Scuderia Ferrari, Siena joined him in the early 1930s, doing mechanical work, but also racing from time to time. In June 1932, Siena drove a Ferrari-entered Alfa Romeo in the Italian GP, but retired. The following month he partnered Brivio in the winning works 2.3 Alfa Romeo in the Belgian 24 Hours race at Spa. At the end of the year he crashed, and broke a leg, in practice for the Czechoslovakian GP.

The following year, Siena drove a 2.3-litre for Scuderia Ferrari in the Monaco GP, but retired because of clutch problems. Later in 1933 he again drove a Ferrari-entered Monza in the Belgian GP and finished fifth, while in the Italian GP at Monza his car was taken over by Brivio to finish fifth. At the end of 1933 Siena left Ferrari and set up his own Scuderia Siena at Como. This permitted him to pursue his own career as a racing driver, and also to prepare cars for private owners.

During 1933, Tazio Nuvolari had fallen out with Ferrari, partly because of the factory's failure to release the Monopostos to Scuderia Ferrari, and he was now driving Maseratis in Grands Prix. It seems that Siena's decision to start his own business was encouraged by Nuvolari, who was able to offer him some business. For 1934, Siena bought the two-seater Maserati 8C 3000 that Campari had driven to a win in the 1933 French GP. Then, for 1936, he bought from Scuderia Subalpina the Tipo 34 that they had raced in 1935, and he fitted this car with Tecnauto 'twisted coil' independent front suspension.

When he first started Scuderia Siena, he prepared a special 2336cc Alfa Romeo Monza for Tazio Nuvolari to drive in the 1934 Mille Miglia. The modifications to this car had been designed by Vittorio Jano himself. Eugenio Siena rode in the race with Nuvolari, and the race took place in sustained and heavy rain. Nuvolari's Alfa Romeo was less powerful than the 2632cc Monza driven for Ferrari by Varzi, and its Dunlops had less grip than Varzi's Pirelli Pneugrippa tyres. Varzi won the race, and Nuvolari finished second, nearly nine minutes behind.

By 1937, Siena was back with Scuderia Ferrari as a reserve driver, but it seems that Ferrari had little opportunity to use him as a driver, so he carried out mechanical work, and was released to drive Maserati Voiturettes. He achieved one worthwhile success, a win with a 6CM Maserati in that year's 75-mile (120km) race at Milan, and he also finished fifth at Naples. Siena joined Alfa Corse in 1938 and was entered as part of the works team in the Tripoli GP on 15 May. On lap nine he was passing Cortese's Maserati 6CM, then leading the Voiturette category (which was held concurrently with the GP), when he lost control of his 8C 312 and crashed into a house, with fatal results.

Below: *Eugenio Siena was head mechanic to Scuderia Ferrari in the 1930s, but his ambition was to race. He set up his own organisation, Scuderia Siena. He was killed at the wheel of an Alfa Romeo in the 1938 Tripoli GP when his car went out of control while he was lapping Franco Cortese's Maserati Tipo 6CM. He is seen on the left in this photograph, with Carlo Sozzi.* (Spitzley/Zagari Collection)

Sighinolfi, Sergio

Driver
Born: (Modena, Italy)
Died: September 1956 (Modena)

A very successful driver of Stanguellini cars from 1949 to 1951, and again in 1953, Sighinolfi became very closely associated with the Stanguellini family, especially Francesco. He was recommended to Enzo Ferrari as a possible works driver by both Vittorio Stanguellini and Alberto Ascari. This never happened on a regular basis because of a series of crashes, although he drove works cars in the 1952 Modena GP and the 1956 Mille Miglia. It was because of his technical knowledge that Ferrari employed him, and he eventually became chief of the testing staff. He took part in the development driving of all new models until he was killed in a collision with a lorry near Modena in September 1956.

Below: *Seen here, centre, in white linen helmet, holding the winner's trophy, is Sergio Sighinolfi after taking first place in the 1950 Aerautodromo GP at Modena with his works Stanguellini. He moved on to become a Ferrari test driver, but he was killed in an accident. On Sighinolfi's right, wearing braces, is Vittorio Stanguellini.*
(Author's collection)

Simon, André

Works driver
Born: 5 January 1920 (Paris, France)

Even at the time he was racing, Simon never made a strong impression, although he was obviously a very able driver. From 1950 he was a regular member of the Simca team, taking second places in several F2 races, including the F2 German GP and the Coupe des Petites Cylindrées at Reims (both behind Ascari with a V12 Ferrari), and second to Fangio (Maserati) in the Circuit des Ramparts at Angoulême. He stayed with Simca for 1951 and won the F2 race at Les Sables d'Olonne from Manzon and Behra with other Simcas, and finished sixth in the Italian GP at Monza, albeit six laps in arrears.

For 1952, Simon was signed up by Ferrari, but he made only a small number of appearances. He drove in the Swiss GP, where Farina took over his Tipo 500, but retired because of magneto failure, and he took over Farina's car in the Paris GP at Montlhéry to finish second. He took a good second place to Farina in the non-Championship Autodromo GP at Monza, and his car was taken over at Comminges by race-winner Ascari. Another sixth place followed in the Italian GP at Monza. He also shared a 4.1-litre Ferrari with Vincent at Le Mans and, although they finished down in fifth place, they led the race for the first two hours.

At this time Simon looked as though he had the makings of a leading GP driver, but he was seriously ill towards the end of 1952. When he returned to racing, it was on an occasional basis only. From 1952 onwards he drove for what became Gordini, and he finished third in the final of the 1954 International Trophy at Silverstone behind team-mate Behra. His skills were appreciated by Mercedes-Benz, and when Herrmann crashed heavily in practice for the 1955 Monaco GP, he drove a W196 in this race, but retired because of mechanical problems. At the end of May 1955 he won the poorly supported Albi GP with a Maserati 250F entered by Écurie Rosier, and le patron Louis Rosier finished second with another 250F.

In the British GP at Aintree he was entered with a works Maserati, but retired because of gearbox trouble. He had been in the Mercedes-Benz 300SLR team at Le Mans where he co-drove with Karl Kling, but the team withdrew following Levegh's fatal accident with another of the team's cars. He co-drove with von Trips in the Tourist Trophy on the Dundrod circuit, and they completed a Mercedes-Benz 1–2–3 behind Moss/Fitch and Fangio/Kling.

Simon drove for Gordini again in the 1956 Caen GP, a very wet race, and he drove smoothly and steadily to finish second to Harry Schell with a works Maserati. Subsequently, he drove regularly in GT races with a Ferrari belonging to his friend Jo Schlesser, and successes included third place with Schlesser in the Paris 1,000km race at Montlhéry, winning the Tour de France with Dupeyron in 1962, and as late as 1965 finishing 12th with Schlesser at the wheel of a Cobra entered by Ford France in the Nürburgring 1,000km race. At the end of 1966 he was badly injured in a road accident, but made a full recovery and continued to run his garage business until 1984 when he retired.

Simon, Gilles

Engine designer
Born: 14 June 1958 (Oujda, Morocco)

Gilles Simon graduated with a thesis on materials, and between 1984 and 1988 he worked in Renault's research department on production engines. He joined Peugeot Sport in 1989, and worked in their research department until 1993 on the Peugeot 905 and the first F1 V10 engine. He joined Ferrari in 1994, working in the research department in charge of engine projects, and in 1997 he became Ferrari's chief engine designer under

Paolo Martinelli. He has been responsible for the design of the first Ferrari V10 engine in 1996 and all Ferrari competition engines since then. He took over as head of the engine department in the racing division of the company in 2006. He is married, with three children.

Sivocci, Ugo

Racing driver, friend of Enzo Ferrari
Born: 29 August 1885 (Salerno, Italy)
Died: 8 September 1923 (Monza circuit, Milan, Italy)

In his early days, Sivocci was a successful racing cyclist, and after the First World War he worked as a car mechanic at Costruzioni Meccaniche Nazionali (CMN) in Milan. During the war, CMN had manufactured car and aircraft parts, but in 1919 it turned to the manufacture of cars. The first products had 2.3-litre four-cylinder and 2.6-litre six-cylinder side valve engines with no features of particular merit. Sivocci knew Enzo Ferrari, and they ran into each other again when Ferrari was delivering a car chassis to the coachbuilders for a body to be fitted. Sivocci used his influence to help Ferrari obtain a job at CMN.

Both Sivocci and Ferrari joined Alfa Romeo in 1920, and while Sivocci had a brief, but proven, racing record, Ferrari had considerable potential. In 1921–2 Sivocci drove consistently for Alfa Romeo, and achieved a modest level of success. He drove an RL in the Autumn GP over a distance of 249 miles (400km) at Monza in 1922, taking second place in the up to 3-litre class behind Alfieri Maserati, who was at the wheel of a 2-litre GP Diatto.

The following year, Sivocci was a member of a strong Alfa Romeo team in the Targa Florio. Sivocci and Ferrari had cars with engines enlarged to 3.6 litres and ran in the 4½-litre class. Sivocci won the race with his RL from Antonio Ascari with a 3-litre. It was at this race that Sivocci ran his Alfa Romeo for the first time with what was to become the famous green quadrifoglio (four-leaf clover) on a white background painted on the red bonnet. It is not clear whether Sivocci conceived the design.

In September 1923, Alfa Romeo entered a team of Tipo P1 cars in the Italian GP at Monza. These cars, which were the work of Giuseppe Merosi, had a 1991cc (65 x 100mm) twin overhead camshaft engine with a power output of 115bhp at 5,000rpm and a claimed maximum speed of 115mph (185kph). In practice for the Monza race, Sivocci crashed and was killed. The team was withdrawn from the GP and the cars were never raced. It seems that this was

Above: *Sivocci is seen at the wheel of one of the Merosi-designed Alfa Romeo P1 Grand Prix cars at Monza in 1923. The photograph was taken during practice and not long afterwards Sivocci crashed with fatal consequences. The P1s were withdrawn from the race and broken up, mainly because they were only too obviously underpowered and uncompetitive. (Automobilismo Storico Alfa Romeo, Centro Documentazione)*

quite simply because the P1 was so much less powerful than the supercharged Fiat 805s. For 1924, Jano designed the supercharged P2 that had a power output, in original 1924 form, of 134bhp at 5,200rpm.

Smedley, Robert

Race engineer
Born: 28 November 1973 (Manchester, England)

After graduating in 1996 with a degree in mechanical engineering and mathematics, Robert Smedley worked as a design and race engineer on touring cars for Peugeot, and then in 1989 he joined Williams in the same role. In 2000 he became race engineer at Benetton to Alonso, who was competing in F3000. He moved to Jordan in 2001, and stayed there two years as race engineer for Heinz-Harald Frentzen, and later for Giancarlo Fisichella. Smedley went to work for Ferrari as a test team race engineer in 2004, and since 2006 has been engineer for Felipe Massa.

Sommer, Raymond

Works driver
Born: 31 August 1906 (Mouzon, Ardennes, France)
Died: 10 September 1950 (Cadours, France)

Raymond Sommer was born into a family of carpet-makers who were, it seems, considerably wealthy. Initially, he drove an American Chrysler in European events, and in the 1931 Belgian 24 Hours Touring race at Spa-Francorchamps, he and Delamar covered the fourth longest distance, but in front of them on distance were three Alfa Romeos. The Spa race was always run on a class basis and there was no outright winner.

The following year, he and Chinetti were partners at the wheel of an 8C 2300 Alfa Romeo. This is how Peter Hull and Roy Slater described the race in their book *Alfa Romeo, a History*:

'At 3am Birkin found his Alfa Romeo had blown its cylinder head gasket, so he and Lord Howe went to bed. Then things began to drop off the remaining Alfas, such as mudguard stays, exhaust pipe clips, headlamp brackets and windscreens… Cortese and Guidotti had practically to refabricate their wings, and when Guidotti was asked if his works car would be fighting the private car of Sommer and Chinetti for the lead to the bitter end, he replied, "I must not win, because my wings, they are no longer the right shape for the regulations. If I win, the other driver he make a protest. Then I am disqualified. Not so good!"'

And so it was that Raymond Sommer crossed the line as the winner in a race which first brought his name to the fore. He drove for 21 hours, as his co-driver Chinetti was unwell, and (as recorded in Peter Hull and Roy Slater's book) said for the last few hours he handled the gear lever 'as if the pinions were made of glass'.

In 1933 Sommer teamed up with Nuvolari at Le Mans, and they were at the wheel of an 8C 2300 car that looked very similar to the one with which the Frenchman had won the previous year. They ran steadily with the front-runners all the way, but they were delayed by a leaking fuel tank and at the finish they were in front by only ten seconds from the similar car of Chinetti/Varent. At Spa-Francorchamps the winners were Chiron/Chinetti, but Sommer, partnered by Henri Stoffel, drove very well again to take second place.

Sommer had been racing a private Alfa Romeo Monza in Grands Prix, and he achieved a reasonable measure of success. He drove for Maserati in 1934, but accomplished very little, and he raced a private Alfa Romeo Monoposto in 1935. In that year his greatest success was a win in the Comminges GP, defeating the Scuderia Ferrari entries. He also drove his Monoposto to fourth place in the Vanderbilt Cup race on Long Island, New York. Sommer was still competing in endurance racing, and in 1936 he and Severi covered the greatest distance in the Spa 24 Hours race at a speed not beaten until 1949 when Chinetti/Lucas with a 2-litre Ferrari exceeded this distance.

In 1937 Sommer was a reserve driver for Scuderia Ferrari, but the Italian cars were now outclassed, and he achieved no worthwhile successes. Sommer was an occasional driver for Alfa Corse in 1938, but it was another largely fruitless year. At Le Mans in 1939 Sommer asked 'B. Bira' to share his 6C 2500 Alfa Romeo. The cylinder head gasket failed after only 24 laps. Sommer, with assistance from a mechanic, changed the gasket in just over an hour, but he and Bira retired on the Sunday morning by when they had climbed up to tenth place. Sommer's last pre-war success was fifth place with his rather tired 8C 308 Alfa Romeo in the 1939 French GP.

Sommer drove 4CL Maseratis in immediate post-war races, and he was entered by Ferrari in a small number of events with the latest V12 sports cars. He also won the Formula 2 Coupe des Petites Cylindrées at Reims with a V12 2-litre Ferrari. When Ferrari introduced his new GP cars at the Italian race held at Turin, Sommer was included in the team and, in a very wet race, he drove very well to finish third behind Wimille's Tipo 158 Alfa Romeo and Villoresi's Maserati. Sommer also drove a GP Ferrari in the Autodromo GP at Monza the following month, but was forced to pull out because he was feeling unwell.

Two very odd, similar experiences occurred in Sommer's post-war GP career. Raymond was due to drive

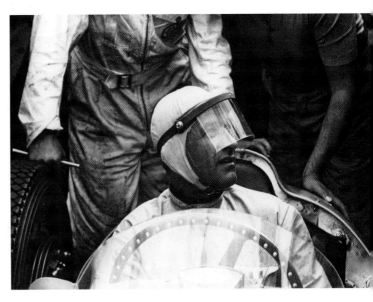

Above: *Raymond Sommer was one of the greatest of all French drivers, and in pre-war days was a very successful member of Scuderia Ferrari. He is seen here at the wheel of the BRM V16 at its race debut at the International Trophy meeting in August 1950. There was a minor catastrophe when the BRM broke a drive shaft at the start of its heat.* **(Guy Griffiths Collection)**

the great French racing hope, the CTA-Arsenal, in the 1947 French GP at Lyon, but the clutch seized on the starting grid, and when he fed in the pedal the engine power snapped a driveshaft. It was a great disappointment and very upsetting for this exceptionally courageous driver.

During 1949, Sommer finished third with a Talbot-Lago in the Swiss GP. He continued to drive a Talbot-Lago in GP racing in 1950, finishing fourth at Monaco and Pau. He was still driving for Ferrari in Formula 2, and won the races at Marseille, Roubaix, and Aix-les-Bains. In August, Raymond Mays invited Sommer to drive the new V16 BRM on its debut in the International Trophy race at Silverstone. Oddly enough – and sadly enough – at the start when Sommer let in the clutch, a component in the drive shafts failed, and the new British car jerked forward a few inches and that was that.

Although Sommer was not in the least responsible for this failure or that of the CTA in 1947, which in both cases was attributable to mechanical fragility, he received considerable criticism. In September he drove a 500cc Cooper, with motorcycle engine, at a race meeting at Cadours in the Haute Garenne. For some reason that was never properly explained – cockpit error is unlikely for a man of such consummate skill and experience – he lost control on a gentle fast bend, crashed, and was killed.

Sopwith, Tommy

Entrant
Born: 15 November 1932

The son of Sir Tom Sopwith of Sopwith Aircraft, Hawker Siddeley and America's Cup fame with *Endeavour*, Thomas Edward Brodie Sopwith was an apprentice at Hawker Siddeley's car and aviation subsidiary, Armstrong Siddeley at Parkside, Coventry. He raced MG and Jaguar XK 120 cars before building his own sports-racing car, the Sphinx; this was a 'special' that combined an Allard J2R chassis, a developed Armstrong Siddeley Sapphire engine, and a sleek body designed by Sopwith and built in Coventry by Motor Panels, a company that did a lot of specialist work for British manufacturers, including the prototype Jaguar D-type body.

Sopwith raced the Sphinx in 1954, and then ran a number of different British competition cars, including a Cooper-Jaguar, a Cooper-Climax, a Lotus Eleven, and a Cooper-Climax F2 car. From the Boxing Day meeting at Brands Hatch in 1957 Tommy and his good friend Sir Gawaine Baillie raced Jaguar 3.4 saloons. He retired from racing at the end of 1958 and he then concentrated on

Below: *Tommy Sopwith is seen here at the wheel of his Sphinx on the starting grid of the Members' meeting at Goodwood in late 1954. This car combined an Allard J2R chassis with an Armstrong Siddeley Sapphire engine, and was very successful in club events. It was some years later that Sopwith's Équipe Endeavour entered Jaguar saloons and Ferrari GT cars. (Author's collection)*

entering Jaguars under the name Équipe Endeavour.

Tommy had owned an early Ferrari 250GT which he bought off Mike Hawthorn's stand at the 1957 London Motor Show, but he was never happy with this car, which he thought always ran badly, and sold it to Colonel Ronnie Hoare. Hoare loved the car and went to a great deal of effort in getting it to run properly. This was how Hoare first became involved with Ferrari, and it ultimately led to the setting up of Maranello Concessionaires.

In 1961 Équipe Endeavour was still racing Jaguar saloons, but also competed with a Ferrari 250GT SWB owned jointly with Maranello Concessionaires. After achieving substantial success in British events in 1961, they sold this at the end of the year and bought a 250GTO, which was again owned in partnership. The 250GTO was usually driven by Mike Parkes, and it too achieved a good measure of success. Sopwith was becoming increasingly interested in powerboat racing, and he withdrew from car racing. They sold the 250GTO for £6,500, which was more than they had paid for it.

Of his Ferraris, Tommy remembers:

The 250GT SWB was great fun, very fast, and the only road car that was anywhere near it in performance was the Jaguar E-type. The original E-type that we raced in 1961 was almost a straightforward production car. It was nearly as fast as the 250GT SWB and I think that it stimulated Ferrari into building the 250GTO. On the road the E-type was a nicer car to drive because of its independent rear suspension. The 250GT SWB had a better power to weight ratio than the Jaguar – and the 250GTO was a much harder car to drive than the SWB.

Stepney, Nigel

Chief Mechanic, Race Technical Manager
Born: Ufton, Warwickshire, England

Nigel Stepney took a mechanical engineering apprenticeship at Broadspeed, and from 1975 to 1978 he worked on Broadspeed sports car projects. In the years that followed, he worked for a number of F1 teams: Shadow (1979–80), Lotus (1981–8), Benetton (1989–91), and then in 1992 he worked for the Piquet F3000 team. Stepney joined Ferrari at the start of the 1993 season as Chief Mechanic, and at that time he was the only English-speaker on the technical staff. He was

Above: *Nigel Stepney was the man accused in 2007 of passing a dossier of technical information to the McLaren team.* (Author's collection)

brought into the team by John Barnard, who had worked with him at Benetton.

Barnard was, of course, working from his specially set-up headquarters at Guildford, and it is not surprising that Stepney's role expanded into that of being the principal means of liaison between Guildford and Maranello. At this time Barnard's chief assistant on the Ferrari project at Guildford was Mike Coughlan, another former Benetton technician, and there was constant communication between Stepney and Coughlan.

When Stepney joined Ferrari, team morale was very low and many of the staff lacked motivation. Although foreigners at Ferrari have, notoriously, been resented in the highly charged and highly political atmosphere that has always existed at Maranello, Stepney seemed to become steeped in the atmosphere very easily and was soon on excellent terms with the Ferrari technical staff. According to Richard Williams of *The Guardian*, he talked Italian in the Modenese dialect spoken on the workshop floor.

He found a house in a village just outside Maranello, and this was a bare hour to the nearest ski resort, and only a little further from the beaches on the Adriatic. It was not long before Ferrari realised that its experiment of having a technical office in Guildford was not working, and Barnard and Coughlan were dismissed.

This was a severe blow for Stepney, who saw his job on the line as well, but it soon became obvious that this was not the case when another group of ex-Benetton employees, that included technical director Ross Brawn, joined the Ferrari team. Stepney's position was strengthened, and when he was promoted to technical co-ordinator in 2002 it seemed that he was the most likely candidate for the role of technical director when it became vacant.

At the end of 2006, Brawn decided to take a year's sabbatical, and Stepney was badly upset by Ferrari's refusal to give Brawn's job to him. Instead, the role of technical director went to Italian Mario Almondo, and it has been suggested that this was part of an attempt to restore the Ferrari team's Italian character. It was announced that Stepney would be responsible for coordinating the technical aspects of the Ferrari racing and test team from the sporting administration at Fiorano with the technical staff at the factory. While this was clearly an important position, it was also very low profile – something to which Stepney was unaccustomed.

In the week between the French and German Grands Prix in 2007, Ferrari made the claim that a dossier of technical information running to 780 pages had been passed to McLaren. It emerged that Nigel Stepney was responsible for passing on the information, and that the recipient was Mike Coughlan of McLaren. It is known that Ron Dennis and other senior McLaren executives had no direct or personal knowledge of the matter. What is not known is whether any or how much of the contents of the dossier would be of use to a rival.

The Féderation Internationale de l'Automobile announced, on 13 September 2007, that McLaren would forfeit all constructors' points scored in 2007 and, in addition, would pay a fine of $100m. It was a sum totally disproportionate to the offence, and indeed to any offence that could conceivably be committed in F1 racing. What the penalty revealed was a prejudice against McLaren by officials, and the attitude of Ferrari reflects that, after many years in the doldrums, Ferrari had become the most consistently successful GP team, and it feared that McLaren would usurp its position.

The financial situation of Italy and Fiat, which owns 56 per cent of Ferrari shares, is very uncertain and volatile. Certain Fiat executives will pressure for extreme sanctions if there is any breach of rules – potentially, if not actually – detrimental to their position. Mike Coughlan was dismissed by McLaren, and in 2008 Stepney worked for Gigawave, a company whose expertise is in digital wireless technology (that is, the making of on-board camera footage).

Stewart, Jackie

Driver
Born: 11 June 1939 (Milton, near Dumbarton, Scotland)

John Young 'Jackie' Stewart narrowly missed becoming a works Ferrari driver. He came up through the ranks of lesser formulae driving for Ken Tyrrell, and became a member of the works BRM team in 1965. In his first F1 season he won the Italian GP and finished third in the Drivers' Championship. During the next two seasons, the BRM team struggled to make their cumbersome, excessively complex H16 cars competitive, and for much of 1966 and for three races in 1967 he had to drive the old V8 1500cc cars with engines enlarged to 2/2.1 litres.

Jackie's first Ferrari drive was with Scarfiotti, at the wheel of a 250LM entered by Maranello Concessionaires in the

Below: *Seen here at the 1967 Mexican Grand Prix, when he was driving for BRM, Jackie Stewart was negotiating to drive for Ferrari in 1968. His only drive for Maranello was in the BOAC 500 race at Brands Hatch in 1967. He partnered Chris Amon at the wheel of a P4, and their second place behind the Chaparral of Phil Hill/Mike Spence was good enough to clinch Ferrari's win in the Prototype Championship. (LAT Photographic)*

1964 Paris 1,000km race at Montlhéry. After holding second place, they dropped back because a steering link failed, and they finished in seventh place. In 1966 Stewart shared David McKay's 250LM Ferrari with Andy Buchanan to win the Surfer's Paradise 12 Hours race. It was the inaugural race on this new circuit in Queensland. Many involved with the meeting believed that the organisers rigged the results, and that the real winner was Peter Sutcliffe, who was sharing his Ford GT40 with Frank Matich.

During 1967, Stewart became increasingly disenchanted with BRM. He travelled to Maranello to meet Enzo Ferrari, and at a second meeting in August 1967 he agreed terms for driving for the team. In the meantime he had made his only appearance with a works Ferrari, a 330P4 Sports Prototype, in the BOAC 500 at Brands Hatch at the end of July 1967. His co-driver was Chris Amon, and with a car that was clearly unsuited to the circuit they took an excellent second place behind the Chaparral of Phil Hill/Mike Spence.

Following the second meeting, Stewart travelled on to drive a Tyrrell in the F2 race at Enna, where Jacky Ickx, also a Tyrrell driver, told him that he had been offered a place in the Ferrari team. Stewart concluded that Enzo Ferrari was playing the two drivers off against each other, and he changed his mind about joining Maranello. Instead, Ken Tyrrell set up a Formula 1 team, and Stewart won the Drivers' Championship three times – in 1969 with Matra cars, and in 1971 and 1973 with cars of Tyrrell's own construction.

Surtees, John

Works driver
Born: 11 February 1934 (Tatsfield, Surrey, England)

Surtees was probably the most versatile, conscientious, and hard-working of racing drivers. He was the son of a south London motorcycle dealer, Jack Surtees, who raced motorcycle combinations and was a Vincent dealer and enthusiast. Young John was apprenticed to the Vincent company, he started racing motorcycles in 1951, and in

Opposite: *This photograph shows Surtees during the years of the Ferrari V12 3-litre cars. He left Ferrari at Le Mans in 1966, and there is no doubt that both, in later days, regretted the split. The fortunes of Surtees and Ferrari would have been very different and probably very much more successful if they had not split. (Ford Motor Company)*

his early days he rode a rare Vincent 500cc Grey Shadow. In 1955 Joe Craig of Norton brought him into the works team, and he beat the reigning World Champion Geoff Duke at both Silverstone and Brands Hatch.

Because of the financial instability of Associated Motor Cycles, owners of Norton, he decided to leave the team for MV Agusta, for whom he rode from 1956 onwards. That year, Surtees won his first 500cc World Championship, although it was facilitated by the fact that Geoff Duke (Gilera) was suspended for six months for supporting a riders' strike for higher starting money.

Persistent mechanical problems resulted in a hopeless 1957 season, but Gilera and Moto Guzzi pulled out of racing at the end of 1957 and Surtees and MV Agusta dominated the sport. Surtees won 32 out of 39 races entered, he became the first man to win the Senior Isle of Man TT three years in succession, and he won both the 350cc and 500cc Championship in each year.

In 1959 Surtees was tested in works Aston Martin DBR1 and Vanwall F1 cars, but he rejected offers from both teams. He did, however, agree to drive Ken Tyrrell's FJ Coopers, which were not very competitive cars, and with one of these he took second place in the FJ race at the international meeting at Silverstone in May 1960. He then took a second place at Oulton Park with his own F2 car, and after being given a trial in a

Below: *Young John Surtees, still a schoolboy, is seen here with father Norman and mother who were competing with a Vincent Rapide and sidecar at a motorcycle grass-track meeting.* (Guy Griffiths Collection)

works Lotus, Colin Chapman offered him a drive in F1 whenever his motorcycle commitments permitted. He retired in the Monaco and Portuguese races, but took an excellent second place in the British race behind Brabham (Cooper).

At the end of the 1960 season he retired from motorcycle racing, and he originally planned to stay with Lotus, but he was invited to Maranello with a view to driving for the team in 1961. However, John concluded that the team already had too many drivers, and he could not see where he would fit in. He told them, 'No, I'll come back when I have more experience.' He also turned down Lotus because there were difficulties with Innes Ireland, and he did not want to get involved in controversy.

So, John joined the Yeoman Credit team run by Reg Parnell, but the problem was that the team had to race uncompetitive customer Coopers. Nevertheless, Surtees won the Lombank Trophy at Snetterton and the Richmond Trophy at Goodwood. He also drove the rear-engined Vanwall in the International Trophy at Silverstone in May and finished fifth after a spin in the wet, and he was third with a Cooper in the British Empire Trophy in July, again at Silverstone. His best performances in Championship races were fifth places at Spa and the Nürburgring.

Surtees suggested that Eric Broadley should build the Lola T4 and that Parnell's team, now known as Bowmaker Racing, should race them. John put a lot of effort into the project and he, in fact, signed the contract with Broadley that he then assigned to Bowmaker. The 1962 season proved outstanding for a team with a completely new car but, although they were close to winning races, the only victory was Surtees's first place in the 2000 Guineas race at Mallory Park. In World Championship races John's best performances were second places at Silverstone and the Nürburgring.

At the end of the year, Coventry Climax told Parnell that they couldn't continue to supply engines. In fact, after a bit of a rumpus and financial jiggery-pokery, they did go on supplying their V8 units, but Surtees was a cautious, one might say pessimistic, man and accepted a further approach from Ferrari. Maranello had just endured one of their worst seasons ever, and John was impressed by the fact that the team was a shambles and could only get better! At this time Forghieri's most pressing objectives were to redevelop the V6 GP car in competitive form and to develop the V12 rear-engined 3-litre 250P as a race-winning GT Prototype. He was to succeed on both scores.

While he was at Ferrari, Surtees was also responsible for giving the cars their final test and passing them out.

The first race of the year was the Sebring 12 Hours, and there was a frantic rush to complete the 250Ps. When he arrived at Sebring, he found that the last car he had tested had been given to NART, and John and Scarfiotti were driving a completely untried car. John recalled:

'They said I had done all the testing of the 250P, and I had to sort it out. So we just got on with it in practice. Obviously, I wasn't happy, and this was, I suppose, the first time that I crossed swords with Dragoni.

It was an eventful race. One of the problems that we'd encountered in testing had been fumes, which blew back in under the rear engine cover and over the cockpit, as the engine cover tended to lift. We had modified the sealing round the top of the body and the way it was held down, except on the last car. Ludovico and I were getting gassed, so we were consuming large quantities of liquid, and it was very uncomfortable. We won the race, despite some brake trouble and other niggling little problems.

Then we found that Dragoni, our own team manager, had protested us and suggested that the NART car had won. My then wife Pat, who was probably the best time-keeper and lap chart-keeper at the race, had kept an immaculate lap-chart and a record of lap times. It so happened that the official lap-chart coincided perfectly with my wife's. NART didn't have a proper chart – they'd been on the vino and the pasta.'

With the benefit of hindsight it is so very easy to see how the hostility between Dragoni and the drivers grew. Surtees, partnered by Mairesse, won the Nürburgring 1,000km race, and they were leading at Le Mans with Mairesse at the wheel when the car caught fire. John Surtees recounted:

'The fuel sloshed over and, as far as we understand it, the stop-light switch ignited the fuel as he braked to go under the Dunlop Bridge. He was badly burned, and it very nearly brought his career to an end. In some ways I think that it contributed to him committing suicide a few years later. He drove a few times more, but he was devastated by losing his racing career, the thing he lived for.'

Throughout 1963 the V6 F1 cars gradually improved. Forghieri had produced in May a completely new car with lighter chassis, redesigned rear suspension, and Bosch fuel injection. After fourth at Monaco, third at Zandvoort, and second at Silverstone, Surtees won the German race. Surtees drove a new monocoque car at Monza and was leading the Italian race when the engine failed. Fourth place in the Drivers' Championship with 22 points was a marked improvement on Phil Hill's sixth place and 15 points in 1962.

In 1964 the team raced two new designs of Prototype, the 3.3-litre Tipo 275P and the 4-litre Tipo 330P, both with a single overhead camshaft per bank of cylinders. Surtees was partnered by Bandini with a 330P at Sebring, and after a long delay while brake pads were changed and defective rear lights repaired, they took third place. Ferrari missed the Targa Florio that year to concentrate on preparations for the Monaco GP. Surtees was again partnered by Bandini at the Nürburgring 1,000km, and they were leading when a wheel came off. At Le Mans Surtees/Bandini drove the more lithe and more reliable 275P, and finished third after delays caused by fuel pick-up problems.

Although the V6 cars were still used in a few races in 1964, Forghieri and his engineering colleagues had developed new F1 cars with V8 and flat-12 engines. Both Surtees and Bandini drove V8s in most of the year's races. After winning the non-Championship Siracusa GP, Surtees drove consistently and successfully in the face of the very strong British opposition. He took second place in the Dutch race at Zandvoort, third at Brands Hatch, second at Solitude (non-Championship) and then won the German, Austrian, and Italian races.

Ferrari's rather fatuous argument with the authorities culminated in him returning his competition licence, repainting the cars in American white and blue racing colours, and NART entering them in the last two Championship races of the season. Surtees achieved another second place at Watkins Glen, and as the teams arrived at Mexico City for the last round, the outcome of the Championship was still very much in doubt: Graham Hill (BRM) had 39 points, Surtees 34, and Clark 34 – and any one of them could win it.

Clark, with the Lotus, was fastest in practice, and in the race he built up a lead over Gurney (Brabham), followed by Graham Hill, and Bandini, while Surtees was well down the field. For several laps, as Hill and Bandini went through the hairpin bend at the far end of the circuit from the pits, the Italian was very close to the BRM driver, pressing him so hard that there was a danger of the two cars colliding, and Hill was shaking his fist at the Ferrari driver. Then Bandini, holding a very tight line, collided with the BRM, crumpling its exhaust system.

Bandini may not have acted in a calculated manner, but he must have been well aware that if he and Hill collided, then Surtees would benefit. Maybe Dragoni put him up to it. Both cars spun off, but they rejoined the race. The BRM began to run so roughly that Hill had to stop at the pits for the exhaust pipes to be cut away. Surtees was now in third place and, just as Clark seemed all set to win the race, a rubber oil pipe split on the Lotus and he eased back to finish fifth. Gurney won for Brabham, Surtees came through to take second place and win the Championship by a margin of one point.

In 1964 Ferrari had, for the first time, faced a challenge from Ford in endurance racing, but the GT40s, although fast, had been unreliable. However, in 1965 they proved more successful. The latest Ferraris were the Tipo 275P2 and 330P2 models, similar to the previous year's models, but with twin overhead camshafts per bank of cylinders. Surtees/Rodriguez retired their 330P2 at Daytona (a Ford won) and then Ferrari missed the Sebring race because the organisers permitted Appendix C sports cars to run (Jim Hall and Hap Sharp won with a Chaparral).

The works Ferraris took the first two places at Monza in the order Parkes/Guichet and Surtees/Scarfiotti (delayed by tyre trouble) with 330P2s, and a Ford finished third. Surtees missed the Targa Florio, but Vaccarella/Bandini won for Ferrari. The Ferraris proved dominant yet again in the Nürburgring 1,000km race, and Surtees, partnered by Scarfiotti, led almost throughout to win the race from team-mates Parkes/ Scarfiotti. All the works Ferraris and Fords failed at Le Mans (a NART-entered 250LM Ferrari driven by Jochen Rindt/Masten Gregory won the race).

Formula 1 was pretty disastrous for Ferrari in 1965 and the successes of 1964 were not sustained. Coventry Climax had developed a more potent 16-valve version of their V8 engine, which was supplied to their leading customers, Lotus and Brabham. That year, the last of the 1500cc unsupercharged formula, there were ten rounds in the Drivers' Championship. Clark won six to achieve maximum points; Hill (BRM) won two, Stewart (BRM) one and Ginther (Honda) one. Surtees's best performances were second place in South Africa and third in the French race at Clermont-Ferrand.

Because of the tie-up with Fiat, Ferrari was concentrating on developing the V8 engine, which was to power a version of the Dino. This engine was not a match for the Coventry Climax V8, and Surtees thinks that for political reasons development of the flat-12 was neglected. Throughout the year he only once had an engine that he believed to be truly competitive, and

that was at the Italian GP where his flat-12 Tipo 1512 car had a revised cylinder head with improved induction developed by Ing. Rocchi. He finished fifth in the Championship with 25 points.

From 1965 onwards Surtees had been racing Lola T70 Group 7 sports-racing cars, and a bad crash in practice for the sports car Canadian GP, the result of a broken stub axle, injured Surtees to the point that it seemed that he would not survive, and he of course missed the last two F1 races of the season at Watkins Glen and Mexico City.

When John returned to Europe after his accident, he had been due to compete at Indianapolis with a Lola, but he passed the drive over to Graham Hill. Surtees had no personal injury insurance cover and Ferrari met all his expenses.

John concentrated on recovering from the accident and making himself fit, but he found himself in constant conflict with Dragoni. Because Ferrari did not attend races, he relied on what he was told by Dragoni, Lini and, rather more frankly and honestly, by Forghieri. The first real problem with Dragoni was at Monaco where the race manager insisted that Surtees drove the 3-litre V12 car. Surtees told him:

'The 2.4-litre Dino [built for Surtees to drive in the 1966 Tasman series, but unused because of the accident] was two seconds a lap faster round Modena than the current Formula 1 car.

You are denying me the use of it and I am the fastest driver. I came to Monaco to win. The V12 will break its gearbox, you have to row it along because it doesn't have enough power, and it's too heavy. I led the race, but predictably retired because of gearbox failure. Bandini finished second and if I had been driving the V6, we would have won. Three weeks after Monaco, I won the Belgian GP with the V12 to which a modified cylinder head had been fitted.

Then I went to Le Mans where I was to drive for Scarfiotti. When I arrived, Dragoni told me, "Mr Agnelli [President of Fiat] is coming and so we are going to put Ludovico for the start."'

John told him that if they hoped to beat the Fords, there was only one way that they were going to do it: he was a minimum of a second a lap faster than Scarfiotti, and he had to go flat-out right from the start as though it were a GP. With the other two team cars, they should play for safety and they should run at a steady pace.

Surtees said to him:

'What are you trying to do? I've just come back from winning at Spa and you didn't even congratulate me.'

He left Le Mans and drove to the factory where he saw Enzo Ferrari. They discussed the problem, and it was agreed that Surtees should leave the team. They agreed that they would never actually spell out the final reason for the break. It was a blow to both Surtees and Ferrari, but the basic reason was that Dragoni had vital contacts with Agnelli and the other Fiat directors in Turin. Ferrari desperately needed Fiat's financial support and he was not going to get it so long as Surtees was in the team, urging that Ferrari should break its isolation from other racing car manufacturers and pall up with the likes of Lola.

After he left Ferrari, Surtees joined Cooper and won the 1966 Mexican GP, and he continued to drive Lolas through 1967. He drove for Honda in 1967–8 (still working with Lola), and joined the hopeless BRM team for 1969. That year he started building Formula 5000 cars at his workshops in Edenbridge, Kent, and from 1970 he raced his own Surtees F1 cars. Surtees retired from racing in 1972, but continued to field F1 cars until 1978. He also entered a Formula 2 team, with sponsorship from the 'Matchbox' toy car company.

Above: *Peter Sutcliffe used this studio portrait as a hand-out to enthusiasts, possible sponsors, and anyone who showed interest in his racing activities.* (Peter Sutcliffe)

Sutcliffe, Peter

Works driver
Born: 1 December 1936 (Huddersfield, Yorkshire, England)

The son of the co-owner of a large woollen mill employing some 500 people, Sutcliffe decided to leave the family company and become a professional racing driver. He had previously raced MG TD, Frazer Nash Le Mans Replica, and Jaguar D-type cars, but in 1963 he acquired a 'Lightweight' Jaguar E-type, followed this with an ex-David Piper Ferrari 250GTO, and then in 1965 raced his own Ford GT40.

His last season of racing was 1967, when he was asked at very short notice to drive a works Ferrari P4 at Le Mans with Günther Klass. They retired at Le Mans because of the failure of a gear in the camshaft drive. Sutcliffe was asked again by Ferrari to drive a P4 in the BOAC 500 race at Brands Hatch in July and, co-driving with Scarfiotti, finished fifth. He then emigrated to South Africa, and for some years he has split his time between that country and the UK.

Swaters, Jacques

Private driver, entrant and Ferrari dealer
Born: 30 October 1926 (Woluwe-St-Lambert, Brussels, Belgium)

Driving with Paul Frère, Swaters made his racing debut at the wheel of his special-bodied 939cc PB MG entered in the name of Écurie Francorchamps in the 1948 Spa 24 Hours race. The engine had blown up shortly before the race (and had been rebuilt by Frère) and, despite very real doubts as to whether it would last the distance, it finished fourth in the class ahead of a number of larger-capacity cars. There is great confusion over Belgian team names. Later in 1950, Swaters, Frère, and André Pilette formed Écurie Belgique to race in sports car and single-seater events.

There were two things very much in their favour: Swaters had money and Frère had great technical skills. Swaters bought an unblown 4½-litre Talbot GP car, already painted Belgian racing yellow because 'Johnny'

Above: *This recent photograph shows Jacques Swaters (on the right) with Piero Lardi Ferrari.* (Roberto Piccinini and Spitzley/Zagari Collection)

Claes had previously owned it. He raced this in the 1951 German GP (tenth) and the Italian GP (retired). Ferrari announced that he would be selling a small number of the new Tipo 500 F2 cars, sometimes called for obscure reasons the 'Starlet'. Swaters decided to buy one of these and, just to confuse matters, he raced this in partnership with Charles de Tornaco under the name Écurie Francorchamps.

Owners generally claimed that the private Tipo 500 Ferraris were less powerful than the works cars, and this was undoubtedly true, but the owners themselves were also slower than the works drivers. Swaters's performances were unexceptional, but he did win the poorly supported 129-mile (208km) Avusrennen in 1953 from German Veritas cars driven by Klenk and Helfrich. His friend and colleague Charles de Tornaco had raced the Tipo 500 on a few occasions without success.

De Tornaco was due to drive the Tipo 500 in the 1953 Modena GP, but in practice rolled the car and suffered very serious head and neck injuries. There were no adequate medical facilities at the circuit and de Tornaco died while being taken to hospital in a private car. Swaters raced the car through 1954 on an occasional basis.

By this time he had become increasingly interested in racing sports cars, which gave a rather better chance of success to the private owner, even if starting and prize money was abysmal. At Le Mans in 1953 Écurie Francorchamps (a team jointly run by de Tornaco and Swaters) had a C-type Jaguar prepared at the works and this was driven by Laurent/de Tornaco into ninth place in the 24 Hours race. The following year, still with a works-prepared C-type, Laurent/Swaters finished fourth at Le Mans. By 1955 the team possessed a D-type Jaguar, which Swaters/Claes drove to third place at Le Mans that

year, and in the 1956 race Swaters/Rousselle finished fourth with the D-type.

By 1957, Swaters had given up racing and he had become the Brussels agent for Ferrari. The racing team retained the name Écurie Francorchamps and concentrated on entering Ferraris. In the 1950s it owned a Tipo 750 Monza and then a Tipo 250 Testa Rossa. The team continued entering cars after the introduction of the category for GT Prototypes and Competition Sports Cars. It achieved mixed results and only some of the best efforts are mentioned here.

Swaters also managed Équipe Nationale Belge, which raced F2 Coopers and Emerson single-seaters until 1962. In that year it built up the ENB-Maserati, which Lucien Bianchi drove without success, but the team soon lost interest in the project. At Le Mans in 1962, the team's 250GTO, driven by 'Elde' (Léon Denier)/'Beurlys' (Jean Blaton), finished third, second in its class. In 1963 the 250GTOs of 'Beurlys'/'Langlois' (Langlois van Ophem) and 'Elde'/'Dumay' finished second and fourth overall at Le Mans and also took first two places in their class.

In 1965 Écurie Francorchamps performed magnificently at Le Mans after the retirement of the works cars. The NART Ferrari 250LM of Gregory/Rindt won, but Belgian entries took the next two places; Dumay/Gosselin finished second with the team's 250LM after leading until three hours before the end of the race when the right rear tyre burst and wrecked the glass-fibre wing on that side. The car spent a long time in the pits while repairs were carried out. The third-place car was the lightweight 275GTB driven by Mairesse/'Beurlys'. Écurie Francorchamps owned several 250LMs and raced them extensively in minor international events with some success.

During 1967, ENB had raced a Ferrari 330P3/4, the 1966 P3 updated for selected private teams and also known as the Tipo 412. Mairesse went off the road in the wet during the Spa 1,000km race and had completely wrecked this car. It was partly because of this that at Le Mans that year a yellow-painted 330P4 was entered in the name of ENB, but was in reality a works entry, and Mairesse/'Beurlys' drove it into third place overall. Ferrari withdrew from Prototype racing at the end of 1967.

When the works entered racing in the Competition Sports Car category with the 512S in 1970, the Belgian team acquired one of these cars and ran it without success at Spa and Le Mans. Écurie Francorchamps finally ceased racing in 1982, but Swaters's Garage in Francorchamps has retained the Belgian Ferrari agency and has also developed a Ferrari centre, emphasising all aspects of the marque.

Tadini, Mario

Pre-war Scuderia Ferrari driver
Born: 1905 (Bologna, Italy)
Died: August 1993

Tadini was one of a number of Italian drivers who were well to the fore in their home country in the 1930s and, as members of Scuderia Ferrari struggled, largely unsuccessfully, against the overwhelming German opposition. He owned a chain of clothing stores, but whether he built it up himself or it was the family business is unknown. He had met Enzo Ferrari through motor sport, and provided much of the initial capital for the setting up of Scuderia Ferrari. Having put so much money into the racing business, he drove regularly, persistently and with considerable ability as an amateur, but only as hard and as frequently as he wanted, because he was never a professional driver.

When he was in the mood, he drove like the wind, and with Scuderia Ferrari he regularly drove GP Alfa Romeos, but with limited success. In the 1934 Mille Miglia road race, Tadini, partnered by Barbieri, was at the wheel of a 2.6-litre Alfa Romeo Monza entered by Scuderia Ferrari, and he drove a scintillating race in persistent, heavy rain, leading at Florence with about a third of the race covered, a minute ahead of Varzi. He was still leading at Rome, but gradually fell back because of gearbox problems, and by Ancona he was out of the race after struggling with only two gears. This was Tadini at his best, fighting hard in a race that he loved.

His successes in 1934 were limited to thirds at Bordino, Modena, and Naples, all parochial races in which there was no German opposition. The following year, partnered by Chiari, he finished second in the Mille Miglia, with his Alfa Romeo Monza, to Pintacuda at the wheel of an Alfa Romeo Monoposto, who was accompanied by diminutive jockey, the Marquis della Stufa.

For the time being, Tadini had fallen out with Ferrari, and in this race he drove a 2.6-litre Monza that had previously been modified by Ferrari, and he had bought this from Ippolito Berrone. Tadini always dressed smartly when racing, but his natty suit under a raincoat provided inadequate warmth, and he had to stop on the Futa Pass to eat in an effort to raise his blood-sugar levels. Tadini was also a brilliant hill climb driver, and in 1935 he won the Stelvio mountain hill climb, as well as finishing second in the Circuit of Modena and winning the very minor Lucca race. In addition, of course, he won minor Italian hill climbs.

Above: *Refuelling himself, Tadini swigs a bottle of beer at the wheel of his Alfa Romeo Monza during a pit stop in the 1935 Mille Miglia. Tadini, partnered by Chiari took the lead in the early stages of the race and eventually finished second, behind the Scuderia Ferrari Alfa Romeo Monoposto of Pintacuda and Marchese.*
(Spitzley-Zagari Collection)

The following year Tadini, as a member of the Alfa Romeo GP team, was the centre of a debacle at the Monaco GP, which was held in stormy conditions with torrential rain. On the starting grid a mechanic noticed that Brivio's Alfa Romeo was dripping oil, so he and Tadini swapped cars. For much of the first lap there was no problem, but at the chicane after the tunnel Tadini dropped a large quantity of oil. The leading cars avoided the trouble on the next lap, but Chiron triggered off a multi-car pile-up that eliminated his car and seven others. Scuderia Ferrari was responsible for allowing Tadini to start the race.

It was, generally, a poor year, but Tadini finished fourth at Budapest and he finished second to Nuvolari at Milan. In the race in Sempione Park he was taking copious sips of lemonade to counter the effects of the Shell 'Dynamin' fuel mix with 85 per cent methanol that the Scuderia used in many races that year. With an 8C 2900A he again set FTD in the Stelvio hill climb at the end of August, and in early September he won the minor 'round the houses' Circuit of Lucca from Brivio.

Tadini was rarely seen in circuit racing in 1937, but he continued to drive regularly in hill climbs. With a 12C Alfa Romeo he won the Parma–Poggio di Berceto hill climb in May, and later the same month took second place to Trossi in the Genoa race. He set FTD at Susa–Montcenisio on 18 July, and won his class at Freiburg on 1 August. In both these events he drove an 8C 2900A. The full takeover of Scuderia Ferrari by Alfa Corse was completed on 1 January 1938, and Tadini was no longer a member of the works team. His racing career was to all intents over, but he did make a brief appearance at the wheel of a V12 Ferrari in post-war days.

Tambay, Patrick

Works driver
Born: 25 June 1949 (Paris, France)

Above: *Patrick Tambay was brought into the Ferrari team after the death of Gilles Villeneuve, and during his less than two seasons with Maranello he won two races and took some good places. Later, he drove for the Renault and the Beatrice Foods-sponsored Lola teams.*
(LAT Photographic)

Patrick Tambay joined Ferrari at one of the most difficult times in its racing history. He performed magnificently, winning three races and taking fourth place in the 1983 World Championship, but it was not good enough for Ferrari, who terminated his services after 18 months. Some would say that Tambay was far too easy-going (he was that, and wonderfully smooth and courteous too) for the cut and thrust of motor racing politics in general. Others would conclude that he was not given a fair chance by the Ferrari team. Probably both are true.

His career in motor racing started to take off with a win in the Pilote Elf scheme, which took him into 1973 Formula Renault. He was runner-up, which was good enough to give him a place in the Elf team that was contesting the European F2 Championship. He performed well enough to gain a place in the Elf-backed March F2 team the following year. On the credit side, he scored a win and four second places (and some people commented 'only one win?'). In his third year in F2 in 1976, driving for Martini, he again only scored one victory, compared with three by Arnoux.

They took second and third places in the European Championship, but Tambay was dropped from the team in favour of Pironi. At the start of 1977, he lacked a future, but that was provided when Brian Redman crashed his Lola CanAm car and temporarily put himself out of racing. Entrants Carl Haas and Jim Hall had a problem that they solved by offering the drive to Tambay. The opposition was fairly weak, and Tambay won six of the seven rounds and the Championship.

It was now that he moved into the bottom rungs of F1. From the British GP until the end of the 1977 season, he drove Ensigns for Teddy Yip's Theodore Racing, and in three races scored points, which was quite something in itself. He then was offered – and accepted – a place in the McLaren team. It sounds better than it was, for the team was going through a dismal patch. In two seasons, 1978–9, his best performance was a fourth in the 1978 Swedish race, and in 1979 he failed to score a single point.

Tambay was out of F1 in 1980, and that year he competed in the CanAm series again, driving Lolas for Carl Haas, and won the Championship for the second time. Teddy Yip was still struggling with his Theodore Racing Team, and although Tambay took a sixth place at

Long Beach, driving beyond the car's realistic potential, it was the only finish in the points. In mid-season Jabouille decided to retire from the Ligier team, and Patrick filled his place. Tambay drove for Ligier in eight races and finished none. After he crashed in several races, the season ended in recriminations and near-despair.

So, Tambay was cast into the wilderness, but tragedy at Ferrari revived his F1 career. He joined the Maranello team at the 1982 Dutch race and soon showed that, with a car that was half-good, he was very good. He started with eighth place at Zandvoort, slowed by an engine misfire that was probably linked to the new water-injection system developed by Agip engineers. Then Pironi and Tambay took second and third places at Brands Hatch, followed by third and fourth in the French race at Paul Ricard, where they were outpaced by the Renaults.

Next came the German race at Hockenheim and, after Pironi's dreadful practice crash, Tambay was the sole Ferrari starter, and he achieved a superb win from Prost (Renault). In the Austrian race he was delayed by a puncture, but recovered to finish fourth. He had to miss the next race, the Swiss GP at Dijon-Prenois, because of severe neck and arm pains caused by the excessively firm ride of ground-effect suspension.

In the Italian GP, Arnoux was the winner for Renault,

but Tambay and Andretti (who had joined Ferrari for the last two races of the season) took second and third places. Tambay missed the final race at Caesars Palace because of a recurrence of the arm and neck problems, and Andretti retired because of suspension problems. Remarkably, Ferrari won the Constructors' Championship with 74 points to the 69 of McLaren and 62 of Renault.

There were important changes for 1983 because FISA had decided, without consultation, to ban ground-effect, that is, more precisely, to require a flat under-body within the wheelbase. Postlethwaite modified the 1982 126C2 cars to comply with these changes, and the team had to make do with these cars for half the 1983 season before the new 126C3 cars were ready. Tambay remained with the team, and he was joined by René Arnoux from Renault. Greater sensitivity was required in driving cars without ground-effect, notably to conserve the tyres. Arnoux was expected to be able to adjust to the changed handling characteristics of the cars more readily, but this proved not to be so.

After a poor start to the season, Tambay won the San Marino GP at Imola ahead of Prost (Renault), with Arnoux in third place. Throughout the season, Tambay proved a consistent finisher in the first four, although he failed to win another race that year. Postlethwaite's new 126C3, with carbon-fibre composite monocoque, was ready by the British GP. Already Arnoux had won the Canadian GP, and he went on to achieve a better record than Tambay, with wins in the German and Dutch races, and second places in Austria and Italy.

Ferrari won the Constructors' Cup for the second successive year, and Arnoux and Tambay were third and fourth in the Drivers' Championship. Maranello had decided that one of their drivers would be replaced for 1984, and the axe fell on poor, undeserving Tambay. Ferrari always expected, but never understood, loyalty. Tambay spent two largely fruitless seasons with Renault (best results second in the 1984 French race and thirds in 1985 at Estoril and Imola) and then, along with Alan Jones, wasted a year with the uncompetitive Beatrice Foods-sponsored Lolas in 1986.

Later, Tambay drove Jaguars with Jan Lammers for the TWR team; he worked as a TV commentator, and for a short while in 1994 carried out public relations for the Larrousse team. Despite his achievements, he was, sadly, another driver whom Ferrari used and discarded. He raced in the Masters series for retired F1 drivers when it was introduced in 2006, and in 2008 Patrick's son Adrien competed successfully in the Formula BMW Europe series with Eifelland racing, and was the pre-season favourite. He is also deputy mayor of the suburb of Cannes in which he lives.

Taruffi, Piero

Works driver
Born: 12 October 1906 (Rome, Italy)
Died: 12 January 1988 (Rome, Italy)

An exceptionally versatile driver and engineer, author and team manager, Taruffi's greatest days were with Ferrari and the Gilera motorcycle team. In pre-war days he raced both motorcycles and cars. As early as 1932 he and D'Ippolito had finished second with a works 8C 2300 Alfa Romeo in the Belgian 24 Hours race, and the following year, partnered by Pellegrini, he finished third in the Mille Miglia. By this stage he was driving

Below: *Piero Taruffi had a long and successful racing career that dated back to the 1930s. In 1951–2 he drove for the Ferrari GP team. He is seen at the wheel of his Tipo 500 Ferrari before the start of the 1952 British GP. He drove a superb race and took second place behind team-mate Alberto Ascari. He finished third in that year's Drivers' World Championship.* (Tom March Collection)

regularly for Scuderia Ferrari, but in 1934 he became a member of the Maserati works team.

In that year's Mille Miglia he finished fifth overall, partnered by Maserati head mechanic Guerino Bertocchi, winning the 1100cc class and beating the MG Magnettes. He drove the Tipo V5 4,905cc 16-cylinder Maserati in the 1934 Tripoli GP, but the brakes locked on the fourth lap, he went off the track, demolished a hoarding, and the Maserati was a write-off; and he was lucky to escape with just a broken arm. Piero returned to racing in 1935, and raced for Bugatti without much success. By 1938 he was a member of Alfa Corse, but he was back to works Maseratis the following year. He was also a Gilera rider, development engineer, and team manager in late pre-war days.

Taruffi's close involvement with Gilera continued after the Second World War; he had significant involvement in the development of the team's very successful four-cylinder racing motorcycles, and he was responsible for signing up Geoff Duke, Reg Armstrong,

and Dickie Dale as works Gilera riders. In early post-war years he was also involved in development of Cisitalias, and raced the 1100cc single-seaters. In 1950 he drove an Alfa Romeo 158 into third place in the GP des Nations at Geneva behind other Alfa Romeo drivers, Fangio and de Graffenried.

He started to drive works Ferraris on a regular basis in 1951, and with a 4.1-litre V12 GP car he finished third behind team-mates Ascari and Serafini in the Penya Rhin GP on the Pedralbes circuit at Barcelona in October 1950. In 1951 Taruffi finished second to Fangio (Alfa Romeo) in the Swiss GP, a fine performance, and he was due to drive in the European GP at Reims, but Gilera were also expecting him to attend the motorcycle Belgian GP. He became unwell shortly before the race and although not fit enough to drive, he was up to attending as chief engineer with the Belgian team.

So Froilán González took his place at Ferrari, worked his way up to second, and then handed his car over to Ascari. González was again in the Ferrari team at the British race, and scored the first real defeat of the Alfa Romeos. Taruffi's season with Ferrari continued with a fifth place in the German GP, and another fifth in Spain. Luigi Chinetti arranged a Ferrari drive for him, and rode with him in the Carrera Panamericana Mexico in November, and they won the race from Ascari and Villoresi with another Ferrari.

Taruffi stayed with Ferrari in 1952, and among his

Below: *At the British GP meeting in 1952 Taruffi also drove Tony Vandervell's Ferrari Thin Wall Special in the Formule Libre race. He set fastest lap and, despite being penalised one minute for jumping the start, won the race from other 4.5-litre Ferraris driven by Luigi Villoresi and Brazilian Chico Landi.* **(Guy Griffiths Collection)**

other commitments was his Tarf record-breaking car. He finished second for Ferrari in the Tour of Sicily, and in the Mille Miglia he was at the wheel of a Vignale-bodied Ferrari Tipo 340MM 4.1-litre car. Although he was very much in contention, he was eliminated by broken transmission. Ascari missed the Swiss GP because he was competing at Indianapolis, and in his absence Taruffi won the race. Later he finished third in the French GP at Rouen, second in the British race and third in Germany. He took third place behind Ascari and Farina in the Drivers' World Championship.

During 1952 he had won the Ulster Trophy at Dundrod and the Formule Libre race at Silverstone in July with Tony Vandervell's Ferrari Thin Wall Special. For 1953, he signed up to drive Lancia sports-racing cars, and his best performance was second place in the Mexican road race. He stayed with Lancia in 1954 and, despite retiring in the Mille Miglia, the race that he most wanted to win, he won both the Tour of Sicily and the Targa Florio for the Turin team. He also drove a Ferrari into sixth place in the German GP.

Although his racing career was coming to an end, Mercedes-Benz brought Taruffi into their F1 team as 'a safe pair of hands' following Herrmann's bad practice crash at Monaco in 1955. He finished in the British race at Aintree behind three other Mercedes-Benz W196 cars, and took second place in the Italian GP. He joined the Maserati sports car team in 1956, and among his successes was second place in the Targa Florio.

'The Silver Fox', as he was sometimes known, arranged to drive a Ferrari in the 1957 Mille Miglia, and on this occasion, his 13th attempt, he won the race after the retirement of Peter Collins with his Ferrari. After this race he retired from racing and started a racing drivers' school. He had also written two very successful books, *Works Driver*, the story of his days with the big Continental entrants, and *The Technique of Motor Racing*, a superb guide to the sport for motor racing beginners.

Tavoni, Romolo

Race Director
Born: 30 January 1926 (Modena, Italy)

Educated in accountancy, Romolo Oscar Tavoni hoped to go into banking, but there was little work available immediately after Italy left the Axis side in the Second World War and joined the Allies. In September 1945 Romolo succeeded in obtaining a job with Maserati, and

Above: *A fine view of Tavoni and Mike Hawthorn in the pits at Le Mans in 1958. Behind them is 'Lofty' England of Jaguar.* (LAT Photographic)

he became the transport administrator. Modena was pretty evenly divided between the supporters of communism and supporters of the Christian Democrats. Maserati, run by the very independent and forceful Adolfo Orsi, was strongly challenged by the Communists, and their sanctions forced suspension of car production at Modena. Tavoni was left without any work, he resigned from the company, and in January 1950 he joined Ferrari.

Enzo Ferrari engaged the young Tavoni as his private secretary, a position that demanded not just total commitment to the 'Old Man', but (because Enzo Ferrari kept two separate families) it also required delicacy and discretion to the point of secretiveness. Following the departure of Ugolini in 1955, Sculatti, who was a journalist, agreed to manage the Ferrari racing team for a season. There was little wrong with Sculatti's management, save for the fact that he failed to realise that he should not claim credit for himself but rather that all credit (but not criticism!) should go to the boss.

So, Sculatti's contract was not renewed and Tavoni took on the role in addition to that of private secretary. Tavoni proved a very effective and able team manager, and held the position between 1957 and 1961. He was very much Ferrari's man, and when he was at race meetings he reported to Ferrari twice a day. Generally,

Above: *Another view of Tavoni – apparently dozing – in the pits at Le Mans, 1961. That year, the works Ferrari TR61 Testa Rossas with twin-nostril 'shark nose' took the first two places. Tavoni was an outstandingly able racing manager, although there were times when he was quite incapable of maintaining team discipline.* (Author's collection)

drivers liked him, but had no respect for him because of his complete lack of independence.

Cliff Allison commented:

'Tavoni was OK, but he was always working under orders from the factory, and you were never quite sure what might be going on. If anything went wrong, he would be on the telephone to Enzo, and Enzo would say, 'Pull yourself together man and do this or whatever.' My impression of Tavoni was that he was a genuine chap and he would like to help you, but he was always on a lead from the factory. He just didn't go that extra bit on his own, as it were.'

Laura Ferrari meddled increasingly in the running of the team, and Enzo Ferrari (who was far from well – and failing to take his medicine on a regular basis) proved incapable of handling the situation. The leading members of Ferrari staff sent him a 'round robin' letter about the problem. On the last Tuesday in October 1961 there was the usual 5pm meeting of senior staff, at which Enzo Ferrari made no reference to the letter. As the staff members went down to the next floor to leave the building, each was handed an envelope containing notice of dismissal and the money due to them. Such was the reward for loyalty.

Tavoni was desperate to find employment as he had a family to keep, and eventually, along with Carlo Chiti, he was offered a job by the newly formed ATS (Automobili Turismo e Sport) company, the main aim of which was to develop a high-performance production car, but in addition a new GP car complying with the current 1500cc formula was built. ATS was jointly owned by Count Giovanni Volpi, Bolivian tin millionaire Jaime Ortiz Patino, and Tuscan industrialist Giorgio Billi. A vast amount was spent on new factory premises near Bologne.

The GP car was the work of Chiti, and was powered by a 90° V8 four-cylinder overhead camshaft 1494cc (66 x 54.6mm) engine, said to develop 190bhp at 10,000rpm, and used a six-speed Colotti gearbox. There was a multi-tubular space-frame chassis, and as the engine was mounted well forward in this it has been argued that it was the first mid-engined (as opposed to rear-engined) car. Former Ferrari drivers Baghetti and Phil Hill signed up to drive the ATS, while Jack Fairman carried out much of the testing.

The cars first appeared at the 1963 Belgian GP where they were slow and looked distinctly tatty and ill-prepared. The cars ran in only three races, and after the Italian GP, where they finished at the tail of the field, ATS withdrew from racing. The reason was not simply that the funds ran out, but – according to Romolo – each of the three founders claimed that he should be 'President', and the failure to agree led to a stop on the funds. Volpi took away the design of the V8 GT/sports-racing car, that was later raced ineffectually under the name Serenissima. After a short period of unemployment, Tavoni became General Manager of Monza circuit, a post that he held until his retirement.

Terletti, Davide

Head of Structures Department
Born: 3 February 1959 (La Spezia, Italy)

Terletti graduated from Milan Polytechnic in 1983 and joined Piaggio Aerospace in 1985, working on stress analysis on the P180 Avanti. He moved to Alenia Aerospace in 1986, where he worked until 1987 on the Spacelab modules for the Shuttle. In 1988 he joined Ferrari working in the Structures Department, carrying out safety crash tests, working on composite design and structures, and performing stress analysis on gearboxes, suspension, and wings. He is married with one daughter.

Todt, Jean

Sporting Director
Born: 25 February 1946 (Pierrepont, France)

In his early days, Todt competed in rallies and co-drove a Talbot-Lotus in the Rally World Constructors' Championship. He set up Peugeot Talbot Sport, and in 1990 he became director of all the sporting activities of PSA Peugeot-Citroën, but he left the group because of their reluctance to enter F1. Todt was appointed Sporting Director of Ferrari in July 1993.

He took over at a time when, as so often in Ferrari history, things were in technical and political disarray. Initially, he worked with Technical Director John Barnard, who had insisted on being based at Guildford in Surrey. In 1996 Todt recruited Michael Schumacher into the team from Benetton. After the Barnard-designed F310 F1 car proved slow and unreliable, both Rory Byrne and Ross Brawn left Benetton for Ferrari, and Barnard left Ferrari.

Under Todt's leadership, Ferrari produced a succession of race-winning cars for Schumacher, who dominated the Drivers' Championship during the period 2000–5. At the end of the 2007 season, Todt stepped down as Sporting Director and was replaced by Stefano Domenicali. He remains at Ferrari in a leading role that has yet to be disclosed.

Below: *After many years with the Peugeot group and heading their competition division, Jean Todt joined Ferrari in July 1993 and, although he resigned as Chief Executive Officer in 2007, he remains the driving force behind Ferrari in F1.*
(LAT Photographic)

Tombazis, Nikolas

Chief Designer
Born: 22 April 1968 (Athens, Greece)

After graduating in engineering studies at Trinity College, Cambridge in 1986, he gained a PhD in aeronautics at Imperial College, London. In November 1992 he joined Benetton as a junior aerodynamicist, and in August 1994 he was promoted to Chief Aerodynamicist. In February 1997 he joined the Aerodynamics Department at Ferrari, and in July 1998 he was promoted to Chief Aerodynamicist in charge of the wind tunnel and CFD (Computational Fluid Dynamics). In April 2004 he joined McLaren, initially as Chief Engineer, and subsequently as Vehicle Project Director. In March 2006 he returned to Ferrari as Chief Designer.

Trintignant, Maurice

Works driver
Born: 30 October 1917 (Sainte-Cécile-Les-Vignes, Vaucluse, France)
Died: 13 February 2005 (Nîmes, France)

Maurice Bienvenu Jean Paul Trintignant was a vintner by profession. His elder brother, Louis, was killed in practice with his Bugatti for the 1933 Picardy GP at Péronne. He was the uncle of distinguished film actor Jean-Louis Trintignant. He did not race until post-war days when he first appeared and retired in the Coupe de la Liberation held in the Bois de Boulogne in 1945 to mark victory in the Second World War. He was invited to join the Simca team run by Amédée Gordini, and stayed with the team after Gordini became solely responsible for it and raced in his own name. Gordini was a magnificent, impoverished effort, even though the cars were fragile, often unreliable, and frequently uncompetitive.

In the 1948 Swiss GP, Trintignant spun his Simca, was thrown out on to the middle of the track, and Farina, 'B. Bira', and Manzon all went off in avoiding his prone body. It was a terrible race in which three other drivers were killed. It was nearly four, for Maurice was in a coma for eight days, and although at one stage his pulse stopped and he was pronounced dead, he thereafter gradually recovered. He stayed with Gordini until the end of 1953, and it was obvious that, however much it was regretted, the team was going nowhere but bust.

With best performances for Gordini of a fifth place in the French GP at Rouen in 1952, coupled with sixth in Holland and fifth in Italy in 1953, Trintignant did not take much persuading when he was asked by Louis Rosier to drive one of his Tipo 625 Ferraris in 1954. He was a strong nationalist, and it helped that, even if the car was Italian, it was painted blue and French-entered. In South

Left: *For some years Maurice Trintignant was a stalwart of the French Gordini team. He moved to the works Ferrari team in 1954 after he had won the Formule Libre Buenos Aires City GP with a Ferrari Tipo 625 belonging to Louis Rosier. Trintignant's greatest success for Ferrari was a win with a Tipo 625 in the 1955 Monaco GP. Here, Trintignant is seen at the wheel of a Gordini at Silverstone in 1953. (Guy Griffiths Collection)*

America, Trintignant finished fourth in the Argentine GP and won the Formule Libre Buenos Aires City GP. Ferrari invited him to join the works team ('Why now?', he must have asked himself), and Rosier urged him to accept.

It was a difficult year for Ferrari, for F1 was dominated by Fangio, first with the Maserati 250F, and then with Mercedes-Benz, and when Fangio was driving for Mercedes-Benz, Stirling Moss inherited the role of supremo at Maserati. In a year in which the leading Ferrari drivers were González and Hawthorn, the French driver was pretty low down in Maranello priorities. Even so, he displayed good, sound, and sensible driving, and his results were more than adequate: fifth in the British GP, third in Germany, and fifth in Italy. His great success that year was at Le Mans, where he co-drove with Froilán González to win the race by a narrow margin from Tony Rolt and Duncan Hamilton with a works Jaguar D-type.

Trintignant stayed with Ferrari in 1955, and in some ways it was his best season ever. The Argentine GP was run in incredibly hot conditions, with drivers coming into the pits overcome by the heat and constant swapping between cars. Today, there is no clear record of driver swaps. Driving solo, Fangio won the race for Mercedes-Benz; Trintignant co-drove with González and Farina, the second-place car, and with Farina and Maglioli, the third-place car. Shortly afterwards he shared the third-place Ferrari with González in the Formule Libre Buenos Aires City GP.

The first European Championship race was the Monaco GP, where Trintignant was at the wheel of an uncompetitive Tipo 625 Ferrari. The level of retirements was high, including all three Mercedes-Benz entries, and through steady and restrained driving he came through to win the race from Castellotti (Lancia, slowed by brake problems). He finished sixth in the Belgian GP a fortnight later and, being realistic, it has to be said that he achieved nothing of importance during the rest of the year, save for a win with Castellotti at the wheel of a Ferrari in the Messina Ten Hours night race.

In 1956 Trintignant continued to drive works Ferrari sports cars, and he won the Agadir, Dakar, and Swedish GP races with these cars. He drove for Vanwall in four GPs in 1956, but they all ended in retirement, and his most significant F1 appearance was in the French GP at Reims. Here he drove the new Bugatti Type 251 designed by Giaocchino Colombo, and with a specification that at the time seemed plain mad, but now seems a new and very sensible way forward.

The Bugatti was powered by a straight-eight twin overhead camshaft engine, which was mounted transversely at the rear, the suspension was by de Dion axles front and rear, and other features were a full-width nose, and the fuel tanks alongside the cockpit each side. The car proved slow at Reims, and retired because of throttle problems. It was never raced again, which was a great shame because it was a car of the near future that craved investment and development – even if many self-appointed experts laughed at it at the time.

Trintignant again drove for Ferrari in 1957, and in F1 he finished fifth at Monaco, albeit five laps in arrears, he retired in the French GP at Rouen, and in the British GP at Aintree he handed his Tipo 801 Lancia-Ferrari over to Collins, who finished fourth. In addition, he won the F2 Coupe de Vitesse at Reims with the new Dino V6 car, and he also drove a works BRM to third place in the non-Championship Moroccan GP.

Although his best days were almost over, the Frenchman was to stay in F1 for many years. He drove rear-engined Cooper-Climax cars for Rob Walker in 1958 and, apart from achieving his second World Championship race win, once again at Monaco, he finished third in the German GP. He stayed with Walker in 1959 (third at Monaco, second at Sebring), drove various cars in 1960, including the very unsuccessful Aston Martins, and drove for another four years in F1, achieving very little.

Over the years he had proved himself to be an adequately fast driver who was completely consistent and reliable. He rounded his career off by co-driving a Ford GT40 with Guy Ligier in the 1965 Le Mans race, but they retired early because of gearbox trouble. He was mayor of his village, and he concentrated his efforts on his vineyard. He was a low-key person of great charm and common sense, who was respected by all in the motor racing world.

Trips, Wolfgang von

Works driver
Born: 4 May 1928 (Horrem, near Cologne, West Germany)
Died: 10 September 1961 (Monza circuit, Italy)

Wolfgang Alexander Albert Eduard Maximilian Reichsgraf Berghe von Trips, usually called simply 'Taffy', was an aristocrat of considerable wealth and, in a social sense, of considerable arrogance. It always seemed tactful not to probe too deeply into the pre-war and wartime activities of members of the von Trips family. He started his racing career with private Porsche cars, and later drove works Porsche entries. In 1955 he

joined the Mercedes-Benz team in the Tourist Trophy at Dundrod and, sharing his 300SLR with Simon and Kling, finished third. In 1956 he drove a works 300SL Gullwing in the Mille Miglia, and was a serious contender for outright victory until he crashed at speed.

He also started to drive for Ferrari, and there was no conflict of interest. He was due to drive a Lancia-Ferrari in the 1956 Italian GP, but crashed in practice and non-started. Initially, the accident was attributed to inexperience and over-exuberance, but when the car was examined after the race it was realised that the cause was a broken track-rod caused by tyre stress.

At the beginning of 1957, von Trips went to South America with the Ferrari team and with a Lancia-Ferrari, subsequently taken over by Perdisa and Collins; he finished sixth in the Argentine GP. He subsequently drove a few Lancia-Ferraris that year and took a good third place in the Italian GP. He shared the third-place Ferrari in the Buenos Aires 1,000km race, finished third with Hawthorn in the Targa Florio, and then non-started in the Nürburgring 1,000km race after crashing a works Ferrari 250GT in practice.

Throughout 1958, von Trips drove works Ferrari Dino 246 GP cars, but he was still very much on a learning curve. After retiring at Monaco, he finished third in the French GP, retired at Silverstone, took fourth place in Germany, fifth in Portugal, and in the Italian GP at Monza he collided at the start with Harry Schell (BRM). He also competed in the 1958 European Mountain Championship, which at this time had a 1500cc capacity limit, with works Porsche RSK Spyders. He gained the Championship, having won three of the six rounds.

In 1959 von Trips drove regularly for Porsche, but his performances were inconsistent. At Monaco he drove the F2 car, but triggered off a multi-car accident that eliminated all four F2 runners. With Porsche sports cars, he finished third at Sebring with Bonnier, he won the Berlin GP (the sports car race at Avus in which Behra was killed), and with Bonnier he finished second in the Tourist Trophy at Goodwood.

He rejoined Ferrari for 1960 when the team was still running front-engined Dinos, which were no match for the British rear-engined cars. Even so, he performed consistently and, in the circumstances, very well. After a

fifth in Argentina and a hopeless eighth at Monaco, the rest of the season produced quite reasonable results: fifth in Holland, sixth in the British race, and fourth in Portugal. He also drove Ferrari F2 cars, in effect prototypes for the 1961 season, and his results were fast and skilful. He won at Siracusa in March with a new front-engined car, but thereafter drove a rear-engined car in the Solituderennen (1st), Italian GP (fifth and first F2 car), and Modena (third, slowed by brake problems).

In 1961 the new V6 1500cc GP Ferraris were almost all-conquering. That has to be said with two caveats: first, Moss beat the Ferraris at Monaco and the Nürburgring; second, although the Ferraris were more powerful than the British opposition, their roadholding was poor and this would become obvious in 1962. After his engine failed on the last lap, von Trips was classified fourth at Monaco, but thereafter he had a great run of success, winning in Holland, finishing second at Spa, retiring at Reims, but then winning at Aintree, and finishing second in Germany.

He led the World Championship as the teams lined up for the Italian GP at Monza. The young German made a poor start, and both he and Jim Clark (Lotus) were on the straight approaching the Parabolica when they collided, causing von Trips's Ferrari to veer off the track up the narrow grass bank and into the wire-mesh fence where it reared up and spun in the air among spectators before crashing back on to the track.

The German was flung out and killed instantly, and 14 spectators were also killed by the car. Jim Clark was wandering about, clearly in a state of shock. Eventually, he made his way back to the pits, stopping on his way to apologise to Tavoni (the Ferrari racing manager) for the accident. That Clark was still in a state of shock is beyond dispute, and Tavoni was little better. The race carried on, won by Phil Hill, who took the World Championship with 34 points to the 33 of the deceased von Trips.

Trossi, Felice

Pre-war Scuderia Ferrari driver, a shareholder in Scuderia Ferrari in its early days
Born: 27 April 1908 (Biella, Italy)
Died: 9 May 1949 (Milan, Italy)

Part of the education of Count Carlo Felice Trossi of Biella and Portofino occurred at Leeds University, where he studied the wool trade, a business on which the family fortunes were partially founded. It is believed that his first event was in the Pontedecimo–Giovi hill climb in 1931. At this time he regularly drove Alfa Romeo sports cars, and he also owned and sometimes competed with a massive 7-litre Mercedes-Benz SSKL.

In 1932 he bought out the shareholding of Alfredo Caniato in Scuderia Ferrari, using funds provided by the private Banco Sella, owned by his family. Because of his family's business background, Trossi was able to bring into the business considerable expertise in addition to capital. Trossi was very much a hands-on President, spending much of his time at Scuderia's premises, and even working on the cars himself, although it is recounted that he insisted on always wearing gloves.

Trossi contributed much to the acceptance of Scuderia Ferrari as suitable to act as Alfa Romeo's works team once the Milan manufacturer found itself in a situation similar to administration today. But for Trossi, it is doubtful whether Scuderia Ferrari would have been the team to battle out GP racing with the Silver Arrows.

One of the advantages of Trossi's position was that it gave him the opportunity to race Scuderia Ferrari cars. That he was talented and very able is undoubted, and his successes included second place with Brivio in the 1932 Mille Miglia, second place behind Nuvolari with a Monza in the 1933 Circuit of Bordino, wins in that year's sports car Circuit of Florence and Targa Abruzzo, together with fastest times in the Pontedecimo–Giovi and Gaisberg hill climbs.

Successes were fewer in 1934, although Trossi won the

Below: *Count Felice Trossi was an early President of Scuderia Ferrari, and in post-war days he drove for the Alfa Romeo works team. Seen here at the wheel of an early post-war Tipo 158 Alfa Romeo, and with the habitual pipe in his mouth. Trossi had a brain tumour and died in a Milan clinic in 1949.* (Author's collection)

Vichy GP, finished third at Nice, and won the Circuit of Biella. In 1935 Trossi driving a Tipo B Monoposto finished third in the Coppa Ciano. The following year, with a 6CM Maserati, he was the winner of the Eifelrennen Voiturette race at the Nürburgring. Trossi tended to race less frequently in the late 1930s. He remained President until Alfa Romeo acquired an 80 per cent interest in Scuderia Ferrari in 1937.

In 1934 Trossi was persuaded to become a partner with designer Augusto Monaco who was building an advanced GP car. Trossi made available the workshops at the family home, Gaglianico Castle near Biella, which in those days was famed for its electrically operated drawbridge. The Trossi-Monaco had a chassis frame of aviation style, made from small-diameter tubing (what later was called a space-frame) with a 7ft 8in (2,335mm) wheelbase and independent suspension front and rear. The power unit was a radial, air-cooled, two-stroke with twin pistons, which doubled what would otherwise have been a capacity of 1991cc (65 x 75mm).

Two Zoller-type superchargers were fitted, and power was taken to the front wheels by a four-speed gearbox. Work had started on the car in 1934, it was seen during tests at Monza in 1935, and the project was finally abandoned in 1936. It was not such a crackpot idea, but there were problems with the engine and weight distribution. Trossi controlled the money, and when he lost interest the project was dropped. The only car built is still exhibited in the Turin Automobile Museum.

In post-war days, Trossi became a member of the Alfa Romeo GP team. He was an immensely safe and experienced driver and he was consistently successful. His most important results with the 158s were second at Geneva and a win at Turin in 1946. In 1947 he was third in the Swiss and Belgian Grands Prix, and won the Italian GP; and in 1948 he won the Swiss race (the European GP) and in the wet Italian GP he was unwell and handed his car over to Sanesi, who retired due to a supercharger problem. Alfa Romeo temporarily withdrew from GP racing at the end of the 1948 season.

During 1948 Trossi frequently felt unwell, and at the end of the year he was diagnosed as suffering from lung cancer. There was no question of treatment, and Trossi died in a clinic in Milan the following May. The obituary in *The Motor* Year Book 1950 said:

'In manner and appearance he was English, with his inseparable pipe, his ready smile, his boyishness, and, above all, he was a modest and retiring driver, who shrugged off his victories with greater embarrassment than his failures. He was prominent in the affairs of Italian motor sport. His death left a great gap in the ranks of sportsmen.'

Ugolini, Nello

Team manager
Born: 9 August 1905 (Vignola, Modena, Italy)
Died: 20 February 2000 (Modena)

An outstanding figure in Italian sporting circles, Ugolini became Secretary of Modena Football Club in 1923, but he attracted the attention of Enzo Ferrari and, at the 'Old Man's' invitation, he took on the role of sporting director of Scuderia Ferrari in 1934. Following Alfa Romeo's decision in 1938 to take over running the works team from Scuderia Ferrari, he joined Alfa Corse as Secretary, and later he became personnel director at the Portello, Milan, factory.

During the war years, Ugolini worked in a factory in Florence. He returned to Modena in 1948, and was at that time a correspondent of the *Gazzetta de la Sport* and he still managed Modena Football Club, which was remarkably successful. He then went on to manage Fiorentino (Florence) Football Club, but in 1950 he approached Ferrari and asked him if there were prospects of him returning to work for him. At the time it was not possible because Giberti was race director,

Above: *Seen here in 1951 are a very dour-looking Lampredi, Ugolini, and Mercedes-Benz Racing Manager Alfred Neubauer.* (Author's collection)

but later it was decided that Giberti should work in the factory at Maranello.

So, Ugolini rejoined Ferrari as racing manager. He was pressured to return to football to become sporting director of Internazionali, but instead he became racing manager of Maserati in 1955, allegedly at twice the salary he received from Ferrari. Following Maserati's withdrawal from racing at the end of the 1957 season, Ugolini managed Bologna Football Club for a season, and then took on the same role at Turin. The once top-line Turin team had been relegated to Italy's Second Division following the deaths of most of the team in an aircraft crash in the Superga Mountains near Turin in 1949. After the team had spent a long period in the doldrums, Ugolini restored it to its glory days.

During the 1960s, the Maestro managed Scuderia Serenissima di Reppublica Venezia belonging to Count Volpi di Misurata and the Venice Football Team. He joined Scuderia Filipinetti in 1966, and then worked for the De Tomaso company until he retired in 1976. Ugolini had a fantastic reputation as a timekeeper, and could time some ten to a dozen cars with a single stop watch.

He was responsible for timekeeping in the Allen Guiberson pit at the 1955 Sebring 12 Hours race when Guiberson, entrant of the second-place Ferrari, protested the winning Jaguar D-type of Hawthorn/Walters on the grounds that his car had covered a greater number of laps. Either Ugolini was aware of the true situation and turned a blind eye to Guiberson's protest, or his timekeeping was not all that it was cracked up to be!

Below: *In his long career 'Maestro' Nello Ugolini managed several different football clubs, the Scuderia Ferrari team in pre-war days and after the war the Ferrari team and, later, Maserati. He is here at the 1954 Syracuse GP, resetting the tachometer 'tell-tale' while he talks to young Mike Hawthorn.* (Author's collection)

Vaccarella, Nino

Works driver
Born: 4 March 1933 (Palermo, Sicily)

As a local man, Vaccarella had an intimate knowledge of the 44.7-mile (72km) circuit on Sicilian roads used for the Targa Florio. Academically, he holds a Dottore Juris Prudensa (Doctor of Jurisprudence – the science and philosophy of law – but he never practised or taught law). Instead he bought a private school, which he used to run with his sister, and his role was that of headmaster.

Vaccarella started his competition career in 1956 with a Fiat that belonged to his father. The following year he moved on to a Lancia Aurelia GT2500 (which he was at the wheel of when he competed for the first time in the Targa Florio in 1958), and then he acquired a Maserati sports-racing car.

He competed regularly in the major Italian hill climbs, but Nino's serious racing career started in 1960. That year he drove a Maserati Tipo 60 'Bird-cage' entered by the Camoradi Team in the Targa Florio, and he co-drove with Umberto Maglioli. At this time the Tipo 60s were plagued with problems, and the car was not expected to last the race. Although they led initially, they retired after three laps. In 1962 Vaccarella joined the Porsche team for the Sicilian road race, and he and Joakim Bonnier finished third with an RS61 coupé powered by a flat-eight engine.

Although Vaccarella competed in some F1 races, mainly with uncompetitive cars entered by Count Volpi's Scuderia Reppublica, his most successful period was as a member of the works Ferrari team, driving Prototypes. In 1963 he shared a 250P with Mairesse at Sebring, and they finished second to Surtees/Scarfiotti with another 250P. Nino missed the Targa Florio because of a driving disqualification, and he next appeared at the Nürburgring for the 1,000km race in which he was to co-drive with Bandini. He crashed in practice and broke an arm, and he did not race again until 1964.

Vaccarella partnered Scarfiotti at the wheel of a 275P at Sebring in 1964, and they drove a good race to finish second to team-mates Parkes/Maglioli. Ferrari missed the Targa Florio and next appeared in the Nürburgring 1,000km race where he and Scarfiotti scored a magnificent win with a 275P. At Le Mans he was partnered by Guichet, and they scored a superb win with a 275P at 121.563mph (195.59kph), and also won the Index of Performance.

Vaccarella was due to share a 330P2 with Bandini in the 1965 Monza 1,000km race, but Bandini crashed in practice and the car had to be rushed to the factory for repairs. Bandini started the race, but after only a few laps a rear suspension wishbone broke and he narrowly avoided colliding with one of the Shelby-entered Ford GT40s. So, in this race, Vaccarella was deprived of a drive. Ferrari returned to the Targa Florio, and Vaccarella partnered Bandini in a 275P2. The other two works Ferraris retired, and Vaccarella/Bandini won by a margin of over four minutes from Davis/ Mitter (Porsche).

At the Nürburgring there was a 1.6-litre Dino V6 car for Vaccarella/Surtees, and they drove an excellent race to finish fourth. In the Le Mans 24 Hours race, Vaccarella, partnered by Pedro Rodriguez, drove a NART-entered 365P and, although they had clutch and gearbox problems, they eventually finished seventh. The Sicilian drove in one more race for Ferrari in 1965, the Italian GP, where he was at the wheel of a Tipo 158 V8 car (which it was originally intended that Scarfiotti should drive). The V8's engine failed, but Vaccarella was classified 12th.

In 1966 Vaccarella did not drive for the team until the Targa Florio in which he and Bandini were at the wheel of the latest P3 4-litre car. They were in third place when Bandini crashed out of the race. His only other appearance for Ferrari that year was at Le Mans, but it was another disappointing race; he was entered at the wheel of a 2-litre Dino with Casoni, and they retired early in the race because of engine problems. Early in the year, Nino had shared a Ford GT40 with Maglioli in the Sebring 12 Hours race, and they finished fifth.

Vaccarella's first drive for Ferrari in 1967 was in the Targa Florio, in which he shared a 4-litre P4 with Scarfiotti, and this was the only works entry. The Sicilian led on time at the end of the first lap, but on lap two he misjudged his speed into the left-hand bend in the village of Collesano and slid into a low wall, wrecking the front suspension and the right-hand wheels. At Le Mans he shared a works P4 with Chris Amon, but the car punctured a tyre with Amon at the wheel and caught fire while the young New Zealander was trying to nurse it back to the pits.

Ferrari withdrew from Prototype racing at the end of 1967, and Vaccarella drove Alfa Romeo 33s for the works Autodelta team in 1968–9, but failed to register any conspicuous successes. He rejoined Ferrari in 1970 and raced the 5-litre Competition Sports Cars. Partnered by Giunti, he drove a 512S, a totally unsuitable car for this race, to third place in the Targa Florio behind two very nimble Porsche 90/03s. The following year, driving with

Above: *A Sicilian school teacher, Vaccarella was a superb sports car driver, especially on the Little Madonie circuit.* (**LAT Photographic**)

Toine Hezemans, he won the Targa Florio for the second time at the wheel of an Alfa Romeo 33/3. He retired from racing in 1972.

Vandervell, Tony

Bearing supplier to Ferrari and purchaser and entrant of Ferrari F1 cars

Born: 8 September 1898 (Westbourne Park, London W2, England)
Died: 10 March 1967 (Stoke Poges, Buckinghamshire, England)

Son of an electrical engineer who founded and developed the CAV industrial electrical empire, Guy Anthony Vandervell competed as an amateur with motorcycles and cars, and founded, and built into a mighty empire, the Vandervell 'Thin Wall' bearing company. Thin Wall bearings were built under licence from a United States company, but Vandervell became the dominant partner in the relationship. Vandervell's company was based on the Western Avenue in Park Royal, Acton, London NW10, and during Vandervell's post-war motor racing days it acquired additional

Above: *In the centre, about to accept a free fag, is Tony Vandervell, best known because his Vanwalls beat the Ferraris and Maseratis. Before he built his own cars, however, he ran a series of Ferraris, the last of which was extensively modified, and was the fastest racing car in Europe. Vandervell raced these Ferraris painted green and named 'Thin Wall Special' after the bearings which he manufactured in his works on the A40 at Park Royal. Users of Vandervell Thin Wall bearings included Ferrari.* (Author's collection)

premises in Maidenhead, to which it eventually moved the whole business.

Vandervell was an enthusiastic supporter of the BRM, the F1 project of Raymond Mays, backed and supported by his lover Peter Berthon. In addition to supporting the BRM, Vandervell sought and obtained the necessary import licence to buy a Ferrari GP car, which could be used for research purposes and which he could race against the BRM. In all, there were four of these Ferraris and the original aim was lost after Vandervell abandoned his support for the BRM V16 because of the slow progress of this project and the incompetence of the project's leaders.

He became a racing entrant purely for the love of racing, and then decided to build his own GP cars. It must be pointed out that, although the name of these cars was originally 'Thinwall Special' (and on the second car, through a mistake in Italy, the camshaft covers were inscribed 'Thinwell Special'), the name developed through 'ThinWall Special' (no space) to 'Thin Wall Special' (with a space).

These Ferrari-based cars started with a supercharged 1.5-litre model of the type that first appeared in the 1948 Italian GP, and this was entered with Raymond Mays at the wheel in the British GP at Silverstone in May 1949. He handed the car over to Ken Richardson, the BRM head mechanic who had never driven in a race previously. It is, of course, incredible that a man with no racing experience should make his debut in an international GP. Richardson went off the track and ran into a group of spectators, none of whom – fortunately – was seriously injured.

It was an unsatisfactory car in most respects and was returned to the factory. The second 'Thin Wall Special' was one of the improved cars with twin-stage supercharging and longer wheelbase that had first run at Monza in September 1949. It was driven in the International Trophy at Silverstone in August 1950 by works Ferrari driver Alberto Ascari (World Champion in 1952–3). This car, too, was returned to Maranello, and

what eventually came back from Italy was a rebuilt car powered by a 4.5-litre unsupercharged V12 engine.

Reg Parnell was at the wheel of this car when he was leading the field and was adjudged the winner in the International Trophy at Silverstone in May 1951. Just as the race started, torrential rain began to fall and flooded the circuit, leaving the all-conquering Alfa Romeo 158s trundling round, coughing and spitting because their superchargers were sucking in water. The fourth and final version of the 'Thin Wall' had a twin-plug engine and was extensively modified by the Vandervell team, including Firestone aircraft-type disc brakes.

Vandervell had decided to build his own F1 car, known as the Vanwall, which was influenced to a considerable extent by the four-cylinder Ferraris raced from 1952 through to 1955 – despite the fact that it had become his avowed intent to 'best the bloody red cars'. During the development of the car, Colin Chapman of Lotus, acing as consultant, designed a new multi-tubular space-frame, and de Havilland aerodynamicist Frank Costin (responsible for Lotus bodies) produced a startlingly new and uncompromising body.

The Vanwall team of drivers in 1957 consisted of Stirling Moss and Tony Brooks, later joined by Stuart Lewis-Evans, and the cars, although plagued by irritating faults, were very fast and handled well. In the European

Above: *Here, Tony Vandervell is with Farina when the former World Champion came to England in 1952 to drive the Ferrari Thin Wall Special at two meetings. At Goodwood in late September he finished second to González (BRM) after the Thin Wall broke its final drive on the last lap of the five-lap Woodcote Cup, and as a result he failed to start in the 15-lap Goodwood Trophy. A fortnight later he retired the Thin Wall in the Formule Libre race at Charterhall near Berwick-upon-Tweed after the gearbox broke.* **(Guy Griffiths Collection)**

GP at Aintree, Moss took over from Brooks and brought his car through to Vanwall's first major victory, and then won the Pescara and Italian Grands Prix, both rounds in the World Championship.

The following year, Moss and Brooks each won three rounds of the World Championship, and for the second year in succession Moss was second in the Drivers' Championship, in 1958 beaten by Hawthorn by a single point. Tragedy had, however, struck Vanwall, and a bad crash by Lewis-Evans when his engine seized caused him terrible burns and a dreadful lingering death. Vandervell's own health was deteriorating, and the team withdrew from serious racing after the end of the 1958 season, and was finally wound up in 1961.

Varzi, Achille

Scuderia Ferrari driver
Born: 8 August 1904 (Galliate, Milano, Italy)
Died: 3 July 1948 (Bremgarten, Bern, Switzerland)

That Varzi was one of the greatest drivers in the history of the sport is debatable, but it is beyond argument that he was one of the greatest drivers of the 1930s. Flawed by his drug dependency, and with an incredibly Saturnine expression, when all was well he was remarkably courteous, affable and friendly; he had a distinct talent for smart dressing and appearance. For racing he wore immaculate white overalls and linen helmet, and otherwise he was usually seen wearing exceptionally well-cut suits, formal shirts, and silk ties. When life was going badly, he was taciturn, introspective, moody, and guilt-ridden.

His racing career started with motorcycles, and he rode British Sunbeam 500cc bikes and Italian Garelli machines powered by 350cc single-cylinder, double-piston, two-stroke engines. After a largely fruitless season in 1926 with one of the new 1496cc Bugatti Type 37 cars, he and Tazio Nuvolari teamed up to race a pair of Bugatti Type 35 cars in 1927. It was not a successful venture, although these two drivers were very good friends. So, Varzi bought from Campari, at a price of £800 (75,000 lire), one of the P2 Alfa Romeos with some of the money loaned by the Sunbeam motorcycle agent for whom he raced.

Varzi had found his feet, and he raced the P2 with great success in Italian events in 1928–9. After finishing second to Chiron in the 1928 European GP at Monza, the following year he won the Monza GP, together with the Rome GP, the Coppa Ciano, and the Circuit of Alessandria, and he was second in the Circuit of Cremona. The net result was that he was Champion of Italy.

At the end of the year, Varzi sold his car back to the factory, as did Brilli Peri, and these cars, together with a third, were rebuilt with modifications that included 6C 1750 Grand Sport front and rear axles, suspension, and brakes. Engine capacity was slightly increased to 2020cc, power output rose from 134bhp to 145bhp, and maximum speed was now around 140mph (225kph).

The P2s were again raced by the works, and the drivers were Campari and Varzi. Varzi won the Circuit of Alessandria, but the works thought that they were too fast and difficult to handle in the Targa Florio. Varzi insisted on running his car, and despite losing the spare wheel and the back of the car catching fire while the mechanic tried to refuel while they were racing, Varzi won at record speed, and set a new lap record. No other victories were achieved by Varzi with the car that year, although Nuvolari continued to race a P2 very successfully. Varzi did, however, win the Spanish GP at the wheel of a Maserati, and he took second place in the Mille Miglia with an Alfa Romeo 6C 1750 Gran Sport.

For the next two seasons, Varzi drove for Bugatti, and in 1933 he played a leading role in the Italian state lottery swindle at the Tripoli GP. Of the many tickets sold, 30 bore the names of the 30 starters in the race. If a 'punter' drew a ticket with a driver's name, and that driver won the race, the punter won the lottery. It was a swindle waiting to happen. An Italian lumber merchant had drawn Varzi's ticket, and he flew to Libya to offer Varzi half the prize money if he won the race. Varzi, Borzacchini, Campari, and Nuvolari rigged the results, and Varzi won by a foot or two from Nuvolari in a staged finish.

Varzi drove for Scuderia Ferrari in 1934 and enjoyed a tremendous run of success. His performances that year included wins in the Mille Miglia (with Bignami who became his life-long mechanic and friend), in the Bordino GP at Alessandria, the Tripoli GP, the Targa Florio, the Penya Rhin GP, the Coppa Ciano, and the Nice GP, as well as second place to Chiron in the French GP at Montlhéry.

Then Varzi received an exceptionally generous offer from Auto Union that was too high for him to sensibly refuse. He was paid a retainer of £4,000 for the 1935 season, plus a share of starting money and prize money, together with the latest and most expensive Horch, painted a gleaming white. Overall he had a poor season in a year largely dominated by Mercedes-Benz, partly because Auto Union had tyre problems, and his wins were limited to the Tunis GP and the Coppa Acerbo.

There was a new woman in Varzi's life, the beautiful, blonde Ilse, on her second marriage to Paul Pietsch. It seems that he was glad to be rid of her and that she was already a morphine addict. Early in 1936, Varzi won the Tripoli GP and, apparently, the result was fixed by slowing down Stuck in second place. Libya was an Italian colony and it seems that the aim was to ensure that an Italian won on Italian territory.

Opposite: *Achille Varzi was a great enigma. He was, apparently, the immaculately dressed, strong man of motor racing, a man of brilliant judgement and masterly expertise, who sank from greatness to drug addiction – and then climbed back to finish his career as a top driver. It does not make sense.* **(Guy Griffiths Collection)**

When he found out about this, it is said that he was distraught. For a man who had been involved in the Tripoli swindle, that does seem rather far-fetched, although he may have been a trifle 'miffed' that no one told him what was going on. That Ilse introduced him to the mixed pleasures of a snort, coupled with sex, is undoubted, but it is most likely that he simply did what she wanted. He crashed heavily a week later at Tunis, and it was the perfect excuse for another snort.

Throughout 1936, Varzi was overshadowed by Rosemeyer, and Auto Union decided not to renew his contract for 1937. He disappeared from the racing scene – albeit temporarily – but made a fleeting appearance with an Auto Union at Brno. He drove one of the very fast Maserati Tipo 8CTF supercharged 3-litre cars in the Tripoli GP in May 1938, but retired because of engine problems. He then disappeared once more from the racing scene, but he and Ilse had split up, and she had returned to Germany where she had managed to come off drugs altogether. She married an opera singer, and it seems that they had a very contented marriage.

In 1941 Varzi married Norma, a woman whom he had known for many years. Very much against the odds, he succeeded in giving up drugs, and when Alfa Romeo resumed racing in 1946 he became a member of the team. The cars from Portello were vastly superior to the opposition. He first appeared with a Tipo 158; in the Turin GP, which he won, and he took second place behind team-mate Trossi in the Milan GP.

That he had recovered most of his old form was undoubted. In the 1947 Swiss GP he finished second behind Wimille with another Alfa Romeo 158, he was second again in Belgium, he won at Bari, and finished second in the Italian GP held in Sempione Park, Milan.

Alfa Romeo's first race of 1948 was the Swiss GP at Bremgarten. During practice in the wet he drove the Tipo 158/47 with larger low-pressure supercharger and other modifications. On a winding downhill section of this superb, testing circuit, poor Varzi lost control and crashed. With only his linen helmet as protection, he suffered fatal head injuries. It was a very sad end for a man who fought his way back from despair and drug dependence, and a severe blow to Italian motor racing. When the Argentinian government sponsored a team for European racing in 1949, it consisted of Maserati 4CLT/48 San Remo cars painted Argentine blue and yellow racing colours, and known as Squadra Achille Varzi. The chief mechanic to this team was Bignami, who had been Varzi's personal mechanic, and the new team was based at Varzi's former home at Galliate near Milan.

Vernor, Brenda

Personnal Assistant to Enzo Ferrari
Birth details not known

A long-term figure at Maranello has been Brenda Vernor, who was born in Ireland, and lived in England until she moved to Italy in the 1960s. She was closely attached to Mike Parkes and this was the main reason that she went to Italy. Their relationship broke down, and he was proposing to marry someone else when he was killed in a road

Above: *Brenda Vernor is seen here during a Ferrari reception at Maranello.*

accident. She never married and she worked at Ferrari for many years, where she was regarded as an essential member of the team and is remembered with great affection. At Maranello she was initially employed in the press office and she later became Enzo Ferrari's personal assistant, a position she until his death in 1988. Thereafter she became secretary to his son Piero Lardi Ferrari. Although she has retired from Ferrari, she still lives in Modena.

Villeneuve, Gilles

Works driver
Born: 18 January 1950 (Saint Jean sur Richelieu, Quebec, Canada)
Died: 8 May 1982 (Zolder circuit, Belgium)

Joseph Gilles Henri Villeneuve became a legend in his own lifetime. He was dramatically emotional, incredibly highly skilled, passionate, emotive, sometimes irrational, and, despite many shortcomings, so very popular in Maranello and throughout Italy. He was a man who lived everything that was legendary about Nuvolari. Of him, Niki Lauda said, 'he was the craziest devil I ever came across in F1'. Gilles raced snowmobiles, had a go at drag racing, and then in 1973 took up Formula Ford. He soon moved on to Formula

Atlantic, and fractured a leg racing at Mosport, but was racing again within a month. In 1976 he soundly beat James Hunt in a F2 race at the Trois Rivières circuit, and James, with his great generosity, urged McLaren, for whom he was driving, to snap up Villeneuve before someone else did.

McLaren signed up Villeneuve for five races, and entered him in the British GP. No one before, in the history of motor racing, has spun so many times in so few laps. Villeneuve supporters hold that he was probing his limits in a GP car, and that he could only ascertain the limit of adhesion by going beyond it. Other, more restrained personalities argued that that was not how you learned about motor racing, and this writer would agree. Villeneuve's approach frightened the horses and just about everyone else. At Silverstone he finished 11th, two laps in arrears after being delayed by a faulty temperature gauge.

Teddy Mayer of McLaren concluded that Villeneuve was not a driver for them. It was arranged for Villeneuve to meet the 'Old Man' during August. Enzo Ferrari said that Villeneuve reminded him of Nuvolari, and promptly signed him up. Lauda had already announced that he would be driving for Brabham in 1978, so there were only two cars in the North American races, one of which was driven by Villeneuve. These were poor

outings by the team, and not aided by Villeneuve's moronic driving. He retired because of drive-shaft failure in Canada.

In the Japanese race, Villeneuve was eliminated in a frightening accident; he collided with Ronnie Peterson's Tyrrell, riding over the back wheels, with the result that the Ferrari was launched into a succession of cartwheels, during which two spectators, watching from a prohibited area were killed. Afterwards, Villeneuve, who had walked away from the accident unscathed, simply said to Peterson, 'Sorry, but I didn't seem to have any brakes.' What bothered this writer is that Villeneuve showed no apparent compassion or grief for the two people who had been killed.

For Villeneuve, the 1978 season was a massive learning curve. In South America the team was still racing the previous year's 312T2 cars, and in the Brazilian GP, run in exceptionally torrid conditions, Reutemann, who was perfectly happy in the heat, won easily. This win was

Below: *Gilles Villeneuve, seen here with Ferrari team manager Danielle Audetto, was one of the most exciting drivers to watch, and he had sublime confidence in himself to drive out of any difficulty. Sadly, this let him down and he crashed with fatal results in practice for the 1982 Belgian GP at Zolder.* (LAT Photographic)

assisted by the fact that the cars, now running on Michelin radial tyres, were handling well.

Forghieri's new 312T3s appeared in South Africa and, although the season was dominated by the ground-effect Lotus 79s, the Ferraris performed well. Villeneuve had too many crashes, but both drivers acheived good results, and Villeneuve scored his first GP victory on the Île Notre Dame circuit at Montreal after the leading car developed an incurable oil leak.

Jody Scheckter joined Villeneuve at Ferrari for 1979, and again the latest flat-12 Ferrari, the 312T4, was not ready to race until Kyalami. The new car was the most successful of the year and won Ferrari the Constructors' Championship. Although Scheckter won the Drivers' Championship, it was very close between him and Gilles all year. Three times they finished 1–2, Villeneuve leading Scheckter across the line twice (Kyalami and Long Beach), Scheckter leading Villeneuve once (Monza). Scheckter also won at Zolder and Monaco, while Villeneuve won the final race of the year at

Below: *Gilles Villeneuve applies opposite lock in his 126CK to correct one of his trademark drifts during practice for the 1981 Canadian Grand Prix. He finished in third place in the wet race, nearly two minutes behind winner Jacques Laffite and second-place John Watson, despite losing his front wing.* (LAT Photographic)

Watkins Glen. Scheckter won the Championship with 51 points, Gilles was second with 47.

By 1980, Forghieri was hard at work on the 1981 turbocharged 126CK, and in the last year of the flat-12 the team raced the 312T5s. These were rebuilt 1979 cars that proved mechanically unreliable and were plagued by problems with their Michelin tyres. Scheckter gave up the fight and retired at the end of the year, while Villeneuve battled all year. His best performances were at Monza where he worked his way up to fourth place before a tyre failed and the Ferrari crashed, writing itself off, and at Île Notre Dame where he took fifth place (Scheckter failed to qualify).

Villeneuve the rearguard fighter, was a side of the French-Canadian that the 'Old Man' admired so much. It also endeared him to the Tifosi, who were quite convinced that he was fighting for them. Throughout 1981 Villeneuve was still fighting, but now at the wheel of a car that had immense potential, yet was very underdeveloped. After a poor start to the season, Gilles won at Monaco. Four laps from the finish he squeezed past Alan Jones's Williams, which had a good lead, but because of an engine misfire Jones had had to make a very quick stop for extra fuel which reduced that lead over the Ferrari from thirty to six seconds. Jones then dropped back, as his engine was still misfiring. After the race Villeneuve told the press (as reported by Alan Henry in *Ferrari: The Grand Prix Car*:

'I tell you, my car was very hard to drive … suspension so stiff it was like a go-kart. I bumped my head all the time on the rollover bar and now I ache all over. It was one of the most tiring races of my life. My brakes were finished and when they started to go, I had to be very brutal with the gearbox, but it lasted OK … I'm very lucky!'

Then Villeneuve won again in the Spanish race at Jarama, battling throughout the race to hold off the opposition, and at the flag only two seconds covered the first five cars. He finished third in pouring rain at Montreal after hitting the rear of de Angelis's Lotus and damaging the Ferrari's one-piece front wing; this was angled down at one end and up at the other until the upward angled part fell off. In the Drivers' Championship Gilles finished a poor ninth.

The tragedy of Villeneuve and Pironi during the 1982 season is recorded on page 189. Suffice it to say here that Villeneuve is remembered in Italy, and you do not need to drive many miles before you find a roadside café decorated with posters and photographs of the French-Canadian.

Villoresi, Emilio

Alfa Corse driver
Born: 1914 (Milan, Italy)
Died: 20 June 1939 (Monza, Milan)

Younger brother of Luigi Villoresi (see below), Emilio shared a Fiat Balillas 508S with Luigi in the Mille Miglia in 1935–6, but in the latter year they also raced a Maserati Voiturette. Emilio joined Scuderia Ferrari in 1937, racing both single-seaters and sports cars. After the founding of Alfa Corse, he drove for the works team and achieved a reasonable degree of success.

On 20 June 1939 Alfa Romeo held a reception at

Below: *Emilio was the younger of the Villoresi brothers who was so very sadly killed during a private demonstration at Monza in 1939. Brother Luigi refused to race Alfa Romeos because Enzo Ferrari dissuaded Alfa Corse from pursuing compensation from the company's insurers. Even so, Villoresi was willing to race for Ferrari. Make sense of it if you can!* (Author's collection)

Monza circuit for Alfa Romeo trade representatives and dealers. Emilio was present, with other members of the Alfa Corse team. Enzo Ferrari asked him to take a 158 for a few demonstration laps for the benefit of the guests. He refused because he had drunk too much wine at lunchtime, but Ferrari pressured him, and finally he agreed. After a few laps, Emilio went off the track and was killed. In most books on Alfa Romeo, Villoresi's death is reported as a practice accident, but David Venables is a notable exception. There was an insurance policy on Emilio's life, but the insurers refused to pay out because the policy was voided by his inebriation.

It is claimed (and this is the part of the story that this writer challenges) that Enzo Ferrari would do nothing to support the Villoresi family's claim against the insurers. Allegedly, according to the two versions of the story, Luigi would never forgive Alfa Romeo, but that does not have a strong ring of truth because he did nothing to prevent Ascari, his amanuensis, if one may use the word in this context, from driving an Alfa Romeo in the 1948 French GP. And if Luigi had really felt so bitterly about Enzo Ferrari he would not have driven for the works team for the five seasons 1949–53.

Below: *In early post-war days Luigi Villoresi raced Maseratis for Scuderia Ambrosiana, which was to all intents and purposes the works team. He joined Ferrari for 1949 and stayed with Maranello until 1954 when he and Ascari moved on to Lancia. This photograph was taken at the Jersey Road Race in April 1948 (Guy Griffiths Collection)*

Villoresi, Luigi

Works driver
Born: 16 May 1909 (Milan, Italy)
Died: 24 August 1997 (Modena, Italy)

Luigi Villoresi was one of the greatest of Scuderia Ferrari drivers. The Villoresi family had considerable status in Milan, for Luigi's grandfather had built a canal running from the River Ticino, at a point near the present Malpensa Airport, for the purpose of irrigating agricultural land in that part of Lombardy. His father generated electricity for the city of Milan. Luigi's parents, Gaetano and Esther, had five children, but apart from Emilio (above), one brother committed suicide, another died of cancer, and his sister Rosa was killed in a road-traffic accident.

Along with his brother Emilio, Luigi (known as 'Gigi'), rallied an old Lancia Lambda in 1931, and then moved on to Fiats. In 1936 Luigi acquired an ex-works Maserati 4CM 1500 Voiturette, which he drove to sixth place in the Voiturette race at the 1936 Monaco GP meeting. In 1937 he was a partner with Count 'Johnny' Lurani in Scuderia Ambrosiana, and with a 6CM 1500 he scored a win in a weak field in the 1937 1500cc Circuit of Masaryk. As a result of his successful 1937 season, in general and this race in particular, he was brought into the works Maserati team for 1938.

During 1938, his successes included a win in the Voiturette races at Albi and Pescara. Although he could win in the face of Maserati opposition only, the 6CM 1500 was no match for the very fast and generally very reliable Alfa Romeo 158s. Luigi's successes overall were good enough for him to win the Italian 1500cc Championship. He also drove one of the very fast, but exceedingly fragile, 3-litre supercharged 8CT 3000 cars in that year's Donington GP, but retired because of engine problems.

Luigi travelled out to South Africa for the country's 1939 National GP, which was held that year as a race for 1500cc cars, and he won with his Maserati from Cortese with another of these cars. He drove a streamlined four-cylinder Maserati in the Tripoli race and, although he could match the lap speed of the new Mercedes-Benz W165 cars, he retired on the first lap because of gearbox failure. Another Villoresi victory that year was in the Targa Florio (held as a Voiturette race), a success that he repeated in 1940.

After Italy entered the war, Luigi fought in the army, but was captured and he spent most of the war in a

prisoner-of-war camp. What would have been his most successful racing years were wasted. When racing resumed in 1946, Villoresi drove Maseratis for Scuderia Milano, and, in addition to winning the Nice GP, he travelled out to Indianapolis to drive an 8CL 3-litre Maserati into seventh place. Luigi was still driving for Milano at the beginning of the 1947 season, and in the Argentine races he finished second in the Rosario GP, and won the Juan Perón and Eva Perón Grands Prix at Buenos Aires.

Alfa Romeo dominated the small number of races in which they competed, and Maserati won most of the remainder. In 1947 Count 'Johnny' Lurani re-formed his Scuderia Ambrosiana, which was in reality the works Maserati team, and the drivers were Villoresi and the young Albert Ascari. Generally, the Maseratis were unreliable, but Villoresi won at Strasbourg and Lausanne. The following year, he finished third behind

Above: *Villoresi raced in pre-war days and, like many of his generation, his career was ruined by the Second World War. Before the war he drove Maseratis and he is seen here with his works Maserati Tipo 6CM at the 1940 Targa Florio held for 1500cc racing cars in Palermo Park.* **(Spitzley/Zagari Collection)**

two Alfa Romeos in the Swiss race, and won at Comminges and Albi; he finished second in the very wet Italian GP at Turin, and rounded off the season with a win in the RAC GP at Silverstone in October.

Ferrari had introduced his new single-stage supercharged V12 GP cars at the Italian race, and both Villoresi and Ascari joined the Maranello team. Alfa Romeo temporarily withdrew from racing in 1949, so the year was fought out between the ponderous, heavy unblown Talbot-Lagos that were light on fuel and tyres

and could run through most races without refuelling. The Ferraris were marginally competitive, and Villoresi's best performances in Formula A were second in Belgium (Rosier won with a Talbot), second in Switzerland (Ascari won), and a win at Zandvoort.

In an effort to improve the team's F1 competitiveness, Ferrari had introduced longer-wheelbase, twin-stage supercharged cars in the Italian race at Monza. Ascari won the race, but Villoresi retired because of gearbox failure. Villoresi won Formula B races for Ferrari at Brussels, Luxembourg, Rome, and Lake Garda. During the year Ferrari had been the strongest and most successful of racing teams, but that all changed in F1 when Alfa Romeo returned to racing. Alfa Romeo ran in ten F1 races in 1950 and won them all.

Technical director Aurelio Lampredi persuaded Ferrari that he would have a better chance of beating Alfa Romeo with an unsupercharged 4500cc car, so the team started on the development work that led to the appearance of the Tipo 375 at the 1950 Italian GP. With supercharged cars, Villoresi finished second at Pau, San Remo, and Zandvoort, won the Eva Perón Cup and the Rosario GP in Argentina, and also won F2 races at Marseille, Erlen, and Monza.

Villoresi crashed heavily in the F1 GP des Nations at Geneva in July, skidding on a patch of oil into the crowd, killing four spectators, and injuring 27 others. Villoresi suffered a broken leg, and he was out of racing for the rest of the season. By 1951, Villoresi, 42 years of age, had ceased to be a leading F1 driver, although he remained in the GP team. In the very wet Swiss race he crashed heavily, blinded by spray, but he then scored a succession of good places, thirds at Spa, Reims, and Silverstone, and fourth places at the Nürburgring and Monza. In F2 he won at Marseille, finished second in the Autodromo GP at Monza, and won the Genoa race.

Another outstanding performance was in the Mille Miglia road race in 1951, in which Ferrari had wanted him to drive an open 4.1-litre car. Villoresi had insisted on driving a coupé, and being partnered by Cassani, and after a very difficult drive in wet conditions and an off-

course excursion near Ferrara, he won the race by a margin of just under 20 minutes from Bracco/Maglioli with a Lancia Aurelia GT. He partnered Ascari to second place with a Ferrari in the 1951 Carrera Panamericana road race, and he and Ascari won the Sestrière Rally with a Lancia Aurelia saloon.

In 1952–3, World Championship races and most other Grands Prix were held to F2 rules. Both Villoresi and Ascari stayed with Ferrari, and he took third places in the Dutch GP and the Italian GP, the only Championship races in which he competed. He ran in a number of non-World Championship F2 races and won at Les Sables d'Olonne in July, and finished second to Ascari at La Baule – both of these races were rounds in the French F2 Championship. 'Gigi' raced for the works Ferrari team more frequently in 1953 and, after taking second places at Buenos Aires and Spa-Francorchamps, he finished third in the Italian race.

When Ascari joined Lancia for 1954, so did Villoresi. As previously mentioned, the D50 GP cars were not ready to race until the Spanish GP in October, so Villoresi drove works Lancia sports cars, and also appeared in four races for Maserati, taking fifth place in the French GP at Reims with Moss's car that had been loaned back to the works. Earlier, he had non-started in the 1954 Mille Miglia because of a practice crash. He won the Porto sports car GP at the end of June after Ascari ran into mechanical problems.

Because of brake trouble, Villoresi was an early retirement with the new D50 GP car in Spain, and he had little luck with these cars in 1955. After retiring in the Argentine GP, he took third place at Turin, fourth at Pau, and third at Naples. He took fifth place in the European GP at Monza. Following Ascari's death, and the withdrawal of Lancia from racing, Gigi was entered by Ferrari with a Lancia at Monza in September, but the entry was scratched because of problems with the Englebert tyres to which Ferrari was contracted.

Subsequently, Villoresi drove private Maseratis in a few races in 1956, and rounded off his F1 career with a works Maserati in that year's Italian GP, but stopped to hand the car over to Bonnier. He crashed very heavily, breaking a leg, in an OSCA at the Castelfusano circuit at Rome in October 1956. At long last, he gave in to his family's wishes that he should retire from racing. His last appearance was in the 1958 Greek Acropolis Rally, which he won with Basadonna. He was very impoverished in his later years, and there was a public fund to help keep him. He died in the Santa Caterina Nursing Home in Modena at the age of 88.

Wharton, Ken

Driver
Born: 21 March 1916 (Smethwick, near Birmingham, England)
Died: 12 January 1957 (at the wheel of a Ferrari Monza at Ardmore Circuit, New Zealand)

Poor Ken Wharton was a garage proprietor by trade, but he was also an immensely versatile and able racing driver. I have written 'poor', because his talents were never properly appreciated, and team managers tended to regard him as a man of limited ability. He was addicted to motor sport: he competed in British 'mud' trials with a car of his own construction, he rallied a Ford Pilot V8 saloon, winning the Dutch Tulip Rally three times, and he won the RAC British Hill Climb Championship in four successive years from 1951 onwards.

He enjoyed a fine career in circuit racing that started with a supercharged Austin Seven at Donington Park in pre-war days. After racing a Cooper-JAP from 1950 onwards, he appeared in World Championship events in 1952 with a Frazer Nash entered by wealthy amateur

Peter Bell, and finished fourth in that year's Swiss GP. He raced a lighter, faster, but still far from competitive Cooper-Bristol in the following year's World Drivers' Championship.

Ken drove the works Frazer Nash, in effect the manufacturer's development car, between 1952 and 1955. In 1954 he drove a works Daimler Conquest Century in the Touring Car race at the May Silverstone meeting (retiring after a collision with Tony Crook's spinning Lancia), and he was also a member of the works Jaguar team, winning the 1954 Reims 12 Hours race with Peter Whitehead. William Lyons regarded

Wharton's nominal role as Daimler racing manager as incompatible with his place in the works Jaguar team, so Ken lost his place in the team for 1955.

There is no doubt that the most important part of Wharton's career was his time with BRM, driving the monstrous V16 cars during the years 1952–4. During 1954 he also drove the Maserati 250F that the Owen Organisation had bought to race while the new 2.5-litre BRM was being developed. For 1955, he signed up as number two at Vanwall, but it was with the Park Royal team that everything fell apart. The cars were not raceworthy and he crashed in the International Trophy race at Silverstone, and suffered burns on the arms and neck.

He raced Vanwalls twice more, in the Championship British and Italian races, plus a minor race at Snetterton, and he was dropped by Vandervell at the end of the 1955 season. No single-seater team wanted Wharton, and he had to take whatever sports car drives he was offered. He had co-driven Jonneret's Ferrari Monza in the 1955 Goodwood Nine Hours race, and he raced and rallied Austins in 1956. He drove Bonnier's ex-works rebodied 3.6-litre Alfa Romeo in a couple of events, and continued to drive the famous black ex-Mays ERA R4D in hill climbs.

The same year, Jaguar brought him back into their D-type team at Le Mans, but on only the second lap Jack Fairman spun the D-type that he and Wharton were sharing, in his efforts to avoid Frère's Jaguar and de Portago's Ferrari that had already spun off, and he bent the car against the barriers; so Ken missed out on a drive in this race. Ken realised that the new 1500cc F2 was going to be very popular, and he ordered one of these cars from Cooper. He drove it into fifth place in the Gold Cup race at Oulton Park, and at the same meeting he also won his class with a Ford Zephyr in the saloon car race.

Although Wharton was now 40, he thought that his driving was just going through a bad patch. He was delighted when wealthy alcoholic entrant, John du Puy, scion of a Pittsburgh steel family, offered him drives in both a Ferrari Monza and a Maserati 250F in the 1957 Tasman Series. He set fastest lap for the GP and joint fastest lap for the sports car race, both held on the Ardmore airfield circuit on 12 January.

Wharton was leading the sports car race from Jack Brabham with a 1500cc Climax-powered Cooper when he lost control of the Ferrari and crashed into the barriers in front of the control tower. The Monza was hurled into the air, while Wharton was flung out and suffered injuries to which he succumbed an hour later. Wharton is probably Smethwick's most famous son, and the Art Gallery and Museum has a permanent display in his memory.

Whitehead, Peter

Driver
Born: 12 November 1914 (Menston, near Ilkley, Yorkshire, England)
Died: 21 September 1958 (Lasalle, near Nîmes, France)

For most of his career, Whitehead drove as an amateur, funding his own very expensive racing programme, and racing for pleasure. He was, however, an exceptionally good driver, and his successes included a win in a fairly major European GP, a win at Le Mans as a works Jaguar driver, and seven years later second place in the 24 Hours race with an Aston Martin co-driven by half-brother Graham. Whitehead was a very wealthy man, who took over the family business, which included involvement in the wool trade.

Below: *During his later race days, Peter Whitehead raced mainly sports cars. In 1954 and 1955 he had new Cooper-Jaguars. He is seen here at the wheel of his 1955 Cooper-Jaguar at the International Trophy meeting at Silverstone in 1955.* (Tom March Collection)

While at university in the early 1930s he bought an Alta 1100cc sports car, and also let his close friend Peter Walker drive it. He soon moved on to an ERA, and shipped it out to Australia in 1938 and won the handicap Australian GP from local opposition on the Bathurst circuit. He continued to race the ERA in post-war days, and finished second in the 1947 British Empire Trophy on the Douglas, Isle of Man circuit behind Bob Gerard with his ERA.

Like many other drivers, Whitehead was captivated by the V12 Ferraris raced from 1947 onwards, and in 1948 he decided to buy one. He was going to fly to Milan from Croydon, but the aircraft crashed on take-off and Peter suffered injuries that put him out of racing until 1949. By then Peter had acquired his Ferrari and he was able to circumvent the British government's currency restrictions by using overseas funds. The price would have been about £10,000, an immense sum in those days. The new car was a V12 short-chassis single-seater of the type first raced by Ferrari in the 1948 Italian GP.

Whitehead's car was supplied with two engines, a

1497cc supercharged unit for GP racing, and an unblown 1995cc engine for F2. It was painted British Racing Green. In blown 1.5-litre form it was a formidable piece of machinery, but not as powerful as the rival Alfa Romeos that dominated GP racing from 1946 to 1951 (but the Portello team withdrew from racing for 1949), or the better-driven 4CLT/48 Maseratis, but it had superb acceleration. The biggest shortcoming was the short wheelbase, which meant that the handling was very tricky, especially in the wet, and spins were easily provoked. Another shortcoming was that the brakes tended to fade badly in long races.

Peter drove gently in the early part of 1949, as he learned the qualities and quirks of the Tipo 125. His first race was the San Remo GP on the Ospedaletti circuit at the beginning of April, and he drove cautiously to finish sixth. At the end of April, Whitehead ran the car in the Jersey International Road Race on the St Helier circuit, and here, for whatever reason, it was entered in the name of Scuderia Ferrari. The race was run in torrential rain, and Whitehead, who had no one to please but himself, drove a very wary race to take seventh place. An eighth place, co-driving with Dudley Folland, followed in the British GP at Silverstone.

Shortly afterwards, Whitehead gave clear indication that he had mastered the handling difficulties of the Tipo 125 by finishing fourth in the Belgian GP behind Rosier (Talbot), Villoresi, and Ascari (the latter two both with works Tipo 125s). A poor ninth followed at Bremgarten, and then, in the GP de France at Reims (that year the French GP proper was a sports car race on the St Gaudens circuit at Comminges), Whitehead took the lead near the finish of the race, but with only a lap to go the Ferrari's gearbox seized up, leaving him only fourth gear, and he dropped back to finish third behind Chiron (Talbot) and 'B. Bira' (Maserati) after the finest drive in his career to date.

In the next few races Whitehead was out of luck, but in the last GP of the season, the Czechoslovakian at Brno, three of the fastest Maserati drivers crashed, and Whitehead scored a well-deserved win ahead of Etancelin (Talbot). By 1950, substantial changes had taken place in F1. Alfa Romeo returned to racing and

Ferrari started development of a new unsupercharged car. Both the 1.5-litre blown Ferraris and the 4.5-litre unblown Talbots were obsolete. Even so, Whitehead finished third in the absence of works Ferraris behind two Alfa Romeos in the French GP at Reims, and won the Jersey Road Race from the private Maseratis of Parnell and de Graffenried.

Later, he took fourth place in the Dutch GP at Zandvoort, and he won the Ulster Trophy at Dundrod. Another success followed in the International Trophy race at Silverstone in August when he took third place behind the works Alfa Romeos of Farina and Fangio. At the end of 1950, Whitehead sold this Ferrari and bought from the works one of the long-chassis blown cars that had first appeared in the 1950 Italian GP. He raced this car in only a few races in 1951, and his best performances were fifth places in the Pescara and Bari Grands Prix.

Peter was entered with Tony Vandervell's Tipo 375 unblown 4.5-litre Ferrari, known as the Thin Wall Special, in the British GP, but he drove a slow race and finished ninth. Whitehead's greatest success in 1951 was a win co-driving a Jaguar C-type with his old friend Peter Walker at Le Mans. He retained the long-chassis Ferrari for 1952, and his best performances were both in F1 races, fourth at Siracusa and Turin. He had enjoyed, and well deserved, success with the Ferrari, but his single-seater career was slipping away from him. He raced an Alta F2 car in 1952 alongside the Ferrari.

In 1953 he raced a F2 Cooper with an Alta engine, and teamed up with American Tom Cole to race under the name Écurie Atlantic. The partnership ended when Cole was killed at Le Mans. Peter was a member of the works Jaguar team through to the end of 1954, and in 1953 he raced his own C-type, winning the Hyères 12 Hours race with Cole, and the Reims 12 Hours with Moss. At Le Mans he and Ian Stewart drove a works C-type into fourth place. Partnered by Ken Wharton at the wheel of a works D-type, he won the Reims race in 1954 for the second year in succession.

At the beginning of 1954 he finished second with a Ferrari Tipo 625 F1 car powered by a 3-litre engine in the New Zealand GP. In 1954–5 he raced his own Cooper-Jaguar sports cars, drove a Maserati 300S in 1956, and then raced an Aston Martin DB3S in 1957–8. His great success with a private Aston Martin was to finish second in the 1958 Le Mans race with half-brother Graham. It was a remarkable performance with an obsolete car. Three months later, Peter was killed when Graham crashed the Jaguar, that they were sharing in the Tour de France, over the parapet of a bridge and into a ravine.

Opposite: *Wealthy privateer Peter Whitehead with his first, short-chassis, GP Ferrari is seen nearest camera on the starting grid for the International Trophy at Silverstone in August 1950. The nose of the Alfa Romeo of Giuseppe Farina can be seen in the bottom left corner of the photograph. Alongside Whitehead are T. C. Harrison (ERA) and Reg Parnell (Maserati).* (Shell Photographic Unit)

Williams, Jonathan

Driver
Born: 26 October 1942 (Cairo, Egypt)

Educated at Cheltenham College in England, Williams started racing Minis in 1960–1 and progressed to an Austin A40, which he drove to second place in the Molyslip Saloon Series at Brands Hatch. He moved up to Formula Junior, driving for the Merlyn team, but was injured in an accident at Monaco in 1963. After a spell racing on the Continent with Lotus cars from a base at

Below: Williams was a close associate of the denizens of the famous flat in Pinner Road, Harrow, that included Charles Lucas, Piers Courage, and Frank Williams. He was given some works drives by Ferrari in 1967, and he was very much involved in the making of Steve McQueen's Le Mans *film. (LAT Photographic)*

Lausanne in Switzerland, Williams became number one driver in F3 for the Italian De Sanctis works team, and achieved a succession of wins.

These achievements led to an invitation to join Ferrari for 1967. He was entered with a Dino 166-powered F2 at Rouen in July 1967, but the car was all too obviously uncompetitive, and after seven laps he retired because of engine problems. He shared a Dino with Casoni of the Brescia Corse team in the Sebring 12 Hours (they retired because of engine problems); he drove an elderly Dino with Günther Klass in the Monza 1,000km race (they retired because of overheating); and then he joined private owner Venturi in his Dino in the Targa Florio (they finished fourth).

In the 1967 BOAC 500 race at Brands Hatch he shared a works P4 with Paul Hawkins, and they finished sixth. Later in the year he drove a P4 subsidised by Bill Harrah in the CanAm series. Following Bandini's death at Monaco in 1967, Williams had expected that he would be brought into the F1 team, but this did not happen until the last Championship race in Mexico City, where he took eighth place. Shortly after the Mexican race he was asked to test the V12 F1 car at Modena, but crashed, seriously damaging it. That was the end of his relationship with Ferrari.

Plans for a F1 drive with Abarth evaporated, and he later drove in a few F2 races and sports events. At Le Mans in 1970, Williams and Herbert Linge drove the 908/02 camera car of Solar Productions, filming for Steve McQueen's film, and he also played a small part in the film. With Michael Keyser, he co-authored the book about the making of the film, *A French Kiss with Death*. He qualified as a commercial pilot and flew corporation jets, and subsequently lived in a motor home with his partner, Linda, travelling, writing, and photographing.

Woodgate, Rex

Mechanic
Born: 2 July 1926

Rex was a mechanic with the HWM team in 1949–50, and he then went to work with Gordon Watson on his Alta. In 1954 he joined the staff of Leslie Hawthorn's Tourist Trophy Garage at Farnham in Surrey, and here he looked after Reg Parnell's Ferrari. As a side issue, it is said that after Parnell battled with Trintignant's works Ferrari in their heat of the International Trophy at Silverstone, Ferrari refused to supply Parnell with spare parts! Leslie Hawthorn was killed in a road accident on

Whit Monday 1954, but Woodgate worked for Mike Hawthorn until after Parnell disposed of the Ferrari at the end of 1954.

Above: *Rex Woodgate sits in the cockpit of Roy Parnell's Ferrari Tipo 625, checking the instrument readings, while Leslie Hawthorn watches.* (Rex Woodgate)

Zagato, Ugo

Coachbuilder
Born: 25 June 1890 (Gavello, Italy)
Died: 31 October 1968 (Milan, Italy)

After the death of his father in 1905, Zagato, who was one of six male children, went to work in Germany and found employment with a panel-beating firm in Cologne. He returned to Italy in 1909 for his compulsory military service, and subsequently worked for a coachwork company in Varese. He moved to Turin in 1915 and worked for the Pomilio aircraft company who were developing a single-seater fighter known as the Gamma.

The aircraft was approved for production too late, and the Pomilio brothers moved to the United States. Zagato, however, benefited from his time with the company by learning about lightweight construction methods. In 1919 Zagato founded Carrozzeria Ugo Zagato based in Milan, and it constructed car bodies that were built on aircraft industry principles; they were very light, but they were also flimsy, and their main advantage was the dramatic styling.

The company built bodies on Alfa Romeo chassis in substantial numbers throughout the 1920s and 1930s.

Interestingly, however, in 1933, by way of an example, the Alfa Romeo works entered three cars with Touring bodies in the Mille Miglia road race, but Zagato bodies were fitted to the five cars fielded by Scuderia Ferrari. In addition, Zagato built cars on a small number of Lancia chassis.

Like Touring, Zagato was forced to switch increasingly to military contracts. The company's premises were destroyed by Allied bombing, and the company was reconstructed as La Zagato outside Milan. Here Ugo was joined by his sons Elio (born 1921) and Gianni (born 1929). In post-war days, the company tended to build the more extreme body styles, notably the Fiat-Abarth and Lancia sporting models with 'double-bubble' roofs, together with the SZ and TZ variations on Alfa Romeo Giulia, 2000 and 2600 chassis.

Ferrari rarely commissioned Zagato to build bodies, but they were fairly frequently ordered by private customers, especially on the 250GT chassis. There were also a small number of bodies on Bristol chassis, and Aston Martin commissioned bodies on the DB4GT chassis. As the demands for traditional coachbuilding declined, Zagato's financial situation deteriorated. The company had been bolstered by small production runs by Alfa Romeo and Aston Martin, and outside finance had been injected. Increasingly the company became dependent on work on concept cars and on prototypes.

Chronology of the Life and Times of Enzo Ferrari

1898

Enzo Ferrari was born on 18 February 1898, but because of heavy snow his birth was not registered until 20 February. His father owned (or, at least, worked from) a small workshop adjoining the family home, and there he did metalwork for Italian railways.

1914

Following the German attack on neutral Belgium, Britain declared war on Germany on 4 August 1914, and Italy entered the war on the Allies' side in May 1915. Enzo Ferrari was conscripted into the Italian army and was posted to the 3rd Mountain Artillery. During this period, both his father and his elder brother Alfredo died, and Enzo became ill and was operated on in the Italian military hospital in Brescia.

1919

Enzo obtained employment with a small firm overhauling ex-military Lancias, and Ferrari's job was testing these vehicles and driving the chassis to the coachbuilder to be fitted with passenger car bodies. Later that year he met Ugo Sivocci, who introduced him to the management of CMN (Costruzioni Meccaniche Nazionali) and he obtained a job with this company in Milan.

1920

Ferrari's first competition outings were in the 1920 Parma–Poggio di Berceto hill climb (in which he finished third), and in that year's Targa Florio. Later that year he joined Alfa Romeo.

1923

It was claimed that on 17 June 1923 Ferrari competed with an Alfa Romeo in the Circuit of Savio at Ravenna – he won the race and set a new lap record. It is said that it was after this race that Ferrari was presented by Francesco Baracca's father with the emblem from his late flying ace son's fighter plane, the prancing horse. Ferrari later added the canary yellow background, the colour of Modena.

It was during this year that he married Laura.

1925

Antonio Ascari was killed at the wheel of his Alfa Romeo P2 when he crashed on 26 July in the French GP at Montlhéry.

1929

On 29 November, the Court in Modena gave approval for the establishment of Società Anonima Scuderia Ferrari with shareholdings by Alfa Romeo and Pirelli each of 200,000 lire. Apart from Enzo Ferrari (the Alfa Romeo agent in Emilia Romagna), the directors were Augusto and Alfredo Caniato (dealers in hemp in Ferrara), Mario Tadini (textiles and sand packaging business), and Ferruccio Testi. Although Ferrari took over the entry of competition cars on behalf of the Alfa Romeo factory, it was not a complete transfer, as right through the 1930s the works continued to enter cars alongside Scuderia Ferrari.

1931

During this year Alfa Romeo introduced the new 8C 2300 model, and these cars first appeared in the Mille Miglia held on 11–12 April. The 8C 2300s were too new, they proved unreliable, and they were too fast for their tyres, so victory went to the gigantic Mercedes-Benz SSKL of Caracciola/Sebastian.

At the Italian GP the Alfa Romeo organisation raced both the short-chassis Monza version of the 8C 2300 and the Tipo A, powered by two supercharged 6C 1750 engines. Luigi Arcangeli was killed in practice for the GP with the Tipo A. The race was held as a ten-hour event and was won by a Monza driven by Nuvolari/Campari.

1932

Alfa Romeo introduced the new 2.6-litre Monoposto single-seaters at the Italian GP in June and these cars were entered by the works. Nuvolari won the race with a Monoposto. In July, Nuvolari and Borzacchini drove Monopostos into the first two places in the French GP at Reims. Subsequently, Nuvolari won four races with Monopostos – the German GP, the Coppa Ciano, the Coppa Acerbo, and the Circuit of Avellino.

Ferrari's legitimate son Dino was born this year.

1933

Alfa Romeo withdrew from racing, and the Monopostos were put into cold storage. So, although Scuderia Ferrari was now the leading team entering Alfa Romeos, these were the obsolete Monza models. Initially, Nuvolari drove for Scuderia Ferrari, but he was unhappy that the Monzas were uncompetitive and he joined Maserati for the Belgian GP held on 9 July. Nuvolari won the race for Maserati, and Campari had already won the French GP at Montlhéry the previous month with the two-seater 8C 3000 Maserati, so the Bologna team was emerging as a dominant force.

By the Coppa Acerbo in August the Alfa Romeo factory had decided to release the Monopostos to Scuderia Ferrari. On 10 September 1933, Trossi was at the wheel of the Scuderia Ferrari's new 4.5-litre Duesenberg in the first heat, but the oil tank split and spilt a large quantity of oil on Monza's South Curve. Efforts were made to clear

this up, but in the next heat both Campari (Alfa Romeo Monoposto) and Borzacchini (8C 3000 Maserati) crashed with fatal results.

It has always been believed that the oil dropped by Trossi had not been properly cleared up, but it has recently been stated that the committee appointed to investigate the accident could find no trace of oil. Whatever the precise truth, the deaths of these drivers was a terrible blow to Italian motor racing and, in particular, to Scuderia Ferrari and Officine Alfieri Maserati. In the heat that followed, Count Czaykowski was also killed at the South Curve at the wheel of his 4.9-litre Bugatti Type 54.

1934

In October 1932 the Association International des Automobile Clubs Reconnus (the AIACR) announced that there would be a new GP formula from 1934, with the requirement that the weight of cars should not exceed 750kg (1,654lb) without driver, fuel, oil, water or tyres. There had been growing concern about the very high speeds attained by such cars as the 4.9-litre Tipo 54 Bugatti, the twin-engined Tipo A Alfa Romeo, and the

Above: *At the Gare de Lyon in Paris at the end of June 1934, doyen of motoring journalists W. F. Bradley is seen accompanied by his West Highland terrier meeting Italian drivers who were competing in the French GP at Montlhéry. On Bradley's right are Scuderia Ferrari drivers Count Trossi and Guy Moll, and on his left Tazio Nuvolari (driving for Bugatti). The figure on Nuvolari's left is probably Eugenion Siena.* (Author's collection)

twin-engined cars from Maserati, the 4-litre V4 and the V5. The aim was to stabilise design in a way that would limit the engine size of GP cars to 2.5/3 litres.

Other changes were that the bodywork should present a minimal cross-sectional area of 85cm x 25cm (33.5in x 9.8in) at the driving seat. In addition, races were to be run over a minimum distance of 500km (311 miles). This formula was originally intended to run for three seasons until the end of 1936, but it was extended until the end of 1937 because the AIACR had been so slow in reaching agreement on a successor formula.

It seemed that racing would continue much as before, a three-party battle between Alfa Romeo, Maserati, and Bugatti, but that failed to take account of the new and technically very advanced cars that were being developed in Germany. Alfa Romeo would continue to fight against the odds and achieve the occasional improbable win, but increasingly the Italian and French teams would become also-rans.

At the Coppa Acerbo race on 15 August 1934, the Algerian driver Guy Moll was in second place with his Alfa Romeo Monoposto. At a routine pit stop, Enzo Ferrari urged him to try harder and catch the race leader, Luigi Fagioli (Mercedes-Benz). On the long, fast Montesilvano Straight, Moll was alongside Henne (Auto Union) whom he was passing at about 160mph (260kph) as they entered the timed kilometre.

The rear of Moll's car broke sideways out of control, uprooted some palm trees and crashed against the side of a house. Moll was fatally injured. It was most likely that Moll's car was caught by a gust of wind. Enzo Ferrari blamed himself for the accident because he had been urging Moll to drive faster, and he never again attended a motor race.

1935

Scuderia Ferrari built the 'Bimotore' Alfa Romeo designed by Luigi Bazzi and powered by two Monoposto engines. Tazio Nuvolari had returned to Scuderia Ferrari and he drove the example with two 3.3-litre engines, while Chiron raced the one with two 2.9-litre engines. Remarkably, they proved very reliable, fairly tractable, decently handling cars, but their biggest weaknesses were the excessive tyre and brake lining wear.

These cars were well over the 750kg weight limit and could only be run in Formule Libre events. Chiron drove the 5.8-litre car to second place in the 1935 Avusrennen, and on 16 June of that year, on the Firenze (Florence)–Lucca Autostrada, he covered the flying mile at a speed of 200.80mph (323.09kph).

In the German GP held at the Nürburgring, Tazio Nuvolari scored one of the most important wins in 1930s GP racing, defeating the might of the German teams with his 3.2-litre Monoposto.

1936

Ferrari continued the uphill battle with the German teams, using the 4.1-litre 12C36 Alfa Romeos, and one of the few successes was Nuvolari's defeat of the German cars in the Penya Rhin GP at Barcelona on 7 June 1936.

1938

For 1938 the AIACR imposed a new GP formula with minimum weight commensurate with engine size for capacities from 666cc to 4500cc, and a maximum capacity of 3000cc for supercharged cars and 4500cc for unsupercharged cars. For these capacities there was a minimum weight of 850kg (1,874.25lb) including tyres.

In 1937, Vittorio Jano had been none too gently eased out of Alfa Romeo, and he joined the Lancia company in Turin. Alfa Romeo once again ran all its own racing activities, and this was done under the name Alfa Corse, which took over Scuderia Ferrari. The Scuderia

Ferrari premises in Modena, in effect, became a branch of Alfa Corse, and it was here that the Colombo-designed Tipo 158 straight-eight Voiturette was built and developed under Enzo Ferrari's supervision.

During 1938, Ferrari split from Alfa Corse and went his own way. There were two principal reasons for this. First, he had been self-employed, running his own business too long to be able to fit comfortably into a management structure. He was unhappy with the fact that Ricart was, in effect, Alfa Romeo chief engineer and, however much Enzo Ferrari exaggerated the Spaniard's shortcomings, the resentment was genuine and strongly felt. When Ferrari left Alfa Corse, he had to enter into a covenant that he would not re-form Scuderia Ferrari for a period of five years.

1939

Ferrari set up a new business to manufacture machine tools, which he called AutoAvio Costruzioni, and this was based in the viale Trento Trieste in Modena. Towards the end of the year he was commissioned to build two cars to run in the 1940 Mille Miglia, to be revived as a road race over a closed circuit. The cars were built with engineering input from Enrico Nardi and Alberto Massimino.

1940

The two new AutoAvio cars were driven by Alberto Ascari/Minozzi and the Marquis Rangoni/Enrico Nardi in the 1940 Mille Miglia, held on 28 April, but both cars retired.

On 10 May, Italy entered the Second World War on the side of the Axis, and motor racing ceased in Italy until 1946.

1945

Enzo Ferrari's illegitimate son, Piero Lardi Ferrari, was born this year.

1946

The November/December issue of the magazine *Inter Auto* published details of the new V12 1.5-litre sports Ferraris.

1947

At the start of this year there was a new Formula 1 (originally known as Formula A) for supercharged cars up to 1500cc and unsupercharged cars up to 4500cc. Although this formula was legally in force until the end of 1953, it was superseded for World Championship events in 1952–3 by a Formula 2 (originally Formula B) introduced in 1948 with capacity limits of 2000cc unsupercharged and 500cc supercharged.

Ferrari introduced the new Tipo 125 1489cc V12 sports cars that incorporated many features from Alfa Romeo design practice, and the marque Ferrari competed for the first time at Piacenza on 11 May 1947. Thereafter they were raced regularly.

1948

Clemente Biondetti/Navone and Tazio Nuvolari/Scapinelli drove 2-litre Ferraris in the Mille Miglia. For Nuvolari, it was one of his last races and he retired after over-driving his car, but Biondetti, with his Ferrari, won the race for the third time, and he won it again in 1949.

The new Ferrari Tipo 125 GP cars with supercharged, single overhead camshaft per bank V12 engines made their debut in September 1948 in the Italian GP. Of the three cars, only one finished, that of Raymond Sommer in third place.

1949

Ferrari won the first post-war Le Mans 24 Hours race with a 2-litre V12 Tipo 166 car driven by Luigi Chinetti, briefly relieved at the wheel by Lord Peter Selsdon.

In September, Ferrari endeavoured to resolve the shortcomings of the team's efforts in GP racing by introducing new longer-wheelbase cars with twin-stage supercharged V12 engines having twin overhead camshafts per bank of cylinders. Alberto Ascari drove one of these cars to a win on their debut in the Italian GP at Monza.

Below: The works Ferraris lined up in the paddock at the International Trophy meeting at Silverstone in August 1949 are the supercharged Tipo 125 cars of Ascari (Number 28) and Villoresi (Number 27). Ascari won the race from Farina (Maserati) and Villoresi took third place. (Guy Griffiths Collection)

1950

Alfa Romeo had returned to racing in 1950. The team had withdrawn in 1949 after dominating Grands Prix in 1946–8 with the Tipo 158 Alfettas, and in 1950 entered ten races and won them all.

After Monza in 1949, the twin-staged supercharged Ferraris disappointed in GP racing, Colombo returned to Alfa Romeo, and the new Ferrari Technical Director Aurelio Lampredi started development of an unsupercharged 4500cc GP car. The 4500cc versions of this design first appeared in the 1950 Italian GP at Monza in September. Ascari took over one of the cars driven by Serafini to finish second to Farina (Alfa Romeo).

1951

In the 1951 British GP at Silverstone a new member of the Ferrari team, Froilán González, at the wheel of an older, single-plug V12 4500cc Ferrari, defeated the works Alfa Romeos for the first time.

After winning the German and Italian Grands Prix, Ascari finished second to Juan-Manuel Fangio (Alfa Romeo) in the Drivers' World Championship. At the end of the year Alfa Romeo withdrew from GP racing.

1952

Because it was believed that there would be no serious opposition to the 4500cc Ferraris in 1952, all World Championship races were held to Formula 2 2000cc unsupercharged rules. In late 1951 Ferrari had introduced the new Lampredi-designed four-cylinder 1980cc F2 Tipo 500 car. With this model, Alberto Ascari

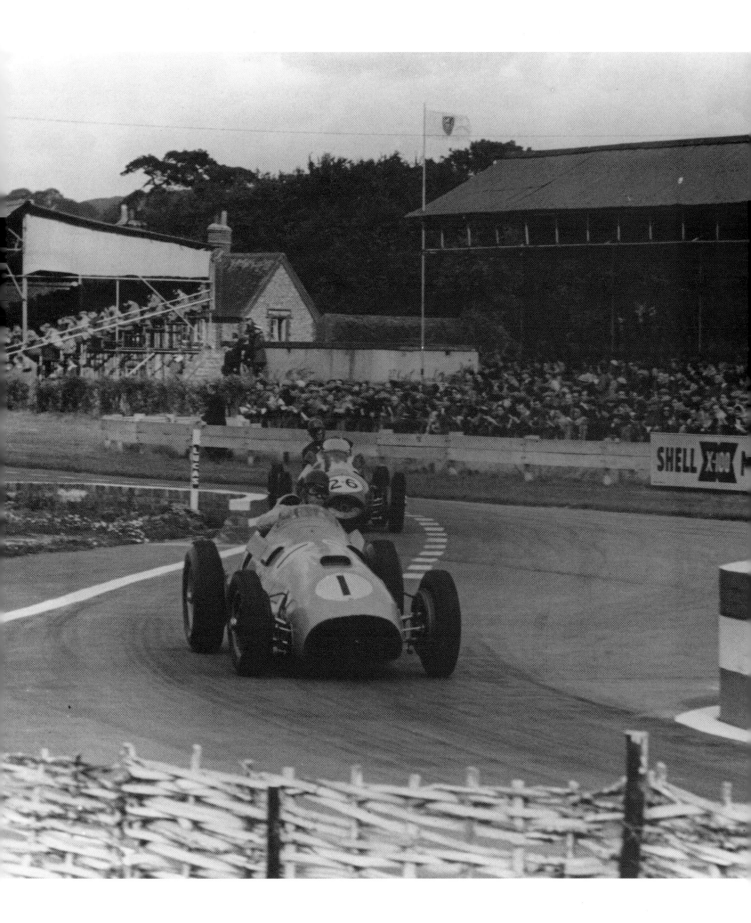

FERRARI: THE MEN FROM MARANELLO

Above: *This is a works Ferrari transporter at the 1953 British GP at Silverstone. Two of the team's Tipo 500 four-cylinder Formula 2 cars have been unloaded. Number 8 was driven by Mike Hawthorn, and Number 7 by Luigi Villoresi.* (Guy Griffiths Collection)

won the Drivers' World Championship in both 1952 and 1953, and works Tipo 500 cars won 17 races in 1952 – every race except the Reims GP won by Jean Behra with a Gordini that may have had an oversize engine.

Mercedes-Benz entered sports car racing in 1952 with their new 300SL Gull Wing coupés. Their first race was the Mille Miglia, and Giovanni Bracco, with a new 3-litre V12 Tipo 250 Sport Ferrari, drove a lunatic race sustained by cognac and cigarettes to beat them.

1953

The World Sports Car Championship was held for the first time in 1953 and was won by Ferrari, although the Ferraris failed at Le Mans where the works Jaguars finished first, second, and fourth.

In September 1953 Ferrari announced that he was withdrawing from racing because the team could not afford the high level of expenditure necessitated by a full racing programme. It was, in fact, a cri de coeur for greater financial support from Fiat – and Fiat duly obliged.

1954

For 1954 there was a new Formula 1 with maximum capacity limits of 2500cc unsupercharged and 750cc supercharged (but no serious contender built a 750cc supercharged car). This formula remained in force until the end of 1960, with just one major change for 1958 when the use of aviation fuel (100/130 octane) became compulsory. Ascari and Villoresi had left Ferrari to drive the new Lancia F1 car that was not raced until the Spanish GP at the end of the 1954 season.

Ferrari again won the World Sports Car Championship in 1954, and at Le Mans there was a titanic struggle between the enormous 4.9-litre Ferrari 375 Plus of González/Trintignant and the Jaguar D-type of Rolt/Hamilton. At its last pit stop the engine of the Ferrari proved very difficult to fire up and, certainly, there were more mechanics working on the car than permitted under the race regulations. At the finish the Ferrari was only 2½ miles ahead of the Jaguar. The organisers invited William Lyons of Jaguar to appeal the win – but, very wisely, he declined to do this.

In F1, Ferrari faced very stiff opposition from the new Mercedes-Benz W196 cars, which made their racing debut in the French GP on the very fast Reims circuit and took the first two places. Despite the strength of the Mercedes-Benz organisation, Ferrari did manage to win two races in 1954: González/Hawthorn in a 1–2 in the British GP and Hawthorn in the Spanish race at Barcelona.

Above: *This superb photograph was taken during a test session with the Tipo 553 Squalo at Modena in February 1954. Enzo Ferrari is on the extreme right of the photograph. Also wearing a trilby, with a pullover under his jacket, is Technical Director Aurelio Lampredi, and behind him is Harry Schell, who was the test driver. In the centre (in the background) wearing a beret is Cavaliere Luigi Bazzi and, with woolly hat, peering into the bonnet is engineer Alberto Massimino.* (Spitzley/Zagari Collection)

Below: *A fine view of the Lancia D50 driven by Luigi Villoresi on the model's debut in the 1954 Spanish GP. This is one of a series of photographs taken in the paddock and nearby by the great and much-missed Denis Jenkinson. After Ascari's death and Lancia's withdrawal from racing, Ferrari took over the D50s and raced them under his own name. They were very successful in near-enough original form in 1956, but the following year, after Ferrari had made substantial changes from the original specification, very little success was gained.* (LAT Photographic)

1955

The Lancia company became impoverished by a competition programme that it could ill-afford. During the Monaco GP, Ascari plunged into Monte Carlo harbour when a brake locked on his Lancia D50 and, although he escaped from this accident largely unscathed, he was killed on 26 May at the wheel of a 3-litre Ferrari Monza during practice for the sports car Supercortemaggiore GP on the Monza circuit. Lancia ran a single D50 for Castellotti in the Belgian GP on 5 June 1955, but he retired because of gearbox trouble.

The following Saturday, 12 June, that terrible accident happened during the Le Mans 24 Hours race when Pierre Levegh's Mercedes-Benz 300SLR collided with the Austin-Healey of Lance Macklin; it was launched into the abutment of a bridge and rebounded

into a spectator area. More than 80 spectators were killed. It has to be stressed that Ferrari was uninvolved in the Le Mans disaster, but the repercussions affected the whole of the motor racing world, and a large number of races were cancelled.

On 7 July it was announced that Ferrari would be taking over the Lancia équipe, and the Italian Automobile Club issued the following statement to the press:

'With the intention of promoting the technical advancement of the building of racing cars, which are a glorious tradition of the Italian motor industry and add prestige to Italian products throughout the world, the President General of the Italian Automobile Club decided to intervene personally with Fiat and Lancia to enlist their aid in sustaining the efforts of the Ferrari Automobili of Modena to which Enzo Ferrari has dedicated his life's work. This development will also serve in the formation and improved efficiency of Italian racing drivers.

The suggestion of the Italian Automobile Club was cordially accepted. Lancia place their racing cars at Ferrari's disposal, cars which have already earned for themselves a brilliant reputation in international competitions, while continuing to devote their activities from now on exclusively to the manufacture of touring cars and commercial vehicles.

Fiat, which treasures the proud laurels won by its great drivers of the past, offers Ferrari an annual contribution of 50 million lire [approximately £28,500 at the time] for a period of five years.'

On the same day, Enzo Ferrari sent the following telegram to Fiat's President, Vittorio Valletta:

'News just received surprises me and evokes my gratitude. I have only recently explained to President Prince Caracciolo my present situation consequent upon prolonged stubborn isolated technical efforts in competition work. Glad to hear of warm comprehension and prompt generous and significant gesture of solidarity made to me by Lancia's offer of substantial technical contributions which comprises fruits of their latest experiments and by Fiat, fountain-head of all modern technical sports progress, which will generously enable my small firm to continue working.

I earnestly hope that old and new collaborators will work happily together, sharing sacrifices and anxieties in order to render even more worthy products of Italian work in the world, thus honouring all those who have fallen in the extreme effort to keep the tricolour to the fore. With respectful gratitude – Enzo Ferrari.'

After the Lancia D50s and all the team's equipment had been handed over to Ferrari, and the technical staff had moved to Maranello, the cars were entered in – and withdrawn from – the Italian GP (the withdrawal being because the Englebert tyres were throwing treads). On 24 September, two Lancia D50s ran in the *Daily Dispatch* Gold Cup race at Oulton Park, and although Moss won with a works Maserati, Hawthorn finished second with his Lancia; Castellotti with his D50 was a poor seventh after a pit stop because of handling problems.

1956

Three of the Lancia D50s, now officially described as Ferraris, ran in the Argentine GP on 22 January 1956 and were entered by Scuderia Ferrari throughout the 1956–7 seasons. Fangio drove for Ferrari this year and he won the Drivers' Championship for the fourth time.

Enzo Ferrari's son Dino died of muscular dystrophy on 30 June 1956.

In 1955, Mercedes-Benz had won the World Sports Car Championship, but Ferrari bounced back in 1956 to win it for the third time.

1957

Castellotti had joined the Ferrari team following Lancia's withdrawal from racing. In March 1957 he was called back from holiday for a testing session at Modena Aerautodromo and crashed with fatal results. He was one of Italy's most promising young drivers and there was never any satisfactory explanation for this terrible accident.

On 12 May, Marquis Alfonso de Portago, accompanied by Eddie Nelson, crashed in the Mille Miglia, almost certainly as the result of a tyre being damaged by a metal object in the road. In addition to the driver and passenger, ten spectators were killed. The Mille Miglia was banned and there was a government inquiry into the accident.

During this time, Ferrari's passport was seized by the authorities. And, with the investigation being deemed to be sub judice, he was in effect muzzled,

Above: *At the start of the 1956 Italian GP at Monza, the V8 Lancia-Ferraris are well to the fore, headed by Luigi Musso (Number 28), Castellotti (Number 24), and Fangio (Number 22). Number 36 is Stirling Moss, who won the race with his Maserati 250F. Fangio finished second and clinched his fourth Drivers' World Championship after taking over Peter Collins's car.* (Author's Collection)

and lost all opportunity to explain whether the accident was caused by the tyres or the car itself. Despite this accident and a Jaguar victory at Le Mans for the third successive year, Ferrari again won the World Sports Car Championship.

At Naples at the end of April 1957 the Ferrari team had revealed the new V6 Dino F2 car that formed the basis of the 1958 F1 cars. The latest F2 had been introduced for 1957 (although there had been some races to the formula in 1956) and was for unsupercharged cars up to 1500cc. Commercial 'pump' fuel was compulsory in 1957, but 100/130-octane 'Avgas' aviation fuel became compulsory for 1958–60.

In F1, Ferrari was still racing the Lancia-Ferraris, but these were no longer competitive and the only wins were in non-Championship races: Collins at Siracusa and Musso at Reims.

1958

Although his only World Championship race victory was in the French GP at Reims, Mike Hawthorn won that year's Drivers' Championship by one point from Stirling Moss (Vanwall). It was, however, another tragic year

Above: *In June 1958 the second 'Two Worlds' Trophy, intended to provide a duel between Indianapolis drivers and cars and their European counterparts, was held at Monza. This photograph shows the start of the second of the three heats in which the race was run. As in 1957, the race was dominated by the Indianapolis cars, but Ferrari entered a Dino with a 4.1-litre V12 engine (Number 12) seen here with Luigi Musso at the wheel. With the driving shared by Hawthorn, Phil Hill, and Musso, it finished third overall.* (Author's collection)

because two drivers were killed: Luigi Musso in the French GP at Reims and Peter Collins in the German GP at the Nürburgring.

1959

The threat from rear-engined cars had been growing steadily. In 1958, rear-engined Coopers entered by Rob Walker's private team had won two major races – Buenos Aires (Moss) and Monaco (Trintignant) – and now, in 1959, Brabham with his works Coopers won the Drivers' Championship with 31 points to the 27 of Ferrari-driver Tony Brooks.

In 1959, Frenchman Jean Behra had joined the Ferrari team, but he did not settle in, and his relations with both Ferrari and racing manager Tavoni were bad.

Behra constantly complained that his car was down on power. Of Behra, Tavoni has said, 'If you had a circuit with lap speeds of around 100mph (160kph), then Behra would be faster [than the other drivers], but he was not fast on difficult, high-speed circuits such as Spa, Reims, and Monza.'

There was an altercation at Reims following Behra's inevitable complaint that his car was down on power, and during the course of this Behra struck Tavoni. The Frenchman was sacked from the team. On the day of the German GP, held on the banked Avus track, he drove a Porsche in a sports car race that preceded the GP. He crashed with fatal results.

Ferrari also won the World Sports Car Championship in 1959 for the sixth time.

1960

By this time, engineer Carlo Chiti had persuaded Enzo Ferrari that the way forward was with rear-engined cars. Although Ferrari raced the obsolescent front-engined Dino cars throughout the 1960 season, the team built both F1 and F2 rear-engined prototypes during the year.

In sports car racing, Ferrari won the World Sports Car Championship yet again, entering the latest version of the Testa Rossa 3-litre front-engined cars that the team had been racing regularly since a 3000cc engine capacity Championship was introduced for 1958.

1961

For 1961 there was a new GP formula, to all intents and purposes a slightly modified version of Formula 2 with a minimum capacity of 1301cc and a maximum capacity of 1500cc unsupercharged; other stipulations were a minimum dry weight of 450kg (992.25lb), commercial 'pump' fuel was compulsory, and cars had to be fitted with a self-starter; no replenishment with oil during a race was permitted.

In Formula 1, Ferrari raced his new and very fast (but not particularly well-handling) rear-engined V6 cars. The British teams had opposed the introduction of the new formula and, mistakenly confident that their demands for the retention of the existing formula would be met, they were slow to start development of new power units. The result was that they had to rely on the old Formula 2 four-cylinder Coventry Climax FPF engines and, apart from Monaco and the Nürburgring (won by the brilliant Stirling Moss with an obsolete Rob Walker-entered Lotus 18), the year was dominated by Ferrari.

When the teams travelled to Monza for the Italian GP, German driver Wolfgang von Trips was leading the Championship. Tragically, he and Jim Clark collided on the second lap, and in the ensuing mêlée von Trips and 14 spectators were killed. Phil Hill, another Ferrari driver, won the race and the Championship, with von Trips a posthumous second.

The year 1961 was the last in the World Sports Car Championship, which Ferrari won yet again, and one of the team's most successful sports-racing cars was another rear-engined design, the 246SP with a V6 2417cc engine.

For 1960, Ferrari had introduced the 250GT SWB ('short-wheelbase') Gran Turismo car, the latest development in the long line of the company's 250GT 3-litre V12 cars that dated back to 1956. These cars were immensely successful, and the 1961 'Competizione' version was a fine lightweight racer.

As recounted on page 99, there was friction arising from Laura Ferrari's interference in the running of the team. Ferrari's response to a letter sent to him by senior management in December 1961 led to their dismissal, and at the end of the year Ferrari was desperately short of engineering and administrative staff.

1962

For 1962, a rather hard-pressed Ferrari appointed the young and relatively inexperienced Mauro Forghieri as Technical Director. Forghieri concentrated on the development of the chassis of the V6 F1 Ferraris, and design was put in hand of both V8 and flat-12 cars. Outclassed in F1, the highest-placed Ferrari driver in the

1962 World Championship was Phil Hill in sixth place with 14 points to the 42 (net) of winner Graham Hill (BRM).

A new category of GT Prototype racing started in 1962 and, in the absence of strong opposition, Ferrari dominated this. Likewise, Ferrari was strong in the GT category where the company was racing and selling the very potent and very stylish 250GTO cars.

1963

For 1963, John Surtees joined Ferrari, and a very satisfactory working relationship developed between him and Forghieri. The team faced an uphill struggle to compete on even terms in F1, with the British teams using their new and very successful V8 engines. However, Ferrari's fortunes were improving, and Surtees won the German GP, as well as the non-Championship Mediterranean and Rand GPs.

There had been protracted negotiations between Ford and Ferrari for the sale of the Maranello company for 12.5 billion lire plus share options to Ford, but these finally foundered in May 1963 because Ford would not allow Enzo Ferrari budgeting discretion in relation to the racing programme. At this time Ferrari was constantly struggling because of lack of adequate financial resources, and these were not resolved until Fiat bought into Ferrari.

In Prototype racing there was no serious opposition, and with the 250P cars that had rear-mounted V12 3-litre engines Ferrari won the 1963 Prototype Championship from Porsche (72 to 30 points). Ferrari also won the GT Championship.

1964

After an interval of six years, the Drivers' Championship returned to Maranello with John Surtees winning by a single point from Graham Hill (BRM).

Ferrari continued to be the strongest force in Sports Prototype racing, and although Ford had raced the GT40, it was far from being reliable enough to win races.

In late 1963, Ferrari had built the first 250LM (250 Le Mans Berlinetta) that was in effect a 1963 250P Sports Prototype with roof, and in April 1964 Ferrari sought homologation of the 250LM as a GT car. Although the first of these cars had a 3-litre engine, all later examples had a 3.3-litre unit.

For homologation in the GT category, it was necessary to build 100 cars. The Commission Sportive Internationale (CSI) had homologated other cars, such as the Aston Martin P214 works GT model, the Ferrari 250GTO, and the 'Lightweight' Jaguar E-type, because they were developments of production models, and the homologation rules specifically covered mechanical developments and the fitting of different bodywork.

By way of contrast, the 250LM was a production version of a works competition car, and production fell well short of 100 cars (only 32 were manufactured). The CSI duly refused homologation of the 250LM, and this led to a row with the Italian Automobile Association because it failed to support Enzo Ferrari in his dispute with the CSI. Ferrari, in a most terrible rage, announced that he was relinquishing his entrant's licence and would not field cars in his own name on Italian soil again.

This had no immediate effect in Europe because racing was over for the year, but the works Ferraris in the United States and Mexican Grands Prix were entered by the North American Racing Team and painted in United States white and blue racing colours. By the start of the 1965 season everyone had forgotten about the dispute, although there was a delay in Ferrari getting his licence back and the cars were entered in Dragoni's name at the South African GP. In Italy, race organisers allowed 250LMs to run as GT cars and, in any event, the model achieved many successes running in the Prototype category.

1965

Ferrari had a bad season in F1 in 1965. Although the improved Fords won at Daytona, overall it was another very successful season for Ferrari in Sports Prototype racing. Both Ford and Ferrari failed at Le Mans, and all the works cars retired, but the 24 Hours race was won by a private Ferrari entered by the North American Racing Team.

In 1965, Ferrari announced that it was pulling out of GT racing, but this meant very little as Ferrari had usually left this category to private owners. What it did mean in the simplest terms was that the factory made no serious effort to build competition GT cars, apart from a small number of 'Competizione' versions of the 275GTB. The Shelby American Cobra Team won the GT Championship in 1965, but it did not ever beat Ferrari – Ferrari simply did not compete. This is correct, and it is something that every Shelby American Cobra supporter needs to have rammed down his/her throat!

Enzo Ferrari was now 67, and in June 1965 he decided to shed some of his responsibilities at SEFAC Ferrari. Although he remained President (but, of course, still ruled the company with a rod of iron when it suited him), he appointed Dottore Piero Gobbato from Fiat as General Manager with overall control, except in the vital area of the company's racing activities; Cavaliere Federico Giberti took over control of racing. Both were members of an executive committee along with Ragioniere Della Casa, the company's accountant.

John Surtees had been racing a Group 7 sports Lola, and he crashed badly with this in practice for the CanAm Canadian GP because of a broken hub carrier. Initially, it seemed unlikely that he would ever race again.

1966

There was a new formula with a maximum capacity of 3000cc unsupercharged and 1500cc supercharged, and a minimum weight limit of 500kg; otherwise regulations were unchanged. Although the new V12 Ferrari was unveiled to the press as early as December 1965, and it looked like a winner, it proved to be too heavy (despite claims to the contrary, it was over 100kg above the minimum permitted weight) and insufficiently powerful (it developed only 300bhp or so compared to the claimed 360bhp).

Surtees made a superb recovery from his crash and shared the winning 330P3 Ferrari with Mike Parkes in the Monza 1,000km race in April; he then won the non-Championship Syracuse GP, and went on to win the Belgian GP with an underpowered V12 car. Already, Ferrari was planning to sack Surtees. There was no rational reason, although there was prejudice about his involvement in racing with Lola (Surtees argued that it benefited Ferrari), and racing manager Dragoni disliked him. Surtees left the team at Le Mans where the Ferraris failed and the Fords finished in the first three places.

1967

A very tired Lorenzo Bandini crashed his V12 Ferrari on lap 82 of the 1967 Monaco GP and suffered terrible burns to which he succumbed after three days.

Mike Parkes crashed his V12 Ferrari in the Belgian GP, and his injuries included breakages of both legs. He never raced for Ferrari again.

Although Ford won the Le Mans race with the 7-litre cars for the second year in succession, Ferrari with the superb 330P4 cars won at Daytona and Monza, took second places at Le Mans and Brands Hatch, and won the Prototype Championship.

During 1967, Ferrari introduced the new Dino 206 four-cam V6 mid-engined coupé (it was not badged as a

Above: *Seen in the paddock at the 1969 British GP at Silverstone are two V12 3-litre GP cars. By this time, the V12 was obsolete and was only being raced because the 312B flat-12 cars were not ready. On Chris Amon's car (on the right) the oil cooler was mounted high at the back between the split wing, which was modified in practice so that the right-hand side was mounted at a steeper angle because Silverstone had almost all right-hand corners. Both Ferrari drivers retired in this race.* (Tom March Collection)

Ferrari) and this was followed in 1969 by the Dino 246GT – the first large-production Ferrari model (nearly 2,500 coupés and over 1,200 spiders were built).

Between 1967 and 1971 there was a new Formula 2 with a maximum capacity of 1600cc unsupercharged; the engines had to be derived from a production unit of which no fewer than 500 units had been built, and had to have not more than six cylinders. Ferrari competed in this formula, running in one race in 1967, regularly in 1968, and during the early part of 1969 with limited success.

1968

Following a change in the Prototype regulations, not announced until after the Le Mans race in June 1967, there was a 3000cc capacity limit for Sports Prototypes from 1968 onwards, and Ferrari temporarily withdrew from this category of racing.

In F1, Ferrari drivers Chris Amon and Jackie Ickx struggled with the uncompetitive V12 cars. The best performances were a win by Ickx in the wet French GP at Rouen and second place by Amon in the British GP.

In practice for the Canadian GP held on 22 September,

young Jackie Ickx crashed heavily, breaking a leg below the knee. He returned for the last F1 race of the year at Mexico City, but joined the Brabham team for 1969.

Introduced in 1968 and built until 1974, the 365GTB/4 Daytona was an exceptionally handsome 4.4-litre V12 coupé with 170mph (270kph) performance and outstanding competition record.

1969

By this stage, Ferrari's financial problems were serious, and the team was forced to race the old V12 F1 cars because the new flat-12 was not ready until 1970. Chris Amon stayed with the F1 team until the British race, but left – very unwisely – because he had lost all confidence that Ferrari could again build a F1 race-winner.

Ferrari returned to Prototype racing with the 312P V12 cars, which were faster than the Porsche opposition, but lacked reliability; in addition they were underdeveloped, and Ferrari team organisation was much inferior to that of Porsche.

In June, Enzo Ferrari travelled to the Fiat headquarters in Turin to confirm the details of the agreement whereby Fiat took 50 per cent of Ferrari's issued share capital and acquired the balance on his death. The most important part of the deal for Ferrari was that he retained control of the racing section, and Fiat assumed control of the road car division. For some while, Ferrari had been under severe financial pressure because of his extensive racing programme, and there was now adequate finance for this.

Ferrari's one successful effort in 1969 was in the European Hill Climb Championship, every round of which was won by Peter Schetty at the wheel of the Ferrari Tipo 212E Montagna flat-12 2-litre car.

1970

The new flat-12 312B car made its racing debut in South Africa in 1970 and Ferrari relied on this basic design, the work of Mauro Forghieri, for 11 seasons. A full account of these cars, which were so important to Ferrari, is given in Appendix 5, primarily as a tribute to the work of Mauro Forghieri.

In 1969 there had been an important amendment to the rules in sports car racing. After the decision had been made to limit Prototypes to 3 litres, it was realised that this would be unfair to owners of cars such as the Ferrari 250LM, Ford GT40, and Lola T70 GT Mk III, so the CSI provided an additional Group 5 for Competition Sports Cars, provided that 50 examples had been built and these were limited to 5 litres, whether they had been built with engines of greater capacity than 5 litres or less.

The works Alfa Romeo team, Autodelta, had requested

the CSI to reduce the number of cars that had to be built for homologation purposes to 25 (as this would prove beneficial for their customers who wanted to compete in the Group 5 category with Tipo 33/2 cars). The CSI agreed, and the effect was to make it possible for any constructor to build 25 5-litre cars and for them to be homologated as Group 5 Competition Sports Cars.

Porsche did this with the 917 that first appeared in the Spa 1,000km race in 1969, and Ferrari responded with the 512S that was raced by the works throughout 1970. Unfortunately, the 512S was no match for its German rival and won only one race in the Championship series, the Sebring 12 Hours.

That the new Tipo 312B F1 car had immense promise became obvious during 1970, although the most successful car was the Ford DFV-powered Lotus 72. Jochen Rindt was leading the World Championship for Lotus when he was killed during practice for the Italian GP. Ickx was unable to close the gap for Ferrari, and after three GP wins he finished second to the posthumous winner.

1971

Despite the immense promise shown by the 312B in 1970 – and the fulfilment of this promise in later years – it was a great disappointment that Jacky Ickx, who was an exceptional F1 driver by any standards, could achieve so little in the years 1971–3. During this time he won only two Grands Prix (Zandvoort in 1971 and Germany in 1972).

For 1971, Enzo Ferrari decided to abandon the latest 512M Group 5 Competition Sports Car, at least as far as the works team was concerned. Instead, he decided to

concentrate on development under racing conditions of the 312PB flat-12 Prototype. Group 5 cars were abolished at the end of 1971, and the development programme that Enzo Ferrari adopted paid immense dividends.

Throughout the year, Ferrari fielded only a single 312PB, and this first appeared in the Buenos Aires 1,000km race where it was driven by Ignazio Giunti and Arturo Merzario. Giunti was killed in a horrible, disgusting accident for which he bore absolutely no responsibility. He was Italy's most promising driver. For most of the rest of the year the 312PBs were driven by Ickx/Regazzoni, but their only finish was at Brands Hatch where they took second place.

1972

Benefiting from the experience gained in 1971, and in the face of weak opposition, the Ferrari Prototype running the flat-12 312PBs won ten of the 11 rounds in the World Championship for Makes. The team had scored the maximum 160 points (there were 20 points for a win and only the best eight results counted) compared with the 85 points of Alfa Romeo, who failed to win a single race. Ferrari missed Le Mans, and the French Matra team entered only this race and won it.

Below: *This photograph was taken at the opening of Ferrari's test track and other test facilities at Fiorano in 1972. Left to right (ignoring people behind the front row) are Clay Regazzoni, Jacky Ickx, unidentified, Ronnie Peterson, and Tim Schenken.* (LAT Photographic)

1973

Forghieri left working with the main Ferrari team to concentrate on his own developments; the latest and very unsuccessful version of the flat-12 GP car, the 312B3, was the work of an engineer from Fiat, Sandro Colombo. Forghieri was brought back into the team and hastily produced a much revised and improved version of the 312B3.

In 1973, Ferrari competed in Prototype racing for the last time, but the latest versions of the 312PB had handling problems and the rival V12 Matras were faster. Matra won the World Championship for Makes.

First seen in 4.4-litre form in 1973, and built from 1976 with a 4.9-litre engine, the 365GT4BB (Berlinetta Boxer) was another landmark production Ferrari with horizontally opposed engine and a body beautifully styled by Pininfarina and built by Scaglietti.

1974

Niki Lauda joined the Ferrari team, and Luca di Montezemolo, whose job it was to act in a liaison role between the team, Ferrari, and Fiat, also acted as team

Below: *Taken at Fiorano in 1976, this photograph shows Niki Lauda at the wheel of the latest version of the flat-12, the 312T with transverse gearbox. Clay Regazzoni is second from the left, Mauro Forghieri fourth from left, and Enzo Ferrari in raincoat standing behind the car.* (LAT Photographic)

manager. The F1 season was marred by the debacle at Brands Hatch when Lauda made a late stop for a wheel-change and was unable to rejoin the race because the pit road was blocked. Ferrari fortunes were improving, and Regazzoni and Lauda took second and fourth places in the Drivers' Championship.

1975

For the 1975 season, Forghieri introduced the 312T with transversely mounted gearbox. Lauda won his first World Championship for Ferrari (the first by a Ferrari driver since 1968), and Ferrari won the Constructors' Championship.

1976

Although Niki Lauda survived his crash with the 312T2 at the Nürburgring, the accident was disastrous for Ferrari. The young Austrian made a recovery that was mainly attributable to the most determined resolution on his part. His withdrawal from the torrentially wet Japanese GP allowed James Hunt to win the Championship with 69 points to his 68, but Ferrari still won the Constructors' Championship.

1977

This was Lauda's last year with Ferrari, and his relations with the team were steadily deteriorating. He won the World Championship with two races in hand, and then declined to drive in these last races of the season. Ferrari won the Constructors' Championship again.

1978

The Ferrari F1 team drivers were now Argentinian Carlos Reutemann and French-Canadian Gilles Villeneuve. Reutemann was never happy or secure in the team, and Villeneuve was wild and inexperienced. The latest flat-12 cars were no match for the Lotus 79 'ground-effect' cars, but Reutemann took third place in the Championship behind Lotus drivers Andretti and Peterson (the latter posthumously second after his fatal crash in the Italian GP).

Laura Ferrari died on 27 January 1978.

1979

Forghieri's 1979 312T4 was the ultimate Ferrari flat-12 car and resulted from detailed investigations and developments carried out in the Pininfarina wind tunnel. Ferrari regained predominance, and Scheckter and Villeneuve took the first two places in the Drivers' Championship – and Ferrari won the Constructors' Championship.

1980

Although complete failure after such a brilliant year seemed impossible, the 312T5s, the last manifestation of the flat-12 design, proved an unmitigated disaster because of mechanical unreliability and problems with the Michelin tyres.

1981

Throughout 1980, Forghieri had been working on a turbocharged F1 car, and the result was the six-cylinder Tipo 126CK that performed with such promise in 1981, although there was a conspicuous absence of solid success. Ferrari was only fifth in the Constructors' Championship, and the highest-placed driver was Villeneuve, seventh in the Drivers' Championship. Villeneuve did, however, win two races, at Monaco and Jarama.

1982

The team retained the same drivers in 1982: Gilles Villeneuve and Didier Pironi. Although relationships between the two drivers had seemed fine in 1981, they totally disintegrated the following year. The 1982 F1 Ferrari was the 126C2, highly developed and very competitive, while the drivers represented the strongest pairing in F1 at the time. The San Remo GP was boycotted by the mainly British FOCA-aligned teams. Gilles Villeneuve was leading as they started the last lap and, according to Ferrari team instructions, he should have been allowed to win. Instead Pironi passed Villeneuve and held the lead to win the race.

Above: *Enzo Ferrari at his desk in about 1982. In this photograph, he is making a special effort for the camera, but like many very old people he would sit for long periods, oblivious to his surroundings, his mind full of memories of a great past.* (LAT Photographic)

Villeneuve never spoke to Pironi again. Thirteen days later, during qualifying for the Belgian GP at Zolder, Villeneuve went out for a final effort to take pole position and collided with Jochen Mass's March 821. The Ferrari catapulted over the right rear wheel of the March, and came nose-down into the sand at the side of the circuit. Villeneuve was killed instantly, his neck broken by the deceleration.

Later that year, in practice for the German GP at Hockenheim, Pironi ran into the back of Alain Prost's Renault and suffered two broken legs. He never returned to racing. Despite these tragedies, Ferrari won the 1982 Constructors' Championship, and newcomer to the team Patrick Tambay won the German GP (where Pironi had crashed in practice).

1983

The Ferrari drivers were now Tambay and René Arnoux (who had joined the team from Renault). Tambay won at Imola, while Arnoux finished first at Montreal, Hockenheim and Zandvoort (and was third in the Drivers' Championship). Ferrari again won the Constructors' Championship.

1984

For 1984, Tambay was replaced at Ferrari by Alboreto, and the team was entering a barren, unsuccessful period. With the latest 126C4, Alboreto won at Zolder and, because of consistent finishes, the team took second place to McLaren-TAG in the Constructors' Championship.

Below: *René Arnoux is seen here at the wheel of the turbocharged Tipo 156/85 on test at Rio in 1985. On lap 27 of the Brazilian race, de Cesaris (Ligier) slammed into the back of the Frenchman's car, puncturing a tyre. After a pit stop, Arnoux drove a storming race back up through the field to finish fourth, but it was to be his last race for the team.* **(Tom March Collection)**

1985

The Ferrari management was very unhappy about the fluctuations in Arnoux's racing performances, and it has been reported that Enzo Ferrari conducted a lengthy and candid interview with Arnoux at the beginning of the 1985 season. This does seem very unlikely because most of those who knew Enzo Ferrari during his last two to three years regard him as being incapable of any sustained effort.

In any event, by negotiation, Arnoux left the team before the second race of the season in Portugal, and was replaced by young Swedish driver Stefan Johansson. That year, Alboreto won the Canadian GP (Johansson second) and also the German race. Prost and McLaren-TAG were the top combination in 1985.

1986

There were no major changes at Ferrari and it was a very poor year for the team. Ferrari failed to win a single race, and the team's fourth place in the Championship with 37 points contrasts strongly with the 141 points of the winning Williams-Honda team. The point has to be made, however, that GP success tends to be cyclical; most contenders who stay the course for a reasonable time have years that are dramatically exciting and successful, and others that are abysmal.

'The Old Man'

Born: 20 February 1898 (Modena, Italy)
Died: 14 August 1988 (Modena)

This is just a brief mention of how he led his life on a daily basis in Modena, and reflects what his one-time personal secretary Romolo Tavoni has said about him (see Appendix 4).

Enzo Anselmo Ferrari led a very quiet life, and ate and drank very moderately. In the morning he would visit the cemetery where his parents, wife Laura, and son Dino were buried, and he then visited Antonio D'Elia's barber's shop for a shave. After he had drunk a cappuccino, he would go to the factory to start his working day. He would have lunch in a small restaurant in Maranello, and in the evening he had dinner with his family.

They lived very modestly in a small house. All the money that he made he invested in the factory. He was paranoid about borrowing money from banks. He told Tavoni that if he borrowed from any of the three banks in Modena, then the managers could discuss his borrowings over lunch, and before he knew what was happening they would be foreclosing on the factory.

1987

Gerhard Berger replaced Johansson at Ferrari in 1987. It proved another year of Williams success – the Didcot team won the Constructors' Championship, and its drivers Piquet and Mansell took the first two places in the driver rankings. For most of the year the F1-87 achieved little, but Berger gave the team great cause for hope by winning the last two races of the season at Suzuka in Japan and Adelaide in Australia.

1988

Ferrari was still racing its V6 turbocharged cars, and these were restricted to 2.5 bar pressure and only 150 litres of fuel, as the racing authorities once more favoured normally aspirated cars. The 1988 season was largely dominated by McLaren and its drivers Senna and Prost. Ferrari's only substantial success was at Monza where Berger and Alboreto delighted the Tifosi by taking the first two places. There were a few other places during the year, and Berger was third in the Drivers' Championship with Ferrari finishing second among the constructors, but the team's total of points was 65 compared to the 199 of McLaren-Honda.

Enzo Ferrari had been seriously ill with kidney trouble and, although he fought to the end, his life had slowly been ebbing away for some time, and he died at the age of 90 on 14 August 1988. His death was not registered for two days, at his request, because his birth was registered two days late. After his death, Fiat took full control of the company.

Footnote

Over twenty years have elapsed since Ferrari's death, and the team continued to struggle for some years. Now, following Michael Schumacher's seven World Championships (two at Benetton and five at Ferrari) Ferrari is very different. It is an international (as opposed to a narrowly Italian) team and it has become one of the two teams consistently at the top. Racing went through a period when Ferrari was unbeatable, but this ended with Schumacher's last win in the Drivers' Championship in 2004. Now there is increasingly a situation where racing is fought out between several major manufacturers, Mercedes-Benz (part-owners of McLaren), BMW, Ferrari (Fiat), Renault and Toyota.

'The Organisation of Ferrari'

by Mike Hawthorn

(Works driver)

(from *Autosport*, 23 October 1953, in edited form)

Although I expect that readers of *Autosport* are familiar with the technical aspects of the works Ferrari cars, possibly they are not so informed on the general make-

Below: *Mike Hawthorn is seen at the International Trophy meeting at Silverstone in May 1953 when he drove both a Tipo 500 car in the Trophy race and a Tipo 340 sports car in the Production Sports Car race. In this photograph he is in conversation with Giulio Ramponi (on the right). Leslie Hawthorn (partly hidden) is on the left, and Luigi Bazzi has his back to the camera.*
(Guy Griffiths Collection)

up of the firm's racing organisation. Ferrari has always been reticent in disclosing details of its behind-the-scenes activities, but, in view of its sensational withdrawal last September from active participation in racing [see Appendix 1], I feel that a short description would now be in order, and enable a comparison to be made with other great teams of the past.

The firm has two establishments, one in Modena itself, which deals with the sales and repair of the standard products, and the other about ten miles outside the town (near Maranello) that is the main works. The Maranello establishment is an ultra-modern structure, and with the exception of the front office, is a single-storey building. The area occupied is of very modest proportions, but the space available is utilised to the full, and apart from the usual offices, houses body, machine, chassis, and final assembly shops, a drawing office, and an engine test house.

The foregoing departments deal with both standard and racing designs as part of the normal programme, but a special racing department handles the assembly, maintenance, and testing of the racing cars. This department has its own mechanics who are, of course, carefully picked. Enzo Ferrari also has an office at Maranello, but his main business is conducted from Modena.

Ferrari does not manufacture its own castings, and even the majority of chassis are made elsewhere. The policy seems to be to leave basic manufacturing processes to the individual specialists, and to me this seems very sound. Ferrari is thus able to concentrate on the finishing and assembly of the parts, and the machine shop is magnificently equipped to cope with the intricate problems called for in their design.

Perhaps the greatest contrast between Ferrari and any British firm making racing cars is the way the former plans its future programme. A modified design for even the current formula is under discussion by the chief designer, Lampredi, and Enzo Ferrari about two years before the car is required. In some cases two engine designs may have equal merits, and the decision is then taken to build both. The final choice is only made after the two engines have been thoroughly tested.

In the case of last season's cars, the first engine was running and the rest of the car was well under way by mid-summer of last year. It should be realised that this car was not very different from its predecessors; a totally new design might be ready even earlier, as indeed happened last February when the 2.5-litre was raced some 15 months before it was expected to be needed.

Having tested the engine to the firm's satisfaction, the car is assembled in the racing department, and the initial tests take place on the long straight road that the works stand on, and at the nearby Modena aerodrome. Testing on the open road is viewed benevolently by the local authorities and, of course, the local citizenry are delighted whenever a red car appears. Comparisons are reputed to be odious, but sometimes it makes one a little wistful.

I went to the works in November and was measured for my car, which was finally ready the following month. It says much for the quality of the test-bed work that I climbed into the completed car for the first time at Modena aerodrome, drove about ten laps and then the car was sent back to the works for a final check-over before being wrapped in a protective covering for shipment to Argentina.

We were usually escorted by a large OM lorry, which held all four cars, and one smaller lorry carrying a workshop, spares, and a complete spare engine. The exception to this was Argentina, where no lorries accompanied the team. If a

Above: *Seen here at the presentation of the awards at the May 1953 Silverstone meeting are Stirling Moss (who won the Touring Car race) and Mike Hawthorn.* (Guy Griffiths Collection)

spare practice car was considered necessary, this was transported in another lorry.

Enzo Ferrari never goes to races as he says he cannot stand the strain, and therefore when 'on the road' we were all under the orders of the team

Below: *Mike Hawthorn drove this Superleggera Touring-bodied Tipo 340 4.1-litre Ferrari to a win in the Production Sports Car race at the Silverstone meeting in May 1953.* (Guy Griffiths Collection)

Above: *In early 1953 Enzo Ferrari was critical of Mike Hawthorn's driving, and did not think that he was trying hard enough. All doubts were overcome when Hawthorn drove this Tipo 500 car to a win in the French GP, finishing fractionally ahead of 1951 World Champion Juan Fangio (Maserati).* (LAT Photographic)

manager Ugolini, who had complete control of the équipe at a race, made all arrangements, gave the drivers their race instructions, and he also lap-scored. The drivers are left to their own devices between races and do not travel with the team; they make their own way to the venue, using their own transport, or sharing with each other.

Normally, the team has two mechanics per car, the chief mechanic being Meazza, but this season [1953] Parenti took over at most meetings because the former was required at the works. Parenti, as I expect readers know, may be recognised by his magnificent corporation, which was frequently the butt of lurid jokes by the rest of us. He took it all very well, though. He is a most excellent mechanic and his excitement during the heat of battle never quite got the better of his mechanical training.

In addition to the mechanics and the trade representatives, we had several other personnel with the team. Amarotti's job was to make a note of the cars' fuel and oil consumption, the various temperature readings, and any faults reported by the drivers. This he did during practising and at the conclusion of every race. Bucci, who is a master of the mystical art of taking plug readings and tuning Weber carburettors, attended to the actual tuning of the cars. With the four cars to look after, he was kept very busy.

I feel that when any comparison is made with the great Germans of pre-war days, it should be remembered that last season Ferraris were racing very nearly every weekend, frequently at places further apart than those with which the Germans had to contend.

When our racing commitments would not permit sending the cars back to Modena for inspection, a suitable garage was hired locally, and the cars were completely stripped and reassembled before the next race. Considering the enormous racing mileages covered by each car, I think that reliability was one of the most outstanding features of the design, and was one which certainly gave me great confidence as a driver.

I am often asked if we will ever see the 'prancing horse' on a car's scuttle again. I have read in the newspapers that Enzo Ferrari has decided to re-enter Grand Prix racing next year, but, as everyone knows, we drivers are the last to be told anything, and until I do hear it from Maranello, I will assume that nothing has been finally fixed. Anyway, I can only give thanks to Ferrari for giving me the opportunity to gain such priceless experience, driving with the world's best.

Memories of a Works Ferrari Driver

by Gino Munaron

I was born on 2 April 1928 in Turin – so I am in my 81st year [this discussion took place in June 2008]. My father, Ramiro Munaron, was born on 19 January and every year my father and mother used to go for a drive to celebrate his birthday. On his birthday in 1928 my mother, who was a very good driver, was at the wheel of a Lancia Lambda. There was a fast road between Turin and Monte Carlo and they had been to Monte Carlo and were now returning.

At that time, Lancia used the road for test purposes. Of course, the manufacturers produced the chassis of the car and coachbuilders built the body. Lancia's chief test driver was Gismondi, and suddenly he overtook my mother with the Lancia chassis that he was testing. My father said, 'Put your foot down', and after some miles she caught up with Gismondi, and on overtaking him she went off the road. So my career with cars started *en ventre de ma mere*. Fortunately, my parents were not injured and the accident did not hasten my birth.

Back in 1924, Enzo Ferrari was working with my father at Alfa Romeo. My father was offered the general management of Alfa Romeo at the main factory at Portello in Milan – provided that he joined the Fascist party. He told them he had nothing against Mussolini, but he would be no better a manager whether or not he was a member of the party.

But they insisted, so he left and was given the Alfa Romeo agencies for Piemonte and Emilia Romagna. Enzo Ferrari went with him and they worked together for seven months in 1924. Then they fell out and Enzo Ferrari went back to Alfa Romeo. Ferrari started Scuderia Ferrari some years later, while my father continued to run his own company.

My father and Enzo Ferrari were the same sort of person, with the same determination and long memory. They did not speak again until 1949, 25 years later. Both he and Enzo Ferrari were at the Motor Show in Turin. Pininfarina and most other important people in the Italian Motor Industry were there and persuaded them to resume relations.

My father drove regularly in the 1927 Mille Miglia road race. The first time that the event was held, in 1927, he finished eighth in general classification with a Merosi-designed push-rod RLSS Alfa Romeo. The following year he drove a Lancia Lambda to 19th place, and then, in 1929, he was eighth in general classification with an Alfa Romeo 6C 1750SS. His final appearance in the race was in 1932 when he drove an Alfa Romeo 8C 2300, but retired.

My ambition was to become a sailor, and in 1942 when I was 14 my father obtained a place for me in the Livorno Naval Academy, but the Academy moved temporarily to Tarento in the south of Italy and stopped taking any more students. My mother died, and after my father and I had discussed the family position, I decided to stay at home, and I went to the University of Turin. As a family we had strong motor racing connections. My father knew Nuvolari well – he was often at our house – and Count Trossi was my godfather.

There was an occasion when we were in the Dolomite Mountains with Nuvolari; I was about eight years old, and he was driving a big eight-cylinder Alfa Romeo with twin superchargers. He said to me, 'Come on Gino, let's go for a drive in the mountains.' We went round a few corners and I told him, 'You are not driving very fast.' So Nuvolari gave me a demonstration of his speed, power-sliding through corners. That was my first experience of high-speed motoring.

I first competed in 1949 when I ran in the Gran Saint Bernardo hill climb with a 'special' that a good friend,

Above: *This is the very peculiar Nardi that Gino Munaron co-drove at Le Mans in 1955. Here the car is seen during practice, but a number of modifications were made before the race.* (Tom March Collection)

Below: *Another view of the twin-boom Nardi, with Gino Munaron at the wheel shortly after the start of the race. There is now a series of slots to draw air to the radiator, and a vent in the left front wing for the discharge of hot underbonnet air. The Nardi survived until the third hour when it was blown off the road by the slipstream from Hawthorn's Jaguar that passed too closely.* (Tom March Collection)

Count Paolo Cordero di Montezemolo, and I had been building since 1947 – he was a cousin of my father and also, of course, the father of Luca di Montezemolo, who is now the President of Ferrari.

This car had a Ford V8 side-valve engine with an Ardun overhead inlet valve cylinder head designed by Zora Arkos-Duntov (who later worked for General Motors on the development of the Chevrolet Corvette). We used a Lancia Astura gearbox and a Fiat final drive, and it had a two-seater sports body. About three-quarters of the way up the course, there is a small village with a very tight hairpin bend. The road changed from tarmac to a loose surface, and there I crashed.

After that I started racing with Enrico Nardi, who provided me with a car powered by a twin-cylinder BMW engine. He was a very nice man and you could see that in Italy he was the alternative man to Ferrari. The BMW engine was modified and the car was very light. With the Nardi I scored many successes in my class. In 1951 Franco Rol asked me to ride with him in the Mille Miglia in his Alfa Romeo. The car was one of the experimental 2443cc six-cylinder cars that appeared regularly in the 1,000-mile race between 1948 and 1952. They were very fast, but reliability was something of a problem, and, although we were going well, we retired after the Rome control.

As late as Le Mans in 1955 I drove the twin-boom Nardi with Damonte, who had designed it together with the architect Carlo Mollino. This had a 735cc twin overhead camshaft Giannini engine with the transmission in the left boom, and the driver seated in

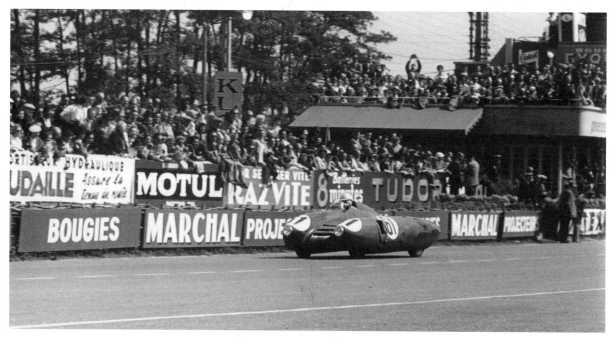

FERRARI: THE MEN FROM MARANELLO

the right boom. The radiator was mounted between the booms. Although this Nardi was criticised by many people, I thought that it went well for such a small car, and that it had handled nicely. Unfortunately, it retired in the third hour when it was blown off the track by the slipstream from Hawthorn's D-type Jaguar, that passed me too closely on the Mulsanne Straight.

It was earlier that year that Nardi took me to meet Enzo Ferrari. Enrico told Ferrari, 'Gino is a young boy and he is very fast, but he is also very safe.' Ferrari said to me, 'Your father doesn't mind you talking to me? There has been enough of us not talking.' This had been going on for so long because my father was like an elephant and never forgot anything – and Ferrari was worse.

So Ferrari gave me the opportunity to test a car, which proved very successful. This was a Mondial four-cylinder 2-litre sports car. This and the 3-litre Monza were identical apart from the engine size. The 2-litre Ferrari was heavy compared with the rival Maserati A6GCS, which was a fantastic car, light and stable. They were very powerful, very fast cars, but the handling was poor. Lampredi had no racing experience and he had no experience at all behind the wheel of faster cars, which explains why Ferraris designed by him handled so badly.

I became an official driver for Ferrari in 1955. During the first two years I was, in effect, a special customer. I had to buy my car – on very favourable terms – but everything else, including preparation of the car, transport to the race, and accommodation was paid by Ferrari. I received 50 per cent of the starting money and prize money. I appeared for the team mainly in Italian races. One of my very first drives for Ferrari was in the Hyères 12 Hours in which I partnered André Canonica, who was a restaurateur in Geneva. We drove steadily and won from the three private DB3S Aston Martins of the Australian Kangaroo Stable.

Then I drove a Monza again in the Imola Grand Prix, where I took fifth place; the opposition was strong and Perdisa (Maserati) and Maglioli (with another Monza) took the first two places. Another fifth place followed at Caserta, but as I was young and relatively inexperienced, Ferrari was satisfied. In July I drove in the Messina 10 Hours night race in Sicily, but I retired because the differential seized up, causing me to do a complete spin.

Castellotti was leading the race with his Tipo 750 Monza, and I was in second place with my Tipo 500 Mondial, leading the 2000cc class. At the Targa Florio in October I co-drove with Carroll Shelby a private Monza entered by American Tony Parravano. We were going

Above: *Gino Munaron, partnered by Geneva restaurateur André Canonica, drove this Ferrari Tipo 750 to a win in the 1955 Hyères 12 Hours race. He is seen, here, at the wheel of the car that was a standard production model with Scaglietti-built body. (Gino Munaron)*

Below: *Gino is seen here at the wheel of the Tony Parravano-owned Tipo 750 Ferrari Monza that he shared with Carroll Shelby in the 1955 Targa Florio. Munaron was holding fifth place with this works-supported car when he crashed because of a seized final drive. The body of the car was built by Scaglietti, and it was a special style that was also used on Parravano's Tipo 121LM. (Gino Munaron)*

very well in a race dominated by the Mercedes-Benz team, and I was holding fifth place when I crashed because of a seized final drive.

My 1956 season followed much the same pattern. In June I was entered in the Paris 1,000km race on the 4.38-mile (7km) road circuit at Montlhéry that incorporated part of the banking. Again, I was driving a 3-litre Monza, and my co-driver was a chap called Pierre Meyrat. The race was run in foul weather, heavy rain and strong winds, and I had completed 40 laps. I was in second place behind Behra/Rosier with a Maserati, and I was due to hand over to my co-driver.

The section of the circuit through the Ascari Curve was very bumpy. It was named for Antonio Ascari who had crashed his P2 Alfa Romeo there with fatal results in the 1925 French Grand Prix. The road was very bumpy and it was followed by a left-hand curve where you had to brake heavily. When I got there, I was going flat-out in fifth gear.

When the car took off over the bump, I crashed heavily, finishing upside down. Trintignant was following me and saw the accident. He went back to the pits and told them that I must surely be dead. The Monza was a terrific car to drive, but it was absolutely lethal because it was much too fast for the road-holding. Many drivers were killed with these cars, including the great Alberto Ascari, and the French called it 'Le Tuer'.

In the 172-mile (277km) Bari Grand Prix held on the Lungomare circuit along the Adriatic coastline in July, I drove the new and improved Testa Rossa, which got its name from the fact that the camshaft covers were painted red. It was for me a very good race and I finished third, close behind Jean Behra and Cesare Perdisa with their works Maseratis.

Once again I was at the wheel of a 2-litre Ferrari Testa Rossa in the sports car race at Pescara in August. Because of the heat on the Adriatic coastline, the race started at nine in the morning, and I drove well to finish third behind Manzon (with a French Gordini) and Taruffi (Maserati). After 500km (310 miles) only four seconds covered the first three finishers.

The following year I drove the 2-litre Testa Rossa model frequently, and in April I finished fourth overall and won my class in the very wet 670-mile (1,078km) Tour of Sicily. It was a very hard, demanding course, and as usual I drove solo. The first three places in this race were taken by Olivier Gendebien (works Ferrari 3780cc Tipo 315S), Piero Taruffi, and Giorgio Scarlatti; the second- and third-place drivers were both at the wheel of 3-litre Tipo 300S Maseratis.

I then drove the Testa Rossa in the Mille Miglia – the only time that I drove in the 1,000-mile race – and it was one of my most successful races. I had, of course, previously ridden as a passenger in the race. Before Verona I had ignition problems caused by magneto trouble, and the car was firing on only one set of sparking plugs. I lost 500rpm in fourth gear, which was the equivalent of about 19mph (31kph). With the rear axle ratio fitted, the car should do 157mph (252kph) at 7,500rpm, but with the 6,900/7,000rpm that I was getting I could do little more than 138mph (222kph), not much more than a 2000cc GT car.

At my first stop at Ravenna, the Ferrari Technical Director, Mino Amorotti, told me that I was lying second in my class, and I explained the problem to him. I was away in less than 25 seconds with strict instructions to look for the missing revs under my right foot! After the fastest stretch of the race to Pescara I had averaged 104mph (168kph) and had a painful right foot that had been bent backwards by my pressure on the accelerator pedal.

On the run from Cremona to Mantua I saw a red car in my mirror, and when it closed up right behind me I recognised Alfonso de Portago. He drew level with me, slowed a little as we crossed Castellucchio, a small village, before we reached Goito, site of the famous battle of 30 May 1848. It was fought between the Piedmontese and the Austrian army, and was won by the Piedmontese during the First Italian War of Independence. De Portago looked across at me questioningly. I replied by making an inelegant gesture at the bonnet of my car; he smiled, nodded his head in a goodbye gesture and accelerated away.

It was his last smile. I arrived on the scene of Alfonso's fatal accident at Guidizzolo, 23 miles (36km) from Brescia, a minute or so after the disaster happened. The road was blocked and my speed was reduced to a crawl; a cable hung down in the centre of the road from a broken telegraph pole. I had no choice but to pass under the cable, which dragged along the bonnet and tail of my Ferrari. Overall, I finished eighth and I won the 2000cc class. It was a satisfactory result in a tragic race. With my other successes in Italian races that year I was Italian Champion in the 2-litre class.

In 1957, the Reims 12 Hour race was run as an event for Grand Touring cars, and I drove our Ferrari 250GT single-handed during the last eight hours after my co-driver Madere refused to touch the steering wheel. Reims was a very fast circuit, and the 12-hour races started at midnight, and I think that he had become afraid of it after something had happened in the dark. So I finished third behind two similar Ferraris driven by Paul Frère/Olivier Gendebien and Phil Hill/Wolfgang

Seidel. In all the circumstances, from my point of view, it was a very good result.

At the 1957 Swedish Grand Prix meeting at Kristianstad I drove a 2-litre Testa Rossa in the 2000cc race in the morning, and finished second. Then, later that day, came the 1,000km sports car Grand Prix in which I was partnered in the same car by one Batista, a nephew of Fulgencio Batista, the Cuban dictator who was overthrown by Fidel Castro in 1959. We finished second in the 2000cc class behind another Ferrari.

With the imposition of the 3-litre capacity limit for sports cars in World Championship events in 1958, the works Ferrari team raced the Tipo 250 Testa Rossa cars. These were V12s based on Colombo's original engine design with improvements. I still took part in fairly minor Italian races as well as international events.

My co-driver in the 1958 Targa Florio was Wolfgang Seidel, and we were holding fourth place at half-distance. All went well until the last lap when Seidel shot off the circuit into a field. He split the sump without realising what had happened and retired when the engine seized. It was a very disappointing outcome after we had driven so well for so long.

In the Nürburgring 1,000km race I was again partnered by Wolfgang Seidel. We had problems at this race because the organisers insisted on supplying their own fuel that was not of the same quality as the Shell normally used by Ferrari. Ferrari threatened to withdraw from the race, but eventually relented and agreed to let his cars run. Despite all the efforts by the mechanics, our Testa Rossa was running especially badly, far worse than the other team cars, and we did well to finish fifth.

Lancia had asked Ferrari whether they would release me so that I could drive a Lancia Aurelia B20 GT car in the Rally of the Midnight Sun held in Sweden in early June. It was a round in the European Rally Championship. I was partnered by Ciro Basadonna, an Italian resident in Geneva. He had partnered Louis Chiron when he won the Monte Carlo Rally in 1954 and, later, in 1958 he partnered Luigi Villoresi on his winning drive in the Greek Acropolis Rally.

I had a bad crash when I lost control of the car. I was thrown out of the Lancia that landed on top of me and trapped me underneath it. No one tried to rescue me – they assumed I was dead – until I shouted for help. I crushed my pelvis and broke it in four places. As a result I spent 106 days in hospital lying flat on a wooden board. It was absolutely terrible – it was soul-destroying – but there was no alternative.

The first 21 days were in Sweden and they used my body like an experiment. I was then flown to Italy where an Italian surgeon carried out two operations. When I

was in hospital in Turin I was visited by a doctor sent by Enzo Ferrari. He told me, 'I am afraid that I have to tell you that in my opinion you will never walk again.' To begin with I could only move my arms, but gradually my condition improved, and eventually I was able to walk, although one leg was 3cm shorter than the other and I had to have another operation.

Despite all these problems, I was fit enough to drive a Ferrari 250GT in the fourth and last Venezuelan Grand Prix at Caracas on 23 November 1965. The event was run over a distance of 469 miles (755km) as a road race, with the cars departing at intervals of one minute from Caracas, traversing mountain roads and main roads, with a final stretch from Valencia back to Caracas. Jean Behra won the race with a Ferrari 250GT from local driver Julio Pola with a similar car, and I finished third with my 250GT.

It had become obvious that I had no future with Ferrari, and I left at the end of 1958. I had entered with a 2-litre Testa Rossa in the Naples Grand Prix that was held in April 1958 as a sports car race. If the car is properly geared for the circuit, you should be able to achieve maximum revs in top gear on the straight, but I found with this car that it was so over-geared that I could not get out of third.

Tavoni was there, and I said to him, 'Romolo, the gearing is all wrong and I cannot engage fourth.' 'No,' he said, 'don't worry. That is the decision of the boss.' What Ferrari was trying to do was to give the impression that I was no longer good enough to be a works driver. So, Giulio Cabianca with an OSCA MT4 won the race, with other OSCA drivers second and third, although it was a race that the Ferrari should have won.

During the 1959 season I twice entered Formula 2 races with an OSCA that I bought myself. The OSCA was not a very competitive car and I had mechanical problems with it. In the Syracuse race in April, I was still running at the finish, but I was too far behind, because of two long pit stops, to be classified as a finisher. I also entered the car in the Pau race held over a course in the streets of the city in May, but again I had mechanical problems and I retired early in the race.

I shared a new Ferrari 250GT Berlinetta with Lino Fayen at Le Mans that year. Fayen was quite a good Parisian driver who had moved to South America to live in Caracas. The works Testa Rossas failed, and works Aston Martin DBR1s took the first two places, and we finished sixth, which was quite a respectable result. At the end of July I drove an OSCA in the two-hour race on the Circuit des Charades at Clermont-Ferrand. The race was won by Peter Ashdown, who was sensationally quick with his 1100cc Lola, but I took third place overall behind Jean Behra with a works Porsche, and second in our class. It was poor Behra's last race before his fatal crash at the German Grand Prix meeting at Avus.

The following January I travelled out to Buenos Aires to drive a 250GT with Todaro in the 1,000km race. Todaro was a Sicilian from Palermo, and he was a very good customer of Enzo Ferrari. The car was an old 1957 model, and although we finished back in ninth place, it was good enough to win the GT category.

In sports car racing in 1960 I drove Tipo 'Bird-cage' Maseratis for the Camoradi team (the name was an abbreviation of Casner Motor Racing Division) and it was run by American motor trader Lloyd Casner with some financial support from the Goodyear tyre company. There really wasn't enough money to run the team, and Casner had advertised in the American *Road & Track* magazine for contributions of not less than $10! I joined the team and I paid a nominal sum for my drives. These Maseratis proved very fast, but they were unreliable.

The Camoradi entry retired in the Buenos Aires 1,000km race in January, and then three of these cars with American drivers ran at Sebring. Moss and Gurney had led the race with a Camoradi car, and built up an enormous lead, only to retire four hours from the finish because of rear axle failure. The other two Camoradi Tipo 61s also retired. There were doubts about running in the Targa Florio, but eventually it was decided to run a single car for Nino Vaccarella and me. We worked our way into the lead, but two laps from the finish Nino went off the road. He had holed the fuel tank, and when he ran out of fuel on a bend, the engine cut out, he lost control, and crashed.

At the Nürburgring 1,000km race, the Camoradi team entered 'Bird-cage' cars for Moss/Gurney and Masten Gregory and myself. The weather was dreadful, with drizzle at the start, and mist that gradually thickened until visibility was reduced to less than 100yd by rolling

Below: *Munaron was partnered by Wolfgang Seidel at the wheel of this works Testa Rossa Ferrari in the 1958 Targa Florio. They were holding fourth place when Seidel went off the road, splitting the bottom of the engine and losing the engine oil. He rejoined the race, but retired almost immediately because of a seized engine.* (Gino Munaron)

FERRARI: THE MEN FROM MARANELLO

Above: *At Le Mans in 1960 Gino shared this Camoradi Team Maserati Tipo 61 with Giorgio Scarlatti, but they retired during the third hour because of electrical problems.* (Gino Munaron)

banks of fog. Because it was cold, the oil was not heating up, and the Maseratis were running with excessive oil pressure. This caused a fractured oil pipe on the Moss/Gurney car, but despite the time lost in the pits while the pipe was changed, they regained the lead and won the race. Masten and I were rather slower, but we finished fifth, and that was quite satisfactory.

The 'Bird-cage' cars failed at Le Mans. I was sharing a car with Giorgio Scarlatti, and I started the race. During the second hour I noticed smoke in the cockpit and I was naturally worried whether the car was likely to catch fire. I stopped on the Mulsanne Straight and I could find nothing wrong. In fact, the starter motor had burnt out, so I was unable to restart. The other two Tipo 61s entered in this race also retired.

I also drove in Formula 1 with a Cooper-Castellotti. This was a private venture in which I paid my way, and the cars consisted of Cooper chassis into which Ferrari four-cylinder SuperSqualo engines and Colotti five-speed gearboxes had been squeezed. These cars took a long time to sort out, and the Cooper company gave us no help at all.

At Monaco I failed to qualify as a starter, but I did start in the French Grand Prix, only to retire because of gearbox failure. We arrived late at the British race at Silverstone, but I was allowed to start from the back of the grid. Not that it did much good, because the car was plagued by mechanical problems and I finished 15th, all

of seven laps in arrears. We stayed in England to compete in the Silver City Trophy at Brands Hatch on what in England was August Bank Holiday Monday, and it was another poor race in which I finished right at the tail of the field.

We missed the Portuguese race and then ran in the Italian Grand Prix on the combined banked track and road circuit at Monza. The British teams boycotted the race, and Giulio Cabianca finished a good fourth, but I retired because of loss of oil pressure when I was holding third place behind the works Ferraris of von Trips and Mairesse.

During 1961, Count Volpi di Misurata wanted me to drive his 250 Testa Rossa 3-litre V12 in the Rhodes Grand Prix in Greece. I agreed and I won the race easily. It was about this time that one of my friends convinced me that I should give up racing because of my family commitments. I had driven in 41 races with Ferraris; I had retired ten times, and I was classified in the other 31 races. My first victory for Ferrari was in the 12 Hours race at Hyères in 1955 and my last at Rhodes in 1961. All in all, a surprisingly good record.

Memories of Enzo Ferrari

by Romolo Tavoni

(Secretary 1950–61/Team Manager 1957–61)

Enzo Ferrari's reluctance to attend races (although he liked to be at the circuit during practice) dated back to the 1934 Coppa Acerbo. In this race, young Algerian Guy Moll, one of the most promising drivers of his generation, crashed at high speed and suffered fatal injuries when his car was caught by a gust of wind and went out of control, hitting the side of a house. In the Scuderia Ferrari pit, when Moll made a routine stop, Enzo Ferrari had urged the young man to drive harder, and afterwards he held himself responsible for the accident that ensued.

What Ferrari needed was a team manager who would do everything that he wanted and in the way he wanted; who would report from the circuit by telephone twice a day, and who would not argue with him; in other words, a complete sycophant. Nello Ugolini, who is regarded in Italy as one of the greatest racing managers of all time, had been team manager in pre-war Scuderia Ferrari days. After the war, between 1947 and 1951, it was Federico Giberti, who had been with Ferrari since 1930 and was one of his closest collaborators. Ugolini returned to Ferrari in 1951 and he held the post of Sport Director through to May 1955.

Relations between Enzo Ferrari and Ugolini were always difficult. Ugolini was a supremely confident team manager, with vast experience and great ability. He succeeded in running the team with a good measure of autonomy, but when he left Ferrari, it may not have been because of friction between them, but because he wanted more money, which Enzo Ferrari stubbornly refused to pay, claiming that he could not afford it. Tavoni has hinted that if Ugolini had stayed he would have got his extra money, and that Ugolini knew that. The reason for leaving may have been deeper.

So, in late 1955, when Scuderia Ferrari's fortunes were at a very low ebb in the face of immensely strong opposition – that year the team won only one World Championship GP (Maurice Trintignant with a 625 at Monaco) and one round in the World Sports Car Championship (the Buenos Aires 1,000km race) – the team was faffing around trying to find a new race director.

Ferrari was persuaded that journalist Eraldo Sculati from Rome was a suitable man to take on the job, and he did it with considerable competence until after the Argentinian races in January 1957. The original arrangement had been for just the one season, and although Sculati would have stayed on, Enzo Ferrari did not want him. Sculati talked to his friends and claimed too much personal credit for the team's successes, and that was totally unacceptable to Enzo.

There was one man who Ferrari could trust: Romolo Tavoni, who had been his private secretary and secretary to Scuderia Ferrari since January 1950. Tavoni had learned a great deal from Ugolini about team management, and he had regularly attended races from 1951 onwards so that he could report back to the 'Old Man'. When Ferrari first interviewed Tavoni eight years previously, he saw a man who was intelligent, able, but pliable and would do his complete bidding. Now Tavoni had considerable experience of both Ferrari and the job, and he was the obvious choice for team manager.

The drivers liked Tavoni, but they never respected him and certainly never trusted him. As for Ferrari, the opposite seemed to apply in that one could go so far as to say that he never liked the tall, thin, swarthy Tavoni, but trusted him completely. During the time that he was racing manager, Tavoni was deeply distressed by the deaths of so many drivers – Castellotti, de Portago,

Musso, Collins, Behra, von Trips – and it is doubtful whether he would have been able to carry on in that post had he not been sacked along with other senior management in the autumn of 1961.

Romolo Oscar Tavoni was born on 30 January 1926 in Modena, and his father owned and worked a small farm about 100m from the family home. He was educated in Modena, first for five years in a primary school at Casenava and then at a school in Modena, and finally at the Modena Technical Institute. He was trained in book-keeping and accountancy and his first job was at Maserati. He joined that company in September 1945.

'I was very happy at Maserati because it was a big factory, making mostly machine tools after the war, but there was a small competition department and it was there that I met the surviving Maserati brothers, Ettore, Bindo, and Ernesto Maserati who had left in 1947 to set up their own company again, OSCA in Bologna. I also came to know other Maserati racing personnel, including Guerino Bertocchi, Luigi Parenti and Alessandro Tomasini. I met for the first time Luigi Villoresi and Alberto Ascari who raced Maseratis in 1946–8. I also came to know Adolfo and Omer Orsi. My main work at Maserati was as a transport administrator.'

The early post-war years were a very difficult time for Maserati because of the Communist unions. A national referendum was held in Italy in 1946 when 50.2 per cent voted for a republic and 49.8 per cent voted for retaining the monarchy. So Italy became a republic by a very fine margin. The Communist party in Emilia Romagna held 94 per cent of the elected seats and wanted to make the Maserati company a co-operative, but Adolfo Orsi, who controlled Maserati, resisted the Communists and was in total confrontation with them. There was no room for compromise. The factory was blockaded, the sports car programme was abandoned and there was no work for Tavoni, who left Maserati in September 1949.

'We were a poor family and I desperately needed a job. I had hoped to get work in a bank, Credito Italiana in Modena, but I was unable to, even with the help of the Orsis, so I wrote to a number of companies, including Ferrari. The Ferrari factory wrote back and said that they might have a position for me. In the ordinary way, the rivalry was such that no one who had worked at Maserati would get a job at Ferrari. When Enzo Ferrari interviewed me, he instructed me: 'You will say nothing, you will only answer my questions.'

I joined Ferrari on 16 January 1950, but my job was terrible at first. Enzo Ferrari was a strong man and an intelligent man, and at first he was very difficult to deal with.'

Even so, when Tavoni and Ferrari first met, there seemed to be an instant recognition, an understanding of their ability to work together.

'Ferrari said to me, 'You are my Secretary and you are also Secretary of Scuderia Ferrari. Fifty per cent you work for me personally and fifty per cent you work for Ferrari. Today it is for me. The two must be separated. When I talk to you, there are two situations: one is private, one is factory.'

It was difficult: Ferrari had his mother, he had family – Laura Ferrari and Dino – and he had a second family of which Laura Ferrari knew nothing. It was very difficult also for me, for whatever Ferrari told me in relation to the family, I could not repeat. Some, but only some, of what Ferrari told me about the factory I could repeat.

I was very poor and I had no bank account or cheque book. I had no real knowledge of financial matters other than book-keeping, but I soon learned. Ferrari explained that he would give me money to pass on to his mother, his family, and to the other person. He always said 'other person' and not second wife or anything similar. At the time his other son was known as Piero Lardi and not Piero Lardi Ferrari. In any case, it was impossible in Italy at this time for Ferrari to recognise his illegitimate son.

Ferrari said to me, 'Your name is Tavoni, your first name is Romolo; you are a bookkeeper and understand accounts. I will give you instructions, and these must be followed very closely. What I want, you will know because I shall tell you clearly. You must do only what I want and not change what I have told you.' But there are, of course, times in life when even if you are someone else's employee or their representative, you have to exercise your own judgement and to get that judgement right. I managed to get that judgement right or else I would have been out of Ferrari.

It was, of course, very difficult to ensure that Ferrari was satisfied. In any case, after three months in my first year at Ferrari in 1950, he added 5,000 lire to my salary. It was his way of saying that he was satisfied, but after another two months he reduced my salary by 7,500 lire, that's a half. He told me, 'I'm not satisfied, so you will get less money.'

I told him that I was making my best efforts for him, but he said, 'You must understand, that it is not good enough.' Ferrari owned the factory, but the way he saw it, he also owned the men who worked there. Ferrari could be very kind and friendly, but he was like a bomb waiting to go off, and he would suddenly explode. He was a typical Modenese man.'

There was a very peculiar bond and understanding between Ferrari and Tavoni, and it is indeed odd the way that Tavoni was able to accept and be content with the way that Ferrari behaved.

'My job at Ferrari was fantastic because it introduced me to so many fascinating people – Ascari and Villoresi, whom I had met briefly before, Raymond Sommer, Piero Taruffi, and Giuseppe Farina, together with all the younger drivers with whom I later worked. I had detailed instructions from Ferrari, and typed up all the instructions for these drivers, which Ferrari signed. I also typed up all the letters sent to the Ferrari organisations in France, England, and Switzerland, as well as in Italy. I also made all the travel arrangements for the team, not just the details for going to race meetings.

Every Tuesday at 5pm, Ferrari had a meeting with the eight top managers. At the meeting he would talk about the factory, the team cars, production, staff, all the problems that the company faced. He would talk to each of us in turn. He would say to Bazzi, 'What is your opinion' about whatever was concerning him. Or, for example, he would ask about the readiness of a second engine. Bazzi would say, 'Mr Ferrari, I do not have the second engine ready yet.' Ferrari would explode, 'Why Luigi, is it not ready?'

Bazzi would say, 'Mr Ferrari, I worked on the engine ten or twelve hours every day and there has not been enough time to have it ready.' Ferrari would shout at him. 'But there are 24 hours in each day!' Ferrari would say the factory is not the building, not the machinery; it is the minds of the people – Bazzi, Forghieri or whoever, what they think, their opinions, and how they worked for

him. 'We have created the car, but before that we had to create the men to build it.' Sometimes Ferrari would also say what we had done was fine, it was very good, but the next day he would say that it was all wrong! Ferrari was simpatico e terribile – terribile e simpatico!

As Secretary to Scuderia Ferrari, I knew Aurelio Lampredi, the Project Engineer, very well. When the Ferrari company was first set up, it made machine tools, but as the war was coming to an end in Italy, Bazzi and others who had stayed with Ferrari after he left Alfa Romeo urged him to build cars. Ferrari told them, 'Yes, we will try', so he arranged for Giuseppe Busso, a designer and mathematician, who had become Satta's assistant in 1939, to work on a design for him. Busso started work at Maranello, but he was not happy and returned to Alfa Romeo.

So Giaocchino Colombo designed the first Ferraris, but a problem was that Ferrari and others were not convinced that the basic Colombo V12 design was suitable for production in substantial numbers. In addition, of course, the original supercharged engine proved incapable of beating the Alfa Romeo 158s, so that is why Lampredi replaced Colombo. In his early years when he was heading design, 1950–3, Lampredi was very successful, both with his 4500cc unsupercharged cars that defeated the Alfa Romeos, and then the four-cylinder 2-litre cars with which Ascari won two World Championships.

The situation changed in 1954 when Maserati was racing the new six-cylinder 250F and Mercedes-Benz introduced their new straight-eight W196. Ferrari was struggling for success and there were many discussions about the need for a new engine. In 1952, when Lampredi was at Indianapolis with Ascari, he had carefully examined the four-cylinder Offenhauser engine. He was very impressed with the design of this and wanted to build a new four-cylinder engine with similar valve gear. He had a phenomenal memory and he could recall all the details.

Ferrari listened to his advisers and they all wanted something different: Rocchi – six cylinders; Bazzi – eight cylinders; Amorotti – 12 cylinders. But Lampredi said, 'I am responsible. Leave me to develop a special engine. This engine should be a new experience.' Lampredi decided to build a Formula 1 car for slow circuits, and proposed the two-cylinder engine. Ferrari was fascinated by this idea. It was completely original and it would be sensational.

Everyone else disagreed with the proposal, but Ferrari said, 'Why not? You will build this new engine for me, Ferrari. If it is successful, I will give you a great bonus. If this engine does not work, you will be sacked within 24 hours. One year later, in 1955, the engine ran. It was a complete failure, it developed too little power and it vibrated terribly. Ferrari sent for his employment manager and told him: 'Lampredi must leave the company within one hour and take nothing with him, not even a pencil.'

Ferrari had a disastrous year in 1955 and, having sacked Lampredi, he had no projects. After Lancia was forced to withdraw from racing, there was discussion as to whether the D50 GP cars should go with financial support from Fiat to

Ferrari or Maserati. Maserati were not interested because their 250F was so good, so the cars, equipment, and technicians all went to Ferrari. The great Vittorio Jano joined Ferrari as a consultant, but he was a complete gentleman and he would say nothing at meetings. At the end of the meeting Ferrari would ask Jano to join him for coffee, and then they made their decisions together.

Below: *Tavoni rated Mike Hawthorn as the greatest driver since the Second World War. He also rated Aurelio Lampredi very highly as a designer. Here, Hawthorn is at the wheel of the Tipo 625 car, designed by Lampredi, that he drove to second place behind team-mate González in the 1954 British Grand Prix at Silverstone.* (Tom March Collection)

Andrea Fraschetti, from Lancia, became project leader, and it was Fraschetti who led and drove every new project, notably the V12 Tipo 290 MM and its derivatives, and the V6 Dino cars. Jano would not interfere, but would give his advice when Fraschetti asked for it before others. He would always approve what Fraschetti was doing, but then would make suggestions which the project leader adopted.

Fraschetti was killed in a testing accident at Modena in 1958. He was not totally concentrating, but looking at the instruments; he put two wheels on the grass, lost control, and the car turned over, crushing him. He was a very talented designer and his death was a great loss to Ferrari. He had a racing licence and he had a project for a Formula Junior car that Ferrari would probably have built if Fraschetti had not been killed. In testing he was always only a second or so slower than the official testers.

My years as race director were my most satisfying with Ferrari. Before I took on the job, I learned everything that I could from Ugolini, who was very much my teacher and mentor. Ugolini was a very important man in Modena. He was vastly experienced; he had worked for Scuderia Ferrari in pre-war days; he had been a correspondent for Gazzetta del Sport, he knew all the factory owners in Modena, and he could smooth relationships between sub-contractors and Ferrari.

In dealing with drivers, Ugolini acted as an intermediary between them and Ferrari.

Below: *Another view of Hawthorn, seen here at the wheel of the V6 Dino 246 that was the work of Fraschetti with Jano acting as consultant. This photograph was taken during practice for the 1958 Moroccan Grand Prix (in the race Hawthorn wore a tinted visor).* (Tom March Collection)

Because of his great experience, Ugolini as well as Ferrari signed drivers' contracts. One of the things that I learned from Ugolini was the need to keep a full record. At the Tuesday meetings he produced notebooks that contained all the details of what had happened at the previous weekend's race.

These included practice and race lap times, power outputs, tyre pressures, adjustments made to the cars in practice, comments made by drivers, details of pit stops in the race, the length of these, how much fuel was taken on board, and details of problems with the cars in the race. Everything was there, so Ugolini could answer every question that Ferrari asked, and when I became race director I kept the same records.

The heads of each department – engine, gearbox, chassis, electrics – were all at the meetings. If, for example, there was an engine problem, then Ferrari asked Lampredi, who was technical director, about the problem. Ferrari was always brief, and he would ask Lampredi what he had done. When he had heard what Lampredi had to say, then Ferrari would respond, 'That is not good enough' or 'That is fine.' If he were dissatisfied, he would give terse instructions as to what should be done. A discussion on any topic rarely lasted longer than three minutes.

So, after the Argentinian races in 1957, Ferrari told Sculati that he wanted him to go because he was claiming too much of the credit that should have gone to the 'Old Man'. So, after 1 February, Ferrari had no team manager. Ferrari asked Della Casa, who was an administrative director, to take on the post. He declined because he didn't want to travel. He wanted to go on working at the factory – he had children at school, and so on. So then he asked another man at Maranello, who turned him down, and then he asked me.

Ferrari said to me, 'Do you have to stay at home all the time? I have no one else but you. Amorotti looks after the technical side and you can go as my representative and look after the organisation. You will be Sport Manager, but always remember that you will be my representative. You will also continue with your secretarial work as before.' So, when I was at the factory, I would go to work at seven in the morning and carry out my work as Sport Manager until ten. I then started my work as Secretary.

On top of this I had my wife, three daughters, and my mother to look after! The family kept quiet, because this terrible man was also very kind and he paid me 135,000 lire per month in place of the 105,000 that I received previously. If I had asked him, he would have said, 'You ask me for money? I have no money for you! If you want more money, you must work harder and longer.' Ferrari would automatically refuse to pay more money, then give it, and then say you have to work more.

As Secretary of Scuderia Ferrari, I already knew all the drivers. When he was dealing with the drivers, Ferrari was always very gentle and there were never any explosions. He told me, 'I used to be a driver, I know the stresses and pressures, and I saw my friends killed in racing accidents. Drivers take big risks, and they have families to worry about. I am not going to harass them and add to their problems. Take it easy, speak to them gently and listen to their problems, then they will always do their best.

Because Ferrari never attended a race, only practice, it was important for him to have his own ears and eyes at races, so that he would always know precisely what was happening. When he was away at a race, Giberti made a telephone call to Ferrari at 1pm and 8pm in the evening. Sculati and Ugolini also did this, and when I became Sport Manager, I did the same; so did Dragoni. Ferrari said to each of us, "You are the Sport Manager, but remember I am Ferrari."'

What follows is an example of the sort of problem that Tavoni had to discuss with Enzo Ferrari. Ferrari would lay down a minimum sum for starting money and, of course, starting money in those days was the life-blood of any racing team. What Tavoni says here is an example of a constant problem, and the race concerned matters not.

'Sometimes I would talk to Ferrari about a problem. For example, I had a problem relating to starting money for the French Grand Prix. The Automobile Club de France had offered Ferrari the equivalent of one million lire. It was not what Ferrari had asked for, which, as I reminded him, was 1.5 million lire.'

Ferrari told Tavoni, 'I will not settle for less than 1.35 million lire. When you arrive at Reims, you talk to the French Automobile Club and you tell them that the starting money must not be less than 1.5 million. If it is

1.35 million, you have to accept, but then you Tavoni will have the difference deducted from your salary. And you tell the club that Ferrari will not return next year.' When Tavoni told Ferrari that the Club had agreed to pay 1.5 million, he said, 'Tavoni, that is fantastic, I am very pleased with you.'

'In my opinion the greatest driver since the Second World War was Mike Hawthorn, and I say this because of his mechanical sympathy, his ability and also his glamour. He was a fantastic guy. Peter Collins was an absolute gentleman. I also had the highest regard for Louise Collins, and the compatibility in their marriage was exceptional. They had a wonderful relationship. Peter Collins's behaviour at Monza in 1956 when he handed his car over to Fangio is unforgettable. In Formula 1 no one else has ever voluntarily handed their car over to another driver.'

Here Tavoni is referring to the Italian GP held on the combined banked track and road circuit at Monza. The Lancia-Ferraris were plagued by problems with the Belgian Englebert tyres to which Ferrari was contracted, and in addition there was a spate of broken steering arms. Fangio was hoping to win his fourth World Championship, but he had dropped well down the field because of tyre problems and a broken steering arm. Collins, who eventually finished third in the Championship, had prospects of winning it, but voluntarily handed his car over to Fangio when he was called in for a tyre change.

The Argentinian finished second, taking three points for the shared drive, and won the Championship by a margin of one point from Stirling Moss. Whether Collins handed his car over to Fangio completely voluntarily is arguable because, according to Fangio's manager Marcello Giambertone (*My Twenty Years of Racing* in which Giambertone collaborated with Fangio – English edition, Temple Press Books, 1961), he asked Collins to hand over his car to Fangio, and Collins 'jumped out of his seat, not even stopping to think that if Stirling Moss, out in front, should break down, he might become World Champion'.

'Because of a mistake in negotiations before he joined Ferrari, Fangio had a difficult relationship with Enzo Ferrari. In 1954–5 Fangio had raced for Mercedes-Benz, who withdrew at the end of 1955. Fangio was a very intelligent man and he always succeeded in driving for the factory that had the best car. For 1956 the choice was between Ferrari

and Maserati. Fangio came to Modena and said to Ferrari, 'I will drive for you, but I expect 50 per cent of starting money, prize money, and bonuses. I was also supplied by Mercedes-Benz with a car for my use and I received one million lire each month.'

Ferrari's response was, 'I cannot pay you one million lire each month because I am Ferrari not Mercedes.' Fangio said that he understood what Ferrari was saying, and that he needed a week to think over the deal. He would come back to see Ferrari the following week. A week later, not Fangio, but Giambertone arrived to see Ferrari, and Ferrari was very angry because he would never talk to a manager, only directly to the driver. Giambertone told Ferrari, 'Either you sign this agreement with me or Fangio will go to Maserati.' [This was probably a bluff because Moss had already agreed to drive for Maserati, and the Modena team would not have wanted both drivers.]

Ferrari agreed to Fangio's terms, save that he paid him 500,000 lire a month, but the agreement was for one year only. At one of our Tuesday meetings in December 1955, Enzo Ferrari told us about his negotiations with Fangio. He made it clear that he did not like Giambertone, and that the agreement was only for 12 months. We knew that at the end of 1956 Fangio would join Maserati. Although Giambertone – and Fangio – later complained that the Argentinian had an inferior car, I know that is not the case, and all the cars were prepared to exactly the same standards.'

At the end of 1956 Juan Fangio duly left Ferrari to drive for Maserati in 1957. The Scuderia still had a superb team of drivers in Formula 1 – the two British drivers, Hawthorn and Collins, and two Italian drivers, Castellotti and Musso, plus de Portago, while Trintignant, Gendebien, Frère, André Pilette, and von Trips also made odd appearances for the team. In Formula 1, Ferrari raced the latest derivatives of the V8 Lancia D50, known as the Tipo 801. These were no longer competitive, and the team failed to win a single World Championship race.

For sports car racing, Ferrari had new V12 cars, the 3783cc Tipo 315 Sport and the 4023cc Tipo 335 Sport. Ferrari won the rounds of the World Sports Car Championship at Buenos Aires, the Mille Miglia (but see below), and at Venezuela. Jaguar won at Le Mans for the third year in succession, while Maserati was the winner at Sebring and in Sweden. Ferrari won that year's World Sports Car Championship.

'The European season started with a very big disaster. This happened in March. Castellotti had broken off his holiday with his fiancée, actress Delia Scala, at Enzo Ferrari's request to attend a test session with the latest Formula 1 car at Modena. I was not there because I had travelled to Florence to the United States Consulate to obtain visas, as we were about to fly to America for the Sebring 12 Hours race. I arrived at the Modena Aerautodromo just as the ambulance was taking Castellotti's body to hospital.

He had been in a very difficult position with his mother and his fiancée. He was a great driver, a fine man, and he was also wealthy, but he was being pulled in different directions and stressed by these women. He recognised that life was short, and he wanted to enjoy his life doing what he wanted. Instead he faced great conflicts, especially as Delia Scala wanted him to give up racing.

Why the accident happened was never understood. After the pits at Modena there was a series of bends, but Castellotti made no attempt to take these corners, and carried straight on and hit a spectator stand. He was killed outright. What may have happened is that he was so concerned by the conflicts in his personal life that he completely lost his concentration. I do not think that he was mature enough to cope with the pressures of the family situation.

There was another major tragedy in 1957 when de Portago crashed in the Mille Miglia. I was in Brescia when the accident happened. Following the disaster, we at Ferrari conducted an intensive study of the race, investigating the condition of the roads, the fuel, and the tyres. There were six refuelling points, and the times between each were thoroughly investigated.
De Portago had changed the tyres at Florence and Bologna, and what happened to the car was not a tyre problem as such. There was a layer of protective material over the fuel tank, which worked loose and detached itself at Mantua.

This, said some people – wrongly – caused a puncture by rubbing on the inside wall of the tyre, but this was not supported by our investigations. Our investigation showed that a tyre was punctured by something lying in the road, maybe a piece of metal. While the accident was being investigated, the authorities seized Ferrari's passport for three months, and the investigation was sub judice so he was in effect muzzled and he lost all opportunity for giving his explanation as to whether the accident was caused by the tyres or the car itself.

There were also suggestions that the cars were too powerful for the tyres, but this was not true. Ferrari said, 'No, we have 350bhp in those cars and the tyres are more than adequate to cope with the power. This is proved by Taruffi whose 4-litre Tipo 335S won the race and was identical to the car driven by de Portago.'

There was never a proper explanation published of what happened. With another of these cars, Peter Collins, accompanied by photographer Louis Klemantaski, was leading when he retired because of transmission failure at Parma. As in 1955, it was a dry race and, as Tavoni pointed out, until he retired Collins was faster than Moss had been in 1955. Ferrari had originally used Pirelli tyres, but he had changed to Belgian Englebert tyres for 1957.

'After the Mille Miglia accident he wanted to change back to Pirelli, and although they had stopped making racing tyres, it was possible that they would start again for Ferrari. In fact, they couldn't have said no if Ferrari had persisted. Through an introduction from Chinetti, Ferrari tried American Goodyear tyres, but he did not think that they were of sufficiently high quality. Ferrari continued to use Englebert tyres in 1958, but he changed to using Dunlop tyres in 1959, and it was a convenient arrangement because this company also supplied the disc brakes adopted that year.

There are always small differences in power output between the cars in a team, but at Ferrari they were never substantial. When Mike Hawthorn was driving the Dino in 1958, he said to me, 'The power output of the engine in my car is 40bhp less than the others.' I assured him that this was not the case, but he said, 'The acceleration is not what it should be.' Hawthorn was an intelligent man, and I showed him the test results for the engine and gearbox of his and the other cars. I pointed out to him that it was impossible for us to make two engines with identical power outputs, but the difference was not 40bhp, but 10bhp – and that was a lot by our standards.

Hawthorn was a very sensitive man and he knew his ability and limits. After practice, we would sit and discuss our prospects in the race, and he would calculate very accurately how high up he would

Above: *At Le Mans in 1959, the Ferrari drivers wrecked their cars by over-revving them, and Tavoni found it impossible to impose team discipline. Tavoni, on the right of this photograph taken at Le Mans, is making a point to two of the more amenable drivers, Gendebien (on the left) and Gurney (centre).* (Author's Collection)

typical Roman man. He was a fantastic driver, but very excitable, and by 1958 Mike Hawthorn and Peter Collins were superior drivers. Musso tried very hard, and although he was very close in speed and skill to Michael and Peter he was not fast enough. Once, Musso went to Ferrari and said to him, "I am struggling with my car. I have a good chance of winning the Italian Championship, but I need more power."'

This was in 1956 when both Castellotti and Musso were in the Ferrari team. Ferrari told him, 'All my cars have the same power and the same handling; the only changes that we can make for you are small ones. If you want, we can change the seat, and you know that we will do that for you.' Tavoni confirmed that the power differences between Ferrari cars was about 2.5 per cent, so if the cars developed about 270bhp, as they did in 1956–7, that meant about 6/7bhp.

'In some races Musso was very strong, very competitive, but he would say of some other races, 'This is not an important race.' Peter Collins and Mike Hawthorn were very different, more professional, and for them every race was important. Musso was killed during the 1958 French Grand Prix at Reims, and this happened because of the way that he took Gueux, the sweeping corner after the pits. Michael was very clear how this corner should be taken, and he explained this to Musso and the other drivers.

He urged that the driver should take this long corner smoothly and evenly, keeping the car to the left of the centre of the road, and then moving further to the left at the apex and dropping 400rpm. This helped to keep the car on a tight line through the corner. Musso took the corner too fast and he was on the wrong line, entering it wide so that he was too close to the apex and then running wide at the exit and going off the course. When this accident happened, I was at Reims, but I was in the stands.'

There were always stories suggesting that when Musso was killed he was very worried because of his gambling debts and the pressure from those to whom he owed money. Tavoni was very clear that Musso did not gamble, as such, but he played poker, especially with Behra (who was driving for BRM) and Cesare Perdisa, a wealthy young man who had been very close to Castellotti and had given up racing after his death.

finish. I always thought that Collins was a complete gentleman, and he was a very fast driver. He and Mike were very close, and this was largely because their opinions were so simpatico; they thought about the cars and the circuit the same way, and they came to the same conclusions.

Musso was from Rome and behaved like a

'Musso came from a very rich family that owned two of the largest buildings in Rome, and he was not short of money. However much he lost, it was immaterial. Musso had a friend in Rome, ex-racing driver Franco Bornigia, and he worked for him, selling expensive cars. He lost some money over this, but it was not of significance.

Mike Hawthorn is the greatest driver that I worked with. He was a champion because he had character, as well as outstanding ability. He was the most satisfactory driver to race for Ferrari. Although he won only one Grand Prix in 1958 and went on to win the Drivers' Championship by a single point, in my opinion he was a better driver than Moss in 1958. Apart from other factors he was at the wheel of an inferior car.

I was in the pits at the 1958 German Grand Prix when Peter Collins crashed with fatal results. After Peter Collins's death, Michael Hawthorn and Enzo Ferrari met at a restaurant in Modena. Michael said to Ferrari, 'As racing drivers, we take risks. We lost Musso and now we have lost Collins. But we must complete the season.' Ferrari told Hawthorn, 'Michael, if it is your wish, we stop racing now. Because for me, two drivers killed in one season, is too much.' Michael insisted on carrying on to the end of the season and then he retired from racing.'

Throughout his period as Sport Manager, Tavoni worked with Carlo Chiti who had joined Ferrari in 1957 as Technical Director; he replaced Andrea Fraschetti, a former Lancia engineer who had been killed at the wheel of a Formula 1 car in a testing accident at Modena. At Maranello the ex-Alfa Romeo engineer carried out some of the later development work on both the Formula 1 Dino 246 and the Testa Rossa sports-racing cars, both of which were raced by the works team in 1958. Chiti constantly urged Enzo Ferrari to update his cars, and he met with stiff resistance.

'Through a relation of Peter Collins he introduced telescopic shock absorbers in place of the Houdaille vane-type, and Dunlop disc brakes in place of the drums, and these were adopted in 1959. Then he talked to Ferrari about the success of the rear-engined Coopers and pointed out to him that this was the way forward.

Enzo Ferrari told him, 'The Berlinettas and the sports cars must have front engines, for that is what my customers expect and want. They pay a very good price for them, and I cannot change

them.' Chiti was allowed to build an experimental rear-engined car in 1960 and this was raced at Monaco in Formula 1 form and later in 1960 in Formula 2 1500cc form. As a Formula 2 car it was very successful and won at Solitude in Germany, and it won its class in the Italian Grand Prix at Monza.

The rear-engined layout became standard for Formula 1 cars in 1961, and in the same year Chiti's brilliant and very successful rear-engined V6 2.4-litre Dino 246S sports car appeared. Ferrari was right about production Berlinettas, and rear-engined Ferraris of this type were not built until 1967 when the first Dino 206 appeared at the Turin Show.'

For 1959, the works Formula 1 drivers included Tony Brooks, Phil Hill, Jean Behra, and Dan Gurney, while on occasion both Olivier Gendebien and Cliff Allison drove for the team. Sports cars were excluded from Brooks's contract, so he did not drive at Le Mans, although he relented and agreed to drive in the Targa Florio, the Nürburgring 1,000km race, and the Tourist Trophy at Goodwood.

'After his experiences with Musso, Ferrari liked to have British drivers in the team, as they were especially good at circuit racing, while Italian drivers were better in long-distance road racing, but by then there were very few of this sort of event.

We liked Tony Brooks; he was the same as Peter Collins – a gentleman. He was a very fast driver and he is a very open personality. Cliff Allison was not as fast as Collins or Hawthorn, but I remember him as a very nice person – another gentleman. Jean Behra was a Frenchman and a very different personality. We had seen and timed Behra with Maseratis, and we had tested him at Ferrari, so we knew exactly what he could achieve. Of the other drivers, Gendebien was superb in sports cars, and one of the very best drivers was Wolfgang von Trips, who won nine races in 1961.

He was very experienced, very brave, and very successful. Between 1950 and 1961 Ferrari had a total of 28 drivers, but between 1957 and 1971 there were 14 drivers. There were always three Formula 1 drivers, but more were needed for sports car races, as two per car were necessary for endurance races. Sometimes Ferrari entered four Formula 1 cars, and the fourth car would be driven by Gendebien (in Belgium) or, maybe, Phil Hill, but the American became a regular member of the Formula 1 team in 1959.

When Behra joined Ferrari, he went to see the 'Old Man' and said, 'I am very happy to be racing for your team, but this year I want to win the World Championship.' Ferrari said to him, 'I hope you will. We will see what has happened at the end of the season.' But Behra was completely overconfident and said, 'No, no, I'm sure that this year I shall win the Formula 1 Championship for you.' With Behra's mentality, every race was a drama.

A reporter at the French newspaper, L'Équipe, wrote, 'This is the year of the Blue of France, and this year we will have a French Champion.' The Italian reporters adopted exactly the same attitude with Musso, and it was not a constructive attitude.'

Behra was a very disruptive figure in the team, and he was a bad influence on the other drivers. Cliff Allison has related what happened at Le Mans in 1959. Because of an error at the factory, the cars were undergeared, so Tavoni instructed the drivers to restrict their revs to 7,500rpm. But, egged on by Behra, they took not the slightest notice, and they were coming into the pits with the 'tell-tales' indicating 8,000rpm plus. As the fastest team driver, Behra claimed the privilege to choose his co-driver, and insisted that Dan Gurney shared his car.

When Behra came in with his 'tell-tale' showing 8,900rpm, Tavoni exploded into a well-justified rage. The other drivers supported Behra. Tavoni threw in the towel, warned them that the engines would not last for 24 hours, and stormed off to sulk in a corner of the pit. So far as Cliff and the others were concerned, they professed to hate Le Mans, and all they wanted to do was break the cars and go home. Tavoni's long telephone conversations with Enzo Ferrari gave rise to plenty of shouting, but little in the way of help and support. The Sports Manager had little alternative but to ignore the drivers, who were behaving like a bunch of irresponsible kids.

That year, Ferrari faced stiff opposition from a well-organised Aston Martin team with a trio of beautifully prepared DBR1s. After stalling his engine twice at the start, Behra then tore round the circuit like a man possessed. Tavoni hung out the 'go-slow' signal, but all he got for his pains was Behra shaking his fist as he passed the pits. The high revs, that the Ferrari drivers insisted on using, caused overheating and expansion

of the cylinder blocks of the works Testa Rossas. This resulted in water leaking past the gaskets, and bearing failure.

At pit stops, around half-a-gallon of water was poured into each car, and the Testa Rossas were struggling to complete the necessary 30 laps before they could take on more. Chaos was added to confusion when all three works cars came into the pits at the same time. It was during this stop that Tavoni looked at the 'tell-tale' on Behra's car and saw that it was reading 9,300rpm. He just walked away, looking miserable and shaking his head. Despite the total abuse of the car, the last of the three Testa Rossas, driven by Phil Hill/Gendebien, did not expire until shortly after 11am on the Sunday. Aston Martin scored the win that they had been trying to achieve for ten years, and their cars finished in first and second places.

'When we were at Reims and Modena, Jean Behra set very fast laps. We timed Behra round Modena in 59sec, but it was a very ragged, untidy lap. Then we tested with Tony Brooks at Modena, and we timed him not in 59sec, but one minute, but he was beautifully balanced and smooth through the corners. Behra was not a fast driver compared with Brooks. Behra was struggling to achieve his time, while Brooks was completely relaxed.

If you had a circuit with lap speeds of around 100mph (160kph) then Behra would be faster, but he was not fast on difficult, high-speed circuits such as Spa, Reims, and Monza. So, when his times were slower than Brooks, he would come into the pits and blame his car! I promised Behra on my honour that all the cars were the same. Before the French Grand Prix we had asked Dan Gurney to drive all the cars at the Modena circuit. At the first corner at Modena, where Castellotti had his fatal accident, Gurney touched a kerb, spun and broke a suspension wishbone.

Ferrari instructed the mechanics to transfer the engine and gearbox to a new chassis with new suspension for the race at Reims. Behra then drove this car at Reims, where we had entered a total of five cars. Brooks was fastest in practice and in the race, which was run in incredibly hot weather. He led throughout to win from Phil Hill with another Ferrari, and Jack Brabham (works Cooper) took third place. Behra stalled at the start, but came up through the field to hold third place on lap 32 when a piston in the Ferrari's V6 engine broke after he had trailed blue smoke for some laps.

Behra had over-revved his engine yet again. The drivers of the Dino 246 were given a limit of 7,500rpm, but the 'tell-tale' on Behra's tachometer showed that he had taken the engine up to 8,000rpm. He denied that he was at fault, and he told the press, 'My engine went up to 8,000rpm only after the piston had failed – not before.' Obviously, this was impossible. He also told the press that the factory had given him the car with the damaged suspension not repaired. So, we had the car inspected by a technical steward, who confirmed that the suspension was undamaged.

Ferrari telephoned me at Reims and instructed me to ask Behra to go to see him at Modena the next Tuesday. I explained this to Behra and he was very unpleasant.'

It is a matter of history that during this altercation Behra hit Tavoni. When this was mentioned, Tavoni simply shrugged his shoulders dismissively and said, 'It is not important.' Tavoni and other Ferrari people talked to Behra's wife about the situation at dinner after the race, and she said, 'Well, Behra is Behra; he is difficult with me.'

Tavoni declined to comment to the press, and when Behra met with Ferrari, the 'Old Man' said to him, 'You have told a newspaper reporter that I gave you a car with a bent wishbone. We fitted your car with a new chassis and suspension. Now I am asking you to explain the true situation to a newspaper reporter in Modena for the benefit of the Italian public.'

Behra replied, 'I am sorry for talking to the French newspaper, but I will not talk to your newspaper reporter in Modena.' Ferrari had expected Behra to put the record straight, and when he refused he told his Administration Manager to give Behra the money that was due to him, and the Frenchman's contract was terminated.

The Porsche company had a close relationship with Behra, and for that year the Frenchman had built by Valerio Colotti's workshop in Modena an open-wheel single-seater Formula 2 car known as the Behra-Porsche. The German GP in 1959 was held in Berlin at the Avus banked track on 2 August, and Behra was entered to drive his single-seater. Tavoni commented on the dangers of Avus, saying, 'We had problems with the drivers at Avus because the banked corners were not designed properly, and they concluded that it was

Above: *Moss won the 1961 Monaco race with Rob Walker's outdated four-cylinder Lotus, but Richie Ginther drove magnificently with the new 120-degree Ferrari to finish three seconds behind the winner. Here, Tavoni congratulates Ginther, while Gozzi looks on and Denis Jenkinson passes.* **(Author's Collection)**

too dangerous to drive higher up the banking than about halfway.'

Earlier in the day, Behra raced a Porsche RSK in the wet sports car race, and he lapped at the top of the banking. He lost control and was killed when he hit one of the flagpoles mounted on Second World War gun emplacements lining the top of the banking, and was thrown out of the car. Behra was never a top driver. Ferrari made no comment on Behra's death and sent no wreath or flowers to his funeral.

Le Mans in 1960 proved to be another fraught race.

'We had a disaster at Le Mans in 1960 because of a mistake made by Luigi Bazzi. He was a very nice man, but he was old. After all, he had been a mechanic and friend to Antonio Ascari more than 30 years previously and, of course, he had been a friend of Enzo Ferrari for many years. At this time he was chief of the Sport Department, but he was from the older school. At Le Mans we had Chiti who was head of the Technical Department, and Luigi Bazzi had been responsible for the assembly of the Le Mans cars.

Before the race, Bazzi had made some modifications to the works Testa Rossa cars, including fitting a new exhaust system that improved pick-up out of corners, and there were also changes to the carburation. Chiti said that this would increase fuel consumption and it was his opinion that the cars needed to refuel every 23 laps. 'To be safe,' Chiti said, 'we should refuel every 21 laps.' Bazzi would not accept this and said, 'I assembled the cars and I know my cars; they will run for at least 25 laps.'

Chiti was unhappy with this, and he persuaded me to call all the cars in for refuelling after 23 laps. On lap 22, not long before the end of the second hour and before there was time to put out a signal for the drivers, the works Testa Rossas of Phil Hill/von Trips and Pedro Rodriguez/Scarfiotti ran out of fuel on the circuit. Von Trips stopped at Tertre Rouge, and Scarfiotti ran out of fuel at White House. Having seen what had happened, I was able to put out a signal to the other two drivers to come in immediately.

Willy Mairesse, co-driving with Ginther, reduced his speed to a crawl, reaching the pits with only a couple of pints of fuel left. The leading car, driven by Olivier Gendebien/Paul Frère, also made it back to the pits. Even so, it was a disaster because the original schedule of pit stops had to be abandoned, as the two remaining cars would be making more pit stops, and this would take time for which we had made no allowance. Bazzi and I discussed the situation, and we agreed that we should take a risk by driving the cars as quickly as possible and opening up a lead over the rest of the field.

When I reported to Ferrari on the telephone on the Saturday evening, I told him what had happened and that I had decided to take a risk in running the cars as quickly as possible. Ferrari exploded, but let me do what I wanted. Frère/Gendebien won by a little over 30 miles from the North American Racing Team-entered 1958 Testa Rossa of Ricardo Rodriguez/André Pilette. Fortunately, the 'Bird-cage' Maseratis entered by the American Camoradi team retired, and third place went to the ex-works Aston Martin DBR1 of Jim Clark/Roy Salvadori, followed across the line by four GT Ferraris.

At the meeting at the factory the next Tuesday, Ferrari said to Bazzi, 'Luigi, explain to me what happened at Le Mans.' For about 15 seconds, Bazzi was silent and then he said, 'Mr Ferrari, I am not in a position to give you an explanation.' Ferrari said, 'We will talk after the meeting, Luigi, we will talk afterwards. I will make my decision.' Quite what Ferrari said to Bazzi remains a mystery, but after this meeting Bazzi became a consultant without any responsibility in the factory.'

In 1961 Ferrari was exceptionally successful in Formula 1 with a team of cars designed by Chiti and powered by rear-mounted V6 engines. The Ferrari team was very strong and included two American drivers. Phil Hill won the World Championship for Ferrari after the death of von Trips, and Tavoni has fond memories of Hill:

'He was the best American driver to be part of the Ferrari team and he was an excellent test driver.

He would test for just five laps and then come in and discuss all the characteristics of the car. Phil preferred high-speed circuits, and he drove equally well in Formula 1 and sports cars. He respected the mechanical aspects of his cars and did not over-drive them. Every driver at Ferrari would have liked him as their partner.

We had three Formula 1 drivers, but when we entered a fourth car, it was given to Richie Ginther who was the regular test driver. He was a very small man, and when he drove sports cars we had to put another seat on top of the original seat. His team-mates were rather concerned about his height, and they pleaded with him to wear elevated shoes with platform soles so that it made it easier to share a driving position. He was chosen as a tester because he had such great sensitivity for the cars.

At the end of 1961 he was fired while he was waiting confirmation of his new contract from Ferrari. I know this, although I had left the company by this time. Ferrari had planned to meet the drivers after the Italian Grand Prix, but after von Trips's death, the meetings did not take place as planned. By the end of November, Ferrari had still not met Ginther to discuss contracts.

Dragoni had been appointed Sport Manager in mid-November and, at around the end of November or the beginning of December, Dragoni went into a restaurant in Modena and saw Ginther talking to Tony Rudd of BRM. Dragoni telephoned Ferrari and asked whether he had yet met Ginther. He described what he had seen, and Ferrari sacked Ginther.

How I managed to cope with the deaths of so many drivers is something that I have asked myself many times. Drivers have said to me, 'You are the link between Enzo Ferrari and ourselves, and can convey our opinions to him.' I continued until the end of 1961.'

When Jim Clark and von Trips collided going into the Parabolica curve in that year's Italian GP, von Trips's Ferrari was hurled up the grass bank, throwing the driver out, and crashing into the wire-mesh fence against which so many spectators were leaning. Eleven were killed, and many others were injured. Von Trips died without regaining consciousness.

'When the accident occurred I was in the pits and we could not see what had happened. After about ten minutes, while we waited anxiously for news, Jim Clark came into the Ferrari pit and said, 'I'm sorry, Romolo, it was a big mistake.' He did not explain what had happened, but it was obvious that he thought that he was responsible for the accident. The Clerk of the race took me to the corner so that we could see what had happened. I went to the hospital where von Trips was.

The whole situation was getting too much for me, and I started to talk in my sleep. I was becoming more and more affected by the stress of managing the racing team. The accident at Monza, the worst of all accidents involving Ferrari cars, was all the sadder because von Trips would almost certainly have won that year's Drivers' World Championship. Phil Hill won the race

for Ferrari and took the Championship by a single point, with von Trips a posthumous second. After Monza I would have said I could remain Sport Manager no longer, if I had been given the chance to continue.

The decision to give up being Sport Manager was taken away from me. We sent a letter about the problems with Laura Ferrari on the Saturday before the last Tuesday in October 1961. On that Tuesday we had our usual 5pm meeting with Enzo Ferrari. Our letter was not discussed, but as we left the building, the Assistant Secretary, who worked for me, stood at the door and he told each of us, 'This is your money and you must sign for it, or if you wish it will be paid into your bank. Then you are out of Ferrari.' Each of us was handed a letter terminating our employment, together with a cheque for what we were owed. This man, Valerio Stradi, took my job as Secretary. I told him that I wanted to talk to Ferrari, but this was refused. [A couple of weeks later both Giberti and Della Casa asked Ferrari if he would take them back, and he agreed.]'

After he left Ferrari, Tavoni had to work because he had no income and a family to support. He tried to find work, but without success, and did not obtain a job until January 1962. Both he and Chiti joined a new organisation called Automobili Turismo e Sport (ATS) , and there was also to be a Gran Turismo version with a 2500cc engine. Originally, it was planned that the cars would be called the Serenissima (from Volpi's Scuderia Serenissima racing team), but when the Formula 1 cars were raced they bore the ATS name. Later, Gran Turismo and Sports Prototype versions were raced as Serenissimas. Large sums of money were spent on expensive factory premises at Sasso Marconi, a village near Bologna.

When the Formula 1 cars appeared, they were scruffy, badly prepared and uncompetitive. The drivers were former Ferrari team-members Phil Hill and Giancarlo Baghetti, who had left Maranello after a desperately unsuccessful 1962 season. The ATS cars' debut was in the 1963 Belgian GP, and they made four more disappointing appearances that year before the team was wound up. Later, Tavoni worked in the Sports Department of the Milan Automobile Club, and then he became a member of the Italian Motor Sport Committee. Finally, from 1972 to 1996 he worked as Manager of Monza race circuit.

Tribute to a Technical Director

Mauro Forghieri and the development of the flat-12 cars

The longest-serving of Ferrari engineers over the years (and probably the most successful) was Mauro Forghieri. His chief claim to fame was the origination

Below: *The 1964 season was closely fought between John Surtees (with Forghieri-designed Ferraris that steadily improved as the season progressed), Graham Hill (BRM), and Jim Clark (Lotus). Here, Surtees is seen with the very handsome V8 Tipo 158 Ferrari in the British GP at Brands Hatch. He finished third behind Jim Clark and Graham Hill.* **(Tom March Collection)**

of the 312B flat-12 series of cars, development of which was protracted, but which had a racing life spread over a period of 11 years. The flat-12 was a completely new concept introduced by Forghieri, an exceptionally able designer and a very practical race engineer, who frequently also adopted the role of team manager.

Forghieri was born in Modena on 13 January 1935. His family were very politically aware and active. His father, Reclus, worked at the Scuderia Ferrari premises in Modena on the development of the Alfa Romeo 158 Alfetta. Because of his Socialist attitudes, he was forced to leave Italy and he stayed out of the country most of the time until Mussolini was unseated. Even so, Reclus and Enzo Ferrari had a close friendship.

Mauro studied mechanical engineering at Bologna University and he graduated in 1959 as a doctor of engineering. The complications of the Italian academic system do not register with the Anglo-Saxon mind, but

his qualification does not, apparently, allow him to call himself 'Dottore'. He was a great enthusiast for gas-turbine engines, and his ambition was to emigrate to the United States and work for a company like Northrop or Chance Vought. At this time, most Italian aerospace companies had ties with North American companies, but no gas-turbine engines were manufactured in Italy.

While he was waiting to hear that he had found employment with an American company, Enzo Ferrari telephoned him and offered him a job. Mauro told him that he was waiting to go to the United States. The 'Old Man' responded, 'Waiting! Come here and work with me.' So he joined Ferrari in 1960 and initially he worked in the engine test department. Following the departure of many of the company's executives in late 1961, Forghieri was the only engineer remaining in the factory.

When he was summoned to see the 'Old Man', he told him that he was leaving, as he felt unable to carry on alone. Ferrari tugged the emotional heartstrings and said to Mauro, 'You cannot leave me, because then I shall be alone. I need you. I will give you responsibility for the racing department.' Mauro thought that Ferrari was crazy, and told him that he lacked the experience. Ferrari responded, 'You look after the technical side and I will look after the political side. You tell me what you would like to do and I will tell you whether economic circumstances will permit it.'

So, Mauro was appointed Technical Director, despite his youth and very limited experience. Initially, Forghieri developed improved versions of the Chiti-designed V6 engine for F1, but for 1964–65 he initiated the 1500cc V8 and flat-12 GP engines. For Prototype racing, Forghieri oversaw the development of a range of cars of exceptionally high performance, from the 250P 3-litre of

Above: *John Surtees is seen with Enzo Ferrari during practice for the 1964 Italian GP at Monza, where he took pole position and won the race from McLaren (Cooper) and team-mate Bandini. Surtees also won the 1964 German GP, and was that year's World Championship driver by a margin of one point from Graham Hill, after Clark retired his Lotus because of engine failure caused by an oil leak. (LAT Photographic)*

Below: *Seen before the start of the 1965 International Trophy at Silverstone in May 1965 is John Surtees at the wheel of his V8 Tipo 158 Ferrari. Crouched on the right of the photograph is Ferrari Technical Director Mauro Forghieri. Jackie Stewart won this 152-mile (245km) race with his BRM, but Surtees drove a good race to finish second, three seconds behind the winner. (Guy Griffiths Collection)*

Above: *In 1965 Ferrari fortunes faded once more and the team failed to win a single race. One of Surtees's better performances was in the British GP at Silverstone (seen here) where he took third place behind Jim Clark (Lotus 33) and Graham Hill (BRM).* (Tom March Collection)

1963 through to the exquisitely beautiful 330P4 that battled with the Fords and won the Prototype Championship in 1967.

Design and development of the 312B

When the 3000cc GP formula came into force for 1966, the team produced another V12 engine. These were manufactured in a number of different forms: two inlet and one exhaust valve (September 1966); exhausts inside the 'V' (March 1967, an arrangement favoured by Forghieri because of the good heat dissipation); 48 valves (September 1967); and reversed gas flow with the inlet ports in the 'V' and the exhausts outside (March 1969). In some ways the Ferrari engineer had been struggling to squeeze too much power out of what was basically an old and traditional design.

Another flat-12 car was the 212E 'Montagna' that Peter Schetty drove to a win in the 1969 European Hill Climb Championship. The design of this engine was delegated by Forghieri to engineer Jacaponi. The concept of a flat-12 engine had originated from a contract with the American Franklin aero-engine

company who had wanted a very low engine that could be incorporated into the wing of an aircraft.

When Forghieri decided that Ferrari needed a completely new F1 engine, the flat-12 engine was the obvious route to take. It was lighter than the V12, it enabled the centre of gravity of the car to be kept closer to the ground, and it permitted a smaller frontal area, although there were problems with the use of the engine in sports cars, as will be discussed later. Generally, it was an exceptionally neat and compact engine.

Various figures were published for the dimensions of the original 312B engine. Retrospectively, what seems to be correct is a cylinder capacity of 2994.82cc (78.55mm x 51.5mm). The twin overhead camshafts per bank of cylinders were driven by a train of spur gears from the rear of the engine, and were enclosed in a single cam cover for each bank. The 48 inlet and exhaust valves were at an inclined angle of 20°, the smallest used in any F1 engine of the time. Because of the layout of the engine, the inlet trumpets for the Lucas fuel injection were above the engine, and the exhaust ports below. Ignition was by the Marelli 'Dinoplex' transistorised system. There were inserted wet cylinder liners.

A number of problems were encountered during development and, as a result, the first race appearance of the new car was delayed from late 1969 until the South African GP in March 1970. (Because of Ferrari's continual failure to provide him with a competitive car,

Chris Amon left the team and drove for March in 1970.) One of the early problems was engine failure during testing. Initially, the engine bearings were made as narrow as possible by the use of roller bearings, but the engine failures necessitated a re-think.

The original built-up crankshaft was abandoned, and instead Forghieri decided to use a one-piece crankshaft machined from a special alloy-steel billet imported from the United States. There were inserted bearings at the two centre mains, and roller bearings at the ends only, but crankshaft failures still occurred during pre-race testing. So, Ferrari adopted special Pirelli-developed rubber couplings between the crankshaft and the flywheel. These shifted the flexing stresses to a part of the crankshaft that could withstand them.

Another of the early problems with the flat-12 engine was excessive oil consumption, and at the first race at Kyalami an extra tank was mounted on top of the gearbox. This was connected to the main tank by a large-bore pipe, and the driver activated it by means of a piano-wire control near his left shoulder.

By the middle of 1970 it was reckoned that the 312B1 was developing a reliable and consistent 460bhp at 11,600rpm, compared with 430bhp from the Ford DFV in its latest form. Transmission was via a five-speed gearbox and a dry multi-plate clutch.

As was usual Ferrari practice, the chassis was a multi-tubular structure stiffened by aluminium panelling – best described as a semi-monocoque. Forghieri told the writer that he had adopted this form of construction because of the difficulty of training staff in the intricacies of monocoques. The engine was suspended from a backbone-type 'beam' extension that carried an additional nine gallons of fuel. The front of the chassis

Below: *This superb photograph shows the original Tipo 312B flat-12 car, with Ignazio Giunti locking a wheel on cement dust put down on a patch of oil in the 1970 Belgian GP at Spa-Francorchamps. Giunti finished fourth on the same lap as the winner, Pedro Rodriguez with a BRM P153, but he was over a minute and a half behind. (LAT Photographic)*

was wedge-shaped for mounting the radiator, and the steering rack was bolted to the front bulkhead.

At the front, the suspension incorporated upper rocking arms, inboard-mounted coil spring/damper units and wide-based lower wishbones. The rear suspension was a conventional double wishbone and coil spring arrangement. The outboard front brakes had cooling ducts cast into the front suspension uprights, and the rear brakes were mounted just inboard of the hub-carriers. The rear aerofoil was mounted well forward on the rear stay of the rollover bar and was fully adjustable, with both leading- and trailing-edge slots. The 312B1 was an exceptionally well-styled car with an NACA duct in the sloping nose for cooling the cockpit.

In 1970, Ferrari also competed with the Tipo 512S in the Competition Sports Car category. This project had originated when Ferrari learned that Porsche was building the 917 and, because of his F1 commitments, Mauro delegated the design work to Ing. Giacomo Caliri, but he attended the various rounds of the Sports Car Championship as Race Director. The strain of running both teams was an almost impossible burden for Forghieri, and there can be no doubt that it contributed to the mediocre performances of the 312B in many races in 1970.

The 1970 racing season

The prototype, 001, had been extensively tested by Amon, and it was driven by Ickx at Kyalami. It retired because of loss of oil from a cracked sump pan. At the Spanish race on the bleak Jarama circuit, Oliver's BRM lost a wheel on the first lap and, brakeless and out of control, he collided with Ickx. Both cars caught fire, Ickx's 002 was destroyed and the young Belgian suffered burns on his arms and legs. Petrol from the Ferrari's ruptured fuel tank soaked through his overalls and, as the medical attendants failed to remove these, he incurred further petrol burns. Ferrari built a replacement car that carried the same chassis number.

Steady development work was carried out during the season, and both Ignazio Giunti (Belgian, French, Austrian, and Italian races) and Regazzoni (the Dutch race and every race from Brands Hatch onwards) joined the team. Overall, Ickx enjoyed a good season, with victories in Austria, Canada, and Mexico, and second place at Hockenheim, while Regazzoni won the Italian GP. Ferrari took second place in the Constructors' Championship with 52 points to the 59 of Lotus, and Ickx was second in the Drivers' Championship with 40 points to the 45 of posthumous Champion Rindt, killed at the wheel of his Lotus in practice for the Italian race.

Racing in 1971 with the improved 312B2

For 1971, Forghieri developed the 312B2, which was similar to the original concept, but with so many detail changes that the two models shared very few components. The car had a much more pronounced wedge shape, with a smaller frontal area, and although the construction of the chassis was similar, there were fewer tubes. The alloy skin was of heavier 16-gauge to comply with the deformable structure regulations that were to come into force for 1972.

Mainly because Forghieri wanted to have the rear suspension and brakes fully inboard, there was completely new rear suspension. The Koni coil spring/damper units were mounted almost horizontally across the back of the car; they were actuated by a bell-crank upper wishbone, and there were wide-based lower wishbones with single upper radius rods each side. There were detail changes to the oil tank, and modified gearbox side-plates to facilitate the mounting of the inboard disc brakes.

The engine now had revised cylinder dimensions of 80mm x 49.6mm (2991.80cc) and Forghieri gave as the reason 'bigger piston area, bigger valves, and better combustion'. Changes to the block castings meant that the new engine would only fit under the pontoon of the 312B2 chassis, which had been modified for the repositioned fuel injection metering unit. Likewise, the 312B1 engines fitted only the 312B1 chassis. In their revised form the 312B2 engines usually had both roller and shell bearings, and although it is known that some engines had roller bearings throughout, it is not known how many.

American-resident Italian Mario Andretti drove for the team in many 1971 races, but the team's 'full-time' drivers were Ickx and Regazzoni. After the considerable level of success achieved by the flat-12 cars in the latter part of 1970, Ferrari was expecting an exceptional 1971, but the season proved most unsatisfactory. It had started well with Andretti's win at Kyalami after Hulme's McLaren ran into problems, and there were wins in non-Championship races by Regazzoni at Brands Hatch and Andretti in the Questor GP in California, but both of these successes were aided by the right choice of tyres when their rivals chose the wrong ones.

Throughout the year the Ferraris failed to match the performance of the new Tyrrell, and the drivers could not match the skill of Jackie Stewart. Development plans for the year went awry because of a succession of industrial disputes that affected the Maranello works, and the team suffered more than its fair share of bad luck. During the European season, the only World Championship race win was by Ickx in the wet at Zandvoort, although he finished second in the Spanish race and won the non-Championship Jochen Rindt Gedächtnis-Rennen at Hockenheim.

In the Drivers' Championship, Ickx finished fourth equal with Jo Siffert (who drove in F1 for the BRM, but was killed at Brands Hatch late in the season) on 19 points. In July Forghieri had left the team for a second time and retreated to his design studio to work on a new version of the 312B that he refers to as 'the snowplough'. The team manager during 1971 was Peter Schetty.

Design of the 312PB Prototype

Ferrari had also contested the Prototype category during 1971 with a new and very compact car that was a sports two-seater version of the 312B. This was again the work of Mauro Forghieri, who designed and developed it before once more quitting front-line management at Ferrari. When the first car was built, it was an exact copy of the 312B apart from the body. In December 1970, Forghieri and his team took the car to Kyalami in South Africa for testing, and spent around two weeks there. On his return, Forghieri completely redesigned the car and produced the definitive 312PB.

The 312PB had the latest 2991.80cc version of the flat-12 engine detuned to develop 440bhp at 10,800rpm in the interests of reliability in endurance races. As on the F1 car, the gearbox was at the rear and the short gear-change moved in a small gate situated on the right side of the driver's seat. The construction of the chassis was similar to that used in the single-seater, with right-hand drive, and behind the cockpit there was a tubular structure over the engine.

At the front, the suspension was by double wishbones with outboard coil spring/damper units, and the cast alloy hub carriers extended rearwards to form the steering arms and carried the disc brake calipers. The rack-and-pinion steering passed across the driver's knees. At the rear, suspension was by lower wishbones, single upper transverse links, twin radius rods each side, and coil spring/damper units. Many of the engine ancillaries were moved from the front of the engine to the top.

There were wide sponsons each side of the cockpit: the one on the left contained the 120-litre fuel tank (the maximum permitted by the regulations). This counterbalanced the weight of the driver. The sponson on the right was empty. The larger filler was positioned at the front of the right-hand sponson, and from this a pipe ran down and across the cockpit floor to the fuel

tank. Another filler protruded from the tank on the left, and this had an Avery-Hardoll bayonet-type attachment similar to that on the right.

When the car made refuelling stops, a mechanic clamped a plastic container on the left filler cap. The air was forced out of the fuel tank under pressure as the gravity-fed house pumped the petrol in, and when it was observed that petrol was moving into the container on the left side, it indicated that the tank was full. When the container and hose were removed, the connectors self-sealed and the car headed back into the race. Twin water radiators were mounted each side at the rear of the sponsons, with the oil tank mounted behind the left-hand radiator and the oil cooler mounted on the top of the clutch housing.

The wedge-shaped body was moulded in two fibreglass sections: the front section consisted of the nose, cockpit sides, and doors, and it was hinged on pivots by the lower front wishbone mountings. The rear section formed the tail and was hinged behind the cockpit. Both body sections were painted the usual Ferrari red, but the sponsons were left unpainted. The 312PB was remarkably small and compact compared with the opposition, and it made both the Alfa Romeo 33/3s and Matra MS670s look extremely bulky.

The 1971 Prototype season

In the early days of racing the car, it suffered from tyre vibration that neither Firestone nor Goodyear could cure. Forghieri introduced a special damping device, but it was not successful. The team raced only one 312PB in 1971 because of their limited resources. Following Giunti's terrible death with car 0882 in Buenos Aires, a new car was built with the same chassis number, although following the accident the team initially raced the first car 0880.

From the point of view of testing and development, the year was a great success in preparing Ferrari to run a full team in 1972. At Sebring, 0880 was driven by Ickx/ Andretti, and was leading the race by a margin of three minutes when the gearbox failed in the third hour. Despite a collision with a small British 'special', called the Dulon, in the Brands Hatch 1,000km race, and later delays caused by a jammed starter solenoid, Ickx and Regazzoni took second place to the Alfa Romeo T33/3 of de Adamich and Pescarolo. It was the best performance of the year, because retirement followed retirement.

Ickx collided with Merzario's spinning Ferrari 512M at Monza, Regazzoni was at the wheel when the 312PB again collided with the Dulon at Spa, and the team chose to miss the Targa Florio. Ickx and Regazzoni were at the wheel again at the Nürburgring, and the 312PB was the

fastest car in the race – but plagued by a myriad of problems, among which failure of a cylinder sealing ring caused the car's retirement when water poured into the header tank ran straight out of the car's exhausts.

Le Mans was another race which Ferrari missed; then Regazzoni crashed in the Austrian 1,000km race at the Österreichring, and at Watkins Glen the 312PB retired because of a jammed starter motor. The team tested at Imola in September, and then stayed on at the circuit for Regazzoni to drive the car in the Interserie race. He won his heat, but retired in the final because of fuel pump failure.

In November, Ferrari entered two 312Bs in the Kyalami Nine Hours race. Regazzoni/Redman won with the old car, but Ickx/Andretti, who had a new car with sleeker body and cockpit modifications to comply with the 1972 regulations, took second place after engine problems – it was badly delayed at the start after the engine cut out, and after it cut out on the circuit later – and was 25 laps behind the winner at the finish.

The 1972 Formula 1 season

By 1972, the Fiorano test circuit was open and possessed all the necessary computers and video cameras to monitor testing in the fullest and most comprehensive detail. It was to pay dividends in abundance, especially when Lauda joined the team, but meanwhile the team had to make do with the 312B2. It was reckoned that power output was now 490bhp, but the major changes were to the suspension. At the front the track was 4.8in (120mm) wider, but the changes at the rear were much more substantial.

There was a new layout with conventional outboard coil spring/damper units, located by single upper links and twin parallel lower links. The rear track was increased by 6.3in (160mm). Although Ickx had previously been unhappy with the 312B2, he was substantially (if not completely) satisfied with the car in its latest form, and only this version was raced during the year.

It had been hoped that the season would bring Ferrari the success that the team had worked so hard to achieve, but it was not to be. The year's racing was dominated by Emerson Fittipaldi and the Lotus 72. The

Opposite: Here, Jacky Ickx is seen at the wheel of his Tipo 312B2 Ferrari in the 1972 German GP at the Nürburgring). The Ferrari team was struggling, despite possessing the most powerful cars, but in this race both Ickx and Clay Regazzoni drove magnificently to take the first two places ahead of Ronnie Peterson (March). (LAT Photographic)

Brazilian won the Spanish, Belgian, British, Austrian, and Italian races. He won the Drivers' Championship with 61 points to the 45 of Jackie Stewart, who had suffered badly during the year with stomach ulcer problems, and had missed the Spa race.

Ickx frequently showed tremendous form in practice (he took pole position in Spain, Britain, Germany, and Italy), but all too often his performance in the race fell short of expectations. There were criticisms of all the team: Forghieri spent too much time dreaming up magic solutions; Team Manager Peter Schetty spent too much time playing with the very expensive computer equipment which Heuer had supplied to Ferrari; and Ickx was reluctant to spend much time testing. These were factors, but there was a foolish assumption that the flat-12 cars had lost all chance of being consistent race-winners.

Ickx finished fourth in the Championship with 27 points; Regazzoni was joint sixth with Cevert on 15 points. In the early part of 1972, Ickx had turned in some reasonable, but not outstanding, performances, starting with a third in the Argentine race, and second places in both the Spanish race at Jarama and Monaco. Monaco was a race that Ickx was expected to win after the sky suddenly blackened, and torrential, flooding rain inundated the circuit, and the cars were throwing up so much spray that there was almost no visibility.

The young Belgian was second fastest in practice, but at the fall of the flag Beltoise (BRM P160) accelerated through from the second row and jostled his way into the lead at Ste Devote. At the end of this thoroughly miserable race, Ickx finished second, 38.2sec behind and admitting freely that there was no way in which he could challenge the French BRM driver. Prior to the French GP, the team went tyre-testing with Firestone at the Nürburgring, and this may have had a major influence on the performance of the Ferrari drivers in the German race.

The French race was held at Clermont-Ferrand, and Ickx fell to the tail of the field because of tyre trouble. He had been second fastest to Amon in practice, and the Ferrari was fitted with further revised rear suspension intended to give better driver control, and featured a new triangulated lower wishbone and a single upper radius rod each side that located modified uprights. Regazzoni missed the race because, at the Austrian 1,000km race, he had been playing football in the paddock when he fell and landed awkwardly, breaking a bone in his left wrist. 'Nanni' Galli took his place, but his driving was wild, slow and unpromising.

Regazzoni was back in the team at the German race held at the beginning of August on a slightly emasculated (and safer) Nürburgring. Ickx was fastest in practice, 1.7sec faster than Stewart (Tyrrell), and he and Regazzoni dominated the race to take the first two places. The young Belgian turned in a fantastic drive, but there was controversy over Regazzoni's second place, for Jackie Stewart claimed that the Swiss driver repulsed his overtaking move by pushing him off the track. It proved to be Jacky Ickx's last World Championship race win.

Forghieri had been working on the 312B3 with distinctive 'snowplough' nose, and the original plan had been to run the model at Monza. It should be clarified that the Italian term 'spartineve' (snowplough) was used by critics, but Forghieri himself always uses the term 'snowplough' when he refers to the car. It proved to have very twitchy handling that both Ickx and Merzario, who did most of the testing, disliked intensely. Ickx also had the misfortune to collide with a rabbit at Monza, so there was blood and mess everywhere, and that became his abiding memory of the car.

Below: *After he had seen the new 312PB Prototype, Franco Lini suggested to Enzo Ferrari that the car should have been designated '312 Boxer Prototipo' and not '312 Prototipo Boxer'. This would have been in accordance with usual Ferrari practice. Ferrari is said to have replied, 'It has to be the 312PB – how can I call it the BP, when my cars are contracted to run on Shell fuel.'* (LAT Photographic)

Prototype racing in 1972

Ferrari had decided to contest all the rounds of the World Championship for Makes in 1972, and was expecting strong opposition from both Alfa Romeo and Matra. It did not work out that way, for Matra decided to run only at Le Mans, the Alfa Romeos proved no serious match for the Ferraris – and after tests at Monza convinced the team that 312PBs would not last 24 Hours, Ferrari withdrew the cars from the Le Mans race only seven days before it was due to take place.

In addition to Ickx, Regazzoni and Andretti (only available when there was no conflict with his USAC commitments), the team signed up Brian Redman, Ronnie Peterson, Tim Schenken, and Arturo Merzario, the last-named only brought into the team when there was a vacant slot. Peter Schetty remained as team manager, while Forghieri had disappeared off to work in his design centre at Modena. Although the Ferraris were far from faultless during the year, they looked magnificent compared with the rather tatty Alfa Romeos.

Six new cars had been built and, since Kyalami, Ferrari had adopted wider wheel rims: 11in (280mm) in place of 10in (255mm) at the front and 17in (430mm) in place of 16in (405mm) at the rear. Weight had risen by 40lb (18kg) to 1,430lb (648.5kg). There had also been an increase in power output, and it is believed that this had risen to 460bhp, still at 10,800rpm.

The season started with the Buenos Aires 1,000km race, and there had been serious doubts as to whether

the team should compete in the race following the 1971 tragedy. It seems that some pressure was brought to bear on Ferrari, and Peterson/Schenken and Regazzoni/Redman took the first two places. The Daytona race, now reduced in length to six hours, a sensible decision as, in the past, 24 hours with small fields had been catatonically boring. In Florida, Ickx/Andretti won with a car that had gone on to 11 cylinders, and in second place, staggering round because of gearbox troubles, were Peterson/Schenken.

In the Sebring 12 Hours the Buenos Aires cars ran for the second time, and they had been fitted with modified gearboxes, which enabled a gear cluster to be taken off the back and the ratios to be changed very quickly. There were also bigger brake calipers. Because of the lack of serious opposition, the Ferrari drivers were becoming increasingly tempted to treat an endurance race as a GP sprint. Andretti and Regazzoni battled for the lead, while Schetty made despairing signals and vain requests for them to slow off.

It was just like Tavoni and the Testa Rossa drivers at Le Mans in 1958–60. After a number of silly problems, some caused by over-driving, Ickx/Andretti, whose car was leaking oil badly, won by two laps from Peterson/Schenken. It seems that no one dared tell Enzo Ferrari about the drivers' antics, mainly because it would have shown Schetty in a bad light and undermined his authority. Ickx drove a long-tail car at the Le Mans Test Weekend and lapped faster than the fastest Matra.

The next race was the BOAC 1,000km at Brands Hatch, where the cars were far from trouble free, but still took the first two places in the order Ickx/Andretti and Peterson/Schenken. Alfa Romeo missed the Monza 1,000km race and, following imposition of the rule that every starter had to lap within 23 per cent of the best time of the fastest competitor, there were only 23 starters. In practice, all the Ferrari drivers were complaining about their gearboxes, and it was discovered that in error these had been assembled with fourth where fifth should have been, and fifth where fourth should have been. On this circuit the Ferraris were fitted with slightly longer tails.

Torrential rain fell throughout race day and, because of the conditions, the drivers were allowed out for a familiarisation session just over half an hour before the 11.30am start. Peterson slid off at the Parabolica, and Schetty persuaded the organisers to delay the start while the nose-section was changed. The Ferraris were far from trouble-free; for some of the race the elderly Porsche 908/03 of Jöst/ Schüller led, and this car eventually took second place behind Ickx/Regazzoni, with Peterson/Schenken third.

There was another poor entry in the Spa 1,000km race, and the Alfa Romeo team was absent, as Chiti had decided to concentrate on preparations for the Targa Florio. In the Belgian race, the Ferraris ran with long tails to improve downforce on this very fast circuit. Ickx/Regazzoni dominated the race, and it was of course Jacky's home circuit – and his favourite. They would have won easily, but Clay had a tyre start to deflate as he came out of La Source hairpin, and he was not aware until he had passed the entrance to the pits, so had to carry on for another lap. Redman/Merzario won the race, a victory especially well deserved by the Lancashire driver. Ickx/Regazzoni eventually finished second, a lap in arrears.

Then came the Targa Florio, for which Alfa Romeo entered four cars as they were desperate and determined to win. Ferrari sent a single entry for rally driver Sandro Munari and Arturo Merzario. This was chassis 0884, the car which had caught fire at Sebring where it was driven by Regazzoni/Redman. For the Sicilian race, the right sponson bulged out to accommodate an 8in-wide spare wheel.

The softest possible suspension was used, and the engine, fitted with a F1 exhaust system, had an engine that had a smooth power range between 5,000 and 11,800rpm. Despite all Autodelta's efforts with the Alfas, the Ferrari was fastest in practice and won by 15.9sec from the leading Alfa Romeo of Helmut Marko/'Nanni' Galli, who had driven unbelievably hard and well in their effort to beat the Ferrari. It was a great (and one can add, an undeserved) humiliation for Chiti and his team.

In the Nürburgring 1,000km race, Derek Bell led briefly with his Mirage, but Peterson/Schenken and Merzario/Redman took the first two places for Ferrari. Regazzoni had crashed the car that he was sharing with Ickx when he lost control at Hohe-Acht, some nine miles from the start, because his car was still on wet-weather tyres on a circuit that had dried out. In the absence of Ferrari, the Matras took the first two places at Le Mans (and Graham Hill, driving for Matra, had the unique distinction of winning the Drivers' Championship, Indianapolis, and Le Mans).

With the Championship in the bag, Ferrari entered four 312PB cars with 'Monza' tails in the Austrian 1,000km race in late June, and took the first four places in the order Ickx/Redman, Marko/Pace, Schenken/Peterson, and Merzario/Munari. Regazzoni was out of the race following his accident playing football. The opposition was again very weak, with just one Ford-powered Mirage and no Alfa Romeos because Autodelta had withdrawn from racing until 1973, but the Ferraris performed incredibly well.

Above: *This is a fine view of Ickx with the unsuccessful 312B3 GP Ferrari in the 1973 British GP at Silverstone. He finished a poor eighth, and he drove only once more for the Formula 1 team, in that year's Italian GP when he again finished eighth.* (Klemantaski Collection)

The final round of the Championship was the Watkins Glen Six Hours race in July, and the drivers of the three Ferraris were allowed to battle among themselves. Ickx/Andretti won from Peterson/Schenken. It had been too easy, and the 312PBs had never been pushed to the limit. As some drivers suspected, it was to prove a much tougher year in 1973 when the 312PBs were struggling all season and eventually falling victim to Matra power.

F1 doom and gloom in 1973

Testing of the 312B3 F1 car in its original form had revealed that it was deficient in most respects. Largely because of the influence of Fiat, Sandro Colombo, an engineer from Turin, was transferred to Ferrari to design a redesigned 312B3. In Forghieri's words, 'He was only the organiser, and the design work of the original 312B3 was given to Rocchi and Salvarini.' Colombo disliked the so-called 'Aero' semi-monocoque, and designed a full monocoque. The skills were lacking to build this at Maranello, so Colombo came to the UK to find a suitable

constructor. He settled on TC Prototypes run by John Thompson at Weedon in Northamptonshire, and this firm supplied three monocoques.

Enzo Ferrari had foreseen an unsuccessful year, and he had informed Clay Regazzoni that the team could run only one F1 car for Ickx, so the Swiss driver joined BRM. Ferrari had made it clear that he hoped to re-engage Regazzoni for 1974, and signed him up again as early as August 1973. Because of Firestone's intransigence in deciding to stay in F1, Ferrari signed with Goodyear, as did Lotus. Until the new car was ready, Ickx continued to race the 312B2, with some degree of effectiveness.

The Belgian finished fourth in Argentina (Merzario was also in the team and finished ninth), fifth in Brazil (Merzario was fourth), and retired at Kyalami where he was involved in a multi-car accident triggered by local driver Dave Charlton, who spun in front of Reutemann's Brabham on the second lap (Merzario took fourth place again).

Although two 312B3s appeared at the Spanish race, Ickx was the only driver entered. The cars were very different in some respects from anything designed by Forghieri. The front suspension was an established 312B layout, with fabricated upper rocking arms and wide-based lower wishbones operating inboard coil spring/damper units. At the rear, however, the car was very different, for the flat-12 engine was used as a stressed member mounted on a cast magnesium-alloy sandwich plate, and with a substantial bridging piece that located the rear suspension.

Construction complied with the new deformable structure regulations. To improve accessibility, the alternator was now mounted with the fuel-metering unit on the top of the engine. The radiators were originally side-mounted, but early tests revealed overheating problems, so one 312B3 (chassis number 010) was hastily modified to a front mounting of the radiator, using modified 312B2 nose panels. Overall, the 312B3 looked a big, bulky car, and the more perceptive critics predicted that it would be uncompetitive.

Ickx raced the car with front-mounted radiator at Montjuich Park, holding sixth place until he stopped to have the brakes bled, after which he rejoined the race to finish in 12th and last place. He then retired in Belgium and Monaco, finished sixth in the Swedish race at Anderstorp, fifth in the French race on the Paul Ricard circuit, and eighth in the British race. At this point he was close to despair, and quit the team.

Forghieri was called back to Maranello, and Ferrari asked him, 'Do you believe that you can modify the F1 car so that it is quicker than the B3 that we are racing.' Mauro responded, 'Of course I do, but it will take a month.' He had been designing the 312T with transverse gearbox, so he modified the 312B3 the same way.

> 'I moved the radiator forward to increase the weight at the front; I designed side pontoons; I developed a high air intake; and I improved the rear wing. I altered the weight distribution, and the aerodynamics were altered in accordance with what I had learned from wind-tunnel testing in Stuttgart. [Forghieri used the wind tunnel belonging to Stuttgart University.]
>
> It took me only three weeks, and when it was completed, Merzario, who was certainly not better than Jacky Ickx, beat the lap record on the Fiorano circuit by almost two seconds.'

Ferrari missed the Dutch and German Grands Prix. Merzario finished seventh in Austria, and Ickx was sufficiently interested in the car to accept an invitation to drive it in the Italian race, in which he finished a poor eighth, while Merzario retired after a front rocker arm broke when he hit a chicane on the second lap. Just to keep face with the public, Merzario was entered in two North American races, but nothing was achieved. For 1974 there was to be a complete shake-up, and Forghieri would be back with the F1 team.

Sports Prototypes in 1973

Forghieri had nothing to do with the 312PB racing programme in 1973, save that he designed a long tail at the request of Colombo. However, without a brief account of the team's performances, this section of the book would be substantially incomplete. Peter Schetty had relinquished the post of racing manager and returned to Switzerland to work in the family textile business, so Ing. Giacomo Caliri acted as technical director and racing manager for the sports car team. The only serious opposition came from the French Matra team whose V12 cars proved exceptionally formidable.

The cars raced by Ferrari in 1973 had been modified very extensively, and not very successfully by Caliri. They had the longer wheelbase and wider track of the cars raced at Kyalami in late 1972. Engine modifications resulted in a safe rev limit for the sports cars of 11,600rpm, with a slightly higher power output. Part of this was because of a new exhaust system, which contributed to an improvement in engine torque. An air-box was mounted between the struts of the roll bar, and the rear wing was integral with the body.

Ferrari had adopted the F1 gearbox for the Prototypes. The brakes were larger, with ventilated discs, and at many races these were mounted inboard at the rear, which necessitated deletion of the triangular wishbones in the rear suspension and the substitution of parallel rods. The handling remained difficult and unpredictable, moving without warning from pronounced oversteer to pronounced understeer. In addition, the power output was slightly lower than that of the Matras. All season the Ferrari drivers were struggling at the limit to match the lap times of the faster Matra drivers.

As late as February 1973 Brian Redman was testing the latest version of the 312PB at the Paul Ricard circuit near Marseille (ideal for winter testing because of the fairly high temperatures in the South of France). He and Ickx, together with Schenken and Merzario, remained in the team, and they were joined by Carlos Reutemann (an Argentinian who drove in F1 for Brabham) and Carlos Pace (a Brazilian who was a member of the Surtees F1 team).

Both Ferrari and Alfa Romeo missed the Daytona race, now – regrettably – restored to the original 24 hours, and after the retirement of the sole Matra, this race was won by a Porsche 911 Carrera. Both the Sebring 12 Hours and the BOAC 1,000km races were cancelled. Ferrari made a poor start to the season, for Matra won the Vallelunga Six Hours race near Rome, with Schenken/Reutemann in second place.

Enzo Ferrari was so concerned about the situation that he telephoned Peter Schetty in Basle and asked him to act as racing manager on a one-off basis at the Dijon 1,000km event that came next. Schetty imposed a fair degree of calm and order on the Ferrari Prototype team at Dijon, but there was nothing directly that he could do to improve Ferrari engine performance or handling; and to add to the problem, preparation had been affected by the metalworker's strike in Italy.

Ickx was partnered by Brian Redman at Dijon, but they were badly delayed, first because a new nose-section to reduce understeer ground itself away on the road and had to be changed; then Redman had a rear tyre puncture in front of the pits and he had to complete a full lap before he came into the pits for the wheel to be changed. Ickx drove extremely hard in the later stages of the race, but at the finish he and Redman were still one and half laps behind the winning Matra of Pescarolo/Larrousse.

At the Monza 1,000km race there were three long-tail cars from Ferrari, prepared to a very high standard, despite the labour problems in Italy. Ickx/Redman charged throughout the race and won for Ferrari after the Matra of Cevert/Beltoise retired because of a broken stub axle.

Ferrari sent only two cars with longer 'Monza' tails to the Spa 1,000km event. Much to everyone's surprise, including that of the Mirage team, the British cars took the first two places. Again there were only two Ferraris at the Targa Florio, and with two of the latest flat-12 Alfa Romeos; Matra had the good sense to miss this very Italian race. The Ferraris had a spare wheel in the body on the driver's side, single-rate coil springs that gave maximum deflection on the very bumpy roads, and a longer exhaust system. Ferrari also had a two-way radio system with an aerial mounted on the roll bar. After the Ferraris and the Alfa Romeos fell by the wayside, the race was won by a Porsche Carrera RSR.

At the Nürburgring, Ferrari, Alfa Romeo, and Matra each entered two cars. In an effort to close the gap in performance with the Matras, Merzario/Pace were entered with an experimental car. At the rear there was a lower centre section and a large F1-style air box. Of necessity, the oil cooler had to be mounted lower and was just in front of the right rear wheel, while there was a cooling duct in the sill instead of the two normally positioned on top of the tail. The pick-up points for the rear suspension links were mounted to reduce the height of the car. Neither driver was convinced that there was an improvement in the car's performance and handling.

Both the Matras, with their incredible, high-pitched screaming exhaust, retired because of engine failure,

and Ickx/Redman won the race by a short head from Merzario/Pace after the diminutive Arturo had put on a wonderful display of indiscipline. During the final quarter of the race he struggled to pass Ickx and take the lead and he ignored 'come in' signs. When he eventually came into the pits, Caliri had to haul him out of the car. Merzario stormed off and left his co-driver to finish the race.

At Le Mans there were three 312PBs, four Matras, and prospects of a duel which, if Ferrari won, would clinch the Championship for Maranello. All three Ferraris were in long-tail form, but these sloped at the rear and had an adjustable lip on the trailing edge of the tail. The space behind the rear wheels was boxed in to reduce turbulence, and they had a modified nose with four headlamps and outboard rear brakes. Both Ferrari and Matra claimed a power output of 450bhp at 10,500rpm. Ferrari's problem was that the flat-12 cars were insufficiently reliable. The Matra of Cevert/Beltoise won the race from Merzario/Pace, while the other two Ferraris retired.

Despite defeat at Le Mans, Ferrari still led the Championship by a narrow margin when the teams arrived at the next round at the Österreichring. There were only 19 starters, and the two Matras held the first two places for almost the whole race. Ickx/Redman finished third, while Pace/Merzario, who drove a car with a new nose-section that curved smoothly upwards and was imitative of the latest Alfa Romeo, finished sixth after a host of minor problems.

There were three Ferraris at Watkins Glen. Matra won and Ickx/Redman took second place despite being rammed by Cevert's Matra. Ferrari withdrew from the Buenos Aires 1,000km race, which was ultimately cancelled, and Matra won the Championship with 124 points to the 115 points of Ferrari. From this moment onwards Ferrari competed only in F1, and the next few years were to see the works fight its way back to supremacy under the guiding technical hand of Mauro Forghieri.

Revival in Formula 1

By late 1973 Mauro was firmly back at the F1 helm at Maranello. Regazzoni had signed up with Ferrari once more, and he was joined by Niki Lauda. Enzo Ferrari had been very impressed by the young Austrian's drive for BRM at Monaco in 1973, and he had all the fighting spirit and determination that the team so desperately needed.

Luca di Montezemolo had been seconded from Fiat's management structure to act in an unobtrusive, almost inconspicuous liaison role between the Ferrari F1 team, Enzo Ferrari, and the Fiat directors at Turin. He was, however, soon fronting the team and acting as team manager. Although Regazzoni was not officially number one driver, the team expected him to occupy that position. Instead, however, Lauda proved the quicker driver, but he had some difficulty in coping with (let alone understanding) Ferrari in-house politics over the three seasons that he and Regazzoni raced together, but their relationship was friendly and uncomplicated.

Forghieri had been Technical Director for 12 years, and some critics regarded him as a burnt-out case, but he proved over the next few years that nothing could be further from the truth. He had returned to the team full of enthusiasm, bounding with energy, and with many new ideas. The team was all too aware that the goal was not simply to restore the cars to the performance level vis-à-vis the opposition that they had possessed in 1970–1, but that the team had to become dominant.

The 312B3s that ran at Buenos Aires in January 1974 incorporated close to 30 changes from the versions raced at the end of the previous season. The most notable change was that the driving seat and fuel tank had been moved 5in (125mm) forward as part of Forghieri's aim to achieve a low polar moment of inertia. At the front there was a new wing mounted on a gently sloping nose and, from the South African race, smoothly rounded cockpit sides and a new air box that was equally smooth. The aim of this last feature was to enhance the airflow over the rear wing.

Engine development included modified cylinder heads, and power output was increased to 495bhp at 12,600rpm, together with a significant improvement in torque. By this stage Forghieri had already completed the development of the 312T with transversely mounted gearbox, but the team had decided that this would not be raced until 1975. In the words of Lauda, 'Forghieri was a tremendous engineer.'

At the first 1974 race, held at Buenos Aires, the winner was Hulme (McLaren) after Reutemann's Brabham dropped out on the last lap because of major engine trouble. Lauda took second place, and Regazzoni came third after a first-corner coming together with Jarier (Shadow). It was an encouraging start to the season, but there was a long way to go. The next round of the Championship, the Brazilian race at Interlagos, was stopped short because of a heavy thunderstorm, and Regazzoni finished second behind Fittipaldi (McLaren). Lauda retired because of electrical problems.

Both Ferraris retired in South Africa: Lauda because of an engine misfire caused by electrical problems, while Regazzoni's car lost its oil pressure. At this stage in the season the Ferraris were looking well short of being race-winners. That all changed in the Spanish GP at Jarama. The race started in heavy rain, but this soon stopped and the circuit began to dry out. So much depended on how much time was lost in the pits when the drivers changed to slicks. Ferrari pit work was exceptional, and Lauda and Regazzoni finished 1–2. It was the first Ferrari GP win since Ickx's victory at the Nürburgring in 1972.

The teams now moved on to Spa-Francorchamps for the Belgian GP on 12 May and held for the second time on the bleak, uninspiring Nivelles circuit. Regazzoni, officially at least, took pole position, but everyone – except the timekeepers – knew that there had been a complete 'cock-up' and the man who had been fastest in practice was Scheckter (Tyrrell). Regazzoni led initially, but soon he had slowed and was holding back the following pack. When he was held up by a back-marker on lap 39 of this 85-lap race, Fittipaldi and Lauda shot through. They went on to take the first two places, while Regazzoni, whose engine started to misfire as it ran low on fuel, fell back to finish fourth.

Although Lauda and Regazzoni took first two places in practice at Monaco, once again success evaded the team. Lauda was all set for his first Monaco win when he was forced to retire because of a repetition of his Kyalami electrical problems, while Regazzoni finished fourth. The Tyrrells of Scheckter and Depailler took the first two places in the Swedish GP; both Ferrari drivers were again out of luck – Regazzoni retired very early in the race because of gearbox problems, and Lauda was holding third place ten laps from the finish when the final drive broke because it had become overstressed by the failure of a broken rear suspension top link.

In the Dutch GP at Zandvoort the Ferrari drivers ran away from the rest of the field to finish 1–2, and it was becoming obvious that both were contenders for the 1974 World Championship. Lauda finished second in the French GP at Dijon–Prenois, and then came the British race at Brands Hatch. Lauda was leading the race when everything went disastrously wrong for Ferrari.

Jackie Stewart was in the commentary box with Murray Walker, and the eagle-eyed reigning champion (now retired) spotted that Lauda, comfortably leading the race with about eight laps to the finish, had a deflating right rear tyre, punctured when he ran over debris from Stuck's crashed March. Lauda realised that the back end of the car felt loose, but, although Mauro Forghieri, standing on the pit counter, was urging Lauda to come into the pits, the young Austrian had decided to carry on, hoping to reach the finish without wasting time on a wheel-change. On lap 74, a lap short of the finish, the tyre disintegrated, and Niki had no alternative but to pull into the pits.

Scheckter took the lead with his Tyrrell, and after a quick wheel-change Lauda accelerated away to rejoin the race and finish in what would now be a poor fifth place, a lap in arrears, but worth two points in the battle for the Championship. Through sheer stupidity, the RAC marshals had allowed the exit road to be blocked by spectators and hangers-on. So Lauda was unable to complete the race, and only a couple of months later the Commission Sportive Internationale awarded him fifth place and two points. Regazzoni finished fourth. It was Lauda's loss of eight points that materially affected the Championship outcome.

The next Championship round was the German GP at

the Nürburgring where Niki made a poor start. Coming up behind the pits he was in third place behind Scheckter and Regazzoni, and as they braked for the North Curve, he slewed into Scheckter and spun into the catch fencing. Regazzoni took the lead and won the race. In his book *Flat 12 Ferrari* Alan Henry quotes Lauda's comments on how the results in these two races cost him all hope of winning the World Championship:

'… as far as Brands Hatch was concerned, I reckoned it was a gamble, a real 50/50 situation. The tyre might well have lasted, and who's to say that the wheel nut wouldn't have jammed if I had come [earlier] into the pits. No, I honestly don't feel I made a mistake at Brands – it was a gamble that didn't come off.'

About the German race, Niki commented:

'Obviously, I couldn't expect Jody to give me much room, but I still tried to get through. As I went on the brakes, I realised that they were pulling me to the right, towards the Tyrrell. In an instant, I'd tapped his car, spun across his front wheels and went smashing into the catch fencing. That was just stupid, I made a complete fool of myself by trying to pull a manoeuvre which I could quite well have managed at any other time round that 14-mile lap.'

Regazzoni scored a superb win at the Nürburgring, but after that it was downhill all the way. At the Austrian race Lauda took pole position in practice, but retired in the race because of engine problems. In this race Clay finished fifth after a long pit stop to change a deflating rear tyre. In the Italian race at Monza the Ferraris ran 1–2 in the order Lauda–Regazzoni, but both retired because of engine problems. Lauda crashed at Mosport Park (the Canadian GP) where Regazzoni finished second to Fittipaldi, who was about to clinch his second World Championship.

In the final round of the Championship at Watkins Glen the Ferraris were plagued by handling problems and a severe vibration. It was believed to be caused by using suspension dampers of the wrong specification, although this has never been established beyond doubt. Lauda retired, while the never-say-die Regazzoni raced on pointlessly but determinedly to finish 11th. Fittipaldi won the Drivers' Championship with 55 points; Regazzoni was second on 52 points; and Lauda fourth with 38. In the Constructors' Championship McLaren won with 73 points net, and Ferrari was second with 65 points.

Flat-12 Transversale in 1975

Ferrari used the 312B3s for the first races in 1975 (and one was also the spare car at Kyalami). These 312B3s incorporated a number of modifications, most notably cast brackets to locate the ends of the coil spring/damper units (in place of the former tubular bridge over the gearbox). The 312B3s were rapidly becoming obsolete, and in Buenos Aires at the start of the year Regazzoni finished fourth, and Lauda, whose car was handling very peculiarly and weaving on the straight, took sixth place. Two weeks later in Brazil it was much the same story; Regazzoni finished fourth and Lauda was fifth.

Although the 312T retained many features of the earlier flat-12 cars, its appearance was distinctive and different. The adoption of a transverse gearbox reflected Forghieri's determination to achieve the lowest possible polar moment of inertia. Because the gear clusters were aligned across the car, ahead of the rear axle line, the shafts were at right angles to the centre line of the car (instead of parallel to it as in the normal longitudinal arrangement), and the power was transmitted by bevel gears on the input side of the gearbox to a spur-bevel final drive.

Part of Forghieri's efforts was to produce a car that was overall more compact than its predecessors. At the front, the chassis was much slimmer, and the very slim water radiators were nacelled behind the front wheels, with the oil radiators mounted ahead of the rear wheels. Forghieri had redesigned the front suspension: attached to the front bulkhead was a magnesium-alloy casing on which very small coil spring/damper units were mounted inboard, and these were operated by long fabricated upper rocking arms.

At the rear, the coil spring/damper units were mounted inboard with single top links, upper radius arms and lower wishbones. The brakes were mounted outboard at the front, but within the wheel rim offset and inboard at the rear. Whereas the 312B had a tendency to understeer that could not be adjusted out, the 312T was much more flexible in how it was set up. It was very sensitive in its handling, and its response to sudden changes of direction was exceptionally positive. It was a delightfully sure-footed car in every respect.

Although the 312T was first seen by the press just after the United States GP East at Watkins Glen in 1974, the development programme was delayed after Regazzoni wrote off one of the first cars during a testing accident on the Vallelunga circuit, and the team used the 312B3 at the first two races in 1975. The 312B3s were outpaced at Buenos Aires and finished fourth (Regazzoni) and sixth (Lauda); it was much the

Above: *Clay Regazzoni had a long and very successful career with the Ferrari Formula 1 team. Seen here with a 312T in the 1975 Italian GP at Monza, the Swiss driver scored his only World Championship race victory of the year.* (LAT Photographic)

same story at Interlagos with Regazzoni fourth and Lauda fifth.

The new cars were first raced at Kyalami, but during qualifying Lauda slid off the course backwards after hitting an oil slick dropped by Fittipaldi's McLaren. Intensive work by the mechanics had the car repaired for the race, but the outcome was disappointing. Regazzoni retired because of a broken throttle linkage, while Lauda soldiered on with a car down on power to finish fifth. Back at Maranello it was discovered that the fuel injection metering unit was slipping badly.

Morale at the factory was poor, but Lauda persuaded Forghieri and di Montezemolo that he should be allowed to do back-to-back tests of the 312B3 and the 312T at Fiorano. The results showed that the new car was significantly faster. Shortly afterwards Lauda won the minor International Trophy at Silverstone, but the team's performance in the Spanish race on the Montjuich Park circuit was very disappointing. The two Ferrari drivers collided at the first corner. Lauda retired immediately, but Regazzoni carried on, finishing unclassified. The race was stopped short after Stommelen's Hill had the rear wing

support fail, causing the car to go off the circuit, killing four spectators and badly injuring the driver.

At Monaco the tide turned in Ferrari's favour. Steady development work was paying off, and the performance of the cars was both improved and more consistent. Most important, the team's confidence and morale was on the up-and-up. In the Monaco race, which started in heavy rain, Lauda benefited from good Ferrari pit-work when the circuit dried out and he changed to slicks. Regazzoni crashed, but Lauda scored a good win from Fittipaldi (McLaren) and Pace (Brabham).

By the Belgian race the Ferraris had a new exhaust system, which improved pick-up at low speeds. Lauda drove another good race at Zolder to win from Scheckter (Tyrrell), with Regazzoni fifth. Although the 495bhp developed by the flat-12 engine gave the Ferraris power advantage over the Brabham, Lotus, McLaren, and Tyrrell with the Ford DFV, the leading cars were evenly matched in terms of steering, braking, and suspension. What advantages the Ferrari had, Lauda exploited to the full in 1975.

Lauda achieved another victory in the Swedish GP at Anderstorp after a tough battle to catch and pass Reutemann (Brabham BT44B) in the closing laps of the race. In the wet Dutch GP the winner was James Hunt at the wheel of the Hesketh. It was a result that the team from Towcester thoroughly deserved, and Lauda was far from displeased with his second place that made him top contender in the pursuit for the World Championship. Regazzoni finished third at Zandvoort. Another Championship race win, Lauda's fourth, followed in the French GP on the Paul Ricart circuit.

The British GP was a shambles because of the weather, and a fiasco for Ferrari. Regazzoni led between laps 13 and 19 when he spun off, damaging his rear aerofoil and was forced to stop at the pits. Very shortly afterwards a torrential thunderstorm inundated the circuit, and most of the drivers headed to the pits to change to wet-weather tyres. Lauda, desperate to rejoin the race, accelerated away from the Ferrari pit with a loose rear wheel that promptly fell off. The race was stopped at the end of lap 56, with the Ferrari drivers well out of the points – Lauda eighth, Regazzoni thirteenth.

The winner was Fittipaldi, so there was a dent in Lauda's World Championship prospects: the Austrian had accumulated 47 points, while Fittipaldi had gained 33, but any reduction in the lead was enough to worry Maranello. Practice for the German GP at the Nürburgring was dominated by Lauda, who lapped in 6min 58.6sec right at the end of practice so that there was no chance of his time being bettered. The Austrian led for the first nine laps, but then a front tyre deflated and Lauda arrived back at the pits with the front wing wrecked by flailing rubber. He rejoined the race to finish third, while Regazzoni retired because of engine problems.

Lauda was fastest again in practice at the Österreichring, scene of his home GP. Rain was falling at the start and, although Lauda's Ferrari was on wet-weather tyres, he had a dry-weather suspension set-up. The circuit gradually dried out, but the rain started again and the race was stopped at half-distance. The winner was Vittorio Brambilla (March), and Lauda's sixth place was worth only a ½-point. The next race was the non-Championship Swiss GP at Dijon–Prenois, and Regazzoni went ahead to take the lead from Jarier (Shadow) when his transmission failed, and he won from Depailler (Tyrrell).

That Lauda had won his first World Championship was confirmed at Monza where Regazzoni scored a resounding win, and towards the end of the race Lauda was able to slow off to finish third behind Fittipaldi. The Canadian GP was cancelled and the final race of the year was the United States GP at Watkins Glen. Lauda set fastest time in all four practice sessions, and won the race from Fittipaldi by a margin of just under five seconds.

This was despite a deplorable display by the Ferrari team who seemed afflicted by a collective madness. After he had been lapped by Lauda, Regazzoni persistently obstructed a front-running Fittipaldi until he was black-flagged. In the pits there was a scuffle between di Montezemolo and Burdette Martin, the self-opinionated, bumptious head of the Sports Car Club of America. Luca was an arrogant young man who still needed to mature, and while he quite rightly thought that Martin should keep his snout out of the trough, he should obviously have acted with greater restraint. The ruckus was settled, but not before the whole Ferrari team came close to being ejected from the circuit.

Lauda had won his first Championship with 64.5 points to the 45 of Fittipaldi, and 37 of Reutemann, and it was Ferrari's first win in the Drivers' and Constructors' World Championships since Surtees in 1964. Despite the stupid behaviour at Watkins Glen, the whole Ferrari team had matured and was well placed to deal with the trials and tribulations of the coming year.

A disastrous year – 1976

Although they did not come into force until the Spanish race, there were amendments to the regulations in 1976 that prohibited the use of high-mounted air boxes. Mauro Forghieri had been working on the improved 312T2 that featured many changes, and the new car was first seen at Ferrari's annual press conference held in December 1975. Under the skin the wheelbase had been increased by 2.2in (55mm) to 8ft 4.8in (2,560mm).

More significant were the external changes and the redesigned suspension. Gone, in accordance with the new regulations, was the high air box, and its place had been taken by a double-skinned cockpit top which featured triangular nostrils either side of the windscreen; these ducted cold air down the sides of the cockpit to the banks of cylinders of the flat-12 engine. Power output was around 500bhp, more than enough to be competitive.

A surprising feature of the prototype 312T2 was the de Dion rear suspension. This seemed a retrograde step because modern IRS systems had proved vastly superior to de Dion systems, which reacted more slowly to road conditions. A tubular bridge located the rear hub carriers transversely and, from the bottom of the hub carriers, transverse tubular links, together with another short link, formed a Watts linkage, while fore and aft movement was limited by the usual forward-facing tubular radius rods. A novel feature was the adoption of aerodynamic deflectors ahead of the front wheels that turned with them – a feature that was held to be illegal when Ferrari tried to race with them.

Early in 1976 Ferrari team-tested and developed the de Dion system, but it remained marginally inferior to the fully independent rear end. Both Lauda and Regazzoni remained with the team. Di Montezemolo had returned to the Fiat management structure, and the sartorially elegant Danielle Audetto, former Lancia rally team chief, became racing manager. Under his management, testing lacked the sharp edge of di Montezemolo's days and it soon became obvious that the Michelin tyres that had been so effective on the Ferraris in 1975 now seemed better suited to the McLaren M23s which, together with Tyrrell, provided the strongest opposition in 1976.

Lauda started the season with a fine win at the wheel of a 312T at Interlagos, over 20sec ahead of Patrick Depailler (Tyrrell 007), and he followed this up with another win with a 312T in South Africa – but it was a close-run thing at Kyalami because of a deflating rear tyre, and at the finish he was only 1.3sec ahead of Hunt (McLaren M23). Lauda was at the wheel of the 312T2 in its first event, the Race of Champions at Brands Hatch, but after qualifying second he retired because of a leaking brake pipe.

Thirteen days later Regazzoni won the United States GP West, with Lauda in second place. It seemed that the season would be another Ferrari flat-12 benefit, but it was to prove a year of drama and disaster. Lauda arrived at Jarama for the Spanish GP on 2 May suffering from

the agony of two cracked ribs, the result of an accident at his new lakeside home at Hof near Salzburg. Despite very considerable pain, he finished second to Hunt, who was subsequently disqualified because the rear track of his McLaren exceeded the maximum permitted. What had happened was bulging of the side-walls caused by the tyres heating. On appeal, a fine of $3,000 was substituted.

Lauda went on to win both the Belgian GP at Zolder (with Regazzoni second) and the Monaco race (Regazzoni was eliminated in an accident, but classified 14th). In the Swedish race at Anderstorp, the handling of the Ferraris was poor and, after qualifying fifth, Lauda came through to finish third (Regazzoni took sixth place). After the hearing of Hunt's appeal, Lauda led the Championship with 53 points to the 26 of Hunt. It was not an unbeatable advantage and it was not that good, for fortune turned against Ferrari.

The long, flat straights of the Paul Ricart circuit, scene of the French GP, should have suited the engine characteristics of the Ferrari flat-12, but the team had engine problems in practice, and in addition the Commission Sportive Internationale determined that the aerodynamic brake scoops were illegal movable aerodynamic devices because they moved as the wheels turned. In the French race both Ferraris retired because of seized engines, and back at Maranello these failures were traced to incorrect machining which had caused very slight cracks that enlarged under the stress of racing conditions.

Once again the British GP, held at Brands Hatch, proved to be another shambles, triggered by a collision between Lauda and Regazzoni on the first lap that caused the race to be stopped and restarted for the original distance. There were arguments as to whether Hunt should have been allowed to join the restart. The rules said that anyone who was running at the time that the red flag was shown to stop the race had a right to join the restart.

Hunt's car had not been running at the red flag, so, strictly, he should not have been allowed to restart, but the Royal Automobile Club succumbed to the vociferous, near-hysterical clamour of the British fans and allowed Hunt to join the restart. The British driver drove his spare car, benefiting from a pain-killing injection for what subsequent investigation revealed as a broken thumb.

Lauda led away at the restart, but his 312T2 developed an engine misfire, so Hunt shadowed the ailing Ferrari and then roared through to win from Lauda by a margin of just under a minute. Ferrari, of course, appealed and eventually – two months later – Hunt was disqualified. After this race, and prior to Hunt's disqualification, Lauda led the Championship with 61 points to the 35 of the British driver. It was a year of protests, coupled with near-tragedy at the Nürburgring.

The next race was the German GP where Lauda crashed and suffered terrible injuries. Hunt won this race from Scheckter (Tyrrell) and Jochen Mass (McLaren). Following Lauda's accident, Ferrari missed the Austrian race and then returned to racing with a single car for Regazzoni in the Dutch race. Hunt was building up a score that made him a Championship contender, and he won at Zandvoort with Regazzoni in second place.

By the Italian race Lauda had forced on himself a regime of exercises that made him fit enough to race, and at Monza there were cars for Lauda, Regazzoni, and newcomer to the team Carlos Reutemann. Regazzoni took second place to a fantastic, superb Peterson (March), Lauda displayed immense courage and depth of moral resources to finish fourth, and Reutemann, cramped in the cockpit of his car, was a very disappointed ninth.

The Ferraris were in trouble in the Canadian GP at Mosport Park where they handled badly on this bumpy circuit, and the shortcomings of their Goodyear tyres were obvious. Hunt scored an impressive win, while Lauda drove hard in his Ferrari until a rear suspension top link worked loose, causing handling problems that forced him to drop back to finish eighth. Hunt won again at Watkins Glen, against Niki's third place for four points, but he still led in the World Championship with 68 points to Hunt's 65 points.

The final round of the 1976 Championship was the Japanese GP on the Mount Fuji circuit, the backdrop of which was the most beautiful of all the races in the Championship series – except that in 1976 the weather was appalling: wet, gloomy, and dangerous. Niki's own comments about his decision to withdraw from the race are recorded in his entry in the alphabetical listing, and it suffices to say here that he pulled out of the race at the end of the second lap. Hunt led for much of the race, but as the track was drying out, one of his tyres started to deflate.

Hunt stopped for the front wheels to be changed, and rejoined the race to finish third, a lap in arrears.

Opposite: *This superb photograph shows Niki Lauda with the 312T2 with flat-12 engine and transverse gearbox in practice for the 1976 Monaco GP. He took pole position and led the race from start to chequered flag.*
(LAT Photographic)

This was good enough for him to win the World Championship by a single point. All year the Championship had been fought out between Hunt and Lauda but, while no one would begrudge Hunt his win (the reward for a combination of brilliance and persistence), it was sad that the outcome was materially affected by Lauda's terrible accident.

Lauda's final year with Ferrari – 1977

For 1977 the drivers were Lauda and Reutemann, and a totally unsympathetic and ungrateful Ferrari team had cast Regazzoni into the wilderness. At Maranello the team regarded Reutemann as the number one driver, and one of Lauda's first aims was to dispel this misapprehension. The team went into the new season with no major changes to the cars – power output was around 8/10bhp higher and the 312T2s now displayed the Fiat badge on the cockpit surrounds.

The season started in Argentina, where both drivers were aware of a lack of grip from their Goodyear tyres. To counteract this, the 312T2s were running so much wing that they lost straight-line speed. Lauda retired because of a fuel-injection metering problem, while Reutemann spun and stopped to change a blistered front tyre; somehow, he reckoned, this had sorted out the loss of grip, and he stormed back up through the field to finish third.

In Brazil the Ferrari struggled throughout qualifying because of handling problems, and Forghieri resolved this on Reutemann's car by fitting a new, modified rear wing. Reutemann drove a fine race, helped by a high level of retirements, to win from Hunt, with Lauda in third place. It was a remarkably good result following the poor showing in qualifying.

Back at Maranello, Lauda urged that the team should hold full test sessions on a regular basis, and he should personally test every 312T2 chassis – testing was the greatest tenet of Lauda's motor racing faith. He tested at Fiorano and then again at Kyalami before the South African race. He had ensured that the 312T2s, without exception, were set up the way that he wanted.

The South African GP proved to be another dreadful, tragic race. The facts need to be related so as to keep the accident and the race in focus. On lap 20, Shadow driver Renzo Zorzi's engine cut, and the car rolled to rest just over the brow of a small hill. As Zorzi climbed out of the car, a small fire started. Inadequately trained, unthinking, and totally ignorant of what was about to come over the brow, two marshals started to run across the track. Nineteen-year-old Jansen van Vuuren was carrying a fire extinguisher that weighed about 40lb.

Tom Pryce, a driver of immense promise, came over the brow of the hill at around 170mph (274kph), ran into van Vuuren, and both marshal and driver, the latter hit fully in the face by the extinguisher, were killed instantly. With the driver dead at the wheel, the Shadow carried on until it hit Laffite's Ligier-Matra and smashed into the catchfence. Lauda ran over debris from the Shadow's rollover bar and this dented the underside of the Ferrari's front wing. Lauda felt a bump, but drove on steadily, then easing off in the closing laps of the race when the oil pressure fell and the oil warning light was flashing. He crossed the line for his first win of the season, 5sec ahead of Scheckter (Wolf).

At Long Beach, scene of the United States GP West, Lauda took second place to Andretti (Lotus 78) despite a vibrating flat-spotted tyre. Reutemann had been delayed by a first-lap pit stop, but resumed the race, later colliding with Brett Lunger's March 761. Lauda was forced to withdraw from the Spanish GP because a rib, that had failed to knit properly following his accident, broke and he was in agony. Andretti (Lotus 78) won the race, but Reutemann finished a sound second for Ferrari. Not long afterwards, Lauda and Reutemann finished second and third at Monaco behind Scheckter (Wolf).

Forghieri was experimenting at around this time with a 312T2 fitted with twin rear wheels. During 1976–7 Tyrrell raced the P34 cars with four small wheels at the front, and this led to experiments by other constructors. Both March and Williams had built cars with four wheels at the rear mounted in tandem, but Forghieri built a car with four rear wheels mounted transversely, as on British hill climb cars through to the 1950s. Apart from other factors, it exceeded the F1 maximum permitted width by a considerable amount and, although grip was fantastic, handling was diabolical.

Ferrari's tyre problems were persistent, as the Goodyears could not be brought up to a satisfactory tread temperature, and the drivers were constantly complaining about lack of grip. Throughout the summer of 1977 Ferrari performances were mediocre. The Belgian GP at Zolder in June started in heavy rain, but when the rain stopped and the track dried out, Lauda benefited from quick Ferrari pit work when he changed to slicks, and he finished second to Swedish driver Gunnar Nilsson who scored his only GP win with a Lotus 78. Reutemann was third in the Swedish race where Lauda retired because of handling problems, and the Austrian was a poor fifth in the French race at Dijon–Prenois.

While the Ferrari drivers struggled, Ferrari negotiated to use Michelin tyres. Despite all the problems, Lauda

Above: *Niki Lauda with the experimental Ferrari with twin rear wheels, seen at Fiorano in 1977. It was an interesting experiment, but it could never have raced in Formula 1 as it exceeded the maximum permitted width.* (Author's collection)

continued to turn in some good performances, and he remained a Championship contender. He was second to Hunt in the British race at Silverstone, won the German race at Hockenheim, and finished second in Austria. With a win in Holland, a second place at Monza and fourth at Watkins Glen, Lauda clinched his second Drivers' Championship with 72 points.

Lauda had decided to join Brabham for 1978 and now, with the Championship in the bag, he thanked Ferrari for his help in his second World Championship win, and expressed his regrets that he was not well enough to drive in the Canadian and Japanese races. Even Bernie Ecclestone tried – unsuccessfully – to persuade Lauda to fulfil his contractual obligations to Ferrari. Gilles Villeneuve joined the Ferrari team at Mosport Park, but both he and Reutemann retired.

Villeneuve was eliminated by a terrible accident at Mount Fuji. With his 312T2, he ran into the back of Peterson's Tyrrell, was catapulted over the top of the six-wheel car and somersaulted down the escape road, killing two spectators watching from a prohibited area. Later, Villeneuve said to Peterson, 'Sorry, but I didn't seem to have any brakes.' The unfortunate deaths left him, it seemed, unaffected. Following Lauda's departure, Ferrari had sunk to a depressing nadir and once again faced an uphill struggle to re-establish its reputation and success.

Villeneuve's first full season with Ferrari – 1978

After the 1977 Monza race, Reutemann had conducted a major test session on Michelin radial tyres, and was 2½sec faster on Michelin qualifiers than he was on comparative Goodyear tyres. Adoption of the Michelin tyres for 1978 was inevitable. For the new season Forghieri had designed the 312T3, an almost completely new chassis that was intended to exploit the performance range of the new tyres to the full.

This did not appear until the Kyalami race, and Ferrari used the existing 312T2 model at both Buenos Aires and Brazil. Most of the year, however, proved an uphill struggle, as the latest Lotus 79 'ground-effect' cars driven by Andretti and Peterson were pretty well unbeatable. At the first races, however, Lotus, like Ferrari, were relying on the 1977 cars.

The Ferraris turned in a mediocre performance in Argentina, with Reutemann finishing seventh after a collision and a fight back up the field, while Villeneuve took eighth place after a determined effort to keep out of trouble.

The Brazilian race was run in oppressive heat, and in these temperatures Reutemann flourished. He was third fastest in practice, but at the start he accelerated through into a lead that he had soon extended to ten lengths. It was a race in which the European drivers were – generally – very badly affected by the heat. Reutemann won for Ferrari, and Emerson Fittipaldi finished second, one of his few decent performances with the car bearing his own name. Villeneuve struggled to keep up with his team-mate, but collided with Peterson and then spun into the catch fencing and out of the race.

In designing the new 312T3 Forghieri evolved new front suspension, which consisted of tubular rocker arms that operated much more substantial coil spring/damper units mounted on the sides of the footwell. At the rear, Forghieri retained the usual arrangement of transverse links and radius arms, with outboard coil spring/damper units. There were significant aerodynamic changes, for the overall effect was to form a flat surface, but with fairly high edges to ensure that the air flowed over the top body and was prevented from spilling over the sides.

For reasons that defied explanation, the Ferrari team suffered tyre problems in practice for the South African race that had not been encountered in tyre testing at the circuit. The race proved completely unsuccessful, for Villeneuve's car leaked oil because of a broken union, and Reutemann slid off on oil that his team-mate had dropped. At West Beach, scene of the United States GP West, Villeneuve accelerated ahead at the start and settled down to lead the race, with Reutemann in fourth place. He drove magnificently, coolly, and forcefully, holding off the rest of the field until he collided with Regazzoni's Shadow which he was lapping and rebounded off a wall into a barrier of old tyres.

In the Monaco race, Reutemann was eighth after a pit stop because of a puncture, but Villeneuve had a tyre deflate in the tunnel, smacked into the guard-rail and emerged on three wheels. At Zolder, after holding second place when a tyre punctured, Villeneuve came back to finish a rousing fourth, behind Reutemann in third place. The performance of the T3s remained mediocre, and the cars were markedly inferior to Lotus and other teams; they also had more than a fair share of bad luck and frustration. In the British race at Brands Hatch the Ferrari team achieved a rare success.

Both the Lotus 79s ran into problems, Lauda (Brabham) assumed the lead and 17 laps from the finish Reutemann squeezed past him when the Austrian found

Giacomelli's McLaren on his line through Paddock Bend. Despite all Lauda's efforts, Reutemann went on to win by just over a second. Villeneuve finished third in Austria and sixth at Zandvoort. Then Reutemann took third place at Monza and achieved a well-deserved win at Watkins Glen. Villeneuve scored his first race victory for Ferrari on home territory in the Canadian GP at Montreal.

Although Lotus drivers Andretti and Peterson (the latter posthumously) took the first two places in the Championship, Reutemann was third, a far from poor result with a mediocre car, and Ferrari was second in the Constructors' Championship. There were yet again major changes in the Ferrari team at the end of the season. Reutemann left to drive for Lotus (for reasons that are difficult to pinpoint, the Argentinian never fitted well in the Ferrari team) and Villeneuve was joined at Maranello by Jody Scheckter.

Ferrari regains predominance – 1979

For 1979 Forghieri succeeded in producing the most successful flat-12 car, the 312T4, after a lot of work had been carried out in the Pininfarina wind tunnel. There was, however, an insuperable problem that could only be resolved by redesigning the flat-12 engine as a V12 (which is what Chiti did with the Alfa Romeo engines used by Brabham) – and, of course, this was not going to happen at Maranello. The width of the engine prevented Forghieri from using side-pods with sufficient surface area to match the downforce created on the Lotus.

Instead he was forced to use the wind tunnel results to produce a body with the smoothest possible upper surface, coupled with reliance on the greater power of the Ferrari engine and the fact that the team possessed – probably – the two fastest F1 drivers. Although they were not yet ready to race, the 312T4s were first seen in Italy in January. The main changes were that the wheelbase had been increased to 8ft 10.4in (2,700mm) from 8ft 4.8in (2,560mm).

The cockpit area was moved closer to the front of the car, with the fuel tank, housing the total fuel capacity, immediately behind it. Underneath the monocoque, the car was shaped with two underbody panels sweeping in to meet a central backbone, rather like the underside of a boat, where the underside curves inwards to form the keel. There was a very smooth upper surface with just small NACA ducts drawing in cooling air that was fed to the fuel pump and the electrics.

Behind the driver the bodywork was abbreviated,

leaving exposed the five-speed transversely mounted gearbox and the inboard coil spring/damper units; these had specific channels on a casting right at the back behind the rear axle and were actuated by tubular rocker arms similar to those at the front. The brakes were mounted inboard at the rear.

At the beginning of the year the team had to rely on the 1978 cars. In Argentina there was a multi-car pile-up at the first corner, and this necessitated a restart. Scheckter sprained a wrist and was unable to join the restart, while Villeneuve had a difficult race; he was battling for sixth place, when he spun, stopped for new tyres, and later retired because of engine failure. Villeneuve and Scheckter finished fifth and sixth in Brazil, and then it was the Kyalami race, coupled with a transformation in Ferrari fortunes on the racing appearance of the new 312T4 cars.

Lotus introduced the new type 80 for 1979, and it was unsuccessful mainly because, as Lotus engineer Peter Wright has commented, 'We took the view that if some was good, more was better, and we came up with the 80 which, in theory, had yet more ground-effect – but still had the flaky structure of the 79.' In addition, of course, the 312T4 was a vastly improved car and proved to be much better in almost every respect than the latest Lotus.

So, as Lotus (rather surprisingly) failed to achieve expectations, Ferrari did achieve them; and two drivers, not reckoned to be able to work together, did so with consistent success. The brilliant performances early in the season ebbed away, but the Ferraris regained form in the last few races of 1979 and the results reflect a very exceptional season. The performances of the 312T4 may be summarised as follows:

South African GP, Kyalami, 3 March, 198.908 miles (320.112km)

1st   G. Villeneuve, 117.197mph (188.611kph)
2nd   J. Scheckter

United States GP West, Long Beach, 8 April, 162.616 miles (261.706km)

1st   G. Villeneuve, 87.808mph (131.313kph)
2nd   J. Scheckter

Spanish GP, Jarama, 29 April, 158.636 miles (255.300km)

4th   J. Scheckter
7th   G. Villeneuve (The Michelin tyres lost their effectiveness as soon as oil and rubber was spread over the track; Villeneuve had braking problems and spun off.)

Belgian GP, Zolder, 13 May, 185.380 miles (298.340km)

1st   J. Scheckter, 111.237mph (179.018kph)
Retd G. Villeneuve (Car ran out of fuel.)

Monaco GP, Monte Carlo, 27 May, 156.407 miles (251.712km)

1st   J. Scheckter, 81.338mph (130.902kph)
Retd G. Villeneuve (Held second place, transmission problems.)

French GP, Dijon–Prenois, 1 July,
188.897 miles (304.000km)

2nd   G. Villeneuve (After an exciting battle with Arnoux [Renault].)

7th   J. Scheckter (Delayed by pit stop to change tyres.)

British GP, Silverstone, 14 July,
199.4376 miles (320.865km)

5th   J. Scheckter

14th   G. Villeneuve
(Classified but not running at the finish.)
(Fuel vaporisation problems.)

German GP, Hockenheim, 29 July,
189.832 miles (305.505km)

4th   J. Scheckter

8th   G. Villeneuve

Austrian GP, Österreichring, 12 August,
199.378miles (320.868km)

2nd   G. Villeneuve

4th   J. Scheckter

Dutch GP, Zandvoort, 26 August,
196.944 miles (3165.950km)

2nd   J. Scheckter

Retd   G. Villeneuve (Deflating tyre damaged rear suspension.)

Italian GP, Monza, 9 September,
180.198 miles (290.000km)

1st   J. Scheckter, 116.616mph (187.675kph)

2nd   G. Villeneuve

Canadian GP, Montreal, 30 September,
197.298miles (317.520km)

2nd   G. Villeneuve

4th   J. Scheckter

United States GP East, 7 October,
199.243 miles (320.651km)

1st   G. Villeneuve,
106.456mph (171.325kph)

Retd   J. Scheckter (Burst rear tyre.)

Drivers' World Championship:

1st   J. Scheckter, 51 points (net)

2nd   G. Villeneuve, 47 points (net)

Constructors' World Championship:

1st   Ferrari, 113 points

The last year of the flat-12 – 1980

After this phenomenally successful year, Ferrari did not quite expect a repeat in 1980, but the team most certainly did not anticipate the total disaster of a season that followed. Forghieri's efforts were mainly concentrated on the development of a 1500cc six-cylinder turbocharged car for Grands Prix racing in 1981. The final version of the flat-12 was the 312T5, and the cars raced were rebuilt T4s. The principal changes were that the monocoques had slimmer front ends, there was modified bodywork, and suspension and aerofoil changes were coupled with a small boost in power output.

Although the latest Ferraris were lapping about a half-second faster than the 312T4s in 1979, the problem was that the fastest opposition, Williams, Renault, Brabham and Ligier, were all a full second faster. On top of this, the 312T5 proved unexpectedly unreliable, with a succession of mechanical failures, and they were plagued by tyre trouble all year. The best performances in a dismal season were three fifth places, by Scheckter at Long Beach and by Villeneuve at Monaco and Montreal. Ironically, the team's worst performance was also at Montreal where Scheckter failed to qualify as a starter.

After 22 years as Technical Director – interrupted by short breaks – Mauro Forghieri resigned from the Racing Department of Ferrari at the end of the 1984 season. At the insistence of Fiat, he stayed with Ferrari for another two years, but as the head of the advanced engineering department. At the end of this two-year period he switched to a new Ferrari engineering division and developed an advanced Ferrari four-wheel-drive car.

There was a great friendship between Ferrari and Forghieri, and while the ageing 'Il Drago' knew that Mauro could not stay with the Maranello company forever, he did not want to let him go. In 1986 when Fiat had agreed that they could no longer hold on to Forghieri, he went to see the 'Old Man' and said, 'I can leave now.'

Mauro signed a contract with Iacocca, the then President of Chrysler, in 1987. He founded Lamborghini Engineering and was Technical Director of Lamborghini until December 1991. He designed a Formula 1 engine, which was used by Lotus in 1990, but Chrysler had financial problems during the time that Forghieri was with Lamborghini and this prevented the F1 engine from being fully developed.

Later, Forghieri designed a concept electric minivan for the Italian National Electricity Board and he was Technical Director of Bugatti Automobili SpA from May 1993 until December 1994. He set up and still runs Oral Engineering based in Modena, and this company undertakes research and development projects for various motor manufacturers.

Le Ferrari Automobili – 1956 Staff Directory

(This is an English translation of an official 1956 senior staff directory kindly supplied by Romolo Tavoni.)

GENERAL MANAGEMENT FERRARI, E.
    Production Adviser BAZZI, L.
    Technical Adviser BELLENTANI, V.
    Project Adviser MASSIMINO, A.
    Secretary* TAVONI, R.

DIRECTOR OF COMMERCE &
ADMINISTRATION GIARDINI, G.
    DELLA CASA, E.**

ORDERS AND SUPPLIES GIBERTI, F.***
    Secretary**** ROSI, A.
    Personnel SELMI, E.
    Accounts BENZI, C.
    GAVIOLI, C.
    RADIGHIERI, G.

CUSTOMER SUPPORT MONTANI, A.
    RANUZZI, L.

PRODUCTION FERRARI, D.
    Tooling FORGHIERI, R.
    Forging SALA, G.
    Machine gear-cutting GOZZI, R.
    Machine boring and punching MAZZETTI, G.
    Stock CORRADINI, L.
    Rectification OLIVIERI, L.
    Electrics ASCARI, V.
    Assembly FRANCHINI, A.

PLANT AND WORK OFFICE FERRARI, A.
    Service MARI, G.
    Storage DAL RIO, G.

DRAWING OFFICE AND
DESIGN FRASCHETTI, A.
    ROCCHI, F.
    SALVARINI, W.
    CASOLI, E.

FOUNDRY FRANCHI, A.

INSPECTION GAZZOTTI, C.

EXPERIMENTAL AND RACING
DEPARTMENT TADDEI, D.
    LUCCHI, A.
    FLORINI, G.
    PARENTI, L.

SCUDERIA FERRARI FERRARI, ENZO
    Management SCULATTI, E.
    Technical AMOROTTI, G.

* Male secretary, became Racing Manager, sacked October 1961.
** Later accountant, financial director, sacked October 1961, but reinstated by Ferrari.
*** Racing manager, 1934 and 1947–51, sacked October 1961, but reinstated by Ferrari.
**** Female secretary.

NOTE: The foundry had only recently been installed, and prior to this Ferrari contracted foundry work to Maserati.

Scuderia Ferrari and Ferrari Racing Managers

1930–1	Saracco Ferrari	1971–2	Peter Schetty
1932–3	Mario Lolli	1973	Sandro Colombo
1934	Federico Giberti	1974–5	Luca di Montezemolo
1935–40	Nello Ugolini	1976	Guido Rosani
1947–51	Federico Giberti	1976	Daniele Audetto
1952–5	Nello Ugolini	1977	Roberto Nosetto
1956	Eraldo Sculati	1978–88	Marco Piccinini
1957	Girolamo Amorotti	1989–91	Cesare Fiorio
1958–61	Romolo Tavoni	1991	Claudio Lombardi
1962–6	Eugenio Dragoni	1992–3	Sante Ghedini
1967	Franco Lini	1993–2006	Jean Todt
1968–70	Franco Gozzi	2006–9	Stefano Domenicali

Ferrari Formula 1 World Champions

The Constructors' Championship did not start until 1958. These results show how Ferrari drivers and cars fared in Formula 1 over the years, and it is very clear that the team's performances were highly inconsistent, and successes were very patchy.

* = Awarded posthumously

Drivers' Championship

1950
1st   G. Farina (Alfa Romeo 158) 30 points
2nd   J. M. Fangio (Alfa Romeo 158) 27 points
3rd   L. Fagioli (Alfa Romeo 158) 24 points (net)

1951
1st   J. M. Fangio (Alfa Romeo 158 and 159) 31 points (net)
2nd   A. Ascari (Ferrari Tipo 375) 25 points
3rd   J. F. González (Ferrari Tipo 375) 24 points

1952
1st   A. Ascari (Ferrari Tipo 500) 36 points
2nd   G. Farina (Ferrari Tipo 500) 25 points (net)
3rd   P. Taruffi (Ferrari Tipo 500) 22 points

1953
1st   A. Ascari (Ferrari Tipo 500) 34½ points
2nd   J. M. Fangio (Maserati A6GCM) 28 points
3rd   G. Farina (Ferrari Tipo 500) 26 points

1954
1st   J. M. Fangio (Maserati 250F and Mercedes-Benz W196) 42 points (net)
2nd   J. F. González (Ferrari Tipo 625) 25 points
3rd   J. M. Hawthorn (Ferrari Tipo 65) 24½ points

1955

1st　　J. M. Fangio (Mercedes-Benz W196) 40 points
2nd　　S. Moss (Mercedes-Benz W196) 23 points
3rd　　E. Castellotti (Lancia D50 and Ferrari 555) 12 points

1956

1st　　J. F. Fangio (Lancia-Ferrari) 30 points
2nd　　S. Moss (Maserati 250F) 27 points
3rd　　P. J. Collins (Lancia-Ferrari) 25 points

1957

1st　　J. M. Fangio (Maserati 250F) 40 points
2nd　　S. Moss (Vanwall) 25 points
3rd　　L. Musso (Lancia-Ferrari) 16 points

1958

1st　　J. M. Hawthorn (Ferrari Dino 246) 42 points　　　1st　　Vanwall 48 points
2nd　　S. Moss (Vanwall) 41 points　　　　　　　　　　　　**2nd　　Ferrari 40 points**
3rd　　C. A. S. Brooks (Vanwall) 31 points　　　　　　　　3rd　　Cooper-Climax 31points

1959

1st　　J. Brabham (Cooper-Climax) 31 points　　　　　　1st　　Cooper-Climax 40 points **2nd**
2nd　　C. A. S. Brooks (Ferrari) 27 points　　　　　　　**2nd　　Ferrari 32 points**
3rd　　S. Moss (Cooper-Climax) 25½ points　　　　　　　3rd　　BRM 18 points

1960

1st　　J. Brabham (Cooper-Climax) 43 points　　　　　　1st　　Cooper-Climax 48 points
2nd　　B. McLaren (Cooper-Climax) 34 points　　　　　　2nd　　Lotus-Climax 34 points
3rd　　S. Moss (Cooper-Climax and Lotus 18-Climax) 19 points　　**3rd　　Ferrari 26 points**

1961

1st　　P. Hill (Ferrari Tipo 156) 34 points　　　　　　**1st　　Ferrari 40 points**
2nd　　W. von Trips* (Ferrari Tipo 156) 33 points　　2nd　　Lotus 32 points
3rd　　S. Moss (Lotus 18-Climax) 21 points and　　　　3rd　　Porsche 22 points
　　　　D. Gurney (Porsche) 21 points

1962

1st　　G. Hill (BRM P57) 42 points　　　　　　　　　　1st　　BRM 42 points
2nd　　J. Clark (Lotus 25) 30 points　　　　　　　　　　2nd　　Lotus-Climax 36 points
3rd　　B. McLaren (Cooper-Climax) 27 points　　　　　3rd　　Cooper-Climax 29 points

1963

1st　　J. Clark (Lotus 25-Climax) 54 points　　　　　　1st　　Lotus-Climax 54 points
2nd　　G. Hill (BRM P57 and P61) 29 points and　　　　2nd　　BRM 36 points
　　　　R. Ginther (BRM P57 and P61) 29 points　　　　3rd　　Brabham-Climax 28 points

1964

1st　　J. Surtees (Ferrari Tipo 156 and 158) 40 points　　**1st　　Ferrari 45 points**
2nd　　G. Hill (BRM P261) 39 points　　　　　　　　　　2nd　　BRM 42 points
3rd　　J. Clark (Lotus 25 and 33) 32 points　　　　　　3rd　　Lotus 37 points

Drivers' Championship	Constructors' Championship

1965
1st	J. Clark (Lotus 25 and 33) 54 points		1st	Lotus-Climax 54 points
2nd	G. Hill (BRM P261) 40 points		2nd	BRM 45 points
3rd	J. Stewart (BRM P261) 33 points		3rd	Brabham-Climax 27 points

1966
1st	J. Brabham (Brabham BT19 and BT20-Repco) 42 points		1st	Brabham-Repco 42points
2nd	**J. Surtees (Ferrari Tipo 312** and Cooper T81-Maserati) 28 points		**2nd**	**Ferrari 31 points**
3rd	J. Rindt (Cooper T81-Maserati) 22 points		3rd	Cooper-Maserati 30 points

1967
1st	D. Hulme (Brabham BT19, BT20 and BT24-Repco) 51 points		1st	Brabham-Repco, 63 points
2nd	J. Brabham (Brabham BT19 and BT24-Repco) 46 points		2nd	Lotus-Ford 44 points
3rd	J. Clark (Lotus 49-Ford) 41 points		3rd	Cooper-Maserati 28 points

1968
1st	G. Hill (Lotus 49 and 49B-Ford) 48 points		1st	Lotus-Ford 62 points
2nd	J. Stewart (Matra MS10-Ford) 36 points		2nd	McLaren-Ford 49 points
3rd	D. Hulme (McLaren M5A-BRM and M7A-Ford) 33 points		3rd	Matra-Ford 45 points

1969
1st	J. Stewart (Matra MS10 and MS80-Ford) 63 points		1st	Matra-Ford 66 points
2nd	J. Ickx (Brabham BT26A-Ford) 37 points		2nd	Brabham-Ford 49 points
3rd	B. McLaren (McLaren M7A and M7C-Ford) 26 points		3rd	Lotus-Ford 47 points

1970
1st	J. Rindt* (Lotus 49C and 72-Ford) 45 points		1st	Lotus-Ford, 59 points
2nd	**J. Ickx (Ferrari 312B) 40 points**		**2nd**	**Ferrari, 52 points**
3rd	**G. Regazzoni (Ferrari 312B) 33 points**		3rd	March-Ford, 48 points

1971
1st	J. Stewart (Tyrrell 001 and 003-Ford) 62 points		1st	Tyrrell-Ford 73 points
2nd	R. Peterson (March 711-Ford) 33 points		2nd	BRM 36 points
3rd	F. Cevert (Tyrrell 002-Ford) 26 points		**3rd**	**Ferrari** and March-Ford **33 points**

1972
1st	E. Fittipaldi (Lotus 72D-Ford) 61 points		1st	Lotus-Ford 61 points
2nd	J. Stewart (Tyrrell 003, 004, and 005-Ford) 45 points		2nd	Tyrrell-Ford 51 points
3rd	D. Hulme (McLaren M19A and M19C-Ford) 39 points		3rd	McLaren-Ford 47 points

1973
1st	J. Stewart (Tyrrell 005 and 006-Ford) 71 points		1st	Lotus-Ford 92 points
2nd	E. Fittipaldi (Lotus 72E-Ford) 55 points		2nd	Tyrrell-Ford 82 points
3rd	R. Peterson (Lotus 72E-Ford) 52 points		3rd	McLaren-Ford 58 points

1974
1st	E. Fittipaldi (McLaren M23-Ford) 55 points		1st	McLaren-Ford 73 points
2nd	**G. Regazzoni (Ferrari 312B3) 52 points**		**2nd**	**Ferrari 65 points**
3rd	J. Scheckter (Tyrrell 006 and 007-Ford) 45 points		3rd	Tyrrell-Ford 52 points

Drivers' Championship	Constructors' Championship		

1975
1st	**N. Lauda (Ferrari 312B3 and 312T) 64.5 points**	**1st**	**Ferrari 72.5 points**
2nd	E. Fittipaldi (McLaren M23-Ford) 45 points	2nd	Brabham-Ford 54 points
3rd	C. Reutemann (Brabham BT44B) 37 points	3rd	McLaren-Ford 53 points

1976
1st	J. Hunt (McLaren M23-Ford) 69 points	**1st**	**Ferrari 83 points**
2nd	**N. Lauda (Ferrari 312T and 312T2) 68 points**	2nd	McLaren-Ford 74 points
3rd	J. Scheckter (Tyrrell 007 and P34) 49 points	3rd	Tyrrell-Ford 71 points

1977
1st	**N. Lauda (Ferrari 312T2) 72 points**	**1st**	**Ferrari 95 points**
2nd	J. Scheckter (Wolf WR1/2/3-Ford) 55 points	2nd	JPS/Lotus-Ford 62 points
3rd	M. Andretti (JPS/Lotus 78-Ford) 47 points	3rd	McLaren-Ford 60 points

1978
1st	M. Andretti JPS/Lotus 78 and 79-Ford) 64 points	1st	Lotus-Ford 86 points
2nd	R. Peterson* JPS/Lotus 78 and 79-Ford 51 points	**2nd**	**Ferrari 58 points**
3rd	**C. Reutemann (Ferrari 31T2 and 312T3) 48 points**	3rd	Brabham-Romeo 53 points

1979
1st	**J. Scheckter (Ferrari 312T3 and 312T4) 51 points**	**1st**	**Ferrari 113 points**
2nd	**G. Villeneuve (Ferrari 312T3 and 312T4) 47 points**	2nd	Williams-Ford 75 points
3rd	A. Jones (Williams FW06 and FW07) 40 points	3rd	Ligier-Ford 61 points

1980
1st	A. Jones (Williams FW07 and FW07B-Ford) 67 points	1st	Williams-Ford 120 points
2nd	N. Piquet (Brabham BT49-Ford), 54 points	2nd	Ligier-Ford 66 points
3rd	C. Reutemann (Williams FW07B-Ford) 42 points	3rd	Brabham-Ford 55 points

1981
1st	N. Piquet (Brabham BT49C-Ford) 50 points	1st	Williams-Ford 95 points
2nd	C. Reutemann (Williams FW07C-Ford) 49 points	2nd	Brabham-Ford 61 points
3rd	A. Jones (Williams FW07C-Ford) 46 points	3rd	Renault 54 points

1982
1st	K. Rosberg (Williams FW0C and FW08-Ford) 44 points	**1st**	**Ferrari 74 points**
2nd	**D. Pironi (Ferrari 126C2) and**	2nd	McLaren-Ford 69 points
	J. Watson (McLaren MP4B-Ford) **39 points**	3rd	Renault 62 points

1983
1st	N. Piquet (Brabham BT52 and BT52B-BMW) 59 points	**1st**	**Ferrari 89 points**
2nd	A. Prost (Renault RE30C and RE40) 57 points	2nd	Renault 79 points
3rd	**R. Arnoux (Ferrari 126C2B and 126C3) 49 points**	3rd	Brabham-BMW 72 points

1984
1st	N. Lauda (McLaren MP4/2-TAG) 72 points	1st	McLaren-TAG 143.5 points
2nd	A. Prost (McLaren MP4/2-TAG) 71.5 points	**2nd**	**Ferrari 57.5 points**
3rd	E. de Angelis (Lotus 95T-Renault) 34 points	3rd	Lotus-Renault 47 points

Drivers' Championship	Constructors' Championship

1985
1st A. Prost (McLaren MP4/2B-TAG), 73 points

2nd M. Alboreto (Ferrari 156/85), 53 points

3rd K. Rosberg (Williams FW10-Honda), 40 points

1st McLaren-TAG 90 points

2nd Ferrari 82 points

3rd Williams-Honda 71 points

1986
1st A. Prost (McLaren MP4/2C-TAG) 72 points

2nd N. Mansell (Williams FW11-Honda) 70 points

3rd N. Piquet (Williams FW11-Honda) 69 points

1st Williams-Honda 141 points

2nd McLaren-TAG 96 points

3rd Lotus-Renault 58 points

1987
1st N. Piquet (Williams FW11B-Honda) 73 points

2nd N. Mansell (Williams FW11B-Honda) 61 points

3rd A. Senna (Lotus 99T-Honda) 57 points

1st Williams-Honda 137 points

2nd McLaren-TAG 76 points

3rd Lotus-Honda 64 points

1988
1st A. Senna (McLaren MP4/4-Honda) 90 points

2nd A. Prost (McLaren MP4/4-Honda) 87 points

3rd G. Berger (Ferrari F1-87/88C) 41 points

1st McLaren-Honda 199 points

2nd Ferrari 65 points

3rd Benetton-Ford 39 points

1989
1st A. Prost (McLaren MP4/5-Honda) 76 points

2nd A. Senna (McLaren MP4/5-Honda) 60 points

3rd R. Patrese (Williams FW12C and FW13-Renault) 40 points

1st McLaren-Honda 141 points

2nd Williams-Renault 77 points

3rd Ferrari 59 points

1990
1st A. Senna (McLaren MP4/5B-Honda) 78 points

2nd A. Prost (Ferrari 641 and 641/2) 71 points

3rd N. Piquet (Benetton B189B and B190-Ford) and
G. Berger (McLaren MP4/5B-Honda) 43 points

1st McLaren-Honda 121 points

2nd Ferrari 110 points

3rd Benetton-Ford 71 points

1991
1st A. Senna (McLaren MP4/6-Honda) 96 points

2nd N. Mansell (Williams FW14-Renault) 72 points

3rd R. Patrese (Williams FW14-Renault) 53 points

1st McLaren-Honda 139 points

2nd Williams-Renault 125 points

3rd Ferrari 55.5 points

1992
1st N. Mansell (Williams FW14B-Renault) 108 points

2nd R. Patrese (Williams FW14B-Renault) 56 points

3rd M. Schumacher (Benetton B192-Ford) 53 points

1st Williams-Renault 164 points

2nd McLaren-Honda 99 points

3rd Benetton-Ford 91 points

1993
1st A. Prost (Williams FW15C-Renault) 99 points

2nd A. Senna (McLaren MP4/8-Ford) 73 points

3rd D. Hill (Williams FW15C-Renault) 69 points

1st Williams-Renault 168 points

2nd McLaren-Ford 84 points

3rd Benetton-Ford 72 points

1994
1st M. Schumacher (Benetton B194-Ford) 92 points

2nd D. Hill (Williams FW16 and FW16B-Renault) 91 points

3rd G. Berger (Ferrari 412TI) 41 points

1st Williams-Renault 118 points

2nd Benetton-Ford 103 points

3rd Ferrari 71 points

Drivers' Championship	Constructors' Championship

1995

1st   M. Schumacher (Benetton B195-Renault) 102 points   1st   Benetton-Renault 137 points

2nd D. Hill (Williams FW17-Renault) 69 points   2nd Williams-Renault 112 points

3rd   D. Coulthard (Williams FW17-Renault) 49 points   **3rd   Ferrari 73 points**

1996

1st   D. Hill (Williams FW18) 97 points   1st   Williams-Renault 175 points

2nd J. Villeneuve (Williams FW18) 78 points   **2nd Ferrari 70 points**

3rd   M. Schumacher (Ferrari F310) 59 points   3rd   Benetton-Renault 68 points

1997

1st   J. Villeneuve (Williams FW19) 81 points   1st   Williams-Renault 123 points

2nd H-H. Frentzen (Williams FW19) 42 points   **2nd Ferrari 102 points**

3rd   D. Coulthard (McLaren MP4/12-Mercedes) and   3rd   Benetton-Renault 67 points
      J. Alesi (Benetton B197-Renault) 36 points

1998

1st   M. Häkkinen (McLaren MP4/13-Mercedes) 100 points   1st   McLaren-Mercedes 156 points

2nd M. Schumacher (Ferrari F300) 86 points   **2nd Ferrari 133 points**

3rd   D. Coulthard (McLaren MP4/13-Mercedes) 56 points   3rd   Williams-Mecachrome 38 points

1999

1st   M. Häkkinen (McLaren MP4/14-Mercedes) 76 points   **1st   Ferrari 128 points**

2nd E. Irvine (Ferrari F399) 74 points   2nd McLaren-Mercedes 124 points

3rd   H-H. Frentzen (Jordan 199-Mugen Honda) 54 points   3rd   Jordan-Mugen Honda 61 points

2000

1st   M. Schumacher (Ferrari F1 2000) 108 points   **1st   Ferrari 170 points**

2nd M. Häkkinen (McLaren MP4/15-Mercedes) 89 points   2nd McLaren-Mercedes 152 points

3rd   D. Coulthard (McLaren MP4/15-Mercedes 73 points)   3rd   Williams-BMW 36 points

2001

1st   M. Schumacher (Ferrari F2001) 123 points   **1st   Ferrari, 179 points**

2nd D. Coulthard (McLaren MP4/16-Mercedes) 65 points   2nd McLaren-Mercedes 102 points

3rd   R. Barrichello (Ferrari F2001) 56 points   3rd   Williams-BMW 80 points

2002

1st   M. Schumacher (Ferrari F2001 and F2002) 144 points   **1st   Ferrari 221 points**

2nd R. Barrichello (Ferrari F2001 and F2002) 77 points   2nd Williams-BMW 92 points

3rd   J. P. Montoya (Williams FW24-BMW) 50 points   3rd   McLaren-Mercedes 65 points

2003

1st   M. Schumacher (Ferrari F2002 and 2003GA) 93 points   **1st   Ferrari 158 points**

2nd K. Räikkönen (McLaren MP4/17D-Mercedes) 91 points   2nd Williams-BMW 144 points

3rd   J. P. Montoya (Williams FW25-BMW) 82 points   3rd   McLaren-Mercedes 142 points

2004

1st   M. Schumacher (Ferrari F2004) 148 points   **1st   Ferrari 262 points**

2nd R. Barrichello (Ferrari F2004) 114 points   2nd BAR-Honda 119 points

3rd   J. Button (BAR 006-Honda) 85 points   3rd   Renault 105 points

Drivers' Championship	Constructors' Championship

2005

1st	F. Alonso (Renault R25) 133 points	1st	Renault 191 points
2nd	K. Räikkönen (McLaren MP4/20-Mercedes) 112 points	2nd	McLaren-Mercedes 182 points
3rd	**M. Schumacher (Ferrari F2004M and F2005) 62 points**	**3rd**	**Ferrari 100 points**

2006

1st	F. Alonso (Renault R25) 134 points	1st	Renault 206 points
2nd	**M. Schumacher (Ferrari F2006) 121 points**	**2nd**	**Ferrari 201 points**
3rd	**F. Massa (Ferrari F2006) 80 points**	3rd	McLaren-Mercedes 110 points

2007

1st	**K. Räikkönen (Ferrari F2007) 110 points**	**1st**	**Ferrari 204 points**
2nd	L. Hamilton (McLaren MP4/22-Mercedes) 109 points	2nd	BMW 101 points
3rd	F. Alonso (McLaren MP4/22-Mercedes) 109 points	3rd	Renault 51 points

(The McLaren-Mercedes team was disqualified from the 2007 Constructors' Championship.)

2008

1st	L. Hamilton (McLaren MP4/23-Mercedes) 98 points	**1st**	**Ferrari 172 points**
2nd	**F. Massa (Ferrari F2008) 97 points**	2nd	McLaren-Mercedes 151 points
3rd	**K. Räikkönen (Ferrari 2008) 75 points**	3rd	BMW Sauber F108 135 points

Below: *New Zealand driver Chris Amon was one of the most promising members of the Ferrari team, but his three years with the team, from 1967–69 proved unsuccessful because Ferrari's V12 F1 cars were by then both obsolete and unreliable.*
(LAT Photographic)

Pole Positions in World Championship Grand Prix

by Ferrari drivers

(Inspired by *Autosport* 26 June 2008)

ALBORETO, Michele	**1984:**	Belgian
	1985:	Brazilian
ALESI, Jean	**1994:**	Italian
AMON, Chris	**1968:**	Spanish, Belgian, Dutch
ANDRETTI, Mario	**1982:**	Italian
ARNOUX, René	**1983:**	San Marino, USA (Detroit), Canadian, British
ASCARI, Alberto	**1951:**	German, Spanish
	1952:	Belgian, French, German, Dutch, French, British
	1953:	Argentine, Dutch, French, British, German, Italian
BANDINI, Lorenzo	**1966:**	French
BARRICHELLO, Rubens	**2000:**	British
	2002:	Australian, Austrian, Hungarian
	2003:	Brazilian, British, Japanese
	2004:	Italian, Chinese, Brazilian
BERGER, Gerhard	**1987:**	Portuguese, Japanese, Australian
	1988:	British, German
	1994:	Portuguese
	1995:	Belgian
BROOKS, Tony	**1959:**	French, German
FANGIO, Juan Manuel	**1956:**	Argentine, Monaco, Belgian, French, German, Italian
FARINA, Giuseppe	**1952:**	Swiss, British
	1954:	Argentine
GONZÁLEZ, José Froilán	**1951:**	British
	1954:	Swiss
	1955:	Argentine
HAWTHORN, Mike	**1958:**	Belgian, French, German, Italian
HILL, Phil	**1960:**	Italian
	1961:	Dutch, Belgian, French, British, German

ICKX, Jackie	**1968:**	German
	1970:	French, German, Italian, United States
	1971:	Spanish, Dutch
	1972:	Spanish, British, German, Italian
LAUDA, Niki	**1974:**	South African, Spanish, Monaco, Dutch, French, British, Austrian, Italian
	1975:	Spanish, Monaco, Belgian, Dutch, French, German, Austrian, Italian, United States
	1976:	Belgian, Monaco, British
	1977:	United States West, Austrian
MANSELL, Nigel	**1990:**	French, British, Portuguese
MASSA, Felipe	**2006:**	Turkish, Japanese, Brazilian
	2007:	Malaysian, Bahrain, Spanish, French, Turkish, Brazilian
	2008:	Malaysian, Turkish, Monaco
PARKES, Mike	**1966:**	Italian
PIRONI, Didier	**1982:**	Canadian, German
RÄIKKÖNEN, Kimi	**2007:**	Australian, European, Belgian
	2008:	Spanish, French
REGAZZONI, Clay	**1970:**	Mexican
	1971:	British
	1974:	Belgian
	1976:	United States West
REUTEMANN, Carlos	**1978:**	United States West, Monaco
SCHECKTER, Jody	**1979:**	Monaco
SCHUMACHER, Michael	**1996:**	Monaco, French, Hungarian
	1997:	Canadian, French, Hungarian
	1998:	Italian, Luxembourg, Japanese
	1999:	Canadian, Malaysian, Japanese
	2000:	Spanish, Monaco, Canadian, French, Hungarian, Italian, United States, Japanese, Malaysian
	2001:	Australian, Malaysian, Brazilian, Spanish, Austrian, Canadian, European, British, Hungarian, United States, Japanese
	2002:	Malaysian, San Marino, Spanish, German, Belgian, United States, Japanese
	2003:	Australian, San Marino, Spanish, Austrian, Italian
	2004:	Australian, Malaysian, Bahrain, Spanish, European, German, Hungarian, Japanese
	2005:	Hungarian
	2006:	Bahrain, San Marino, United States, French
SURTEES, John	**1963:**	Italian
	1964:	German, Italian
	1966:	Belgian
TAMBAY, Patrick	**1983:**	United States West, German, Austrian, South African
VILLENEUVE, Gilles	**1979:**	United States West
	1981:	San Marino
VON TRIPS, Wolfgang	**1961:**	Italian

Bibliography

Blunsden, John, *Formula Junior*, Motor Racing Publications, 1961

Borgeson, *The Alfa Romeo Tradition*, Haynes Publishing, 1990

Clutton, Cecil, Posthumus, Cyril, and Jenkinson, Denis, *The Racing Car, Development & Design*, B. T. Batsford, 1956

Collins, Peter and McDonough, Ed., *Alfa Romeo Tipo 33, The Development and Racing History*, Veloce Publishing, 2007

Conway, H. G., *Bugatti: Le Pur-Sang des Automobiles*, G. T. Foulis & Co., 1963, reprinted 1965

de Agostini, Cesare, *La Saga dei Marzotti*, Giorgio Nada Editore, 2003

Fangio, Juan Manuel (in collaboration with Marcello Giambertone), *My Twenty Years of Racing*, Temple Press, 1961

Fitzgerald, Warren W. and Merritt, Richard F., *Ferrari: The Sports and Gran Turismo Cars*, Bond Publishing, 1968

Fraichard, Georges, (translated by Louis Klemantaski), *The Le Mans Story*, Bodley Head, 1954

Frère, Paul, (translated by Louis Klemantaski), *On the Starting Grid*, B. T. Batsford, 1957

Fusi, Luigi, *Alfaromeo, All Cars From 1910*, Emmeti Grafica Editrice, Third Edition, 1978

Gauld, Graham, *Reg Parnell*, Patrick Stephens, 1996

Gozzi, Franco, *Memoirs of Enzo Ferrari's Lieutenant*, Giorgio Nada Editore, 2002

Hamilton, Duncan, with Lionel Scott, *Touch Wood!*, Barrie & Rockliff, 1960

Hawthorn, Mike, *Challenge Me The Race*, William Kimber, 1958, reissued by Aston Publications, 1988

———, *Champion Year*, William Kimber, 1959, reissued by Aston Publications, 1989

Hayhoe, David and Holland, David, *Grand Prix Data Book*, Haynes Publishing, Fourth Edition, 2006

Henry, Alan, *Flat-12, The Racing Career of Ferrari's 3-litre Grand Prix and Sports Cars*, Motor Racing Publications, 1981

———, *Ferrari: The Grand Prix Cars*, Second Edition, Hazleton Publishing, 1989

Hodges, David (edited and with contributions by Mike Lawrence), *A–Z of Formula Racing Cars, 1945–90*, Bay View Books, 1990

Hull, Peter and Slater, Roy, *Alfa Romeo, A History*, Cassell & Co., 1964

Jenkinson, Denis, *The Racing Car Pocketbook*, B. T. Batsford, 1962

———, and Posthumus, Cyril, *Vanwall, The Story of Tony Vandervell and his Racing Cars*, Patrick Stephens Ltd, 1975

Marzotto, Giannino, *Red Arrows, Ferraris at the Mille Miglia*, Giorgio Nada Editore, 2001

McDonough, Ed, *Alfetta: The Alfa Romeo 158/9 Grand Prix Car*, Crowood Press, 2005

Moity, Christian (translated and adapted by D. B. Tubbs), *The Le Mans 24-Hour Race, 1949–73*, Edita Lausanne/
    Patrick Stephens, 1974

Monkhouse, George and King-Farlow, Roland, *Grand Prix Racing: Facts and Figures*, G. T. Foulis, Third Edition, 1964

Nixon, Chris, *Mon Ami Mate*, Transport Bookman Publications, 1991

Nye, Doug, *Dino: The Little Ferrari: V6 and V8 Racing and Road Cars, 1957 to 1979*, Osprey Publishing, 1979

Orsini, Luigi and Zagari, Franco (English text edited by Doug Nye), *The Scuderia Ferrari*, Osprey Publishing, 1981

Pritchard, Anthony, *The World Champions*, Leslie Frewin Publishers, 1972

————, *Grand Prix Ferrari*, Robert Hale, 1974

————, *Maserati: A History*, David & Charles/Arco, 1976, reissued by Mercian Manuals, 2001

————, *Scarlet Passion, Ferrari's Famed Prototype and Competition Sports Cars, 1962–73*, Haynes Publishing, 2004

————, *Mille Miglia, The World's Greatest Road Race*, Haynes Publishing, 2007

Ramirez, Jo, *Memoirs of a Racing Man*, Haynes Publishing, 2005

Seymour, Miranda, *The Bugatti Queen*, Simon & Schuster, 2004

Sheldon, Paul with Rabagliati, Duncan, *A Record of Grand Prix and Voiturette Racing*, Volume 4, 1937–49; Volume
    5, 1950–53; Volume 6, 1954–59, St Leonard's Press, 1987

Small, Steve, *Grand Prix Who's Who*, Third Edition, Travel Publishing, 2000

Tanner, Hans with Nye, Doug, *Ferrari*, Haynes Publishing, Fifth Edition, 1979

Thompson, John, with Rabagliati, Duncan, and Sheldon, Dr K. Paul, *The Formula One Record Book*, Leslie Frewin, 1974

Trow, Nigel, *Lancia Racing*, Osprey Publishing, 1987

Venables, David, *First Among Champions, The Alfa Romeo Grand Prix Cars*, Haynes Publishing, 2000

Wyer, John, *The Certain Sound*, Edita SA, 1981

Magazines, annuals, etc.

Autocourse, Autosport, Motor Racing, The Autocar, The Motor, The Motor Year Books

Index